Canon Law Society of America

Proceedings of the Seventy-Seventh Annual Convention

Pittsburgh, Pennsylvania
October 12-15, 2015

Canon Law Society of America

ISBN 978-1-932208-42-9
ISSN 0277-9889
SAN 237-6296

The Canon Law Society of America's programs and publications are designed solely to help canonists maintain their professional competence. In dealing with specific canonical matters, the canonist using Canon Law Society of America (CLSA) publications or orally conveyed information should also research original sources of authority.

The views and opinions expressed in this publication are those of the individual authors and do not represent the views of the CLSA, its Board of Governors, staff or members. The CLSA does not endorse the views or opinions expressed by the individual authors. The publisher and authors specifically disclaim any liability, loss or risk, personal or otherwise, which is incurred as consequence, directly or indirectly, of the use, reliance, or application of any of the contents of this publication.

Unless otherwise noted, all canons quoted are from the *Code of Canon Law, Latin-English Edition* (Washington, DC: Canon Law Society of America, 2012) and the *Code of Canons of the Eastern Churches, Latin-English Edition* (Washington, DC: Canon Law Society of America, 2002).

Printed in the United States of America.

Canon Law Society of America
Office of the Executive Coordinator
415 Michigan Avenue NE, Suite 101
Washington, DC 20017-4502

Table of Contents

Foreword

The Canon Law Society of America (CLSA) is pleased to present the Proceedings of the Seventy-Seventh Annual Convention held in Pittsburgh, Pennsylvania, October 12-15, 2015. The CLSA annually publishes for its members, and others in the canonical community, the major addresses, seminars and reports presented at the annual meeting.

We are grateful to the presenters who provided their final texts in a timely fashion. Texts have been edited for consistency in conformity with the CLSA Style Sheet and Publication Guidelines including capitalization, use of footnotes, gender-inclusive language, and citation of canons. Included in this edition of *CLSA Proceedings* are the Tribunal Statistics collected from participating (arch)-dioceses and (arch)eparchies along with a listing of the participants who attended the convention in St. Louis.

The CLSA, established on November 12, 1939 as a professional association dedicated to the promotion of both the study and the application of canon law in the Catholic Church today, numbers over 1,400 members who reside in the United States and 37 other counties. *CLSA Proceedings 77* (2015) should take its place among previous volumes as a professional resource. Additional copies of this volume may be purchased from the CLSA website: www.clsa.org.

For information on how to become a member of the CLSA, please visit the CLSA website (www.clsa.org) or contact the Office of the Executive Coordinator.

Reverend Roger H. Keeler
Executive Coordinator
Canon Law Society of America
415 Michigan Avenue NE, Suite 101
Washington, DC 20017-4502

Keynote Address

Become What You Are: Doctrinal Insights and Practical Applications of *Communio* Following the Second Vatican Council

Most Reverend Joseph W. Tobin, C.Ss.R.

Introduction

Nearly two years ago, the Board of Governors of the Canon Law Society of America proposed as the theme for its 77th Convention: *Church Structures Fifty Years After Vatican II: Present and Future*. Recognizing the contemporary emphasis on the notion of the Church as a *communio,* the Board observed that:

> *communio* is not a description of the Church structures. For the structures of the Church are not ends in themselves but a means for helping the Church to be more clearly the sign and instrument of fellowship or communion with God and with others.[1]

Experience teaches that the means that have been employed in a given era may not remain adequate for the mission in another. Hence, the Board posed a question: what are and what should be the structures of the Church and the norms that express, promote and sustain the bond of *communio*?[2] In this modest contribution, I hope to point towards an answer by returning to the first day of the Second Vatican Council, exactly fifty-three years ago yesterday. A deeper understanding of the words of the Bishop of Rome on October 11, 1962 will help to unlock the meaning of the "event" of the Council and demonstrate how, fifty years later, the program of Pope Francis is rooted fundamentally in the renewal begun by his predecessor, St. John XXIII.

1 Canon Law Society of America (CLSA), *Statement of the Board of Governors* (November 2013).

2 Ibid.

Gaudet Mater Ecclesia

The Council opened on October 11, 1962 with a liturgy in the Basilica of St. Peter that reportedly lasted over seven hours.[3] The allocution of Pope John XXIII came near the end of that marathon, and the first words pronounced by the pontiff were *Gaudet Mater Ecclesia* – Mother Church rejoices! A noted historian of the Council emphasizes that John XXIII wrote the text personally and began outlining it more than three years before.[4] We can believe that his words were carefully crafted to communicate an argument for joy.

Pope John used the allocution *Gaudet Mater Ecclesia* to inform the Council Fathers and a curious world regarding his hopes for the Council. Historians note that listeners heard what they wanted to hear, and, from the very beginning, a proof-texting approach to the opening address, or any of the sixteen documents of the Council itself, produces an impressive array of apparently contradictory interpretations. The day following the opening ceremonies of the Council (i.e., October 12, 1962), the front-page of *L'Osservatore Romano* announced, "Chief Aim of the Council is to Defend and Promote Doctrine," whereas the headline in the leading Parisian daily, *Le Monde* was "Pope Approves Research Methods in Modern Thought."[5] The parable of the blind men and the elephant comes to mind!

Since it is true that Pope John identified as "the greatest concern of the ecumenical council … that the sacred deposit of Christian doctrine should be guarded and taught more efficaciously,"[6] one might be tempted to congratulate *L'Osservatore* for getting it right! However, those listening carefully to his words on that historic day would have noted how Papa Giovanni understood the nature of "guarding" and "teaching," as well as the means that the pope was suggesting in addressing those objectives. In fact, the Holy Father described the duty of the Council:

> not only to guard this precious treasure, as if we were concerned only with antiquity, but to dedicate ourselves with an earnest will and without fear to that work which our era demands of us.[7]

---

3 Richard R. Gaillardetz, "Vatican II and the Humility of the Church," in *The Legacy of Vatican II* [henceforth *Legacy*], edited by Massimo Faggioli and Andrea Vicini (New York: Paulist Press, 2015) 91.

4 Giuseppe Alberigo, *A Brief History of Vatican II*, trans. by Matthew Sherry (Maryknoll, NY: Orbis Books, 2006) 21.

5 John O'Malley, *What Happened at Vatican II?* (Cambridge, MA: The Belknap Press, 2008) 94.

6 *Gaudet Mater Ecclesia: Allocutio Ioannis PP. XXIII in Sollemni SS. Concilii Inauguratione, (*die 11 octobris mensis a. 1962) 5.

7 Ibid., 6.

The Church has always opposed errors and often condemned them in the severest manner; however, at this moment in the history of salvation, "the spouse of Christ prefers to make use of the medicine of mercy rather than that of severity."[8]

While his intention in convening the Council was "to assert once again the Church's magisterium, which is unfailing and remains until the end of time," the pope recognized that the Church must "bring herself up-to-date where required," in order to make her mission more effective.[9] The Church should "never depart from the sacred patrimony of truth received from the Fathers," however, she must "ever look to the present, to the new conditions and new forms of life introduced into the modern world which have opened new avenues to the Catholic apostolate."[10]

Three principal points

At the risk of following the venerable tradition of proof-texting, it seems to me that three important points for the question of ecclesial structures and norms that promote *communio* emerge from the allocution:

1. The opening address of John XXIII not only indicated a new set of tasks for the Council, providing also a new style in which the work would be accomplished, it began a process of structural reform that Pope Francis continues today with renewed urgency.
2. *Gaudet Mater Ecclesia* reminds us that the Church's law is grounded in and to be measured by the Church's faith, not only by her self-understanding but also by what she believes about God, about Jesus Christ, and about the human person.
3. Both the content and the tone of the allocution lay a foundation for the present insistence of Pope Francis that mercy is not simply a benevolent pastoral attitude, but the very substance of the Gospel of Jesus. Hence, the various theological disciplines, including law, must reflect its centrality.

From a "Pastoral Approach" and *Aggiornamento* to Pastoral Conversion

The renowned historian, Father John O'Malley, points out that *Gaudet Mater Ecclesia* was "was strikingly different from the scolding and grief-stricken

8 Ibid., 7.

9 Ibid., 3 (The reference is precisely to the following text: "Huius ergo Concilii lumine illustrata, Ecclesia spiritualibus divitiis, ut confidimus, augebitur atque, novarum virium robur ex illo hauriens, intrepide futura prospiciet tempora. Nam, opportunis inductis emendationibus ac mutua auxiliatrice opera sapienter instituta, Ecclesia efficiet, ut homines, familiae, nationes reapse ad ea, quae supra sunt, mentes convertant").

10 Ibid., 5.

tone of the correlative document of Vatican I."[11] By emphasizing the Council's pastoral orientation, moreover, the pope essentially countered those who wanted Vatican II to be "doctrinal," a code word for restricting its agenda to producing further specifications of church teaching.[12]

What did John XXII mean by the "pastoral approach" of the Council? According to an eyewitness, the Holy Father chose to avoid the

> classical pairing of doctrine and discipline, or faith and morals that were used to indicate the topics that fell under Church teaching. Instead, he preferred an overall consideration of what was needed in the life of the Church now, both within itself and in its relationship to society.[13]

Pope John XXIII insisted that the Second Vatican Council would not tinker with the sacred deposit of faith, but would help the Church to update herself, where necessary, and "by making appropriate changes and by the wise organization of mutual cooperation, [the Church will] make individuals, families and peoples really turn their minds to heavenly things." Hence, the Church would not hesitate to "bring herself up to date, where required" in service of her salvific mission.[14]

In the decades that followed the Council, the pastoral concern articulated by Papa Giovanni found enthusiastic expression in a movement popularly known as *aggiornamento*, an Italian word that means "bringing up to date." Interestingly, John XXIII used the word *aggiornamento* three years before the beginning of the Council, but, in that context, the word referred only to the updating of the *Pio-Benedictine Code* of 1917.[15]

One does not hear the word *aggiornamento* much nowadays, unless it is accompanied by the nostalgic sighs of someone my age or older. Nevertheless, the pastoral dynamism that is rooted in the content of *Gaudet Mater Ecclesia* and subsequently unleashed by the style and content of Vatican II continues under a new name: *pastoral conversion*. If you have been paying attention to the magisterium of the present successor of Peter, you know that pastoral conversion is a

---

11 O'Malley, 96.

12 Ibid.

13 Alberigo, 14.

14 See footnote 9.

15 *Allocuzione del Santo Padre Giovanni XXIII con la quale annuncia il Sinodo Romano, il Concilio Ecumenico and l'aggiornamento del Codice di Diritto Canonico*, Sala capitolare del Monastero di San Paolo Domenica, 25 gennaio 1959, at: http://w2.vatican.va/content/john-xxiii/it/speeches/1959/documents/hf_j-xxiii_spe_19590125_annuncio.html.

consequence of Pope Francis' call to the Church to become more missionary in her life and methods.

In the first programmatic statement of his papacy, the apostolic exhortation *Evangelii Gaudium*,[16] Pope Francis makes an urgent appeal for renewal in the contemporary Church. He seeks a:

- "path of a pastoral and missionary conversion which cannot leave things as they presently are" (*EG*, 25),
- and adds that "even good structures are only helpful when there is a life constantly driving, sustaining and assessing them" (*EG*, 26),
- hence, he calls for a "renewal of structures [that is demanded by pastoral conversion]"(*EG*, 27).

If we want to appreciate the value that Francis assigns to the notion of pastoral conversion, it is helpful to visit briefly a crucial ecclesial event that took place nearly six years before his election. The Fifth General Conference of the Bishops of Latin America and the Caribbean took place in May 2007 at the national shrine of Brazil, the Basilica of Our Lady Aparecida (Basílica do Santuário Nacional de Nossa Senhora Aparecida). At Aparecida, his brother bishops elected the archbishop of Buenos Aires, Cardinal Jorge Bergoglio, to chair the important committee charged with drafting the final document, a doctrinal statement that Benedict XVI approved for publication in 2008.

In the Aparecida document, pastoral conversion can have several meanings:

- the conversion of the People of God, which entails "listening attentively and discerning what the Spirit is saying to the churches (Rev 2:29) through the signs of the times in which God is made manifest";[17]
- the conversion of the shepherds that leads bishops to live and promote a "spirituality of communion and participation";[18]
- the conversion of ecclesial communities to become "communities of missionary disciples around Jesus Christ, Master and Shepherd" through "attitudes of openness, dialogue, and willingness to promote the stewardship and real participation of all the faithful in the life of Christian communities."

16 Apostolic exhortation, *Evangelii Gaudium*, (November 24, 2013); henceforward *EG*.

17 *Aparecida,* 366.

18 *Aparecida* 368.

However, pastoral conversion can also mean the missionary renewal of ecclesial structures. Perhaps it is not simply a coincidence that this understanding of pastoral conversion precedes the others in the text:

> All ecclesial structures and all pastoral plans of dioceses, parishes, religious communities, movements, and any Church institution must be imbued with this firm missionary decision. No community should excuse itself from entering decidedly with all its might into the ongoing processes of missionary renewal and from giving up outdated structures that are no longer helpful for handing on the faith.[19]

It is clear that this last understanding of "pastoral conversion" is the sense in which Pope Francis uses the term in *Evangelii Gaudium*. The call in the apostolic exhortation is frequently understood as a shift from maintenance to mission, that is, a movement from keeping the machinery of the institutional church grinding along, to a renewed focus on missionary outreach and conversion, one person at a time.

Recalling the allocution of Pope John XXIII, we can see another possible reading of Francis' use of "pastoral conversion." Among his reasons for convoking the Council, Papa Giovanni noted a need for the Church to bring herself "up to date where required." This is an apparently tame statement today, but spoken before two thousand prelates in October, 1962, such an admission could not help but shock more than a few, since it was clearly at odds with the dominant view of the Church as a *societas perfecta*, a Church hovering serenely above the turmoil of human history. As Richard Gaillardetz points out, "perfect" in the Neo-Scholastic sense of the claim meant simply that the Church possessed all that was necessary for the fulfillment of its mission, but the pope chose to emphasize the Church was also a historical reality in need of reform and renewal.[20]

In a similar way, the way Pope Francis uses "pastoral conversion" can suggest a similar idea: that the church's missionary difficulties do not stem exclusively from external problems, such as active persecution, secularism, or a hostile media, but also from its own internal defects and failures. In that sense, the call for "pastoral conversion' can betoken "a self-critical spirit and a willingness to concede that perhaps the church needs some internal housecleaning."[21]

---

19 *Aparecida*, 365.

20 Richard R. Gaillardetz, "Vatican II and the Humility of the Church," in *The Legacy of Vatican II*, edited by Massimo Faggioli and Andrea Vicini (New York, NY: Paulist Press, 2015) 91.

21 An observation by John Allen in his online blog; cf. his entry entitled "Synod notebook: Catechists and 'pastoral conversion'," at: http://ncronline.org/blogs/ncr-today/synod-notebook-catechists-and-pastoral-conversion.

What's the fuss about mercy?

Gaudet Mater Ecclesia reminds us that the Church's law is grounded in and to be measured by the Church's faith, not only by her self-understanding but also by what she believes about God, about Jesus Christ, and about the human person. Papa Giovanni chose to close his allocution with a reference to the Acts of the Apostles, which revealed abundant sympathy for the people of his time:

> To the human race, oppressed by so many difficulties, [the Church] says like Peter of old to the poor man who begged alms from him: 'Silver and gold I have none; but what I have, that I give thee. In the name of Jesus Christ of Nazareth, arise and walk' (Acts, 3, 6). In other words, the Church does not offer to the men of today riches that pass, nor does she promise them a merely earthly happiness. But she distributes to them the goods of divine grace which, raising men to the dignity of sons of God, are the most efficacious safeguards and aids toward a more human life.[22]

In his opening address to the bishops assembled in St. Peter's on October 11, 1962, Pope John XXIII deliberately set a conciliatory tone and task for the Council. In fact, reconciliation is a key to understanding the subsequent doctrine of the Council in such areas as the Divine Liturgy as well as the Catholic Church's relationship with other Christian Churches, non-Christian religions, and the modern world.[23]

The compassionate vision articulated by Papa Giovanni resonates anew in the image of the Church as a "field hospital," frequently proposed by Pope Francis.[24] Together with reconciliation and closely related to it, mercy is a hermeneutical principle for a correct understanding of the event of the Second Vatican Council. For it was mercy that impelled Peter and Paul to dialogue with the lame man begging at the Beautiful Gate. It was mercy that led them to share the divine healing, which they communicated "in the name of Jesus Christ the Nazorean," by offering the poor man that which they themselves had received.

According to Ladislas Örsy, the best definition of ecclesiastical law is given by its purpose: "it is a system of structures and norms to secure freedom for the people so that they can receive, without impediment, the gifts of the Spirit. *And it is a system of structures and norms to secure freedom for the Spirit to dispense,*

22 *Gaudet Mater Ecclesia*, 7.

23 See the excellent reflection by John W. O'Malley in "Modernity Made Manifest," in *The Tablet*, (13 October 2012) 8-10.

24 Pope Francis first used the image in his extensive interview with Fr. Antonio Spadaro, published online at: www.w2.vatican.va/content/francesco/en/speeches/2013/september/documents/papa-francesco_20130921_intervista-spadaro.html.

without impediment, God's gifts."[25] Ecclesiastical legislators are called to create freedom for the citizens of God's kingdom *and* for God's Spirit – a vocation judged by Örsy to be "an awesome task."[26]

Such an instrumental function for ecclesiastical law was highlighted by St. John Paul II at the time of the promulgation of the present Code, which, in no way, was intended as a "substitute for faith, grace and the charisms in the life of the Church and of the faithful."[27] The revision of the Code seeks to create "such an order in the ecclesial society that, while assigning the primacy to faith, grace and the charisms, it at the same time renders easier their organic development in the life both of the ecclesial society and of the individual persons who belong to it."[28] The revision itself can be seen as an exercise in "pastoral conversion," which was necessary in order that "the doctrinal riches of the Council [might] have their consequences and necessary impact on canonical legislation."[29] The application of the "medicine of mercy," deliberately chosen by John XXIII to describe *modus operandi* he envisioned for the Council, guided the revision of the Code.[30]

Some practical considerations

Gaudet Mater Ecclesia not only proposed a new set of tasks for the Council, it began a process of structural reform for the Church. The allocution of Papa Giovanni reminds us the Church's law is grounded in and to be measured by the Church's faith, not only by her self-understanding but also by what she believes about God, about Jesus Christ and about the human person.

Novo Millenio Ineunte: now a work in progress

John Paul II understood the need for continuing reform of Church structures as well as the need to connect that to the insight of the Council. At the close of the Great Jubilee, he proposed that the new century

---

25 Ladislas Örsy, "Law for Life," in *Receiving the Council: Theological and Canonical Insights and Debates*, (Collegeville, MN: Liturgical Press, 2009) 78-79.

26 Ibid.

27 Apostolic constitution *Sacrae Discipliane Leges* of the Supreme Pontiff Pope John Paul II for the Promulgation of the New Code of Canon Law (January 25, 1983).

28 Ibid.

29 *Code of Canon Law*, prepared under the auspices of the Canon Law Society of America, (Washington, D.C., 1998), "Preface to the Latin Edition", xxxvi.

30 The centrality of mercy was evident in principles that guided the revision, approved almost unanimously by a general assembly of the Synod of Bishops in 1967. These principles called for the revision to "take cognizance of charity, temperance, humaneness and moderation" as well as justice. Another example of how mercy would condition the principles is the preference in revised Code for *ferendae sententiae* penalties and the reduction of *latae sententiae* penalties. Cf. "Introduction to the Latin Edition," xxxvi-xxxvii.

> will have to see us more than ever intent on valuing and developing the forums and structures which, in accordance with the Second Vatican Council's major directives, serve to ensure and safeguard communion.[31]

John Paul indicated some very concrete structures that called for further development, including the Petrine ministry and episcopal collegiality, the ongoing reform of the Roman Curia, the organization of Synods and episcopal conferences, as well as relations within the particular Churches.[32] The widespread consultation in preparation for the two most recent Synods answered John Paul's call to "make our own the ancient pastoral wisdom which, without prejudice to their authority, encouraged Pastors to listen more widely to the entire People of God." John Paul II remembered the urgent plea of Saint Paulinus of Nola: "Let us listen to what all the faithful say, because in every one of them the Spirit of God breathes."[33] Critics of Pope Francis' program of reform fail to realize that many of his initiatives plainly respond to the situations that Pope John Paul II highlighted in his vision for the Church at the dawn of the Third Millenium.

Mitis Iudex Dominus Iesus as a result of pastoral conversion

The "medicine of mercy," called for by Pope John XXIII at the beginning of the council, informs the priorities of the present pontiff. For Francis, "mercy is not simply a pastoral attitude, but it is the very substance of the Gospel of Jesus." He encourages us to study how the various disciplines – the dogmatic, morality, spirituality, law and so on – may reflect the centrality of mercy.[34]

Because mercy is not a theory, but rather concrete and conscientious behavior, Francis published two *motu proprii* that reformed the canonical processes for the declaration of nullity of marriage: *Mitis Judex Dominus Jesus* and *Mitis et Misericors Jesus*. Besides an anxiety for the salvation of souls, which remains a perennial concern for the Church, particular circumstances also motivated the decisions of the Holy Father:

> The desire for this reform is fed by the great number of Christian faithful who, as they seek to assuage their consciences, are often kept back from the juridical structures of the Church because of physical or moral distance. Thus char-

31 John Paul II, apostolic letter *Novo Millenio Ineunte*, (January 6, 2001) 44.

32 Ibid., 44-45.

33 Ibid.

34 Francis' address to the University of Argentina is cited by Kevin E. McKenna in "The First Canon: Mercy," in *America* (October 12, 2015) 19.

> ity and mercy demand that the Church, like a good mother, be near her children who feel themselves estranged from her.[35]

While leaving untouched the traditional doctrine on the indissolubility of marriage, Pope Francis has enacted a structural reform that applies the "medicine of mercy" to those who have suffered the trauma of civil divorce. Those of you who have worked in ecclesiastical tribunals already see the potential healing that these new norms offer.

Make provision for the shadow side of the Church

The pastoral conversion of ecclesiastical structures is driven by the doctrine of the Council. In at least one instance, however, the call to conversion comes from what the Council neglected to say. Ladislas Örsy has demonstrated how the Council displayed a certain naiveté regarding the shadow side of the Church and this apparent ingenuity has left the Church without adequate structures to address her shadow side:

> Vatican Council II in the Dogmatic Constitution on the Church *Lumen gentium*, gave a lasting exposition of the divine gifts in the church and of the divine qualities that mark the community. But the Council never really elaborated on the presence of human limitations and of sinful behavior in the same church. By stressing the one, and saying little about the other, the Council left behind an image of the church, which can be misleading if it is not completed by further information arising from the history of the Christian community.[36]

More than a decade before the widespread disclosure of the extensive sexual abuse of minors by clergy and religious, Örsy worried that the little attention paid to a correct understanding of the "limitations, weaknesses, and sinful tendencies" in the community would not only leave justice without adequate support, but also "keep us from an adequate perception of God's mercy."[37] After the tsunami of accusations that paralyzed the Church, especially her pastors, Örsy would point to "the inability of our legal system to respond in a prompt, fair and efficient way to such a crisis" as a call for the ongoing renewal of the legal structures of the Church.[38]

---

35 Pope Francis, apostolic letter *motu proprio Mitis Judex Dominus Jesus*, (August 15, 2015).

36 *From Vision to Legislation: From the Council to A Code of Laws*, the 1985 Père Marquette Theology Lecture, (Milwaukee: Marquette University Press, 1985) 58, n. 11.

37 Ibid.

38 "Law for Life," 89.

Conclusion: the "Lex Suprema"

In this modest contribution to the work of the 77th Annual Convention of the Canon Law Society of America, I have tried to reflect on the instrumental character of Church structures and trace a line of continuity that links the opening address to the Second Vatican Council by John XXIII to the pastoral priorities of Pope Francis. The allocution of Papa Giovanni reminds us that the Church's law is grounded in and measured by the Church's faith, not only by her self-understanding but also by what she believes about God, about Jesus Christ and about the human person. Francis has modified structures that prevented the Church from sharing what she had received.

Canonists are no strangers to the necessity for pastoral conversion, since the final canon of the Code exhorts the Church to measure all her structures against the mission she has received in faith.[39] With the valuable assistance of your particular ministry, the Church will more unmistakably be the visible face of her Lord, risen and glorified, who is the "visible face of the invisible Father, of the God who manifests his power above all in forgiveness and mercy."[40]

---

39 Canon 1752, "The salvation of souls, which must always be the supreme law in the church, is to be kept before one's eyes."

40 From Pope Francis's *Prayer for the Jubilee of Mercy.*

Major Address

Cardinal Momentum in Marital Theology

Very Reverend Anthony Kerin

While we are gathered here in Pittsburgh this week, the fourteenth Ordinary Synod of Bishops is meeting in Rome. This institution was created by Blessed Pope Paul VI fifty years ago to perpetuate the dynamic of the Second Vatican Council. As this paper unfolds chronologically, various Cardinals and their contribution to the developing expression of marital theology will appear. At the outset it is important to remember that there are no heroes or villains in this story. There are just sincere, distinguished churchmen of varying vision and capacity. As Cardinal Oscar Maradiaga said only yesterday at the Synod, there are no opposing camps here. Even in their differing views, they are all playing on the same team.

The twenty-first century is but a decade and a half old. From what we have seen so far, it is very different from what was imagined by forecasters in the twentieth century. The Church, like many other institutions of long standing, is still recognisable and continues to play its part in the public square, but even she has been influenced by factors unforeseen, such as social media, blogging, and the immediacy of the internet. No longer are we constrained to read reports of events overseas through the filter of news agencies and editors. We can log on to read overseas local newspapers or simply confine our browsing to like-minded news feeds that present life as we like it. This can have the effect of amplifying and even distorting our own perceptions and prejudices.

Think of the recent reporting of the Same-Sex Marriage campaign. News editors carefully filtered stories of same-sex marriage referenda and judgements, giving air time to only those which furthered their purpose. In Australia, Ireland's referendum result was widely disseminated, while Austria's resounding defeat went unreported. This distorts our perceptions of reality.

The pretext, subtext, and context of this Synod and its dialogue dynamic are indicative of the wider Church at this time. Predictions of a looming battle between conservative and progressive elements were widely reported in the secular media. While the fourth estate appears to thrive on stories of conflict, such reports are frequently posted by commentators whose experience is with factional struggles in political parties. For all this experience, they demonstrate little comprehension of the *modus operandi* of the Holy Spirit. Indeed, the vocal presentation of widely divergent views, by sincere, prayerful, and committed Catholics from all around the world, is not the weakness they describe so much as a guarantee of our Catholicism.

With all this Catholic diversity, the twenty-first century is not a comfortable place for many in the Church. The number of Christian martyrs so far this century rivals that of the worst centuries of persecution. The secular agenda in western societies is often presented as the death knell for religion. The mistaken belief that if we remove religion from the public square we will just be left with the "reality of life," is propagated by many commentators whose senses are dulled to the sacred. However, the removal of religious underpinnings in society has been replaced imperceptibly by an "atheology" even more dogmatic than the tenets it sought to banish. Just think of the progressive intolerance for views which espouse traditional values.

We should be grateful that it is an uncomfortable age, for no progress, no breakthrough, no advance of any worth is made by those who are comfortable. Comfortable people are not provoked or inspired to make any conversion of lasting significance.

How does the teaching of Vatican II influence the institution of marriage in such a milieu? What can we as canonists, teachers, and tribunal staff learn from this? We shall see as we first explore the lead up to the event of Vatican II; next, the impact it had last century; and third, what needs to and yet may happen in the twenty-first century. We will finish with a few remarks about the fourteenth Synod of Bishops by way of conclusion.

1. The Event of Vatican II

The lead up to Vatican II

Four hundred years before the Second Vatican Council, the Council of Trent proclaimed the doctrine of the sacrament of marriage,[1] clearly enunciating the teaching of the Church to be based on Sacred Scripture in the book of Genesis, the Gospels, and the Pauline letters. The scriptural basis of Church teaching on marriage is its essence and strength. Such was the confidence of popes and theologians that by the nineteenth century they felt all the Church had to do was point out the errors in modern society and declare that the Church had the answers.

The encyclical *Arcanum*[2] which Pope Leo XIII issued in the second year of his papacy addressed Christian marriage in reaction to contemporary trends threat-

1 The 24th Session of the Council of Trent, 11 Nov 1563.
2 *Arcanum*, 10 Feb 1880, Pope Leo XXIII.

ening to undermine the institution.[3] Leo was determined to defend the traditional understanding of marriage based on sacred scripture.[4] *Arcanum* reaffirmed that the original intention of marriage revealed in the Bible, thwarted by the sinfulness of humans, had been redeemed by Christ. The nature of marriage is evident in the scripture and tradition and the nuptial image of Christ as bridegroom. The Church as his bride is the pattern by which we are to understand the relationship between God and his people and the natural reality as lived by husband and wife in matrimony.

The Church asserted its right to protect the institution of marriage from assaults by secular legislators whose laws might concede to allow polygamy, divorce, adultery, prostitution and a disregard for procreation. *Arcanum* restated the decrees of the council of Trent but also made clear the Church's right to speak for marriage. It insisted that it was not interfering in the marital relationship of couples, rather just telling it like it is.

In 1904[5] Leo's successor, St Pius X, in response to requests by the bishops at the First Vatican Council decades before, announced plans to codify the canon law of the Church and appointed Cardinal Pietro Gasparri as the Commission President. Gasparri had taught canon law at the Catholic Institute in Paris from 1879 until 1898. According to Dr. Ed Peters, Gasparri's *Tractatus Canonicus de Matrimonio*[6] is the most influential treatise on marriage since Gratian. Among many erudite comments, Gasparri made three major points about marriage. First, marriage was a contract, second, the object of the contract was the *ius in corpus*, and third the primary end of marriage was the *bonum prolis*.

The 131 canons on marriage in the Code promulgated in 1917 by Pope Benedict XV, made no attempt to portray a particular theological vision with regard to marriage.[7] This code largely concerned itself with juridical determination of the nature of valid consent to marriage and the factors impeding such consent. The canons explicitly state that the primary purpose of marriage was the begetting and education of children. The secondary end of mutual help for the spouses

---

3 We note that the first encyclical of Leo XIII's pontificate (20 Feb 1878 – 20 July 1903) was *Inscrutabili Dei Consilio*, promulgated on 21 April 1878 on the evils of civil society. "Now, the source of these evils lies chiefly, We are convinced, in this, that the holy and venerable authority of the Church, which in God's name rules mankind, upholding and defending all lawful authority, has been despised and set aside," *Inscrutabili Dei Consilio* §3.

4 *Arcanum* was issued eleven years before Leo's ground breaking social encyclical, *Rerum Novarum,* on Capital and Labour, but it was one of a number of his encyclicals drawing attention to the perceived errors in current philosophy and social theory.

5 Pius X, m.p. *Arduum sane munus*, 19 March 1904.

6 Pietro Gasparri, *Tractatus Canonicus de Matrimonio* (2 Vol. Paris – Lyon 1891).

7 W. Urbine and W. Seifert, *On Life and Love: A Guide to Catholic Teaching on Marriage and Family* (Mystic, CT: Twenty Third Publications, 1993) 19.

and the remedying of concupiscence was acknowledged but it was just as clearly subordinate[8].

The other notable feature of the codification was the defined insistence that between baptized parties, the valid contract must be a sacrament[9].

On 31 December 1930 Pius XI issued the encyclical *Casti Connubii*. While it coincided with the fiftieth anniversary of the Leo XIII's *Arcanum*, this document is better understood as a rebuttal of the softening of the Anglican line on artificial contraception. At the sixth Lambeth Conference in 1920 resolution 68 reiterated the primary purpose of marriage as the begetting and educating children and it railed against contraception.[10] But ten years later at the Seventh Lambeth Conference, resolution 15 began to waver on the methods and motives for contraception.[11]

Pius XI insisted that marriage is not just a private matter. The nuptial calling encompasses the dignity and obligations of parenthood. While a couple exercise

8 Can 1013 §1. Matrimonii finis primarius est procreatio atque educatio prolis: secundarius mutuum adiutorium et remedium concupiscentiae.

9 Can 1012 §1. Christus Dominus ad sacramenti dignitatem evexit ipsum contractum matrimonialem inter baptizatos. §2. Quare inter baptizatos nequit matrimonialis contractus validus consistere, quin sit eo ipso sacramentum.

10 Resolution 68 – Problems of Marriage and Sexual Morality, Lambeth Conference Archives, 1920: "We utter an emphatic warning against the use of unnatural means for the avoidance of conception, together with the grave dangers – physical, moral and religious – thereby incurred, and against the evils with which the extension of such use threatens the race. In opposition to the teaching which, under the name of science and religion, encourages married people in the deliberate cultivation of sexual union as an end in itself, we steadfastly uphold what must always be regarded as the governing considerations of Christian marriage. One is the primary purpose for which marriage exists, namely the continuation of the race through the gift and heritage of children; the other is the paramount importance in married life of deliberate and thoughtful self-control."

11 Resolution 15 – The Life and Witness of the Christian Community: Marriage and Sex, Lambeth Conference Archives, 1930: "Where there is clearly felt moral obligation to limit or avoid parenthood, the method must be decided on Christian principles. The primary and obvious method is complete abstinence from intercourse (as far as may be necessary) in a life of discipline and self-control lived in the power of the Holy Spirit. Nevertheless in those cases where there is such a clearly felt moral obligation to limit or avoid parenthood, and where there is a morally sound reason for avoiding complete abstinence, the Conference agrees that other methods may be used, provided that this is done in the light of the same Christian principles. The Conference records its strong condemnation of the use of any methods of conception control from motives of selfishness, luxury, or mere convenience."

free will in marrying, this freedom does not extend to their altering the nature of marriage.[12]

Prior to this encyclical, the only justification offered for engaging in sexual congress was the attempt to conceive offspring. This encyclical does mention the link between sex and procreation[13] but it introduced an allowance for seeking the unitive benefit of intercourse for its own sake.[14]

Pope Pius XII spoke to the Catholic Union of Midwives on 29 October 1951. While not an encyclical, this address builds on *Casti Connubii* and is a forerunner to *Humanae Vitae* and *Donum Vitae*. In this address Pope Pius XII goes further to state that the pleasure encountered by couples in their sexual activity is a God-given gift and couples who seek this pleasure are doing no wrong.[15] These teachings were the impetus to research that saw the advances and refinement of natural family planning methods which have proliferated since this time.

---

12 Pius XI, *Casti Connubii* §6: "Yet although matrimony is of its very nature of divine institution, the human will, too, enters into it and performs a most noble part. For each individual marriage, inasmuch as it is a conjugal union of a particular man and woman, arises only from the free consent of each of the spouses; and this free act of the will, by which each party hands over and accepts those rights proper to the state of marriage, is so necessary to constitute true marriage that it cannot be supplied by any human power. This freedom, however, regards only the question whether the contracting parties really wish to enter upon matrimony or to marry this particular person; but the nature of matrimony is entirely independent of the free will of man, so that if one has once contracted matrimony he is thereby subject to its divinely made laws and its essential properties."

13 Pius XI, *Casti Connubii* §54: "But no reason, however grave, may be put forward by which anything intrinsically against nature may become conformable to nature and morally good. Since, therefore, the conjugal act is destined primarily by nature for the begetting of children, those who in exercising it deliberately frustrate its natural power and purpose sin against nature and commit a deed which is shameful and intrinsically vicious."

14 Pius XI, *Casti Connubii* §59: "Nor are those considered as acting against nature who in the married state use their right in the proper manner although on account of natural reasons either of time or of certain defects, new life cannot be brought forth. For in matrimony as well as in the use of the matrimonial rights there are also secondary ends, such as mutual aid, the cultivating of mutual love, and the quieting of concupiscence which husband and wife are not forbidden to consider so long as they are subordinated to the primary end and so long as the intrinsic nature of the act is preserved."

15 Pius XII, Address to Catholic Union of Midwives, 29 Oct 1951, §326: "The same Creator, Who in His bounty and wisdom willed to make use of the work of man and woman, by uniting them in matrimony, for the preservation and propagation of the human race, has also decreed that in this function the parties should experience pleasure and happiness of body and spirit. Husband and wife, therefore, by seeking and enjoying this pleasure do no wrong whatever. They accept what the Creator has destined for them."

What might have been: the impact of Ottaviani

Cardinal Alfredo Ottaviani, the secretary of the Holy Office,[16] had for some time been encouraging Pope Pius XII to summon a Second Vatican Council to complete the work of the rudely adjourned First Vatican Council and to arrest the seeming slide into chaos and despair experienced in Europe in the aftermath of the Second World War. That pope chose not to call a Council but rather to address these issues through his encyclical *Humani Generis*.

When after his passing, Angelo Roncalli was elected as Pope John XXIII, it still surprised many that he should call an Ecumenical Council. When one reads his apostolic constitution *Humanae Salutis*[17] convoking the Second Vatican Council, we cannot help but be struck by his optimism. Clearly, in Saint John XXIII's view this was not a Council called to address a crisis, but a proposed fillip for an already energetic and active Church called to meet new challenges and to assist the secular world to move on from the devastation of the Second World War.

Subsequently, there was a feverish endeavour by prelates allied to Ottaviani, such as Enrico Dante and Ernesto Ruffini, to prepare the *schemata* for the Council to vote on and approve.[18] These followed a familiar pattern. They restated Church teaching and then with paternal affection, instructed the modern world about what was wrong with it. In the eighteen-page brochure prepared by the Holy Office as an outline for Vatican II there was but one paragraph on marriage.[19]

In reading the Council diaries of Australian Archbishop Matthew Beovich,[20] it is clear to me Beovich shared Saint John XXIII's optimism. His Archdiocese of Adelaide had never had it so good. Abundant vocations to priesthood and religious life staffed a Church comprising a thriving Church school system, which was expanding at mind-boggling speed. Sunday observance among Catholics was at all time highs.[21] Like most other Australian bishops, educated in Rome by professors who were now officials of various dicasteries, Beovich expected to attend the Council, catch up with classmates from Propaganda Fide College, and then to formally assent to the *schemata* prepared by their respected teachers.

16 The Pope was traditionally understood to be the head of the Holy Office dicastery.

17 December 25, 1961.

18 E.g., *Draft of a Dogmatic Constitution on Chastity, Marriage, the Family and Virginity*, translated by Joseph A. Komoncha, 2012. Available through search engines on the internet.

19 Section IV, 2. (f) of *An Outline for the Ecumenical Council* (1960), translated by Joseph A. Komonchak, 2012.

20 Josephine Laffin, "An Australian Bishop at Vatican II: Matthew Beovich's Council Diary,"*Australasian Catholic Record* 91, No. 4 (Oct 2014) 387-495.

21 Laffin, 389.

Again, to the surprise of many, that is not what happened.

Vatican II

When Archbishop Pericle Felici, the Secretary General of the Council, began proceedings by outlining the method and manner of the Council workings on the 13 October 1962, he called for:

> ... the fathers to fill in the names of 16 bishops for each of the 10 Commissions. Cardinal Achille Liénart, Bishop of Lille, rose to his feet to ask that the election of commission members should be postponed for a few days, so the bishops from different countries could get to know each other better.[22]

This was arguably the most significant intervention of the Council. It not only saw the first Session adjourned after just fifty minutes, it also afforded national hierarchies the opportunity to canvas and offer their best and brightest members for service in roles that had seemed predestined for dicasterial nominees. The Council had taken control of the process and eliminated the possibility of simply endorsing prepared texts. Eventually it cast aside the various *schemata.*

The documents of the Second Vatican Council changed the tone of theological discourse when they employed a personalist rather than an institutional approach in the discussion of marriage and family. The distinguishing feature of this new approach is the openness for dialogue with the contemporary world. There is optimism evident in this approach. The focus is on marriage as a vocation, with conjugal love having a sanctifying and redemptive role.[23]

In December 1965, the *Pastoral Constitution on the Church in the Modern World* was promulgated and it made a further refinement when it gave equal

---

22 Alain Woodrow, "Diary of an Insider: How Vatican II Changed the Church: 3," *The Tablet* (26 Oct 2002) 12.

23 Dogmatic Constitution on the Church *Lumen Gentium*, 21 Nov 1964, n. 11: "Christian spouses, in virtue of the sacrament of Matrimony, whereby they signify and partake of the mystery of that unity and fruitful love which exists between Christ and His Church,(Cf. Eph. 5, 32) help each other to attain to holiness in their married life and in the rearing and education of their children. By reason of their state and rank in life they have their own special gift among the people of God. From the wedlock of Christians there comes the family, in which new citizens of human society are born, who by the grace of the Holy Spirit received in baptism are made children of God, thus perpetuating the people of God through the centuries. The family is, so to speak, the domestic church. In it parents should, by their word and example, be the first preachers of the faith to their children; they should encourage them in the vocation which is proper to each of them, fostering with special care vocation to a sacred state."

priority to the two ends of marriage. The mutual help of the spouses was now ranked equal to the procreative purpose.[24]

Gaudium et Spes devotes paragraphs 48 – 52 to marriage. Its treatment gave new prominence to the personal dimension of the conjugal society of marriage. This presented Catholic teaching on marriage in a manner better understood by couples living it.

It was not a smooth development, nor immediately accepted, however. In a 1944 decree of the Holy Office on the ends of marriage, the question was put:

> whether the opinion of certain modern writers can be admitted, who either deny that the primary end of marriage is the generation and education of children, or teach that the secondary ends are not essentially subordinate to primary end, but are equal principal and independent. The response was in the negative.[25]

While Pius XII in his address to the midwives in 1951 allowed for couples to seek pleasure in the relationship as their main purpose, he insisted this aim was still subordinate to the primary end which must remain the generation of children.

It is most important to note that Vatican II documents did not reverse or contradict these former teachings. Instead they side stepped the discussion by omitting reference to a hierarchy of ends in marriage. The presentation of marriage was now couched in descriptions of covenant rather than contract and defined as an intimate partnership of conjugal life and love. This was not to say marriage was not a contract, but rather that the concept of contract was an impoverished description that fell well short of doing justice to the rich reality of matrimony. Despite many *modi* from concerned bishops who feared diminishing the contractual language would see a slide to the acceptance of dissolving 'said contracts' in divorce, other bishops argued that the concept of covenant was more a sacred concept and less vulnerable to personal whim and withdrawal of consent, than a contract which was something of a secular description.

---

24 Pastoral Constitution on the Church in the Modern World *Gaudium et Spes*, 7 Dec 1965, n. 48: "The intimate partnership of married life and love has been established by the Creator and qualified by His laws, and is rooted in the conjugal covenant of irrevocable personal consent. Hence by that human act whereby spouses mutually bestow and accept each other a relationship arises which by divine will and in the eyes of society too is a lasting one. For the good of the spouses and their off-springs as well as of society, the existence of the sacred bond no longer depends on human decisions alone. .... As a mutual gift of two persons, this intimate union and the good of the children impose total fidelity on the spouses and argue for an unbreakable oneness between them."

25 SCOf, decree 1 April 1944, *AAS* 36 (1944) 103; *CLD* 3, 401-402.

Where the 1917 Code had described the object of consent as the perpetual *ius in corpus,* Vatican II explained that consent was a mutual giving and acceptance of each other. In setting aside the strict pre-conciliar assertions of the hierarchical ordering of the ends of marriage, the Council Fathers had opened the possibility to new expressions of the doctrinal truth. Now procreation was described as the fruit of a couple's fruitful love: not subordinate to their expression of love, but the Creator's blessing upon that love expressed. The intimate connection of the two ends is thus preserved, but the description is more comprehensible to the couples living this vocation.

Birth Control

The discussion by the Council fathers prompted some to seek a precise treatment of responsible parenthood and the moral regulation of birth. The imminent development and release of the birth control pill amplified this desire. Pope John XXIII had asked the council to forego this topic, promising instead to form a separate pontifical commission to explore the matter in depth. The Council obliged and made some general reference to the regulation of birth in a manner contrary to the *magisterium* but without specific mention of methods[26].

Gaudium et Spes

It is important to acknowledge that the topic of *Gaudium et Spes* was not one of the original 51 questions in the *schemata* produced by the ten commissions. Less than twenty of these questions actually got to the floor of the council in session. During Session I on 4 December 1962 Cardinal Leo Suenens gave a well-received speech about how the *schema* should be grouped around two poles; *ad intra et ad extra.* In January 1963 a new mixed commission[27] was formed to draft a new schema. The first draft was issued on 25 May that year; "On the presence of the Church in the world of today." It was revised September 6-8, 1963, in Louvain by a team led by Suenens. "On the active presence of the Church in building the world" was produced in late September before the Second Session of the Council convened at the end of that month.

A third draft, dated 3 July 1964 and entitled "On the Church in the Modern World," followed various meetings in Zurich and Rome, and it was discussed at the Third Session (Sept-Nov. 1964) from October 20 to November 10. In the first week of February 1965, seven subcommittees met in Ariccia, outside of Rome, and worked on a fourth draft which was approved for distribution on 11 May 1965. It was discussed at the Fourth Session (Sep 14-Dec 12, 1965) from September 21 to October 8. A revised fifth draft was presented to the fathers in Council from November 12-17 with voting on each paragraph. There were 20,000

26 *Gaudium et Spes*, n. 51.

27 "Mixed" in that it comprised commission members from the Doctrine Commission and the Laity Commission.

interventions and *modi*. The final text was presented to the Council fathers on 4 December and two days later they voted on the complete text with 89% in favor. It was promulgated on 7 December 1965 with 97% in favor.

I recite these details[28] to highlight that the working document, the discussion, and the final resulting text developed through the course of this process. The preliminary topics for discussion, drawn up by curial officials, were scrutinized by the mood of the times, and in prayerful discourse, were moved to a new framework and purpose more suited to the needs of the Church in the modern world. There arose from this process a new expression of the Church teaching on marriage. We should expect the current Synod process will do likewise.

Humanae Vitae

After considering the report of three years' work by the Pontifical Commission on Population, Family and Birth established by his predecessor, Pope Paul VI sought further counsel from another group before he promulgated *Humanae Vitae* on 25 July 1968. This document also surprised many. Markedly different from the approach suggested by leaked copies of the Commission's report, the document began by reflecting on the pressing issues of rapid population growth and increasing scientific control over the natural order with regard to fertility and family life. The document set out the principles at play in such discussions. It asserts that procreation is essentially linked to the dignity of marriage. It listed the characteristics of marital love as a) fully human, b) total gift, c) faithful and exclusive, and d) fruitful.[29] Conjugal acts must be mutually and freely entered into respecting the capacity to transmit life. Unlawful means of birth control are direct abortion, direct sterilization, and any act directly intended to prevent procreation.[30] Lawful means of birth regulation comprise recourse to infertile periods of the cycle and therapeutic means to remedy diseases.[31] The sad legacy of this document sees most of its wisdom disregarded, as it is unread and ignored. Instead it became the certain trigger for an argument on the controversy of personal conscience and theological dissent - not the topic the encyclical was addressing.

In our present age, when the conceiving of children, now totally separated from the conjugal union, is commonly turned on by in vitro fertilisation, artificial insemination, and surrogacy, but far more frequently turned off by artificial contraception, sterilization, and abortion, a rereading of the wisdom *Humanae Vitae* is now sorely needed.

28 These dates are taken from an unpublished lecture by Dr. Peter Matheson, STD, who wrote his doctoral dissertation at the Gregorian University on truth texts in *Gaudium et Spes*.

29 *Humanae Vitae,* n. 9.

30 *Humanae Vitae,* n. 14.

31 *Humanae Vitae,* nn. 15-16.

2. The Impact of Vatican II

The damage to Church credibility occasioned by those who insisted on the authority of *Humanae Vitae* in the dissent debate rather than utilising the sound reasoning of its arguments contributed to an environment that began to sideline Church moral teaching. The message of *Humanae Vitae* was rarely well explained and often misrepresented. It became fashionable in many places around the world to omit reference to this teaching rather than risk alienating those who were struggling to understand it, let alone live out its precepts.

Further damage would later be done to the hierarchy's credentials for moral teaching by the patent failure to address clergy sexual abuse with justice and compassion for victims. But even before this more recent blow to their credibility as moral leaders, bishops' conferences around the world sought to redress the problem.

The United States Catholic Conference responded five months after *Humanae Vitae* with a statement that addressed both the theological dissent about birth control and the concerns of their society about the war in Vietnam. It restated the theological framework for understanding the encyclical and listed norms for legitimate theological dissent. But it was a lost opportunity because this document was not focused on *Humanae Vitae* but on dissent.

The Congregation for the Doctrine of the Faith also contributed to this discussion in 1975 with its Declaration on Certain Questions regarding Sexual Ethics.[32] This document dealt with issues such as pre-marital sex, masturbation, and homosexuality, but should perhaps be better characterized for its confirmation of the use of natural law methodology as the objective basis for morality. The real gem of a topic 'Natural Law' was buried in the dissent occasioned by the issues addressed.

It appears from this document that the 1960's and 1970's were for some a time of licentious hedonism. The release from the risk of conception afforded by artificial contraception saw uninhibited rejection of moral behaviour.[33]

As the Church responded to this moral decay, it drew criticism from secular sources for appearing to be obsessed with sex. The irony of celibate males pronouncing definitively on matters of sex and sexuality did not pass unremarked.

32 *Persona Humana*, CDF, 29 Dec 1975.

33 *Persona Humana*, n. 1: "In the present period, the corruption of morals has increased, and one of the most serious indications of this corruption is the unbridled exaltation of sex. Moreover, through the means of social communication and through public entertainment this corruption has reached the point of invading the field of education and of infecting the general mentality."

When some professed celibates were later proven not to be chaste, the remaining respect for the teaching authority of Church was further eroded.

Psychologists, sociologists, and anthropologists were tendering explanations of married life that differed markedly from those contained in moral theology and sacred scripture. The role of the family within society had changed. The extended family, which had provided social, recreational, educational and financial support to the parenting partners, had diminished. The couple were now often alone in their parenting and most frequently raising fewer children, either alone or with other partners.

In 1977 the International Theological Commission issued its Propositions on the Doctrine of Christian Marriage and the Christological Theses on the Sacrament of Marriage.[34] In noting the history of the institute of marriage and its diverse development in the eastern and western traditions, the Commission acknowledges very different approaches are possible within the reality of matrimony. They pointed out that Jesus disclosed marriage as the Creator intended, then restored it through his death and resurrection. There is a unique bond between indissolubility and sacramentality.[35] They also argued that while personal faith does not constititute the sacrament of marriage, its absence does certainly compromise the sacrament.[36]

The 1980 Synod of Bishops

The following year Saint John Paul II was elected Pope. He had been a staunch defender of *Humanae Vitae*. Although a member of the Pontifical Commission on Population, Family and Birth, he had never attended a meeting. The Polish authorities in the early 1960's would not permit him a travel visa[37]. On 16 December 1978, he confirmed 'The Role of the Christian Family' as the theme for the next Ordinary Synod of Bishops in 1980. There was much media speculation about whether the Synod would advise the Pope to alter the teaching of *Humanae Vitae*. Unfortunately, this misguided speculation not only misunderstood how a Synod works, but it hijacked the public discussion and reporting of the event. A better question is not 'what did the Synod do?' but 'what has the Synod begun?'[38]

On the first morning, Archbishop John Quinn of San Francisco raised the issue. He stated immediately that he accepted the teaching of *Humanae Vitae*, but

34 In 1977 the propositions were approved *in forma specifica* and sixteen Christological theses were approved *in forma generica*.

35 International Theological Commission, 2.2.

36 Ibid., 2.3.

37 John Marshall, "My Voyage of Discovery, How Vatican II Changed the Church: 7," *The Tablet* (23 Nov 2002) 9.

38 David M. Thomas, "Marginal Man at the Synod," *Marriage and Family Living Magazine* (Dec 1980/Jan 1981) 25.

that its arguments are underdeveloped. He was calling for deeper insights to be more easily explained in a manner sensitive not only to the laity but to pastors as well. The press reported in a manner to imply Quinn was confronting the pope by calling for a new teaching. Archbishop Joseph Bernadin of Cincinatti also called for a more positive and better developed theology of sexuality.[39]

The Synod method was at that time was quite restricted. The first two weeks comprised day after day of four minute interventions by the bishop delegates. The two English bishops, Basil Hume and Derek Worlock, chose their intervention topic carefully. An extensive consultation with parishes and dioceses coordinated by Father (now Cardinal) Vincent Nichols throughout 1979, culminated in his *Report on Marriage and Family Life*, dated 14 July, which set out the Church's vision, as well as the reality, of marriage and family life and practical steps towards creating a sustainable pastoral ministry.

The English delegates cut to the chase. Worlock spoke to the pastoral care of the divorced and remarried. Cardinal Hume spoke about the reception and understanding of *Humanae Vitae.* He shared with the Synod Fathers his dream.

> I saw with great clarity that the insight of Paul VI in the Encyclical *Humanae Vitae*, confirming the traditional teaching of the Church, was surely right. But alas we did not know how best to speak to the people.[40]

While the media reported these and other interventions as if they were dissenting from the teachings of Pope Paul VI, Saint John Paul II did not see it that way. He had heard the plea for a better expression of the Church teaching and the need to communicate Church teaching more sensitively. It had long been a practice in the Church to focus fastidiously on saying exactly what the Church meant concerning complex matters, while largely ignoring how such expression might be heard and understood in different parts of the world.[41] It seemed only important that the Church knew what she meant, not how others would understand it.

This dissonance was evident in the questionnaire for last year's extraordinary synod. While Church people know that the term 'natural marriage' distinguishes it from 'sacramental marriage,' most people responding to the questions saw it as a distinction from "unnatural" marriage. References to irregular marriage were perceived as insulting by some, but interpreted by others as specifying same-sex

39 Ibid., 26.

40 Hume, 2nd Intervention, 14 Oct 1980.

41 Consider the insensitive expression of a moral and a doctrinal matter in the one communication. The norms on *Delicta Graviora* 21 May 2010 referred both to the delicts of clergy child abuse and attempted women's ordination. Critics misread the Vatican as arguing that these delicts because they were in the same document were equivalent.

unions. How we express Church teaching is important, but how it is understood is even more important.

The 1980 Synod members could not wait for the customary post-synodal exhortation and they published a Message to the Christian Families in the Modern World in the week after the Assembly adjourned. They also presented to the Pope a request for and draft of a *Charter of the Rights of the Family*. This was later formally approved and issued 22 October 1983. It develops an argument from natural law for the rights it proposed and is modelled after the United Nations Charter of Human Rights.[42]

The post Synodal Apostolic Exhortation *Familiaris Consortio* issued 15 Dec 1981 is clearly written in the personalistic[43] language style characteristic of Saint John Paul's writings. The theological structure of the document is also reminiscent of his earlier writings. Married couples are cooperators with the Creator in creation of new life. The unitive and procreative meanings of conjugal love cannot be separated. Natural family planning is a tool to assist couples in living this.[44]

During this time, the final redaction of the revision of the *Code of Canon Law* was also taking place. The delivery of 129 Wednesday reflections by Saint John Paul II, now known as the *Theology of the Body*, also continued.[45] These activities and influences undoubtedly interacted with the Code revision, as well as the preparation of the post Synodal Exhortation and the Charter of Rights. Each affected the other and informed the pope's future Wednesday reflections.

Theology of the Body

Saint John Paul had for some time been a foremost scholar and defender of *Humanae Vitae*.[46] On 5 September 1979, Saint John Paul began the first of 129 Wednesday reflections. In the 114th reflection on 11 July 1984, while discussing the morality of the marriage act, he noted the connection between the two significances of the marriage act, the unitive and procreative elements. He spoke that day of the promised fidelity manifest in the language of the body, reread in truth.

The *Theology of the Body* is an innovative treatment of marriage by Saint John Paul. It is founded in the philosophy of Immanuel Kant, Max Scheler and Edmund Husserl. John Paul accepted the terms of sexual ethics as defined by

42 Its content may be found in an earlier form in paragraph 46 of *Familiaris Consortio.*

43 *Familiaris Consortio,* n. 31.

44 *Familiaris Consortio,* n. 32.

45 Wednesday reflections were disrupted during 1983 when reflections on the Holy Year of Redemption took precedence.

46 Karol Wojtyla, *Reflections on Humanae Vitae: Conjugal Morality and Spirituality.* Latin text, *Acta Apostolica Sedes* 60 (1968) 487-503.

Kant but argued for a different conclusion. Where Kant excused the pleasure of sexual congress because the couple were reduced to accepting that which diverts their attention from higher things, John Paul saw it rather as the fulfilment of their love.

There are six cycles in the series, each of them introduced by a scriptural reference. Please note the importance of reaffirming the scriptural basis for the theology of marriage. Departing from the scriptural basis diminishes the effectiveness of doctrinal truth.

The first cycle concerns the original plan. The response to the Pharisees questions on divorce sees Jesus refer back to Genesis. The original solitude of Adam, identified by his naming the animals and not finding a partner is answered by the gift of Eve and their original unity. Before original sin the first purpose of marriage is to orient the couple together toward God.

The second cycle is after the fall. The lust and adultery committed in the heart and referred to by Christ in the teachings on the mount, is the setting off point for these reflections.

The third cycle concerns the end of time. The text about the woman who marries seven brothers moves to an exploration on why marrying is a transitional state for making the divine present to the couple and thus in eternity is no longer necessary.

The fourth cycle is an exploration of how celibacy and virginity give some hint to the love of God present and incarnate in the human lives of the unmarried.

The fifth cycle is specifically about marriage and its sacramentality. The couple, in living out their sacrament, make Christ's grace present to their family, their community, and their world.

The final cycle addresses the procreativity of the couple, and in restating *Humanae Vitae's* teaching, enumerates the benefits to the couple by using the Natural Family Planning approach.

The *Theology of the Body* is not without its critics. While conceding that the phenomenological approach may be innovative, some argue the scriptural exegesis is naïve and ignores more recent scholarship. Others bemoaned that the reflections are too complex to be understood by those attending the Wednesday audiences. They do not have the authority of more structured papal teaching *motu proprio* and of encyclicals. There are also aspects of human sexuality that are not completely addressed, such as the little said about the significance of an unmarried and unprofessed single life, or of a chaste life by those of homosexual orientation.

For our purpose it is important to acknowledge that this teaching presents the issue of marriage and family with a new approach, a new expression, and thus expands our understanding. We are clearly not to be constrained to look at age-old doctrines always from the same angle.

CIC83 as the canonical expression of Vatican II

When the revised *Code of Canon Law* was promulgated in 1983, it lay claim to being the final document of Vatican II. Christian teaching on marriage has always been founded on scriptural descriptions of the connection between love, sex, and reproduction. Initially expounded by Gasparri as the linking of the Contract, the *Ius in Corpus* and the *Bonum Prolis,* it is this same interrelation which we find newly expressed in canon 1055 of the 1983 Code.[47] Theological reflection on the nature of the sexual act, the *ius in corpus,* was later displaced by exploration of the nature of marriage itself. This seemed to favour the argument of the French, Canadian, and Belgian bishops in their responses to *Humanae Vitae*, conceding that although childbearing is integral to family life, in any given marriage a couple can be morally sincere even if not all of their sexual acts were open to reproduction.

Increasingly reliable birth control methods, both natural and artificial, saw a newly manageable gap emerge between sexual activity and procreation. Artificial insemination and test tube conception further widened this disconnect. Nowadays conception can be totally removed from the sexual congress. Arguments for the intrinsic connection of love, sex, and procreation have in secular society's estimation been considerably weakened. But what might be the alternative to simply restating this link as before?

Taking Saint John Paul's hint,[48] what if fidelity, rather than sexual activity, were the abiding focus for Christian marriage? The scriptural image of marriage as Christ's fidelity to his Church would provide the pattern. If the pursuit and demonstration of fidelity were seen as the distinguishing mark of Christian love in all of its expressions (celibate, pre-marital, and marital), it would also mean that sexuality, while still important, would become secondary and thus subordinate to a higher principle of fidelity. Indissolubility, also an important and valued element in marriage, would be consequent on the pursuit of fidelity. This could be a new manner of explaining the truth of marriage. It would soften the carnal emphasis of current theology. Could such a change of emphasis, like the change

47 Can. 1055 §1: "The marriage covenant, by which a man and a woman establish between themselves a partnership of their whole life, and which of its own very nature is ordered to the well-being of the spouses and to the procreation and upbringing of children, has, between the baptised, been raised by Christ the Lord to the dignity of a sacrament. §2 Consequently, a valid marriage contract cannot exist between baptised persons without its being by that very fact a sacrament."

48 114th Wednesday reflection, 11 July 1984.

concerning the hierarchy of the ends of marriage, offer a way forward in the theology of marriage? I do not know. We shall have to wait and see.

The Catechism of the Catholic Church

In 1992 Saint John Paul II promulgated the *Catechism of the Catholic Church*, a document dealing with faith and morals. Marriage features in the Creed section (faith) and in the Moral section (Commandments). Subtle refinements of expression are evident, and the text deals with explicit accommodation of the innocent party in divorce proceedings. As authentic teaching, it affords us the chance to visit new expressions of age-old truths.

3. The Twenty-First Century

The profound advances at Vatican II in inter-Church and Inter-Faith relations are also clearly demonstrated by the manner in which documents such as the *Decree on Ecumenism* and the *Declaration on Religious Freedom* motivated the Congregation for the Doctrine of the Faith to issue the instruction on mixed marriages, *Matrimonii Sacramentum,* on 18 March 1966. The document displayed a more supportive attitude toward mixed marriages and suggested pastoral support for Christian/non-Christian marriages. The change of approach toward the impediments of mixed religion and disparity of worship was later refined in the Apostolic Letter *Matrimonia Mixta,* issued on 1 October 1970.

Baptized unbelievers

Because the marital union of two baptised persons is a sacrament, there was considerable discussion in the meetings of the Code Commission regarding the marriages of separated brethren whose comprehension of marriage did not include the sacramental understanding or intention presumed of Catholics. When Christians see themselves as part of an ecclesial community that permits divorce and remarriage, can they be said to intend permanency in the same manner as a Catholic? In all events the Code Commission determined this to be a theological, rather than a canonical, question.[49] The International Theological Commission had addressed this issue in its *Propositions* in 1977, but in stating that a lack of faith compromises the validity of the Sacrament of Marriage, they also acknowledged "this gives rise to new problems for which a satisfactory answer has yet to be found."[50]

49 *Communicationes* 9 (1977) 122.

50 I.T.C., *Propositions on the Doctrine of Christian Marriage*, n. 2.3.

In his 2015 address to the Rota, Pope Francis confirmed that "ignorance of the content of faith could lead to what the Code calls error determining the will."[51] The Pope also mentions how many people demonstrate an increased tendency to fashion their marital commitment to suit themselves rather than the purpose of the sacrament. Fancying marriage to be a 'do-it-yourself' project, couples insist they are free to first fashion, and then "try before they buy," any personal arrangement of their circumstances. The nature of the marriage thus intended is private, personal, and self-focused. It intentionally ignores the communal and ecclesial responsibilities of marriage, and so discussion of marriage is considered to be a private matter for each couple, rather than a community or a Catholic concern. Each couple seems to want to negotiate their own terms for the contract, often excluding essential elements and properties. They sometimes approach a Church wedding only after they are already happy with every aspect of their union.

In addressing these trends, the Pope sees ready access to tribunals and their well trained staff as part of the solution to the problem.[52]

Marriage and Eucharist

Since the Synod on the Eucharist in 2005, the link between Eucharist and Matrimony has been a central focus of current theological research.[53] Family is the relationship that God gives us. Marriage is the addition we make with a decision of the will. Eucharist is the spiritual nourishment for this journey. Matrimony and Orders are the sacraments that ensure the continuity of this dynamic. Diminishing numbers responding to the call of these vocations of Matrimony and Orders undoubtedly subdue the impact that family and Eucharist have on the world today. They are both agents of grace and conversion in our world. These and many other issues are being addressed at the synod as we speak.

---

51 Pope Francis, Address to the Rota, 23 January 2015: "Therefore, the judge, in evaluating the validity of consent given, must take into account the context of values and faith – or of their scarcity or absence – in which the matrimonial intention was formed. In fact, ignorance of the contents of the faith could lead to what the Code calls error affecting the will (cf. c. 1099). This eventuality is no longer held exceptional as in the past, given in fact the frequent prevalence of worldly thought on the teaching of the Church."

52 "I greet all of you who have come from local Churches in various parts of the world and have actively participated and shared the experiences of your local tribunals. Your large number and qualifications are of great consolation: it seems to me to be a generous response to the solicitations that every authentic ministry of the Church's tribunals receives for the good of souls." Pope Francis to participants at International Congress on 10th anniversary of *Dignitas Connubii*, 24 January 2015.

53 Post Synodal Apostolic Exhortation, *Sacramentum Caritatis*, 22 February 2007, nn. 27-29.

Conclusion: The 14th Ordinary Synod of Bishops

This is perhaps the best prepared, most widely consulted, and most widely followed Synod of Bishops ever. This is a blessing afforded by the internet. When consulting bishops concerning the issue of marriage and the family, Archbishop Baldisseri at the outset specifically asked that they not simply repeat Church teaching. If restating Church teaching were all that was needed, there would be no need to hold a synod. The synod should explore a new expression of that teaching.

We have already seen an extraordinary dress rehearsal in October 2014. At that time, the 2014 *lineamenta* focused on:

1. Natural Law as the basis for Understanding Marriage,
2. The Pastoral Care of People in Difficult Circumstances,
3. Openness to New Life and Procreativity.

The 2014 *Instrumentum Laboris,* which followed, also had three sections:

1. Communicating the Gospel of the Family in Today's World,
2. A Pastoral Program for Addressing the Challenges,
3. Openness to life and parental responsibility in the upbringing of children.

The 2015 *lineamenta* includes:

1. Listening: The Context and Challenges of the Family
2. Looking at Christ: The Gospel of the Family
3. Confronting the Situation: Pastoral Perspectives

The Jocist "See, Judge, and Act" of the Young Christian Workers method is evident in this ordering.

The *Instrumentum Laboris* for the 2015 Synod is a much-critiqued document. Last weekend, Cardinal Tagle described it as a "martyr document." He expressed hopes that it would "die for the faith." It is a framework open to revision, but a starting point nonetheless. Again, it is in three parts:

1. Considering the Challenges of the Family,
2. The Discernment of the Family Vocation,
3. The Mission of the Family Today

We can discern from the refinement in expression from one document to the next how the dialogue is developing as the process progresses. This is to be expected. It is every bit as likely that the *Instrumentum Laboris* of this synod, like the *schemata* of Vatican II, will have large swathes of it set aside and may be unrecognisable at the finish. Already we see a discernable shift from last year when the extraordinary synod documents seemed to concentrate on addressing difficult circumstances and pastoral challenges to family life. The expression of authentic Church teaching is surely at its best in presenting the glory of marriage and family life. Confining synodal outcomes to addressing problems reduces its scope and purpose. We ought to expect a presentation of the connected seamlessness of Catholic moral teaching, not just accommodations to pastoral aberrations. Enthusing young couples with the challenge and blessing a courageous commitment to married life brings is surely a better approach to take in this century.

Pope Francis clearly favours presenting the joy of living the gospel message rather than condemning those who have set it aside.[54] True happiness and authentic freedom comes from living in accord with the Creator's plan. The personal security and serenity that derives from committed, faithful, and fruitful marriages is amply evident in those with the discipline to live it. Conversely, the misery and insecurity of people who hedonistically choose to do otherwise in their relationships is likewise easily observed.

We can expect that the move away from troubleshooting single issues and challenges in family life, to discerning the family's purpose, mission, and calling, will better reflect the outcome of this synod. The family is not the problem; it is the agency of evangelising.

To expect any change in doctrine or discipline is to misread, misunderstand, or misconstrue what is taking place in Rome. We should rather pray for the enlightenment of the Spirit to afford a change of expression of the age-old discipline and doctrine that may make the joy of a self-sacrificing, disciplined, life-long, marital commitment apparent and appealing to a post-modern community living on the roller coaster of feelings, fads, and fancies. The interference of humans in God's creation does not always produce pretty results. Just because we can do something does not make it a good idea to do so.

Joy and hope are our point of difference, our competitive advantage in the marketplace. Committed, faithful, and fruitful love is our alternative to the misery of the godless world.

And just when pre-synodal posturing by prelates from far and wide was reaching a crescendo in the media, Pope Francis issued *motu proprio,* game-changing, new procedural rules for nullity cases[55] that take much of the steam out of the

54 Pope Francis, Address to Bishops at St. Charles Borromeo Seminary for the World Meeting of Families (Philadelphia), 2015.

55 Pope Francis, m.p. *Mitis Iudex Dominus Iesus*, August 15, 2015, and m.p. *Mitis et Misericors Iesu*s, August 15, 2015.

issues that threatened to monopolise discussion at the 2015 Synod. To facilitate such an immense pastoral change without any alteration to doctrine or jurisprudence is surely an indication of the Holy Spirit's presence in this process. This *novus habitus mentis* for processing marriage nullity cases demands no change to doctrine.

At first glance it may mean that two-thirds of our trials will now take half as long to process. For the other third, there will be fewer changes to how they are handled now. Using the plaintiff's domicile for competence will no doubt help expedite some cases.

While these provisions are not just about U.S. tribunals – and perhaps are more directed to Churches without such organised tribunal structures – they are also an implicit endorsement of American tribunal praxis. Onetime European conjecture that American efficiency enabled the granting of too many annulments has been implicitly refuted by the Pope's teaching. The confidence Francis places in diocesan bishops and in the integrity of their tribunal personnel is amply evident. This is frightening for some. The safety net of mandatory review is removed. It is also quite humbling as we continue our trials "having only God before our eyes."

We will see an increase in the number of annulments granted all around the world, partly because the new process is that much less a deterrent, but also because there are many more invalid marriages in this century than in the past. Rotal jurisprudence now confirms that the former expectation that every couple intends to wed as the Church understands marriage is demonstrably no longer true.[56]

The barque of Peter is setting sail on a journey that excites some and intimidates others. Some cardinals have come aboard with maps and charts depicting where they would like the voyage to explore. Others have just as clear an idea of where danger lies and where we just should not go. Others still are taking the role of a sea anchor slowing the pace of progress. Before anyone starts making judgements about the motives or sincerity of any of the bishop delegates, I must state that I have no problem with sea anchors. They are a valuable piece of safety equipment that steadies a passage in turbulent winds and waters. While they do not stop progress, they do slow the passage, and most importantly, they also prevent us being knocked off course.

I have far less affection for those admirals who stride the dock in full dress uniform yet refuse to put to sea. A ship in the harbour is safe but that is not for what ships are built. Refusing to embark and set sail means they will miss the boat.

---

56 Pope Francis, Address to Roman Rota, 23 January 2015.

It is difficult for us to conceive ever embarking on this journey, had it not been for the courage and immense faith in the Holy Spirit displayed by Pope Benedict XVI, whose towering intellectual contribution from Vatican II onwards is now eclipsed by his innovative wisdom in conceiving the possibility of a Pope Emeritus.

This is a voyage to the new world, to a new twenty-first century world. It is a world where African, South American, and Asian churches are ascending. They are losing patience with western churches and our fixation with communion for the divorced and remarried and homosexual unions. Greater issues for them include war, domestic violence, child sexual abuse within families, absent fathers working overseas, poor nutrition, and short life expectancy.

In this new century, communities are digitally configured and gathered, and yet individuals are more easily isolated and lonely.

Pope Francis' desire is for a synod that dialogues rather than debates these issues. For me, the difference between dialogue and debate is best displayed in the episode in John's Gospel with Jesus dialoguing with the Samaritan woman at Jacob's well.[57] There is no argument here, just growth in understanding through the discussion. There is first a companioning, then a gentle correction, and ultimately a liberating conversion. It describes a pattern for my hopes for this month's synod.

Jesus engages her with an exchange that at first resembles a Tribunal Assessment Interview (perhaps like the *processus brevior* of *Mitis Iudex*). The dialogue progresses to a theological/liturgical catechesis that reveals the path to be taken. The encounter concludes with the commissioning of a new evangeliser. The Samaritan woman's life and the lives of those who listened to her[58] were transformed. May it ever be so for all of us. It is a difficult time to be a canonist, but it is an exciting time to be a faithful canonist aboard the barque of Peter.

---

57 Jn 4: 1-26.

58 Jn 4: 39-42.

Major Address

The Reciprocal Impact of the Local Church and the Universal *Communio*: A Global Perspective Offered through the Lens of the Pontifical Council for Legislative Texts

Most Reverend Bernard Hebda

In the context of this gathering dedicated to examining the impact that the Second Vatican Council has had on Church structures, I was asked to offer a global perspective on the ways in which the present canonical ordering of the Church, fifty years after the closing of the Council, seems to be both expressing and fostering the conciliar vision of a Church that is at the same time universal and local. I realize that I was not invited to address this topic because of any scholarly credentials in this area, but rather because of my experience as an official of the Pontifical Council for Legislative Texts (hereinafter "PCLT" or "the Pontifical Council") from 1996 to 2009.

Accordingly, what follows are principally reflections flowing from that experience, most of which will focus on the Pontifical Council's role in the granting of the *recognitio*. This is admittedly a very narrow window into a very broad topic. The presentation in no way pretends to offer an explication of the theological notion of the Church as *communio*,[1] nor is there any intention of making a contribution to the famous "conversation" that has taken place between Pope Emeritus Benedict and Cardinal Walter Kasper "on whether the universal church (*ecclesia universalis*) is in its essential mystery a reality that takes precedence, ontologically and temporally, over the individual local churches." [2]

1. Vatican II and the configuration of the Pontifical Council for Legislative Texts

When I began working at the Pontifical Council, its title had only recently been shortened to "The Pontifical Council for the Interpretation of Legislative

1 Cf. Congregation for the Doctrine of the Faith, Letter on Some Aspects of the Church Understood as Communion *Communionis Notio*, 28 May 1992, *AAS* 85 (1993).

2 For a succinct treatment of this discussion, see W. Kasper, "On the Church: A Friendly Reply to Cardinal Ratzinger," *America* 184 (April 23-30, 2001) at: http://americamagazine.org/issue/333/article/church; J. Ratzinger, "A Response to Walter Kasper: The Local Church and the Universal Church," *America* 185 (November 19, 2001) 7-11.

Texts." The length of its name, however, was disproportionate to the size of its staff. As a result, the Pontifical Council had to share its offices in the *Palazzo delle Congregazioni,* just outside St. Peter's Square, with the Archives of the Second Vatican Council. While it seems that the arrangement was at that point in history primarily a matter of convenience,[3] it visually helped me to recognize the very real connection that existed between the work that had been entrusted to the PCLT and what had transpired at the ecumenical council recorded in those archives. I am convinced that the Pontifical Council has served, and continues to serve, an important role in facilitating the creative dialogue that the Second Vatican Council intended between the universal and local expressions of the Church.

1.1 A Brief History of the Pontifical Council and its areas of competence

To appreciate the depth of the connection between the Pontifical Council and Vatican II, one needs to know a little about the history of the PCLT and its organizational antecedents. A good place to start is the historical description presented each year in the *Annuario Pontificio.* The *2016* edition indicates that the PCLT can trace its modern heritage to the Pontifical Commission for the Authentic Interpretation of the Code of Canon Law that was established by Pope Benedict XV with the *motu proprio Cum iuris canonici*[4] on 15 September 1917, just a few months after the promulgation of the *Codex Iuris Canonici* (*CIC* 1917). As its title suggested, the primary purpose of the Commission was to perform the function of authentic interpretation, paralleling the work of the group of Cardinals who had been entrusted with the responsibility of authentically interpreting the decrees of the Council of Trent.[5]

While there were no such authentic interpretations issued after 1952, that Commission formally continued in existence until it was replaced on 28 March 1963, by Pope John XXIII's Pontifical Commission for the Revision of the Code of Canon Law, which, as once again suggested by the title, was created to reform the 1917 Code in the light of the decrees of the Second Vatican Council – a revision called for by the Council itself.

Four years later, on 11 July 1967, Pope Paul VI established the Pontifical Commission for the Interpretation of the Decrees of the Second Vatican Council, and named as its first president Cardinal Pericle Felici (who earlier that year had also been put at the helm of the abovementioned Pontifical Commission for the

---

3 The Archives of the Second Vatican Council were transferred to the Secret Archives of the Vatican in March of 2000, on the threshold of the 80th birthday of their curator, Msgr. Vincenzo Carbone. Cf. P. Doria, "L'Archivio del Concilio Vaticano II: Storia e sviluppo," *Anuario de Historia de la Iglesia*, 21 (2012) 135-15.

4 Pope Benedict XV, m.p. *Cum Iuris Canonici*, 15 September 1917, *AAS* 9 (1917) 483-484.

5 The Pontifical Commission was also tasked with making any necessary modifications to the code as later legislation was issued.

Revision of the Code of Canon Law as well). In 1969, the mandate of the Commission was broadened to include the interpretation not only of the conciliar decrees but also of the documents subsequently issued by the Holy See to implement those decrees.

Both of those Commissions passed out of existence on 2 January 1984, just a few weeks after the 1983 Code went into effect, when Pope John Paul II established the Pontifical Commission for the Authentic Interpretation of the Code of Canon Law. [6] The new Pontifical Commission was given competence to issue authentic interpretations (subject to confirmation by papal authority) regarding not only *CIC* 1983 but also the other universal laws of the Latin Church.

The function of the Pontifical Commission for the Authentic Interpretation of the Code changed significantly with the reorganization of the Roman Curia that came with the issuance of the Apostolic Constitution *Pastor bonus* on June 28, 1988.[7] The office was restructured as one of the twelve Pontifical Councils, the Pontifical Council for the Interpretation of Legislative Texts. While the title of the dicastery no longer included the word "Authentic," the Council retained "authentic interpretation" as one of its core areas of competence[8] and to this were added three other areas of responsibility: assisting the other dicasteries in the preparation of general executory decrees and instruction;[9] examining from the juridical perspective the general decrees of episcopal conferences;[10] and determining the legislative conformity of particular laws and general decrees.[11] The other modification in the title (the loss of the reference to the *Code of Canon Law*) more accurately reflected the scope of the Council's purview, stretching beyond the *Code of Canon Law* to include all of the Church's Legislative Texts.

---

6 John Paul II, m.p. *Recognito Iuris Canonici* (2 January 1984), *AAS* 76 (1984) 433-434.

7 John Paul II, Ap. Const. *Pastor bonus,* June 28, 1988, AAS 80 (1988). English translation provided in Constitutio apostolica "Pastor bonus," 28 iunii 1988, editio latina-anglica curante Michaële Thériault (Ottav, Facultas iuris canonici, Universitas sancti Pauli, 2000) 80.

8 *Pastor bonus*, Art. 155: "With regard to the universal laws of the Church, the Council is competent to publish authentic interpretations confirmed by pontifical authority, after consulting the dicasteries concerned in questions of major importance."

9 *Pastor bonus,* Art. 156: "This Council is at the service of the other Roman dicasteries to assist them to ensure that general executory decrees and instructions which they are going to publish are in conformity with the prescriptions of the law currently in force and that they are drawn up in a correct juridical form."

10 *Pastor bonus,* Art. 157: "Moreover, the general decrees of the conferences of bishops are to be submitted to this Council by the dicastery which is competent to grant them the *recognitio*, in order that they be examined from a juridical perspective."

11 *Pastor bonus,* Art. 158: "At the request of those interested, this Council determines whether particular laws and general decrees issued by legislators below the level of the supreme authority are in agreement or not with the universal laws of the Church."

The scope of the Pontifical Council's areas of competence was subsequently broadened when Pope John Paul promulgated the *Code of Canons of the Eastern Churches* and suppressed the Pontifical Commission for the Redaction of the Code of Canon Law of the Eastern Churches. Shortly after the effective date of the *Code of Canons of the Eastern Churches*, a letter from the Secretariat of State clarified that the purview of the Pontifical Council extended not only to the Latin Church's legislative texts but also to the *Code of Canons of the Eastern Churches* and any laws common to all the Eastern Catholic Churches.[12]

While the core areas of competence of the Pontifical Council have remained constant since *Pastor bonus*,[13] it should be noted that on the occasion of the twenty-fifth anniversary of the *Code of Canon Law*, Pope Benedict spoke of an area of competence sourced more in common sense than in *Pastor bonus,* namely, that the Pontifical Council had a role to play when norms become obsolete and should be abrogated, or when a lacuna was discovered that needed to be addressed.[14] The website of the Pontifical Council now lists that "implied competence" first among its areas of competence[15] and it would seem that a high percentage of its work and time has, in recent years, been devoted to this type of work.

Whether or how the Pontifical Council will be reconfigured in the reform of the Curia initiated by Pope Francis has not yet been indicated.

12 Letter of the Secretariat of State, Prot. N. 278.287/G.N., (27 February 1991).

13 It should also be noted that there was one further change to the title of the Council. Sometime in 1999 the title was changed from "Pontifical Council for the Interpretation of Legislative Texts" to "Pontifical Council for Legislative Texts." The change was not formally announced and received little intention and did not indicate any structural change in the areas of competence; rather, it was hoped that the change would correct the mistaken assumption that the bulk of the Pontifical Council's work was related to Art. 155 of *Pastor bonus*.

14 Benedict XVI, "*Discorso di sua Santità Benedetto XVI ai partecipanti al convegno di studio organizzato dal Pontificio Consiglio per i Testi Legislativi in occasione del XXV anniversario della promulgazione del Codice di Diritto Canonico*, January 25, 2008, 40 *Communicationes* I (2008) 26-28. An English translation appears on the Vatican website: "It is therefore necessary to abrogate norms that prove antiquated; to modify those in need of correction; to interpret – in light of the Church's living Magisterium – those that are doubtful, and lastly, to fill possible *lacunae legis*. As Pope John Paul II said to the Roman Rota: 'The very many expressions of that flexibility which has always marked canon law, precisely for pastoral reasons, must be kept in mind and applied' (*Address to the Roman Rota*, 18 January 1990, n. 4). It is your task in the Pontifical Council for Legislative Texts to ensure that the work of the various bodies in the Church that are required to dictate norms for the faithful always reflects, all together, the unity and communion that are proper to the Church."

15 "1. *Proposta legislativa al Santo Padre - La proposta legislativa rivolta al Papa in caso di "lacuna legis" oppure di obsolescenza della norma, relativamente al Codice latino e a quello delle Chiese orientali, nonché relativamente alle altre norme della Chiesa universale*.," http://www.delegumtextibus.va/content/testilegislativi/it/competenze.html

While this summary of the organizational genealogy of the dicastery might not give much evidence of a direct correlation between the Second Vatican Council and the Pontifical Council, the connection can be seen indirectly in two areas: the impact of the Council on the Code (which would be the primary focus of the Pontifical Council's work) and the impact of the conciliar ecclesiology on the Curia and its relationship with particular Churches.[16]

---

16 A third connection to be explored would be at the level of personnel. When Archbishop Pericle Felici was named in 1967 as head of the Pontifical Commission for the Revision of the Code of Canon Law and of the Pontifical Commission for the Interpretation of the Decrees of the Second Vatican Council, two of the organizational predecessors of the present Pontifical Council for Legislative Texts, he would have brought with him his extensive experience not only as a Council Father but also as a General Secretary of the Council. From that vantage point, he had a thorough knowledge of the debates and discussions that ultimately resulted in the conciliar documents. While historians of the Council, not surprisingly, may have differing evaluations of the contribution of Felici, depending on their general perspective on what occurred at the Council, few would deny that Felici was one of the "key figures" at the Council. See Vincenzo Carbone, *Il "diario" conciliare di Monsignor Pericle Felici,* Agostino Marchetto, ed. (Vatican City: Libreria Editrice Vaticana, 2015). On the occasion of the publication of Felici's council diary, Pope Francis referred to him as "a most qualified source," at: https://it.zenit.org/articles/francesco-scrive-a-mons-marchetto-il-suo-volume-frutto-di-un-insigne-studio-ermeneutico. While Felici is frequently recognized as being one of the architects of the Code, his long tenure as head of the relevant Pontifical Commissions would provide ample reason to see him as one of the architects of the Pontifical Council as well.

That lived connection to the Second Vatican Council was very much kept alive in the person of Cardinal Julian Herranz. As a young priest and canonist in Rome, he was brought to the Holy See by Cardinal Pietro Ciriaci to work at the Congregation for the Council in 1960. Cardinal Ciriaci was also serving as the President of the Pontifical Commission for the Interpretation of the Code of Canon Law. When, two years later, Cardinal Ciriaci was elected at the Council to head its Commission for the Discipline of the Clergy and of the Christian People, Father Herranz assumed responsibility as an *aiutante di studio* for that Commission, giving him the privilege of being a witness to the Council. He was subsequently brought on as part of the Staff of the Pontifical Commission for the Revision of the Code, a commission also under the direction of Cardinal Ciriaci when it actively began its work after the close of the Council 1965. He would continue in that office, and its future iterations, until he retired as President of the Pontifical Council in February of 2007, having served as a living historical link to the conciliar period. His personal reflections on that experience provide great insight into the impact that the Council had on the Code. Julian Herranz, *Nei dintorni di Gerico*. Edizioni (Ares, Milan 2005).

1.2 The PCLT and Vatican II are linked through their ties with the CIC

On the feast of the Conversion of St. Paul in 1959, the newly elected Pope John XXIII announced to the Cardinals assembled (only seventeen) that he intended to do three things: convoke a Synod for the Diocese of Rome, call an ecumenical council, and update the *Code of Canon Law*. In one address, he managed to touch on the three major focal points of this presentation: the local Church, the Universal Church, and the Code.

It was clear that it was Pope John XXIII's intuition that both the Synod and the Council would have an impact on the Code – his discourse that day spoke of the revision of the Code "which should accompany and crown these two tests of the practical application of the provisions of ecclesiastical disciplines, as the Spirit of the Lord will suggest to us little by little along the way."[17]

Almost a quarter of a century later, Pope John Paul II would suggest that his predecessor's intuition was only partially correct. In the Apostolic Constitution promulgating the revised *Code of Canon Law*, he wrote:

> Of these two events [the Synod and the Council], the first was not closely connected with the reform of the Code, but the second, that is, the Council, is of supreme importance in regard to the present matter and is closely connected with it.[18]

The connection that Pope John Paul II recognized went beyond Vatican II's influence on the content of the new legislation. He insightfully realized that the Second Vatican Council had had an impact on the very process of revision, which in some ways reflected the collegiality of the Second Vatican Council:

> Therefore, in promulgating the Code today, I am fully aware that this act is an expression of pontifical authority and, therefore, it is invested with a 'primatial' character. But I am also aware that this Code in its objective content reflects the collegial care of all my brothers in the episcopate for the Church. Indeed, by a certain analogy with the Council, it should be considered as the fruit of a collegial collaboration because of the united efforts on the part of specialized persons and institutions throughout the whole Church.[19]

---

17 John XXIII, Allocution (January 25, 1959) 51 *AAS* 1959, 65-69.

18 John Paul II, Ap. Const. *Sacrae Disciplinae Leges* (January 25, 1983) 75/II AAS 1983, vii-xiv. English translation found in *Code of Canon Law: Latin-English Edition* (Washington, DC: Canon Law Society of America, 1983) xi-xvi.

19 Ibid., xiii.

Recognizing that the impact of the Second Vatican Council on the content and revision of the *Code of Canon Law* is a rich motherlode that has already been tapped extensively[20] and continues to be tapped,[21] the present discussion will be limited to a brief explanation of the way in which the connection recognized by Pope John Paul II necessarily roots the everyday work of the Pontifical Council in the experience and documents of the Second Vatican Council.

While the competence of the Pontifical Council extends to all legislative texts, it should not be surprising that the bulk of its work concerns the *Code of Canon Law* and the *Code of Canons of the Eastern Churches*. Whether in evaluating requests for authentic interpretation, in assisting the other dicasteries, in reviewing the general decrees of episcopal conferences and particular councils, or in evaluating questions of legislative conformity, the work of the Pontifical Council almost always focuses on a correct understanding of the canons. Given the rules for interpretation set forth in canon 17, and the potential relevance of the canons' purpose and circumstances, as well as the relevant *mens legislatoris*, the work of the Pontifical Council requires a constant return to the archives of the Pontifical Commission for the Revision of the Code or the Pontifical Commission for the Redaction of the Code of Canon Law of the Eastern Churches. These in turn almost inevitably lead the researcher back to robust discussions of the Second Vatican Council.

In this context, it was logical that one of the first tasks of the Pontifical Commission for the Authentic Interpretation of the Code of Law was to prepare an edition of the new code that made reference, as a helpful research tool, to its *fontes*, greatly facilitating the linkage to the conciliar and post-conciliar docu-

---

20 See, e.g., J. Alesandro, "Law and Renewal: A Canon Lawyer's Analysis of the Revised Code," in *Proceedings of the Annual Convention of the Canon Law Society of America* 1982, 1-40; Eugenio Corecco, "La réception de Vatican II dans le Code de droit canonique," in G. Alberigo and J. Jossua, eds., *La réception de Vatican II* (Paris: Cerf, 1985) 327-91; Thomas J. Green, "The Revised Code of Canon Law: Some Theological Issues," in *Theological Studies* 47 (1986) 617-652; J. Komonchak, "The Ecumenical Council in the New Code of Canon Law," in *Concilium* 167 (1983) 100-105; J. Komonchak, Vatican II and the New Code / *Vatican II et le nouveau code. Archives de sciences sociales des religions* 62/1 (1986) 107-117; Ladislas Örsy, *From Vision to Legislation: From the Council to a Code of Laws* (Milwaukee, WI: Marquette University Press, 1985) 76; G. Thils, "Le nouveau Code et l'ecclésiologie de Vatican II," *Revue théologique de Louvain 14*, 289-301.

21 On 25 January 2013, the 30th Anniversary of the promulgation of the Code, the PCTL, for example, co-sponsored a study day at the Vatican on the theme, "*Il Codice: una riforma voluta e richiesta dal Concilio.*" The texts of the presentations offered on that occasion can be found in *Communicationes* (Vol. 45, No. 1) 61-104. Later that year, the Faculty of Canon Law of the Cardinal Stefan Wyszynski University in Warsaw sponsored a conference in June 2013 on the theme "*Il Concilio Vaticano II come fonte del Codice di diritto canonico.*"

ments.[22] The Pontifical Commission for the Redaction of the Code of Canon Law of the Eastern Churches similarly published an edition of the *CCEO* that included its *fontes*, including references where applicable to the conciliar and post-conciliar documents.[23]

Along similar lines, the Pontifical Council has sustained its commitment to publishing in *Communicationes* the historical materials from its archives concerning the revision of the *CIC* and the redaction of the *CCEO*, including the *Acta* from the various working groups. This has required a Herculean effort from successive generations of staff, but it has had the collateral effect of serving to acquaint them with the extensive work that was embraced after the Council to ensure that the laws of the Church would be rooted in what had transpired at the Council.

It would be rare for a significant question to be posed to the Pontifical Council that did not ultimately require the type of historical research that would root the Code in the Second Vatican Council. The official assigned to the question would trace the *iter* of the canon, beginning with any precedent in the 1917 Code and following the discussion throughout the various sessions of the working groups up to the promulgation of the Code. The informal collection of those "legislative histories," shared among the staff, became a valued commodity.

2. The work of the PCLT reflects the conciliar understanding of the relationship between the Universal Church and the Particular Churches

While the daily work at the Pontifical Council would necessarily take its staff back to the Second Vatican Council, there is a somewhat less obvious, but equally important, connection that relates to the Pontifical Council's very existence and areas of competence. I would contend that the present configuration of the Pontifical Council is itself an expression of the ecclesiology of the Council and plays a key role in fostering the universal *communio*.

2.1 The reason for the creation of the PCLT is fundamentally ecclesiological and rooted in the Council.

In an often-quoted volume on the Roman Curia issued shortly after the promulgation of *Pastor bonus*, the then-Secretary of the new Pontifical Council, Msgr. Julian Herranz, suggested that the primary ecclesiological reason for the creation of the Pontifical Council was rooted in the teachings of the Second Vatican

22 Pontificio Commissio Codici Iuris Canonici Authentice Interpretando, *Codex Iuris Canonici Fontium Annotatione et Indice Analytico-Alphabetico Auctus* (Vatican City: Libreria Editrice Vaticana, 1989) 669.

23 Pontificium Consilium de Legum Textibus Interpretandis, *Codex canonum ecclesiarum Orientalium: fontium annotatione auctus* (Vatican City: Libreria Editrice Vaticana, 1995) 617.

Council, which spoke of unity as being both a desire and an obligation not only of the Pope but of all bishops.[24] In support of that conclusion, he quoted Umberto Betti, who had indicated that the overall reform of the Curia was essentially rooted in the affirmation found in *Lumen Gentium* 23 that refers to "the duty of all bishops to promote and to safeguard the unity of faith and the discipline common to the whole Church."[25]

For Msgr. Herranz, who would later go on to become the President of the Pontifical Council – and like Betti, a member of the College of Cardinals – the conciliar teaching on the importance of preserving *communio* made it essential that the structure of the Curia would work for both a preservation of the unity of faith and a preservation of the unity of discipline. In explaining the work of the Pontifical Council, Cardinal Herranz would frequently speak of a parallel between the Congregation for the Doctrine of the Faith's preservation of the "unity of faith" and the Pontifical Council's role in preserving the "unity of discipline," seeing both as a service to the Holy Father in his service to hierarchical unity.[26] The work of the Pontifical Council, as set forth in *Pastor Bonus* 155-158, is best understood in that ecclesiological context: preserving the unity of discipline in a *communion ecclesiarum.*

2.1.1. The ecclesiological foundation for the PCLT is reflected in its make-up.

Even a cursory examination of the entry for the PCLT in the *Annuario Pontificio 2015* reveals an intentional diversity that gives evidence of a dicastery that is structured to facilitate a reciprocity between the universal Church and the local Churches. Looking at the fifteen "Members" of the Pontifical Council, one sees that while the majority are Europeans, there is also representation from Asia and North and South America. Six of the fifteen are diocesan bishops and five others had experience as diocesan bishops before receiving curial assignments. While the listing of the "Superiors" of the Pontifical Council reveals that the President, Secretary, and Under-secretary are all European, they come from three different countries with three different juridical traditions.

Even more revealing is the list of consultors. One notes immediately that the list is bifurcated, with one part including experts in the law of the Eastern Churches, and the other, experts in the law of the Latin Church. While there is a heavy representation from those European countries with strong traditions of maintaining ecclesiastical faculties of canon law, there are also canonists from Asia, Africa, and the Americas. There is a mix as well between diocesan bish-

24 Julian Herranz, "Il Pontificio Consiglio della Interpretazione dei Testi Legislativi" *La curia romana nella costituzione apostolica «Pastor bonus,»* Piero Antonio Bonnet and Carlo Gullo, eds. (Vatican City: Libreria Editrice Vaticana, 1990) 467-481.

25 Ibid. See Umberto Betti, *"La collocazione ecclesiologica della Curia romana" L'Osservatore Romano,* 9 July 1988, 1.

26 Herranz, 468.

ops, curial bishops, professors, and other practitioners. Some are members of the laity, some are in consecrated life, and some are ordained to the priesthood. It has been a longstanding practice of the PCLT, moreover, to consult canonists other than those appointed as "consultors," particularly when there is a need to understand the juridical, ecclesial and cultural particularities of a specific area or grouping of local Churches, or in order to assess how a proposal could have an impact on diverse situations around the globe.

2.1.2. The ecclesiological foundation for the PCLT is reflected in the four areas of competence attributed to it by *Pastor bonus*.

While the first of the four areas of competence attributed to the Pontifical Council (Art. 155) can be seen as primarily responding to a juridical need that was recognized long before the Second Vatican Council (i.e., the need to equip a legal system to offer authoritative interpretation *per modum legis*), and the second area of competence (Art. 156), mandating the Council's collaboration within the curia, could be seen primarily as a corollary of basic principles of sound governance or administration not directly related to the Second Vatican Council's ecclesiology and evident even in secular systems. I would argue that the third and the fourth (Art. 157 and Art. 158) were uniquely tied to the conciliar vision of *communio* that had found expression in the 1983 Code's treatment of episcopal conferences, particular councils, and particular laws and general decrees issued by other local legislators. Those two areas of competence, and the texts on which they are based, merit further attention.

3. Determinations of legislative congruency or conformity (*Pastor bonus* Article 158).

Article 158 of *Pastor bonus* specifies that "At the request of those interested, this Council determines whether particular laws and general decrees issued by legislators below the level of the supreme authority are in agreement or not with the universal laws of the Church."

This area of competence is premised on the juridical need for internal consistency in the Church's laws at all levels. It would do a disservice to the *communio*, to the unity of discipline, if there were an irresolvable conflict in the obligations imposed on a member of the faithful at different levels of same Church.

The fifth of the ten principles set forth for the revision of the Code indicated that:

> The Code should be guided by the principle of modified subsidiarity, balancing the need for a unified system of law for the universal Church while also allowing greater weight to be

> given to particular legislation so that the unique characteristics of particular Churches will be apparent."[27]

While the notion of subsidiarity is in some ways more closely associated with the First Vatican Council than the Second, there is a clear connection to the vision of *Lumen Gentium* 27, which spoke of bishops as true "vicars of Christ" and not simply "vicars of the Roman pontiff." As such, "they have the sacred right and the duty before the Lord to make laws for their subjects, to pass judgment on them and to moderate everything pertaining to the ordering of worship and the apostolate." *Lumen Gentium* goes on to state that: "Their power, therefore, is not destroyed by the supreme and universal power, but on the contrary, it is affirmed, strengthened, and vindicated by it."

With more than three thousand ecclesiastical circumscriptions throughout the world, and thousands of diocesan bishops (and those equivalent to them) legislating as Vicars of Christ, the question becomes how can the proper "unity of discipline" be maintained? It was to respond to that challenge that *Pastor bonus* attributed competence to the PCLT to preserve that unity by determining whether particular laws and general decrees conformed to the universal laws of the Church.

From a comparative law perspective, *Pastor bonus*'s attribution of this competence to the PCLT is rather unique. In most legal systems, this role is decidedly judicial and is most often attributed to a tribunal of some form, which the PCLT clearly is not.

The *Code of Canon Law* is silent on this question. Interestingly, those preparing the *Lex Ecclesiae Fundamentalis* had foreseen the need for a mechanism for dealing with the issue of particular laws and decrees that conflicted with the *LEF*, similar to the conflicts that are seen in many legal systems between particular laws and a constitution. They had proposed that the resolution of these conflicts would fall not to a constitutional court but rather to the Roman Pontiff, or to a particular institution that he would designate to declare null particular laws or decrees that were in conflict with the *LEF*.[28]

---

27 See *Pontificia Commissio Codici Iuris Canonici Recognoscendo*, "*Principia quae Codicis iuris canonici recognitionem dirigant*" *Communicationes* 1 (1969) 77-85. See the English translation *Code of Canon Law, Latin-English Edition* (Washington, DC: Canon Law Society of America, 1999) xxxvi-xxxvii.

28 Herranz 478. See also Julian Herranz, "Il Pontificio Consiglio per i Testi Legislativi: Natura, Competenze e Metodo di Lavoro," *Slovenská spoločnosť kanonického práva 12* (2004) at: http://www.vatican.va/roman_curia/pontifical_councils/intrptxt/documents/rc_pc_intrptxt_doc_20040809_pc-intrptxt_it.html.

A mechanism of this sort did not, however, appear in the first proposal for the reform of the Curia prepared by Cardinal Antonelli's commission,[29] which perhaps had perceived it as an issue that related solely to the *LEF* or the presence of a "constitution" of some sort. The mechanism was, however, introduced into the draft prepared by Cardinal Sabbatani's commission in 1985, and the provision remained virtually unchanged in the revision process.[30]

Cardinal Herranz claimed that the attribution of this function to the PCLT by *Pastor bonus* represented the first time in the history of the Church that the function was stably committed to an organ of the Holy See.

While the task, given its importance and technical difficulty, could seem rather daunting for a small office with somewhat limited resources, in practice there have been relatively few laws that have been referred to the PCLT on the basis of Art. 157.

In some ways, the practice of the PCLT in these matters is probably the least developed of the various areas of competence, but the careful evaluation undertaken on those few occasions reflects the respect attributed by the PCLT to particular law and the local legislators and the dicastery's commitment to respecting the modified subsidiarity called for by Guiding Principle #5.[31] In the thirteen years that I served at the Council, instances of questionable normative conformity were often handled by entering into a dialogue with the local legislator. The dialogue aimed to gently prompt a revision of the law in question, before it could or would be declared to be in conflict with a universal law. The matters were often resolved in a manner that allowed for the local law to be "saved" and the local legislator to be respected.

Since a recourse would understandably be rendered "moot" if the law on which it was based was modified, the numbers published in the annual *Attivitá della Santa Sede* might not be the best indicator of the extent or importance of the Council's activity in this area. Nor should they be taken as suggesting a bias in favor of siding with the Legislator.

It should be noted that the Article only applies to "particular laws and general decrees." At times, a party might challenge a "practice" in a diocese: Unless the challenged action was required by a piece of legislation or general decree, the matter would not strictly fall to the competence of the Pontifical Council under Art. 158. Rather, it would need to be addressed to the dicastery with competence for that subject matter, such as the Congregation of the Clergy, or the Congregation for Bishops, or the Congregation for Divine Worship. The first question that is asked of the petitioner by the PCTL is to identify the particular law or general

29 Herranz, 477.

30 Herranz, 479.

31 See fn. 27.

decree that is the basis for the petition and to submit a copy of the same, indicating that it was properly promulgated.

This might seem like an arcane point but it is not. The Pontifical Council would presumably not, for example, be competent under Art. 158 to entertain a question concerning the conformity of a provision of the *Charter for the Protection of Children and Young People*, given that the *Charter* is not a general decree of an episcopal conference. Nor would it be competent under Art. 158 to judge the conformity of a non-promulgated diocesan policy in that area.

One final note on this area of competence: *Pastor bonus* 158 specifies that the question of conformity can only be raised by someone who "is interested" ("At the request of those interested, this Council determines ... "). The person making the request has standing only if he or she has an interest. Generally that would be understood as meaning that the law applies to that person but there certainly could be circumstances where a particular law that is intended to regulate the conduct of pastors, for example, could be shown to have an impact on his parishioners. It would be up to the person claiming standing, however, to demonstrate the "interest."

Note that the Article would not seem to allow the Pontifical Council to act *sua sponte*. It is not envisioned that the Council would be surfing the internet looking for laws to correct. The working presumption is that a promulgated law or decree is in conformity with the universal law unless it is challenged and found to be otherwise. For that reason, the mere fact that a copy of a particular law or general decree was sent to the Pontifical Council for its library does not mean that the law or decree is necessarily in conformity with the universal law. The staff of the Council is very small and cannot be expected to have reviewed from a technical perspective every legislative act that arrives at its office.

4. Examination of general decrees of episcopal bodies (Article 157).

Article 157 provides that "the general decrees of the conferences of bishops are to be submitted to this Council by the dicastery which is competent to grant them the *recognitio*, in order that they be examined from a juridical perspective." In many ways, this is the area of activity of the Pontifical Council that really gets to the heart of the topic of this presentation: It is in the regular examination of general decrees from episcopal conferences (and particular councils) and the granting of the *recognitio,* that the Code, creating juridical structures to deal with the realities desired by the Second Vatican Council, has fostered a genuine reciprocity that I would argue enriches the universal *communio*.

The Second Vatican Council, in promoting a vision of Church that would be marked by the "modified subsidiarity" that was reflected in the "Fifth Guiding

Principle for the Revision of the Code,"[32] also envisioned increased collaboration between Churches at the regional, national, and international levels. This emphasis on collaboration created a need for new and more highly developed universal norms concerning structures for collaboration between particular Churches.

One thinks, for example, of the Council Fathers speaking in *Christus Dominus* of the Church's long tradition of bishops "pooling their abilities and their wills for the common good," as expressed in synods, provincial councils, and plenary councils. They noted that in the modern day, bishops "frequently are unable to fulfill their office effectively and fruitfully unless they develop a common effort involving constant growth in harmony and closeness of ties with other bishops."[33]

The Council Fathers recognized that the collaboration that once took place in synods and councils was more often taking place in national episcopal conferences. With that in mind, they expressed their will that episcopal conferences be erected around the globe – usually national, but multi-national with the approval of the Holy See – so that there would "emerge a holy union of energies in the service of the common good of the churches."[34]

In the practical decisions taken to implement that decision, the Council Fathers called for each episcopal conference to draft statutes and submit them to the Holy See for the *recognitio*. They envisioned the decisions of the episcopal conferences as being binding

> in those cases prescribed by the common law or determined by a special mandate of the Apostolic See, given either spontaneously or in response to a petition of the conference itself ... provided they have been approved legitimately and by the votes of at least two-thirds of the prelates who have a deliberative vote in the conference.[35]

The Council Fathers effectively drafted what would become c. 455, §2.

They explicitly prescribed, moreover, that in the revision of the *Code of Canon Law,* suitable laws be drawn up in keeping with the principles that had just been enunciated in *Christus Dominus*, with due consideration being given to the observations made by the commissions and the Council Fathers.

It should have been no surprise, then, that those drafting the new Code would have set out to put canonical flesh on the bones set forth in *Christus Dominus.*

32 Ibid.
33 *CD,* 37.
34 Ibid.
35 *CD,* 38, no. 4.

Nor should it have been surprising that canonical minds would have begun to wonder how a "unity of discipline" could be preserved even in this new situation. The key would be found in the requirement of the *recognitio*.

When the new Code was promulgated, it specified that the *recognitio* would be essential in five instances: (1) when a particular council, whether plenary or particular, issued decrees;[36] (2) when an episcopal conference drafted its statutes;[37] (3) when an episcopal conference issued a general decree;[38] (4) when an episcopal conference was producing translations of liturgical books;[39] and (5) when an episcopal conference would prepare its own rite of marriage.[40]

4.1. Just what is the recognitio*?*

In a 2006 Explanatory Note[41] signed by Cardinal Herranz, the PCLT indicated that the *recognitio* was tied to the Roman pontiff's power over the entire church (c. 333 *CIC* and can. 45 *CCEO*), which is the guarantee of a "true and healthy ecclesiology of communion," (described as being "a fundamental and central theme of the documents of the Second Vatican Council") and a protection of both the unity and the diversity of the Church.

After considering a whole host of opinions, the Note concludes that the *recognitio* is neither an approval nor an authorization, nor is it a simple "*nulla osta.*" Rather, it is a *sui generis* act of the Holy See that serves as a "*conditio iuris*" imposed by the supreme legislator for the validity of certain acts. From a civil law point of view, it might be called a condition *sine qua non*. If that condition of law has not been met, the particular general decree lacks force. It is an act that seeks both to safeguard that a legislative act is correct from a juridical point of view (both in form and substance), and that it can be seen as the common action of the Church.

---

36 Can. 446 ....decrees issued by a particular council [plenary or provincial] are not to be promulgated until the Apostolic See has reviewed them.

37 Can. 451 indicates that the statutes that every episcopal Conference were to elaborate had to be submitted for the *recognitio*.

38 Can. 455 §2 – as anticipated in *CD*, §2. The general decrees issued by an episcopal conference would not "obtain binding force unless they have been legitimately promulgated after having been reviewed by the Apostolic See."

39 Can. 838 §3, indicates that translations of liturgical books into the vernacular have to be submitted for the *recognitio*.

40 Can. 1120 – If the conference of bishops produces its own rite of marriage, it has to be reviewed by the Holy See.

41 See PCLT, *Nota Esplicativa: La Natura giuridica e l'estensione della "recognitio" della Santa Sede,* 28 April 2006, 38 *Communicationes* (2006) 10-17. An English translation was published in "Studies in Church Law: Pontifical Council for Legislative Texts: Explanatory Note: The Legal Nature and the Extension of *Recognitio* of the Holy See," 4 *Studies in Church Law* (2008) 27-42.

It goes beyond a mere judgment of the absence of non-conformity (i.e., a judgment that the act does not conflict with universal law) or even of the presence of technical and terminological adequacy; rather, it affirmatively expresses a sense that the decree in question is judged to be consonant with the preservation of the Church's unity.

The Note stresses that the concession of the *recognitio* in no way changes the "ownership" of the act. The decree does not become a pontifical act or an act of the relevant dicastery. Rather, it remains a decree of the particular council or episcopal conference that produced it.

Interestingly, one of the most helpful descriptions comes not from the Pontifical Council but rather from the Congregation for Divine Worship and the Discipline of the Sacraments. In the Instruction concerning liturgical translations, *Liturgiam Authenticam* (2001), no. 80, we read:

> The practice of seeking the *recognitio* from the Apostolic See for all translations of liturgical books ... accords the necessary assurance of the authenticity of the translation and its correspondence with the original texts. This practice both expresses and effects a bond of communion between the successor of blessed Peter and his brothers in the Episcopate. Furthermore, this *recognitio* is not a mere formality, but is rather an exercise of the power of governance, which is absolutely necessary (in the absence of which the act of the Conference of Bishops entirely in no way attains legal force).[42]

What makes the description noteworthy is its joint emphasis on technical correctness and on the *recognitio's* potential for "both express[ing] and effect[ing] a bond of communion between the successor of blessed Peter and his brothers in the Episcopate."

4.2. Possible areas for legislative action on the part of Episcopal Conferences.

Before we go any further, please allow me to speak briefly about the conciliar view of an episcopal conference's legislative authority. You will recall from *Christus Dominus* 38, that the Council Fathers had decreed that there would be the possibility of a conference legislating "in those cases prescribed by the common law or determined by a special mandate of the Apostolic See, given either spontaneously or in response to a petition of the conference itself."

42 Congregation for Divine Worship and the Discipline of the Sacraments, Instr. *Liturgiam Authenticam* (28 March 2001) AAS 93 (2001) 685-726.

As for the "cases prescribed by the common law," the 1983 Code identified a whole host of areas that would fall within that scope. The provisions, however, were basically of two types: canons that required an episcopal conference to issue a general decree to address a particular question, and canons that permitted an episcopal conference to issue a general decree.

In a circular letter from the Cardinal Secretary of State to the Presidents of all Episcopal Conferences issued on November 8, 1983,[43] the Holy See provided what has been seen as an indicative listing of the canons making mention of the Conference's legislative authority, identifying twenty-one instances in which an Episcopal Conference was required to issue a general decree, and twenty-two additional instances in which an Episcopal Conference could issue a general decree. Subsequently, there have been a few instances in which the Holy See has authorized or mandated on its own initiative the issuance of general decrees by Episcopal Conferences in addition to those decrees foreseen in the Code as specified in the above-cited circular letter.

The Apostolic Constitution *Ex Corde Ecclesiae*, for example, *requested* that episcopal conferences and other assemblies of Catholic hierarchs issue "ordinances" for the local implementation of *Ex Corde*, specifying that they would need to be submitted for the *recognitio* mentioned in canon 455 §2.[44]

Thereafter, the Congregation for Catholic Education's 1996 *Instruction on the Admission of Seminarians Coming from other Seminaries or Religious Communities*[45] conferred *sua sponte* on episcopal conferences "a special mandate, in conformity with canon 455 §1" and authorized them, "in conformity with §§2-3, to publish the necessary *decreta generalia,*" noting that the norms "would need the *recognitio* of the Apostolic See in order to have a binding character."

---

43 Reprinted in 15 *Communicationes* 1983, 135-139.

44 John Paul II, Ap. Const. *Ex Corde Ecclesiae*, Art. 1, §2 82 *AAS* (1990) 1475-1509, 1502.

45 The Instruction was never promulgated or published in *AAS*. An Italian text can be found at 15 *Enchiridion Vaticanum* (1996) 384-394. An English translation is found at: https://www.ewtn.com/library/curia/cceadmit.htm.

Similarly, the 2002 Apostolic Letter, *Misericordia Dei*,[46] called for episcopal conferences to issue norms complementary to canon 961, a canon not listed among those specified by the Secretariat of State in 1983, which would set forth the conditions for the use of general absolution, indicating that the conferences, "observing Can. 455 §2 of the *Code of Canon Law*," would have to send any norms for the *recognitio* as soon as possible to the Congregation for Divine Worship and the Discipline of the Sacraments.

4.3. Competent Dicasteries for the concession of the recognitio.

That specific reference to submission to the Congregation for Divine Worship for the *recognitio* raises the question of the mechanics for requesting the *recognitio.* While the Pope as Supreme Legislator can obviously grant the competence to a Dicastery for decrees concerning a particular subject that is within their competence, as was explicit in *Misericordia Dei, Pastor bonus* seems to have foreseen only two possibilities when dealing with statutes and decrees:[47] the Congregation for Bishops and the Congregation for the Evangelization of Peoples. Article 82 of *Pastor bonus* provides that the Congregation for Bishops

> ... deals with matters pertaining to the celebration of particular councils as well as the erection of conferences of bishops and the *recognitio* of their statutes. It receives the acts of these bodies and, in consultation with the dicasteries concerned, it examines the decrees which require the *recognitio* of the Apostolic See (emphasis added).

For episcopal conferences in mission territories, however, that same role seems to be attributed by *Pastor bonus* to the Congregation for the Evangelization of Peoples. Article 89 provides that that Congregation "deals with everything

46 John Paul II, Ap. Letter m.p. *Misericordia Dei* (7 April 2002), 94 *AAS* (2002) 452-459. An English translation is found at: http://www.clerus.org/clerus/dati/2005-07/18-13/070402IN.html:
"Given the fundamental importance of full harmony among the Bishops' Conferences of the world in a matter so essential to the life of the Church, the various Conferences, observing Can. 455 § 2 of the Code of Canon Law, shall send as soon as possible to the Congregation for Divine Worship and the Discipline of the Sacraments the text of the norms which they intend to issue or update in the light of this *Motu Proprio* on the application of Can. 961. This will help to foster an ever greater communion among the Bishops of the Church as they encourage the faithful everywhere to draw abundantly from the fountains of divine mercy which flow unceasingly in the Sacrament of Reconciliation."
47 Translations of liturgical books and local adaptations of those books prepared by episcopal conferences are treated differently for the *recognitio* in *Pastor bonus*. In those cases, Art. 64 §3 specifies that it is the Congregation for Divine Worship and the Discipline of the Sacraments that grants the *recognitio*.

pertaining to the establishment and change of ecclesiastical circumscriptions and to the provision of these Churches, and it carries out the other functions that the Congregation of Bishops fulfills within the scope of its competence." That last clause has been understood as attributing to the Congregation for the Evangelization of Peoples competence for examining the statutes of episcopal conferences in mission territories as well as any general decrees submitted for the *recognitio*, presumably with the same requirement that they work in consultation with the other dicasteries involved.

4.4. The particular role of the PCLT in the granting of the recognitio.

In virtue of Art. 157 of *Pastor bonus*, the PCLT would necessarily be included among the "interested Dicasteries" whenever a general decree of a *coetus episcoporum* is involved. While the English translation on the Vatican website translates *coetus episcoporum* in this instance as "episcopal conference,"[48] the other translations appearing on that site all use a more generic term[49] that could arguably include a particular council. The working assumption appeared to be that Art. 157 did indeed give the PCTL competence with respect to the decrees of particular councils. In a 2004 presentation, for example, the then-President of the PCTL, in discussing Art. 157, matter-of-factly stated "episcopal conferences and particular councils" as two specifications of *organismi episcopali*, the expression used in the Italian translation.[50] While the objection could be raised that the Holy See has at other times stressed the distinction between *coetus episcoporum* and *coetus ecclesiarum*, with the former describing episcopal conferences and the latter describing particular councils, as a matter of fact and of curial practice, decrees of particular councils submitted for the *recognitio* by reason on canon 446 have been routinely referred to the PCTL

While the *recognitio* process focuses on both the decree's impact on *communio* and its conformity with the universal law of the Church and "correctness" from a technical point of view,[51] the focus of the PCLT is primarily in the area

48 English-language translation of the Apostolic Constitution *Pastor bonus* on the Vatican website at: http://w2.vatican.va/content/john-paul-ii/en/apost_constitutions/documents/hf_jp-ii_apc_19880628_pastor-bonus-index.html. It was prepared by Francis C.C.F. Kelly (Ottawa), James H. Provost (Washington), and Michel Thériault (Ottawa).

49 Zusammenschlüsse von Bischöfen (German); asambleas episcopales (Spanish); dos organismos episcopais (Portuguese); organismi episcopali (Italian).

50 Julian Herranz, "Il Pontificio Consiglio per i Testi Legislativi: Natura, Competenze e Metodo di Lavoro," *Slovenská spoločnosť kanonického práva* 12 (2004). See http://www.vatican.va/roman_curia/pontifical_councils/intrptxt/documents/rc_pc_intrptxt_doc_20040809_pc-intrptxt_it.html].

51 See PCLT, *Nota Esplicativa: La Natura giuridica e l'estensione della "recognitio" della Santa Sede,* 28 April 2006, 38 *Communicationes* (2006) 10-17. An English translation was published in Studies in Church Law: Pontifical Council for Legislative Texts: Explanatory Note: The Legal Nature and the Extension of *Recognitio* of the Holy See, 4 *Studies in Church Law* (2008) 27-42.

of examining the decree from the technical/juridical point of view, while the prudential question regarding the impact on *communio* would fall primarily on the competent Congregations, presuming their knowledge of the situations existing in the local Churches. That does not mean that the Pontifical Council in its examination would not also be looking at matters with an eye to broader consequence or to factors and experiences outside the confines of the local Church.

The examination by the PCTL would first concentrate on matters that were of a strictly technical nature – indicating areas where, for example, there would be a conflict with the universal law of the Church, or where the decree or statute was addressing matters that went beyond the specific scope of what the canon had authorized the conference to legislate. In the case of the canons that required the conference to act, red flags would go up if the proposed decree or statute failed to really address the substance of the matter raised in the canon or if, rather than legislating, the proposal simply passed the buck back to the individual diocesan bishop. More often than not, where technical difficulties were identified, the Council would propose possible revisions. In other instances, the observation would simply be made that the conference needed to redraft the provision, indicating the reason for that determination.

Observations would also frequently be offered that were juridical in nature but perhaps more prudential than technical. They might reflect pastoral challenges or legal difficulties that had come to the Council's attention from other episcopal conferences or regions in applying similar norms. They might bring to the attention of the Congregation of Bishops or the Congregation for the Evangelization of Peoples information concerning the content of decrees from other episcopal conferences in the region. So too might they highlight for the Congregation the need to make an assessment on the importance of consistency within a region, or raise questions when a formulation that was not approved for one conference or council is then approved for another.

Conversely, the PCLT could bring to the attention of the relevant Congregation reasons why a formulation already approved in a general decree or statutes of another episcopal conference might not be opportune in this particular instance or why a derogation might be justifiable in a particular case. One could imagine, for example, that differences in civil laws in different countries could require a diversity in canonical formulations – or that an episcopal conference with only a handful of bishop members perhaps could not be held to the highly-developed committee structure envisioned by the Code. Essentially the Pontifical Council raised the issues and offered observations, but the prudential decisions were left to the Congregation of Bishops or the Congregation for the Evangelization of Peoples, after they gathered information from all the relevant dicasteries.

It is really in the preparation of those observations, and the evaluation of them by the Congregation that the process facilitates the type of balancing that is necessary to allow for diversity on a local level without unnecessarily sacrificing the unity of discipline that the bishops are called to preserve.

That balancing, admittedly not always perfect, requires that the competent entities in the Curia have, to the maximum extent possible, accurate information concerning the realities of the local Church. While not always true in the smaller Pontifical Councils, most dicasteries divide the world geographically or linguistically, allowing the development of some expertise concerning the local Churches. That was certainly the case with the Secretariat of State, which presumably would have been one of the "interested dicasteries" always consulted.

The process of gathering reliable information about the Church at the local level was certainly advanced by the internationalization of the Curia, not only with respect to those who work in the various dicasteries, but also those who are members or consultors. One can only speculate on the impact that the present hiring freeze at the Vatican might have in this area, especially when coupled with a reluctance among diocesan bishops – facing clergy shortages in their diocese – to release priests for Curial service. One wonders as well how the Holy Father's desire to rotate staff in and out of the Curia, in an effort to avoid the risk of careerism, might have an impact in this area.

The process of gathering essential information about the situation in local churches throughout the world is certainly facilitated by the quinquennial *ad limina* visits of bishops. Many episcopal conferences seem to have recognized that the process can similarly be facilitated by more frequent visits to the Curial offices by conference leadership or delegations, giving the dicasteries a more expeditious opportunity to clarify ambiguities or to provide details about particular circumstances existing in the Churches of the relevant region.

Unfortunately, for many episcopal conferences, and particularly those at a greater distance or with fewer financial resources, those face-to-face exchanges have not always been an option. With advances in telecommunications, however, one can speculate that many more will be able to take part in an easier give-and-take. In the 1990s, questions about a proposed decree would be passed on to the pertinent Congregation, who would forward it to the Nuncio who would forward it to the conference, and then the response would return by the same route. Now, an email could potentially resolve the matter in minutes.

The *recognitio* has by no means been immune to criticism. Some, for example, have claimed that the *recognitio* has been used for ulterior purposes, "including that of imposing on local churches a discipline which they themselves had not voted to assume."[52] It has been argued that "using the process to impose

52 James H. Provost, "Title II: Groupings of Particular Churches [cc. 431-439]," in *The Code of Canon Law: A Text and Commentary*, eds., James A. Coriden, Thomas J. Green, Donald E. Heintschel (Mahwah, NJ: Paulist Press, 1985) 350-377, 362.

on the faithful practices they did not dream of assuming is likely to promote disharmony between the universal Church and the pertinent group of particular churches."[53] Judging from a reluctance that I have perceived among bishops to propose complementary legislation, or to update or modify existing legislation based on a fear of what might come back from Rome, I know that the above-cited critique was not only one commentator's lament.

Others were critical of the amount of time that it would take before a decree or set of statutes would be granted the *recognitio* and drew the conclusion that the delays were indicators that some at the Holy See valued neither the episcopal conferences nor their legislative acts. An examination of the relevant portions of the *Regolamento* for the PCLT[54] would suggest that the opposite conclusion should be reached – i.e., that the amount of time taken in the examination of statutes and decrees actually bespeaks a deep respect for the episcopal conference or particular council and for the decrees and statutes they issue.

The process of review is highly labor intensive. After an initial review by the President of the PCLT, the decree or statute is usually assigned to an official of the Congregation for an in-depth examination and the preparation of a draft response. That proposed response, as well as the text of the decree or statutes, would be ordinarily reviewed by the whole staff and a lively discussion would ensue at the *Congresso*, the weekly meeting of the whole staff. Where an examination at the full *Congresso* was for any reason not going to be feasible, an abbreviated process for examination was put in place, with the decree or statute being once again thoroughly examined by one staff member, then reviewed with a single colleague, then presented to the undersecretary and secretary for comments and, finally, sent to the President for a decision.

When serious questions arose, or the complexity of the subject matter so required (consider, for example, the USCCB's *Essential Norms*), it would not be uncommon for the matter to be referred to two or three consultors who would be asked for written comments.[55] The consultors could be chosen by reason of their

53 John G. Johnson, "Title II: Groupings of Particular Churches [cc. 431-459] in *New Commentary on the Code of Canon Law: A Text and Commentary*, eds., John Beal, James Coriden, Thomas Green (New York/Mahwah, NJ: Paulist Press, 2000) 566-609, 559, fn. 82.

54 See the text of Articles 19-22 and 25 of the *Regolamento del Pontificio Consiglio per i Testi legislativi*, (referring to nn. 19-22) cited in J. Herranz, "Il Pontificio Consiglio per i Testi Legislativi: Natura, Competenze e Metodo di Lavoro," *Slovenská spoločnosť kanonického práva* 12 (2004). See http://www.vatican.va/roman_curia/pontifical_councils/intrptxt/documents/rc_pc_intrptxt_doc_20040809_pc-intrptxt_it.html.

55 See the above-cited text of Article 19 of the *Regolamento del Pontificio Consiglio per i Testi legislativi*, quoted in J. Herranz, "Il Pontificio Consiglio per i Testi Legislativi: Natura, Competenze e Metodo di Lavoro," *Slovenská spoločnosť kanonického práva* 12 (2004). See http://www.vatican.va/roman_curia/pontifical_councils/intrptxt/documents/rc_pc_intrptxt_doc_20040809_pc-intrptxt_it.html.

expertise in the subject matter, or their knowledge of the particular situation addressed by the episcopal conference, or even for linguistics reasons. Whenever the consultors manifested a serious difference in opinion, they would be invited to come to the PCLT for a *consulta*, where the group of experts would be expanded from two to up to six. The amount of time devoted to the process, including that of the staff, the experts, and the superiors of the PCLT, is enormous. What at times can appear to be curial stubbornness or intransigence from one perspective may actually be evidence of a real respect for the local legislator and a deep desire to produce the best result possible as a true manifestation of *communio*.

In writing and speaking about the PCLT, Cardinal Herranz would often stress that the role of the Pontifical Council in the *recognitio* process was purely one of service – the object was not to impose norms but to help a conference to achieve the end it desired and to promulgate decrees that truly complemented the universal norms in a way that respected the local ecclesial context. It might be helpful to remember that not every episcopal conference has available to it the canonical resources that are found in the United States.

Through no fault of their own, many conferences really struggled with the new role given to them by the 1983 Code; they found it difficult to issue statutes and decrees. A chronological examination of the complementary legislation issued in the last thirty years reveals that many of the early norms were technically awkward and suggests something of a reluctance on the part of the conferences to legislate. The early general decrees often seemed more like position papers than legislative acts. While the *CIC* was asking the conferences to enter into discussions that would produce national norms, the temptation was to skirt the more difficult issues by forming norms that simply deferred to the decision of individual diocesan bishops.

While those decrees received the *recognitio* (one can only imagine how difficult it must have been to deal with the onslaught of requests for the *recognitio* in the years immediately following the promulgation of the Code), it seems that there developed a sense that there were advantages to be gained from challenging the conferences to tackle the precise issues at hand (and only the issues targeted by the canons) and to engage in the collaborative dialogue that would allow them to develop a unified normative approach to common pastoral problems.

The results seem to have been positive. While one would hope that the improvement could partially be attributed to the give-and-take with the Holy See in the *recognitio* process, much could be attributed to the work of canonical scholars who have collected, categorized, and commented upon the complementary norms[56] and statutes[57] that have been granted the *recognitio*. Those collections seem to have really helped bishops and conferences to grasp what was being asked of them and the opportunity that was being given to them.

At the same time, there seems to be a growing awareness that it may be counterproductive to insist on a one-size-fits-all approach, especially when dealing with the larger conferences or with countries exhibiting significant internal cultural differences. One wonders how many forests were lost in the effort to get the bishops of the United States to either decide upon a common age of confirmation, or else accept the default norm (confirmation around the age of reason). The norm that resulted – allowing each bishop to decide – is not particularly satisfying from the juridical point of view, but it certainly broke open a logjam that possibly, if not probably, would have continued to dominate discussion for years.

Thirty years into this delicate balancing act, it seems that the conferences and dicasteries may be hitting their stride at both the local and universal levels. One thinks, for example, of local difficulties that have been addressed by conferences taking advantage of the option provided in c. 455 to seek a special mandate to legislate in an area not foreseen in the *CIC* or subsequent universal legislation, but also in areas that are the subject of a special mandate.

Consider, for example, the experience of the USCCB's *Essential Norms*. Prescinding from any judgment on the content of the norms, it would seem fair to state that the exceptional give-and-take that characterized the *recognitio* process in that instance has resulted in a much deeper appreciation of penal law at the local level and a much deeper recognition in Rome (and elsewhere) that the universal law of the Church in that area was in need of revision and/or development. The request of the USCCB for a special mandate to issue a decree in this area, and the process that ensued, seems to have successfully brought the attention of the Holy See to the subject of the abuse of minors in a way that not only resulted in a more fruitful collaboration between the Holy See and the USCCB, but also strengthened the universal *communio* by providing a stimulus and framework for addressing a challenge that was global (even if not initially perceived as such). The process produced consequences not only for the local church but also for the Church universal, with the Holy See finding itself in a better position to be of assistance to other particular Churches, even in circumstances quite distinct from those in the United States.

56 Jose Tomas Martín de Agar and Luis Navarro, *Legislazione delle Conferenze Episcopali complementare al C.I.C,* (2nd ed. updated) Coletti a S. Pietro 2009; complementary legislation of the English-speaking conferences can be found as an appendix of the *Annotated Code of Canon Law*, ed. Caparros et al, (Montreal, PQ: Wilson & LaFleur, 2004).
57 Ivan C. Iban, *Gli Statuti delle Conferenze episcopali*, Padova CEDAM 1989 (the work consists of two volumes: 1 (for European conferences) and 2 (for conferences from the Americas).

While not having the same universal impact, the special mandate envisioned in c. 455 and the *recognitio* process seem to have been used effectively to address an issue that had been creating significant tension between the conferences of Germany, Austria, and Switzerland and the Holy See, stemming from local decisions addressing the status of Catholics who, for financial reasons particular to the civil law of those countries, had declared to civil authorities that they were no longer Catholic.

In September of 2012, the German Episcopal Conference promulgated a decree, having received the *recognitio* of the Holy See, which addressed this matter in a manner that reflected the distinct situation of the *Kirchensteuer* in Germany, without offending the general theological and canonical principles that had been of concern to the Holy See The precision required in the drafting of the decree, as well as the give-and-take and consultation involved in *recognitio* process, seem to have resulted in a situation that promoted understanding and *communio*.[58]

5. Conclusion

At a distance of fifty years from the closing of the Second Vatican Council, and at a time when Pope Francis seems to be speaking so often about synodality and attributing even greater emphasis to episcopal conferences, the canonical structures given flesh in cc. 450-455 can be expected to be of increasing importance in promoting a relationship of reciprocity that concretely preserves and manifests the Church's identity as the *communio ecclesiarum* described by the Council Fathers. With more than thirty years of experience of promulgating norms that address local needs while maintaining the unity of discipline that preserves that *communio*, today's episcopal conferences can be expected to assume the responsibility that has been, or will be, attributed to them.

While it is not yet clear what will happen to the PCTL in the wake of current reorganization of the Curia, the role that it has played in assisting episcopal conferences, in assisting the other dicasteries of the Holy See, and in fostering a unity of discipline, would seem to be essential. While one could imagine that the technical juridical roles described in Arts. 157 and 158 of *Pastor bonus* could be assigned to some other dicastery or office, it would be unfortunate to lose the

58 Since then, not surprisingly, the possibility of following that path has been informally suggested by some in the Curia as an avenue for resolving other issues in which the interest of the local Church seems to diverge from that of the universal Church, particularly when they relate to particular historical circumstances or social phenomena in the territory of a single episcopal conference Recalling the frustration that has been experienced on both sides of the Atlantic over parish closings and the disposition of Church buildings one wonders whether a request for a mandate for a general decree setting forth criteria for parish closings in the particular circumstances of the United States would have any impact in resolving the perceived tension.

PCTL's unique connection to the Code, to the process that resulted in the Code, and ultimately to the Council. Inasmuch as the episcopal conferences have developed an expertise in promulgating appropriate norms since the introduction of the 1983 Code, the PCTL has continued to build upon its experience in a way that maximizes the service that it offers directly to the Holy Father and the Curia that serves him, and indirectly to the local Churches throughout the world.

SEMINAR

INTERECCLESIAL STRUCTURES IN THE EASTERN CODE

Reverend Jobe J. Abbass, O.F.M. Conv.

At the sixty-eighth annual convention of the Canon Law Society of America in Fort Worth, TX (October 9-12, 2006), the theme concerning structures foreseen by the Eastern Code to foster interecclesial communion was treated for a first time.[1] The impetus for the conference came from the 2001 apostolic letter *Novo millennio ineunte* (n. 45), in which Pope John Paul II urged that, to foster and strengthen ecclesial communion, greater use be made of the structures of collaboration foreseen by canon law. His Holiness stated:

> Communion must be cultivated and extended day by day and at every level in the structures of each Church's life. There, relations between Bishops, priests and deacons, between Pastors and the entire People of God, between clergy and Religious, between associations and ecclesial movements must all be clearly characterized by communion. To this end, the structures of participation envisaged by Canon Law ... must be ever more highly valued.[2]

As this passage implies, the pope did not intend to promote only collaborative structures foreseen by the Latin Church's *Code of Canon Law*. In fact, with specific regard to structures for interecclesial collaboration, the Latin Code does not contemplate such possibilities.[3] On the other hand, the Eastern Code has prescribed a variety of norms whereby bishops of different Churches *sui iuris* exercising power in the same territory are to collaborate so as to further a unity of action and interecclesial communion. Building on the same theme already advocated by Vatican II in *Orientalium Ecclesiarum* (*OE*) 4 and *Christus Dominus*

1 J. Abbass, "The Eastern Code at the Service of Interecclesial Communion," *CLSA Proceedings* 68 (Washington, DC: Canon Law Society of America, 2006) 65-86.

2 John Paul II, *Novo millennio ineunte*, January 6, 2001: *Acta Apostolicae Sedis (AAS)* 93 (2001) 266-309. For this English translation, see John Paul II, apostolic letter *Novo millennio ineunte* (Vatican City: Vatican Press, 2001) 60-61. Unless otherwise indicated, foreign language translations are the author's.

3 See also: M. Brogi, "Commento," *Ius Ecclesiae* 6 (1994) 837. Commenting on the participation of Latin bishops in the Assembly of Catholic Ordinaries of the Holy Land, the author states: "Inasmuch as they are Latin, these prelates exercise their functions according to the legislation of the Latin Church, which does not contemplate cases of interecclesial collaboration...."

(*CD*) 38 (6),[4] the norms often invoke and urge interecclesial collaboration among bishops by way of this formula: *collatis consiliis cum episcopis Eparchialis aliarum Ecclesiarum sui iuris, qui in eodem territorio potestatem suam exercent* (after having consulted with the eparchial bishops of the other Churches *sui iuris* exercising their power in the same territory). In the 2006 study, it was argued that these Eastern norms also implicitly involve the collaboration of Latin bishops because, unlike canon 1 of the *Codex Iuris Canonici* (*CIC*), canon 1 of the *Codex Canonum Ecclesiarum Orientalium* (*CCEO*) establishes an interrelationship of the two Codes of the universal Church. *CCEO* canon 1 states: "The canons of this Code affect all and solely the Eastern Catholic Churches, unless, with regard to relations with the Latin Church, it is expressly (*expresse*) established otherwise." The paper focused on twelve Eastern norms which foresee forums of collaboration among all the Churches *sui iuris*, including the Latin Church.[5] It was then argued that, besides the explicit reference to the Latin Church in *CCEO* canon 322 §1, in at least five other cases (*CCEO* cc. 84 §1; 202; 720 §3; 1013 §2; and 1405 §3) the Eastern draftsmen had implied that the Latin Church came within the intended scope of those norms without being, in each instance, explicitly named.[6] Indeed, in two cases (*CCEO* cc. 322 and 720 §3), consultation with bishops of our sister Orthodox Churches was also encouraged.

The argument that *CCEO* canon 1 sets up an interrelationship of the Codes and that the Latin Church is implicitly included when the Eastern Code legislates regarding interecclesial matters was not universally accepted. Over the years, several authors argued that the rule expressed in *CCEO* canon 1 was peremptory

4 *OE* 4 states: "But ordinaries (*hierarchae*) of the various individual (*particularium*) Churches who exercise jurisdiction in the same territory should take care to further unity of action, after taking counsel among themselves in periodic meetings. They should also take care, with united forces, to help common activities for furthering the cause of religion more easily and safeguarding the rule of life of the clergy more effectively." *CD* 38 (6) states: "It is earnestly recommended that, in promoting the discipline of their own Church in their synods, the prelates of the Eastern Churches should, for the more efficacious encouragement of works for the good of religion, also take into account the common good of the whole territory where many Churches of different rites exist, by exchanging views in inter-ritual meetings, according to the norms to be determined by competent authority." Translations from Norman P. Tanner, ed., *Decrees of the Ecumenical Councils* (London and Washington: Sheed & Ward and Georgetown University Press, 1990) 2: 901 and 937, respectively.

5 The *CCEO* norms examined were: cc. 84 §1; 202; 322 §1; 332 §2; 622 §1; 720 §3; 784; 792; 904 §2; 1013 §2; 1068 §1; and 1405 §3.

6 Cf., however, M. Brogi, "Assemblies of Hierarchs of Several Churches *Sui Iuris*," in *A Guide to the Eastern Code (A Commentary on the Code of Canons of the Eastern Churches)*, ed. George Nedungatt (Rome: Pontificio Istituto Orientale, 2002) 252, note 3. The author states: "Therefore, the Latin bishops have CCEO c. 322 as the only codical norm relating to collaboration with bishops of the other Churches *sui iuris*."

and intended to exclude the Latin Church unless it was explicitly established.[7] Other canonists maintained that the interrelationship of the Codes was broader and that the Legislator implicitly established it through the use of the expression "Church *sui iuris*" or even by reason of the nature of the matter (*ex natura rei*).[8] Then, on December 8, 2011, the Pontifical Council for Legislative Texts published an official, Explanatory Note regarding the meaning of *CCEO* canon 1 and the Eastern Code's application in relation to the Latin Church. After recognizing "that the express (*expresse*) mention of the Latin Church in the (*CCEO*) canons can occur both in an 'explicit' and an 'implicit' way," the Pontifical Council concluded:

> According to this distinction, that appears reasonably confirmed by the normative provisions of *CCEO*, besides the canons in which the Latin Church is "explicitly" named, there are also other canons of the same code in which it is included "implicitly", if one takes into account the text and context of the norm, as *CCEO* canon 1499 requires. It is therefore necessary to begin with the expressions contained in the norm to be interpreted and with the context in which it is found to determine if the Latin Church is implicitly included in it or not. This is the case, for example, of the *CCEO* norms that concern juridical relations with the various Churches of the one Catholic Church.
>
> Consequently, one must hold that the Latin Church is implicitly included by analogy each time that *CCEO* explicitly uses the term "Church *sui iuris*" in the context of interecclesial relations. We say "by analogy" keeping in mind that the characteristics of the Latin Church, though not coinciding completely

7 See M. Brogi, "Licenza presunta della Santa Sede per il cambiamento di Chiesa *sui iuris*," *Revista Española de Derecho Canonico* 50 (1993) 645; Peter Erdö, "Questioni interrituali (interecclesiali) del diritto dei sacramenti (battesimo e cresima)," *Periodica de re canonica* 84 (1996) 317-318; and P. Gefaell, "Impegno della Congregazione per le Chiese orientali a favore delle comunità orientali in diaspora," in Luis Okulik (ed.), *Nuove terre e nuove Chiese: Le comunità di fedeli orientali in diaspora* (Venice: Marcianum Press, 2008) 137-138.

8 See D. Salachas, "Problematiche interrituali nei due codici orientale e latino," in *Apollinaris* 75 (1994) 641-648; C.G. Fürst, "Interdipendenza del diritto canonico latino ed orientale," in K. Bharanikulangara (ed.), *Il Diritto Canonico Orientale nell'ordinamento ecclesiale* (Vatican City: Libreria Editrice Vaticana, 1995) 21-24 and 28-30; J. Abbass, "The Interrelationship of the Latin and Eastern Codes," *The Jurist* 58 (1998) 12-20; R. Metz, "Preliminary Canons," in G. Nedungatt (ed.), *A Guide to the Eastern Code (A Commentary on the Code of Canons of the Eastern Churches)* (Rome: Pontifical Oriental Institute, 2002) 72 and L. Lorusso, "L'ambito d'applicazione del Codice dei Canoni delle Chiese Orientali: Commento sistematico al can. 1 del CCEO," *Angelicum* 82 (2005) 471-472.

with those of the Church *sui iuris* described in canons 27 and 28 §1 of *CCEO*, are nevertheless, in this regard, substantially similar.[9]

By this official interpretation, the Explanatory Note allows for a more extensive application of the Eastern Code to the Latin Church at least with regard to those *CCEO* canons in which the expression "Church *sui iuris*" is employed in the context of interecclesial relations.[10] As it happens, with the exception of *CCEO* canon 1405 §3, the Eastern canons examined in the 2006 study referring to interecclesial collaboration contained the expression "Church *sui iuris*." However, in referring to the "other canons of the same (Eastern) Code in which it (Latin Church) is included implicitly," the Note does not limit them to only those canons that mention "Church *sui iuris*." In fact, it would seem that, in opening the door to a broader application of the Eastern Code to the Latin Church, it could be argued that Eastern norms, like *CCEO* canon 1405 §3, which do not contain the expression "Church *sui iuris*," may still implicitly include also the Latin Church by reason of the nature of the matter such as interecclesial collaboration. In those cases, the norms need not necessarily be addressed to the hierarchical authorities of a "Church *sui iuris*" or even contain that expression.

The purpose of this paper will be to outline the many Eastern norms that implicitly include the Latin Church among the Eastern Catholic Churches *sui iuris* in the context of promoting structures for interecclesial collaboration. Regarding the twelve canons examined in the 2006 study, part 1 will review the five which the Eastern draftsmen themselves had implied included the Latin Church. Three more *CCEO* canons will be added to this list that calls for the active collaboration among the hierarchical authorities of the Eastern and Latin Churches. In all these cases, the conclusions drawn in the first study are only supported by the 2011 Explanatory Note. Part 2 will look at other Eastern norms which prescribe interecclesial collaboration by way of consultation among the "Churches *sui iuris*," that is Eastern and Latin, present in the same territory or region. Collaboration by way of mutual assistance among the hierarchical authorities of the different "Churches *sui iuris*" is the subject of part 3 in which three other *CCEO* norms are considered. Finally, in part 4, two Eastern norms that urge collaboration among the laity and religious are mentioned. Although the first canon (*CCEO* c. 405) contains the expression "Church *sui iuris*," it addresses the Churches' laity rather than their hierarchical authorities. The other canon (*CCEO* c. 416) is directed at hierarchical authorities but does not contain the expression "Church *sui iuris*." In both situations, however, it will be argued that the canons encourage collaboration among the Eastern and Latin Churches *ex natura rei*. Besides allowing

9 *Communicationes* 43 (2011) 316.

10 Of course, that does not mean that all 243 mentions of "Church *sui iuris*" in the Eastern Code implicitly include the Latin Church. More than half certainly do not. See J. Abbass, *The Eastern Code (Canon 1) and Its Application to the Latin Church* (Bangalore: Dharmaram Publications, 2014) 14-132.

for collaborative structures among the hierarchies of the various "Churches *sui iuris*," the 2011 Explanatory Note also seems to support the possibility of inter-ecclesial collaborative structures at the level of the Churches' laity and religious institutes because of the very nature and purpose of the matters at issue.

1 - *CCEO* Norms Promoting Unity of Action and Interecclesial Communion

1.1) Fostering Unity of Action in Patriarchal Territories (CCEO c. 84 §1)

The first norm, Eastern canon 84 §1, prescribes that Eastern Catholic patriarchs and their bishops, in consultation with patriarchs and bishops of other Churches *sui iuris* exercising their power in the same territory, are to promote among themselves, as well as their faithful, cooperative efforts and forums that will strengthen Church unity. With *OE* 4 and *CD* 38 (6) as sources, *CCEO* canon 84 §1 states:

> The patriarch is to take the greatest care that both he and the eparchial bishops of the Church over which he presides, after consultation with the patriarchs and eparchial bishops of the other Churches *sui iuris* who exercise their power in the same territory especially in the assemblies foreseen by law, promote a unity of action among themselves and with all the Christian faithful of any Church *sui iuris*, and, through concerted efforts, sustain common works that intend to promote more expeditiously the good of religion, to protect more effectively ecclesiastical discipline, and also to foster more harmoniously the unity of all Christians.

Within the *Pontificia Commissio Codici Iuris Canonici Orientalis Recognoscendo* (*PCCICOR*), the special study group entrusted with the *denua recognitio* of the schema containing this norm had decided to qualify the expression "Churches *sui iuris*" by adding an explicit reference to the Latin Church.[11] Subsequently, however, the *Coetus de coordinatione* omitted this explicit reference from the canon. While the reported proceedings of *PCCICOR* give no reason for the omission, it could hardly have meant to exclude the Latin Church from the collaborative scope and sense canon 84 §1 obviously conveys to all Churches *sui iuris* in the same territory. Indeed, it is more probable that the *Coetus de coordi-*

11 See *Nuntia* 22 (1986) 64 (c. 52 §1). Canon 52 §1 stated: "The patriarch is to take the greatest care that both he and the hierarchs of the Church over which he presides, after consultation with the patriarchs and hierarchs of the other Churches *sui iuris*, also the Latin, exercising their power in the same territory especially in the assemblies established by law, promote a unity of action among themselves, clerics and other Christian faithful ascribed to any Church *sui iuris*, and, through concerted efforts, sustain common works that intend to promote more expeditiously the good of religion, to protect more effectively ecclesiastical discipline, and also to foster more harmoniously the unity of all Christians."

natione considered the explicit mention of the Latin Church to be unnecessary. Given the norms's context and purpose, the inclusion and consultation of Latin bishops is necessarily to be implied.[12] The Pontifical Council's Explanatory Note seems only to affirm this interpretation that would favor a collaborative structure among the Churches *sui iuris*, including the Latin Church, to foster ecclesiastical discipline and unity.

1.2) Interecclesial Collaboration of Bishops in the Same Territory (CCEO c. 202)

Again based upon *OE* 4, *CCEO* canon 202 is essentially a revision of the former Eastern norm in *Cleri sanctitati* (*CS*) canon 4.[13] Urging a collaborative forum for bishops of various Churches *sui iuris* exercising their power in the same territory, *CCEO* canon 202 states:

> The eparchial bishops of several Churches *sui iuris* exercising power in the same territory are to ensure that through the exchange of views in periodic meetings, they foster unity of action and, by combined resources, help advance common works more readily to promote the good of religion and more effectively safeguard ecclesiastical discipline.

Within *PCCICOR*, an initial formulation of this Eastern norm was contained in canon 25 of the 1979 provisional canons *De episcopis*.[14] The study group revised *CS* canon 4 on the basis of the wording contained in *OE* 4, but declined to adopt the proposal of some consultors that the wording be effectively changed to make this type of episcopal collaboration mandatory.[15] It is most probable that the proposal was not adopted in order to safeguard the autonomy of the individual Churches *sui iuris*. In any event, after canon 25 subsequently appeared as canon 200 of the 1986 *Schema Codicis Iuris Canonici Orientalis* (*SCICO*),

12 See also: Dimitrios Salachas, "Le Chiese patriarcali," in Pio V. Pinto (ed.), *Commento al Codice dei Canoni delle Chiese Orientali* (Vatican City: Libreria Editrice Vaticana, 2001) 95. In his commentary on *CCEO* c. 84 §1, the author states: "In various *CCEO* canons, the wish is expressed that, in establishing particular law, one proceed '*collatis consiliis cum Episcopis eparchialibus aliarum Ecclesiarum,*' that is to say, in agreement with the eparchial bishops of the other Churches *sui iuris* involved, including the Latin Church."

13 *CS* c. 4 stated: "Local hierarchs having jurisdiction in the same territory are, by mutual consultation, to foster a unity of action among the clergy of the various rites, and, by combined resources, they are to help advance common works to promote more expeditiously the good of religion and to safeguard more effectively the discipline of the clergy."

14 *Nuntia* 9 (1979) 22 (c. 25).

15 *Nuntia* 9 (1979) 23 (c. 25). Regarding the consultors' proposal, the study group's relator wrote: "Because of its importance, certain consultors wished that the word *curent*, that is found in the conciliar text, should be replaced by the expression *curare debent*. This proposal was voted upon separately, receiving 3 *placet*, 4 *non placet* and 1 abstention."

the *Coetus de expensione observationum,* entrusted with the overall review of the 1986 *SCICO,* accepted one last change to indicate that eparchial bishops are to work collaboratively to safeguard not simply clerical discipline but, rather, ecclesiastical discipline in general.[16]

Within the context of collaborative efforts among the various Churches *sui iuris* to foster a unity of action in patriarchal territories (*CCEO* c. 84 §1), *CCEO* canon 202 only serves to reinforce such a goal on the episcopal level. However, rather than being limited to collaborative ventures within patriarchal territories, such episcopal cooperation can also find structural expression in many nations or regions of the diaspora where individual Eastern Catholic bishops representing various Churches *sui iuris* are present. In Canada, for example, in addition to being members of the Canadian Conference of Catholic Bishops, Eastern Catholic bishops of the Ukrainian, Slovak, Melkite, Chaldean, Syro-Malabar and Maronite Churches *sui iuris* might find the collaborative forum suggested by *CCEO* canon 202 to be quite useful. In either case, whether inside or outside a patriarchal territory, to foster a unity of ecclesial action among Churches *sui iuris* in any particular region, *CCEO* canon 202 would effectively intend the collaborative input of Eastern as well as Latin bishops present there.[17]

1.3) Assemblies of Hierarchs of Various Churches Sui Iuris (CCEO c. 322 §1)

In the light of *OE* 4 and the Eastern norms (cc. 84 §1 and 202) prescribing interecclesial collaboration, *CCEO* canon 322 establishes a unique forum for such cooperation to foster a unity of action in the same region or nation.[18] *CCEO* canon 322 §1 states:

> Where is seems advisable in the judgment of the Apostolic See, periodic assemblies are to be held of patriarchs, metropolitans of metropolitan Churches *sui iuris*, eparchial bishops, and, if the statutes so state, other local hierarchs of various

16 *Nuntia* 28 (1989) 48 (c. 200).

17 See also: René Metz, "Preliminary Canons," in George Nedungatt, (ed.) *A Guide to the Eastern Code (A Commentary on the Code of Canons of the Eastern Churches)* (Rome: Pontificio Istituto Orientale, 2002) 72. The author states: "However, there are also other canons which, without using the formula, include the Latin Church in the expression "Church *sui iuris*"... Certainly, where the legislator prescribes unity of action among the various Churches *sui iuris*, particularly in the same territory, the Latin Church is also intended (see, for example, cc. 84 §1, 202, 330 §2, 622 §1)."

18 See also: Marco Brogi, "Assemblies of Hierarchs of Several Churches *Sui Iuris*," in George Nedungatt, (ed.) *A Guide to the Eastern Code (A Commentary on the Code of Canons of the Eastern Churches)* (Rome: Pontificio Istituto Orientale, 2002) 251. The author states: "It (c. 322) completes the directives and prescriptions of CCEO, as for example in cc. 84, 99 §2, 202, to patriarchs, metropolitans and eparchial bishops to meet with their colleagues of other Churches *sui iuris* who exercise power in the same territory and formulate and coordinate united action."

> Churches *sui iuris*, even of the Latin Church, exercising their authority in the same nation or region. These assemblies are to be convoked at regular intervals by the patriarch or another authority designated by the Apostolic See. The purpose of these meetings is that, by sharing the insights of wisdom born of experience and by the exchange of views, the pooling of their resources is achieved for the common good of the Churches, so that unity of action is fostered, common works are facilitated, the good of religion is more readily promoted and ecclesiastical discipline is preserved more effectively.

Within *PCCICOR*, the *Coetus de sacra hierarchia* proposed the draft of this norm as canon 292 §1 of the 1984 *Schema canonum de constitutione hierarchica Ecclesiarum orientalium* (1984 Schema). While underlining the importance of the conciliar directives in *OE* 4 and *CD* 38 (6) regarding interritual assemblies, the study group's *Praenotanda* to the 1984 Schema highlighted that the work of such assemblies already established in Eastern regions "is of great benefit to the salvation of souls and to each Church *sui iuris* that takes part in these assemblies."[19] During the *denua recognitio* of the norm, the expert study group noted, in particular, the distinction to be made between interecclesial assemblies and Latin episcopal conferences. They stated: "Indeed, we are dealing with a new, atypical institution, common to all the 'Ecclesiae rituales sui iuris,' Latin included, present together in the same territory, and directly dependent only upon that authority which is 'suprema relationum interecclesialium arbitra' (OE art. 4)."[20] Subsequently, the Eastern norm on interecclesial assemblies became *SCICO* canon 320 §1 and was reviewed by the *Coetus de expensione observationum*. Since the canon seemed to confine the establishment of interrecclesial assemblies to patriarchal territories, one consultor questioned whether or not the norm applied to Eastern Catholic bishops in the diaspora. In response, the *Coetus,* while noting that the canon did intend to limit such assemblies "to regions

19 *Nuntia* 19 (1984) 19.

20 *Nuntia* 23 (1986) 103 (c. 292 §1).

where the Eastern rites are prevalent," decided to begin the canon with the clause "Where it seems advisable in the judgment of the Apostolic See."[21]

As a result, it seems logical to argue that *CCEO* canon 322 §1 prescribes the establishment of interecclesial assemblies of hierarchs not only in patriarchal territories but also in regions where, according to the judgment of the Roman See, the Eastern Churches *sui iuris* are prevalent.[22] Until now, however, no assemblies of hierarchs have been established in the West.[23] Besides the participation of hierarchs from other Eastern Churches *sui iuris*, the norm explicitly allows for the collaboration of Latin ordinaries exercising their authority in the same region. Indeed, regarding the possible members of interecclesial assemblies, *CCEO* canon 322 §4 even foresees the participation of hierarchs of those Churches with which the See of Rome is not yet in full communion.[24]

1.4) Deciding upon Grave Necessity for General Absolution (CCEO c. 720 §3)

CCEO canon 720 §3 presents another example of interecclesial collaboration that could conceivably take an institutional or structural form. According to the norm, if there is a "grave necessity," general absolution can be imparted to

---

21 *Nuntia* 28 (1989) 57-58 (c. 320). The consultor's observation, together with the *Coetus'* response stated: "The canon seems to want to create a 'counterpart' to the Latin episcopal conferences. In any case, it does not adequately reflect the situation of the Eastern Catholic bishops constituted outside the territories of the patriarchal Churches. These bishops, according to *CIC* c. 450 §1, if invited to the episcopal conferences, have a consultative vote there; on the other hand, they are excluded from participating in the 'Conventus' described in this canon because they do not exercise their power 'in eadem natione vel regione.' What is the 'mens' of the legislator on this subject? Perhaps Eastern Catholic bishops must have a deliberative vote in local episcopal conferences or does the future CICO (Eastern Code) intend to institute for these bishops their own 'conventus' distinct from the episcopal conferences of the Latin Church?" R. (Response): "We accept the substance of the proposal according to the 'mens' of the canon, which is that of circumscribing it to the regions in which the Eastern rites are prevalent: which is expressed juridically by having the canon begin with the following clause: Ubi id de iudicio Sedis Apostolicae opportunum videtur..."

22 For a detailed treatment of this position, see J. Abbass, "Assemblies of Hierarchs for Eastern Catholic Bishops in the Diaspora," *Studia canonica* 40 (2006) 371-396.

23 For a current list of assemblies, in the sense of *CCEO* c. 322, see *Annuario Pontificio* (2014) 1093. They are as follows: 1) Assembly of the Catholic Hierarchy of Egypt; 2) Assembly of the Catholic Patriarchs and Bishops of Lebanon; 3) Assembly of the Catholic Hierarchy in Syria; 4) Assembly of the Catholic Ordinaries of the Holy Land; 5) Assembly of Catholic Bishops of Iraq; and 6) Iranian Episcopal Conference.

24 *CCEO* c. 322 §4 states: "Every assembly of hierarchs of several Churches *sui iuris* is to draw up its own statutes in which, as far as possible, the participation of the hierarchs of those Churches which are not yet in full communion with the Catholic Church is also to be fostered. The statutes, to have force, must be approved by the Apostolic See."

several penitents together without prior individual confessions.[25] Regarding the competence to decide whether or not such necessity exists, Eastern canon 720 §3 states:

> The eparchial bishop is competent to decide whether such grave necessity exists. He can, after having held consultation with patriarchs and eparchial bishops of other Churches *sui iuris* who exercise their power in the same territory, determine the cases of such necessity even through general prescripts.

Within *PCCICOR*, the draftsmen explained the rationale for the norm. They stated: "Apart from the case of danger of death or another grave necessity, 'general absolution' cannot be imparted except according to the norms of particular law established by the legislative authority of each Church *sui iuris*. In making these norms, regarding the proposed canon, a consideration of both the Catholic faithful's common good and a healthy ecumenism is required, after having consulted with hierarchs of the other rites, the Orthodox hierarchs not excluded."[26] At no point in the canon's reported *iter* was the bishop's consultation with other bishops, including the Orthodox, an issue. Therefore, while the eparchial bishop has the competence to decide the circumstances under which a grave necessity exists in order to impart general absolution, he can also opt to discern those situations after having consulted with bishops of other Churches *sui iuris* who exercise their power in the same territory. From the perspective of a healthy ecumenism, nothing precludes the Eastern bishop from consulting a local Orthodox bishop over the question as to whether or not a grave necessity exists for granting general absolution. If that is true, then certainly the norm has to imply that an Eastern bishop also confer with a Latin bishop, among the other Catholic bishops exercising their power in the same territory, about the same issue. Given this context, which would foster a unity of action regarding an important pastoral question for the entire Catholic Church, the use of the expression "Church *sui iuris*" in *CCEO* canon 720 §3 undoubtedly also implies the Latin Church. The Pontifical Council's 2011 Explanatory Note only affirms that plain meaning.

1.5) Interecclesial Common Fees and Offerings (CCEO c. 1013 §2)

Eastern canon 1013 §2 stipulates that, in the same territory, patriarchs and bishops of different Churches *sui iuris* are to work together to establish a uniform

25 *CCEO* c. 720 §2, 2° states: "There is a grave necessity, that is, if, considering the number of penitents, there is not a supply of priests present to administer the sacrament of penance to individual penitents within a reasonable time so that, through no fault of their own, they would be forced to forego the sacramental grace or the reception of the Divine Eucharist for a long time. The necessity is not considered sufficient when it is not possible for confessors to be available merely because of a large gathering of penitents such as can happen on some great feast day or pilgrimage."

26 *Nuntia* 10 (1980) 9.

rule regarding ecclesiastical taxes and offerings. The norm states: "Patriarchs and eparchial bishops of various Churches *sui iuris* exercising their power in the same territory are to take care that, after mutual consultation, the same norm is established regarding fees and offerings." During the review of this norm within *PCCICOR*, the following proposal was made: "We strongly urge that each rite be responsible for the designating of the taxes and offerings regarding their liturgical services and practices according to their particular custom."[27] While the special study group's response meant to safeguard the competence of each Church *sui iuris,* it also implied that Latin bishops came within the purview of the norm. The group stated: "(The proposal) is not accepted, in principle, maintaining as better *'eadem regula taxarum aut oblationum'* in a given territory and, at the same time, safeguarding the competence of each Church *sui iuris*. So, too, the consultor that observed 'for Easterners in the West, it is appropriate that they consult with the Latin bishops' can be satisfied."[28]

CCEO canon 1013 §2 is therefore another norm that provides a potential forum or structure for interecclesial cooperation. Given its legislative history, it is obvious that the canon implicitly prescribes the united efforts of both Eastern and Latin bishops in the same territory to reach a common agreement regarding taxes and offerings for ecclesiastical services. In this context of interecclesial relations, the use of the expression "Church *sui iuris*" in Eastern canon 1013 §2 is a clear example of where the Explanatory Note would surely infer collaboration and consultation also with bishops of the Latin Church.

1.6) Uniform Penal Laws (CCEO c. 1405 §3)

Inasmuch as the Latin Code affects only the Latin Church (see *CIC* c. 1), the rule in *CIC* canon 1316 that bishops are to see that penal laws in the same city or region are uniform is, at most, an interdiocesan norm in scope.[29] However, the parallel Eastern canon 1405 §3 regarding the establishment of penalties has interecclesial implications. This is by reason of *CCEO* canon 1 which sets up a possible interrelationship of the Codes not only because a norm speaks of "Churches *sui iuris*" but, also, on account of the very nature of the matter the norm regulates. An example of the latter, *CCEO* canon 1405 §3 states: "Insofar as it is possible, patriarchs and eparchial bishops are to take care that penal laws of particular law are uniform in the same territory."

Within *PCCICOR*, the *Coetus de delictis et poenis* formulated and intentionally added this norm among the provisional canons regarding penal sanctions because "it corresponds, among other things, also to the wishes of Vatican Council II, expressed in the decree *Orientalium Ecclesiarum* n. 4 ('*Hierarchae variarum*

27 *Nuntia* 18 (1984) 50 (c. 84 §2).

28 Ibid.

29 *CIC* c. 1316 states: "Insofar as possible, diocesan bishops are to take care that if penal laws must be issued, they are uniform in the same city or region."

Ecclesiarum... curent... unitatem actionis fovere...').''[30] During the *denua recognitio* of the draft norm, a motion was made to specify that, in Latin territories, Eastern bishops must consult with their Latin counterparts. The proposal, together with the response, stated:

> In §3, it ought to be made explicit that Eastern bishops in Latin rite countries must consult, regarding the case contemplated in the canon, together with Latin bishops.
>
> *It is not accepted* because the text is sufficiently clear in that regard, while the clause "*in quantum fieri potest*" safeguards the Eastern bishop from not going, by conforming to the penal discipline of the place, against Eastern penal law.[31]

Therefore, to the extent that it is possible, Eastern bishops, when establishing canonical penalties, are to ensure that penal laws are uniform in the same territory. Given the legislative history of *CCEO* canon 1405 §3, it should be clear that, without expressly naming them, Latin bishops also come, *ex natura rei*, within the scope of the interecclesial consultations intended by the norm. The expert study group entrusted with the review of the norm indicated that the norm is sufficiently clear in that regard without explicitly mandating it. Furthermore, although *OE* 4 is not an official source of *CCEO* canon 1405 §3, it clearly inspired the study group in its formulation so as to provide another forum for unity of action among the Eastern and Latin bishops of the Catholic Church.

1.7) A Common Program for Clerical Formation (CCEO c. 330 §2)

Regarding the elaboration of a program of formation for clerics, the Eastern Code applies the principle of subsidiarity by generally deferring to the superior authorities of the various Churches *sui iuris*. In a norm that is new to the Eastern legislation and unique to the Eastern Code, *CCEO* canon 330 §2 permits that program of clerical formation to be common to a region or nation or even with other Churches *sui iuris*. It states: "The formation program can, by common agreement, be common to an entire region or nation or even with other Churches *sui iuris*, provided care is taken that it is not detrimental to the specific character of the rites."

Within *PCCICOR*, the *Coetus de clericis et de magisterio ecclesiastico* (*Coetus de clericis*) first introduced the draft of this norm for a specific purpose. Its relator, George Nedungatt, stated: "Having regard for unity in diversity, §2 aims

30 *Nuntia* 12 (1981) 45 (c. 6 §3). Canon 6 §3 stated: "Insofar as it is possible, hierarchs are to take care that penal laws in the same city or region are to be uniform."

31 *Nuntia* 20 (1985) 17-18 (c. 5 §3). *Ex officio*, the expert study group also changed "*Hierarchae*" to "*Patriarchae et Episcopi eparchiales*" and specified that "§3 referred not to all penal laws, but only to particular penal laws." See ibid., 18.

at preventing undue fragmentation and waste of ecclesiastical resources in drawing up a Ratio."[32] Although some redactional changes were subsequently made to the norm during the *denua recognitio* of the 1981 Schema, the principle remained that, if needed (*si opus est*), the program of clerical formation could be established by an agreement common to an entire region, nation or even to other Churches *sui iuris*.[33] After the norm became *SCICO* canon 328 §2, it only underwent a minor reformulation before promulgation.[34]

Like many other Eastern norms that caution against harming the ritual expression and heritage of the various Churches *sui iuris* in the context of interecclesial relations, *CCEO* canon 330 §2 also aims to safeguard the Churches' *sui iuris* nature and status regarding any proposed common program for clerical training. Nevertheless, in an area where ecclesiastical resources could be joined to promote the common good and a unity of action, this Eastern norm allows for a collaborative effort among the Churches *sui iuris*, including the Latin Church, of a region or nation in determining a common program for clerical formation.

1.8) Seminary Admission to Students of Other Churches Sui Iuris (CCEO c. 333)

Regarding another example of interecclesial cooperation, *CCEO* canon 333 foresees that seminaries of one Church *sui iuris* can admit students from another Church *sui iuris*. While the norm does not see such a situation as preferable, it concretely helps in areas where eparchies may not be self-sufficient or where a pooling of formation personnel logically amounts to a wiser use of ecclesiastical resources. Unique to the Eastern Code, *CCEO* canon 333 states: "Even if it is preferable that a seminary, especially minor seminaries, be reserved to students of one Church *sui iuris*, on account of special circumstances, students of another Church *sui iuris* can be admitted into the same seminary."

Within *PCCICOR*, the *Coetus de clericis* proposed a first draft of this norm, although its formulation was not identical. Regarding the norm's objective, the study group's relator stated:

> A seminary that is constitutionally monoritual (that is reserved to one rite) may in special circumstances open its doors to candidates representing other rites. In that case, however, their formation in their own rite should be assured, according to canon 21 (now *CCEO* c. 343). The group discussed the pros and cons of monoritual and pluriritual seminary formation; no option was felt to be entirely free of disadvantages or difficul-

32 *Nuntia* 8 (1979) 71 (c. 4 §2).

33 See *Nuntia* 13 (1981) 94 (c. 9 §2) and *Nuntia* 20 (1985) 70-71 (c. 9 §2).

34 *Nuntia* 27 (1988) 46 (c. 328 §2). In reformulating the first part of the norm, the clause *si opus est* was omitted.

> ties. The canon adopts a pragmatic stand in view of the overriding concern for eparchies that are not self-sufficient.[35]

The norm's realistic stance would remain unchallenged and unchanged during its *iter* even though minor redactional changes were made to the canon before promulgation.[36]

Although the purview of *CCEO* canon 333 may more often concern seminaries of different Eastern Catholic Churches who, as wise stewards, need to combine resources and personnel, the canon does not exclude that Eastern seminaries might also admit students from the Latin Church on account of special circumstances. This type of collaboration might well occur in those regions of the world where the Eastern Catholic Churches are predominant or where Latin seminaries are comparatively fewer and farther apart. For example, in Romania, Conventual Franciscan Friars of the Latin Church, whose only seminary is located in the Eastern part of the country (Roman, Bacău), have also been admitted to the Romanian Catholic Seminary at Babeş-Bolyai University in Cluj-Napoca, northwestern Romania.

1.9) Clerics in Common Seminaries Trained in Their own Rite (CCEO c. 343)

Regarding their clerical formation, students may also be admitted to the seminary of another Church *sui iuris* (*CCEO* c. 333) or a common seminary of different Churches *sui iuris* (*CCEO* c. 330 §2). In either case, to safeguard the equality of the rites, Eastern canon 343 prescribes that these students be formed in their own rite. Unique to the Eastern Code, *CCEO* canon 343 states: "Students, even if admitted into a seminary of another Church *sui iuris* or into a common seminary for several Churches *sui iuris*, are to be formed in their own rite; any contrary custom being reprobated."

Within *PCCICOR*, the *Coetus de clericis* gave priority to the principle that clerical training be done in a student's own rite but the members did not feel it could be achieved in practice. In cases where no one on the seminary's formation team belonged to the student's rite, the study group maintained that a policy whereby the student acquired the rite or rites of the seminary might have to be adopted. The group's relator stated:

---

35 *Nuntia* 8 (1979) 72 (c. 7). Canon 7 stated: "Although it is preferable that each and every seminary, especially a minor one, be reserved to one rite, for special circumstances, candidates of other rites can be admitted to the same seminary, especially a major one."

36 See *Nuntia* 20 (1985) 72 (c. 12); *Nuntia* 27 (1988) 46 (c. 331) and *Nuntia* 31(1990) 40 (c. 333).

> If the seminary admits alumni of different rites, it must obviously also be consistent and offer them a formation consonant with their rites. This means, ideally at least, that there are formators who belong to the same rite as the students. This ideal however is not always realizable in practice, as everyone knows. Realistically then, under pain of refusing admission to students not belonging to the rite or rites of the formators, another policy may have to be adopted that is perhaps only the second best: biritualism or pluritualism. The canon, taking into account the difficulties inherent in this practice in certain places, does not authorize biritualism in general, but leaves it to Particular Law as determined in the Statutes.[37]

Accordingly, the *Coetus* proposed the following draft canon:

> §1. Even if students are enrolled in a seminary of a different or of several rites (*plurirituali*), they are to be formed in their own rite; any contrary custom being reprobated.
>
> §2. While they are limited to the seminary mentioned in §1, clerics are to take on the rite of the students, where they can, in accord with the norm of the Statutes.[38]

The special study group subsequently entrusted with the *denua recognitio* of this norm identified a "particularly evident inconsistency" between §§1 and 2 of the proposed norm. Even though a student was to be formed in his own rite, any contrary custom being reprobated, the same student might have to adopt the rite or rites of the seminary's formation team. Instead, given the importance of "safeguarding the juridical equality of the rites," the special group of experts insisted on the principle stated in §1, that is, to be formed in one's own rite. Consequently, the experts decided to omit §2 altogether and, regarding §1, they substituted the word "rite" with "Church *sui iuris*" and eliminated the word "pluritual." [39] When the canon later appeared as *SCICO* canon 341,[40] it was already identical to *CCEO* canon 343.

While many *CCEO* norms encourage interecclesial cooperation, it is not promoted at the expense of a Church's rite. Regarding clerical formation programs, for example, they can be common to different Churches *sui iuris*, including the Latin Church (*CCEO* c. 330 §2). Formation students of one rite can be admitted to the seminary of another Church *sui iuris* (*CCEO* c. 333) or to a seminary

37 *Nuntia* 8 (1979) 78 (c. 21).

38 Ibid.

39 See *Nuntia* 20 (1985) 83 (c. 28).

40 *Nuntia* 24-25 (1987) 65 (c. 341).

common to several Churches *sui iuris*, including the Latin Church (*CCEO* c. 332 §2). In all these collaborative areas, the Eastern Code (cc. 330 §2 and 343) consistently affirms that the common program or host seminary is not to be detrimental to the specific character of the rites, whether they be of the Eastern or Latin Catholic Churches.

2 - *CCEO* Norms Promoting Consultation in a Territory

The next series of seven norms, while directed to superior authorities of the Eastern Catholic Churches, invite those authorities to involve, either in a passive or active sense, the other Churches *sui iuris* in their territory or geographical area. The first two *CCEO* norms mean to involve, at least in a passive sense, the other Churches *sui iuris* of an area by taking them into consideration before decisions are made. The last five *CCEO* norms intend to involve, in an active sense, the other Churches *sui iuris* in a particular region by inviting their participation or counsel regarding other matters for decision. If the Latin Church is present in these territories, it is argued that its involvement is undoubtedly implied in the context of each case.

2.1) Feast Days and Days of Penance for Individual Churches Sui Iuris (CCEO c. 880 §2)

While essentially repeating *OE* 19,[41] *CCEO* canon 880 §2 also recalls the duty of Eastern hierarchs, in any event, to observe accurately their own rite in accord with *CCEO* canon 40 §1.[42] Eastern canon 880 §2 states:

> The competence to constitute, transfer or suppress feast days and days of penance for individual Churches *sui iuris* belongs also to the authority in those Churches that is competent to establish particular law. It may do so, however, only after taking into account the other Churches *sui iuris* and without prejudice to can. 40 §1.

---

41 *OE* 19 states: "To establish, transfer or abolish feast days common to all Eastern Churches belongs henceforth solely to an ecumenical synod or the Apostolic See. However, to establish, transfer or abolish feast days for individual Churches belongs to the patriarchal or archiepiscopal synods, as well as to the Apostolic See, due consideration having been given to the whole area and to the other individual Churches." For the English translation, see Tanner, 905.

42 *CCEO* c. 40 §1 states: "Hierarchs who preside over Churches *sui iuris* and all other hierarchs are to care with the greatest diligence for the faithful and accurate observance of their own rite; nor are they to allow changes to be made in it except by reason of its organic progress; they are nonetheless to keep in mind mutual goodwill and the unity of Christians."

According to canon 880 §2, the competence to establish, transfer, or suppress feast days and days of penance in the individual Eastern Catholic Churches *sui iuris* belongs to the authority competent to make particular law. In concrete terms, it is the synod of bishops in patriarchal and major archiepiscopal Churches (see *CCEO* c. 110 §1), the council of hierarchs in the metropolitan Churches (see *CCEO* c. 167 §1), and the hierarchs responsible for the other Churches *sui iuris* (see *CCEO* c. 176). While these authorities are to take the greatest care to observe their own rites accurately (*CCEO* c. 40 §1), they are to establish, transfer, or suppress feast days or days of penance only after taking into account the other Churches *sui iuris*. Given the context and text of the source to canon 880 §2, it only seems logical that the norm intends the other Churches *sui iuris* that are present in the territory. Besides the other Eastern Catholic Churches *sui iuris*, canon 880 §2 implicitly includes the Latin Church by analogy, as the 2011 Explanatory Note indicates, even though nothing in its legislative history explicitly names the Latin Church or any other Eastern Catholic Church *sui iuris* for that matter. Therefore, while canon 880 §2 requires that the Churches *sui iuris*, including the Latin Church, at least be taken into account, nothing in the norm precludes the Eastern hierarchs from involving the other Churches more actively and collaboratively by way of forums or structures established to solicit their input or opinion regarding changes to that Eastern Church's feast days or days of penance.

2.2) The Patriarchal Assembly and Churches Sui Iuris in a Territory (CCEO c. 140)

Eastern canon 140 establishes the patriarchal assembly as a consultative group to assist the patriarch and synod of bishops of a patriarchal Church to deal with matters of major importance for the common good not only of that Church but, also, for the common good of the entire territory where it coexists with other Churches *sui iuris*. *CCEO* Canon 140 states:

> The patriarchal assembly is a consultative group of the entire Church presided over by the patriarch. It assists the patriarch and the synod of bishops of the patriarchal Church in dealing with matters of major importance especially in order to harmonize the forms and methods of the apostolate as well as ecclesiastical discipline, adapting them to the current circumstances of the time and to the common good of the respective Church, but also taking into account the common good of the entire territory where several Churches *sui iuris* coexist.

It is clear that the patriarchal assembly must also take into account the common good of the whole territory where other Churches *sui iuris* are present. However, this may amount to more than a passive role at the assembly for these

Churches. Given the source that inspired the canon, it may well intend a more collaborative role for the other Churches *sui iuris*. Its source, *CD* 38 (6), states:

> It is earnestly recommended that, in promoting the discipline of their own Church in their synods, the prelates of the Eastern Churches should, for the more efficacious encouragement of works for the good of religion, also take into account the common good of the whole territory where many Churches of different rites exist, by exchanging views in inter-ritual meetings, according to the norms to be determined by competent authority.[43]

Moreover, *CD* 38 (6) is an official source for canon 322 §1 governing assemblies of hierarchs. In that norm, as mentioned in part 1.3, the local ordinaries of the Latin Church are explicitly named among the potential members of such an assembly. In the context of canon 140, it seems reasonable to conclude that the Latin Church, in an analogous sense, is also included among the "Churches *sui iuris*." Strictly speaking, while the norm only requires that the Churches *sui iuris*, including the Latin Church, be taken into account, there is every reason to suggest that the role of the Churches be more collaborative as *Christus Dominus* suggested. In fact, the next norm to be examined, canon 143 §3, expressly provides that persons of other Churches *sui iuris* can be invited to participate actively in a patriarchal assembly.

2.3) Persons of Another Church Sui Iuris at a Patriarchal Assembly (CCEO c. 143 §3)

Regarding participation at the patriarchal assembly of a patriarchal Church *sui iuris*, canon 143 §3 foresees that possibility for persons from another Church *sui iuris*. The unique norm states: "Persons of another Church *sui iuris* can be invited to the patriarchal assembly and can take part in it according to the norm of the statutes." Undoubtedly, the persons from another Church *sui iuris* invited to participate in a patriarchal assembly implicitly include persons from the Latin Church. Interestingly enough, during the *denua recognitio* that regarded this canon, the expert study group introduced the draft to *CCEO* canon 143 §4 "for greater ecumenical openness."[44] That norm now states: "To the patriarchal assembly can also be invited some observers from other Churches or non-Catholic ecclesial communities." Since canon 143 §4 foresees the participation of observers from the Orthodox, Protestant, and other non-Catholic ecclesial communities, then it would only stand to reason that canon 143 §3 intends implicitly the collaborative participation of Eastern, as well as Latin, faithful of the other Catholic Churches *sui iuris* in order to foster ecclesial communion.

---

43 See Tanner, 937.

44 *Nuntia* 22 (1986) 102-103 (c. 115 §4).

2.4) The Patriarchal Territory and Other Churches Sui Iuris (CCEO c. 146 §2)

If a doubt arises regarding the territorial boundaries of a patriarchal Church or if there is a desire to enlarge these boundaries, the synod of bishops of the patriarchal Church is to investigate the matter. As part of the investigation, the synod is to hear the superior administrative authority of the other Churches *sui iuris* concerned before forwarding the matter to the Roman Pontiff for resolution. To regulate this question, Eastern canon 146 §2 states:

> If any doubt concerning the territorial boundaries of the patriarchal Church arises or if it is a question of the modification of boundaries, it is for the synod of bishops of the patriarchal Church to investigate the matter. After hearing the superior authority of each Church *sui iuris* concerned, and after discussing the matter in the synod, it is up to the same synod to present a properly documented petition for the resolution of the doubt or for the modification of the boundaries to the Roman Pontiff. It is for the Roman Pontiff alone to resolve the doubt authentically or to decree a modification of the boundaries.

Within *PCCICOR*, the *Coetus de sacra hierarchia* had proposed a draft formulation of the norm that was already similar to the promulgated norm. The clause that referred to the consultation with the other Churches concerned stated: "having heard the hierarchs of the other Churches concerned."[45] During the *denua recognitio* of the 1984 Schema, no observations were made regarding the norm but, regarding the clause just mentioned, the expert study group, *ex officio*, stated: "Indeed, this clause would have intended too broad a consultation and difficult in practice to accomplish. In this regard, the study group agreed on the advisability of consulting only the '*Superior auctoritas cuisvis Ecclesiae sui iuris, cuius interest*'."[46] Subsequently, only a few redactional changes were made, one of which was the addition of the word "administrative" to qualify "superior authority."[47]

Nothing in the legislative history of *CCEO* canon 146 §2 explicitly names the Latin diocesan bishop to be among those that the synod of bishops of the patriarchal Church has to consult regarding a question about the patriarchal territory. For that matter, no specific administrative authority of any other Eastern Church *sui iuris* is named either. It only seems logical that, in any discussions regarding the limits of a patriarchal territory, the participation of a Latin bishop, if present, would necessarily be implied. It is also worth noting that, in the context of

---

45 See *Nuntia* 6 (1978) 25 (c. 1 §2).

46 See *Nuntia* 22 (1986) 105 (c. 118 §2).

47 For these changes, see *Nuntia* 27 (1988) 40 (c. 146 §2) and *Nuntia* 31 (1990) 38-39 (c. 146 §2).

drafting the provisional norms regarding the territory of a patriarchal Church, the *Coetus de sacra hierarchia* was intent on affirming the fundamental equality of all the Churches, as defined in *OE* 3.[48] Given this fact and the implication that can legitimately be drawn to include the Latin Church among the "Churches *sui iuris,*" *CCEO* canon 146 §2 offers yet another opportunity for interecclesial consultation and collaboration regarding a question that could possibly affect the communion and unity of the entire Catholic Church.

2.5) Bishops of Another Church Sui Iuris at a Council of Hierarchs (CCEO c. 164 §1)

Regarding participation in a council of hierarchs of a metropolitan Church *sui iuris,* the characteristic *CCEO* canon 164 §1 provides that, in addition to the bishops of the metropolitan Church *sui iuris*, bishops of other Churches *sui iuris* can be invited. Eastern canon 164 §1 states:

> All and only the ordained bishops of the metropolitan Church *sui iuris*, wherever they are constituted, must be called to the council of hierarchs, except those (unqualified to vote) mentioned in can. 953, §1 or those who have been punished with the canonical penalties mentioned in cann. 1433 and 1434. Bishops of another Church *sui iuris* can be invited as guests only if the majority of the members of the council of hierarchs agrees.

Within *PCCICOR*, the draft of this norm already contained the provision allowing for bishops of other Churches *sui iuris* to be invited to the council of hierarchs. It stated: "Other bishops of the same Church or even of a different rite are able to be invited only if the majority of the members of the council will have agreed to it."[49] Apart from subsequent, redactional changes, nothing in the reported *iter* of this norm helps to shed any further light on the definition to be given the wording "bishops of another Church *sui iuris*." Still, there is nothing to indicate that the draftsmen meant to exclude bishops of the Latin Church from participating in the council of hierarchs of a metropolitan Church *sui iuris*. Given this context of interecclesial relations, as the 2011 Explanatory Note highlights,

48 See *Nuntia* 6 (1978) 25. *OE* 3 states: "Although individual (particular) Churches of this kind, both of the East and the West, differ somewhat in what are called rites, such as liturgy, ecclesiastical order and spiritual heritage, still they are entrusted on an equal footing to the pastoral guidance of the Roman Pontiff, who by divine right succeeds blessed Peter in the primacy over the whole Church. Thus the same Churches enjoy equal dignity, so that none of them ranks higher than the others by reason of rite, and they enjoy the same rights and are bound by the same laws, even as regards preaching the Gospel throughout the whole world, under the direction of the Roman Pontiff." For the English translation, see Tanner, 901.

49 *Nuntia* 19 (1984) 50 (c. 137 §1).

it seems obvious that, by the wording "bishops of another Church *sui iuris*," the Eastern draftsmen intended that bishops of other Eastern Catholic Churches *sui iuris* as well as the Latin Church could be invited to the council of hierarchs of a metropolitan Church *sui iuris*.

2.6) Persons of Another Church Sui Iuris at an Eparchial Assembly (CCEO c. 238 §2)

Unlike the former Eastern norm (*CS* c. 424 §1) which had excluded lay persons from participating in the eparchial assembly, the current *CCEO* canon 238 §2 foresees their participation and possible active voice in it. Furthermore, the new Eastern norm now expressly establishes that persons of other Churches *sui iuris* can also be invited to the eparchial assembly, again with the right to vote. Eastern canon 238 §2 states: "The eparchial bishop, if he judges it opportune, can invite to the eparchial assembly others also, not excluding persons of other Churches *sui iuris*, to all of whom he can even grant the right to vote."

Within *PCCICOR*, the *Coetus de sacra hierarchia* initially presented the norm in two paragraphs, the first referring generally to the laity and the second to persons of another rite.[50] Subsequently, although one consultative body did object that it "seemed less than correct to grant the right to vote also to persons of another rite or Church," the expert study group reviewing the norm disagreed, noting that the eparchial assembly is purely consultative and that granting the right to vote is left to the bishop's discretion.[51] Otherwise, apart from a minor redactional change, the norm remained unchallenged before promulgation.[52]

Clearly, *CCEO* canon 238 §2 does not explicitly mention inviting persons of the Latin Church to participate in the eparchial assembly. However, as mentioned above, local hierarchs of the Latin Church are explicitly named as possible members of assemblies of hierarchs in *CCEO* c. 322 §1. Since that canon's source (*CD* 38,6) also inspired *CCEO* canon 140 regarding patriarchal assemblies, it was argued that the involvement of the Latin Church can certainly be implied there. If the collaboration of the Latin Church is foreseen in assemblies of hierarchs and potentially in patriarchal assemblies, it only seems reasonable to include the participation of persons of the Latin Church at the level of the eparchial assembly. Moreover, as was argued in the case of patriarchal assemblies, to which observers from non-Catholic Churches can be invited, if the same observers can be invited to an eparchial assembly according to *CCEO* canon 238 §3,[53] then it would seem inappropriate to exclude persons of the Latin or any other

---

50 See *Nuntia* 9 (1979) 37 (c. 50 §§2-3).

51 See *Nuntia* 23 (1986) 53 (c. 209 §2).

52 For this change, see *Nuntia* 27 (1988) 43 (c. 236 §2).

53 *CCEO* c. 238 §3 states: "Some observers from non-Catholic Churches or ecclesial communities can also be invited to the eparchial assembly."

Catholic Church *sui iuris* from being invited to an eparchial assembly if the eparchial bishop deems it opportune.

2.7) Persons of Another Church Sui Iuris on the Pastoral Council (CCEO c. 273 §3)

Regarding the composition of a bishop's pastoral council, Eastern canon 273 §3 allows a bishop even to invite persons from another Church *sui iuris* to participate in this consultative body. After §§ 1 and 2 of this Eastern norm indicate those who, representing the faithful of the eparchy, can be members of the pastoral council, §3 of *CCEO* canon 273 states: "Along with these Christian faithful, if it is opportune, the eparchial bishop can also invite others to the pastoral council, even if they are of another Church *sui iuris*."

Within *PCCICOR*, the *Coetus de sacra hierarchia* proposed a first draft of this norm which was already very similar to the promulgated norm. It stated: "Along with the Christian faithful of his eparchy, mentioned in the preceding paragraph, the bishop can, if opportune, also invite others although of a different rite."[54] Except for a minor reformulation and a couple of redactional changes before promulgation,[55] no observations were made to oppose the norm's intent to invite others ascribed to a different Church *sui iuris*.

Regarding an Eastern bishop's pastoral council, then, *CCEO* canon 273 §3 allows a bishop, if he judges it appropriate, to invite the Christian faithful of another Church *sui iuris* to participate. By implication, this would include the participation of the faithful of the Latin Church. Indeed, like many other Eastern norms seen here, *CCEO* canon 273 §3 aims at promoting ecclesial collaboration and communion among the rich variety of the Catholic Churches *sui iuris*.

3 - *CCEO* Norms that Foresee Assistance (Hiring) from Other Churches *Sui Iuris*

The third category of norms, which effectively amount to another kind of interecclesial collaboration, permits hiring ecclesiastical personnel from other Churches *sui iuris*. This would include the Eastern Catholic Churches *sui iuris* as well as the Latin Church by implication. As consultors within *PCCICOR* often raised the problem of a lack of personnel among the Eastern Churches and eparchies, the three norms considered here are possible ways to alleviate the problem in those specific cases. Even without the formula "eparchial bishops of various Churches *sui iuris* exercising their power within the same territory," the norms can be interpreted to allow for hiring needed personnel from other Churches *sui iuris*. From the same perspective of ecclesiastical collaboration, and supported

54 *Nuntia* 9 (1979) 54 (c. 86 §3).

55 See *Nuntia* 23 (1986) 73 (c. 246 §3) and *Nuntia* 27 (1988) 44 (c. 271 §3).

by the 2011 Explanatory Note, it is obvious that the Latin Church should also be implied by the expression "Church *sui iuris*" in the following norms.

3.1) Eparchy's Protosyncellus/Syncelli from Another Church Sui Iuris (CCEO c. 247 §4)

First, in the context of establishing prerequisites for appointment to the offices of protosyncellus and syncellus, Eastern canon 247 §4 stipulates that the eparchial bishop can take on personnel for these offices from another Church *sui iuris*. *CCEO* canon 247 §4 states: "The eparchial bishop can also take the protosyncellus or syncelli from another eparchy, or from another Church *sui iuris*, however, with the consent of their eparchial bishop."

Within *PCCICOR*, when the *Coetus de sacra hierarchia* initially proposed this norm and then made it part of the 1984 Schema, the possibility of hiring the protosyncellus or syncellus from another Church *sui iuris* was not written into the draft. The proposed rule stated: "The bishop can hire the protosyncellus and the syncellus from another eparchy."[56] It was not until the *denua recognitio* of the 1984 Schema that the expert study group, *ex officio*, decided to specify that, if the eparchial bishop wanted to appoint as protosyncellus or syncellus a priest of another eparchy, he had to have the consent of his eparchial bishop. Furthermore, the experts expressly added that this priest could also be ascribed to another Church *sui iuris*.[57] Subsequently, apart from a minor reformulation,[58] the rule went unchanged and unchallenged.

In applying *CCEO* canon 247 §4, an Eastern bishop may well decide to appoint his protosyncellus or syncellus not only from another eparchy but even from another Church *sui iuris*, including the Latin Church. As the rule states, however, the bishop must also have the consent of the candidate's own bishop. Nothing in the reported legislative history of Eastern canon 247 §4 explicitly points to the possibility of that appointee coming from the Latin Church but such an interpretation is certainly not excluded. Indeed, an interpretation inclusive of the Latin Church is more consonant with the interdependence of the Codes established by *CCEO* canon 1 as well as the theme of interecclesial collaboration present throughout the Eastern Code. Finally, an inclusive interpretation in the context of such interecclesial relations is also consistent with the 2011 Explanatory Note.

3.2) Designating a Pastor from Another Church Sui Iuris (CCEO c. 916 §4)

Secondly, if in a country or region the hierarchy of an Eastern Catholic Church *sui iuris* has been established but groups of that Church's faithful remain isolated

56 See *Nuntia* 9 (1979) 42 (c. 60 §3) and *Nuntia* 19 (1984) 70 (c. 219 §3).
57 See *Nuntia* 23 (1986) 58 (c. 219 §4).
58 See *Nuntia* 27 (1988) 43 (c. 245 §4).

and without a proper pastor, the eparchial bishop for those faithful is to designate a pastor for them from another Church *sui iuris*. In Canada and the United States, for example, where Eastern Catholic bishops are responsible for vast territories, this is often the case. The applicable norm, canon 916 §4, which is unique to the Eastern Code, states:

> If there is no pastor for the Christian faithful of a certain Church *sui iuris*, the eparchial bishop for those same faithful is to designate the pastor of another Church *sui iuris*, who is assume their care as their proper pastor, with the consent, however, of the eparchial bishop of the pastor to be designated.

Within *PCCICOR*, the initial draft of *CCEO* canon 916 §4 was already substantially the same as the promulgated norm. During its *iter*, consultative bodies made no reported observations and the norm only underwent minor amendment.[59] Nor is there any discussion regarding the specific meaning to be given "pastor of another Church *sui iuris*."

Accordingly, of the pastors that an Eastern bishop could designate for his faithful who need one, he could choose one from any number of Churches *sui iuris*, including the Latin Church, that are present where the faithful are. While pastors of many other Eastern Catholic Churches *sui iuris* might also be present, they might not be as available as the more numerous Latin pastors who, more importantly, have received the consent of their diocesan bishops. In fact, in the United States and Canada, Eastern bishops have often obtained biritual faculties for Latin pastors and designated them, with the consent of their own diocesan bishops, as pastors for their Eastern faithful. Within the context of interecclesial relations, *CCEO* canon 916 §4 again serves as a forum for interecclesial cooperation which, in turn, highlights Catholic ecclesial communion.

3.3) Tribunal Personnel from Another Church Sui Iuris (CCEO c. 1102 §1)

Thirdly, *CCEO* canon 1102 §1 provides for the recruitment of judges and other personnel of ecclesiastical tribunals from one's own or even another Church *sui iuris*. It stipulates:

> Judges and other officers of the tribunals may be chosen from any eparchy, religious institute or society of common life in the manner of religious, of one's own or even of another Church *sui iuris*, with the written consent, however, of their own eparchial bishop or major superior.

59 For the *iter* of *CCEO* c. 916 §4, see *Nuntia* 13 (1981) 14 (c. 6 §4); *Nuntia* 18 (1984) 9 (c. 6 §4); *Nuntia* 24-25 (1987) 164 (c. 912 §4) and *Nuntia* 27 (1988) 77 (c. 912 §4).

Within *PCCICOR*, the *Coetus de processibus* initially drafted this norm to state: "Judges and other officers of tribunals can be hired from any eparchy, monastery or institute of consecrated life of one's own or a different rite, provided the written consent of one's own hierarch is given." While "rite" would eventually be changed to "Church *sui iuris*" and "monastery or institute of consecrated life" would be amended to read "religious institute or society of common life in the manner of religious," the underlying rule that tribunal personnel could be taken from another rite, or what is now called, a Church *sui iuris*, remained a constant throughout the *iter* of Eastern canon 1102 §1.[60]

Regarding the interpretation to be given *CCEO* canon 1102 §1 in the context of the recurring theme of interecclesial cooperation, an Eastern Catholic bishop can choose judges and other tribunal personnel from any eparchy of his own Church *sui iuris* or even from an eparchy of another Church *sui iuris*. Given the implicit meaning of the expression "Church *sui iuris*" to include the Latin Church, an Eastern bishop could appoint judges and tribunal personnel from an eparchy of his own Church or from an eparchy (diocese) of another Eastern Church or even the Latin Church. The Eastern bishop can also hire his tribunal personnel from among the religious or the members of societies of common life of his own Church or another Eastern Catholic Church *sui iuris*. However, in the case of the Latin Church, the same Eastern bishop can hire religious or members of societies of apostolic life mentioned in *CIC* canon 731 §2, since the latter are to be equated with Eastern societies of common life, as defined in *CCEO* canon 554 §1.[61] In whichever case, the Eastern bishop will need the written consent of the relevant eparchial (diocesan) bishop or major superior.

4 - *CCEO* Norms on Lay/Religious Collaboration from Various Churches *Sui Iuris*

The 2011 Explanatory Note does allow for a more extensive application of the Eastern Code to the Latin Church at least with regard to those Eastern canons in which the expression "Church *sui iuris*" is employed in the context of interecclesial relations but it does not limit that application only to those canons that explicitly contain the expression "Church *sui iuris*." Indeed, in referring "to the other canons of the same (Eastern) Code in which it (Latin Church) is included implicitly," the Note seems to open the door to a still broader understanding of the interrelationship of the Eastern and Latin Codes. For example, even if an

60 For the legislative history of *CCEO* c. 1102 §1, see *Nuntia* 5 (1977) 26 (c. 40 §1); *Nuntia* 14 (1982) 29 (c. 44 §1); *Nuntia* 21 (1985) 46 (c. 44 §1); *Nuntia* 24-25 (1987) 200 (c. 1117 §1); and *Nuntia* 31 (1990) 38 (c. 1117 §1).

61 For the similarity between Eastern societies of common life in the manner of religious (*CCEO* c. 554 §1) and Latin societies of apostolic life, whose members assume the evangelical counsel with some bond (*CIC* c. 731 §2), see J. Abbass, *The Consecrated Life: A Comparative Commentary of the Eastern and Latin Codes (*Ottawa: Saint Paul University, 2008) 419-425.

Eastern canon does not contain the expression "Church *sui iuris,*" can it nonetheless implicitly oblige the Latin Church just because of the nature of the matter regarding interecclesial relations? Although the Explanatory Note does not address this line of reasoning, it certainly would appear to be open to it. In part 1.6, it was already argued that *CCEO* canon 1405 §3, while addressed to hierarchical authorities without reference to their "Churches *sui iuris*," implicitly included, *ex natura rei*, authorities of both the Eastern and Latin Churches in order to assure that penal laws are uniform in the same territory. This part will examine two other Eastern norms, addressed not only to hierarchical authorities but, rather, to the laity or religious, to determine whether or not, by the use of the expression "Church *sui iuris*" or simply by the nature of the matter, they might also implicitly involve the laity or religious of the Latin Church.

4.1) Collaboration among Lay Members of Different Churches Sui Iuris (CCEO c. 405)

OE 4 urges that Eastern Catholic lay persons be taught about their rites and laws and *OE* 6 establishes that Eastern Catholics are to acquire an ever greater knowledge of these matters and a more perfect practice of them.[62] The conciliar decree, however, does not go on to prescribe that such study be conducted on an interecclesial level, thus encouraging a united effort to show that the variety of the rites does not harm the common good but, rather, enhances it. All these elements are contained in the characteristic Eastern canon 405. Unique to the Eastern Code, *CCEO* canon 405 states:

> Lay persons are to study zealously their liturgical, theological, spiritual and disciplinary patrimony, so that mutual goodwill, esteem and unity of action between the lay members of different Churches *sui iuris* are fostered, and so that the variety of rites does not harm the common good of the society in which they live, but rather may daily contribute to that same good.

Within *PCCICOR*, the *Coetus de laicis et de boni temporalibus* first proposed this norm with substantially the same formulation. The study group made reference to the sources in *OE* 4 and 6, mentioned above, but the members provided no written explanation for adding the collaborative, interecclesial component. During the *denua recognitio* of the norm, a motion was made to either omit this

62 *OE* 6 states: "All Eastern Christians should know and be certain that they may and should always preserve their own lawful liturgical rites and way of life, and that changes should be made only by reason of their proper and organic development. All these things are to be observed with the greatest fidelity by the Eastern Christians themselves. They should indeed, from day to day, acquire greater knowledge of these matters and more perfect practice of them and if for reasons of circumstances, times or persons they have fallen unduly short of this they should have recourse to their age-old traditions." For the English translation, see Tanner, 902.

canon or transfer it to the canons respecting the preservation of the rites (now *CCEO* 39-41). The expert study group decided, instead, to keep the canon in place as a complement to those norms. Apart from the change from "of different rites" to "of different Churches," the canon's formulation remained practically the same. Subsequently, only slight redactional changes were made to the canon before promulgation.[63]

While the sources to *CCEO* canon 405 undoubtedly had Eastern Catholics in mind, the scope of the Eastern norm is evidently broader. By promoting the study of rites among lay persons of "different Churches *sui iuris,*" *CCEO* canon 405 certainly does not mean to exclude the involvement and collaboration of the Latin Church and its laity even though the canon is not principally addressed to them. After all, in the context interecclesial relations, the Latin Church can be implied in the expression "Church *sui iuris.*" While the norm does not go on to define new structures for conducting this interecclesial endeavor, those specifics are evidently left to the originality of the laity. Whether the study is carried out in centers already set up or in newly established ones, the interecclesial communion that *CCEO* canon 405 aims to foster rightly includes the laity of the Latin Church, as the lay faithful from all the Churches *sui iuris* collaboratively work to show that the variety of rites in the Catholic Church does not diminish the common good but, rather, enriches it.

4.2) Meetings with Religious Superiors of Different Religious Institutes (CCEO c. 416)

CCEO canon 416 is entirely new to the Eastern legislation and unique to the Eastern Code. Addressed to patriarchs (in the patriarchal and major archiepiscopal Churches) as well as the local hierarchs of those and the other Eastern Catholic Churches, the norm calls on them to take the initiative to meet with religious superiors to ensure that different institutes' apostolic works are carried out in a collaborative and harmonious manner. The meetings are to be held at fixed times or whenever they appear necessary. Eastern canon 416 states: " Patriarchs as well as local hierarchs are to promote meetings with superiors of religious at fixed times and whenever it appears opportune, in order that the apostolic works that the members exercise be carried out cooperatively and harmoniously."

Within *PCCICOR*, the draft of *CCEO* canon 416 that the *Coetus de monachis* introduced in 1980 was already substantially similar to the promulgated norm. While no reported explanation is given for the canon's introduction, the reasonable aim of promoting harmony among religious institutes in the exercise of the apostolate may well have been thought to be self-evident. At any rate, during the *denua recognitio* of the norm, no objections were raised regarding the norm but

63 For the iter of *CCEO* c. 405, see Nuntia 5 (1977) 42-43 (c. 6); *Nuntia* 13 (1981) 114 (c. 93); *Nuntia* 21 (1985) 18-19 (c. 93); *Nutnia* 24-25 (1987) 77 (c. 403); and *Nuntia* 27 (1988) 49 (c. 403).

the word *concorditer* (harmoniously) was added, it would seem, for emphasis. Subsequently, only slight redactional changes were made before promulgation.[64]

In addition to the presence of religious superiors at patriarchal assemblies (see *CCEO* c. 143 §1, 3°) and eparchial assemblies (see *CCEO* c. 238 §1, 9°), *CCEO* canon 416 provides yet another forum or structure for their collaborative participation in the life of the Church. Although the norm refers specifically to meetings with superiors of religious, it would not seem to preclude hierarchical authorities from convoking assemblies of superiors of all institutes of consecrated life to encourage their collaborative efforts in the apostolate of a given region. Nor does Eastern canon 416 exclude the participation of superiors of Latin religious or other institutes of consecrated life in the interest of a harmonious exercise of apostolic works, for example, in the territory of a patriarchal Church. Such a conclusion seems reasonable simply because of the nature and purpose of this matter. Indeed, soon after the promulgation of the Eastern Code, the Maronite patriarch initiated meetings of Eastern, together with Latin, superiors to encourage the cooperative and harmonious exercise of their apostolates in Lebanon.

Conclusion

In the context of this Seventy-seventh Annual Convention of the Society, whose theme is "Church Structures Fifty Years after Vatican II: Present and Future," this paper examined the Eastern Code regarding the presence of interecclesial structures or forums for collaboration among the Churches *sui iuris* that make up the entire Catholic Church. Such an examination seemed appropriate in order to highlight the fact that such structures are not found in the Latin Code but, rather, in the Eastern Code, which now marks its twenty-fifth anniversary since promulgation. Building upon a first study done in 2006, this paper began by recalling the 2001 apostolic letter, *Novo millennio ineunte*, in which Pope John Paul II underscored the importance and value of "structures of participation envisaged by Canon Law." By this declaration, the pope already implied that, if such structures were not contained in the Latin Code, then they could very well be found in the other Code of the Catholic Church.

Regarding Eastern norms that promote structures for interecclesial collaboration, part 1 reviewed the twelve canons of the 2006 study and selected the one explicit canon (*CCEO* c. 322 §1) and five other norms (*CCEO* cc. 84 §1; 202; 720 §3; 1013 §2; and 1405 §3) in which the Eastern draftsmen themselves had implied collaboration also with the Latin Church. Three more *CCEO* norms were added to the list that calls for active collaboration among the hierarchical authorities of the Latin as well as the Eastern "Churches *sui iuris*." The conclusions drawn here were only confirmed by the 2011 Explanatory Note published by the Pontifical Council for Legislative Texts, which held that the expression "Church

64 For the *iter* of *CCEO* c. 416, see *Nuntia* 11 (1980) 17 (c. 7); *Nuntia* 16 (1983) 17 (c. 7); *Nuntia* 24-25 (1987) 79 (c. 414); and *Nuntia* 27 (1988) 49 (c. 414).

sui iuris" could also imply the Latin Church in the context of interecclesial relations. Part 2 examined seven other Eastern norms which prescribe interecclesial collaboration by way of consultation among the "Churches *sui iuris*," that is Eastern and Latin, present in the same territory or region (*CCEO* cc. 140; 143 §3; 146 §2; 164 §1; 238 §2; 273 §3 and 880 §2). Collaboration by way of mutual assistance among the hierarchical authorities of these different "Churches *sui iuris*" was the subject of part 3 in which three other Eastern norms were considered (*CCEO* cc. 247 §4; 916 §4 and 1102 §1). Finally, in part 4, two Eastern norms that urge collaboration among the laity and religious were mentioned. Although the first canon (*CCEO* c. 405) contains the expression "Church *sui iuris*," it addresses the Churches' laity rather than their hierarchical authorities. The other canon (*CCEO* c. 416) is directed at hierarchical authorities but does not contain the expression "Church *sui iuris*." In both situations, however, the canons encourage collaboration among the Eastern and Latin Churches *ex natura rei*. It was argued that, besides allowing for collaborative structures among the hierarchies of the various "Churches *sui iuris*," the 2011 Explanatory Note also seems to support the possibility of interecclesial collaborative structures at the level of the Churches' laity and their religious institutes because of the very nature and purpose of the matters at stake.

Seminar

Tribunal Management: A Tale of Two Tribunals

Very Reverend Anthony Bawyn
Kelly E. O'Donnell

Part I [Bawyn]

Introduction

Any examination of tribunal management today will surely involve comparing the role of the judicial vicar and the role of at least one other person, whether lay or cleric, who shares in his duties. This comparison raises many questions: When did this structure start to appear in tribunals? How does this relationship work? Who serves in this capacity? By what authority does this other person function in this role? What theological and canonical foundations are in place?

This seminar will address both the foundational material that grounds shared management in tribunals and the current practices that demonstrate how tribunals actually work under this model. I will talk about the foundational aspects of this topic and Kelly O'Donnell will address the practical aspects. We hope that there will be something of interest to all participants. Some may be looking to learn how this configuration works with an eye to establishing it in their own tribunal or considering for their own tribunal some of the ideas presented here. Others may find interesting some of the historical, theological, and canonical roots of this practice.

Although the general theme of this year's convention is "Church Structures Fifty Years After Vatican II: Present and Future," this is not the first time that a convention seminar has looked at ministerial collaboration. In 1992 at the convention in Cambridge, Massachusetts, Sister Theresa Monroe, R.S.C.J., and Father Joseph Koury, S.J., spoke together about cooperation between clergy and laity both as a concept and as outlined in the canons of the *Code of Canon Law*.[1]

1 Theresa M. Monroe, "Part I: The Rhetoric and Reality of Collaboration," *Proceedings of the Canon Law Society of America,* 54 (Washington, DC: Canon Law Society of America, 1992) 147-161; Joseph J. Koury, "Part II: The Code and Collaboration: Recent Literature," Ibid., 162-184.

The Traditional Structure in Tribunals

When first choosing a title for this seminar the two presenters intentionally chose to allude to the work of Charles Dickens, *A Tale of Two Cities*. It was meant to be a light-handed way to make a distinction between tribunals structured in a traditional way and those structured differently because of some form of shared leadership. Upon further investigation, this author realized that "two tribunals" also refers to an important and necessary distinction in the use of the word "tribunal" in the law as pointed out by William Doheny at the beginning of his classical work on matrimonial procedure published in 1938. When referring to Book Four of 1917 Code and the 1936 Instruction *Provida Mater*, Doheny states that sometimes the word "tribunal"

> refers to the entire court or judiciary system of a diocese, thereby including the *Officialis*, the V*ice-Officialis*, the synodal and pro-synodal judges, the auditor, the *Promotor Iustitiae*, the *Defensor Vinculi*, the notaries, the court messenger, and any other members of the court. At other times the word *tribunal* is strictly limited to signify only the collegiate group of three judges under the presidency of the presiding judge. The precise significance of the term in a particular instance is usually clear from the context.[2]

This is still a useful distinction since tribunals, understood in the first sense, employ not only some of the same persons today but also others who are the subject of this work.

Neither the 1917 *Code of Canon Law* nor the 1983 *Code of Canon Law* expressly identifies a leader for the tribunal from a strictly administrative point of view, but both Codes speak about the office of judge that pertains to the diocesan bishop and his judicial vicar, both of whom possess the ordinary power of judging in the diocesan tribunal of first instance. Although the *Code of Canon Law*[3] and *Dignitas connubii*[4] address in detail the officials of a judicial process who are the ministers of the tribunal, the daily operations of the tribunal not directly connected with the judicial process are covered only indirectly in the canons and articles of these two respective documents. The priest who is appointed judicial vicar, therefore, has traditionally directed the tribunal. As noted above in the

2 William J. Doheny, *Canonical Procedure in Matrimonial Cases: Formal Judicial Procedure* (Milwaukee, Bruce, 1938) 34.

3 Unless expressly indicated by the title "1917 *Code of Canon Law*" the titles "*Code of Canon Law*," "Code" and "new Code" refer to the 1983 *Code of Canon Law*.

4 Pontifical Council for Legislative Texts, *Instruction to be observed by diocesan tribunals and interdiocesan tribunals in handling causes of the nullity of marriage, Dignitas Connubii* (Vatican City, 2005: Libreria Editrice Vaticana). Hereinafter also called the Instruction.

quotation from Doheny, under the 1917 Code tribunals were composed of the officialis and, where appointed, the vice-officialis, and other judges, synodal or pro-synodal.

The Development of a New Structure

It is safe to assume that the informal practice of sharing leadership between the judicial vicar and another tribunal staff person arose in particular cases on account of a pastoral need. Furthermore, it is likely that, in some cases, the role of a tribunal leader other than the judicial vicar developed in steps. As a hypothetical example, one can imagine how in a small tribunal with an elderly judicial vicar and no other available priest, a lay administrative assistant began to take on more and more practical tasks so that the judicial vicar could spend his time managing cases and judging them. Before long, that assistant became responsible for more complicated tasks such as personnel and budget and, eventually, case management. Finally, the diocesan bishop recognized the important and supportive role the lay employee had been playing in the life of the tribunal and promoted the lay person to the position of "Executive Assistant," "Director" or another related title.

In view of this example, at what point did the role of tribunal director actually emerge so that it was no longer an employee with sufficient experience to perform important tasks in a tribunal, but rather a church professional who exercised a management role? Furthermore, is it necessary for the tribunal director to perform duties called for by procedural law (e.g., to serve as notary, or even defender of the bond or judge) or only non-canonical management duties such as supervising personnel or preparing a budget? Like many other situations arising from practical and pastoral need, it appears that a formal distinction arose only gradually as tribunals were served by vicars judicial who, perhaps, no longer served in a full-time capacity and by lay persons who began to study canon law and be appointed to ecclesiastical office in tribunals.

To discuss this structure, therefore, under the heading of lay ecclesial ministry is indeed warranted. Of course, not all directors are lay persons; however, this seminar will use the prevalence of lay persons in this position to permit a review of the theological foundation that opened the function of tribunal administration to a broader number of persons.

First of all, what is meant by tribunal director in this presentation is someone who exercises leadership in the administrative task of the Church under the authority of the diocesan bishop and in collaboration with a cleric who is appointed the judicial vicar.

In the absence of canonical structures foreseen by the *Code of Canon Law* for the appointment of a tribunal leader who is not the same as the judicial vicar, what parallel structure exists in canon law? The most helpful concept for comparison is the provision of canon 517 §2 on the leadership of a parish when the diocesan bishop does not appoint a pastor. Care must immediately be taken with this comparison since the person who leads a parish according to canon 517 §2 is appointed to an ecclesiastical office, but not all tribunal directors are so appointed. That being said, there are several points of comparison between the two positions. First, and most obvious, the relationship between a judicial vicar and another leader, whether cleric or lay, is not unlike the lay person or deacon who leads a parish in the absence of a pastor and must relate to the priest who is "provided with the powers and faculties of a pastor."[5] Second, both the appointment of a "non-pastor" to lead a parish and the function of directing a tribunal are relatively new developments in the history of the Church. In both cases a priest still plays an important and necessary role: in the one, a priest is entrusted with the faculties of a pastor; in the other, a priest is appointed judicial vicar. Likewise, despite the role of the priest in both structures, the lay person (or the other cleric) may end up with much on-site "visibility." She or he is the one people see regularly and who makes practical decisions for the parish or the tribunal.

One of the difficulties faced by those who appointed parish leaders was how to name them. In their book researching the application of canon 517 §2 in the United States, Dr. Barbara Anne Cusack and Sr. Therese Guerin Sullivan, S.P., noted in the introduction that "no consistent name or title" could be found for those persons holding either the office of the leader who was not a priest or the priest who supervised the pastoral care of the parish.[6]

Official appointments to the office of leading a parish according to canon 517 §2 came about when the new Code came into effect, but when did directors of tribunals come on the scene? Although this study did not attempt to discover who first held the position, there is evidence that directors of tribunals existed at least

---

5 "*sacerdotem constituat aliquem qui, potestatibus et facultatibus parochi instructus, curam pastoralem moderetur*" (canon 517 §2).

6 Barbara Anne Cusack and Therese Guerin Sullivan, S.P., *Pastoral Care in Parishes Without a Pastor: Applications of Canon 517 §2* (Washington, DC: Canon Law Society of America, 1995) xi.

as early as 1981.[7] Most likely some dioceses already had experiences of informal sharing of authority in the tribunal in cases where the judicial vicar was assisted by another person, even someone who was not a cleric. Administrative assistants with much experience, and even other canonists working in the tribunal, could have been performing administrative tasks well before this time as implied by the example stated above.

Today when one talks about those persons who share the duties of tribunal management with the judicial vicar, there is no consistent title in use. For the sake of this presentation the title "Director" will be used without prejudice to those holding a similar tribunal management position under a different title. By reviewing only a limited, and not random, number of entries for the dioceses listed in *The Official Catholic Directory* for 2015, commonly called the *Kenedy Directory*, the author found several titles: "Director" (Archdiocese of Cincinnati, Diocese of Erie), "Administrator" (Diocese of Tyler), "Coordinator" (Diocese of Norwich), "Administrative Director" (Diocese of Las Cruces) and "Tribunal Chancellor" (Archdiocese of Milwaukee).

It is interesting to note that, in consulting the *Kenedy Directory* in ten-year intervals since the promulgation of the 1983 Code, for the years 1985, 1995, 2005 and 2015, there has been an evolution in both the designation of a "Director" in diocesan tribunals and the titles being used. For example, for the six dioceses listed above, the 1985 *Kenedy Directory* lists "Associate Directors" for Cincinnati, all of whom were priests, whereas Sister Victoria Vondenberger, RSM, was listed as "Director" in 1995, 2005, and 2015. Erie did not list a "Director" in 1985, 1995 or 2005, but did so in 2015. In 1985 and 1995 Norwich had a "Secretary of the Tribunal," but a "Coordinator" in 2005 and 2015. Milwaukee listed an "Executive Secretary" in 1985 and 1995, an "Associate Director" in 2005, and a "Tribunal Chancellor"[8] in 2015. Tyler and Las Cruces had not been established

---

7 *The Official Catholic Directory* (hereinafter called the *Kenedy Directory*) lists the late Sr. Ellen O'Hara, C.S.J. as "Associate Director" of the Boise Tribunal as early as its 1982 volume, and in the 1985 volume she is listed as "Director." As early as 1979 Sr. Lucy Vazquez, O.P. is listed in the Kenedy Directory as "Canonical Consultant" for the Orlando Tribunal, but by 1983 she is listed as "Director." Although other directors may have been functioning before this date, it is interesting to note that this structure already existed before the promulgation of the 1983 Code. Not surprisingly, it was also in 1981 that "Raymond Lucker, bishop of the New Ulm (Minnesota) diocese, named the first non-ordained pastor in the United States." This quote is taken from Dr. Peter Gilmour in his article, "The Non-Ordained Pastor: A Paradigm for Future Church Leadership," in Loyola Pastoral Life Center, *Emerging Forms of Pastoral Leadership: Job Description and Pastoral Guidelines*, 3rd ed. (New Orleans, 1996) 6.

8 This title is very close to that of Moderator of the Tribunal Chancery, a title described in Article 61 of the Instruction, which will be discussed below.

in 1985. In 1995 and 2005 Tyler listed an "Administrator;" in 1995 Las Cruces had no listing, but in 2005 it listed an "Administrative Director."[9]

Although this study did not include a survey of all U.S. dioceses, a casual review indicates that more dioceses have directors now than twenty years ago. Suffice it to say that there are several tribunals with directors and several tribunals that have operated with directors for more than thirty years.

If some tribunals already saw this model of collaboration take shape in the 1980s, how were these foundations laid? Although every institution must from time to time adapt to changing conditions that challenge its existing structures, not all leaders wait until norms change or permission is granted before making the changes they deem necessary. One changing condition that affected tribunals was the declining number of priests being ordained who could staff a tribunal. According to statistics furnished by CARA, the survey conducted in 1970 was the year when the number of priests in the United States was highest, and that number has declined in every survey conducted since.[10] This decline also forced bishops, especially in local churches that were growing, to weigh whether they could set apart a priest to serve in canonical ministry exclusively if at all.

The declining number of priests, although not the only factor in the development of collaboration in many aspects of ministry in the Church, can be viewed as either a routine problem or an adaptive problem.[11] When viewed as an adaptive problem, leaders think, for example, not so much how to call, train, and ordain more priests – a routine solution – but whether the paradigm is changing and a solution will be found only by changing the paradigm.

Even as challenges mounted, bishops were not left without options. Although hardly a seamless transition, lay persons were already being formed in theology and other Church disciplines in the 1970s such that they formed an ever-growing pool of candidates to serve the institutional Church. Asked, more often at first, to work in parishes, especially in religious education or liturgy, trained members of the lay faithful were also recruited by bishops to serve in chanceries, even in leadership positions. This was already happening more than a decade before the promulgation of the 1983 Code.

9 As mentioned earlier in this article, it is important to note that, even today, not all directors are lay persons. Father John Boyle, for example, serves as Director in the Archdiocese of Portland in Oregon. Although it is likely that a lay person is given the task of directing a tribunal because of a dearth of priests or when the judicial vicar has other duties or because the tribunal is large, the function can be exercised by a priest or deacon. Since a priest can be appointed adjutant judicial vicar, it seems less likely that he will be named "Director." Furthermore, some canonists who are appointed judges may, in fact, be managing the tribunal without any extra title.

10 See: http://cara.georgetown.edu/caraservices/requestedchurchstats.html.

11 See the discussion in: Monroe, 150-152.

When the Second Vatican Council brought to the spotlight the importance of baptism for establishing a fundamental equality among the People of God[12] and recognizing the universal call to holiness,[13] many lay persons discerned a call to serve the Church in an official capacity.[14]

What do the changes ushered in by the Second Vatican Council and the 1983 *Code of Canon Law* tell us about how we arrived at lay management in the Church in the first place? Vatican II provided both the theological framework and the suitable environment for the emergence of lay persons to serve in leadership positions in the local church, in parishes, chanceries and social services. Rarely at that time was there an office to which they could be appointed, but the functions lay persons exercised arose according to need and in line with the vision of the diocesan bishop who created structures to satisfy the needs of his diocese.

Eventually the Code formalized some of the changes already taking place in view of the Vatican Council's new way of thinking. In his article Joseph Koury identified various types of inclusion of lay persons on the level of what he calls "horizon." First, what some canons of the 1917 Code identified as a passive right (e.g., to receive spiritual goods from the clergy), the 1983 Code identified more actively by verbs such as "enjoy," "have the right," "are capable," etc.[15] Second, the 1983 Code recognized the particular vocation of the laity in ways not known before. Third, if lay persons were traditionally absent from various structures of collegiate bodies in the Church, the 1983 Code affirmed their presence on and proper gifts for these bodies. Fourth, the 1983 Code expressed the right of laity to be heard.[16]

In several places the Code opened to lay persons the possibility of cooperating in pastoral care, undertaking certain activities previously allowed only to clerics, allowed lay persons to become an extraordinary minister and allowed lay persons to be delegated to perform certain works. More dramatically, other canons allowed lay persons to become chancellors, judges and even persons entrusted with the pastoral care of parishes.

12 "Although by Christ's will some are appointed teachers, dispensers of the mysteries and pastors for the others, yet all the faithful enjoy a true equality with regard to the dignity and the activity which they share in the building up of the body of Christ" *Lumen gentium,* no. 32, *Vatican Council II: The Basic Sixteen Documents*, A. Flannery, gen. ed. (Northport, NY: Costello Pub. Co., 1996) 50.

13 "It is therefore quite clear that all Christians in whatever state or walk in life are called to the fullness of christian life and to the perfection of charity, and this holiness is conducive to a more human way of living even in society here on earth" (*Lumen gentium,* no. 40).

14 "Besides this apostolate which belongs to absolutely every Christian, the laity can be called in different ways to more immediate cooperation the apostolate of the hierarchy ..." (*Lumen gentium*, no. 33).

15 Koury, 178-179.

16 Koury, 179-180.

Part II [O'Donnell]

Introduction

On April 11, 2015, Divine Mercy Sunday, Pope Francis I declared "A Year of Mercy" through *Misericordia Vultus* proclaiming an extraordinary jubilee year to begin on December 8, 2015, on the Solemnity of the Immaculate Conception. It will close on November 20, 2016, the Solemnity of Christ the King.[17]

Changes will be made beginning on December 8, 2015, as well with the processing of marriage cases in ecclesiastical tribunals worldwide. Since the *Codex Iuris Canonici* 1917, the Church has experienced more rapid time statutes in which to process them. Canon 1620 of the *CIC* 1917 states:

> Iudices et tribunalia curent ut quamprimum, salva iustitia, causae omnes terminentur, utque in tribunali primae instantiae ultra biennium non protrahantur, in tribunali vero secundae instantiae ultra annum.[18]

For almost sixty-six years under the 1917 Code, the judges and tribunals completed case within two years in the court of first instance. In second instance, the cases were to be handled not beyond one year.

Canon 1453 of the *CIC* 1983 states: "Iudices et tribunalia curent ut quam primum, salva iustitia, causae omnes terminentur, utque in tribunali primae instantiae ultra annum ne protrahantur, in tribunali vero secundae instantiae, ultra sex menses."[19] Thus, from the *CIC* 1917 until the *CIC* 1983, the adjudication process was shortened by one year in first instance and six months in second instance.

This year marks the tenth year anniversary of *Dignitas connubii.* This legal commentary regarding the new norms governing the marriage nullity process according to the 1983 *Code of Canon Law*, states in *DC* 72: "Judges and tribunals are to see that all causes are finished as soon as possible, while safeguarding justice, and that they not be prolonged beyond *one year* in a tribunal of first instance

---

17 Pope Francis, Bull of Indiction of the Extraordinary Jubilee of Mercy, *Misericordiae Vultus*, April 11, 2015 (Vatican City: Liberia Editrice Vaticana, 2015).

18 *Codex Iuris Canonici Pii X Pontificis Maximi issu digestus Benedicti Papae XV auctoritate promulgatus* (Rome: Typis Polyglottis Vaticanis, 1917).

19 *Codex Iuris Canonici auctoritate Ioannis Pauli PP. II promulgatus* (Vatican City: Liberia Editrice Vaticana, 1983).

and beyond *six months* in a tribunal of second instance (can. 1453) [italics added for emphasis]."[20]

Since the most recent changes regarding matrimonial procedural laws in *Mitis Iudex Dominus Iesus,* if certain criteria are met for the use of the briefer process, a case could be adjudicated in a matter of months.[21] During this year's pre-convention workshop, "Instructing a Tribunal Case," the presenter, Rev. Paul D. Counce, Judicial Vicar for the Diocese of Baton Rouge, Louisiana, stated on October 12, 2015, that if all the criteria were met for the brief process as outlined in *Mitis Iudex Dominus Iesus* (referred to as *Mitis Iudex*), the case could be processed in one hundred and one days. [22]

How Does "Expeditiously" Become a Reality Within a Tribunal?

Setting realistic goals for the short term and long term are necessary. Include all tribunal staff and officers in the process because implementing *Iudex Mitis* will require a transition period for them. There will be older cases to deal with as well as the new cases being introduced after December 8, 2015.

In order to access the situation for every tribunal as far as preparing for more petitions being accepted and processed, it would be prudent to consult the Rome Reports (the numbers of cases processed sent yearly to the Apostolic Signatura). I mention what transpired in the Diocese of Shreveport, Louisiana, because in the year 2000, when Pope John Paul II, declared it a Holy Year, [23] Bishop Friend decided to waive all annulment fees. It was so successful that the bishop decided to waive them again for 2001. The Rome Reports for those two years indicated an increase of almost six times as many cases processed during those years than in 2013. That is an excellent barometer to measure what we may be anticipating in our own tribunals as far as a tremendous increase in our caseloads in light of *Mitis Iudex*.

Take advantage of utilizing the expertise of your in-house canonists to determine grounds and what procedures are to be used to the advantage of the petitioners and respondents. This usually helps save time in the long run and with the case flow. That way, it will cut down on having to rejoin the issues or determin-

20 Pontificium Consilium de Legum Textibus, *Dignitas Connubii*, Instructio Servanda a Tribunalibus Diocecesanis et Interdioecesanis in Pertractandis Causis Nullitatis Matrimonii (Vatican City: Typis Polyglottis Vaticanis, 2005).

21 Pope Francis, *motu proprio*, *Mitis Iudex Dominus Iesus*, August 15, 2015 (Vatican City: Liberia Editrice Vaticana, 2015).

22 Rev. Paul D. Counce, JCD, *Instructing a Tribunal Case*, (Canon Law Society of America Pre-Convention Workshop, October 11-12, 2005, Pittsburgh PA, October 12, 2015).

23 John Paul II, apostolic letter, *Tertio millenio adveniente*, November 10, 1994, at http://w2.vatican.va/content/john-paul-ii/en/apost_letters/1994/documents/hf_jp-ii_apl_19941110_tertio-millennio-adveniente.html.

ing if a case is actually a diriment impediment or not. In many circumstances, the cases do not reach the canonists until a Defender of the Bond's brief is necessary or until writing the sentence.

It is always beneficial to have your operating systems and databases up to date. Otherwise, you minimize your communication with your clients and it also impedes the cases. In order to cut down on errors and manage case flow, the best product on the market is, no doubt, CaseMaster.[24] It was developed in the 1990's with Walt Payne. Other databases, which are not as functional as CaseMaster, are TMS[25] and Tribunal Systems.[26] CaseMaster will be updating their system and apprising all their subscribers of these updates in light of *Mitis Iudex*.

In my thirty years of canonical ministry, I have used all three of the aforementioned databases. The best one by far is CaseMaster. Their technical support is unsurpassed and the multi-functions are worth it. Reports can be run from CaseMaster that inform the tribunal how many outstanding cases are on the docket with a status report on each one. The reports can be modified in any fashion to include any pertinent information needed, for instance, which personnel were assigned to the cases, or which parish in the diocese turned in the most cases during a certain time period. There is no other database out there that is as multifunctional, even in other languages, than CaseMaster, unless there is a tribunal out there that has developed its own system with an expert computer programmer.

It is imperative to have an excellent rapport with the IT (Information Technology) specialists who are employed by the diocese. They are useful and needed each step of the way from upgrading computer systems, assisting as a liaison with acquiring new equipment, or communicating to the outside on any issues related to what it is the tribunal needs in order to accomplish its ministry. It is only smart to seek their expertise before making any final decisions regarding anything associated with computers.

Training all tribunal personnel to actively operate its database and equipment is the only manner in which to successfully operate the processing of annulment cases. How many times have we heard from tribunals that a case could not be advanced because so and so was absent and they were the only person who could perform a certain action on a case (e.g. send a case to the Defender of the Bond, or finalize a case for a decree of nullity).

Cross training of personnel is imperative, especially in light of *Mitis Iudex* or just as an act of mercy to assist others in getting loved ones back to the sacra-

---

24 Tribunal and Chancery Software Experts, Digital Innovation Incorporated, CaseMaster at: https://www.dicorp.com/products/tribunal/.

25 Tribunal and Chancery Software Experts, Digital Innovation Incorporated, TMS at: https://www.dicorp.com/products/tribunal/.

26 Tribunal Systems, at: http://www.tribunalsystems.com/contact.html.

ments as soon as possible. Relying on just one person to advance cases on the docket should be a thing of the past.

Everyone Is Right on Target With Their Caseloads. Right?

In the majority of tribunals, RCIA candidates who have submitted annulment applications are considered *a priori* to be processed ahead of the docket. Since these cases are relative to someone embracing the Catholic faith or receiving sacraments, care should be of primary importance to the tribunal in advancing the cases in a timely manner so the candidates are ready for the Easter Vigil.

Since the date of the Easter Vigil changes yearly, depending where Easter falls, it is the tribunal's duty to apprise all the parishes, missions, as well as RCIA directors, of the cut-off date in which a case may be processed. There are never any guarantees that the candidates' cases will be completed in time, but there should be that monumental effort to make the necessary attempts to do so.

Being pro-active in the diocese as a tribunal just makes sense given the nature of the ministry entrusted to us by the bishop. We need to reach out to parishes by providing annulment workshops, training advocates, or special presentations to RCIA directors.

The most innovative and most outreaching of any tribunal I have heard of by far is the Diocese of San Bernardino, California. Very Rev. David Andel, JCL, Director and Judicial Vicar, spoke about formulating a triage and going out to the parishes, especially the more remote ones or a central one located near a cluster of parishes.[27] This triage consisted of all the tribunal personnel setting up various stations in a parish to assist those who came seeking an annulment. The triage might start Friday evening and end on Saturday evening, depending on how many sign-ups the parish had and then serving walk-ins as well.

Before the triage would visit a certain parish, those coming would be informed way in advance through the sponsoring parish (e.g. church bulletins, RCIA programs, etc.) which documents would be necessary. Even if the person did not have all their documents ready at the time they met with one of the triage members, their petition for an annulment could be accepted. It seems to be working exceedingly well and portrays the tribunal and its ministers in a much better light throughout the diocese.

In summary, execute a plan to make certain all the cases are moving in a timely fashion so that no case becomes waylaid. There is no doubt there will be an onslaught of annulment petitions being sent in to the tribunals shortly compared to the normal amount. However, it can be done simply with constant updates and

27 Very Rev. David Andel, JCL, *Triage in Parishes*, (Western Regional Canon Law Convention, Palm Springs, California, March 2-4, 2015).

communication with tribunal personnel, superb organization skills utilized, and some leeway for making necessary adjustments along the way. At times, it may work out better if a shift in tribunal duties makes for a better case flow.

Remember, if a tribunal has CaseMaster, reports can be run to ease the difficulty of managing cases. Or, if a tribunal has another type of database, check with IT to see if a status report can be run from it. The rationale behind having reports run periodically is important because it is the most useful tool in identifying the tribunal's complete active inventory of cases on the docket and it keeps them moving for the salvation of souls.

Part III [Bawyn]

Canonical Aspects of Sharing Tribunal Management

It is important not only to identify and comment on the fact that, in some tribunals, lay persons or clerics direct the day-to-day operations of the tribunal in relationship to the judicial vicar, but also to examine the canonical basis for doing so. As mentioned above, the *Code of Canon Law* does not speak to this possibility by identifying a function or giving it a title; nevertheless, the Code and the Instruction *Dignitas connubii* both speak to the issue in some way.

The traditional structure for the tribunal of first instance arises from the judicial authority of the diocesan bishop who, as the judge of first instance, exercises judicial power "personally or through others" (c. 1419 §1). As stated in canon 1420 the diocesan bishop "is bound to appoint a judicial vicar, or officialis, with ordinary power to judge, . . ." The judicial vicar "constitutes one tribunal with the bishop but cannot judge cases which the bishop reserves to himself" (c.1420 §2). If they are appointed, assistants to the judicial vicar (c. 1420 §3) "must be priests" (c. 1420 §4). From here the canons address other functions of judges, even the appointment of lay persons to that position [canon 1421 §2], but no mention is made of a tribunal director.

Understandably, the canons of the Code from Book VII *de Processibus* are interested in regulating the canonical trial and do not address the administrative duties of the judicial vicar. Although the Code describes the other offices that comprise the diocesan tribunal and, for the most part, these offices can be exercised by lay persons, a position like "Director" does not appear. What, then, is a diocesan bishop permitted to do with the job description of a judicial vicar in order to accommodate the appointment of another tribunal manager? If the

Code does not clearly lay out all the duties, then there is significant room for the diocesan bishop to build a structure that works within the norm of law.[28]

When trying to discover the canonical foundation in the *Code of Canon Law* for the office of tribunal director, it is helpful to look for this title or those related to it. Book VII, Part I, Title III, Chapter I begins with the heading *De Officio Iudicum et Tribunalis Ministrorum* (The Duty of Judges and Ministers of the Tribunal). Judges are singled out, and other offices treated in Title II, Chapter I are mentioned occasionally by name. Canon 1449 §4 speaks generally of *alios tribunalis administros* (other officials of the tribunal) but does not indicate the scope of its reference. Given the context of this and the previous canon, *administros* likely refers to the notary, assessor, procurator, advocate or auditor, but is this for certain?

At this point one does not expect to see mentioned any other official, but canon 1457 §2 raises questions when it distinguishes between "ministers and personnel of the tribunal" (*tribunalis ministri et adiutores*). Here now are found two more words in the Latin text, *ministri* and *adiutores*, and it is not clear, first, what the distinction is between these two words and, second, how both words differ from *administros*. Even canon 1456 adds to the confusion by distinguishing between "judge and all officials of the tribunal" (*judex et omnes tribunalis administri*). Since the office of judge has been treated in a special way so far, it would not be right to say that, from this phrase alone, judges are not officials. Yes, there are now three titles in use: ministers (*ministri*), officials (*administri*), and personnel (*adiutores*) without a clear indication of who is included under each.[29]

Could it be that this ambiguity presents at least subconsciously the possibility that other officials of the tribunal, such as a director, are covered by these norms even though not all possible officials are named? Without a thorough linguistic analysis and examination of the discussion of the *relatores* of the Code Commission this is a facile conclusion. For this seminar it is sufficient to point out how multiple similar titles invite speculation about where the title "Director" might fit.

If the language of the Code hints at the possibility that "Director" or other titles were envisioned by the legislator, canonists should take seriously the warn-

---

28 I would argue that canon 381 §1 gives the diocesan bishop sufficient authority to organize his tribunal, especially in the exercise of administrative power: "A diocesan bishop in the diocese entrusted to him has all ordinary, proper, and immediate power which is required for the exercise of his pastoral function except for cases which the law or a decree of the Supreme Pontiff reserves to the supreme authority or to another ecclesiastical authority."

29 *Dignitas connubii* rather consistently uses "*ministri tribunalis*" and "*ministri iustitiae*" throughout its articles.

ing found in article 37 of the Instruction which states: "No other minister of the tribunal can be established besides those listed in the Code."[30]

How, then, is it possible to reconcile this with the growing practice in tribunals of identifying tribunal managers other than the judicial vicar? One could return to the observation made by Doheny, cited above, about the two meanings of "tribunal," and try to justify the practice in view of the first definition, but it is more useful to refer to a reputable commentary on the Instruction. In their commentary on *Dignitas connubii*, Ronny Jenkins and Klaus Lüdicke explicitly take up the practice of establishing other ministers as an example of what is not permitted by this article of the Instruction. They say that such a practice was not foreseen by the universal law and that to sustain it runs the risk of confusion when persons communicate with tribunal managers of this sort since they will not understand the scope of the manager's authority. They also warn against using the title "Administrator" since this title "is properly reserved to the bishop moderator of a tribunal."[31]

Does article 37 settle the matter? To answer this question one should look first at article 61. Even though Lüdicke and Jenkins suggest that in a tribunal where someone is named "Tribunal Manager" or "Tribunal Director" she or he is to "fulfill only the tasks assigned to the head of the chancery tribunal,"[32] they seem to equate this person with what article 61 §1 calls the "head of the tribunal chancery" (*cancellariae tribunalis moderatorem*). "Head of the tribunal chancery" (or moderator) is a new title found in an article of the Instruction that has no reference in the Code. The role of modeartor described in this article looks very much like the chancellor of the diocesan curia, and this is intentional given the reference in that article to canon 482 of the Code. Because the list of duties found in article 61 §2 covers many functions found in the procedural law of the contentious trial, it is easy to see how this official might be called "Director" or serve in the capacity of what some tribunals call a director. Paragraph 3 of this article cautions against the moderator interfering in a cause being heard except for those matters that pertain to this job. In their commentary Lüdicke and Jenkins point out that the judicial vicar "is required to give the moderator a mandate for all necessary operations (procedures) that concern the business of the tribunal (outside of matters involved in the hearing of concrete judicial cases)."[33] By their comment the authors indicate the possibility that the moderator will be

30 *Praeter eos qui in Codice recensentur, nullus alius minister tribunalis constitui potest.*

31 Klaus Lüdicke and Ronny Jenkins, *Dignitas connubii: Norms and Commentary* (Washington, DC: Canon Law Society of America, 2006) 82.

32 Ibid., 82. The use of "head of the chancery tribunal" in this part of their commentary is unfortunate given the English translation of *cancellariae tribunalis moderatorem* found in Article 61: "head of the tribunal chancery," a translation that more accurately describes the position and avoids the very confusion against which the authors warn.

33 Lüdicke and Jenkins, 118.

responsible for more than those duties outlined in paragraph 2 of this article of the Instruction.

The question still remains whether the *Code of Canon Law* is really interested in regulating those administrative functions that comprise part of the overall duties of managing a tribunal. This author believes not. The fact that the head of the tribunal chancery, who may in fact be managing tribunal administration to some degree, is listed among the ministers of justice and no other position attached to the tribunal is described either in the *Code of Canon Law* or in *Dignitas connubii* seems to indicate that the legislator is only interested in identifying and regulating those positions directly related to the primary work of tribunals in canon law, namely, the exercise of judicial power. The possibility that a diocesan bishop would appoint someone to manage the operations of a tribunal does not, it seems, violate the spirit of the law so long as the one who is appointed to manage does not take part in the judicial process strictly speaking. Furthermore, if that same manager is also a minister of justice, (e.g., defender of the bond), he or she should be able to fulfill that official function in a trial and still manage the administrative affairs of the tribunal without a conflict of interest.

In their commentary on article 26 of the Instruction Lüdicke and Jenkins state that the judicial power exercised by the diocesan bishop "is to be distinguished from the administrative authority he exercises over a tribunal. He may depute other officials to exercise administrative authority. . . . The deputing of administrative authority is not subject to the same provision of law regarding the reservation by the bishop to himself of the adjudication of causes that come before the tribunal."[34]

In view of this commentary, it is puzzling that the text of article 26 does not speak about either the diocesan tribunal of first instance in the narrow sense, or the task of administration. Article 26 refers, rather, to article 23 on the interdiocesan tribunal of first instance and article 25 on the tribunal of second instance. One does find, however, the phrase "has all the powers which pertain to a Diocesan Bishop in regard to his own tribunal." At this point in the text one might expect a reference to the powers of the diocesan bishop found in Book II of the Code since the procedural law found in Book VII speaks only to judicial power,[35] but the reference at the end of the article is to canons 1423 §1 and 1439 §3, which also refer to the interdiocesan tribunal and second-instance tribunal respectively. At first, it seems out of place that Lüdicke and Jenkins use this article to expand on the notion of administrative power exercised by the diocesan bishop in his tribunal. It is not hard, however, to see this as a logical conclusion

34 Ibid., 65.

35 *In unaquaque dioecesi et pro omnibus causis iure expresse non exceptis, iudex primae instantiae est Episcopus dioecesanus, qui iudicialem potestatem exercere potest per se ipse vel per alios, secundum canones qui sequunter* (c. 1419 §1).

when considering the general context of these articles of the Instruction and the related canons of the Code.

As often happens in the *Code of Canon Law* the administrative authority of the diocesan bishop is rarely mentioned. Apart from the issuing of singular administrative acts, which are considered acts of executive power, administrative power has to be inferred from canon 381 §1, the general canon on the broad authority of the diocesan bishop. This broad authority is tempered by the other norms of the Code that limit his authority in areas reserved to a higher authority, in particular, the norms governing the procedural law on marriage.

These articles and the commentary are key to understanding by what authority a lay person or other cleric who is not the judicial vicar can be appointed by the bishop to direct the administrative activity of a tribunal. So long as the norms of the procedural canons are respected, there is not necessarily a conflict for the tribunal director who, if she or he also holds a judicial office, must make a proper distinction between the exercise of that office and the merely administrative functions that pertain to running the tribunal. The bigger challenge, however, of sharing tribunal administration with the judicial vicar rests with the diocesan bishop's articulating a clear division of duties and the quality of the relationship that the two tribunal leaders create between themselves.

Of course, there are still examples of tribunals functioning effectively under the traditional structure of a judicial vicar who both exercises his judicial power and handles the day-to-day administration; however, it appears that bishops in more and more dioceses are opting to permit the sharing of administrative responsibilities in tribunals as a better use of priest personnel and, very often, the gifts of the lay faithful.

Part IV [O'Donnell]

How "Really" Christian Are We When It Comes To Tribunal Management Tactics?

Dignitas Connubii, art. 33 states:

> In light of the seriousness and the difficulty of causes of the nullity of marriage, it is the responsibility of Bishops to see to it:
>
> 1° that suitable ministers of justice are prepared for their tribunals;
>
> 2° that those selected for this ministry each fulfill their respective functions diligently and in accordance with the law."[36]

Article 33 does not have a parallel canon in the Code. However, the corresponding commentary is a reminder that the bishop is ultimately responsible for assuring that the application of the Code regarding marriage nullity is carried out "correctly, efficiently, and in a dedicated manner." Also, the commentary speaks of the caliber of ministers who should be representing the tribunal and the bishop. Not only should they have suitable formation, but, in addition, they should be able to carry out the tasks to fulfill the ultimate goal of the marriage nullity process.[37]

The need to formulate a collaborative spirit among those with whom we practice tribunal ministry is of paramount importance. Everyone should be treated with equity and be made to feel part of the team that assists those in need of tribunal services. It may not be part of our natural instinct to offer a word or two of praise or thanks, but after the completion of what seemed to be a monumental case or task, we should be gracious and humble enough to offer that to our colleagues.

There is no doubt about it, tribunal ministry can be very stressful. Good management should be able to monitor the stress level within the confines of the tribunal among its personnel. Remember, anyone practicing a form of tribunal ministry can exhibit signs of too much on their plate. Before they burnout, remember it takes a lot of energy and time to train new personnel, so it is better to relieve them of a burden temporarily or make a change, until their situation

---

36 K. Lüdicke and R. Jenkins, *Dignitas Connubii: Norms and Commentary* (Alexandria, VA: Canon Law Society of America, 2006) 76.
37 Ibid., 76-77.

changes.[38] We all could be a bit more sensitive and understanding at times with our coworkers.

The Black Hole in the Diocese Where Money is Concerned, the Tribunal.

It is always a challenge to prove and convince those at the top that effective and efficient tribunal management requires financing. In most tribunals, the budget is increased yearly by an average of ten percent. That appears to be the norm, however, it is not sufficient to explain why the increase is needed or even perhaps adding a new line item in the budget. The best manner possible will take some time when you first introduce a narrative budget, but the chances are, you will receive the funding you requested.

The way to get started on preparing a narrative budget[39] is to request from all the vendors the tribunal utilizes their pricing for the following year. A statement by the vendor, either by e-mail or invoice, will be needed as an appendix to the form or forms utilized by your diocese. This is especially critical if a tribunal needs costly equipment. This is the most effective way to receive the funding the tribunal needs in order to fulfill its ministry.

One year, where I was practicing canonical ministry, the tribunal needed a very expensive piece of equipment. We did procure the necessary funding for it. However, when it came time to purchase the item, the business from which we had received an invoice for the price had substantially raised the price of the equipment. Once they were notified with the copy of their invoice, they were very gracious to charge the tribunal what they had agreed upon. In addition to the price increase was another expense they had added as a maintenance agreement. On the invoice, that was included as well with the original price the tribunal had been quoted previously. The company acquiesced to the prior agreement as well.

The bottom line is that if the tribunal has the vendor's quotes in writing, it should be capable of adequately spending within its budget. In addition to the vendor's quotes, it is advised to find out each year if prices will be raised for membership in canon law societies and the costs of attending conventions if the diocese covers these expenditures. Also, be prudent to seek all costs for each line item requested in the budget.

There are many creative ways in which tribunals have been successful in acquiring financing after fees had been abolished. Two tribunals come to mind. One is located in the Diocese of Dallas and the other in Columbus, Ohio. I have previously worked for both of them, either as a satellite or full-time. Since Pope

38 Mayo Clinic Staff, *Health Lifestyle Management*, July 19, 2013 at: http://www.mayoclinic.org/healthy-lifestyle/stress-management/in-depth/stress-symptoms/art-20050987.
39 Grant Central Station, *Writing a Budget Narrative* at: http://grant-central-station.com/articles/33/.

Francis is requesting tribunals to not charge fees or to reduce them, it might be worth contacting these tribunals or others who have abolished fees, to learn from them how to fund the tribunal and retain qualified personnel while maintaining a high standard of operation.

We all are aware of the biblical adages such "as mercy and kindness shall follow you . . ."[40] the beatitudes[41] and the reference to "offering an olive branch."[42] All of us practicing ministry anywhere should keep in mind how we are to conduct our business as the bishop's representatives of the diocese. We should emulate what we have heard from the pulpit of our Church and have studied in catechism in our youth. Is not that what Pope Francis is asking each of us as followers of Christ?

Conclusion

Applying the Golden Rule[43] will make the tribunal a more manageable operation.

Make every reasonable attempt to stay on track with the processing of cases while at the same time, keeping an eye on tribunal officers and staff to make certain everyone feels part of the team and not alienated. The stronger the cohesiveness of tribunal personnel, the better the productivity.

While the tribunal is concentrating on the processing of cases, it is difficult to keep up the morale in the workplace at the same time. Uniting in prayer is one way to solve this. In the Orange Tribunal, everyone prays the Angelus[44] every day at noon. It has been their custom for many years now and praying together creates a common focal point for why we are there in the first place.

There are other ways in which to unite tribunal personnel apart from the workplace. Some tribunals take the birthday celebrants out to lunch, go to the theatre, visit theme parks, go to museums, attend ball games, and engage in other activities together. The rules are that no one is to discuss work while enjoying each other's company outside the office. These are all effective ways in which tribunal personnel can get to know one another.

Acknowledging someone's birthday or another occasion certainly is a sign of respect towards that person. Too many times, a birthday or Christmas greeting,

40 Ps. 23:6 at: http://www.usccb.org/bible/psalms/23.

41 Mt. 5:1-12 at: http://www.usccb.org/bible/matthew/5.

42 Margaret Minnicks, What it means to 'extend the olive branch', November 14, 2011 at: http://www.examiner.com/article/what-it-means-to-extend-the-olive-branch.

43 Mt. 7:12 at: http://www.usccb.org/bible/matthew/7.

44 *The Angelus* at: http://www.ourcatholicprayers.com/the-angelus.html.

either verbally or through a card, does not get transmitted to those who are dedicated ministers of our Church.

Hopefully, those who attended the seminar have profited from hearing new ideas on how to improve or implement new methods of tribunal management in their dioceses. There are three additional points to remember along the way. First, make certain to keep current with changes emanating from Rome. Employ them accordingly. Second, educate everyone in the tribunal for their ministry and, third, remember flexibility is the key to successful management. Not everything turns out the way we envision or plan it to, so changes and modifications are necessary.

SEMINAR

FINANCIAL IRRESPONSIBILITY AND ITS IMPACT ON THE *COMMUNIO* OF MARRIAGE: FROM SIMPLE FACTS TO JURIDIC FACTS

Timothy J. Cavanaugh

Introduction

In February of 2014, I got an email from Fr. Michael Joyce, then chairperson of the Convention Planning Committee, inviting me to speak at the 2015 convention on the topic of "Financial Irresponsibility and Its Impact on the *Communio* of Marriage."

While I was of course deeply honored by the invitation, I confess to being initially a little puzzled by the topic. I did not doubt that there was plenty to be said about money and marriage from a sociological standpoint, or a therapeutic standpoint, or a pastoral-theological standpoint.

But was there a canonical angle there? That evening I asked my wife why she thought I might have been asked to speak on that topic. She said, "Well, let's see. You quit your job and convinced your pregnant wife to quit her job and go with you to Washington, DC, for six semesters of schooling, all so you could go work for the Church. I guess they thought you must be some kind of expert on financial irresponsibility!" She might have a point.

The topic bounced around in the back of my mind during the next few days and weeks, as I went about my normal daily tasks in the tribunal. I thought back to the very first case I ever worked on as a Defender, the case of Roy and Nina. Roy was the poster boy for financial irresponsibility. They were merely civilly married at first, then divorced, then married *coram ecclesia*. During their civil marriage, Nina learned to live with a number of Roy's quirks, one of which was that he insisted on being the one to get the mail every day. It was only after seven years that she learned why. Roy had accumulated tens of thousands of dollars in overdue bills and other debt, which Nina never saw. Worse still, he had never filed taxes during the whole duration of their civil marriage. After divorce and bankruptcy, Nina found it in her heart to give Roy another chance. Roy got baptized, and they married in the Church. He seemed like a new man. He even let her get the mail herself … but he neglected to tell her about the PO Box. Nor, when he lost his job, did he bother to tell Nina; he just kept driving off in the morning and coming home in the evening. Roy had not actually gotten more responsible; he had just gotten better at hiding his irresponsibility. But all that time, he was never unfaithful, he was an involved father, he never laid a hand on Nina.

I thought about the case of Rob and Patty. They both had glamorous, high paying jobs, but somehow money ended up being a constant problem for them anyway. Patty liked to shop. She shopped to celebrate, she shopped to relax, she shopped for fun. And she had expensive tastes. And it turns out you can only buy so many thousand-dollar handbags before it becomes a drain on your dual income.

I thought about the dozens of cases in which one party or the other says almost these exact words: "It seemed like we never knew where all our money was going, so eventually I asked if I could take over the finances."

In fact, once I got started, I could think of few cases in which some sort of financial issue did not play a part. But I also noticed, once I went back to look more systematically, that there did not seem to be any obvious trends tying these cases together: no obvious patterns in grounds, no obvious patterns in whether the case was ruled in the affirmative or in the negative. I started looking elsewhere for a lead.

There are numerous surveys and studies about the prevalence of various martial problems in general and more specifically about the immediate causes of marital breakdown.[1] These studies, both religious and secular, vary considerably in things like their degree of formality, their methodologies, their sample sizes, and their philosophical approaches. Not surprisingly the results vary considerably from study to study, but there are a few constants that appear on virtually every list. Here are four of the usual suspects, which I have chosen not only for their prevalence but also to help me demonstrate a point:

(1) infidelity
(2) disagreements about having children
(3) lack of a permanent commitment
(4) financial problems

As they used to say on Sesame Street, "Three of these things belong together, three of these things are kind of the same, but one of these things is doing its own thing." The first three relate so clearly to the essential obligations of marriage: the obligations deriving from the *bonum fidei*, the *bonum prolis*, and the *bonum sacramenti*, respectively. That is not to imply that these facts render a marriage

1 One noteworthy example is the Center for Applied Research in the Apostolate's "Marriage in the Catholic Church: A Survey of U.S. Catholics," ed. Mark Gray et al., (Washington, DC: Georgetown University, 2007) 100.

null – naturally they do not. But if these facts were alleged in a marriage nullity case involving a defect of consent, their juridic relevance would be more obvious. It would be clearer what their significance was in a case of marriage nullity. But finances? Their relevance is not so clear. In fact, in the rite of marriage most frequently used in the United States, the spouses explicitly profess that their marital commitment is indifferent to finances: it is "for richer or for poorer."

What, then, is the juridic relevance of financial irresponsibility in a marriage nullity trial? More fundamentally, what is the juridic relevance of financial irresponsibility in marriage?

My contention is that finances *in themselves* have no essential or constitutive relationship to the matrimonial covenant. I am not saying that money has nothing to do with marriage or with a happy married life; no sane married person would try to argue that. Instead I am saying that its relationship to marriage does not derive immediately from the essence of marriage, but only secondarily or contingently.

Here is my reasoning: First, marriage is essentially characterized by its unity, its indissolubility, its ordination to the procreation and education of offspring, and its ordination to the good of the spouses. Money – having it, being able to earn it in sufficient quantities, being able to manage it well – certainly tends to *facilitate* all of these things, but only secondarily and not by intrinsic necessity.

Second, if something is *essential* to marriage, it is true of all marriages in all times and places and cultures. But in a pre-industrial or agrarian culture, money might have no role at all in married life. If it is not essential to those marriages, then it is not essential to marriage in general.

Third, we read in canon 1135 that "Each spouse has an equal duty and right to those things which *pertain* to the partnership of conjugal life."[2] One of the distinguishing marks of the rights and duties that pertain to marriage is that each spouse can and must have an equal share in them. The "contrapositive" of this statement, as the logicians would say, is that anything to which the spouses do not have an equal duty and right does not pertain essentially to the partnership of conjugal life. In many modern, Western marriages, the spouses do assume an equal right and duty over finances. But it is not hard to imagine a marriage in which only one of the spouses assumes the duty of earning or managing money. The same cannot be said of, say, the duty of observing conjugal fidelity: we

2 *Codex Iuris Canonici auctoritate Ioannis Pauli PP. II promulgatus* (Vatican City: Libreria Editrice Vaticana, 1983) c. 1135: "Utrique coniugi aequum officium et ius est ad ea quae pertinent ad consortium vitae coniugalis." This and all subsequent English translations from *Code of Canon Law, Latin-English Edition: New English Translation* (Washington, DC: Canon Law Society of America, 1998), with my own modifications here and throughout for the sake of clarity of argument.

cannot imagine a marriage in which only one spouse has the duty of observing fidelity. The fact that the rights and duties pertaining to finances is capable of arbitrary division among the spouses shows that that these rights and duties do not derive from the essence of marriage. Similarly, a person could totally turn over the management of his or her financial affairs to a third party, which cannot be said of the rights and duties that are constitutive to marriage. The *ius in corpus* is an obvious example of a constitutive right that cannot be turned over to a third party.

It might be countered that, as the Fathers of the Second Vatican Council put it, marriage is a *communio*,[3] that is, a sharing of things in common. Does that not mean that a sharing of finances is essential to marriage? Well, no. Marriage is a *communio*, but it is a *communio* of life and love. What the spouses essentially *share in common* is not possessions but a conjugal life together. Normally and normatively, this includes a common domicile as well, and even that is not an essential requirement. But as for finances, even though I think most of us would agree that shared finances generally contribute to a happy and healthy marriage, there is no obligation for spouses to have shared finances, whether totally or in part.

So for all these reasons, I contend that finances *in themselves* have no essential juridic relevance in the marriage covenant. That means, among other things, that no degree of financial irresponsibility is in itself capable of rendering a marriage invalid. It cannot do so under canon 1095, 2°, in which the defect of discretion must always relate to the matrimonial rights and duties mutually to be handed over and accepted. It cannot do so under canon 1095, 3°, in which the psychic incapacity must relate to the assumption of the *essential* matrimonial rights and duties. A grave defect of discretion about management of money does not make a marriage invalid. An incapacity to assume financial obligations does not make a marriage invalid.

This is generally confirmed in rotal jurisprudence. For example, a 1992 sentence *coram* Burke says that "financial irresponsibility [cannot] be considered a breach of any essential – constitutional – obligation of the married covenant."[4]

Does that mean that financial irresponsibility is always and in every case wholly irrelevant to the question of nullity? Not at all. Just because it is incapable of causing nullity in itself does not mean it cannot be an important fact in the proof of nullity under any number of grounds. But when it is relevant, it is relevant as a "simple fact," and not as a "juridic fact." In order for the judge to discern in a given case whether alleged financial irresponsibility tends to support

3 Vatican II, pastoral constitution *Gaudium et spes* 22 in AAS 58 (1966) 1072: "totius vita [...] communio."

4 Sentence *c.* Burke, *Armachana*, November 26, 1992: printed in English translation in *Studia canonica* 27 (1993) 504.

the juridic fact of nullity, it is necessary to translate the simple facts of the case into juridic facts.

I want to be clear what I *do not* mean when I talk about the need to translate the simple facts of the case into juridic language and juridic facts. I do not mean that a change of terminology and some hand waving will turn a broken marriage into an invalid marriage. Instead I mean the translation that needs to occur before we can even responsibly consider whether or not a marriage is proven invalid. It is always necessary to do this in any marriage nullity case; it is really the *essential* judicial task, but the translation is somewhat more intuitive or effortless when the judge is dealing with a fact like, say, serial adultery.

Simple fact, juridic fact, proof, and doubt.

Before proceeding, it will be helpful to define some terms, but without getting bogged down in philosophical and terminological distinctions. What is a juridic fact? First of all, what is a fact?

- For present purposes, we can define a fact as a proposition to which the intellect assent as being true.
- A juridic fact is a fact to which the law attributes some legal importance or consequence. Age and place of domicile are two basic examples of juridic facts.
- Other facts (again for our present purposes) are simple facts or secondary facts: facts to which *in themselves* the law does not attribute legal importance or consequence.
- A proof is anything that causes the intellect to tend toward certitude regarding a proposition.
- A doubt is anything that causes the intellect to tend away from certitude regarding a proposition.[5]

As I said, I do not want to get too bogged down in terminology, especially because all of these terms can be used equivocally. "Proof," for example, can refer to any substantive act of a case, whether or not it supports the hypothesis of nullity. The testimony of a given witness, for example, is a "proof" in that sense. "Doubt" can refer to the mental state of uncertainty rather than the fact that gives rise to that uncertainty. "Fact" could refer to any proposition, whether or not it is assented to as true; in that sense it would not be contradictory to speak of an unproven fact.

5 These definitions are loosely based on Francis Wanenmacher, *Canonical Evidence in Marriage Cases* (Philadelphia: Dolphin Press, 1935) 3-8.

Canon 1400 lists "the declaration of a juridic fact" as one of the three objects of a trial.[6] The object of a marriage nullity trial is the declaration of the juridic fact of the nullity of a marriage. Any other fact that results by logical necessity in the nullity of the marriage is also a juridic fact: "the Petitioner excluded the good of permanence by a positive act of the will" is a juridic fact.

Other facts of the case may or may not have juridic importance in the broader sense (the age or baptismal status of the parties, for example) but unless this is a case of nonage or disparity of cult, they can be considered "simple" facts for the purpose of the marriage nullity trial. Some of these simple facts will be proofs: they will cause the mind of the judge to tend toward certitude regarding the juridic fact of nullity. Other simple facts will be sources of doubt: they will cause the mind of the judge to tend away from certitude regarding the juridic fact of nullity.

When is the juridic fact of nullity established? Not just when the proof of nullity outweighs the doubt: that would be a mere preponderance of evidence. The preponderance of evidence has never been the standard for proof of nullity of marriage – even, I would argue, under the American Procedural Norms, even though that was not so obvious from the letter of the law.[7] The preponderance of evidence as a standard of proof is explicitly repudiated in Article 12 of the *Ratio procedendi* appended to the two documents issued *motu proprio* revising the marriage nullity process for the Latin and Eastern Churches.[8] The standard of proof for marriage nullity is moral certitude, which is defined as the absence of a positive and prudent doubt.[9] A doubt is positive when it arises from a fact rather than conjecture about an unknown fact, and it is prudent when it would cause a prudent person who knows the law to doubt the nullity of the marriage. In the presence of a single positive and prudent doubt, the nullity of the marriage cannot be considered proven, despite overwhelming evidence to the contrary.

For each ground of nullity, the judge should have a list in his or her mind of the simple facts that would need to be demonstrated in order to prove nullity on that ground – or, more to the point, the simple facts that would demonstrate doubt of nullity on that ground. For example, for the ground of partial simulation, the list of facts would look something like this:

---

6 *CIC83*, c. 1400: "§1. Obiectum iudicii sunt: 1° [...] facta iuridica declaranda."

7 Council for the Public Affairs of the Church, rescript, April 28, 1970, Prot. No. 3320/70, *CLD* 7, 961, American Procedural Norms, norm 21: "the judge will render his decision according to moral certitude generated by the prevailing weight of that evidence having a recognized value in law and jurisprudence."

8 Francis, *motu proprio Mitis Iudex Dominus Iesus*, August 15, 2015, and *motu proprio Mitis et Misericors Iesus*, August 15, 2015, both as yet unpublished in the *Acta Apostolicae Sedis*.

9 See, for example, Pontifical Council for Legislative Texts, instruction of January 25, 2005, *Dignitas Connubii* art. 247 §2.

- The simulator has confessed to simulating.
- The confession is credible.
- The simulator had remote and proximate causes to simulate.
- The simulator also had cause to contract marriage instead of simply not marrying.
- The circumstances and behaviors from before the wedding, at the time of the wedding, and during the course of married life confirm the simulation.

But the first step is ascertaining the simple facts of the case to begin with. The guiding maxim for the judge is that "*facta non praesumuntur sed probantur.*" Facts are not to be presumed but to be proven. As St. John Paul II said in his 1980 allocution to the Roman Rota, "the judge cannot limit himself to giving credence to affirmations alone."[10] I think it is sufficiently appreciated that this maxim applies to the juridic fact of nullity: we all know that nullity has to be proven. But perhaps it is insufficiently appreciated that this maxim applies to simple facts as well. Any fact that is to be relied on as a proof supporting the juridic fact of nullity must be proven. Only then can it be considered a "*probatum*" in the sense contemplated in canon 1608, which requires the judge to derive certitude "*ex actis et probatis*."[11]

Proof of a fact can be either partial or total; total when it suffices in itself to remove prudent doubt about the fact or when it is a "peremptory proof," i.e., the law gives it full probative value regardless of its subjective effect on the mind of the judge. Proof is partial when it leaves room for prudent doubt or when the law regards it as partial regardless of the subjective effect it might have on the mind of the judge. Several partial proofs can cumulatively provide full proof – and in fact, this is the most normal and most common way for a fact to be proven.

The law recognizes six kinds of proof (in the broader sense of the word, meaning sources of evidence): the declarations of the parties, documents, witness testimony, experts, judicial examination and inspection, and presumptions.[12] I want to focus on two of these: the declarations of the parties and witness testimony, not just because they tend to form the bulk of the evidence in marriage nullity trials or because their evaluation poses the most serious difficulties for the judge, but because the recent revision of the marriage nullity process altered the norms for weighing their probative value in marriage nullity cases.

---

10 John Paul II, allocution to the Roman Rota, February 4, 1980: AAS 72 (1980) 175: "il giudice non può limitarsi a dar credito alle sole affermazioni." English translation in *Papal Allocutions to the Roman Rota 1939-2011*, ed. William H. Woestman (Ottawa, ON: Saint Paul University, 2011) 161.

11 *CIC83* c. 1608.

12 *CIC83* cc. 1530-1586.

Probative Value of Witness Testimony

First, I want to discuss the evaluation of witness testimony; or in other words the derivation of facts from witness testimony. Witnesses are the people other than the parties who can attest to facts of relevance to the case, ideally from their firsthand knowledge, but also from other sources.

The norms for evaluating the testimony of witnesses can be traced to the Old Testament. Deuteronomy 19:15 reads: "A single witness shall not suffice to convict a person of any crime or wrongdoing in connection with any offense that may be committed. Only on the evidence of two or three witnesses shall a charge be sustained."[13] Examples of similar norms can be found dispersed through the Old and New Testaments.[14]

From the Deuteronomic Code to the 1917 Code, the norm remains substantially unaltered: canon 1791 of the 1917 Code states:

> §1 The testimony of a single witness does not produce full proof, unless it be a qualified witness who testifies regarding matters done *ex officio*.
>
> §2 If two or three persons beyond all exception, firmly cohering with one another, testify from personal knowledge under oath regarding some matter or fact in the trial, sufficient proof is present, unless in a certain cause the judge, owing either to the great importance of the matter or to indications that give rise to some doubt regarding the truth of the matter asserted, considers fuller proof necessary.[15]

Canon 1573 of the 1983 Code reads:

> The testimony of one witness cannot produce full proof unless it concerns a qualified witness making a deposition concerning

---

13 Deuteronomy 19:15, *NRSV*.

14 E.g., Deut. 17:6, Num 35:30, Mt 18:16, 2 Cor 13:1.

15 *Codex Iuris Canonici Pii X Pontificis Maximi iussu digestus Benedicti Papae XV auctoritate promulgatus* (Rome: Typis Polyglottis Vaticanis, 1917) c. 1791:

"§1. Unius testis depositio plenam fidem non facit, nisi sit testis qualificatus qui deponat de rebus ex officio gestis.

§2. Si sub iuramenti fide duae vel tres personae, omni exceptione maiores, sibi firmiter cohaerentes, de aliqua re vel facto in iudicio testificentur de scientia propria, sufficiens probatio habetur; nisi in aliqua causa iudex ob maximam negotii gravitatem, vel ob indicia quae aliquod dubium de veritate rei assertae ingerunt, necessariam censeat pleniorem probationem." English translation is my own.

> matters done *ex officio*, or unless the circumstances of things and persons suggest otherwise.[16]

Finally, canon 1678 §2 of the 1983 Code as modified by the apostolic letter *motu proprio Mitis Iudex*, which applies only to cases of marriage nullity, states:

> In the same causes [i.e., causes of marriage nullity], the testimony of a single witness can produce full proof, if it is a matter of a qualified witness who testifies regarding matters done *ex officio* or the circumstances of things and persons suggests it.[17]

The most noteworthy legislative development occurs between the 1917 Code and the 1983 Code, the latter of which allows the testimony of a single non-qualified witness to have the force of full proof "when the circumstances of things and persons suggests otherwise." In practice, however, the principle that the requirement of multiple witnesses ought not to be applied too stringently or artificially was already recognized in rotal jurisprudence. For example, a 1951 rotal sentence states:

> It must be remembered that in matrimonial cases … concerning an interior fact which no other person can directly know, it would be idle to raise any question about the number of witnesses – a requirement which, for that matter, is not categorically prescribed by law, but is merely recommended as a norm to be properly applied. … It is the weight of the testimony rather than the number of witnesses which must be attentively considered.[18]

So the development between the 1917 Code and 1983 Code is not so drastic as it might first appear, but it still represents a significant shift. What was implicit in the old law became explicit in the new law, although under both regimes it was exceptional for the testimony of a single witness to have full probative value.

---

16 *CIC83,* c. 1573: "Unius testis depositio plenam fidem facere non potest, nisi agatur de teste qualificato qui deponat de rebus ex officio gestis, aut rerum et personarum adiuncta aliud suadeant."

17 *CIC83,* c. 1678 §2, as modified by *Mitis Iudex*, effective December 8, 2015: "In iisdem causis, depositio unius testis plenam fidem facere potest, si agatur de teste qualificato qui deponat de rebus ex officio gestis, aut rerum et personarum adiuncta id suadeant."

18 Sentence *c.* Mattioli, *Versaliensis*, November 27, 1951: *RRDec* XLIII (1961) 689: Neque obliviscendum est quod in causis matrimonialibus, in quibus [...] de actu interno creaturae nulli directe noto iudicium proferri debet, inepte quaestio institueretur de numero testium, qui ceterum cathegoricis legis praescriptis non decernitur, sed tantum suadetur ut norma, recte quidem exigenda." English translation in *CLD* 3, 604-605.

By contrast, the development between the existing canon 1573 (which remains in force for all cases, concerning either the public good or the private good of the parties, with the sole exception of cases of marriage nullity) and the new canon 1678 §2 is far less momentous. In fact, from a logical or a semantic standpoint, the two canons are identical. The one is phrased negatively and the other is phrased affirmatively, but they mean exactly the same thing.

On the other hand, the drafters of *Mitis Iudex* were likely not just channeling their inner psalmists when they wrote the revised canon, restating the same thing in different words for poetic effect. Obviously, some nuance or difference in emphasis is intended here, especially since canon 1573 will continue to govern all non-marriage nullity cases. By rephrasing the negative rule positively, the legislator has not in any way changed the conditions under which full probative value can be attributed to the otherwise uncorroborated testimony of a single witness; what he has done is to encourage judges to be attentive to those conditions under which it is possible, and to be ready to attribute full probative value when such an attribution is truly warranted.

As we saw in that 1951 rotal sentence quoted earlier, a sentiment emphasized in the new canon, the exhortation against the rigid and formalistic evaluation of witness testimony, is not something new. It is good, sound judicial advice. But can I make the somewhat provocative suggestion that it may not be directed at most of us in the tribunals of the United States? Judging by the tribunal statistics published annually by the CLSA, we are not generally in need of any further inducements to attain moral certitude of nullity. A sizeable portion of tribunals did not issue a single negative during the whole 2014 judicial year.[19] In other words, if there was not a single case that came before them in which the judges held that there was a *single* positive or prudent doubt about nullity. Based on that trend, my guess is that we collectively have very few qualms about attributing the force of full proof to an uncorroborated witness. Or maybe I should rephrase that; maybe it is not that we attribute too much probative value to witness testimony, but that we do not attribute *enough* probative value when (as is so often the case) the witnesses attest to facts that do not support the nullity of the marriage.

The Probative Value of Confessions and Other Declarations of the Parties

A similar but somewhat more drastic development can be seen in the norms regarding the probative value of the declarations and other confessions of a party. Once again, the roots of the norm can be seen in scripture. John 8:13 reads: "The Pharisees said to him, 'You testify on your own behalf, so your testimony cannot be verified.'"[20] Please note, I cite this passage not because it represents anything like the establishment of an authoritative norm, but because it shows that the norm is already presupposed by the Pharisees and presumably the reader as well.

19 Canon Law Society of America, program for the 77th Annual Convention, 73-79.
20 Jn 8:13, *NAB*.

Jesus, as usual, subverts the argument, but without calling into question its basic premise: a person's attestations about himself or herself are not to be relied on as proof of a fact.

The 1917 Code itself does not contain an equivalent positive norm, but the subsequent instruction *Provida Mater* does at number 117, which states: "The judicial deposition of the spouses is not suitable to constitute proof against the validity of the marriage."[21]

Canon 1536 §2 of the 1983 Code reads:

> In cases which regard the public good, a judicial confession and declarations of the parties which are not confessions can have a probative force which the judge must evaluate together with all the circumstances of the case; the force of full proof cannot be attributed to them, however, unless other elements are present which completely corroborate them.[22]

Finally, canon 1678 §1 of the recently-revised 1983 Code states:

> In cases of marriage nullity, the judicial confession and declarations of the parties, supported perhaps by witnesses to the credibility of the same parties, can have the force of full proof, which the judge must evaluate having weighed all of the indications and circumstances, unless other elements are present which weaken them.[23]

The innovations in the 1983 Code regarding the probative value of the declarations of the parties were drastic, at least judging by the letter of the law. Under the regime of the 1917 Code as put into effect through *Provida Mater*, the judicial declarations of the parties were not regarded as proofs at all, not in the proper sense. They did not, as a rule, have probative weight. Now, once again, this norm was not applied mechanically or rigidly; it was recognized that in exceptional

21 Sacred Congregation for the Discipline of the Sacraments, instruction *Provida Mater*, article 117: *AAS* 28 (1936): "Depositio iudicialis coniugum non est apta ad probationem contra valorem matrimonii constituendam." English translation is my own.

22 *CIC83*, c. 1536 §2: "In causis autem quae respiciunt bonum publicum, confessio iudicialis et partium declarationes, quae non sint confessiones, vim probandi habere possunt, a iudice aestimandam una cum ceteris causae adiunctis, at vis plenae probationis ipsis tribui nequit, nisi alia accedant elementa quae eas omnino corroborent."

23 *CIC83*, c. 1678 §1, as modified by *Mitis Iudex*, effective December 8, 2015: "In causis de matrimonii nullitate, confessio iudicialis et partium declarationes, testibus forte de ipsarum partium credibilitate sustentae, vim plenae probationis habere possunt, a iudice aestimandam perpensis omnibus indiciis et adminiculis, nisi alia accedant elementa quae eas infirment."

cases the declarations of a trustworthy party could have probative value.[24] And outside of these exceptional cases, the declarations of the parties always played a crucial role in shaping the instruction of the case: in determining, for example, which facts to ask the witnesses about. But only in the 1983 Code were they given normative probative value, including the possibility of providing the force of full proof in exceptional circumstances.

Once again, by comparison, the development between canon 1536 §2 and the revised canon 1678 §1 is far less momentous. And although it is less obvious here than it is in the norms on witness testimony, I submit that the revised norm is the logical equivalent of the existing norm. Canon 1536 allows for the attribution of full proof "when elements are present which completely corroborate them" – in other words, "when there are no elements present which weaken them." In the presence of weakening elements, the corroborating elements could not be regarded as "completely" corroborating. And once we apply that paraphrase, it becomes clearer that the two canons are logically equivalent; one is phrased negatively, and the other is phrased affirmatively, but they can both be reduced to the same proposition. The difference is a matter of emphasis, not substance. Once again, the legislator is encouraging the judge to be attentive to the circumstances in which the declarations of the party can have full probative value, and to be willing to attribute full probative value to them when warranted. And once again, can I suggest that this sound, common-sense advice or encouragement is *not* mainly directed to American tribunals? There really is a risk of ignoring the probative value of the parties' declarations artificially or formalistically, treating it as a numbers game. But we are far, far more susceptible to the opposite risk: the risk of uncritically accepting the declarations of the parties at face value, not only when they are unsupported by other sources of proof, but even when they are starkly contradicted.

But let us return to the matter of "elements" or "circumstances of persons and things" that can corroborate witness testimony or the declarations of the parties and that can sometimes justify the attribution of full proof. Is it clear that we are not talking about *factual* corroboration, i.e., by attestations to the same facts by other parties or witnesses? If there were factual corroboration, then the question of attributing full probative value to one witness or party would not arise to begin with. Instead, we would be faced with the very normal circumstance of having

24 See, e.g., the quasi-official commentary on American Procedural Norms, norm 21, *CLD* 7, 962: "The reference in the norm to 'evidence having a recognized value in law and jurisprudence' is noteworthy, especially light of a proposed norm originally submitted by the conference but not explicitly included in those which were finally approved by the Holy See. That norm read: 'In exceptional cases the concordant statements of the principals, or even in some instances the statement of one principal, given due consideration to the circumstances of the case, may constitute preponderance of evidence.' It was pointed out with merit by Vatican experts that what was said in the proposed norm was already a recognized principle of law and jurisprudence."

partial proof from one source and partial proof from another source. Rather, this is a question of a certain fact that is attested to in only once source, without being repeated or substantially contradicted anywhere else in the case. So what are these "elements"? A list of some such elements can be found in canon 1572 regarding the trustworthiness of witness testimony. Canon 1572 instructs the judge to take into account:

> 1° what the condition or reputation of the person is;
>
> 2° whether the testimony derives from personal knowledge, especially from what has been seen or heard personally, or whether from opinion, rumor, or hearsay;
>
> 3° whether the witness is reliable and firmly consistent or inconsistent, uncertain, or vacillating;
>
> 4° whether the witness has co-witnesses to the testimony or is supported or not by other elements of proof.[25]

These same criteria can be applied, *mutatis mutandis* to the declarations of the parties. What they really amount to is signs of the deponent's credibility. Credibility is another fact that is not to be presumed; it has to be weighed and evaluated by the judge. There are two important aspects of credibility: subjective credibility and objective credibility. Subjective credibility refers to a person's honesty, integrity, and intention to be truthful. Objective credibility refers to a person's ability to provide an objectively accurate account of facts. A reputation for dishonesty, an intense personal interest in the outcome of the case, or an internal pattern of contradictions are reasons to doubt a person's subjective credibility. Reasons to doubt a person's objective credibility would be any signs of gaps or distortions in their memories, signs of obtuseness or credulousness, signs of unconscious bias, or notable disparities between their accounts and the accounts that appear in other proofs. It is crucial to pay close attention to both kinds of credibility, and not just in assessing the overall credibility of the witness or party, but also in assessing their credibility with regard to each fact attested to.

So when would the "elements" thoroughly corroborate the declarations of a party or the testimony of one witness, such that it would be possible to attribute full probative value even in the absence of any other factual corroboration? Or to put it the other way around, what does a total lack of "weakening" elements look like? When a person is reputed to be honest and reliable, when he or she

25 *CIC83*, c. 1572:

"1° quae condicio sit personae, quaeve honestas;
2° utrum de scientia propria, praesertim de visu et auditu proprio testificetur, an de sua opinione, de fama, aut de auditu ab aliis;
3° utrum testis constans sit et firmiter sibi cohaereat, an varius, incertus vel vacillans;
4° utrum testimonii contestes habeat, aliisve probationis elementis confirmetur necne."

has no personal interest in the outcome of the case (or is at least shown to be willing to attest to facts that are against that interest), when he or she is attesting from firsthand personal knowledge, when his or her account is confident and internally consistent, and when he or she is factually corroborated or at least not contradicted in other important matters, then and only then is the judge justified in attributing full probative value. When even one of those elements is missing, or put conversely, when even one weakening element is present, then prudent doubt remains. The judge has a responsibility to evaluate each of these criteria and, moreover, to be certain beforehand that he or she will have the data to evaluate each of these criteria, such as by always asking the source of the party's or witness's knowledge.

Finally, whether a given proof is partially probative or fully probative, we need to be attentive to what fact it is probative of. The testimony of three witnesses who concordantly testify to the fact that, say, the Petitioner told them the Respondent was unfaithful" is probative of the fact that the Petitioner said the Respondent was unfaithful; it is *not* probative – certainly not fully probative – of the fact that the Respondent was unfaithful.

Case studies

By the same process of evaluation described above, the simple facts of a case accumulate one by one. If time and space permitted, I would discuss the evaluation of the other kinds of proofs, but for now I would like to return to the question of financial irresponsibility. Specifically, I want to use a slightly fictionalized example involving serious financial responsibility as a test case for applying that which has been discussed so far. The goal is to see whether the simple facts suffice to establish the juridic fact of nullity.

The case of Rob and Patty, described at the outset, provides a fitting test case. Rob and Patty, if you recall, were up-and-coming professionals, and Patty had a bit of a shopping problem. Rob is the Petitioner, and he alleges that the marriage is invalid on the ground of 1095, 3°. In his *libellus*, he cites Patty's compulsive shopping as a grave psychic anomaly that he believes gave rise to her incapacity and that eventually brought about the breakdown of the marriage. When there is an allegation of nullity on the ground of 1095, 3°, the juridic fact under doubt is whether the Respondent was incapable of assuming one or more of the essential obligations of marriage for causes of a psychic nature. What are the simple facts that the judge should be looking for, and whose absence would constitute a doubt about the nullity?

- First, did the Respondent suffer from a grave psychic anomaly?
- Second, was the grave psychic anomaly present already at the time of consent?

- Third, was there a link between the psychic anomaly and the essential obligations of marriage?
- Fourth, was the effect of the anomaly to render the assumption of one or more of those obligations impossible, and not merely difficult?

In his deposition, Rob gives numerous examples of seriously irresponsible expenditures that predated the wedding and were a source of conflict starting from early on in their relationship. Rob cites a number of mutual friends as witnesses, and they corroborate him on those points. Patty acknowledges the problem, but she says that Rob exaggerates how serious it was and the impact it had on their finances and their marriage in general. Rob submits verified credit card statements and bank statements as documentary evidence, and these generally confirm his account. The expert examines Patty and confidently concludes that she suffered from compulsive buying disorder, and that it was serious at the time of consent although it became more serious as the marital breakdown progressed. The expert does not see evidence of any more serious underlying disorder, or any serious trauma in her past. From all this, the judge deduces that the Respondent suffered from a grave psychic anomaly, and that it was present at the time of consent. But although it was a source of serious problems in the marriage, the judge does not discern an immediate connection between compulsive shopping and any of the essential obligations of marriage. Moreover, even if there were a connection that was not immediately apparent, the judge does not regard the disorder to have been of sufficient gravity to render it impossible and not merely difficult to take on and fulfill that obligation. Patty was faithful, and she was in other respects a caring and devoted spouse. The judge concludes that there is ample prudent doubt about nullity, and he votes in the negative on that ground.

During his deposition, Rob also mentions something that he had not brought up in the *libellus*. He says that a few weeks prior to their wedding, after one of Patty's shopping sprees, he started to wonder about their financial future. He decided that unless Patty ever got past her shopping problem, they could never have children together. He says he never wavered in that decision, and it actually grew more and more confirmed as the wedding approached. This is news to Rob's advocate, who takes him aside after the deposition and suggests that they propose the addition of a new ground: partial simulation *contra bonum prolis* on his part. After hearing from Patty and the Defender of the Bond, the judge adds the ground.

Now the judge is looking for an additional set of simple facts. He already has a judicial confession, which is rendered slightly less suspect based on the fact that Rob was apparently totally unaware of its possible importance; *nemo gratis mendax.* Patty happily corroborates Rob's confession, saying that in her opinion it was Rob's steadfast refusal to consider having children that brought about the breakdown of the marriage. Did he have motives to simulate? He and his witnesses attest that he grew up poor with lots of brothers and sisters and that as a result he bore a lot of resentment towards his parents for what he regards as their irresponsible decision to have children. He was also ambitious in his career and financial goals. Rob brings in a workbook from the parties' pre-Cana retreat, in which he wrote about being indifferent towards children in general. The judge concludes that these were remote *causae simulandi*. Patty's financial irresponsibility – or Rob's perception of it – was his proximate *causa simulandi*, in particular that one shopping spree that started him towards his alleged decision. As for his *causa contrahendi*, everybody attests that he really did love Patty, and he was hopeful that either Patty would get over her problem or else they would grow rich enough one day that it would no longer matter. Finally, the circumstantial evidence uniformly supports an exclusion of the *bonum prolis*: Rob expressed reservations about children before the wedding. In the process of planning the wedding he asked the priest to exercise the option to omit the question about accepting children lovingly. And immediately after the wedding and throughout the married life, he steadfastly refused non-contraceptive intercourse, even when Patty insisted. The judge concludes that not one positive or prudent doubt remains: the Petitioner placed a positive act of the will indefinitely and unilaterally excluding the right to procreative acts. He votes in the affirmative.

How else might the simple fact of financial irresponsibility gain juridic relevance? Some possibilities might be (1) a sign of a serious underlying psychic disorder that does touch upon the essential rights and duties of marriage; (2) as a *causa contrahendi* for marrying a more financially secure partner despite strong motives to exclude marriage itself or one of its essential properties or elements, or (3) as a motive for perpetrating fraudulent deceit to conceal extensive debt or other signs of financial irresponsibility, which although not essentially related to marriage, can certainly disturb the partnership of conjugal life. Or, in many cases, there might be no juridic relevance at all. But the point is that the simple facts on their own are not enough. And since finances and financial irresponsibility do not have an intrinsic or essential connection to the matrimonial rights, duties, elements, and properties, cases centering on financial irresponsibility are never going to be simple. This leads to a final consideration.

Postscript on the "Etc."

Article 14 of the *Ratio procedendi* appended to *Mitis Iudex* lists a number of circumstances that would permit for a cause to be admitted to the *processus brevior coram episcopo*:

> That lack of faith which can give rise to the simulation of consent or an error determining the will; the shortness of conjugal life; an abortion procured in order to avoid procreation; stubbornly remaining in an extraconjugal relationship at the time of or immediately subsequent to the wedding; fraudulent con-

> cealment of sterility or a serious contagious illness or children from a previous relationship or incarceration; a *causa contrahendi* totally extraneous to conjugal life or the unforeseen pregnancy of the woman [as the *causa contrahendi*], physical violence inflicted in order to extort consent, a lack of the use of reason proven by medical documents, etc."[26]

The possible significance of that striking and open-ended "etc." has been one of the most hotly discussed points of the new *motu proprio*. What other circumstances belong on the list? Naturally, the question I would like to address is: does extreme financial irresponsibility belong on that list? Is it one of the "and the rest" that would permit for a cause to be admitted to the *processus brevior*?

Before addressing that question, it is necessary to take a few steps back to talk about the *processus brevior* in general, and article 14 in particular. If you had to rely solely on the mainstream media for your knowledge of the new *motu proprio*, you would probably conclude that the Church was taking a page from the Pizza Hut playbook: "you get your annulment in forty-five days or it's free." Those who were most vocal in their praise of the shorter process said it heralded a new dawn of mercy in the Church, while those who were most vocal in their criticism of it thought it marked the inauguration of "Catholic divorce," but both groups were in agreement about the underlying premise that the shorter process represented a groundbreaking and revolutionary novelty that would, in practice, almost completely replace the ordinary process. I want to challenge both those premises.

First, as to the contention that the shorter process is completely novel: I will not deny that it is the most major innovation in the new *motu proprio*, not to mention the least expected. But its novelty can be exaggerated.

To begin with, despite some criticisms to the contrary, there is nothing especially novel in the idea that the nullity of a marriage can sometimes be manifest: the law already recognizes this possibility in more than one place, at least implicitly. This is most apparent in canon 1674, whose roots go back well beyond the 1917 Code, and which recognizes the right of the promoter of justice to impugn a marriage whose nullity has already become publicly known. So it is nothing new to suppose that nullity could be known from the outset to be manifest.

26 *Mitis Iudex*, *Ratio procedendi*, art. 14 §1: "is fidei defectus qui gignere potest simulationem consensus vel errorem voluntatem determinantem, brevitas convictus coniugalis, abortus procuratus ad vitandam procreationem, permanentia pervicax in relatione extraconiugali tempore nuptiarum vel immediate subsequenti, celatio dolosa sterilitatis vel gravis infirmitatis contagiosae vel filiorum ex relatione praecedenti vel detrusionis in carcerem, causa contrahendi vitae coniugali omnino extranea vel haud praevisa praegnantia mulieris, violentia physica ad extorquendum consensum illata, defectus usus rationis documentis medicis comprobatus, etc."

Nor is it completely novel that certain of the formalities of the judicial process could safely be omitted when the nullity of a marriage is manifest – provided that the favor of marriage and the right of defense remain completely intact. The clearest example of this is the documentary process, which is as bare-bones a process as could be imagined.[27] In a sense, the omission of formalities in the documentary process is the flipside of the same reason for their inclusion in the ordinary process. Formalities are not just arbitrary hoops to be jumped through; they serve the dual purpose of ensuring that justice is done and that justice is seen to be done. In the marriage nullity process, "justice is done" when the judgment accords with the objective truth. When (as is the case with the documentary process) the truth is obvious beyond a reasonable doubt based on reliable proofs, and when there is no doubt about its being *seen* to be done, then the Church happily dispenses with those formalities that would no longer serve either purpose. As an aside, I want to stress that I am not talking about the judge deciding on his own authority to omit the formalities required by law because he deems them unnecessary; such an arbitrary decision would in itself thwart the purpose of justice being seen to be done. What I mean is a procedural law in which the formalities are tailored toward a "minimally invasive" discovery of the truth.

The shorter process *according to the black letter of the revised canons* follows this logic completely, and in that respect, it is an outgrowth of the logic of the existing tradition. Revised canon 1683 gives two conditions for its use, the first of which is that both spouses present the petition, or if not both, then the other must at least consent, and the second of which is "Circumstances of persons and things recur, supported by testimonies and instruments which do not require a more accurate inquiry or investigation, and render nullity manifest."[28] If you parse it out, that second condition really contains two separate subconditions. The first is that the facts upon which the petition is based must clearly demonstrate the nullity of the marriage, such that if those facts were proven there could be no doubt of law that the marriage was invalid. The second condition, and the one that has to my mind not been sufficiently adverted to in discussions about the *motu proprio*, is that the facts themselves must be certain; they must be easily proven true based on a minimal instruction. These two subconditions are, as the scientists would say, "doubly dissociated;" you can have either one without the other. There are cases in which the facts alleged would clearly demonstrate the nullity of the marriage, but in which the proof of those facts cannot be easily obtained. There are cases in which the facts are at hand, but if they render the marriage null at all they at least do not do so *manifestly*. But when both are present, i.e., when the facts themselves are demonstrated beyond a doubt and when those facts clearly render

---

27 *CIC83*, cc. 1688-1690, as modified by *Mitis Iudex*, effective December 8, 2015.

28 *CIC83*, c. 1683, as modified by *Mitis Iudex*, effective December 8, 2015: "2° recurrant rerum personarumque adiuncta, testimoniis vel instrumentis suffulta, quae accuratiorem disquisitionem aut investigationem non exigant, et nullitatem manifestam reddant."

the marriage null, then, to appropriate a rather ominous quotation, "What further need have we of witnesses?"[29]

When I first read through the *motu proprio*, after reading the description of the shorter process but before reaching article 14, I immediately thought of a handful of cases that would meet the canonical criteria for the shorter process. Each one was a "would be" documentary case: a case in which an impediment was very plausibly alleged even though for whatever reason there was no document upon which to base the documentary process, either because the document was lacking altogether or else defective in some way. One was a ligamen case in which both parties were immigrants. No one could locate the marriage certificate or other document proving the prior bond of one of the parties, but twenty minutes with the parties and a few knowledgeable witnesses would have been enough to prove it beyond a positive and prudent doubt. Another was an impotence case involving a paraplegic man with a progressive neurological disorder. There was no doubt of his current impotence, which could be certified in a medical document, but there was no *documentary proof* of his impotence prior to the marriage. A summary deposition of the parties and a few witnesses would have been enough to eliminate any doubt. The third was a case of a woman from China who had entered a sham marriage with her brother to get a green card. The documents that would have proven their consanguinity had all been doctored. For all these cases, the documentary process was inadequate but the full ordinary process was, frankly, overkill. The shorter process would have been the right tool for the job, and I was glad to see that tool added to the tribunal's toolbox.

So far, so good, at least in theory. But then I came to the *ratio procedendi*, and in particular to its article 14. Article 14 does not in any way rule out the use of the shorter process for the kind of "would be" documentary cases that I just described – and I continue to hold that those cases are a perfect fit for the shorter process – but article 14 clearly envisions that the shorter process will be used in cases based on a defect of consent. Whatever else article 14 might mean, it makes that much very clear. Consent is an internal, invisible act of the will, and its existence is primarily verified by its very clear and public external manifestation in the marriage ceremony. We all know that the internal act of consent can be invalid notwithstanding the external manifestation, but can it be manifestly so? It seems to me, for this reason among others, that article 14 presents a difficult interpretive task.

It is not clear to me exactly what genre of norm the *Ratio Procedendi* falls into – is it law? An instruction? To the best of my knowledge this remains an open question, and I do not want to offer an opinion on it prematurely. But I am still less prepared to offer an opinion on the exact meaning of article 14. There are, however, three things I am fairly confident it does *not* mean.

29 Lk 22:71.

First, there seems to be general consensus at this early stage that article 14 is not introducing new grounds of nullity. Most of those items – including the mention of a lack of faith – refer explicitly or implicitly to one of the existing grounds of nullity: simulation, error determining the will, fraud, force and fear, lack of the use of reason. The sole exception is "shortness of conjugal life," the implication of which is not at all clear to me, but which in any case could never be a ground of nullity.

Second, it seems clear that article 14 is *not* a list of situations that automatically qualify a petition to be admitted to the *processus brevior*. Even if one were to admit for the sake of argument that the all of the circumstances listed in article 14 are facts that result in manifest nullity, there would still remain that other very rigorous subcondition requiring the proofs to be readily available. Only one of the items listed in article 14 mentions anything about the availability of proofs, namely, the medically documented lack of the sufficient use of reason. For all of the other circumstances, it would be entirely possible for the facts to be alleged even while the proofs are lacking, or could not be obtained without a thorough and rigorous instruction. In such a case, the case would have to be admitted to the ordinary process even if an article 14 circumstance were alleged.

Third, leaving aside the question of the availability of proofs, I do not believe article 14 is intended as a list of circumstances that would, if proven, make the nullity of the marriage manifest. None of the circumstances are completely irrelevant to the question of nullity. Some of them surely *can* make nullity manifest: no one would deny that marital consent extorted by physical violence is manifestly null. But other circumstances on the list, such as a short conjugal life (how short?) or a marriage precipitated by an unforeseen pregnancy, are certainly not *prima facie* indications of nullity. They can plausibly be accounted for by any number of explanations that do not entail the nullity of the marriage. We all know this from experience.

So if article 14 is none of those three things (i.e., not a list of new grounds of nullity, not a list of circumstances that automatically qualify for the shorter process, and not a list of circumstances that *per se* make nullity manifest) then what is it? I think the list is meant not as a checklist but as a starting point: a purposely open-ended, suggestive, and general listing of the kind of facts or circumstances that *could* indicate the presence of manifest nullity, when all of the facts and circumstances align and the proofs are within easy reach. If I am right about that, then I would say that financial irresponsibility emphatically does *not* belong in the "etc." As we saw, financial irresponsibility is about six steps removed from the juridic question of nullity; it does anything but make nullity manifest. It does, however, lead to some spectacularly disastrous and bitter marital breakdowns. Article 14 is not meant to be a surrogate or substitute for the prudent discernment of the judicial vicar. In that sense, it is typical of *Mitis Iudex*.

Let me finish my reflections on financial irresponsibility with that note about *judicial* responsibility. To a degree, the modifications to the marriage nullity process contained in *Mitis Iudex* represent a relaxation of certain formal elements of the process. Some have interpreted the procedural moderations to be indicative of a desire on the part of the legislator for a less stringent approach to the question of marriage nullity on the part of tribunal ministers. That is a little like saying that taking away the safety net calls for a more relaxed attitude on the part of a tight-rope walker. Surely the opposite is true; surely a relaxed procedure calls for a *more* diligent or even a more rigorous approach on the part of tribunal ministers. If the safeguards are not in the process, they have to be in us. In that regard, *Mitis Iudex* lays bare what has always been the case: the most important safeguards are not in the process but in the diligence and fidelity of the tribunal ministers. Through *Mitis Iudex*, Pope Francis has placed tremendous trust in the diligence of tribunal ministers, especially judges. If we interpret the document as an invitation to laxity on our parts, whether in our judgments or in our adherence to the procedural law, we will have completely misread the Holy Father's intentions. More than that, we will have undermined them. Instead, we must rededicate ourselves in our responsible fidelity to the law, to justice, and to the truth, so that these reforms might bear fruit in the lives of the faithful and the life of the Church.

Seminar

Elements in Writing a Sentence in Matrimonial Cases

Rev. Thomas E. Cronkleton, Jr.

Introduction

The instruction of a matrimonial case culminates in the rendering of a decision and the writing of a sentence. The sentence, therefore, needs to express how the decision was reached and the law and the facts which serve as the basis of that decision. We will look at the elements that are to be present in the sentence.

On December 8, 2015, the announcement was made that Pope Francis modified the canons on marriage process. The *motu proprio*, *Mitis Iudex Dominus Iesus*, which made these changes, was promulgated on August 15, 2015, and becomes effective on December 8, 2015.[1] When, therefore, reference is made to the canons on matrimonial process, they will be the new ones given in the *motu proprio* unless otherwise noted.

Requirements of the Law and the Guidance of the Instruction:

The law and the instruction *Dignitas connubii* describe the basic form and substance to be utilized in a sentence. Only little guidance, however, concerning the sentence is given in the canons for matrimonial process and the articles of the *Ratio procedendi* of the *motu proprio*. The directions, therefore, in canon 1691 §3 are to be followed; namely, the canons on trials in general and the ordinary contentious trial are to be applied to the sentence in a matrimonial case. We look, then, to these canons and to *Dignitas connubii* to discern what is to be in the sentence.

Basic Format:

The basic format of a sentence is given in canon 1612 and article 253 §§1-4 of *Dignitas connubii*. The sentence is to begin with the following: the invoca-

1 Pope Francis, *Motu propio Mitis Iudex Dominus Iesus,* August 15, 2015. http://w2.vatican.va/content/francesco/la/motu_proprio/documents/papa-francesco-motu-proprio_20150815_mitis-iudex-dominus-iesus.html; translations are from the official English translation, at: http://w2.vatican.va/content/francesco/en/motu_proprio/documents/papa-francesco-motu-proprio_20150815_mitis-iudex-dominus-iesus.html.

tion of the Divine Name, the tribunal before which the case is heard including the principals, namely, the judges or judge, the parties and their procurators and/or advocates, the defender of the bond, and the promoter of justice, if one took part in the process. Next follows a brief statement of facts and the formula of the doubt. The dispositive section follows which begins with the reasons for the decision. The sentence concludes with the date and place where it was rendered and the signatures of the judges or judge and the notary.

This produces a basic format, which is given in the outline below:

I. Introduction
   A. Invocation of Divine Name
   B. Principals in the Case
II. Brief Statement of Uncontested Facts
   A. Information about the Parties
   B. Formulation of the Doubt
III. Dispositive Section
IV. Conclusion
   A. Place, the day, the month and the year in which the decisions was given
   B. Signature of the Judges or Judge
   C. Signature of the Notary

This outline, however, is incomplete and needs to be given content.

Content:

More details about the sentence and its content are found in canons 1611, 1679, 1680 §1, 1687 §§1-3 and 1691 §1, and articles 250, 251, 252, 253 §§2, 3 and 5 and 254 of *Dignitas connubii.*

One of the essential elements in the sentence is that it must decide the matter. If it fails to do so, the sentence is irremediably null.[2] Each of the *dubia,* therefore, needs to be answered.[3] Now some tribunal use subordinate *dubia*, e.g., "Failing to find in the affirmative in the previous ground, whether the marriage was invalid because …" There may be a disadvantage if the court of the first of instance does not answer all of the subordinate *dubia.* If an appeal is made, the appellate court may not agree with the affirmative decision of the first instance

2 *Codex Iuris Canonici Auctoritate Ioannis Pauli II Promulgatus* (Vatican City: Libreria Editrice Vaticana, 1989) canon 1620, 8°; translations from *Code of Canon Law,* Latin-English Edition, New English Translation (Washington, DC: Canon Law Society of America, 2012) unless otherwise noted, Klaus Lüdicke and Ronny E. Jenkins, *Dignitas Connubii, Norms and Commentary* (Washington, DC: Canon Law Society of America, 2006), art. 270, 8°; translations are from this work, unless otherwise noted.

3 Canon 1611, 1°; *DC,* art. 250, 1°; 252 §2.

court on the primary ground, and decide in the affirmative on one of the subordinate *dubia.* This means that the case may have go to third instance.[4] Answering all the subordinate *dubia* is a safer course.[5] The *dubia* are stated at the beginning and the answer to them, preferably with a restatement, is given is at the end of the dispositive section.

According to canon 1612 §3, the dispositive section is to give the reasons for the decision. Canon 1611 3° and articles 250, 2° and 254 §3 state that the reasons for which the decision has been made are to be based in both law and fact. Failure to do so renders the decision remediably null,[6] which if contested allows for correction and if not contested sanates in three months.[7]

The law that is to be used in the argument for a marriage case obviously includes those canons which touch on the *dubia* being examined and the related Rotal jurisprudence and papal allocutions and instructions. There are, however, other matters of law to consider.

The canons on proof are of particular importance. The first of which is canon 1526 §1.[8] Here we are reminded that the burden of proof rests with the person making the allegation, be that the petitioner, respondent or even the defender of the bond. In a marriage case, the principal allegation is that the marriage is invalid, so proof of this lies with the petitioner and, if there is agreement between the parties, the respondent. The judge, of course, can also interrogate the parties, gather documents, call additional witnesses, chose experts and conduct inspections and examinations.[9] The *Ratio procedendi*, however, envisions diocesan, parochial or a combination thereof assisting the petitioner and if participating, the other party, in the collection and presentation of proofs in a preliminary pastoral investigation.[10] While this does not substitute for the collection and presentation of proofs during the trial, the party or parties are to have assistance putting the case together.

4 There is some question whether there needs to be conforming decisions since canon 1679 no longer requires an appeal, but since there is an appeal, a conforming decisions would be needed according to canon 1641, 1° and article 291 §1 of *Dignitas Connubii.* If the appellate court finds on a different ground, then a determination on whether the two decisions are equivalent or substantially conforming according to article 291 of *Dignitas Connubii.*

5 Lüdicke and Jenkins, 406.

6 Canon 1644, 2°; *DC*, art. 272, 2°.

7 See canons 1623; 1616 §2; *DC*, art. 273; 276 §2.

8 See *DC*, art. 156 §1.

9 See canons 1530; 1545; 1547; 1574; 1582; 1678 §3.

10 See *Mitis Iudex Donimus Iesus, Ratio procedendi in causis ad matrimonii nullitatem declarandam*, art. 2-6.

While the burden of proof is with the person who makes an allegation, matters presumed by law do not need to be proved.[11] The principal presumption in a marriage case is expressed in canon 1060, which states, "Marriage possess the favor of the law; therefore, in a case of doubt, the validity of a marriage must be upheld until the contrary is proven."

Other presumptions include that: a couple have consummated their marriage after they have cohabited;[12] the juridic acts placed according to their external elements are valid;[13] conformity between the internal consent and external words used in celebrating marriage;[14] after puberty parties to marriage know marriage is a permanent partnership of a man and woman that involves sexual acts;[15] error alone concerning a quality of a person and error concerning unity, indissolubility or sacramental dignity do not invalidate marriage;[16] consent presumed to persist even if impediments or defect of form present;[17] presumption of husband as father and legitimacy of children of marriage;[18] and, in doubtful matter privilege of faith enjoys favor of the law.[19]

Article 14 §1 of the *Ratio procedendi* has been the subject of much attention. It says:

> Among the circumstances of things and persons that can allow a case for nullity of marriage to be handled by means of the briefer process according to cann. 1683-1687, are included, for example: the defect of faith which can generate simulation of consent or error that determines the will; a brief conjugal cohabitation; an abortion procured to avoid procreation; an obstinate persistence in an extraconjugal relationship at the time of the wedding or immediately following it; the deceitful concealment of sterility, or grave contagious illness, or children from a previous relationship, or incarcerations; a cause of marriage completely extraneous to married life, or consisting of the unexpected pregnancy of the woman, physical vio-

11 Canon 1526 §2, 1°; 1585; *DC*, art. 156 §2.
12 Canon 1061 §2.
13 Canon 124 §1.
14 Canon 1101 §1.
15 Canon 1096 §2.
16 See canons 15 §2; 126; 1097 §2; 1099.
17 Canon 1107.
18 Canon 1138.
19 Canon 1150.

> lence inflicted to extort consent, the defect of the use of reason which is proved by medical documents, etc.[20]

At issue here is whether these circumstances constitute legal presumptions for the invalidity of marriage. I would contend that they are not legal presumptions. Rather, they are circumstances in specific situations that have at times been recognized in Rotal jurisprudence to establish invalidity and that when investigated in a new case may also show that a marriage was invalid. For example, an unexpected pregnancy may, when a couple is casually dating, result in pressure from parents and other to marry thus producing reverential fear in the couple compelling them to marry against their will and better judgment; but an unexpected pregnancy may not invalidate the consent when a couple is engaged to be married and the pregnancy is discovered within a few weeks of the marriage celebration. At best, these circumstances can become presumptions of facts when other evidence indicates that they have affected the consent being given so that the consent is insufficient to provide what is necessary for marriage.

One of the proofs is the declarations and confessions of the parties. The new canon 1678 §1 reworks the former canon 1679 and rewords it so that there is a more positive wording making it more like article 180 of *Dignitas Connubii*, yet even more positive.

---

20 *Mitis Iudex Donimus Iesus, Ratio procedendi*, art. 14 §1: "Inter rerum et personarum adiuncta quae sinunt causam nullitatis matrimonii ad tramitem processus brevioris iuxta cann. 1683-1687 pertractari, recensentur exempli gratia: is fidei defectus qui gignere potest simulationem consensus vel errorem voluntatem determinantem, brevitas convictus coniugalis, abortus procuratus ad vitandam procreationem, permanentia pervicax in relatione extraconiugali tempore nuptiarum vel immediate subsequenti, celatio dolosa sterilitatis vel gravis infirmitatis contagiosae vel filiorum ex relatione praecedenti vel detrusionis in carcerem, causa contrahendi vitae coniugali omnino extranea vel haud praevisa praegnantia mulieris, violentia physica ad extorquendum consensum illata, defectus usus rationis documentis medicis comprobatus, etc."

New Canon 1678 §1	Former Canon 1679	*Dignitas Connubii*, **art. 180**
In cases of the nullity of marriage, a judicial confession and the declarations of the parties, possibly supported by witnesses to the credibility of the parties, can have the force of full proof, to be evaluated by the judge after he has considered all the indications and support factors, unless elements are present which weaken them. *In causis de matrimonii nullitate, confessio iudicialis et partium declarationes, testibus forte de ipsarum partium credibilitate sustentae, vim plenae probationis habere possunt, a iudice aestimandam perpensis omnibus indiciis et adminiculis, nisi alia accedant elementa quae eas infirment.*	Unless there are full proofs from elsewhere, in order to evaluate the dispositions of the parties according to the norm of can. 1536, the judge, if possible, is to use witnesses to the credibility of those parties in addition to other indications and supporting factors. *Nisi probationes aliunde plenae habeantur, iudex, ad partium depositiones ad normam can. 1536 aestimandas, testes de ipsarum partium credibilitate, si fieri potest, adhibeat, praeter alia indicia et adminicula.*	§1. Confessions and other judicial declarations of the parties can have probative force, [which the judge must evaluate] together with other circumstance of the [case]; the force of full proof cannot be attributed to them, however, unless other elements of proof [are present which thoroughly] corroborate them (cf. can. 1536 §2). §2. Unless [there are full proofs from elsewhere], in order to evaluate the depositions of the parties, [the judge, if possible,] is to use witnesses to the credibility of [those] parties, in addition to other indications and [supporting factors] (cf. can. 1679). *§1. Confessiones et aliae partium declarationes iudiciales vim probandi habere possunt, a iudice aestimandam una cum ceteris causae adiunctis, at vis plenae probationis ipsis tribui nequit, nisi alia accedant elementa probatoria quae eas omnino corroborent (cf. can. 1536, §2).* *§2. Nisi probationes aliunde plenae habeantur, iudex ad partium depositiones aestimandas testes de ipsarum partium credibilitate, si fieri potest, adhibeat, praeter alia indicia et adminicula (cf. can. 1679).*

While one might argue that there is basically no difference between the former and new canons, the judicial confessions and declarations of the parties are given in the new canon with a more positive assumption toward having full proof. When, therefore, one party declares a fact and the other admits to it, then with other factors present, such as character witnesses, then full proof can be given. While this change does not remove the need for some form of corroboration, as in other cases involving confessions,[21] the fact that the "unless" (*nisi*) is now for when there is some reason to disbelieve the confession rather than a reason to believe it is a major change.

The other proofs are documents, witnesses, experts and judicial examinations and inspections.[22] One of these is the *ex officio* witnesses. The new canon 1678 §2 reproduces and reworks canon 1573 by putting it in the positive.

New Canon 1678 §2	**Canon 1573**	***Dignitas Connubii*, art. 202**
In the same cases, the testimony of one witness can produce full proof, if it concerns a qualified witness making a deposition concerning matters done *ex officio*, or unless the circumstances of things and persons suggest otherwise.[4]	The testimony of one witness cannot produce full proof unless it concerns a qualified witness making a deposition concerning matters done *ex officio*, or unless the circumstances of things and persons suggest otherwise.[5]	The [testimony] of one witness cannot [produce] full proof, unless it [concerns] a qualified witness [making a deposition] concerning matters [done] *ex officio*, or unless the circumstances of things [and] persons suggest otherwise (c. 1573).[6]
In iisdem causis, depositio unius testis plenam fidem facere potest, si agatur de teste qualificato qui deponat de rebus ex officio gestis, aut rerum et personarum adiuncta id suadeant.	*Unius testis depositio plenam fidem facere non potest, nisi agatur de teste qualificato qui deponat de rebus ex officio gestis, aut rerum et personarum adiuncta aliud suadeant.*	*Unius testis depositio plenam fidem facere non potest, nisi agatur de teste qualificato qui deponat de rebus ex officio gestis, aut rerum et personarum adiuncta aliud suadeant (can. 1573).*

As with the change concerning declarations and confessions, one might argue that there is no difference between the new canon 1678 §2 and canon 1573, the positive wording concerning the testimony of a qualified witness provided *ex officio* gives a more positive assumption toward the testimony having full

21 Canon 1526 §1, 2°.
22 Canons 1539-1586.

proof. The positive statement about giving full proof and the replacement of the "unless" (*nisi*) with an "if" (*si*) emphasizes the probative value of *ex officio* testimony. When, for example, a priest, deacon or pastoral minister testifies about something that arose in marriage preparation for a couple, or an assisting minister or the witnesses to the consent testifies about the marriage ceremony, this testimony has full proof, unless other evidence suggests otherwise.

The dipositive section is to evaluate the proofs in the light of the law. Documents, for example, are to be evaluated on the basis of whether they are public or private, ecclesiastical or civil.[23] Public documents are to be trusted concerning what they directly and principally affirm, unless other evidence indicates that they cannot be trusted.[24] Private documents are treated as either extra judicial confessions or declarations of the author and given the probative value of judicial declarations.[25] In a marriage case, since private documents are to be treated as a judicial confession, then canon 1678 §1 applies. Like confessions, therefore, private documents can have full force of proof when corroborated, unless evidence indicates otherwise. If, for example, the documents are erased, falsified or otherwise defective, the judge can decide that little or no probative value to give them.[26] If other evidence which contradicts the private document is presented, the judge must decide the probative value of the private document based on the contradictory and corroborative evidence.

Testimony of witnesses is to be evaluated based upon: the condition (ecclesial or social position) or reputation (honesty) of the person; source of the knowledge – heard or seen personally, or opinion, rumor or hearsay; when the witnesses learned of the information; whether the witness is consistent or inconsistent, uncertain, or vacillating; and whether corroborated.[27] Expert testimony is to be evaluated on its agreement with other expert testimony, the circumstances of the cases, and the factors about the expert's conclusions which are compelling.[28]

Even though canon 1678 §1 puts a positive emphasis on the declarations and confessions of the parties, these declarations and confessions by themselves are still inadequate for full proof. Documents and the testimony of witnesses are still necessary, even if that supportive element is character witnesses. A careful analysis of all the evidence is needed and to be present in the sentence.

The judges or judge must have moral certainty derived from the acts of the case and his or her own conscience.[29] If the majority of the judges or the single

23 Canon 1540.
24 Canon 1541.
25 Canon 1542.
26 Canon 1543.
27 Canon 1572; *DC*, art 201.
28 Canon 1579; *DC*, art. 212.
29 Canon 1608 §1-3; *DC*, art. 247 §1, 3-4.

judge are unable to arrive at moral certainty that the marriage was invalid, then the sentence is to pronounce in favor of the marriage.[30] The requirements of moral certainty are given in article 12 of the *Ratio procedendi* and article 247 §2 of *Dignitas Connubii*.

Ratio procedendi, art. 12	***Dignitas Connubii, art. 247 §2***
To achieve the moral certainty required by law, a preponderance of proofs and indications is not sufficient, but it is required that any prudent [positive] doubt of making an error, in law or in fact, is excluded, even if the mere possibility of the contrary is not removed.[7]	[To achieve moreover] the moral certainty [required] by law, a preponderance of proofs and indications is not sufficient, but it is required that any prudent positive doubt of making an error, in law or in fact, is excluded, even if the mere possibility of the contrary [is not removed].[8]
Ad certitudinem moralem iure necessariam, non sufficit praevalens probationum indiciorumque momentum, sed requiritur ut quodlibet quidem prudens dubium positivum errandi, in iure et in facto, excludatur, etsi mera contrarii possibilitas non tollatur.	*Ad certitudinem autem moralem iure necessariam, non sufficit praevalens probationum indiciorumque momentum, sed requiritur ut quodlibet quidem prudens dubium positivum errandi, in iure et in facto, excludatur, etsi mera contrarii possibilitas non tollatur.*

This reflects the teaching on moral certitude given by Pope Pius XII. He wrote:

> There is an absolute certainty, in which all possible doubt as to the truth of the fact and the existence of the contrary is entirely excluded. Such absolute certainty, however, is not necessary in order to pronounce the judgment. In many cases it is humanly unattainable; to require it would be to demand of the judge and of the parties something which is unreasonable; it would put an intolerable burden on the administration of justice and would very seriously obstruct it.
>
> In contrast to this supreme decree of certitude, common speech often designates as certain a judgment which strictly speaking does not merit to be so called, but should rather be classed as a greater or lesser probability, because it does not exclude all reasonable doubt, but leaves a foundation for the fear of error. This probability, or quasi-certainty, does not afford a sufficient basis for a judicial sentence regarding the object truth of the fact.

30 Canon 1608 §4; *DC*, art. 247 §5.

In such a case, that is, when the lack of certainty regarding the fact at issue forbids pronouncing a positive judgment on the merits of the case, the law, and especially the rules of procedure, supply the judge with obligatory norms of action, in which *presumption of law* and rules regard the *favor of the law* have a decisive importance. The judge cannot afford to ignore these rules of law and of procedure. Yet it would be an exaggerated and wrong application of these norms, and as it were a false interpretation of the mind of the legislator, were the judge to seek recourse to them, when there is not only a quasi-certainty, but certitude in the proper and true sense. Against the truth and sure knowledge thereof, there are no presumptions nor favors of law.

Between the two extremes of absolute certainty and quasi-certainty or probability, is that *moral certainty* which is usually involved in the case submitted to your court, and of which We principally wish to speak. It is characterized on the positive side by the exclusion of well-founded or reasonable doubt, and in this respect it is essentially distinguished from the quasi-certainty which has been mentioned; on the negative side, it does admit the absolute possibility of the contrary and in this it differs from absolute certainty. The certainty of which We are now speaking is necessary and sufficient for the rendering of a judgment, even though in the particular case it would be possible either directly or indirectly to reach absolute certainty. Only thus is it possible to have a regular and orderly administration of justice, going forward without useless delays and without laying excessive burden on the tribunal as well as on the parties.

Sometimes moral certainty is derived only from an aggregate of indications and proofs which, taken singly, do not provide the foundation for true certitude. But which, when taken together, no longer leave room for any reasonable doubt on the part of a person of sound judgment. This is no sense a passage from probability to certainty through a simple culmination of probabilities, which would amount to an illegitimate transit from one species to another essential different one: "Είς άλλο γένος μετάβασις"; it is rather to recognize that the simultaneous presence of all these separate indications and proofs can have a sufficient basis only in the existence of a common origin or foundation from which they spring, that is, in objective truth and reality. In this case, therefore, certainty arises from the wise application of a principle which is absolutely secure and universally valid, namely, the principle of sufficient

> reason. Consequently, if in giving the reasons for his decision, the judge states that the proofs which have been adduced, considered separately, cannot be judged sufficient, but taken together and embraced in a survey of the whole situation, they provide the necessary elements for arriving at a safe definitive judgment, it must be acknowledged that such reasons is in general sound and legitimate.
>
> In any event, this certainty is understood to be objective, that is, based on objective motives; it is not a purely subjective certitude, founded on sentiment or on this or that merely subjective opinion perhaps even on personal credulity, lack of consideration, or inexperience. This moral certainty with an objective foundation does not exist if there are on the other side, that is, in favor of the reality of the contrary, motives which a sound, serious, and competent judgment pronounces to be at least in some way worthy of attention, and which consequently make it necessary to admit the contrary as not only absolutely possible, but also in a certain sense probably.[31]

Pope John Paul II especially stressed the need for moral certainty in reaching a decision.[32] This moral certainty is a judgment based upon objective facts and the law which leads the judge or judges to conclude beyond reasonable doubt that the marriage was invalid. The sentence, therefore, must show by connecting the law and the facts presented in the case how moral certainty was arrived and if not, then must state that the presumption in favor of the validity of marriage remains.[33] A simple statement of the facts is insufficient to show how moral certainty was reach, but the law and the facts must be joined together. This "bridging" of law and facts is an essential element of a well-crafted sentence.

In the course of explaining the connection between the law and the facts of the case, the judges, judge or diocesan bishop need to consider and answer concerns raised in the animadversions of the advocates and especially the observations of the defender of the bond. Failure to address this concerns will likely result in an appeal if the parties or the defender of the bond judge themselves aggrieved by the decision. These concerns can either be taken care of directly in their own section, or indirectly in the course of the argumentation.

31 Pius XII, Address to the Roman Rota, October 1, 1942, 1-3: *AAS* 36 (1944) 281-290; translation from Papal *Allocutions to the Roman Rota, 1939-2001*, ed. Willian H. Woestman, OMI (Ottawa: Faculty of Canon Law, Saint Paul University, 2011) 18-19.

32 See John Paul II, Address to the Roman Rota, February 4, 1980: *AAS* 72 (1980) 172-178; idem, February 26, 1983: *AAS* 75 (1983) 544-559; idem, February 10, 1995: *AAS* 87 (1995) 1013-1019; idem, January 29, 2005: *AAS* 97 (2005) 164-166.

33 Lüdicke and Jenkins, 395-398.

After the signatures, several matters are to be addressed. They include reminders of obligations to one another and to their children;[34] a *vetitum*;[35] a determination about judicial expenses;[36] how to challenge the decision;[37] and how the decision will be communicated to the parties.[38]

Canon 1071 §1, 3° requires the permission for a marriage where there are natural obligations to another party or children arising from a previous union. The sentence, therefore, is to remind the parties that they are to fulfill their moral and those obligations which can bind them both toward one another and toward their children to furnish support and education.[39] Here is a sample wording for this reminder.

> The Petitioner and Other Party are to be reminded they need the permission of the local ordinary before marrying in the Catholic Church. In order to obtain this permission they will need to demonstrate they have faithfully complied with the provisions for the support, education and formation of their children and with the provisions concerning their obligations to each other as specified in the civil divorce decree and the canons of the 1983 *Code of Canon Law*.

A *vetitum* is to be placed when a party is found absolutely impotent[40] or incapable of marriage,[41] and it is removed by the tribunal; a *vetitum* is also placde when there is deceit[42] or simulation,[43] and it is lifted by the local ordinary of the place of the marriage.[44] If there is an issue which does not warrant a *vetitum*, but still causes concern to the judges or judge, a *monitum* may be placed in order to give some guidance to the parties and any minister helping them prepare for marriage. The party or parties on whom the *vetitum* is placed needs to be given sufficient direction in order to know what needs to be done for the *vetitum* to be lifted.

Pope Frances has called for annulments to be as free as possible, considering the need to support tribunal personnel.[45] Many diocese have chosen to no longer

34 Canon 1691 §1; *DC*, art. 252.
35 Canon 1682 §1; *DC*, art. 250, 3°; 251.
36 Canon 1611, *DC*, art. 250, 4°; 304.
37 See canons 1614; 1680 §1; 1683 §3; *DC*, art. 253 §5; 257 §2.
38 See canon 1615; *DC*, art. 258; "Ratio procedendi," art. 13.
39 See canon 1691 §1; *DC*, art. 252; see also canons 1071 §1, 3°; 1059; 1650 §2; 1655; 1671 §2.
40 See canon 1084.
41 See canon 1095.
42 See canon 1098.
43 See canon 1101.
44 See *DC*, art. 250, 3°; 252 §§1-2.
45 *Mitis Iudex Dominus Iesus*, VI.

charge; some still have to do so. Here is a statement about how the fees are paid, and a reminder that the expense of the tribunal have been paid by either the annual diocesan collection or taxes paid by parishes.

> Fees are to be paid according to the agreement entered into by the Petitioner (and the Other Party) at the beginning of this process.
>
> OR;
>
> The Petitioner and the Other Party are reminded that due to the generosity of the People of God of the Diocese through their contributions to the annual appeal that this process has been able to be conducted without any expense to the Petitioner and Other Party. They are, therefore, requested to remember the intention of the donors in their prayers.

Now that there is no longer an automatic appeal,[46] informing the parties how they may contest a decisions is even more important. A short note is to be given that if they judge themselves aggrieved, then they can contest the decision either to the usual appellate court or to the Rota by notifying this Tribunal of the desire to appeal, and if the decision is not appealed in fifteen useful days, the decision will become effective.[47] They should also be informed that a merely dilatory appeal will not be accepted by the appellate tribunal.[48] Here is an example:

> The Parties and the Defender of the Bond, if they judge themselves aggrieved by this decision, are entitled to appeal this decision within fifteen days by notifying this Tribunal of the desire to appeal. The normal appellate court is the Tribunal of the Archdiocese of X, but an appeal to the Roman Rota may also be made. Merely dilatory appeals will not be accepted by the appellate tribunal. If no appeal is received within fifteen days of notification, this decision becomes executable.

Lastly, there should be a direction as to how the decision will be given to the parties. They can technically be required to come to the Tribunal to receive the decision or it can be mailed to them.[49] The party who objects to receiving notices does not have to be given a copy, but may be notified of the dipositive part of the sentence.[50] Here are a couple of examples:

---

46 Canon 1679.

47 See canon 1628; 1679; 1680 §1; *DC*, art. 279; see also canons 1415; 1438, 1° and 2°; 1439; 1630; 1632; *DC*, art. 18; 25; 281; 283.

48 Canon 1680 §2.

49 See canon 1615; *DC*, art. 258 §§1-2.

50 See *DC*, art. 258 §3; *Ratio procedendi*, art. 13.

A copy of this sentence is to be communicated to the Parties and to the Defender of the Bond.

OR;

A copy of this sentence is to be communicated to the Petitioner and the Defender of Bond; but since the Other Party requested no further communications, this request is to be honored and nothing is to be communicated.

Comment about *Processus Brevior*:

Even though the diocesan bishop renders the judgment in the *Processus Brevior*, a sentence is still required.[51] While article 20 §1 of the *Ratio procendendi* states that "The diocesan bishop determines according to his own prudence the way to pronounce the sentence," this does not eliminate the sentence. This article does, however, give the bishop great latitude in how he will explain the reasons he judges the marriage invalid. He may, for example, explain his rationale to the instructor or another and allow them to draft the sentence with its normal structure so that the bishop may review, edit and then sign the sentence. Since this process is only to be used when invalidity is readily apparent,[52] the sentence may be shorter than a sentence in the ordinary process because less analysis of the facts would be required.

Rotal Practice:

According to canon 19, one of the places we turn to interpret the law is the practice of the Roman curia. We, therefore, look to the practice of the Roman Rota for some direction on the composition of a sentence. Their published sentences are in the *Decisiones Seu Sententiae*.[53]

The published cases in the *Decisiones Seu Sententiae* omit some of the introductory formalities the actual sentences. The published decisions sometimes start with the uncontested facts of the cases and the procedures that have been followed. Here are a few things that appear in the sentences sent to the parties.[54]

The actual sentence is printed on Rotal letterhead, or at least a title page with the Rota's seal is the upper left-hand corner. At the top of page, just below the Rotal seal, the ponens is identified. On the next line is the diocese of origin, and on the line below this the statement that the case is a marriage invalidity

51 See canon 1687 §§1-2; *Ratio procedendi*, art. 20 §1.

52 Canon 1683, 2°.

53 For an illustration, please see the published cases in *Decisiones Seu Sententiae* XCVII (Vatican City: Libreria Edictrice Vaticana, 2014).

54 Coram Monier, February 20, 2013, Prot. N. 19.607, Sent. 49.2013 (unpublished; copy at Tribunal, Diocese of Cheyenne).

case. The parties' last names are then provided. On the next line, which is also underlined on the left margin, is the protocol number, and on the right margin, the sentence number. Below this in all-capitalization, bold and larger font is the statement "Definitive Sentence" (*Sententia Definativa*).

The actual sentence begins on the line below the title with the invocation of the Divine Name, often, "In the Name of the Lord" (*In nomine Domini*).

The first paragraph states the year of the pontificate of the Holy Father, and then the auditors are listed. The second paragraph states the petitioner's name, date of birth, religion, domicile and patron. The third paragraph states the same for the other party. The fourth paragraph provides the name of the defender of the bond and any other person involved in the case. The fifth paragraph states the grade of tribunal, e.g., second instance, third instance, etc.

There are three sections to the sentence: *Facti species* (Outline of the fact); *In iure* (In law); and *In facto* (In fact). The *Facti species* begins with the undisputed facts of the case such as when the couple met, were engaged, married and separated (civilly divorced), and other facts such as children and elements of the relationship not in dispute. The second part is the procedures which were followed in the case and includes the *dubium*. The *In iure* states the law and jurisprudence as it applies to the *dubium*. The *In facto* presents the argument based upon the law and facts, and concludes with the decision.

The Rotal sentence concludes with the date, and signatures of the judges and notary. Afterwards follows the directions, such the manner in which the decision can be appealed, the way it is to be executed, and if appropriate, a *vetium*.

Detailed Outline:

From the analysis above the earlier outline can be expanded to give a more complete representation of the elements of a sentence.

- I. Introduction
  - A. Initial Identification of the Tribunal
  - B. Type of Case
  - C. Parties and Case Number
  - D. Definitive Sentence
  - E. Invocation of Divine Name
  - F. Principals in the Case
    - 1. May state Pope and Bishop and the Parties
    - 2. Judge(s)
    - 3. Auditor and/or Assessor(s)
    - 4. Defender
    - 5. Promoter of Justice, if present

6. [Notary]
7. Parties
    a. Domicile
    b. Date and Place of Birth
    c. Religion
    d. Date, Church and Place of Baptism
    e. Advocates/Procurators of Parties
    f. Others, such as Guardians

II. Brief Statement of Uncontested Facts
    A. Position of the Parties
        1. Dates of Meeting, Engagement, [Cohabitation], Marriage, Separation and Divorce.
        2. Children, or lack thereof
        3. Other Undisputed Facts
    B. Procedural Actions
        1. Date of Reception of Petition
        2. Date of Determination of Competence and Acceptance
        3. Date of Citation of Defender and Other Party, if not co-petitioning
        4. Date of Second Citation of Other Party, if did not respond to first citation
        5. Date of Decree Formulating the Doubt and Deciding to assign to Ordinary Process or *Processus Brevior*
            a. Note that a decision to assign to Ordinary Process has the effect of opening the case for instruction, so no degree is needed.
            b. The judges, judge, auditor, and accessor(s) are also assigned at this point.
            c. Note that the date for the instruction session for the *Processus Brevior* is set by this decree.
        6. Dates of Expert Citation and Reception of the Report (for Ordinary Process)
        7. Date of Publication (for Ordinary Process)
        8. Date of Closure and Call for Animadversions and Observations
        9. Dates of Animadversions of Advocates and Observations of Defender
        10. Dates of Responses, if any (for Ordinary Process)

III. Dispositive Section
    A. Law Section

B. Fact Section/Argument Section

IV. Conclusion
  A. Place and Date of Decision
  B. Signatures
    1. Judges or Judge (includes Bishop)
    2. Notary
  C. Additional Matters
    1. Reminder of Obligations to Each Other and to Children
    2. *Vetitum/Vetita* and/or *Monitum/Monita*
    3. A determination about judicial expenses
    4. How to Challenge Decision and If Not Challenged, Becomes Executable in 15 Days
    5. How the Decision and Sentence will be Communicated to Parties

Conclusion

A matrimonial case concerning the invalidity of a marriage culminates in the decision rendered by the judges, judge or diocesan bishop. The sentence, therefore, needs to express how the decision was reached and the law and the facts which serve as the basis of that decision. If the decision is that the marriage is invalid, then the sentence needs to explain how moral certitude was reached. If moral certitude was not attained, the sentence needs to describe this too. If the detailed outline given above is followed, all the structural elements required by law will be in the sentence. Writing a well-crafted sentence is even more important come December 8, 2015, because the amount of review has been reduced since there is no automatic appeal to second instance. Judges and even diocesan bishops have even more responsibility to be thorough in writing their sentences to clearly show how the decision was reached. Lastly, the role of the defender of the bond has grown in importance, because the defender and the right for him or her to appeal a decision is the final safeguard for the integrity of the matrimonial process.

Seminar

Parish Membership and Territoriality

Very Reverend Lawrence DiNardo

May I first express my thanks to the Board of Governors and the Convention Planning Committee for inviting me to offer a seminar on the question of Parish Membership and Territoriality. At first glance the subject seems rather simple, parishes are divided by territory and people become members by living within the territorial boundaries. But is this truly reality? We have all heard of the confusion with clergy and laity over the question of parish membership, enrollment and participation. Stories abound from people who cannot believe that the "church" is forcing people to be members of a certain parish, or that a child cannot attend a parish school since they are not members of the parish, or worse, need to pay non-parishioner tuition. There is no doubt that there is clearly a division between the law and the real life situations of the people who participate in our parishes.

If you came to this seminar to hear a scholarly presentation on the canons related to parishes and membership, you came to the wrong place. If you came to this seminar to walk away with all the answers about parish membership, you might be disappointed. If you came to this seminar to explore a possible different way that we might look at parish life and the principle of territoriality, then you have chosen the right seminar.

Introduction

Pope Francis reminds us that the Church does not exist to maintain structures but for the proclamation of the Gospel. We live in a different society than the one envisioned by the *Code of Canon Law* of 1917 or 1983. We have become a mobile society that travels distances to attend our favorite concert, sporting event, shopping mall and even our church. For most people worship is an action of the heart and it is relational. It deals with individual people making choices about why they attend Mass and where they attend Mass. People, as well as clergy, are often confused by the law on territoriality. We often hear stories of people being told that they cannot join a parish because they live outside the boundaries, or that that they cannot have their children attend a particular Catholic elementary school because they belong to another parish. All of these examples separate people from the Church and can create barriers to the salvation of souls, the supreme law of the Church.

Purpose of This Seminar

This seminar will explore four elements in our discussion of parishes and territoriality. First, we will examine the relevant canons as they apply to this topic. Second, we will explore the present situation that we find ourselves in as leaders in our dioceses. Third, we will examine trends regarding the participation of people in parishes and finally, we will explore a possible future consideration for parish membership.

The Relevant Canons

The foundational canon regarding parishes and membership is found in canon 374 §1 which states: "Every diocese or other particular church is to be divided into distinct parts or parishes."[1] It is clear from the canon that the creation of parishes within a diocese is obligatory not optional. It would seem that parishes are a constitutive part of a diocese. But what is a parish?

Canon 515 offers us a clear definition of what constitutes a parish. The canon states: "A parish is a certain community of the Christian faithful stably constituted in a particular church, whose pastoral care is entrusted to a pastor as its proper shepherd under the authority of the diocesan bishop."[2] The canon offers clear constitutive parts that are necessary to establish a parish. From my reading of the canon there are four main points for consideration. First, a parish is a *certain community of the Christian faithful*, second, a parish is *stably constituted*, third, a parish is *entrusted to a pastor*, and fourth, a parish is *under the authority of the diocesan bishop*. It is clear that all of these elements must exist for a parish to be established. One cannot establish a parish without the consent of the diocesan bishop, nor can a parish be created without a pastor – either one appointed to the parish or responsible for the parish.

In past times many of us were familiar with the term "mission parishes." These were parishes which usually did not have a resident pastor, generally cared for by the pastor of a neighboring parish, which was hopeful that one day it might be erected as a parish and have a resident pastor. While some of these types of "parishes" remain, the 1983 *Code of Canon Law* envisioned such a situation that might exist in parts of the world and in our country. Thus canon 516 speaks to us

1 Canon 374 §1. Quaelibet diocesis allave Ecclesia particularis dividatur in distinctas partes seu paroecias. *Codex Iuris Canonici auctoritate Ioannis Paulis PP. II promulgates* (Vatican City: Libreria Editrice Vaticana, 1983). Translation: *Code of Canon Law, Latin-English Edition*; New English Translation (Washington, DC: Canon Law Society of America, 2001). All subsequent translations will be taken from this source unless otherwise noted.

2 Canon 515. Paroecia est certa communitas christifidelium in Ecclesia particulari stabiliter constituta, cuius cura pastoralis, sub auctoritate Eposdcopi dioecesani committitur parocho, qua proprio eiusdem pastori.

of what we have come to know as quasi-parishes. Canon 516 §1 states: "Unless the law provides otherwise, a quasi-parish is equivalent to a parish; a quasi-parish is a definite community of the Christian faithful in a particular church, entrusted to a priest as its proper pastor but not yet erected as a parish because of particular circumstances."[3] Several interesting comments need to be made about this canon. First, the notion of *equivalent to a parish.* The canon makes it clear that a quasi-parish is juridically the same as a parish defined in canon 515. Second, a quasi-parish might be within a certain geographic area or for a certain group of people such as a hospital staff, travelers at major airports, and the like.[4] Third, that a quasi-parish *has not yet been erected as a parish due to circumstances*. These circumstances might be insufficiency of members, financial considerations, or long-term viability.

For the purpose of this seminar, the heart of our discussion rests within the context of canon 518. The canon states: "As a general rule a parish is to be territorial, that is, one which includes all the Christian faithful of a certain territory. When it is expedient, however, personal parishes are to be established determined by reason of the rite, language, or nationality of the Christian faithful of some territory, or even for some other reason."[5]

The canon clearly indicates that mere attendance at a parish does not constitute membership, nor does registration in a parish constitute membership. Membership is constituted by either having a domicile or quasi-domicile (cf. canons 102 and 107) within a defined region (established in the decree of erection of the parish), or if a parish is decreed as being a personal parish, by belonging to the group for which the parish was established. What is important to note is that a parish can be both territorial (part of a defined portion of the People of God) and also personal (a specific group that is part of the parish). For example, a parish could be established and given a certain territory, but also be for a certain group of people such as Latino ministry. The canon, while seemingly strong in its direction concerning territory as the basis for a parish, is also somewhat elastic in offering various ways by which a parish can be established by the diocesan bishop.

Why would the Church establish such a norm? Should not people be able to belong to whatever parish they desire? Does not this law seem arbitrary and not pastoral in nature? Does the law serve the care of the souls of people? These

3 Canon 516. Nisi aliud iure caveatur, paroeciae aequiparatur quasi-paroecia, quae est certa in Ecclesia particulari communitas christifidelium, sacerdoti uti pastori proprio commissia, ob peculiaria adiuncta in paroeciam nondum erecta.

4 Gordon Read, "The Internal Ordering of Particular Churches," in *The Canon Law; Letter and Spirit*, Gerard Sheehy (gen. ed.), (Collegeville, MN: Liturgical Press, 1995) [hereafter *Letter and Spirit*] 286.

5 Canon 518. Paroecia regula generalii sit territorialis, quae scilicet omnes complectatur christifideles certi territorii; ubi vero id expediat, constituantur paroeciae personales, ratione ritus, linguae, nationis christifidelium alicuius territorii atquae alia etiam ratione determinatae.

and many similar questions are heard daily by pastors and chancery officials. In addition, members of the Christian faithful often seek from the diocesan bishop a "dispensation" from this norm. How do you explain to the average parishioner that the norm on territoriality is a constitutive norm and thus not part of the power of the diocesan bishop to dispense?

In reality the law exists for three important reasons. First, the Church is a community of believers that comes together to celebrate the Eucharist. It would seem that people who have other common interests such as similar school districts, shopping, civil jurisdiction and the like, would also desire to come together to share in the important sacramental reality of a parish. Second, organizationally, the law envisions that each person (Catholic or non-Catholic) knows who their pastor is and thus who is responsible for the care of their soul. Finally, people who live in the same community would view the parish as the center of both ecclesial as well as social life.

While these are admirable principles on which to base a universal law, the reality of our present day situation would indicate the contrary. In present society, rural parishes generally have a model that comports to both the intention and letter of the norm of canon 518. Suburban parishes see more of an *a la carte* approach to membership not based on territory but based on services that a parish may provide. This could include whether or not a parish has a school, the quality of the catechetical program, the liturgical music, the schedule of Masses, and available youth programs. City parishes seem to have a combination of both the traditional, model of parish life and people coming into the parish because they were "former" parishioners when they lived in the city, or because of some special ministry that is being provided in the parish. All of these variations clearly indicate that the norm established in the law, while organizationally sound, is not being adhered to in present parish life.

Some Parish Membership Examples

[Editor's Note: Visual aides were distributed on-site in Pittsburgh, Pennsylvania. The graphics accompanying Examples 1-6 are available, upon request, from the Office of the Executive Coordinator.]

One of the tools available to dioceses and parishes to assist in parish planning is Missioninsite. Missioninsight are community engagement specialists that "empower faith-based organizations with the tools they need to visualize and cultivate their current and prospective members, donors and volunteers and solve their most difficult challenges."[6] One of the aspects which might assist in our conversation about *Parish Membership and Territoriality* is the Congregant Plot for several parishes in the Diocese of Pittsburgh. These examples present the

6 Missioninsite product and information can be found at: http://missioninsite.com.

lived realities for parishes as they work to proclaim the Gospel to those who are part of their parishes.

[Graphic 1]

Example 1 is Saint Ignatius of Antioch Parish, Bobtown, located in Greene County in the Diocese of Pittsburgh, established in 1928. It is a very small and relatively poor rural parish. From the congregant plot we can determine that almost all of the parishioners (98%) reside within the parish territorial boundaries. The people in this region do not have significant access to larger parishes outside their territory and are very territorial about their community. Most parishioners were born and raised in this community and the parish continues to be the center of their religious and social life.

[Graphic 2]

Example 2 is Saint John Neumann Parish, a suburban parish in Franklin Park, located in Allegheny County in the Diocese of Pittsburgh, established in 1979. The residents of this area are middle to upper income and very transitory. The parish was created from several other surrounding parishes. Given the proximity to neighboring parishes, the excellent highways and roadways, the parishioner base has choices as to the parish they may desire to attend. The congregant plot indicates that the Christian faithful who are members of at least twelve other parishes (territorial) are enrolled in this parish. Thus, only 48% of the faithful in the territory of Saint John Neumann reside within the territorial boundaries.

[Graphic 3]

Example 3 is Holy Angels Parish, in the City of Pittsburgh in Allegheny County of the Diocese of Pittsburgh, established in 1903. The territorial boundaries of this parish are very small, given that the community of Hayes is a small inner-city community, once the home of many immigrants who worked in the mills formerly located just across the street from the parish. While the parish is located within one of the poorest regions of the City of Pittsburgh, the congregant plot indicates that only 20% of the people who are enrolled in this parish live within the territory of the parish. This 20% represents most of the Catholics who reside in this area. The remaining 80% enrolled in the parish live in at least seventeen (17) other parishes, many that are neighboring parishes but some that are suburban parishes. Historically, this parish is best known for having a small church building which people see as more intimate than the large suburban churches, where the people know the pastor and he knows each of them by name. The parish is also known for its response to the various needs of the faithful who enroll in the parish.

[Graphic 4]

Example 4 is Saint Camillus Parish in New Castle (Neshannock Township) in Lawrence County in the Diocese of Pittsburgh, established 1959 from another parish located in the City of New Castle. At the time it was erected, Neshannock Township was a growing suburb in the Lawrence County area. While 75% of the parishioners of the parish reside within the parish boundaries, this represents only 40% of the Catholics in the territory. The remaining Catholics are enrolled in several neighboring parishes. Some families remained in the original parish from which this parish was established while others remained in personal (nationality) parishes that were present in the region. At one time there were at least four personal parishes in the region, and at the present there is only one which represents the largest parish in the region. This parish is an Italian personal parish which has enrolled parishioners from all the parishes in the region.

[Graphic 5]

Example 5 is Saint Patrick-Saint Stanislaus Parish in the City of Pittsburgh (Strip District) in Allegheny County that is a merger of two parishes (Saint Patrick and Saint Stanislaus). The merger occurred in 1993. However, both of these parishes have been in this part of the City of Pittsburgh since the late 1800's. The Strip District is a section of the City of Pittsburgh known for its many produce stores, wholesale shops, restaurants, and entertainment venues. In its history it was the location for the produce yards for the City of Pittsburgh and its environs. At present the area has very low housing stock since most of the area is taken up by businesses. Thus, the congregant plot indicates that only 7% of the enrolled faithful live within the territory of the parish. The remaining members of the parish represent over thirty (30) different parishes in City of Pittsburgh and suburban region.

[Graphic 6]

Example 6 is Saint Mary of the Mount in the City of Pittsburgh (Mount Washington) in Allegheny County, erected in 1873. The congregant plot is an example of a parish in which 60% of the enrolled members reside within the territory of the parish, while the remaining 40% are spread across more that forty-five (45) different parishes. This parish has historically been known as the church which resides atop the hill that overlooks the City of Pittsburgh, but more especially for its quality liturgical celebrations and engaging homilies. Recently a neighboring parish merged into Saint Mary of the Mount which has increased its enrollment from outside the new territorial boundary.

What can be ascertained with regard to these examples? A careful analysis would indicate that at least three realities exist. First, the examples indicate that people are very transitory, that is, because they can easily move from place to place with ease. Most people are commuters. They travel to work each day, and drive to shop for food, clothing and entertainment. They also drive to church, whether that church is within their civil community, or a church in the neighboring community, or a church several miles from their home. Second, people who live in the suburbs do not generally see the parish as part of the civil community like people in rural areas do, and thus they are less likely to choose a parish based on geography. Thus, the local community (and by extension the local parish) does not have the same cohesiveness that may have existed in past times. Third, individuals are more interested in informative homilies, the quality of the liturgy (including the music), parish or regional schools, formation programs for children, youth ministry and adult formation than they are with being members of a parish within a given territory. Therefore, the choice of which parish to enroll and become members in is based on many factors, which includes geography, but for the most part other important factors as well.

Three Definitions for Our Considerations

For our consideration it might be wise to make clear distinctions between three important terms: Membership, Enrollment and Participation. While we might use these terms interchangeably, they do have distinct meanings.

Membership implies the Christian faithful who have a domicile or quasi-domicile within a given territory whether they are enrolled or not. Thus, every person who lives within the canonically defined territory is a member of a parish and has a proper pastor. This is critical so that at all times the Christian faithful know who has responsibility for their sacramental care and the care of souls.

Enrollment (registration) implies the Christian faithful who have registered in the parish and are part of the census of the parish. They are the people who actually desire to participate in the parish. They may also be people who are part of the parish by territory, but might also be individuals who are from another territory who desire to participate in the parish due to some reason that has touched their spiritual welfare.

Participation implies the Christian faithful who are neither members of the parish by territory nor members by registration, but participate in the parish on a regular basis. While we may not be aware of who they are, every parish has such participants. They believe that their participation is in fact membership.

Pastoral Solution

Pope Francis has asked us to be pastoral in our approach to people since the goal that we are trying to achieve is to lead people to the eternal kingdom. In order to have this pastoral approach we must first deal with reality. That is, we must recognize the change in the understanding of a parish by the faithful. While the law of the church offers a very important theological and organizational view of how a parish should be viewed, the reality is that our people envision a parish as something not simply defined by boundaries, but as a place where they believe that their spiritual needs are being nourished. Additionally, it is imperative that clergy also understand this change in the view of the people regarding parish enrollment. But how can we deal with the issue in some canonical manner?

To this end, I would propose that we consider the establishment of every parish as both territorial and personal without distinction. In this way each member of the Christian faithful would be cared for by the pastor of a territory and at the same time by the pastor of their choice. In some cases they will be one and the same. In others, they would become two distinct pastors. The basis for this proposal can be found in the final words of canon 518 which indicates that personal parishes can be established "even upon some determining factor." It is my belief that this consideration may remove the many canonical problems that exists in the present system, which while useful, do not meet the present circumstances that we find in present-day society.

From my vantage point, the issue for all of us is how do we bring people closer to the Church and to Jesus Christ? While the historical (and present day legislation) has served, and continues to serve a needed purpose, we must be willing to broaden our horizons so that the pastoral care of the faithful is not inhibited by the laws of Parish Membership and Territoriality.

Seminar

Archdiocesan/Religious Review Board: Structures of *Communio* in the Life of the Local Church

Sr. Sharon A. Euart, R.S.M.

Introduction

The establishment of (arch)diocesan/eparchial and religious review boards (review board) is a relatively recent phenomenon in our country. The clergy sexual abuse crisis in the United States, Europe, Australia, and indeed elsewhere in the world for over two decades – especially so in the United States since 2002 – has highlighted the need for review boards, the importance of consultation in the Church, the role of participative structures and the urgency to use them effectively.

The tragic and painful events in the Church since that time have provided many lessons for the entire Church, including challenges to Church leadership, especially to bishops and religious superiors to be more open, collaborative, transparent and accountable with their people, and to lay men and women to assume their rightful place in the life and mission of the Church.[1] During his recent visit to Philadelphia, Pope Francis offered compassionate support to those who suffered sexual abuse and to their families. He apologized for the priests and bishops who failed in their responsibility to protect children, and asked that during this Jubilee Year of Mercy, the "Door of Mercy" be opened wide in our dioceses, parishes, homes and hearts, to accompany those who have been abused. He promised always to be vigilant in protecting children today and tomorrow.[2]

This morning, I want to focus my comments on three areas: 1) the nature of consultation in the Church and its importance in the life of the local Church today; 2) the nature and role of the review board, and 3) the relationship of the review board to the diocesan bishop or major superior. Finally, I will offer some practical suggestions for the operation of review boards.

---

1 See Sharon A Euart, RSM, "A Canonical Perspective on the Sexual Abuse Crisis," *Origins* 37:8 (July 5, 2007) 113-119.

2 Pope Francis, "Francis meets with the Victims of Sexual Abuse," Vatican Information Service (VIS), September 28, 2015.

Nature of Consultation in the Church

First, the nature of consultation in the Church. In one form or another, consultation has been a part of Church governance since the early days of the Church. It usually involved bishops consulting the diocesan clergy, for example, through the chapter of canons which was a legal/corporate body of priests whose purpose was to assist the bishop as an advisory council.[3] Later the First Plenary Council of Baltimore established the structure of diocesan consultors which ushered in a new approach to consultation in the Church.[4]

The Second Vatican Council's ecclesiology of the Church as *communio* has led to the development of new forms of "common responsibility" at all levels of the Church's life.[5] Moreover, the idea of "active participation in the Church" has reached far beyond the area of liturgy and deepened the faithful's awareness that we are *all* the Church.[6] The theological notion of *communio* reflects the nature and mystery of the Church and its participation in the Trinitarian communion (*LG* 4). The 1985 Extraordinary Synod of Bishops cautioned that the "ecclesiology of communion cannot be reduced to purely organizational questions."[7] It is not a description of the Church's structure[8] for such structures are not ends in themselves; but, rather, a means to assist the Church in its mission to be the sign and instrument of communion with God and with others.

Theological basis

Consultation in the Church is rooted in the theological principles reflected in *Lumen gentium*, the Second Vatican Council's Constitution on the Church, that the Church is the people of God, a people gathered around their bishop, a holy people incorporated into the body of Christ (*LG* 11) with a share in the threefold mission of Christ to teach, to sanctify and to govern (*LG* 31). All members of the Church share a common dignity and the same vocation to holiness. They enjoy a fundamental equality that arises from baptism in Christ (*LG* 32), an equality that precedes all differences of function, charism, or office (*LG* 32). They are called, each according to his or her own particular gifts, to exercise the mission which God has entrusted to the Church to carry out in the world (*LG* 30, 32).

---

3 For a historical summary of cathedral chapters, see J. Abbo and J. Hannan. *The Sacred Canons*, vol. 1 (St. Louis: Herder Book Co., 1960) 400-401.

4 See Gerald Fogarty, "Canon Law in American History and the History of American Canon Law," *CLSA Proceedings* 5 (Washington, DC: Canon Law Society of America, 1988) 7-8.

5 Walter Kasper, *Theology and Church* (New York: Crossroad, 1989) 149-150.

6 Ibid., 150.

7 The Final Report of the 1985 Extraordinary Synod, II. C.1.

8 Kasper, p. 151.

Canonical principles

This theological framework for consultation in the life of the Church is reflected in fundamental principles found in several canons of the *Code of Canon Law*. For example, canon 211 states the duty and right of all the Christian faithful "to work so that the divine message of salvation more and more reaches all people in every age and in every land." This call to communion and mission is repeated specifically for lay persons in canon 225 and is the basis for the rights affirmed in other canons to form associations (c. 215), to assemble (c. 215), to take initiative in apostolic activity (c. 216), and to a Christian education (c. 217).

Canon 212 further details the duty and right of the Christian faithful to participate in the inner life of the Church. While obliged to follow what bishops declare as teachers of faith or determine as leaders of the Church, canon 212 expresses the rights of the faithful to make known their needs and desires to their bishops and to express opinions on matters which pertain to the good of the Church. *Lumen gentium* suggests that making known such opinions "should be done through the institutions established by the Church for that purpose" (*LG* 37).

Now, fifty years after the close of the Second Vatican Council, it is impossible to overestimate the theological significance of the council's teaching on the mystery of the Church, the universal call to holiness, and the laity's participation in the life and mission on the Church. How have post-conciliar papal, episcopal and canonical documents shaped the vision put forth by the council and how do they provide a context for the role of diocesan and religious review boards?

John Paul II: *Pastores gregis*

St. John Paul II, in the 2003 apostolic exhortation *Pastores gregis*,[9] characterizes a bishop's pastoral style of governance, when developed in the context of a "lived ecclesial communion," as increasingly "open to collaboration with all" (*PG* 44). The apostolic exhortation describes the interplay between the personal responsibility of the bishop for the good of the Church entrusted to him and the contribution offered by the faithful through consultative structures as a reciprocal one (*PG* 44). He refers to the sharing of responsibility for the life of the particular Church on the part of the bishop and the faithful as an essential element of the organic structure of ecclesial communion (*PG* 44).

John Paul II: *Novo millennio ineunte*

The relationship between shared responsibility and ecclesial communion was also addressed by St. John Paul II at the beginning of the new millennium in

9 John Paul II, Apostolic exhortation *Pastores gregis*, October 16, 2003; English translation published in *Origins* 33:22 (November 6, 2003) 353-392.

the apostolic letter *Novo millennio ineunte,*[10] in which he states that "the new century will have to see us more than ever intent on valuing and developing the forums and structures that, in accordance with the Second Vatican Council's major directives, serve to ensure and safeguard communion" (*NMI* 44). He goes on to describe the theology and spirituality of communion as encouraging a "fruitful dialogue between pastors and the faithful" (*NMI* 45).

Francis: *Evangelii gaudium*

Pope Francis, in his 2013 apostolic exhortation *Evangelii gaudium* (Joy of the Gospel), describes the Church which goes forth as a "community of missionary disciples who take the first step, who are involved and supportive, who bear fruit and rejoice" (*EG* 24). He refers to ecclesial structures that "can hamper efforts at evangelization," and says that new structures will prove to be ineffective without the infusion of "new life and an authentic evangelical spirit" (*EG* 26).

How do the faithful actually participate in the life of the Church? Do participative structures truly reflect the principle of shared responsibility in the governance of a diocese, religious institute, or society of apostolic life?

Shared Responsibility

In a well-known and often cited article on "Shared Responsibility in Ecclesial Decision-Making,"[11] Rev. Robert Kennedy points out the need for a critical analysis of the process of administrative decision-making in the Church. The notion of shared responsibility imparts to the believer responsibility for carrying forward the mission of the Church in partnership with other members of the Church, according to the gifts and functions of each person. Kennedy points out that discussion on decision-making in the Church often seems focused not so much on shared responsibility but on the notion of "power." Persons who make decisions affecting the life and direction of an ecclesial community are said to have power; while those who have no part in making such decisions are said to be powerless, or without influence in the life of the Church.

For many, shared responsibility comes to mean shared power; and attempts to implement shared responsibility come to be viewed as efforts to take power from

10 John Paul II, Apostolic letter *Novo millennio ineunte*, January 6, 2001; English translation published in *Origins* 30:31 (January 18, 2001) 489-508. John Paul II also speaks of the close relationship between communion and structures of participation in the apostolic exhortation *Ecclesia in America*, January 22, 1999, no. 44; English translation published in *Origins* 28:33 (February 14, 1999) 565-592.

11 Robert T. Kennedy, "Shared Responsibility in Ecclesial Decision-Making," *Studia canonica* 14 (1980) 5-23, p. 7. See also John P. Beal, "Consultation in Church Governance: Taking Care of Business by Taking After Business," *CLSA Proceedings* 68 (Washington, DC: Canon Law Society of America, 2006) 29-32.

those who are considered to possess it, namely, those who hold ecclesiastical office in the Church such as bishops, pastors, and leaders of religious institutes.[12]

The tension surrounding the notion and practice of decision-making in the Church might be lessened by a clearer or more nuanced understanding of what it means to share power and responsibility in the making of decisions. Decision-making power can be narrowly viewed as "choice-making" power, the power to make the final choice or at least participate by deliberative vote in making the final choice. Consultation, on the other hand, can be viewed as something altogether different with little or not enough definitive voice in choosing the final course of action.

Decision-making, however, whether undertaken by an individual acting alone or by a small group or a large community, is a complex process. It involves several stages, only one of which is the making of a final choice, and all of which entail an exercise of influence and power.

Practically speaking, it is within the framework of ecclesial communion and shared responsibility that the review board receives its meaning and its mandate.

Consultative Structures in the Code of Canon Law

What does the Code of Canon Law *say about consultative structures?*

The *Code of Canon Law* presents consultation as a fundamental activity in the Church in service to *communio*.[13] The code requires that certain consultative structures be established in each diocese to assist the bishop in the governance of the diocese and in his pastoral ministry to the local Church. These include the presbyteral council (c. 495), college of consultors (c. 502), diocesan (c. 492) and parish finance councils (c. 537). At the same time, the code leaves to the judgment of the diocesan bishop the establishment of other structures such as diocesan synods (cc. 460-468), and diocesan and parish pastoral councils to the extent that pastoral circumstances warrant such structures (c. 511).

In addition, the episcopal conference might determine that a particular consultative structure be established for all dioceses within its region. Such an action requires at least a two-thirds vote of the members of the conference with a deliberative vote and the *recognitio* of the Holy See (c. 455 §2). Once the Holy See has granted the required *recognitio*, the action may be promulgated as particular law for the region. The review board is such a structure established by the United States Conference of Catholic Bishops (USCCB) and required for each diocese, eparchy, and clerical religious institute and society in the United States.

12 Ibid., p. 7.

13 Oscar Andres Rodriguez, "Consultation in the Life of the Church," *CLSA Proceedings* 68 (Washington, DC: Canon Law Society of America, 2006) 3.

(Arch)diocesan /Religious Review Board[14]

USCCB

In November 2002 the bishops of the United States approved a revised text of the *Charter for the Protection of Children and Young People* (hereafter *Charter*) and the *Essential Norms for Diocesan/Eparchial Policies Dealing with Allegations of Sexual Abuse of Minors by Priests or Deacons* (hereafter *Essential Norms*).[15] Following the grant of the *recognitio* by the Congregation for Bishops (*CIC* c. 455§2), *Essential Norms* was promulgated by the president of the USCCB in December 2002 as particular law[16] for the dioceses and eparchies of the United States.[17]

In June 2005, the *Charter* and *Essential Norms* were revised with *Essential Norms* approved by the Congregation for Bishops in 2006 *donec aliter provideatur* (until provided for otherwise), and promulgated as particular law for the dioceses and eparchies of the United States.

Apostolic See

Meanwhile at the level of the universal Church, in April 2001, John Paul II promulgated the *motu proprio Sacramentorum sanctitatis tutela* (hereafter *SST*). This significant papal document clarified and updated the list of canonical crimes that had traditionally been dealt with by the Congregation for the Doctrine of the Faith (crimes against the faith, that is, heresy, apostasy and schism; as well as most serious crimes, or *graviora delicta*, against the sacraments). These *delicta* included crimes connected with solicitation in confession, and grave crimes of sexual abuse of minors by clerics. The *motu proprio* thus required all cases involving sexual abuse of minors by clergy to be reported to the Congregation for the Doctrine of the Faith (CDF) for its guidance and coordination of an equitable response on the part of Church authorities.

In 2010, after nine years of experience applying the norms of SST to thousands of cases, the Congregation for the Doctrine of the Faith proposed modi-

14 See Diocesan Review Board Resource Booklet, prepared by the USCCB, available at: http://www.usccb.org/issues-and-action/child-and-youth-protection/upload/2012-Diocesan-Review-Board-Resource.pdf.

15 See *Origins* 32:25 (November 28, 2002) for the text of both the *Charter* and the *Essential Norms*.

16 As required by canon law (*CIC* c. 455 §2) for actions of episcopal conferences, the bishops submitted *Essential Norms* to the Congregation for Bishops for the required *recognitio*. Particular laws are those enacted for a particular territory and bind those for whom they are made. Territorial particular laws generally apply to dioceses, provinces, and the nation(s) that comprise an episcopal conference. See *CIC*, cc. 12-13; *CCEO*, c. 1491.

17 See *Origins* 32:29 (January 2, 2003) 476 for text of the letter to then-Bishop Wilton Gregory from Cardinal Giovanni Battista regarding the granting the *recognitio*.

fications to the 2001 legislation to enable the law to deal more effectively with the complexities of the cases. The revised norms were promulgated by Pope Benedict XVI in May 2010. A year later, in May 2011, the *Circular Letter to Assist Episcopal Conferences in Developing Guidelines for Dealing with Cases of Sexual Abuse of Minors Perpetrated by Clerics* was promulgated by the Congregation for the Doctrine of the Faith.[18] The letter invited the episcopal conferences throughout the world to address various aspects of this issue: e.g., the canonical discipline of clergy who are guilty of such crimes; standards to evaluate the suitability of clergy and other persons who minister in Church institutions; oversight for educational programs to ensure the protection of children and young people from the crime of sexual abuse; and how to be pastors to victims of sexual abuse among their flocks who may appeal for remedy or help.[19]

In June 2011, the U.S. bishops approved additional revisions to the *Charter* and *Essential Norms* to conform to the 2010 *motu proprio Sacramentorum sanctitatis tutela* and the 2011 *Circular Letter to Assist Episcopal Conferences in Developing Guidelines for Dealing with Cases of Sexual Abuse of Minors Perpetrated by Clerics.*

Charter and *Essential Norms*

There are several elements regarding the canonical authority of the *Charter* and *Essential Norms* that relate directly to the nature and authority of the review board:

- Together they form a unity but are different in nature.
- The *Charter* contains an extensive declaration of intent on the part of the bishops regarding future policies and provides a framework for the implementation of *Essential Norms.*
- *Essential Norms* is canonical legislation approved by the bishops and the Apostolic See and promulgated as particular law for the dioceses, eparchies, and clerical religious institutes and societies of the United States.

18 John Paul II, Apostolic letter *motu proprio, Sacramentorum sanctitatis tutela;* revised May 21, 2010 *Normae de gravioribus delictis* at http://www.vatican.va/resources/index_en.htm., and Congregation for the Doctrine of the Faith, Circular Letter "To Assist Episcopal Conferences Regarding Guidelines for Dealing with Cases of Sexual Abuse of Minors Perpetrated by Clerics," May 3, 2011, *Roman Replies and CLSA Advisory Opinions 2011* (Washington, DC: Canon Law Society of America, 2011) 35-41. See also USCCB website for the revised *Charter* and *Essential Norms* at: www.usccb.org/ocyp/charter.pdf.

19 See Cardinal William Levada, "The Sexual Abuse of Minors: A Multi-faceted Response to the Challenge," presented at "Toward Healing and Renewal," Symposium for Catholic Bishops and Religious Superiors on the Sexual Abuse of Minors" sponsored by the Pontifical Gregorian University, Rome, Italy, February, 2012.

- While the bishops bound themselves to follow the provisions of the *Charter*, it is *Essential Norms* that is legally (canonically) binding on each diocesan bishop/eparch/major superior.

- Both the *Charter* and *Essential Norms* require each diocesan bishop, eparch and major superior of clerical religious institutes and societies to establish a review board as a confidential, consultative body in his handling of matters relating to allegations of sexual abuse of minors by priests and deacons.

Application of the *Charter* and *Essential Norms* to Clerical Religious Institutes

Following the approval of the *Charter* and *Essential Norms* in 2002 there was much discussion among religious superiors as to the application of *Essential Norms* to clerical religious institutes and societies. Footnote 1 of *Essential Norms* (2002) stated that the term "religious ordinary" shall be substituted for the term bishop/eparch *mutatis mutandis* (the necessary changes having been made) though nowhere in the document was provision made to address distinctions between religious and diocesan clergy. In the 2006 revision of *Essential Norms* clerical religious institutes and societies of apostolic life were added explicitly to the list for which the norms applied. In addition, footnote 1 was revised to read: "when a major superior of a clerical religious institute or society of apostolic life applies or interprets [the norms] for the internal life and governance of the institute or society, he has the obligation to so according to the universal law of the Church and the proper law of the institute or society."[20]

In 2002, the members of the Conference of Major Superiors of Men (CMSM) pledged their commitment to the protection of children and young people. Though not bound by the then-recently approved *Charter* of the U.S. bishops, they declared: "we honor the values and principles of the Dallas *Charter* and we seek to apply them to the unique situation of men's religious institutes in the

20 *Essential Norms,* footnote 1: "These norms constitute particular law for the dioceses, eparchies, clerical religious institutes, and societies of apostolic life of the United States with respect to all priests and deacons in the ecclesiastical ministry of the Church in the United States. When a major superior of a clerical religious institute or society of apostolic life applies and interprets them for the internal life and governance of the institute or society, he has the obligation to do so according to the universal law of the Church and the proper law of the institute or society." http://www.usccb.org/issues-and-action/child-and-youth-protection/upload/Charter-for-the-Protection-of-Children-and-Young-People-revised-2011.pdf. In the 2002 approved version of *Essential Norms*, footnote 1 simply stated: "In applying these Norms to religious priests and deacons, the term 'religious ordinary' shall be substituted for the term 'bishop/eparch' *mutatis mutandis*."

Church."[21] The CMSM developed the *Instruments of Hope and Healing Program* which provided standards for the protection of minors from sexual abuse, outreach to victims, development of review boards, and supervision of members credibly accused of sexually abusing minors. It hired Praesidium Religious Services to develop accrediting standards and an independent accreditation program for religious institutes. In 2013, the members of the CMSM documented improvements in their protection of children and acknowledged that their efforts have been done in "full cooperation with the guidelines, procedures and documents of the Catholic Church, including the *Charter for the Protection of Children and Young People* adopted by the United States Conference of Catholic Bishops in June 2002."[22]

Thus it became clear that the requirement in the *Charter* and *Essential Norms* for a review board applies not only to dioceses and eparchies but also to clerical religious institutes and societies of apostolic life in the United States. Local circumstances and the availability of resources, however, influence how this requirement is implemented in institutes and societies. Some join with other institutes or societies to form inter-congregational review boards or regional review boards. Others bring provinces together for service by a single board. Larger institutes and societies may have their own review boards while smaller institutes and societies may utilize the services of diocesan review boards as needed. Review boards that serve clerical religious institutes and societies are similar to diocesan review boards in nature and function though they may differ in structure and responsibilities.

Nature and Authority of the (Arch)diocesan Review Board

The *Charter* and *Essential Norms* refer to the review board as a "confidential, consultative body to the [diocesan] bishop [major superior] in discharging his responsibilities" (art. 2; norm 4). It has a responsibility to offer advice to the diocesan bishop and major superior. Its task is an advisory one. It is extra-judicial, that is, it is outside the ordinary judicial process.

The May 2011 Circular Letter from the Congregation for the Doctrine of the Faith *To Assist Episcopal Conferences Regarding Guidelines for Dealing with Cases of Sexual Abuse of Minors Perpetrated by Clerics*, provides suggestions to both diocesan bishops and major superiors on various procedures in Part III of the letter. When emphasizing the consultative nature of review boards, the letter offers an important observation in stating that "consultative bodies of review and

21 Conference of Major Superiors of Men, "Improving Pastoral Care and Accountability in Response to the Tragedy of Sexual Abuse," Annual Assembly, Philadelphia, PA, August 10, 2002.

22 Conference of Major Superiors of Men, "*Instruments of Hope and Healing*: Eleven Years of Work and Reflection by the United States Male Religious on the Tragedy of Sexual Abuse within the Catholic Church," Annual Assembly, August 2013.

discernment" are not to take the place of the diocesan bishop's or major superior's discernment and his power of governance (*potestas regiminis*) in individual cases.[23] In other words, the diocesan bishop or major superior cannot relinquish or hand over his authority to the review board in cases of clerical sexual abuse of minors.

Functions of Review Board

The *Charter* and *Essential Norms* assign three functions to diocesan review boards but neither document indicates that the list is all-inclusive or exhaustive.[24] The functions include advising the diocesan bishop or major superior in his assessment of allegations of sexual abuse of minors and in his determination of suitability for ministry; reviewing diocesan or institute policies for dealing with sexual abuse of minors; and offering advice on all aspects of these cases, whether retrospectively or prospectively.

Language of Essential Norms

Whatever functions the bishop or major superior assigns to the review board, however, should be consistent with the board's role as a consultative body with the responsibility to offer advice to the diocesan bishop or major superior regarding cases of sexual abuse of minors by priests and deacons. Other appropriate functions might also include, for example, advising the diocesan bishop or major superior on a program for the protection of children or on the pastoral response to those who allege to have been sexually abused by a cleric. For superiors, it might also include review of the safety plans for members when the sexual abuse of a minor has been established, the appropriate work and activity suitable for members on safety plans, members' compliance with their safety plans, as well as any proposed changes in existing safety plans, and an annual report to the major superior.

Role of Review Board

In practice, the function of the review board is to review and evaluate the findings and facts presented to it in a particular case and to assess whether the proofs are sufficient to support the probable nature of the allegation, and to make recommendations regarding the accused cleric's suitability for ministry (*EN*, norm 4).[25] The role of the review board is not investigatory in nature; that responsibil-

23 Circular Letter, III, f., 41.

24 *Essential Norms* states that "the functions of this board may include ... " norm 4.

25 Canon Law Society of America, *Guide To The Implementation of the U.S. Bishops'* Essential Norms for Diocesan/Eparchial Policies Dealing with Allegations of Sexual Abuse of Minors by Priests or Deacons (hereafter *Guide*), (Washington, DC: Canon Law Society of America, 2003) 27. The *Guide* is also available at www.clsa.org/briefs.htm.

ity belongs to the diocesan bishop or major superior, the promotor of justice, or the individuals with investigative experience to whom the bishop or superior entrusts the investigation. The board receives the investigator's report, evaluates the evidence gathered by the investigator(s) and offers advice to the bishop or major superior.[26] The review board is neither a jury nor a courtroom; it is an advisory body to the bishop or major superior.

When an allegation is received the responsibility to investigate the allegation in dioceses and institutes and societies may be assigned to an intervention team, an outside investigator, a member of the institute or society, or other persons. The results of the investigation should be reported to the diocesan bishop or major superior, the promoter of justice and the review board for a recommendation and determination on how to proceed with the case. At times, the investigator might be invited to present the report and respond to questions from the members of the review board.

In order that the board might carry out its functions responsibly, it is important that the diocesan bishop or major superior ensure that members of the board receive the necessary information regarding an allegation and an alleged perpetrator in order to make an informed recommendation regarding both the allegation(s) and the accused cleric's suitability for ministry. It is important that the review board make an independent recommendation apart from the bishop or superior.

After the review board makes its recommendations to the diocesan bishop or major superior, its involvement with a particular case is generally complete. In some instances, the bishop or superior might seek further clarification from the review board regarding its recommendations. If new information concerning a particular case becomes available at a later time, the review board may be asked to review the information.

The diocesan bishop, having received the review board's advice, should not act contrary to it unless there is a reason which, in his judgment, is an overriding one.[27] At the same time, bishops and superiors should exercise caution and prudence in evaluating the recommendations of review boards especially when the recommendations are in support of removing the priest from ministry.[28] If the bishop or superior decides not to follow the counsel of the review board, he might state his reason(s) to the board for not doing so, though the law does not

26 Ibid. See also USCCB, *A Resource for Canonical Processes for the Resolution of Complaints of Clerical Sexual Abuse of Minors* (hereafter *Resource*), distributed to U.S. diocesan bishops/eparchs by the USCCB Canonical Affairs Committee, November 2003 (Washington, DC, USCCB, 2003) 10, available at www.usccb.org.

27 See *CIC*, c. 127; *CCEO*, c. 934.

28 Richard P. Fitzgibbons, "Accusations Against Priests," *Homiletic & Pastoral Review* (January 29, 2015) 7 at: http://hprweb.com/2015/01/accusations-against-priests/.

require him to do so (c. 127). If the bishop's or superior's *votum* differs from the recommendation of the review board, he should indicate this along with his reasons in the cover letter to the Congregation for the Doctrine of the Faith.

After making his determination regarding the credibility of an allegation, the diocesan bishop or superior should proceed as outlined in the canonical process found in the revised norms of the apostolic letter *Sacramentorum sanctitatis tutela* (SST) and the *Normae de gravioribus delictis*. The process is a complex and technical one, yet one that respects the rights of all persons involved. The current praxis in the U.S. is that following the canonical process, many, if not most, offenders who are members of clerical institutes and societies are not dismissed but remain members of the institute or society with restrictions enumerated in the member's safety plan.

Membership, Size and Composition of (Arch)diocesan/Religious Review Board

Let us consider some practical aspects of Board membership, size and composition.

The *Charter* and *Essential Norms* provide some guidance regarding the makeup of the review board in stating that members "will be lay persons who are not in the employ of the diocese" (art. 2; norm 5). *Essential Norms* also specifies that membership include at least five persons of "outstanding integrity and good judgment in full communion with the Church," an experienced pastor of the diocese, and an expert in the treatment of sexual abuse. Beyond these qualities, the *Charter* and *Essential Norms* are silent on further specifications.

Members

Members of diocesan review boards are generally appointed by the diocesan bishop or major superior, perhaps following consultation with the superior's council or others that the bishop or superior consider appropriate. The letters of appointment might include information regarding the members' role, term of office, schedule of meetings, background materials, lists of review board members and contact person(s), and other relevant information. The letter might also indicate whether or not the bishop or superior intends to release the names of the members of the review board to the public and the reasons for his decision.

The number of members serving on review boards varies from very small to somewhat large. Workload and manageability are important considerations in determining the size of the review board. While review boards with fewer members may be more manageable, larger size review boards may be organized into smaller groups (subcommittees) for the handling of cases. Besides workload and manageability considerations, the pastoral needs of the diocese, institute or society and the availability of resources often determine the size of the review board. Though many dioceses had established review boards prior to the approval of the *Charter* and *Essential Norms*, the large number of cases in some dioceses in the early 2000's suggested the need for larger boards to handle the cases in an effective and efficient manner. With the very welcome decrease in the number of new cases, the workload of many review boards has lessened in recent years.

Beyond the membership requirements of the *Charter* and *Essential Norms*, the composition of review boards varies across the country. Some review boards include representation from law enforcement, the judiciary, and health care providers. Some review boards also include attorneys, sex abuse prevention counselors, business executives, mental health practitioners, psychologists, teachers, social workers, parents of victims of sexual abuse, and victims.

On boards where membership exceeds the required five persons in full communion with the Church (*EN*, norm 5), some review boards might also include non-Catholic members or consultants such as, for example, professional persons who are not Catholic but have an expertise that is needed on the board, or leaders of other faiths who bring an experience and objectivity from their respective faith communities.

Ex officio

Diocesan bishops and major superiors have also included *ex officio* participants on review boards. One example is the promotor of justice. The role of the promotor, appointed by the diocesan bishop for individual cases or for all cases in which the public welfare is involved, is to foster and "safeguard the public good" (*CIC*, c. 1430; *CCEO*, c. 1094), that is, for the protection of the rights of all concerned and for the good of the Church. Norm 5 of *Essential Norms* makes it possible, even desirable, that the promotor of justice participate in the meetings of the review board as a resource to ensure and safeguard the integrity of the canonical processes.[29] The procedures for the operation of the review board should clarify the relationship of the promotor of justice to the review board. For example, when the promotor is permitted to speak or offer suggestions to the board. Since religious institutes and societies do not often have a promotor of justice, a major superior might inquire about appointing the promotor of justice for the diocese where the board meets to serve as an *ex officio* (non-voting) member of the review board.

The diocesan bishop or major superior may wish to appoint other *ex officio* (non-voting) participants to the review board such as, for example, the victim assistance coordinator, a canonical advisor, or other resource persons to assist the review board in carrying out its responsibilities. Additionally, the attorney for

29 *Guide*, 28.

the diocese or institute might be invited as a resource in meetings of the review board as appropriate.

What is essential is that the review board be free to carry out its responsibilities within the authority afforded it according to *Essential Norms* and the *Charter*. The process for offering advice and determining its recommendations should be free from intimidation or the appearance of any such pressure.

Diocesan Bishop/Major Superior and Review Board

The authority of the diocesan bishop or major superior is an important consideration in the effective functioning of the board.

The diocesan bishop, according to the universal law of the Church, is the chief pastoral leader and key authority figure in the diocese. He possesses all the "ordinary, proper, and immediate power" (*CIC*, c. 381 §1; *CCEO*, c. 178) he needs to carry out his pastoral ministry in the diocese entrusted to him.[30] However, his power is not absolute. In exercising his pastoral leadership role in the diocese, universal Church law and the particular law of the diocese identify specific structures which the diocesan bishop may be required to consult on certain administrative matters.[31] There are also structures recommended by universal law as well as other structures the diocesan bishop might establish as consultative bodies in the diocese in light of local circumstances.[32] These consultative bodies assist the diocesan bishop in discharging his governance responsibilities and carrying out his pastoral ministry.

Major superiors of clerical institutes and societies possess power by virtue of their office; they exercise their authority according to the universal law of the Church and the proper law of the institute or society. Major superiors have the personal authority to decide and to take action (c. 618), a right that is not diminished by participative pre-decisional processes. Each major superior has his own council (c. 627) which assists the superior in carrying out his responsibilities.

---

30 The diocesan/eparchial bishop's power is ordinary (related to his office as bishop), proper (exercised in his name) and immediate (exercised without mediation of another person).

31 For example, the diocesan bishop/eparch is to consult the presbyteral council on affairs of greater importance concerning the life of the faithful and the governance of his diocese (*CIC*, c. 500 §2; *CCEO*, c. 269 §2). In addition to affairs of great importance defined by the diocesan bishop, matters for which canon law requires that the presbyteral council be consulted are: *CIC*, cc. 461 (convocation of a diocesan synod), 515 §2 (establishment, suppression and alteration of parishes), 1215 §2 (building churches), 1222 §2 (relegating a church to secular use), and 1263 (taxes).

32 See, for example, the canons on diocesan pastoral councils (*CIC*, cc. 511-514).

Relationship of the Review Board and Diocesan Bishop/ Major Superior

How does the review board relate to the diocesan bishop or major superior? As a "confidential, consultative body," the review board assists the diocesan bishop or major superior in his assessment of allegations of sexual abuse of minors and his determination of the priest's or deacon's suitability for ministry (*Charter*, art. 2; *EN*, norm 4). Other advisory functions of the board, as was mentioned earlier, may include review of sexual abuse policies, programs for the protection of children, or review of safety plans for members of institutes or societies.

Among the ways in which the diocesan bishop or major superior exercises his authority in relation to the review board include establishment of the review board, appointment of the members of the review board, appointment of the chairperson (and vice-chairperson, if applicable) of the review board (or delegation of the selection process to the review board), appointment of the promoter of justice, approval and promulgation of the diocesan or institute's policy on sexual abuse of minors following review by the board, approval of review board statutes and/or policies as well as changes in them, and determination regarding allegations of sexual abuse of minors by priests and deacons following review and recommendation by the board.

Interaction

Diocesan bishops and major superiors interact in various ways with their review boards, though they consistently rely on the advice offered by the members of the board and are supportive of the work of their respective boards. Some bishops and superiors, for example, valuing the importance of the objectivity of the review board in making its recommendations, may seldom interact directly with the members of their boards. Others interact directly with their review boards in varying degrees ranging from attendance at review board meetings on occasion (e.g., to receive the board's recommendation on particular allegations or suitability for ministry), to attending every meeting of the review board. Some review boards in dioceses or institutes which have experienced the appointment of one or perhaps more than one new diocesan bishop or major superior since the establishment of the review board, have found it necessary to adapt to the differing policies and/or governance styles of the new bishop or superior. At the same time, newly appointed bishops and major superiors, after considering a variety of factors, might modify past practices of interaction with the review board.

There is no standard for the level of participation by the diocesan bishop or major superior in meetings of the board. He might consider how his presence impacts the work of the board, his confidence in the functioning of the board, his personal style in relating to the board, as well as the needs of the diocese or institute or society. It would seem that since the review board is established to advise the bishop or superior, direct communication and contact between the board and the bishop or superior is important at some point during the board's deliberation on particular cases, in order to avoid misunderstandings and confusion. The responsibility of diocesan bishops and major superiors to ascertain that the safety of minors and vulnerable adults is assured in schools, parishes and other Church institutions is a serious obligation, one that cannot be handed over to review boards, but one in which the competence, expertise, and wisdom of the review board can play an essential role.

Policies

It is critically important that the diocese, institute or society develop policies and procedures to guide the functioning of the review board. These policies might include a statement regarding confidentiality of proceedings, communication with the media (who has authority to speak to the media), record-keeping (minutes, summaries of actions), the process for arriving at recommendations (e.g., by consensus, voting), interviews with victims and the accused cleric or deacon and the requirements for such interviews, use of technology such as teleconferencing/web-conferencing circumstances, frequency of meetings and attendance requirements, non-member attendance at meetings (who and under what conditions), and the nature, scope and retention of the materials distributed for review by review board members.

One policy that I believe is of utmost importance to the effectiveness of the review board is the orientation and training of board members. Most members of review boards are selected for a particular expertise. Diocesan bishops and major superiors should not assume that the people they appoint to their review boards have an adequate understanding of their role and that of the board, the meaning of consultation in the Church, and the canonical processes to be followed in cases of clerical sexual abuse of minors. An orientation program that addresses the nature of the board; its responsibilities; its relationship to the bishop or major superior; the respect to be given the accuser, the accused, and the diocese, institute or society is essential for the proper handling of cases of clerical sexual abuse of minors.

Review boards play a critical role in the handling of cases of sexual abuse of minors by diocesan clergy and members of clerical institutes and societies. Currently, religious institutes and societies seek accreditation from outside agencies that review the handling of cases by major superiors and their respective review boards according to standards developed by the agencies in conjunction with the Conference of Major Superiors of Men. Each institute and society must demonstrate compliance with the standards in order to receive accreditation which is reviewed and renewed every three or five years.

Dioceses, unlike clerical religious institutes and societies, do not participate in a process of accreditation by an outside accrediting agency. They are, however, audited annually by a national firm for compliance with national and diocesan policies for reporting and handling of cases of clerical sexual abuse of minors. Since the initiation of the accrediting process and the annual audits, significant progress continues to be made in addressing clerical sexual abuse of minors in the Church. Though both diocesan bishops and major superiors are strongly urged to participate in the audit and accrediting process, respectively, neither the USCCB nor the Conference of Major Superiors of Men has the necessary jurisdictional authority to require participation in these programs. This lack of oversight for dioceses and clerical institutes and societies has at times led to inadequate functioning of some boards, a lack of proper procedure in others, and infrequent meeting schedules in still others.[33]

While the functions of the review board are enumerated in the *Charter* and *Essential Norms,* the day to day operation of these bodies varies from diocese to diocese, institute to institute, and society to society. Would more common and consistent standards improve the functioning of all review boards? Perhaps so, but not necessarily. It would seem that, given the broad diversity of structure, size, and resources that exists among dioceses and clerical institutes and societies, it may be unrealistic to expect that common policies and procedures could be applied consistently to all review boards.

However, it would seem both timely and appropriate for dioceses, clerical institutes, and societies to undertake what Pope Francis calls "a renewal of structures demanded by pastoral conversion." Assessment of their review boards might highlight issues that continue to arise regarding the precise nature of the board, its canonical relationship to the diocesan bishop or major superior, and the scope of its authority and responsibility. In moving forward to address clerical sexual abuse of minors it will be important for the boards' effectiveness and for the relationship between diocesan bishops, major superiors and their review boards, that a spirit of openness, shared responsibility, transparency, and accountability characterize their collaborative efforts to ensure the protection of children.

Conclusion

I want to conclude with the words of Pope Francis in his February 2015 *Letter to Presidents of Episcopal Conferences & Superiors of Institutes of Consecrated Life & Societies of Apostolic Life Concerning the Pontifical Commission for the Protection of Minors*. In the letter he states that: "everything possible must be done to rid the Church of the scourge of the sexual abuse of minors and to open pathways of reconciliation and healing for those who were abused" ... by taking

33 See for example, 2014 Annual Report: Findings and Recommendations, March 2015, http://www.usccb.org/issues-and-action/child-and-youth-protection/upload/2014-Annual-Report.pdf. See also Joshua McElwee, "USCCB's Clergy Sex Abuse Audit Finds Decline but Major Limitations," *National Catholic Reporter,* April 1, 2014.

the necessary steps "to ensure the protection of minors and vulnerable adults, and to respond to their needs with fairness and mercy."[34] The service of review boards for your dioceses, institutes and societies can be one effective means of providing such protection now and in the future.

34 Letter Of His Holiness Pope Francis to The Presidents of the Episcopal Conferences and Superiors of Institutes of Consecrated Life and Societies of Apostolic Life Concerning the Pontifical Commission for the Protection of Minors, February 2, 2015, at: http://w2.vatican.va/content/francesco/en/letters/2015/documents/papa-francesco_20150202_lettera-pontificia-commissione-tutela-minori.html.

Seminar

Canon 245 and the Powerful Spiritual Leadership of an Intentional Presbyterate

Reverend J. Ronald Knott

I am honored to be here, but in my mind it's close to being yet another sign that the "end times" are coming! I never in my life imagined that I would ever be addressing a canon law convention, but I am very excited about sharing what I have learned in my seventeen years of trying to implement the following canon. Miracles do happen!

CODE OF CANON LAW

TITLE III .
SACRED MINISTERS OR CLERICS
(Canons 232 – 293)
CHAPTER I
THE FORMATION OF CLERICS

Canon 245

> §1. Through their spiritual formation, students are to become equipped to exercise the pastoral ministry fruitfully and are to be formed in a missionary spirit; they are to learn that ministry always carried out in living faith and charity fosters their own sanctification. They also are to learn to cultivate those virtues which are valued highly in human relations so that they are able to achieve an appropriate integration between human and supernatural goods.
>
> §2. Students are so to be formed that, imbued with love of the Church of Christ, they are bound by humble and filial charity to the Roman Pontiff, the successor of Peter, are attached to their own bishop as faithful coworkers, and work together with their brothers. Through common life in the seminary and through relationships of friendship and of association cultivated with others, they are to be prepared for fraternal union with the diocesan *presbyterium* whose partners they will be in the service of the Church.

To begin with, it might be a good idea to place my involvement in implementing this canon in a time line – not a complete time line of course – but it will give you a pretty good idea where my work fits into the bigger scheme of things.

"COMMUNION IN THE PRESBYTERATE"
MY PLACE IN A TIME LINE
1998-2015

St. Ignatius of Antioch – A.D. 35 or 50 – 98 to 117

Vatican Council II – *Christus Dominus, Presbyterorum Ordinis, Optam Totius*, 1965

Pope John Paul II – New *Code of Canon Law,* 1983

Pope John Paul II – *Pastores Dabo Vobis*, 1992

Rev. Ronald Knott – Vocation Director, began 1998

USCCB – *The Basic Plan for the Ongoing Formation of Priests*, 2001

Rev. Ronald Knott – Vocation Director, term ended 2003

Rev. Ronald Knott – *Intentional Presbyterates: Claiming Our Common Sense of Purpose as Diocesan Priests,* 2004

Rev. Ronald Knott – Became founding Director of the Institute for Priests and Presbyterates, 2004

Rev. Ronald Knott – *From Seminarian to Diocesan Priest: Managing a Successful Transition,* 2004

Rev. Gary L Coulter – (License - Canon Law - Rome) – "*Juridical Manifestations of the Presbyterium*," 2004

Rev. Ronald Knott – (editor) – *A BISHOP AND HIS PRIESTS TOGETHER: Resources For Building More Intentional Presbyterates,* 2004

Rev. Ronald Knott – Retired as Director of the Institute for Priests and Presbyterates, while continuing some formation work with seminarians, priests and especially presbyterates.

Next, I would like to share with you where I have presented what I call "initial and remedial formation" in presbyteral theology to bishops, priests and seminarians – either through convocations, retreats, classes, courses, study days or printed and electronic materials.

CONVOCATIONS, RETREATS AND STUDY DAYS

Atlanta, GA
Baltimore, MD
Baton Rouge, LA
Beaumont, TX
Belleville, IL
Birmingham, AL
Boston, MA (2 times)
Bridgeport, CT (2 times)
Buffalo, NY
Chicago, IL
Columbus, OH
Denver, CO
Davenport, IA
Des Moines, IA
Dodge City, KS
Dubuque, IA
Evansville, IN
Fresno, CA
Gary, IN
Grand Rapids, MI
Green Bay, WI
Hartford, CT
Houston-Galveston, TX
Indianapolis, IN
Jefferson City, MO
Joliet, IL
Kansas City, KS
Kansas City, MO
Knoxville, TN
Lafayette, IN
Lansing, MI
Lexington, KY
Little Rock, AR
Louisville, KY
Memphis, TN
Monterey, CA (2016)
New Ulm, MN
New York, NY
Norwich, CT
Ogdensburg, NY
Oklahoma City, OK
Orlando, FL
Owensboro, KY
Pittsburgh, PA
Portland, ME
Portland, OR (2016)
Reno, NV
Richmond, VA
Sacramento, CA
Saginaw, MI
Salina, KS
Salt Lake City, UT
San Bernardino, CA
San Diego, CA
San Francisco, CA (two times)
San Jose, CA
Savannah, GA
Scranton, PA (2015 and 2016)
Sioux City, IA
Sioux Falls, SD
Springfield, IL,
Springfield-Cape Girardeau, IL
St. Augustine, FL
Toledo, OH
Trenton, NJ (two times)
Tulsa, OK (two times)
Winona, MN
Youngstown, OH

International Convocations, Retreats and Study Days

Cardiff, WALES, Hamilton, Ontario, CANADA, London, Ontario, CANADA, Nassau, THE BAHAMAS, Niagara Falls, Ontario, CANADA , Prince Albert, Saskatchewan, CANADA, Saskatoon, Saskatchewan, CANADA
Toronto, Ontario, CANADA (4 convocations - two in 2013 and two in 2014)
Tuam, IRELAND, Winnipeg, Manitoba, CANADA
Kingstown, ST. VINCENT AND THE GRENADINES, Kamloops, British Columbia, CANADA
Kingston, Ontario, CANADA, Regina, Saskatchewan, CANADA
Corner Brook, Labrador, Newfoundland, CANADA , Victoria, British Columbia, CANADA, Nelson, British Columbia, CANADA, Port Harcourt, NIGERIA, Ikot Ekpene NIGERIA (2016)
Sault Ste. Marie, Ontario, CANADA (2016), Pembroke, Ontario, CANADA (2016)

RELATED ADDRESSES AT US BISHOPS MEETINGS

St. Petersburg, FLORIDA, (USCCB Special Spring Meeting – 2010)
Chicago, ILLINOIS, (Catholic Extension Society Meeting – 2014)

SEMINARY RETREATS, STUDY DAYS AND COURSES ON PRESBTERAL THEOLOGY

St. Meinrad Seminary, St. Meinrad, INDIANA
St. Mary Seminary, Houston, TEXAS
St. Augustine Seminary, Toronto, Ontario, CANADA
Redemptoris Mater Seminary, Toronto, Ontario, CANADA
Sacred Heart Seminary, Hales Corner, WISCONSIN
Conception Seminary, Conception, MISSOURI

CONVENTIONS, KEYNOTES, ADDRESSES and WEEK-LONG PROGRAMS

National Federation of Priests Councils:
UNITED STATES: Phoenix, Miami, Minneapolis
CANADA: Toronto
ENGLAND: Leeds
Canon Law Society of America
Pittsburgh

RELATED BOOKS WRITTEN

Intentional Presbyterates: Claiming Our Common Sense of Purpose as Diocesan Priests (Louisville, KY: Sophronismos Press, 2003, ISBN 9-9668969-3-9).

- Spanish Translation – *Presbiterados Intencionales*
- Swahili Translation – *Ubasteri Kusudiwa*

Intentional Presbyterates: The Workbook (Louisville, KY: Sophronismos Press, 2007).

A Bishop and His Priests Together: Resources for Building More Unified Presbyterates (Louisville, KY: Sophronismos Press, 2011, ISBN: 978-0-9800023-4-8).

From Seminarian to Diocesan Priest: Managing a Successful Transition (Louisville, KY: Sophronismos Press, 2005, ISBN: 0-9668969-5-5).

- Spanish Translation – *De Seminarista a Socerdote Diocesano*

The Spiritual Leadership of a Parish Priest: On Being Good and Good at It (Louisville, KY: Sophronismos Press, 2007, ISBN: 978-0-9668969-9-2).

- Spanish Translation – *El Parroco Como Director Espiritual*

Personal Growth Plan: Handbook For Priests (Louisville, KY: Sophronismos Press, 2013, ISBN: 978-1-4912810-4-5).

- All books listed are available on the internet in e-book and hard copy for easier international distribution.

- Many of the books listed are used as textbooks in various seminaries, here and abroad.

BOOKS SENT FREE OF CHARGE TO ALL ARCHBISHOPS AND BISHOPS

- United States and Canada
  - *Intentional Presbyterates*
- United Sates, Canada, England, Wales, Ireland, South Africa and Australia
  - *A Bishop and His Priests Together*

FREE BOOKS SENT TO VARIOUS BISHOPS AND PRIESTS IN OTHER COUNTRIES

India, Philippines, South Pacific Regional Priest Retreat, South Korea, Kenya, Tanzania, Togo, Vietnam, Nigeria, Singapore. Barbados, St. Vincent and the Grenadines, The Bahamas, Austria.

RELATED ARTICLES PUBLISHED

Seminary Journal
The Priest
Origins
Church
Pastoral Review
Deacon Digest

RECOGNITIONS FOR WORK IN THIS AREA

NFPC Touchstone Award, 2008
St. Meinrad Distinguished Alumnus Award, 2010

ADDITIONAL RESOURCES DEVELOPED TO BUILD UNIFIED PRESBYTERATES

PRESBYTERAL CONVOCATIONS, STUDY DAYS AND RETREATS

INTENTIONAL PRESBYTERATES
Claiming Our Common Sense of Purpose as a Body of Priests

CONVOCATION MODEL
"The Powerful Spiritual Leadership of a Unified Presbyterate"
RETREAT MODEL
"Made Holy By Our Shared Ministry"

INTENTIONAL PRESBYTERATES - A
"Claiming Our Responsible Freedom as Individual Priests"

INTENTIONAL PRESBYTERATES - B
"Honoring the Variety of Gifts Within Our Presbyterate"

INTENTIONAL PRESBYTERATES - C
"The Asceticism of Dialogue in the Ministry of Unity: Learning to Talk to One Another More Effectively"

INTENTIONAL PRESBYTERATES – D
"Reclaiming the Four Pillars of Priestly Formation"

INTENTIONAL PRESBYTERATES
Claiming Our Responsible Freedom as Individual Priests

HYMN FOR PRESBYTERAL GATHERINGS
Lord and Teacher You Have Called Us
(in cooperation with Father Harry Hagan, OSB)

PRAYER CARDS
A PRIEST'S PRAYER FOR HIS PRESBYTERATE (English and Spanish)
A SEMINARIAN'S PRAYER FOR HIS PRESBYTERATE (English and Spanish)
A CATHOLIC'S PRAYER FOR THE DIOCESAN PRESBYTERATE

TALKING POINTS FOR BISHOPS

- When a man is sent to the seminary
- When a man is about to be ordained
- When a priest is made pastor for the first time

A PRESBYTERAL EXAMINATION OF CONSCIENCE
(developed by a Canadian priest at the end of an INTENTIONAL PRESBYTERATE convocation)

RITE FOR RENEWAL OF DIACONAL (transitional), PRIESTLY AND EPISCOPAL COMMITMENTS WITHIN A PRESBYTERAL CONVOCATION

Finally, I would like to summarize my work trying to teach and implement canon 245 these past seventeen years by sharing with you some of the most important things I have learned.

SOME THINGS I HAVE LEARNED FROM MY WORK IN TEACHING AND IMPLEMENTING CANON 245

1. Revived at Vatican Council II (*Christus Dominus, Presbyterorum Ordinis, Optam Totius*), the theology of a "presbyterate" has been neglected since the early church.

Writing at the start of the second century, St. Ignatius of Antioch provides a clear idea of the threefold ministry we know today.

> I exhort you to strive to do all things in harmony with God: the bishop is to preside in the place of God, while the presbyters are to function as the council of the Apostles, and the deacons, who are most dear to me, are entrusted with the ministry of Jesus Christ (Magnesians 6:1).

St. Ignatius speaks often of the presbyters, but normally refers to them as a council; in Greek: *presbyterion*, in Latin: *presbyterium*. The primary idea of St. Ignatius concerning the *presbyterium* is that priests remain in close union with one another and have a strong bond with their bishop. Thus his famous analogy: "your presbytery, which is a credit to its name, is a credit to God; for it harmonizes with the bishop as completely as the strings with a harp" (Ephesians 4:1).

His letters frequently indicate that the *presbyterium* acted as a collective body: a band, college, council, or senate. For Ignatius, this collegiality is always characteristic of the *presbyterium*. Indeed whenever the Patristic Fathers of the first three centuries mention presbyters, they almost speak of them in the plural and never in the singular: they always constitute a college.

Notice that the relationship Ignatius describes between the bishop and presbyters is not one of equality: the *presbyterium* is subject to the bishop who presides over them as Christ over the apostles. On the other hand, as the bishop's senate, the college of presbyters shares with him the responsibility for the well being of the ecclesial community. Saints Clement of Rome and Cyprian of Carthage are just two important examples of the many other Church Fathers who describe presbyters as constituting a council and being counselors of the bishop.

From the New Testament and early Christian writings, we see that the ancient church did not think in terms of solitary priests but of a *presbyterium*. United with the local bishop, it was a college that surrounded him and helped him to carry out the work of the church.

The loss of the concept

So what happened to the *presbyterium* and this idea of the collaboration of the presbyters? As the Church expanded after the legalization of Christianity, priests were stationed outside the episcopal city in order to administer the sacraments in rural districts. This physical separation from the city where the *presbyterium* would meet limited the priests' participation in it.

With the spread of the gospel into rural areas, isolated from the episcopal city and the *presbyterium*, the presbyter's role declined as counselors who assisted the bishop in administration. In its place, other bodies developed such as the Cathedral Chapter and the Diocesan Synod, which continued some of the *presbyterium*'s advisory and governing functions.

Another historical factor that encouraged individualism was development of the benefice system, by which priests were ordained for a particular benefice, a ministry to a particular church or benefactor who guaranteed his economic sustenance. This contributed to a decline in the common life and collaboration among priests, as they would feel less of a bond to the bishop than to their benefactor.

Some also see individualism coming from the developing theology of the priesthood that would culminate with the council of Trent. Of course, nothing is wrong with emphasizing the character of the priest as representing Christ, with a special dignity and personal power to celebrate the Eucharist. This idea, however, should not lead to a separation of the priest from the community or to an individualism or competitiveness in pastoral work.

> With the spread of the Church, there was a general breakdown of the early collegiality, and a trend toward an individual, not collegiate, ministry. The conception of presbyteral community, as well as knowledge of the meaning of the word *presbyterium* itself, was slowly lost in centuries of neglect." (Gary Coulter, *Juridical Manifestations of the Presbyterium,* 2004)

2. The American bishops called this a "neglect" in their basic plan for the ongoing formation of priests, saying that this "neglect" has left a vacuum:

   - "To pursue the ongoing formation not simply of (individual) priests, but of a presbyterate as a whole, brings us to new territory." (This calls for individual mentoring, as well as mentoring into the group.)
   - "The corporate sense of priestly identity and mission, although not fully developed even in official documents, is clearly emerging as

an important direction for the future." (This is why I got into this work.)

- "Its neglect favors division and a number of attendant problems within the diocese." ("Nothing gets better by leaving it alone," said Winston Churchill.)

3. When I started this work, I realized very quickly from a show of hands at every presbyteral convocation that *most* US priests have had no formal education in the theology of the presbyterate. As a result of this neglect, many priests have fallen into the habit of a priesthood of "private practice" which flies in the face of the "radical communitarian dimension of ordained ministry" that Pope John Paul II was so adamant about. Even though canon 245 §2 called for seminarians to be trained to take their places in presbyterates, when I started this it had barely been implemented, if at all. As a result of a continuing neglect and lack of a common vision, many of today's young priests are forming "tribes" within their presbyterates, struggling against other priests over who has the right vision. Some of these "tribes" are actively cultivating members from among seminarians. They groom them in secret, advise them how to "get through" seminary formation programs and which bishops deserve respect and obedience. If problems like these are being caused by neglect, imagine what we could become if we were to become more intentional about strengthening presbyteral unity? The biggest misconception priests have had of the "intentional presbyterate" idea is that it is about making priests happy. While that may be an important by-product of the process, the main reason for an "intentional presbyterate" is to offer the People of God a more coherent and effective ministry. Finally, as *Lumen Gentium* taught us, as well as canon 245 §1 and *Pastores Dabo Vobis,* that working for presbyteral unity is an essential part of a priest's spiritual life.

4. From a show of hands at hundreds of presbyteral convocations, I have learned that an even greater number of US priests have had no formal education in the diocesan priest's "promise of obedience." As a result they tend to see obedience mainly in terms of a personal relationship with the bishop that is invoked in cases of interagency, rather than seeing what Pope John Paul II called its "communal relationship with the bishop *and* the presbyterate as a whole." While seminaries are regularly focusing on celibacy programs, many still neglect to teach "that other promise," the promise of obedience which, when understood well, is critical in developing a common sense of purpose in our ministry because it has to do with what Pope John Paul II called "non-attachment to one's own preferences and points of view" for the sake of our common ministry. Obedience helps priests and bishops deliver a unified and coherent min-

istry to God's People and is probably even more important to their shared ministry than the promise of celibacy.

5. Most bishops, where I have made presentations, have indicated to me that US bishops get no training in how to lead presbyterates when they are named bishops. As a result, bishops may not always know how to direct individual ministry accomplishments toward the ministry goals of the diocese as a whole. Priests are waiting, craving really, to be led by shepherds with convincing voices. Bishops are the *designated* leaders of presbyterates, but some may need a lot more help in becoming *real* leaders of presbyterates.

6. Bishops and presbyterates need to pay better attention to the transition of new priests out of seminary and into ministry, to the transition of priests into first pastorates, and to the transition of international priests into new local presbyterates and parishes. Presbyterates need to see themselves as mentoring communities for these newest members which will require learning how to be such mentoring communities. Presbyterates need to understand how risky it is for both sides for new priests to be made pastors without proper training. Presbyterates need to understand as well that it is risky, for both sides, to accept international priests without a plan to receive them well.

7. An intense, complete and ongoing study of the teachings in *Pastores Dabo Vobis* and the implementation document, *The Basic Plan For the Ongoing Formation of Priests,* would do more than anything else to help priests find common theological ground on which to heal ideological differences. As it is, both sides of the divide tend to pick and choose citations from church documents to bolster their, already arrived at, conclusions.

8. A general acceptance of the theology that the ministry of priests consists in helping the bishop carry out *his* ministry and making *him* present in the places where they serve, would do wonders in building a sense of presbyteral unity among priests. This includes more dialogue with priests "on directions to be taken and choices to be made."

9. The best program to promote vocations today, I believe, would be one that is directed at building intentional presbyterates. Young men today will not be attracted to an informal association of "lone rangers," but to the religiously saturated environment of a happy and effective presbyterate with a clear identity and mission. As Vatican II said so many years ago, "Let priests attract the hearts of young men by their own humble and energetic lives, joyfully pursued, and by brotherly collaboration with their brother priests."[1] If this is true, when we pray for more vocations to

1 Paul VI, *Decree on Priestly Training, Optatam Totius*, October 28, 1965, no. 2.

the priesthood, we ought to move away from asking God to change *his* behavior and toward asking God to help us change *our* behaviors – that we might be more humble and energetic in our individual ministry and see it as our share in a collaborative ministry, especially with our bishop and fellow priests.

10. Seminaries need more ways to introduce reality into their curriculums. As seminaries continue to add more and more mandated communal experiences, the numbers of priests living alone continues to rise – some say 58% at present and growing. Seminaries need to prepare young priests to creatively live alone, while working together, by experimenting with small group living and individual living situations while they are still in the seminary. (To that end, I have designed and spearheaded the building of a new "life-skills center" at Saint Meinrad to teach simple healthy cooking, to practice being part of a support group, and to prepare for being part of a prayer group. It is to be finished by year's end.) To build more unified presbyterates, seminaries need to teach seminarians to *respect and negotiate* the various cultures of ecclesial life in today's Church rather than conspiring with them in *protecting* them from those cultures. Seminarians should be taught to identify and distinguish their own preferred learning culture from the learning cultures of other priests and be prepared to respectfully engage the needs and assumptions of other priests.

11. What is needed, ultimately, for presbyteral unity is not a new program, but a new mindset. I believe at the root of things is a need for a radical conversion of mind and heart by priests and bishops toward the good of one another. Likewise, we need to replace our downward spiraling talk of diminishment with some upward spiraling talk of abundance. Believing is different from wishing. Believing leads to positive action on our part. Wishing simply waits for others to act on our behalf.

12. The Church cannot afford infighting and demoralization among its priests. We need "all hands on deck." If we need "all hands on deck," we need to start seeing our diversity as a blessing. We must firmly and consistently reject the Rush Limbaugh approach to presbyterates, where we feel free to demonize and attribute the worst possible motives to those with whom we disagree. If "every snowflake in an avalanche pleads not guilty," we must individually reverse the process and begin to practice the spiritual discipline of blessing each other by intentionally looking for goodness to affirm in each other.

    - The more lay ministry develops the more need there will be for well-formed priests.

- Some statistics say 10% - 15% of our newly ordained priests leave in their first five years.
- 50% of all US priests are scheduled to retire in the next five years.

Let me conclude here. I hope this has been helpful. Doing this work as the founding director of the Institute for Priests and Presbyterates at Saint Meinrad Seminary and School of Theology, and doing work in so many dioceses around the country and around the world, has been the joy of my life for the last seventeen years. Sharing it with you here at this convention has been icing on the cake.

...and just to think I literally came within seconds of deleting all my original work and giving it up when I became despondent and discouraged during the height of the sexual abuse scandal!

SEMINAR

THE USE OF ELECTRONIC MEDIA IN CHURCH STRUCTURES

Michael Nobel

Introduction

The rapid increase in means of social communication requires an awareness of all Christian faithful, especially for the hierarchy in the Church and particular churches. The internet becomes more and more a tool not only to inform all Christian faithful, but also to share, discuss, and learn. The internet is no more considered a tool for IT-experts but with very little effort anyone can share and receive information on a non-stop basis with the danger that not always all information received through the internet is correct, and, furthermore, the danger of dependence and addiction to it: non-stop accessibility through laptops, tablets and smart-phones. All so often the internet is considered a tool where "anything goes"; the reasonable use declines, social relations are transferred to a digital world, cyber friendship has a bigger place in society than personal contact.

Some key features of a reasonable use of the internet and other electronic media related to it in the context of Church structures are to be examined, with reference to selected norms in the *Code of Canon Law*. A detailed study or even reference to civil law cannot be done due to the diversity of all various civil federal, provincial/state laws, and local regulations. A certain awareness of Church hierarchy is necessary especially when it comes to matters that are in the context of the mission of the Church.

1. Internet, Websites, and Online Publications

1.1. Participation in the Teaching Function of the Church

All Christian faithful, by virtue of their baptism participate in the *tria munera* of Christ according to their status in the Church. This principle outlined in c. 204 §1 indeed gives everyone validly baptized the possibility to participate in the teaching function of the Church: the *munus docendi*. But this teaching function cannot be related to all different topics, and it cannot be claimed by everyone to teach "anything on everything I want," hiding and justifying it with the general right outlined in c. 204 §1 and/or by the office or function that a person holds within the particular church. There are certain limitations such as the object of the teaching of the Church (c. 747) and the subject, answering the question, who can teach in the name of the Church.

Canon 747 states:

> §1. The Church, to which Christ the Lord has entrusted the deposit of faith so that with the assistance of the Holy Spirit it might protect the revealed truth reverently, examine it more closely, and proclaim and expound it faithfully, has the duty and innate right, independent of any human power whatsoever, to preach the gospel to all peoples, also using the means of social communication proper to it.
>
> §2. It belongs to the Church always and everywhere to announce moral principles, even about the social order, and to render judgment concerning any human affairs insofar as the fundamental rights of the human person or the salvation of souls requires it.

The first object in the context of the *munus docendi* is the proclamation of the gospel to all people, allowing the use of various means of social communication proper to it. This first paragraph already requires a certain awareness, and needs to be well understood. Certainly, "[h]uman dignity demands that persons should enjoy their use of their own judgment and freedom in making decisions. They should be free to base their own actions on their consciences, and not be coerced by internal (psychological) or external pressure."[1] A proper understanding of c. 748 seems necessary, as it states in §1:

> All persons are bound to seek the truth in those things which regard God and his Church and by virtue of divine law are bound by the obligation and possess the right of embracing and observing the truth which they have come to know.

Therefore, to teach and proclaim the gospel it is necessary that the person has a proper and correct understanding of the object. "All persons also have a moral obligation to seek the truth, especially religious truth, about God and about his Church. Once that quest is complete, once the truth is known, then they are

---

1 James A. Coriden, "Commentary on cc. 747-755," in: John P. Beal, James A. Coriden, Thomas J. Green (eds.), *New Commentary on the Code of Canon Law*, Commissioned by The Canon Law Society of America (Mahwah, NJ: Paulist Press, 2000) 912.

obliged to hold on to the truth and regulate their lives in accord with it"[2] and to proclaim it.

The second object concerns the announcement of moral principles, even about the social order, and any human affairs insofar as the fundamental rights of the human person or the salvation of souls. For this, every one of the Christian faithful has to rely on the teachings of the Church, meaning the pope, college of bishops, and the bishops themselves within their particular church, exercising their magisterium on above mentioned topics.[3] All the Christian faithful are to adhere with reverence and obedience to the authentic magisterium of the Church as stated in c. 212:

> §1. Conscious of their own responsibility, the Christian faithful are bound to follow with Christian obedience those things which the sacred pastors, inasmuch as they represent Christ, declare as teachers of the faith or establish as rulers of the Church.

When the *Code of Canon Law* was promulgated in 1983, the members of the various study groups as well as the supreme legislator could not foresee the development of various means of social communication; it was limited to books and other forms of printed publications, radio and television. The internet was not developed yet for public use, and over the decades it evolved more and more as the main instrument for sharing information. Therefore, the norms on instruments of social communication, cc. 822-832, are to be interpreted in the context of online publications and presentations as well although their adaptation may not be always without conflict.

1.2. Considerations for the Establishment of a Website Subject to the Authority of the Diocesan Bishop

Establishing a diocesan website or any website of a juridic person subject to the authority of the diocesan bishop requires for the diocesan bishop to be diligent in making use of it for the Church's purposes, as outlined in c. 822 §1:

> The pastors of the Church, using a right proper to the Church in fulfilling their function, are to endeavor to make use of the instruments of social communication.

It is also for the diocesan bishop to be sure that people know their duty to try to imbue the internet with an ethos that is truly human and Christian, according to c. 822 §2:

2 Ibid., 912.
3 See cc. 749-750, and 752-754.

> These same pastors are to take care to teach the faithful that they are bound by the duty of cooperating so that a human and Christian spirit enlivens the use of instruments of social communication.

Furthermore, the Christian faithful, especially those who are experts on the internet, are to assist the diocesan bishop with the tasks ahead, meaning, programmers, IT-experts, and web designers to set up websites, legal advisors, and "content supervisors." This can be found in c. 822 §3:

> All the Christian faithful, especially those who in any way have a role in the regulation or use of the same instruments, are to be concerned to offer assistance in pastoral action so that the Church exercises its function effectively through these instruments.

1.2.1. Choosing the Server

Establishing a diocesan website, a parish website or any other website for a juridic person subject to the authority of the diocesan bishop becomes foremost a financial question. Since most dioceses do not have the finances or the technical capacity to have its own server to host all information and data to be published online, this task will often be outsourced to other corporations for a monthly or annual fee, to host all the data to be presented online on their own main server. The selection as to which corporation or company to choose is often times not considered a serious task – the price and costs involved are the only leading arguments for choosing the outsourced servers. And this is the first step where a possible dilemma starts. It may be unknown to the diocesan bishop and the personnel responsible to set up a diocesan website if the chosen server is "without risks," meaning, if the company/corporation chosen hosts other information on their main server which may lead to conflict with civil authorities, such as pornography etc. The designated same I.P. address of the main server will also be provided to the diocese. This may have the effect that either unknown to the diocese its website gets on the "watchlist" of civil authorities, or access to the websites can be denied due to the I.P. address that is registered to be an address that hosts pornography etc.

Most dioceses do not have any policies concerning media, internet presence, websites, etc. and most dioceses do not have a specific office designated for this task. Mostly diocesan media centers are established, with IT-experts, as well as personnel for media liaison and similar affairs. The first question that can arise is simple: Who will decide which server to chose that will host the diocesan, parochial or any other website of a juridic person subject to the diocesan bishop? A clearly outlined diocesan policy can serve as main guideline for this initial task.

1.2.2. Naming the Website

Since the website needs to appropriately represent the judiric person concerned, special attentions need to given also to the name of the website. The *Code of Canon Law* is silent on the use of the name "Catholic" in the context of websites, but reference can be made to canon 216:

> Since they participate in the mission of the Church, all the Christian faithful have the right to promote or sustain apostolic action even by their own undertakings, according to their own state and condition. Nevertheless, no undertaking is to claim the name Catholic without the consent of competent ecclesiastical authority.

as well as canon 803 §3 on Catholic schools:

> Even if it is in fact Catholic, no school is to bear the name Catholic school without the consent of competent ecclesiastical authority.

and canon 808 on Catholic universities:

> Even if it is in fact Catholic, no university is to bear the title or name of Catholic university without the consent of competent ecclesiastical authority.

Therefore, the use of the name "Catholic" for a website of a juridic person subject to the authority of the diocesan bishop requires the consent of the competent ecclesiastical authority. The authority competent to consent to the use of the name "Catholic" would depend on the circumstances, and with reference to canons 300 and 312 which explain that the competent ecclesiastical authority to erect a public association is also competent to allow an association to use the word "Catholic," it can be concluded that the competent ecclesiastical authority for the use of the name "Catholic" on websites of juridic persons subject to the authority of the diocesan bishop is the diocesan bishop.

1.3. The Content of a Website

The above mentioned steps are just a few of the considerations of a diocesan bishop that are usually to be determined once: a webmaster, diocesan office, server, website name, etc. Initially establishing a website as well as its regular and frequent updates are necessary steps to be taken on a regular basis. Furthermore, civil legislation has to be observed when it comes to matters such as copyright and copyright violations, etc. of the material presented. Canonical requirements demand the involvement of the diocesan bishop when it comes to publications of matters concerning faith and morals on websites, as outlined in canon 823 §1:

> In order to preserve the integrity of the truths of faith and morals, the pastors of the Church have the duty and right to be watchful so that no harm is done to the faith or morals of the Christian faithful through writings or the use of instruments of social communication. They also have the duty and right to demand that writings to be published by the Christian faithful which touch upon faith or morals be submitted to their judgment and have the duty and right to condemn writings which harm correct faith or good morals.

Any material concerning morals and faith to be published on the official diocesan website as well as any other website of a juridic person subject to the authority of the diocesan bishop requires the approval of the diocesan bishop since he is the pastor of the Church in his diocese. Furthermore, canon 823 §1 can also be subject of a broad interpretation, that require the mentioned watchfulness of the diocesan bishop to any online publication of all Christian faithful in his diocese when it comes to matters of morals and faith; an almost impossible task with the ever growing accessibility and establishments of new websites. The question of a forum, blog, etc. will be treated separately.

According to canon 824 it seems that any writings destined for public distribution on diocesan websites or any other website require the permission or the approval of the local ordinary, unless it is otherwise evident:

> §1. Unless it is established otherwise, the local ordinary whose permission or approval to publish books must be sought according to the canons of this title is the proper local ordinary of the author or the ordinary of the place where the books are published.
>
> §2. Those things established regarding books in the canons of this title must be applied to any writings whatsoever which are destined for public distribution, unless it is otherwise evident.

Interestingly J. Coriden states that "[e]lectronic "publication" was not envisioned by the canon, e.g., e-mail, servers, websites, CD-ROMs, other Internet or World Wide Web Communications" and, therefore, "they do not require submission for approval."[4]

The use of published material in form of printed books etc. that were already permitted or approved, would definitively fall under Coriden's conclusion. Furthermore, it requires the observance of possible copyrights. If a purely online based publication such as e-books would not require any prior permission or approval remains questionable, but it is strongly recommended that those texts for public distribution on the diocesan website or any other website of a juridic person subject to the authority of the diocesan bishop be at least vetted. Christian faithful accessing the above mentioned websites interpret the presented material as official and in line with the teaching of their diocesan bishop and the universal Church, and, therefore, it is recommended that they be verified to be in accordance with the magisterium of the Church.

Not every content to be made available on a website would require such a permission or approval, such as contact information, presentation of events, historical facts of the diocese etc. A purely online based commentary on the new *motu proprio Mitis iudex* for example would require such a permission to verify whether or not the commentary made available on the diocesan website or any other official website of a juridic person subject to the authority of the diocesan bishop is actually correct and in line with the teaching of the Church, reflecting correctly the intention of the Supreme Legislator.

Although Coriden states that it was not in the mind of the legislator that any writings concerning morals and faith that are purely intended for public distribution on a website do not require a permission, it seems to be necessary for such texts that are intended to be published online only. Since the diocesan bishop himself or the local ordinary may not be an expert on the matter to be made available on a website, reference to canon 830 may permit the use of a censor:

> §1. The conference of bishops can compile a list of censors outstanding in knowledge, correct doctrine, and prudence to be available to diocesan curias or can also establish a commission of censors which local ordinaries can consult; the right of each local ordinary to entrust judgment regarding books to persons he approves, however, remains intact.
>
> §2. In fulfilling this office, laying aside any favoritism, the censor is to consider only the doctrine of the Church concerning faith and morals as it is proposed by the ecclesiastical magisterium.

---

4 James A. Coriden, "Commentary on cc. 747-755," in: John P. Beal, James A. Coriden, Thomas J. Green (eds.), *New Commentary on the Code of Canon Law*, Commissioned by The Canon Law Society of America (Mahwah, NJ: Paulist Press, 2000) 980.

> §3. A censor must give his or her opinion in writing; if it is favorable, the ordinary, according to his own prudent judgment, is to grant permission for publication to take place, with his name and the time and place of the permission granted expressed. If he does not grant permission, the ordinary is to communicate the reasons for the denial to the author of the work.

The use of a censor is recommended for publications destined for any purely online publication made for public distribution, such as websites, e-books, etc. As outlined in canon 830 paragraph 2, this censor is only to verify that the doctrine of the Church concerning morals and faith are observed in the proposed text. If changes to the original text are deemed necessary, the local ordinary can insist on them before the text is published on the official website. A detailed and precise diocesan directory can outline the content that requires permission or approval by the local ordinary. Furthermore, it can give competency to "content supervisors," such as censors. Explicit mention of civil legislation and copyright issues need to be addressed in the diocesan directory as well.

A last important norm in the context of online publications is canon 831 §1:

> Except for a just and reasonable cause, the Christian faithful are not to write anything for newspapers, magazines, or periodicals which are accustomed to attack openly the Catholic religion or good morals; clerics and members of religious institutes, however, are to do so only with the permission of the local ordinary.

This canon treats in its first paragraph the problem of writing in newspapers or magazines which openly attack the Catholic religion, faith and morals. Two other aspects can be added: firstly, it may also include internet websites used for publications that are notoriously known to attack the Catholic Church and its doctrine; secondly, all Christian faithful are not to publish writings to openly attack the Catholic religion, faith and morals. With the recent publication of the *motu proprio Mitis iudex*, on the internet as well as other media various commentaries were submitted and published, and, unfortunately, they were not always in the line with the teaching of the Church and its magisterium. Canon 212 §3 states:

> According to the knowledge, competence, and prestige which they possess, they [the Christian faithful] have the right and even at times the duty to manifest to the sacred pastors their opinion on matters which pertain to the good of the Church and to make their opinion known to the rest of the Christian faithful, without prejudice to the integrity of faith and morals,

> with reverence toward their pastors, and attentive to common advantage and the dignity of persons.

And, although canon 218 allows for a certain freedom in the context of academic research, the magisterium of the Church is always to be respected:

> Those engaged in the sacred disciplines have a just freedom of inquiry and of expressing their opinion prudently on those matters in which they possess expertise, while observing the submission due to the magisterium of the Church.

The prudence in their opinion as well as the observance of the submission due to the magisterium of the Church may sometimes get lost and is forgotten in any kind of publication, online as well as other means of social communication. All Christian faithful are citizens and as such they enjoy, in most countries, a constitutional right of free speech. But especially clerics and those Christian faithful that have an official function or a ministry within the Church also have a moral obligation to respect the magisterium of the Church. Any publication can and will be interpreted as the official position and opinion of the particular ecclesiastical institution, although this may not be always the fact. This becomes more evident in blogs, online chat-rooms, online discussions, etc.

2. Online Discussions, Blogs, and Related Privacy Concerns by Accessing the Internet

2.1. Freedom of Academic Research and Possibility to Express Personal Opinion

The freedom of academic research (c. 218) as well as the possibility to express their opinion which pertain to the good of the Church and to make their opinion known to the rest of the Christian faithful (c. 212) require the respect of the magisterium of the Church. This becomes very present in online discussions, fora, and other blogs. All the Christian faithful, especially clerics and lay people that have an official function within the Church, have the obligation to assist with the needs of the Church, and not to publish contrary to it or create more confusion, according to canon 222:

> §1. The Christian faithful are obliged to assist with the needs of the Church so that the Church has what is necessary for divine worship, for the works of the apostolate and of charity, and for the decent support of ministers.

§2. They are also obliged to promote social justice and, mindful of the precept of the Lord, to assist the poor from their own resources.

The internet and its blogs, discussion rooms etc., are a powerful tool that should be intended to be a helpful tool. But the dangers of the internet are more than evident. Reference can be made again to the recent promulgation of *Mitis iudex*. Within minutes after its promulgation, such online tools were flooded with opinions, commentaries, and translations of the original text that are sometimes worse than Google-translated texts. Blogs and online discussion rooms established and meant to help and assist canonists in their work were reduced to discussions such as found on Facebook and twitter. A true reflection, understanding, and interpretation of the *motu proprio* is not possible within minutes. Although canon 218 guarantees academic research, the "academic" aspect of some commentaries was simply lacking as well as the submission due to the magisterium of the Church. Most of the online discussions are intended for discussion purposes, but the danger of the internet becomes again evident, that the purely discussion-based forum can become a "show off" platform. In the internet, everything is just one mouse click away; anonymity can be insured; "first comes first serve" based publications can become a leading standard etc.

2.2. Limitation Standards Concerning Access and Accessibility

Several other aspects are to be kept in mind when it comes to online discussions etc., especially in non-professional, non-canonical groups reserved to members only. Oftentimes the Christian faithful and clerics in particular, especially the younger generation of clerics, do have internet accounts on various other websites. Especially for clerics it is an obligation to avoid those websites that are not proper to the clerical state. With the leaking of information of people registered on the adult entertainment website Ashley Madison, several hundred priests and clerics have been identified, even causing an increased suicide rate amongst those pastors and ministers who have been notoriously identified.

Diocesan policies should be established to serve as guidelines as to which actions online are permitted and which are not. It is impossible for a diocese to connect all computers in an intranet, so that everyone connected can have online access only through a main server, similar to huge office buildings where all computers are connected to one main server and "special" and "inappropriate" websites are not accessible. Even if it would be the case that a diocese could do it, there are always ways around it to avoid access through the main computer, but through smartphones, or tablets with a data plan etc.

Furthermore, it would be most difficult for dioceses to establish such intranets since there can be a risk of privacy concerns and a violation of privacy legislation, if every action of a cleric, even at home, and every employee of the diocese, can be monitored. Diocesan policies must make raise awareness of the risks and dangers of online activities: each time someone does something online, a digital fingerprint is left behind with every mouse click and can be traced back to the person who did the action – whether on purpose or by "accident." Erasing a computer afterwards does not erase the digital fingerprint left behind because the information is not only stored on the user's computer, but also on the server of the site visited.

Diocesan policies must address this awareness of digital fingerprints and liability concerns since "total control" of internet use of all clerics and employees of a diocese can neither be done nor guaranteed. To avoid scandal and eventually costly lawsuits, it is strongly recommended that such diocesan policies be established.

A drastic example may clarify the problem: A naïve but decent parish priest wants to organize a special event for his altar boys, and he wants to see what other parish priests do as far as fun excursions and activities with altar boys are concerned. Since he cannot simply call every parish priest and ask for advice, he goes online and, with good heart but very naïvely, he gets on Google and searches for "fun with altar boys." He has an entirely different intention than what the internet will provide him with information. And here begins the problem: the Google search itself is already registered and the parish priest has left already a digital fingerprint concerning his "research." In case the naïve priest decides to click on a "special" website unknown to him, he can be, depending on the content of the website, subject to the RCMP or FBI/Homeland Security; not only he has left a digital fingerprint behind concerning his initial research, but an additional digital fingerprint by accessing a website that hosts child pornography, and he can be charged with access and possession of child pornography since the data of each website is automatically downloaded on the computer in the Temporary File folder, it does not matter if the parish priest actively "downloaded" the information or not; the date and content are downloaded automatically so that the computer can "display" it – intended or not – but he accessed the website. Diocesan policies must address the issue of online use and make an awareness of the risks and challenges.

2.3. Social Media Platforms

Social media platforms such as Twitter, Facebook etc. are to be used with great care. Not everything that can be shared, should be shared. Diocesan policies can provide regulations on the use of various means of social communication, especially with regard to various online platforms. Clerics and lay personnel that have an office or function within the diocese, should be alert in sharing information on sites such as Twitter and Facebook. For every other user it is not evident if, for example, the priest is online as priest, or "personal and private."

Can a cleric or a lay person with an office or function within the diocese post and comment on everything on social media platforms? Diocesan policies need to raise awareness on the proper use of such media platforms, especially if a diocese has a shared website on Twitter or Facebook itself. This raises even more questions since those websites would require a more severe supervision on the content being posted and shared on a diocesan Twitter or Facebook page.

2.4. Concerns and Pastoral Approach With Information Gathered from the Internet

A question arises as to how to respond if a certain view is shared on Facebook. A possible scenario may be the following: two weeks before the celebration of the sacrament of confirmation, the parish priest reads an online commentary of one of his parishioners on Facebook, stating that the youth is happy her best friend had an abortion and she totally agrees with it.

It is notorious information, public, and shared on Facebook visible for everyone – the external forum. How should the priest react in such situation? Not admit the teenager to the reception of the sacrament of confirmation? Proceed and go ahead as if nothing has happened? Invite the teenager to the parish office and inform her about the consequences? Have a short follow-up catechesis and instruction on morals and faith of the Church? Unfortunately, it is just a mouse click for the teenager to remove the public commentary, but that does not mean that she is now fully in accord with the teaching of the Church. Even during the additional instruction prior to the reception of the sacrament, the teenager most likely will agree to everything the parish priest tells her, just so that the already prepared celebration can take place; and to avoid any conflict with her parents, family etc. It is a difficult task for a parish priest that requires sensitivity on his part and pastoral engagement. Furthermore, it is also questionable why the parish priest has access to accounts of teenagers and under-aged parishioners on Facebook and other online accounts in the first place.

Consequently, diocesan policies should also address the issue of how to respond to information appropriately that is been received through the internet, and appropriate online behaviour.

3. The Use of Video-Conferences

The internet can also be used for other purposes such as video conferences, which can be helpful tools in a judicial as well as an administrative context. In that case, a precise procedure should be established in a handbook if such procedure is to be applied, and when it is possible to do so.

3.1. Video Conference in the Judicial Context – Interrogation of Parties and Witnesses

In the judicial context, video conferences may be used in two different ways: interrogation of parties and witnesses, and convening the judges to deliberate.

M. Nobel highlighted current problems of interrogating parties and witnesses of a marriage case.[5] According to canon 1528 parties and witnesses are to be interrogated at the diocesan tribunal.

> If a party or a witness refuses to appear before the judge to testify, it is permissible to hear them through a lay person designated by the judge or to require of them a declaration either before a notary public or in any other legitimate manner.

Canon 1558 §1 repeats the necessity of interrogating witnesses at the tribunal itself:

> Witnesses must be examined at the tribunal unless the judge deems otherwise.

Under special circumstances, the interrogation can be held at another location according to canon 1558 §1. In this case the judge has to be aware that the interrogation be done at a public place such as parish office, at a house of a religious institute etc. Never can the interrogation be done at a public place such as bar or restaurant, nor can it be done in the house of the person to be interrogated. If a person is to be interrogated but has residence outside the jurisdiction of the tribunal, the judge has two options: according to canon 1469 §2 the judge of the tribunal can interrogate the person outside the jurisdiction following and observing the conditions attached:

> In addition to the case mentioned in §1, for a just cause and after having heard the parties, the judge can also go outside the territory to acquire proofs. This is to be done, however, with the permission of the diocesan bishop of the place where the judge goes and in the location designated by that bishop.

or the tribunal can ask for legal assistance according to canon 1418:

> Any tribunal has the right to call upon the assistance of another tribunal to instruct a case or to communicate acts.

---

5 Michael Nobel, "The Auditor in a Marriage Nullity Process: His Rights and Obligations for the Instruction of the Case," in *Philippine Canonical Forum* 14 (2012) 47-50.

Oftentimes, to avoid delays because the person to be interrogated cannot present him/herself at the tribunal, the judge orders that the questionnaire to be sent to the person via mail. This practice is to be avoided since there is no guarantee that the person answers the questions diligently and honestly, that there is no "family reunion" to answer all questions together, or that the person concerned actually answered the questions.[6]

Sometimes, judges refer to a telephone conference which may give a bit more guarantee that the person concerned is actually the one who answers the questions. But, if the party or witness is unknown to the judge or auditor, it is unknown if the person on the phone is actually the person to be interrogated.[7]

To avoid this situation, canon 1528 states:

> If a party or a witness refuses to appear before the judge to testify, it is permissible to hear them through a lay person designated by the judge or to require of them a declaration either before a notary public or in any other legitimate manner.

may be interpreted that the judge can allow for a video conference. Canon 1528 speaks of "in any other legitimate manner," therefore, an interrogation via video conference can be conducted.

Canon 1558 §1 may also give the judge the possibility to interrogate witnesses via video conference:

> Witnesses must be examined at the tribunal unless the judge deems otherwise.

Another important norm is canon 1558 §3 that allows judges to decide where to hear the witnesses:

> The judge is to decide where to hear those for whom it is impossible or difficult to come to the tribunal because of distance, sickness, or some impediment, without prejudice to the prescripts of cc. 1418 and 1469, §2.

The notary can request prior to the interrogation a scanned copy of a valid ID; a photo of the ID may be sufficient as well.[8] A video conference can be conducted, even if the person is outside the jurisdiction of the diocesan tribunal. To

6 Ibid., 37.
7 Ibid., 48.
8 Ibid., 62.

avoid any unnecessary complications after the interrogation, it is recommended to use software such as *Adobe Connect* that allows the interrogation to be video recorded. This way, a precise transcript can be done by the notary, and since it is video recorded, proof of the testimony itself is given. But, the link of the video recorded session cannot be send to the party or witness to avoid harm or scandal, i.e. the person forwards the video or makes it public. Even a password protected video that can be reviewed only, cannot be forwarded to the person, since he or she can still video record the instruction from the computer screen. Instead, the person interrogated can be invited to appear at the tribunal to verify its authenticity. It applies the same principle as if the instruction was done at the tribunal: never leave the person interrogated alone in the room with the testimony to avoid photos been taken etc. The same principle applies also in the context of the publication of the acts.

With the promulgation of the *motu proprio Mitis Iudex*, it seems to be possible to interrogate the parties and witnesses via video conference if procedural norms are observed for the ordinary process. In the context of the abbreviated procedure, where the norms of the oral contentious process apply for the interrogation of the parties, it may be questionable if jurisprudence would allow for such interrogation via video conference. A diocesan or national handbook or *vademecum* could address the awareness and usefulness of video interrogations of parties and witnesses.

3.2. Video Conference in the Judicial Context – Judges Convene for Deliberation

A second possibility to make use of video conferences in the judicial context is the stage of the process when the judges convene for deliberation of the definitive sentence. An opinion on this was already published in 2010 by M. Nobel.[9] The main norm for the possibility is canon 1609 §1 which indicates that the collegiate tribunal must convene at the tribunal or any other location determined by the presiding judge.

> In a collegiate tribunal the president of the college is to establish the date and time when the judges are to convene for deliberation; unless a special reason suggests otherwise, the meeting is to be held at the tribunal office.

The norm speaks of "unless a special reason suggests otherwise" which may give the collegiate tribunal the possibility to convene for deliberation via video

9 Michael Nobel, "Canons 1609 and 1610: Procedure for Judges to Convene for Deliberation via Internet-Conference," in: *Roman Replies and CLSA Advisory Opinions 2010* (Washington, DC: The Canon Law Society of America) 183-185.

conference. Certain procedures are to be observed to comply with the law.[10] This opinion may also be applicable to the new changes according to the *motu proprio Mitis Iudex*. This *motu proprio* also states that there is to be a collegial tribunal in the ordinary process, and if a sole judge is nominated, he is to convene for deliberation with two assessors.

3.3. Video Conference in the Administrative Context – Reunion of the Presbyteral Council

In the administrative context, a video conference can be applied, for example, at meetings of the presbyteral council. The statutes of the presbyteral council need to indicate if a possibility of having some members of the presbyteral council – not all of them – participate via video conference at a meeting in order to have the quorum necessary to make decisions. As canon 496 states:

> The presbyteral council is to have its own statutes approved by the diocesan bishop, attentive to the norms issued by the conference of bishops.

It may be recommended, according to canon 496, that the conference of bishops itself should discuss and determine the issue of members of the presbyteral council to participate via video conference, under certain circumstances only.

According to canon 500 §1, it is up to the diocesan bishop to call for a convention of the council:

> It is for the diocesan bishop to convoke the presbyteral council, preside over it, and determine the questions to be treated by it or receive proposals from the members.

It seems that the diocesan bishop is the only person competent to allow for a possible participation via video conference if certain circumstances demand it.

To avoid the possibility that the council cannot convene and does not have the quorum necessary for consulting by the bishop or to give consent in cases expressly defined by law according to canon 500 §2, the bishop may have an option of an online convocation via video conference, to avoid the situation that the council cannot fulfill its function and is to be dissolved according to canon 501 §3.

---

10 The proposed procedure is already outlined in M. Nobels article on the procedure for judges to convene for deliberations in the *2010 CLSA Advisory Opinions*, and is not repeated in this article.

> If the presbyteral council does not fulfill the function entrusted to it for the good of the diocese or gravely abuses it, the diocesan bishop, after having consulted with the metropolitan, or, if it concerns the metropolitan see itself, with the suffragan bishop senior in promotion, can dissolve it but must establish it anew within a year.

Recommended again is the use of software that would video record the session, also for the transcript and minutes of the meeting. A difficulty arises when members are asked for a vote. It needs to be distinguished between a regular vote via handraise mode, or a secret vote. The first option does not seem to create any difficulties since every member of the presbyteral council can be asked to give an oral vote – even the member that participates via video conference. Difficulties may arise if a secret vote is called for. Members present at the councils meeting can cast a vote in writing and a scrutineer can collect the ballots. For participants via video conference this is not possible. Since the vote is secret, the use of chat rooms or email cannot be done; but as alternative prior to the meeting an online survery such as via SurveyMonkey, etc. can be created and the link to be distributed to all online participants. The votes cast are anonymous and immediately visible for all participants – live at the meeting and online. The votes cast in the meeting of all members present at the meeting as well as the online result can immediately be evaluated and the result of the vote is cast.

Conclusion

In 2002 the Pontifical Council for Social Communications published the document "The Church and Internet"[11] which offers guidelines and encourages responsible use of the internet:

> The Church also needs to understand and use the Internet as a tool of internal communications. This requires keeping clearly in view its special character as a direct, immediate, interactive, and participatory medium.
>
> Already, the two-way interactivity of the Internet is blurring the old distinction between those who communicate and those who receive what is communicated, and creating a situation in which, potentially at least, everyone can do both. This is not the one-way, top-down communication of the past. As more and more people become familiar with this characteristic of

11 Pontifical Council for Social Communications, "The Church and the Internet," Vatican City 2002, at: http://www.vatican.va/roman_curia/pontifical_councils/pccs/documents/rc_pc_pccs_doc_20020228_church-internet_en.html (accessed on November 5, 2015).

> the Internet in other areas of their lives, they can be expected also to look for it in regard to religion and the Church.

Furthermore, the document continues:

> Education and training are another area of opportunity and need. 'Today everybody needs some form of continuing media education, whether by personal study or participation in an organized program or both. More than just teaching about techniques, media education helps people form standards of good taste and truthful moral judgment, an aspect of conscience formation. Through her schools and formation programs the Church should provide media education of this kind.'

It concludes that

> Education and training regarding the Internet ought to be part of comprehensive programs of media education available to members of the Church. As much as possible, pastoral planning for social communications should make provision for this training in the formation of seminarians, priests, religious, and lay pastoral personnel as well as teachers, parents, and students.

This calls also for diocesan policies that not only make an awareness of a responsible use of the internet, but also gives guidelines on how to use the new developed form of social communication.

Seminar

Canon 1095, 2°: Lack of Internal Freedom on Matrimonial Consent: An Analysis of Rotal Jurisprudence and American Decisions

Reverend Jaimes Ponce

Canon 1095 is one of the most controversial grounds of nullity, or perhaps the most misunderstood ground of nullity. This presentation will attempt to address some of the discrepancies that exist between the Roman Rota's understanding of c. 1095, n. 2 and the way in which this concept is understood and applied by Tribunals in the United States.

This is what c. 1095 states:

> The following are incapable of contracting marriage:
>
> 1. those who lack the sufficient use of reason;
> 2. those who suffer from a grave defect of discretion of judgment concerning the essential matrimonial rights and duties mutually to be handed over and accepted;
> 3. those who are not able to assume the essential obligations of marriage for causes of a psychic nature.[1]

It is often claimed that grave defect of discretion of judgment is the most widely used ground of nullity.[2] As a matter of fact, it is well known by some tribunal ministers that grave defect of discretion of judgment is the only ground

1 *Codex Iuris Canonici* auctoritate Ioannis Pauli PP. II promulgates (from now on *CIC*), Vatican City: Libreria Editrice Vaticana, (1983). English translation from *Code of Canon Law,* Latin-English Edition: New English Translation (Washington, DC: Canon Law Society of America, 1998). All subsequent English translations of canons from this code will be taken from this source unless otherwise indicated.

2 The Statistical yearbook of the Church, from 1985 to 2013, lists a large percentage of cases under this ground. For instance, in 1985, all the cases around the world on this ground amounted to 46,956, the tribunals in the United States accounted for 78% or 36,803 cases. In 2004, the world handled 60,864 cases under this ground, while the tribunals in the United States accounted for 38,831 cases or 64%. By 2010, while the world was handling 44,512 cases under this ground, the tribunals in the United States accounted for 51% or 22,012 cases.

of nullity accepted by some tribunals of First Instance because the tribunal of Second Instance does not accept any other ground.

It is important to observe that n. 2 refers to grave defect of discretion of judgment, and it is concerned with the essential rights and obligations of the matrimonial covenant. Although there is not an exhaustive list of these matrimonial rights and obligations per se; these rights and obligations can be deduced from the canons themselves. For instance, c. 1055 §1 lists a partnership of the whole of life, the good of the spouses and, the good of children. In addition, c. 1056 lists unity and indissolubility. In addition, some canonists list the right and obligation to the community of life and love of which *Gaudium et Spes (GS)*, n. 48 speaks about.

One important aspect of this ground of nullity that we need to take into consideration is the fact that a defect of discretion of judgment must be *grave* and it must relate to the essential rights and obligation of the marital covenant.

Before looking into the differences between the Roman Rota and the practices of the American Tribunals, it is important to review some very basic concepts regarding marriage.

Matrimonial Consent

In studying the concept of matrimonial consent, whether one takes a theological, canonical, psychological, or philosophical perspective, it is evident that the definition of this concept encompasses the whole human person. Therefore, taking into consideration that the human person is constituted of complex and dynamic elements, there are some basic theological and juridical concepts that need to be specified and applied to the theory of matrimonial covenant. In discerning an accurate understanding of marriage, all persons establishing a marital covenant must be able to pose a human act; that is their consent must be free, deliberate, and conscious. Furthermore, the engaged must be endowed with internal freedom in order to exercise their right to marry (*"ius connubii"*).

Canon Law stipulates that all persons who are not prevented by law are free to marry.[3] Furthermore, as John Paul II asserted when speaking to the Roman Rota:

> The Church and, consequently, canon law recognize that every person has the possibility of contracting marriage (cf. CIC, c. 1058; CCEO, c. 778); a possibility, however, which can only be exercised by those 'who are not prohibited by law' (ibid.). The latter are, first of all, those who have sufficient psychological maturity of intellect and will, along with the ability to

3 *CIC*, c. 1058: "All persons who are not prohibited by law can contract marriage."

> fulfill the essential obligations of the marital institution (cf. CIC, c. 1095; CCEO, c. 818).[4]

It is important to discern that John Paul II did not speak about a perfect or well-developed psychological maturity of intellect and will; rather, he stipulated that a sufficient psychological maturity of intellect and will is all what is necessary for a person to have the possibility of contracting marriage. It is therefore understood that a sufficient psychological maturity of intellect and will, and not a perfect maturity, gives the person the capacity to understand marriage, to resist impulses or pressures, and to make a free choice regarding the establishing of a marital covenant with a particular person at a particular time. Similarly, when a person does not have this sufficient maturity, such a person might be unable to resist the influence of internal or external coercions regarding marriage.

Therefore, in order for a person to manifest consent validly, it is required that there is no situation, condition, or event that might render the person's consent inefficient.[5] Some possible impediments that render the person's consent inefficient are age[6] (the person needs to be of a certain age in order to be able to enter into marriage both civilly and canonically); degree of consanguinity[7] (the person cannot marry one's own brother or sister, etc.); physical or mental incapacities;[8] the reception of sacred orders or sacred vows (such as certain categories of deacons, a priest, or a religious nun or brother);[9] the existence of a previous matrimonial bond, even if the person is divorced civilly,[10] among others. By the same token, from a canonical and theological perspective, freedom, is a preliminary condition for a person to be able to give consent and establish a matrimonial covenant.[11] Furthermore, as Bañares (2009) indicates:

> At the moment of the conjugal pact, the commitment of the partners requires, by its very nature, certain requisites: as it pertains to the subject, an adequate degree of freedom is necessary; as it pertains to the form of manifesting consent, a proper

4 John Paul II, Address to the Tribunal of the Roman Rota, 21 January 1999, in *AAS, XCI* (1999) 622-627, n. 7.

5 *CIC*, c. 1066: "Before a marriage is celebrated, it must be evident that nothing stands in the way of its valid and licit celebration."

6 *CIC*, c. 1083 §1: "A man before he has completed his sixteen year of age and a woman before she has completed her fourteenth year of age cannot enter into a valid marriage."

7 *CIC*, c. 1091 §1: "In the direct line of consanguinity marriage is invalid between all ancestors and descendants, both legitimate and natural."

8 *CIC*, c. 1095, 1°: "Those who lack the sufficient use of reason."

9 *CIC*, c. 1087: "Those in sacred orders invalidly attempt marriage."

10 *CIC*, c. 1085 §1: "A person bound by the bond of a previous marriage, even if it was not consummated, invalidly attempts marriage."

11 *CIC*, c. 1058: "All persons who are not prohibited by law can contract marriage."

form is necessary, so that the necessary juridical certainty may take place; and as it pertains to the object, the effective volition of a true conjugality is necessary.[12]

Freedom is absolutely necessary for the establishment of the matrimonial covenant, because through it, "man and woman accept the intimate community of life and love willed by God himself"[13] as they "give themselves to one another."[14] Nonetheless, it is important to observe that the mere observance of these requisites do not necessarily guarantee the success of the conjugal life, because "Marriage, one and indissoluble, as a human reality is not something mechanical and static; its success depends on the free and conscious cooperation of the spouses."[15]

It is also interesting to observe, however, that "this mutual giving/accepting of the spouses is not limited to certain aspects of conjugal life" [16] because the fact that they become one flesh, one body, does not mean that they belong to each other only at the physical-intimate level, but also at the emotional-intimate level. Ideally, they become one in each other for they acquire the right and the responsibility to nurture each other in all the dimensions of the human person – physical, emotional, intellectual, and spiritual. This understanding is confirmed by Gramunt (1991):

> Through the marriage covenant the spouses enter into a consortium or partnership in which they commit themselves in justice to give to each other, through their free acts, those human goods included in their own masculine and feminine humanity. This includes not only sexual acts but also a sharing of those spiritual goods inherent in their own feminine or masculine modality by which they complement each other.[17]

---

12 Juan I. Bañares, "Antropologia Cristiana e Dimensione Giuridica del Matrimonio," in Hector Franceschi & Miguel A. Ortiz, (eds.), *Verità del Consenso e Capacitàdi Donazione* (Roma: EDUSC, 2009) 39. The text in Italian reads: "Nel momento del patto coniugale, l'impegno delle parti richiede, per natura propria, certi requisiti: per quanto riguarda il soggetto è necessario un grado di libertà adeguato; per quanto riguarda la forma di manifestazione del consenso, è necessaria una forma propria, che possa dare luogo alla necessaria certezza giuridica; e in quanto all'oggetto è necessaria la volizione effettiva di una vera coniugalità."

13 *FC,* n. 11.

14 Ibid.

15 John Paul II, Address to the Tribunal of the Roman Rota, 4 February 1980, in *AAS LXXII* (1980) 172-178, n. 9.

16 Paul Churchill, "Cormac Burke's Vision of Marriage: A Critical Look," in *Canon Law Society of Great Britain & Ireland Newsletter*, 109 (1997) 66.

17 Ignatius Gramunt, "The Essence of Marriage and the Code of Canon Law," in *Studia canonica*, 25 (1991) 377.

Consequently they need to support each other, in all their dimensions, so that they become the best husband or the best wife that they are called to be. For when they consent to marry each other, they accept each other with all their fears, insecurities, strengths, and weaknesses realizing that the life ahead of them may be difficult to navigate, but they will remain together in good times and in bad times. For consenting to marriage means that the parties are embracing each other in their whole personhood, and at the same time they are committing themselves to be with each other "until death do us part."

Pompedda (1993), in postulating his views on marriage, states that the first three canons: 1055, 1056, and 1057 are absolutely fundamental to the definition of matrimony. These canons are essential because they contain the juridical components of marriage as they promote a personalistic notion of matrimony; and as such, they establish:

> — that matrimony *emanates from the consent* of the partners;
> — that the engaged are *a man and a woman*;
> — that the object of *consent* is the reciprocal *"traditio-acceptatio"* of the engaged regarding the *constitution of marriage*;
> — that the marriage covenant ("*matrimonio in fieri*") has its own specific content;
> — that this content is the *consortium totius vitae* between the man and the woman;
> — that such consortium because of its very nature is ordained to the *"bonum coniugum"* and to the *"prolis procreatio et education;"*
> — that the *essential properties* of matrimony are the *unity and* indissolubility;
> — that marriage between the baptized is a *sacrament*;
> — that because of the sacrament the indissolubility acquires a special firmness.[18]

---

18 Mario F. Pompedda, *Studi di Diritto Matrimoniale Canonico* (Milano:1993) 169. The Italian text reads:

"— che il matrimonio sorge del consenso delle parti;
— che nubenti sono l'uomo e la donna;
— che oggetto del consenso è la reciproca 'traditio-acceptatio' dei nubendi in ordine alla costituzione del matrimonio;
— che il patto matrimoniale (il 'matrimonium in fieri') ha un suo contenuto specifico;
— che questo contenuto è il consortium *totius vitae* tra l'uomo e la donna;
— che tale consortium per sua indole naturale è ordinato al 'bonum coniugum' e alla 'prolis procreatio et educatio';
— che proprietà essenziali del matrimonio sono l'unità e l'indissolubilità;
— che il matrimonio fra battezzati è un sacramento;
— che in ragione di esso sacramento l'indissolubilità acquista una speciale fermezza."

The relational dimension of the marital covenant is echoed in the Pastoral Constitution *"Gaudium et Spes"*, approved by Vatican Council II. It states that "God did not create men and women as solitary beings. ... For by their innermost nature men and women are social beings..."[19] Furthermore, upholding the dignity of marriage, it states, "The intimate partnership of life and the love which constitutes the married state has been established by the creator and endowed by him with his own proper laws; it is rooted in the contract of its partners, that is, in their irrevocable personal consent."[20] Consent of the persons then, is a foundational element of marriage; this is why the *CIC* establishes that in order for marriage to become a reality, it is necessary for consent to be legitimately manifested by legally and capable partners who wish to enter into this covenant. Since consent is placed at the center of the essence of marriage, it "cannot be supplied by any human power"[21] because it is an act that takes place in the person's innermost being: the will. It is this act of the will that enables the future spouses to enter into this "intimate union of marriage, as a mutual giving of two persons [which requires] an unbreakable unity between them."[22]

Pompedda (1993) clearly states that Canon 1057 is fundamental for understanding matrimonial consent. He asserts that:

> In this canon there are three clearly distinct elements that concur to bring about marriage; these are the consent [of the partners], the capacity of the persons and the legitimate manifestation [of consent].[23]

Among these elements, consent is considered as of primordial importance because it comes from within the person; it is formed within the will of the person as a "psychological act where the same consent is born as a formal human act."[24] As a consequence, if we accept the premise that consent is born in the innermost core of the person, then the person should possess a certain degree of maturity which will allow him/her to give birth to a valid consent. It is important to note that this degree of maturity does not refer to the idea of maturity as defined by the psychological sciences. Rather, maturity for marriage refers to the basic understanding of this institution, because marriage, under this canonical view:

---

19 *GS,* n. 12.

20 Ibid., 48.

21 *CIC,* c. 1057 §1.

22 *GS,* n. 48.

23 Mario F. Pompedda, *Studi di Diritto Matrimoniale Canonico...*, 63. The original text in Italian reads: "In tale canone si distinguono chiaramente tre elementi che concorrono a fare il matrimonio; si parla cioè di consenso, di abilità delle persone e di legittima manifestazione."

24 Ibid., 163. The original text in Italian reads: "... atto psicologico donde lo stesso consenso nasce quale atto formalmente umano."

> [R]epresents a true vocation for the great majority of the human race ... in assessing the capacity or the act of consent necessary for the celebration of a valid marriage, one cannot demand what it is not possible.[25]

Therefore, the degree of maturity that is required refers to the "minimum capacity sufficient for valid consent."[26] Without this minimum maturity, it cannot be acknowledged that a person has the sufficient capacity to consent to a valid marriage.[27]

Since consent germinates in the mind: in both the will and the intellect of the individual, it is reasonable to expect that consent undergoes a formative period before it can be expressed. This formative period begins with the experiences that a child undergoes with his/her family of origin and continues with his/her socialization process as he/she continues growing and developing.

The experiences that a child has outside his/her family of origin, such as in society in general, in school, in observing his/her extended family, in religious education, etc. influence the formative process of his/her consent. For instance, Viladrich (2001) states, "forming consent is a process of generating it through a time period in the life of the spouses-to-be."[28] This formative process can include both positive and negative experiences; however, the important aspect is that this process shapes the person's understanding of what marriage is. These lived experiences as well as one's education influence not only the perceptions that a person develops about marriage, but also the perceptions of what it means to enter into a community of life and love in which there is a responsibility to assume the essential obligations of marriage: such as fidelity, procreation, and

---

25 John Paul II, Address to the Tribunal of the Roman Rota, 27 January 1997, in *AAS, LXXXIX* (1997) 486-489, n. 5.

26 John Paul II, Address to the Tribunal of the Roman Rota, 25 January 1988, in *AAS, LXXX* (1988) 1178-1185.

27 John Paul II, Address to the Tribunal of the Roman Rota, 1997, n. 5.

28 Pedro J. Viladrich, "Commentary to Canon 1096," in Angel Marzoa, Jorge Miras, Rafael Rodriguez-Ocaña (eds.) and Ernest Caparros (gen. ed. of English translation), *Exegetical Commentary on the Code of Canon Law* (Montreal, PQ: Wilson & Lafleur, 2004) 963.

education of children.[29] Therefore, the formative process of consent "takes place through time in the life of the future spouses"[30] and it affects the choice of a future partner. Consequently, a reasonably formed consent, not a perfect consent, is what allows the future partners to express freely a valid consent at the time of marriage and form a family, knowing that by embracing this particular marriage covenant, they are acquiring some essential rights and obligations that need to be fulfilled. According to Gramunt (1991), those essential rights and obligations acquired through marriage are:

> [T]he mutual, exclusive, perpetual, and irrevocable rights and obligations to the following: **i**– a complementary relationship between persons (a man and a woman) from which derive many acts of mutual help which... belong... to the practice of marriage; **ii** –a sexual relationship which, specifying the nature of that relationship, refers to sexual acts that are human and open to procreation; and **iii** –the receiving of offspring which, completing the sanctification of this relationship is a right exercised by many acts of raising the children to their human development. These are the rights and obligations that are essential to establish marriage, and without the mutual handing over of those rights and obligations, even implicitly, no marriage partnership is formed but another sort of union.[31]

Even though ignorance of the obligations of marriage is not presumed after puberty,[32] it is difficult to ascertain, because of sociocultural and educational factors, that a given person is mature enough to understand fully that the consent that he/she is expressing at the time of marriage includes the knowledge that:

29 It is interesting to observe that: "The legislator has chosen not to commit those rights and duties to a legal formulation and has left it to canonical doctrine and jurisprudence to progressively declare and explain their content and limits. ... we will simply enumerate those essential rights and duties as correlated, in the sense that to each essential right corresponds an equally essential duty. These are the following: *the right/duty to sexual acts, the right/duty to not impede procreation, the right/duty of establishing, preserving, and ordering the intimate conjugal partnership toward its objective ends; the right/duty of fidelity; the right/duty of mutual help in ordering toward the pursuit of the essential ends of marriage those acts and types of behavior that are apt and needed for that purpose; the right/duty to welcome and care for the common children within the married community; and the right/duty of educating the common children.*" Pedro J. Viladrich, "Commentary to Canon 1096," in Angel Marzoa, Jorge Miras, Rafael Rodriguez-Ocaña (eds.) and Ernest Caparros (gen. ed. of English translation), *Exegetical Commentary on the Code of Canon Law* (Montreal, PQ: Wilson & Lafleur, 2004) vol. III/2, 1233.

30 Pedro J. Viladrich, *Il Consenso Matrimoniale* (Milano: Giuffre' Editore, 2001) 171. The Italian texts reads: "... ha bisogno di un certo spazio di tempo nella vita dei futuri contraenti."

31 Ignatius Gramunt, "The Essence of Marriage," 382.

32 *CIC*, c. 1096 §2: "This ignorance is not presumed after puberty."

> [M]arriage is a permanent partnership between a man and a woman, ordered to the procreation of children through some form of sexual cooperation.[33]

The reason for this is that:

> [C]onsent is, first of all, a human act, (...) [and as such, it includes both] the intellect, which is the faculty through which we know, and (...) the will, which is the faculty through which we freely will.[34]

Consequently matrimonial consent emanates from the internal core of the person: the mind; and as such, consent, in order for a man and a woman to give and accept each other as husband and wife, requires a "... previous self-control and self-acceptance in order for a real and true reciprocal giving and accepting [of each other]."[35]

Internal Freedom

Knowing that matrimony is a juridical act between two legally capable persons, it is imperative that this act be endowed with the elements that constitute the essence of the act as well as those elements that make the act valid.[36]

Consequently, when the constitutive or required elements are missing, the act is invalid. For instance, Canon Law indicates that unity and indissolubility are essential properties of marriage;[37] therefore, if those essential properties are excluded from matrimonial consent, the marriage would be null: nonexistent. Similarly, consent is described as the constitutive element of matrimony[38] which is an act of the will by which a man and a woman mutually give and accept one another by entering into an irrevocable covenant and establishing a partnership of the whole of their lives – marriage.[39] Thus, if consent is defective or missing, the juridical effects of consent are not produced and, therefore, matrimony is not considered to be valid.

---

33 *CIC*, c. 1096 §1.

34 Pedro J. Viladrich, "Il Consenso Matrimoniale," 14. The Italian texts reads: "Tale consenso è, prima di tutto, un atto umano, ossia un atto congiunto e armonico dell'intelletto, che è la facoltà per mezzo della quale conosciamo, e della volontà, che è la facoltà per mezzo della quale liberamente vogliamo."

35 Ibid., p. 11. The Italian text reads: "... previo 'dominio e possesso di sè,' affinchè possa esserci una reale e vera donazione e accettazione reciproca."

36 *CIC*, c. 124 §1; *CCEO,* c. 931.

37 *CIC*, c. 1056; *CCEO* c. 776 § 3.

38 *CIC*, c. 1057 §1; *CCEO*, c. 817 §1.

39 *CIC*, c. 1057 §2; *CCEO*, c. 776 §1; 817 §1.

Matrimonial consent is a human act and, thus, it implies the exercise of intelligence and will, as well as the free, conscious, and responsible manifestation of those who are to express it.[40] Consequently, one of the defects that might stain consent so deeply and in such a way as to render it null is that of lack of freedom, which can be internal or external. For this reason, the Catechism of the Catholic Church indicates that consent should be an act of the will of the future spouses, and this act should be free of any type of violence or of any grave external coercion; consequently, if such freedom is missing, the marriage is invalid.[41]

The enjoyment of internal freedom by the subjects exchanging matrimonial consent is of critical importance because expressing matrimonial consent is such a personal and intimate act which involves the whole human person. Furthermore, matrimonial consent is considered to be a "mutual personal gift of two human beings whose well-being is intrinsically linked to the reception or creation of a new life [in their conjugal union]."[42] Consequently, in order for matrimonial consent to be considered a true personal gift between the spouses, it must be exchanged in freedom; as Burke (1993) indicates:

> A true marital gift of the self means all one has to give, and accepting all the other has to give. Insofar as there is a refusal to give or to accept, there is no real marital donation or surrender. There is no full union and there can be no conjugal fulfillment.[43]

The internal freedom of the person entering into a juridical act has been critical to Rotal jurisprudence for a long time, because "in order for the human act to be such and to produce its precise juridical effects, it must be free from any intrinsic predetermination;"[44] and in matrimony, in order for consent to be considered valid it is necessary that it be expressed in freedom, as Aznar Gil (1989) indicates, "it is read in a *c.* Anné of January 26, 1971, "*saepissime iam denotavit ad validum consensum requirit libertatem*," (513). Therefore, in order for matrimonial consent to produce its juridical effect – marriage – canonical jurisprudence requires that consent be expressed in freedom.

---

40 Pedro J. Viladrich, "Commentary to Canon 1095," 1219-1266.

41 *CCC*, n. 1628.

42 Augustine Mendonça, & Patrick S. Morris, "Pathological Gambling and Marital Consent," in *Canon Law Society of Great Britain & Ireland Newsletter*, 143 (2005) 35.

43 Cormac Burke, "Personalism and the Bona of Marriage," in *Studia canonica*, 27 (1993) 406.

44 Federico R. Aznar Gil, "El 'Defecto' o la 'Falta de Libertad Interna' en la Jurisprudencia Canónica Española," in *Revista Española de Derecho Canónico*, 46 (1989) 513. The text in Spanish reads: "...el acto humano, para que sea tal y surta los precisos efectos jurídicos, debe ser libre de toda predeterminación intrínsica."

Rotal jurisprudence requires the internal freedom of those who are to enter into a matrimonial covenant because:

> In the process of deliberation… consent, as a human act, requires that the committing party… should be owner of his/her consent through reason and will; or that he/she possesses the use of reason in such a way as to be able to understand marriage and its essential properties, at least vaguely, and chooses to express consent with full deliberation… the proper internal freedom is equally required.[45]

There is no clear specification regarding the degree of internal freedom required so that a person can give a valid matrimonial consent because it is thought that the person is either free or not free. However, it is expected that the internal freedom of the person should be proportional to marriage. In other words, in positing consent:

> The human person (…) should be owner of his/her actions. It is only in this way that it can be affirmed that his/her act is a truly human act and, consequently, the proper juridical effects can be attributed to it.[46]

There are different situations in which the human person does not have any control of his/her actions; normally, these situations fall within a range of anomalies of a psychic nature, such as obsessive-compulsive disorders. These disorders, according to Mendonça, (2005):

> [D]eprive the victim of the internal freedom and clarity of thought which are indispensable for making weighed deci-

---

45 Federico R. Aznar Gil, "La Inmadurez Psicológica y el Consentimiento Matrimonial en la Jurisprudencia Rotal," in *Anuario Argentino de Derecho Canónico*, 14 (2008) 28. The text in Spanish reads: "En el proceso de deliberación … el consentimiento, como acto humano, requiere que el contrayente … sea dueño de su consentimiento por la razón y la voluntad; o posea tal uso de razón que pueda entender el matrimonio y sus propiedades esenciales, al menos confusamente, y se dirija al consentimiento con la plena deliberación… exigiéndose igualmente la debida libertad interna."

46 Federico R. Aznar Gil, "El 'Defecto'," 517. The text in Spanish reads: "La persona humana … debe ser dueña de sus actos. Sólo así se puede decir que el acto puesto por ella es un acto verdaderamente humano y, por consiguiente, atribuirle los oportunos efectos jurídicos."

> sions concerning important matters affecting one's life [such as marriage].[47]

Other conditions might not have a psychic origin; however, they might also impair the person's affective and reasoning processes, as well as the intellectual and volitive capacities. To this effect, Mendonça and Morris (2005), indicate that:

> [T]he elicitation of the act of consent must be free from any substantial impairment to the affective, intellectual and volitive powers or functions of the person placing it. Thus, for example, a person who suffers from serious alcoholism, schizophrenia or pathological gambling, will be deprived of the psychological capacity to place a valid act of matrimonial consent. In a similar vein, if a person is so afflicted with a mental disorder that he/she is not able to live out married life as a partnership of the whole of life, he/she will be disqualified from placing a valid act of consent because of incapacity related to its object.[48]

Reviewing the approaches that Rotal jurisprudence has taken concerning the effects of pathological gambling on matrimonial consent, Mendonça & Morris (2005) state that pathological gambling has been recognized by the behavioral sciences as a mental disorder because it seriously affects the intrapsychic and interpersonal aspects of the human person. Furthermore, they state that since marriage is a personal and interpersonal communion that involves all the dimensions of the human person, it requires the cooperation of both persons to establish this lifelong and intimate community. Thus, they affirm that:

> [T]he nature of pathological gambling is such that it is likely to render its victims incapable of establishing and sustaining such an intimate conjugal and parental community of life and love.[49]

Consequently, the person with this disorder is not considered capable of exchanging free matrimonial consent because this disorder "involves irrational

47 Augustine Mendonça, & Patrick S. Morris, 34. Other authors also speak to the effects of psychological disorders on marriage; see for instance Gianfranco Zuanazzi, *Psicologia e Psichiatria nelle Cause Matrimoniali Canoniche* (Roma: Libreria Editrice Vaticana, 2006); also, Cristiano Barbieri, *La Coppia Coniugale: Attualità e Prospettive in Medicina Canonistica.* Cristiano Barbieri, (ed.), (Roma: Libreria Editrice Vaticana, *Studi Giuridici LXXIV*, 2007).

48 Ibid., 36.

49 Ibid., 12.

thinking, loss of control and obsessive-compulsive elements"[50] that take away the person's capacity to place a free human act.

Matrimonial Consent as an External Expression of Internal Freedom

Having established that:

a. "The Church and, consequently, canon law recognize that every person has the possibility of contracting marriage (cf. *CIC*, c. 1058; *CCEO*, c. 778); a possibility, however, which can only be exercised by those *'who are not prohibited by law'* (ibid.);"[51] and that

b. Matrimonial consent must originate in a person's free will and intellect, as a free human act, it is necessary to understand that the person should be endowed with the necessary internal freedom to manifest a valid matrimonial consent.

One of the ways in which a person's internal freedom is fully realized is when it is externally expressed in matrimonial consent. In order for this to occur, the person undergoes a formation period in which the intellect, helped by the experiences of the person, identifies and comes to know a person of the opposite sex as a future husband or wife. After this person has been identified, the will, having been illuminated by the intellect, chooses that particular person with whom to enter into a matrimonial covenant. This process presumes that the person is free from any external or internal coercion that might vitiate matrimonial consent; consequently, as John Paul II (21 January 1999) states:

> [M]arriage consists essentially, necessarily and solely in the mutual consent expressed by those to be married. This consent is nothing other than the conscious, responsible assumption of a commitment through a juridical act by which, in reciprocal self-giving, the spouses promise total and definitive love to each other. They are free to celebrate marriage, after having chosen each other with equal freedom.[52]

According to the CIC, all persons have the right to choose their state of life. They have the right of choosing how to live out their vocation/call to love. In matrimonial life, this right necessarily implies that the person is free to choose one's spouse. Freedom, as John Paul II (21 January 1999) indicates:

---

50 Ibid., 13.

51 John Paul II, Address to the Tribunal of the Roman Rota, 21 January 1999, n. 7.

52 Ibid., n. 4.

> [C]onsists in the human being's possibility of conforming responsibly, that is by personal choice, to the divine will expressed in the law, and in this way to become more and more like his Creator (cf. Gn 1:26).[53]

Therefore, in order for the person to respond to the call to love and to establish a community of life and love, the person must enjoy internal freedom so as to be able to choose a particular wife or husband over another. It is important that the person freely chooses whom to marry, because he/she must want to marry a particular individual and embrace the responsibilities and obligations that come with it. Canon 1101 (CCEO c. 824) states that "[t]he internal consent of the mind is presumed to conform to the words or the signs used in the celebration of marriage." The law presumes, therefore, that in the celebration of matrimony, both partners want, by their own free will, to marry each other. Consequently, their matrimonial consent is presumed to be valid and in harmony with their internal freedom. In other words, persons have the right and responsibility to freely chose to marry one another.

Matrimonial consent might be vitiated in multiple situations. One such situation would be in the case of an out of wedlock pregnancy in which the woman, experiencing the fear of revealing her pregnancy to her parents because of the shame that it may cause to her family, does not find any other solution but to marry her boyfriend, something which she would not do if the situation were removed. Or, in the same circumstances, the boyfriend, because of his religious convictions, feels that he has to marry his girlfriend because that is the responsible thing to do, and not because he has a desire to form a community of life and love with her. In both of these cases, the person would not be acting out of a free, rational, and deliberate decision. Rather, they would be acting out of fear. The woman would be afraid to reveal her pregnancy to her parents and the man would be afraid of a punishing God. The interplay of these two factors, external influences pressuring the persons to marry and their internal emotions, provides what Beal (2010) calls a "fertile breeding ground for disagreements about whether force and fear or lack of due discretion is the ground of nullity appropriate to the facts of a particular case."[54]

In these types of situations, where the interplay of internal and external factors make it difficult to differentiate between force and fear or grave lack of due discretion as the true cause for marriage, Ortiz (2003) explains the following:

---

53 Ibid., n. 6.

54 John P. Beal, "From Theory to Practice: Finding Equivalent Conformity Between Sentences Decided on Force and Fear and Lack of Due Discretion or Simulation," in *The Jurist*, 70 (2010) 307.

> If the disturbance arises exclusively on account of a subjective reason, without any objectified external motivation, the case could fall under the ground of consensual incapacity ex can. 1095 (on account of lack of internal freedom, discretion of judgment, etc.).[55]

In this explanation, it is **an internal element**, the mental state of the individual, which is the determining factor in marrying. On the contrary, under force and fear, Ortiz (2003) explains that:

> The determining elements are: the existence of an external and objective action of the other spouse or of a third party (the *"incutiens"*), which provokes a subjective reaction in one of the engaged: a state of disturbance, of anxiety, of fear; consequently, the *"patiens"* chooses in a forced way, not spontaneously, marriage, because [marriage] is perceived as the means to liberate oneself from harm or the threat of damage.[56]

In this paragraph, Ortiz explains that it is **an external and objective influence**, which disturbs the person's sense of control by provoking a fearful reaction to the situation. Therefore, the person chooses marriage to escape the perceived disastrous consequences (i.e., harm to oneself or a family member). As Beal (2010) indicates:

> In force and fear cases, it is ultimately fear, inner trepidation in the person's mind and heart, which prompts him or her to choose marriage as the only available way to avert a threated physical or moral evil.[57]

Consequently, the community of life and love that they would establish would not be based on love but on fear.

---

55 Miguel A. Ortiz, "Il Timore che Invalida il Matrimonio e la Sua Prova," in *Ius Ecclesiae*, 15 (2003) 111. The original text in Italian reads: "Se l'agitazione sorge esclusivamente da cause soggettive, senza alcuna motivazione esterna oggettivabile, il caso potrebbe rientrare magari nelle fattispecie di incapacità consensuale ex can. 1095 (a causa di mancanza di libertà interna, di discrezione di giudizio, ecc.).

56 Ibid., 109. The original text in Italian reads: "Gli elementi determinanti della figura sono: l'esistenza di una azione esterna oggettiva dell'altro coniuge o di un terzo (l'incutiens), che provoca una reazione soggettiva in uno dei contraenti: uno stato di agitazione, d'inquietudine, di timore; di conseguenza, il patiens sceglie in maniera forzata e non spontanea il matrimonio, perché lo percepisce come il mezzo per liberarsi dal danno o la minaccia del danno."

57 John P. Beal, 306.

The case described above does not necessarily imply that the persons are unable to learn to love one another as they grow and mature in their matrimonial relationship. Nor does it imply that their marriage would be a failure because it is very possible for them to develop affectionate bonds of attachment for one another and to learn to work through any problems that they might encounter in their relationship. Furthermore, they may also learn to accept their choice of marrying each other as a free choice and not as the only choice that they had. In which case, even if consent were vitiated at the beginning of the marriage, it would be possible to be sanated *"in radice."*

It is essential that the person, while consenting to marriage, be endowed with internal freedom so that he/she can assume freely, and without reservations, the commitment of his/her decision, because as John Paul II (21 January 1999) states:

> *Amor coniugalis*, therefore, is not only and not primarily a feeling, but is essentially a commitment to the other person, a commitment made by a precise act of will. It is this commitment which gives amor the quality of coniugalis. Once a commitment has been made and accepted through consent, love becomes conjugal and never loses this character. Here the fidelity of love, which is rooted in the freely assumed obligation, comes into play.[58]

Therefore, the human person, through his/her freely assumed obligation, is called to live his vocation to matrimony with the same love that Christ manifested to humanity. The person is called to love, to forgive, and to embrace his/her new reality created through matrimonial consent. As John Paul II (5 February 1987) indicates:

> [T]he realization of the meaning of the conjugal union, by means of the mutual self-giving of the spouses becomes possible only by means of a continuous effort, which also includes renunciation and sacrifice. The love between the spouses must in fact be modeled on the love of Christ who 'loved us and gave himself up for us, a fragrant offering and sacrifice to God' (Eph. 5:2 and 25).[59]

Through their consent, they create a new reality whose validity does not depend on the success of their matrimonial life, but rather on their internal freedom to express a valid consent. This is a new reality in which the spouses can grow and be transformed so that they share with one another and with others the same

58 John Paul II, Roman Rota, 1999, n. 3.

59 John Paul II, Address to the Tribunal of the Roman Rota, 5 February 1987, in *AAS, LXXIX* (1987) 1453-1459, n. 6.

love that Jesus Christ showed for humanity. When difficult situations arise, the spouses, who were endowed with true internal freedom while manifesting matrimonial consent, are more likely to answer positively their call to embrace the cross in order to be transformed with the love of Christ; because:

> [I]n every marriage the mystery of redemption becomes present, brought about by a real participation in the Cross of the Saviour, accepting the Christian paradox that joins happiness with the bearing of suffering in the spirit of faith.[60]

In this way, the spouses grow and mature in their matrimonial life as they grow in their unity with Christ and with one another. They are more likely to be aware of the necessity to assist each other in this journey because only through their mutual help can they grow in love, understanding, and trust for one another. Furthermore, they understand that they are both indispensable components of their new reality. In addition, that new reality can grow stronger through their mutual help and support. This would be an authentic love, a love that acts and strives to attain the greatest good for the other person. This can only become a reality when both spouses have entered into this community of life and love with sufficient freedom.

Right of the Human Person to Marry

God, the creator of all, has created the human person with a natural inclination to marriage. This natural inclination emanates from the fact that the human person was created "in His own image and likeness: calling him to existence through love, He called him at the same time for love."[61] Consequently, it is recognized that God planted the vocation to marriage in the hearts of every human being regardless of time, culture, nationality, race, or creed. Consequently, "Marriage as such has no religion. It is neither Jewish, nor Catholic, nor even civil."[62]

The Natural Right of the Human Person to Marry

The right to matrimony is so integral a part of human nature that it is recognized by both national and international law. For instance, the United Nations in The Universal Declaration on Human Rights, article 16, declares that men and women of a proper age have the right to get married without imposing any limits regarding religion, race, or citizenship as long as they give their free and full

---

60 John Paul II, Address to the Prelate Auditors, Officials, and Advocates of the Tribunal of the Roman Rota, 30 January 2003, in *AAS, XCV* (2003) 393-397, n. 5.

61 *FC*, n. 11.

62 Roch Pagé, "Marriage: Sacrament of Love or Sacrament of Bond?" in *Studia canonica*, 34 (2000) 7.

consent. Similarly, article 12 of the European Convention on the Rights of Man gives men and women of a proper age the right to get married and form a family according to the regulations of state laws. In addition, article 1 of the Charter of the Rights of the Family presented by the Holy See on October 22, 1983 states that men and women of matrimonial age who have the necessary capacity have the right to get married and to form a family without being discriminated.[63]

It is evident that the Church, upholding the dignity of the human person, respects and defends the vocation of every person to marriage. First of all, it defends the right of the person to freely choose their state of life: either to enter into a matrimonial covenant or to remain single; and secondly, it establishes that a person can enter into a marriage covenant only through his/her free and full consent which needs to be free of all pressure, so that he/she is able to choose a certain complimentary person as a spouse.[64] In addition, according to Haring (1969), the first paragraph of Article 48 of GS "describes the conjugal covenant of love as something sacred, and does so in a way accessible to all men whatever religious conviction."[65]

In *FC,* John Paul II indicates, "God has inscribed in the humanity of man and woman the capacity and responsibility for love and communion. Love is therefore the fundamental and innate vocation of every human being."[66] In this document, John Paul II does not specify any group of people; rather, he identifies this capacity for the whole human race. In addition, John Paul II (27 January 1997), speaking about the vocation to marriage states that matrimony "is a possibility open in principle to every man and woman; indeed, it represents a true vocation for the great majority of the human race."[67]

Given the fact that the *"ius connubii"* is the natural right of the person to enter into a marriage covenant with a member of the opposite sex, this fundamental right of the human person "...implies the whole person in his/her different levels: corporal, affective, and spiritual."[68] Consequently, it is imperative that this right be exercised voluntarily and through the free and deliberate consent of the partners involved, because as Franceschi (2009) states:

63 Angelo D'Auria, *Il Matrimonio nel Diritto della Chiesa* (Roma: Lateran University Press, 2003) 48-49. Also, Pontifical Council for the Family, 22 October 1983, Charter of the Rights of the Family, *Communicationes,* XV (1983).

64 Charter of the Rights of the Family, arts. 1 & 2.

65 Bernard Häring, "Some Problems of Special Urgency: Fostering the Nobility of Marriage and the Family," in Herbert Vorgrimler, (gen. ed.), *Commentary on the Documents of Vatican II,* vol. V (New York, NY: Herder and Herder, 1969) 235.

66 *FC*, n. 11.

67 John Paul II. *Address to the Tribunal of the Roman Rota,* 27 January 1997..., n. 5.

68 Hector Franceschi, "El Contenido y la determinación del 'Ius Connubii' y sus Manifestaciones en el Sistema Matrimonial Canónico Vigente," in *Ius Canonicum*, 47/93 (2007) 73. The text in Spanish reads: "... implica toda la persona en sus diversos niveles: corporal, afectivo, y espiritual."

> [T]he Church has always defended the freedom of choice and the necessity of the personal and free consent as the only force capable of founding marriage.[69]

Along these same lines, D'Auria (2003) states that:

> The right to matrimony, even though it is considered a fundamental right that belongs to every man, is neither an absolute nor an arbitrary right in its exercise. First of all, it is not by its own nature: in fact, since in marriage such right belongs to both the engaged and it should be free from both partners, its exercise does not depend exclusively from the one who holds it but it is inevitably subjected to the will and the free consent of the other (…).[70]

The exercise of this right, however, must contain, as its purpose, the free and deliberate consent of both persons to enter into a marriage covenant and establish a community of life and love. In other words, the exercise of this fundamental right belongs to those "who have a concrete project of celebrating marriage and forming a family."[71] This concrete project, however, must contain certain elements that are inherent to the nature of marriage and are considered essential to matrimony. Franceschi (2007) mentions the following natural realities that need to be present in any natural marriage:

a. The right to contract marriage, one, indissoluble, and open to fecundity.
b. The right to form a family.
c. The right to contract matrimony according to the exigencies of one's own religion, logically respecting always the true natural matrimony.

---

69 Hector Franceschi, "Preparazione al Matrimonio e Prevenzione della Nullità," in Hector Franceschi & Miguel A. Ortiz, (Eds.), *Verità del Consenso e Capacità di Donazione* (Roma: EDUSC, 2009) 66. The text in Italian reads: "... la Chiesa ha sempre difeso la libertà di scelta e la necessità del consenso personale e libero come unica forza capace di fondare il matrimonio."

70 Angelo D'Auria, *Il Matrimonio nel Diritto*, 49. The Italian text reads: "Il diritto al matrimonio, pur considerate un diritto fondamentale appartenente ad ogni uomo, non è tuttavia un diritto assoluto o arbitrario nel suo esercízio. Innanzitutto non lo è per la sua stessa indole: infatti, posto che nel matrimonio tale diritto appartiene ad entrambi i nubenti e che deve essere libero da ambo le parti, nel suo esercizio non dipende esclusivamente da chi lo detiene ma è inevitabilmente soggetto alla volontà e al libero consenso dell'altro (...)."

71 Hector Franceschi, "El Contenido," 77. The text in Spanish reads: "… aquellos que tiene un concreto proyecto de celebrar el matrimonio y fundar una familia."

d. The right to structure one's own family according to one's personal convictions, respecting always the same nature of matrimony and of family relationships.[72]

However, when that essential content of natural matrimony is missing, it is impossible to talk about the *"ius connubii"* of the person, because their union would not be a matrimonial union as understood by nature; rather, it would be the exercise of libertinage. Therefore, the *"ius connubii"* is the natural right inherent in the engaged, a male and a female, to enter into a marriage covenant with the desire to form a family through their free and voluntary choice and through their mutual gift of themselves to each other.[73]

The Right of the Church to Regulate the Exercise of the ***Ius Connubii*** of all the Faithful

Since the right to matrimony is a natural right inherent in humanity, it cannot be taken away from any person. However, since it is recognized as a sacrament within the Catholic Church, it is governed by ecclesiastical law; to this effect, Gramunt (1991) affirms that:

> [B]ecause of the sacramental nature of Christian marriage, the Church establishes laws regulating the canonical capacity of the person entering into this juridical situation and precepts concerning the licit reception of the sacrament.[74]

Similarly, Benedict XVI (22 January 2011) states that:

> The right to contract marriage presupposes that the person can and intends to celebrate it truly, that is, in the truth of its essence as the Church teaches it. No one can claim the right to a nuptial ceremony. Indeed the *ius connubii* refers to the right to celebrate an authentic marriage.[75]

---

72 Ibid., 76-77. The text in Spanish reads:

a) El derecho a contraer matrimonio uno, indisoluble y abierto a la fecundidad...

b) El derecho a fundar una familia...

c) El derecho a contraer el matrimonio conforme a las exigencias de la propia religión, lógicamente, siempre respetando el verdadero matrimonio natural...

d) El derecho de estructurar la propia familia según las convicciones personales, siempre en el respeto de la naturaleza misma del matrimonio y de las relaciones familiares

73 Ibid., 77.

74 Ignatius Gramunt, "The Essence of Marriage," 370.

75 Benedict XVI, Address of His Holiness Pope Benedict XVI on the Occasion of the Inauguration of the Judicial Year of the Tribunal of the Roman Rota, 22 January 2011, in *AAS, CIII* (2011) 108-113.

Consequently, when it comes to the celebration of a marriage within the Catholic Church, the Church has the right to establish norms and regulations concerning the licit celebration of an authentic marriage of the faithful.

In addition, the *CIC* specifies that all the Christian faithful have a right to choose a state of life without being coerced in any way.[76] And as Franceschi (2009) indicates, while expressing his views on *"ius connubii"* in light of c. 1057, n. 1:

> That right to marry or not has its own concretizations, one of which is the freedom to form a marriage and a family through a conjugal pact between a man and a woman who are capable and able according to law (...).[77]

Furthermore, expressing his views concerning marriage, Pagè (2000) observes:

> But even if it [marriage] has no religion of itself, it is nonetheless one of those earthly realities which contain within themselves a relationship with the sacred, with the mysterious, with the divine. For in the end, the natural fact that a man and a woman live in a relationship within which existentially they bring about a change, a transformation, becomes by virtue of its own mysterious character a means of recognizing a presence which acts and which transforms.[78]

Therefore, since marriage, within the Catholic Church, is a sacrament instituted by Christ:

> [T]he Church ought to regulate Christian marriage by its own laws for the good of the Christian spouses, of the children born in the Christian family, and of the entire Christian people.[79]

For this reason, the *CIC* indicates that all those who are not prohibited by law can contract marriage.[80] Therefore, the Church has the right and responsibility to insure that this right is exercised properly by indicating the minimum require-

76 *CIC*, c. 219.

77 Hector Franceschi, "Preparazione al Matrimonio," 65. The text in Italian reads: "Quel diritto di sposarsi o meno ha le sue concretizzazioni. Una di queste è la libertà di fondare il matrimonio e la famiglia mediante il patto coniugale tra un uomo e una donna che sono capaci e abili secondo diritto (...)."

78 Roch Pagé, "Marriage: Sacrament of Love," 7.

79 Ignatius Gramunt, "The Essence of Marriage," 367.

80 *CIC*, c. 1058.

ments for the exercise of the *"ius connubii"* such as the minimum capacity as well as the absence of any impediments for marriage. In the words of Bañares (2009), "[each] society—civil or ecclesiastical—should intervene, juridically: not to limit the *ius connubii* of its members, but to fully develop it." [81]

At first glance, it seems as if the *CIC* is restricting this right of the person by granting this right only to "those who are not prohibited by law."[82] However, as Bañares (2004) indicates, "While there is always in every person a juridical capability to contract marriage, a person does not always have the capability to operate with respect to this fundamental right."[83]

The reason for this is that marriage is a communion of persons which involves all the dimensions of the human being, and an adequate development of one's intellectual dimension is critical for entering into a marriage covenant. Moreover, the celebration of an authentic matrimony requires a certain capacity of the person to be able to understand the nature of marriage. It is not enough that the person has reached a certain age,[84] it is also necessary that the person has achieved a certain degree of maturity, both intellectual and psycho-affective, so as to know that he/she is making a free and conscious decision. Consequently, the Church has the inherent right to establish certain norms to regulate the exercise of this right. To this effect, Benedict XVI (22 January 2011) states:

> The right to marry, *ius connubii,* must be seen in this perspective. In other words it is not a subjective claim that pastors must fulfil *(sic)* through a merely formal recognition independent of the effective content of the union. The right to contract marriage presupposes that the person can and intends to celebrate it truly, that is, in the truth of its essence as the Church teaches it. No one can claim the right to a nuptial ceremony. Indeed the *ius connubii* refers to the right to celebrate an authentic marriage.[85]

---

81 Juan I. Bañares, "Antropologia Cristiana," 38-39. The text in Italian reads: "la società – civile o ecclesiale – deve intervenire giuridicament: non per limitare lo ius connubii dei suoi membre, ma puittosto per sviluparlo pienamente."

82 *CIC,* c. 1058.

83 Juan I. Bañares, "Commentary to Canon 1058," Angel Marzoa, Jorge Miras, Rafael Rodriguez-Ocaña (eds.) and Ernest Caparros (gen. ed. of English translation), *Exegetical Commentary on the Code of Canon Law* (Montreal, PQ: Wilson & Lafleur, 2004) 1077.

84 *CIC,* c. 1083 §1. In this canon, the age specified for a man is sixteen, and for a woman, fourteen.

85 Benedict XVI, *On the Occasion of the Inauguration of the Judicial Year of the Tribunal of the Roman Rota,* 22 January 2011.

Faith and *Ius Connubii*

Since marriage cannot be claimed to be the property of any religion nor of any civil society, but rather is a fundamental right of the human person who was created by God with the desire to love and to enter into a conjugal communion with a member of the opposite sex, matrimony, in and of itself, does not require any faith in order to be validly celebrated. It requires, however, that the engaged have "the right intention to celebrate marriage according to the natural reality of matrimony."[86]

Even though the exercise of the *"ius connubii"* does not require any explicit faith on the part of the covenantal partners, an implicit faith is presumed to be present in those who ask to have their marriage recognized by the Church. To this effect, in *FC*, John Paul II states that:

> In fact, the faith of the person asking the Church for marriage can exist in different degrees, and it is the primary duty of pastors to bring about a rediscovery of this faith and to nourish it and bring it to maturity. But pastors must also understand the reasons that lead the Church also to admit to the celebration of marriage those who are imperfectly disposed.[87]

Consequently, the exercise of the *ius connubii* cannot be denied to those who without any indication of having faith, but who having been baptized, are prompted by the Holy Spirit to ask, by their own free will, to be married in the Church. The reason for this is that the intention to celebrate marriage "according to the natural reality of matrimony" necessarily contains the notion that the vocation to marriage is a call from God to enter into a permanent and indissoluble conjugal union with a future spouse and that this permanent conjugal union is ordered to the good of the spouses and the procreation and education of their children:

> The sacrament of Matrimony has this specific element that distinguishes it from all the other sacraments: it is the sacrament of something that was part of the very economy of creation; it is the very conjugal covenant instituted by the Creator "in the beginning." Therefore the decision of a man and a woman to marry in accordance with this divine plan, that is to say, the decision to commit by their irrevocable conjugal consent their whole lives in indissoluble love and unconditional fidelity, really involves, even if not in a fully conscious way, an attitude

86 Hector Franceschi, "El Contenido," 91. The text in Spanish reads: "la recta intención de casarse según la realidad natural del matrimonio."
87 *FC*, n. 68.

> of profound obedience to the will of God, an attitude which cannot exist without God's grace. They have thus already begun what is in a true and proper sense a journey towards salvation, a journey which the celebration of the sacrament and the immediate preparation for it can complement and bring to completion, given the uprightness of their intention.[88]

It must be noted, however, that if the person intends not to celebrate a marriage with its essential properties and the assumption of the acquired rights and obligations, it would not be a genuine matrimony. It would be a mere carnal union and the Church would do well in not admitting them to the celebration of marriage:

> Nevertheless, it must not be forgotten that these engaged couples, by virtue of their Baptism, are already really sharers in Christ's marriage Covenant with the Church, and that, by their right intention, they have accepted God's plan regarding marriage and therefore at least implicitly consent to what the Church intends to do when she celebrates marriage… However, when in spite of all efforts, engaged couples show that they reject explicitly and formally what the Church intends to do when the marriage of baptized persons is celebrated, the pastor of souls cannot admit them to the celebration of marriage.[89]

Therefore, in view of the above, it can be stated that the human person has a natural inclination to marriage because he/she "… is called to love… [and this call] includes the giving of oneself both spiritually and corporally.[90] However, in order for the person to exercise this right, he/she must act in freedom and must have the capacity, and the intention, to celebrate an "authentic" marriage. This is true because only in freedom can the spouses actively participate in building a *"consortium totius vitae,"* a community of life and love founded on their free and deliberate consent to be united with each other "until death do us part."

The Right of the Person to Choose a Suitable Partner

Subsequent to the assertion that consent, as a free human act, is the essential element that constitutes matrimony when it is lawfully manifested between two capable persons (a man and a woman), it must be emphasized that the human person must necessarily be endowed with the freedom and responsibility of choosing a partner with whom to establish a *"consortium totius vitae,"* a community of life and love. As Franceschi (1996) indicates: "The *ius connubii* is

88 Ibid.
89 Ibid.
90 Ignatius Gramunt, "The Essence of Marriage," 366.

not limited to the right to enter into a [matrimonial] contract, but also the right to choose the other party, the right to not enter into marriage, the right to remain immune of any external coercion, etc."[91] Along the same topic, D'Auria (2003) indicates that:

> c. 1058 finding its foundation in the natural inclination of man to the matrimonial union affirms a right which is recognized of every individual: the *ius connubii*, that is the right to matrimony. This right, identified as a fundamental right of every person under which a man and a woman can get married by freely and spontaneously choosing one's spouse, is constantly affirmed by the Magisterium of the Church...[92]

Therefore, since the human person is gifted with the vocation to marriage, and this vocation is recognized as a natural inclination and a fundamental right of every individual, it is a matter of justice to recognize the fact that the person must necessarily be endowed with the freedom to choose with whom to form a *"consortium vitae coniugalis."* This choice is extremely important because the *"consortium vitae coniugalis"* includes not only the sharing of the conjugal life, but also the psycho-affective communion established by the sharing of their interpersonal and intimate relationship.

It must also be affirmed that, even though a person has the right to exercise freely the *"ius connubii,"* he/she does not have the right to impose his/her own choices on another person, because the other person must also be free to choose whether or not to enter into a marriage covenant with a particular candidate. Consequently, the right to choose a partner is limited by the equal right of the other person to express his/her free will and to either accept or decline a choice presented by one's own intellect.

Once the will, without being coerced or influenced in any way, accepts the choice presented, the person is presumed to have expressed a free and deliberate consent. This premise assumes the possibility that the person is capable of engaging his/her intellectual faculties in order to make a reasonable and delib-

91 Hector Franceschi, "Il Diritto alla Libera Scelta del Proprio Coniuge Quale Diritto Fondamentale della Persona," in *Ius Ecclesiae*, 8 (1996) 157. The Italian text reads: "Lo ius connubii non è soltanto il diritto a contrarre, bensì il diritto a scegliere l'altro contraente, il diritto a non contrarre matrimonio, il diritto a restare immune da ogni coerzione esterna, ecc."

92 Angelo D'Auria, *Il Matrimonio nel Diritto*, 48. The Italian texts reads: "Il canone 1058, fondandosi sulla natural inclinazione dell'uomo all'unione matrimoniale afferma un diritto riconosciuto ad ogni individuo: lo ius connubii, cioè il diritto al matrimonio. Questo diritto, ritenuto un diritto fondamentale di ogni persona in forza del quale l'uomo e la donna possono contrarre matrimonio scegliendo liberamente e spontaneamente il proprio coniuge, viene affermato costantemente dal Magistero della Chiesa (...)."

erate choice. Therefore, the absence of any grave psycho-affective anomaly is presumed as well.

It must be emphasized that arranged marriages between a man and a woman, through the mutual cooperation and agreement of their parents, are very special types of cases that must be considered in the context of their culture. This practice is the normal way of establishing marriage between two capable persons in some communities. However, it must be pointed out that although the parents take on the responsibility of choosing a partner for their children, the children have the responsibility of accepting or rejecting the partner proposed to them by their parents. As Franceschi (1996) indicates:

> The Church... has always defended, independently from the diverse cultural and historical perspectives, the centrality of the personal and free consent as the cause for matrimonial union, and it has not condemned the custom of marriages arranged by parents, as long as the freedom of their children is respected, that is that they [the children] come to own the choice presented to them by their parents. This is the central point: to determine, whatever the culture, whether the consent has been free or not.[93]

Consequently, in an arranged marriage, the engaged must be able to choose freely to enter into marriage once they are presented with the possibility of marrying each other. In other words, the engaged must be free to choose the partner chosen for them by their parents. In doing so, they are making the choice their own. Embracing the choice presented to them by their parents is what enables the engaged, in an arranged marriage, to manifest a free and deliberate consent.

In arranged marriages, however, one must not disregard the possibility that, in some cases, one of the engaged chooses to marry a particular person presented to him/her by their parents, not out of a free choice, but because it is expected of him/her to accept this particular person as the only choice. This might happen in cultures where the honor of the family must be preserved by marrying within certain a caste, such as in the Indian or Asian cultures. For instance, Mendonça (1995) indicates that there are some Asian cultures in which:

---

93 Hector Franceschi, "Il Diritto alla Libera," 156. The Italian text reads: "La Chiesa... ha sempre difeso, independentemente dale diverse cornice culturali e storiche, la centralità del consenso personale e libero come causa del vincolo matrimoniale, ma non ha condannato la consuetudine dei matrimoni concordati dai genitori, sempre che sia stata rispettata la libertà dei figli, cioè che questi abbiano fatto propria la scelta loro presentata dai genitori. È proprio questo il punto centrale: accertare, qualunque sia la cultura, se il consenso è stato libero o meno."

> [S]trong family ties in most cases make it almost impossible for children to override their parent's decisions. Family ties are such that parental decisions are not only expected to be respected and accepted by the children but also sustained by the culture of a given community or society.[94]

In cases like this, where the person has no choice but to succumb to the arranged marriage against his/her own free will, a great injustice to the dignity of the person and the constitution of matrimony is committed. It is considered an injustice to oblige a person to enter into a *"consortium vitae coniugalis"* with someone else against one's own will because "the right to matrimony, according to c. 1058, is widely recognized as personal and intangible, whose exercise is free because no one is obliged to get married."[95] Consequently, as John Paul II (28 January 1991) indicates:

> [W]e cannot ignore the fact that such cultures still have a long way to go in the field of the full recognition of the equal dignity of man and woman. Marriage is still, to a large degree, the result of agreements between families which do not take into account the free will of the young people.[96]

Furthermore, as Errázuriz (2009) indicates:

> [I]t has been insisted so much lately about the personal nature of matrimony: marriage unites the persons themselves, and the union encompasses their own actions as persons in a unique rapport of interpersonal love.[97]

In matrimony, the spouses freely accept the union that is formed through their interpersonal love as they willingly consent to marry one another. However,

---

94 Augustine Mendonça, "The Application of the Principle of Equity in Marriage Nullity Cases," in *The Jurist*, 55 (1995) 695.

95 Angelo D'Auria, *Il Matrimonio nel Diritto*, 49. The text in Italian reads: "il diritto al matrimonio, a tenore del canone 1058, viene dunque ampiamente riconosciuto come personale ed intangibile, il cui esercizio è libero poichè nessuno è obbligato a sposarsi."

96 John Paul II, Address to the Tribunal of the Roman Rota, 28 January 1991, in *AAS, LXXXIII* (1991), n. 6.

97 Carlos J. Errázuriz, "Sul Rapporto tra il Consenso e il Matrimonio: Il Consenso quale Atto Umano che Assume l'Altra Persona Nella sua Dimensione Coniugale Naturale," in Hector Franceschi & Miguel A. Ortiz, (eds.), *Verità del Consenso e Capacità di Donazione: Temi di Diritto Matrimoniale e Processuale Canonico* (Roma: EDUSC, 2009) 52. The text in Italian reads: "... si è insistito molto negli ultimi tempi sull'indole personale del matrimonio: esso unisce le persone medesime, e l'unione coinvolge il loro agire in quanto persone in un rapporto unico d'amore interpersonale."

when the personal nature of matrimony is taken away and the choice becomes an obligation rather than a conscious, free, and deliberate expression of the will, the essence of matrimony is empty, nonexistent, and a lie. This would be the case of a person who marries under force or fear (c. 1103). In force and fear, the internal freedom of the person to choose a future spouse is hindered; thus, matrimonial consent is vitiated. Along this line of reasoning, Ortiz (2003) indicates that:

> Protecting the freedom of the engaged when positing [matrimonial] consent is one of the fundamental principles of the matrimonial system of the Church: only the spouses can decide by themselves, and should be able to do it with the freedom that is required by their choice to the state of life that they want to realize.[98]

In a similar vein, Balagapo (2002) observes that "marriage to be valid must proceed from a *free and rational act of the will.-;*"[99] Also, Mendonça (1995) indicates the following:

> Internal freedom to choose marriage or one's marriage partner is one of the essential requisites of a valid matrimonial consent. Lack of a true human act in eliciting consent can happen not only in cases in which force and fear is inflicted by an external agent (cf. c. 1103), but also when it is experienced from within. This can happen when a person marries in order to avoid harm to one's personal reputation or to that of one's family members.[100]

Therefore, without the necessary internal freedom to choose one's spouse, it would be impossible for two persons, who are obliged to enter into marriage, to form an interpersonal relationship of intimate love: a *"consortium totius vitae,"* ordained to the good of the spouses and to the procreation and education of their children. It is important to indicate that this *"consortium totius vitae"* "demands the reciprocal donation of the spouses (*CIC*, can. 1057, n. 2; *CCEO*, can. 817, n.1);"[101] and this reciprocal donation is not limited to their sexuality,

98 Miguel A. Ortiz, "Il Timore Che Invalida il Matrimonio," 102. The original text in Italian reads: "La protezine della libertà dei coniugui quando danno il consenso è uno dei principi fondamentali del sistema matrimoniale della Chiesa: soltanto i coniugi possono decidere su se stessi, e devono poterlo fare con la libertà che richiede la scelta dallo stato di vita che realizzano."

99 Erwin José A. Balagapo, *Lack of Internal Freedom and its Relations to Simulation and Force & Fear,* (Doctoral dissertation, Roma: EDUSC, 2002) 264.

100 Augustine Mendonça, "The Application of the Principle of Equity," 680.

101 Carlos J. Errázuriz, "Sul Rapporto tra il Consenso e il Matrimonio," 53. The text in Italian reads: *"esige la reciproca donazine degli sposi* (*CIC,* can. 1057 §2; *CCEO*, can. 817 §1)."

but it includes their psycho-affective and spiritual dimensions. The interpersonal sharing in these dimensions is what allows them to form a genuine *"consortium totius vitae."* Consequently, the human person, in choosing a sexually complementary partner must be able to act in freedom, because only in freedom, can the human person truly love.

Required Maturity of the Person to Contract Marriage

Inevitably, in order for people to enter into juridical contracts, it is necessary for them to have achieved a certain degree of maturity which enables them to understand the nature of the contract. Along with this maturity, it is necessary for them to possess that sense of freedom which allows them to enter into the contract without any foreign pressure. This is of utmost importance especially in the realm of matrimony; however, it is evident that:

[T]his freedom of human nature, 'wounded in the natural powers proper to it', and 'inclined to sin' (*Catechism of the Catholic Church*, n. 405), is limited and imperfect, but it is not thereby unauthentic and insufficient for carrying out that act of self-determination by the partners which is the conjugal covenant, giving rise to marriage and to the family founded on it.[102]

Consequently, even though the person's sense of freedom may be lightly stained by external or internal influences, these influences may be deemed normal and not strong enough as to have a negative effect on either the freedom or the maturity of the person.

Recognizing the value that the behavioral sciences, such as psychology and psychiatry, have contributed to the understanding of the composition of the human person, especially in the areas that pertain to the development and formation of the intellect, will, sexuality, affective maturity, internal freedom, etc., Pope John Paul II in his address to the Roman Rota of February 5, 1987 stated the following:

> We are well aware of the great progress which has been made by contemporary psychiatry and psychology. It must be appreciated how much these modern sciences have done and are doing to explain the psychic processes of the person, both conscious and unconscious, as well as the help which they give by means of pharmacotherapy and psychotherapy to many people in difficulty.[103]

102 Benedict XVI, Address to the Tribunal of the Roman Rota for the Inauguration of the Judicial Year, 29 January 2009, in *AAS, CI* (2009) 124-128.
103 John Paul II, Roman Rota, 1987, n. 2.

Besides explaining the psychic processes of the human person, the behavioral sciences also shed some light on the development and formation of these processes and on how they are affected by early experiences of the human person. It is widely known in the psychological and medical sciences, for instance, that the first few years of the human person are the most influential and formative of the individual. These early experiences affect the way in which individuals act, think, feel, behave, and relate to others in later years. For instance, the medical field has discovered that neonates are capable of expressing some type of feeling, even in their mothers' womb, as they start forming attachments with their mothers.

Similarly, research in the Psychological field indicates that prenatal twins can be seen interacting with each other in their mother's womb; "[t]hey seem especially interested in the larger environment provided by mother and father, and react to individual voices, stories, music, and even simple interaction with parents."[104] This research demonstrates that the new human being a woman carries in her womb is an individual person able to relate to others; similarly, "university and hospital studies show that unborn children can see, hear and feel in [their mothers'] womb."[105] This fact contradicts "the previous view that prenates did not have the capacity to interact, remember, learn, or put meaning to their experiences."[106] Therefore, it is possible that, even at this early stage, the experiences of an unborn child affect the way in which he/she forms affectional bonds of attachment with others. As a consequence, these experiences would also affect their maturational development and the way in which they form matrimonial consent later on in their lives; because the formation of matrimonial consent is a process that takes time[107] and this time period seems to begin in the mother's womb as the child learns to form bonds of attachment with the mother.

The human person, however, as a being created by God out of love and gifted with the vocation to love, is resilient and unpredictable. The same experiences that might negatively influence the behavior of one person might have a different effect on another person. For instance, even though the field of Developmental Psychology, by studying and analyzing the experiences that the human person undergoes, can make predictions and, up to a certain point, determine the way in which an individual will relate to marriage based on how he/she perceived his/her parent's marriage, it cannot explain why some individuals will develop a

104 The Developmental Psychology Student Netletter, http://www.mc.maricopa.edu/dept/d46/psy/dev/Spring02/prenatal/attachment.htm (accessed 10 October 2015).

105 Ibid.

106 Ibid.

107 Pedro J. Viladrich, "Commentary to Canon 1096," 1267.

healthy attitude toward marriage while others will develop a negative one.[108] For instance, Henry & Holmes (1998) conducted a longitudinal study on the effects of divorce on young adults and found out that the majority of subjects who had experienced the divorce of their parents had developed a distorted understanding of marriage and were more likely to obtain a divorce themselves. However, there were individuals who, even though they also experienced the divorce of their parents, were able to understand the commitment that they were assuming in marriage and accepted the permanence of the matrimonial bond.[109] For this reason, John Paul II (5 February 1987) asserts that:

> The immense research carried out and the remarkable dedication of so many psychologists and psychiatrists are certainly praiseworthy. However, it must be recognized that the discoveries and achievements purely in the fields of psychology and psychiatry are not capable of offering a truly complete vision of the person. They are not capable of resolving on their own the fundamental questions concerning the meaning of life and the human vocation.[110]

Even though the behavioral sciences may be limited in their understanding of the human person as a being created by God and have a different conception of their definition of marriage than Christian anthropology,[111] it is recognized that these sciences offer assistance in understanding how early experiences, especially experiences of attachment, influence the way in which persons understand and relate to matrimony. In light of this, John Paul II (5 February 1987) states that:

> [T]here is no doubt that a profound knowledge of the theories developed and of the results achieved by the aforementioned sciences offers the possibility of evaluating the human response to the vocation of marriage in a more precise and discriminating manner than philosophy alone or theology alone would allow. [112]

It is to be noted, however, that both the behavioral sciences as well as Canon Law indicate that, in order for a person to enter into marriage, it is necessary for

108 Kate Henry & John G. Holmes, "Childhood Revisited: The Intimate Relationships of Individuals from Divorced and Conflict-Ridden Families," in Jeffry A. Simpson & W. Steven Rholes, (eds.), *Attachment Theory and Close Relationships* (New York, NY: The Guilford Press, 1998) 280-316.
109 Ibid.
110 John Paul II, Roman Rota, 1987, n. 2.
111 Ibid., n. 4. Consider, for instance, the following quote: "According to some psychological trends the vision of marriage is such that it reduces the meaning of the marriage union simply to a means of gratification or of self-fulfillment or of psychological release."
112 Ibid.

that person to have attained at least a minimum degree of maturity. However, it must be made clear that both fields diverge on this notion, and oftentimes

> [P]sychic maturity which is seen as the goal of human development ends up being confused with canonical maturity which is rather the basic minimum required for establishing the validity of marriage.[113]

It is essential to point out, however, that in order for a person to be able to express an effective will and enter into marriage, it is necessary for that particular person to be able to know and to discern, at least at a most basic level, what marriage entails. Undoubtedly, through the expression of the free consent to marry, a person enters into a juridical reality by becoming "one flesh" (Gn. 2:24; Mk 10:8; *CIC*, c. 1061, 1) with his/her spouse and forms a *"consortium totius vitae."* Therefore, it is imperative that the person, before entering into a *"consortium totius vitae,"* has attained that degree of minimal canonical maturity that allows him/her to establish a matrimonial covenant. This minimal maturity, besides being necessary, should be such that the individual is capable of knowing, weighing, and choosing, at least at the most imperfect level, that this *"consortium totius vitae"* includes the minimum capacity to be able to enter into a proper relationship: a relationship that encompasses all the dimensions of the human person. Consequently, it is of major importance that the person, in order to enter into this covenantal relationship, must possess the capacity to develop meaningful and affective relationships at least at the most basic level. In other words, the person must know that:

> God inscribed in the humanity of man and woman the vocation, and thus the capacity and responsibility, of love and communion. [And that] Love is therefore the fundamental and innate vocation of every human being.[114]

The person, entering into marriage, needs to be able to have that minimum maturity which, besides being good by its very nature, allows him/her to love others as well as to allow himself/herself to be loved: the good and natural maturity to enter into meaningful and loving relationships.

According to Tassotti, (2010), in order for a person to be able to develop meaningful interpersonal relationships with others, it is necessary for that person to have not a perfect maturity, but a good maturity. According to her, "the criteria that indicate the presence of a good affective maturity are:

113 Ibid., n. 6.

114 *FC*, n. 11.

> – the capacity to love and to receive love, not only give love, but also to accept the love offered by the other person…
> – the empathetic capacity, to be able to establish empathetic relationships, which consists in creating that condition of "harmony" between two subjects…
> – the capacity to be autonomous, the capacity of free choice…
> – the capacity to enter into good interpersonal relations, even if they are not perfect.
> – a sense of humor (…). It is a gift from God that helps us to keep balance in our life.[115]

Matrimonial consent, between a man and a woman, is an individual act of the person's will by which two individuals lawfully manifest their consent to enter into an irrevocable covenant in which they freely give and accept one another with the purpose of establishing marriage[116] Therefore, it is logical to expect that the future spouses have a basic human maturity to be able to grasp the dignity and permanence of their sacramental union. As Viladrich (2001) states:

> The understanding of consensual capacity refers to that degree of self-control and self-acceptance that is needed, in those who are engaged, in order to be able to truly be a gift for the other and to receive, in a no less concrete way, the conjugal gift of the other.[117]

Obviously, this self-control and self-acceptance require the capacity for a human person to be able to form interpersonal relationships with others, and it assumes that a certain degree of affective maturity is present in the individual. This affective maturity is necessary because the person has a fundamental need

---

115 Stefania Tassotti, *Teresa di Gesù e la Formazione alla Maturità Affettiva*, Unpublished manuscript (Rome: Teresianum, 2010) 43-44. The Italian text reads: "I criteri che ci indicano la presenza di una buona maturità affettiva sono:

> –la capacità di amare e di ricevere amore, non solo dare amore, ma anche accettare l'amore offerto dall'altro,...
> –la capacità empatica, saper stabilire relazione di empatia, che consite nel creare quella condizione di "sintonia" fra due soggetti...
> –la capacità di autonomia, la capacità di scelte libere...
> –la capacità di relazioni interpersonali buone, anche se non perfette;
> –il senso dell'umorismo...
> È un dono di Dio che ci consente di mantenere l'equilibrio nella nostra vita.

116 *CIC*, c. 1057.

117 Pedro J. Viladrich, Il Consenso Matrimoniale, 11. The Italian text reads: "... la nozione di capacità consensuale si riferisce a quel grado sufficiente di dominio e possesso di sé di cui ha bisogno il contraente per potersi donare realmente all'altro e accogliere, in modo non meno concreto, la donazione coniugale dell'altro."

to enter into interpersonal relationships with others, and the capacity to form relationships with others:

> [R]eveals his/her maturity in his/her capacity to open up to others in their diversity, and also because one is fulfilled when one is open to interpersonal relationships and discovers the joy of giving oneself.[118]

However,

> This maturity is never achieved in a perfect and definitive way; on the contrary, it is the result of a constant interior dynamic as well as the searching of a balance that is never completely achieved.[119]

Canonical maturity is by no means that maturity explained by the psychological sciences which assert that, in order for a person to be fulfilled as a human being, the individual must attain one's full human potential. However, canonical maturity, besides being the minimum maturity to marry, must include, because of the juridical nature of marriage, that maturity which endows the person with a certain psychosocial and psychosexual development to be able to form affectionate bonds with a suitable partner. In other words, it gives the person the maturity to be able to enter into a loving relationship, which is the maturity to love and to be loved, to give and to receive, to be a gift for the other person and to receive the other person as a God-given gift. Furthermore, this maturity endows the person with the capacity, albeit imperfect, to understand the essential properties of marriage which are unity and indissolubility,[120] the goods of matrimonial covenant, such as the good of the spouses, and the procreation and education of children;[121] as well as the capacity to understand that matrimonial consent is irrevocable.[122] Otherwise, the person would be unable to express a valid matrimonial consent as expressed in canon 1095.

Furthermore, c. 1096 indicates that in order for a person to express a valid matrimonial consent, the person should know that marriage entails entering into a permanent partnership with his/her partner, and that this partnership is ordered

---

118 Stefania Tassotti, *Teresa di Gesú,* 43. The Italian text reads: "rivela la sua maturità nella misura in cui è più capace di aprirsi all'altro nell'alterità, anche perchè egli si realizza pienamente quando si apre a tali rapporti interpersonali e scopre la gioia di donarsi."
119 Ibid., 42, the Italian text reads: "...questa maturità non si realizza mai in modo perfetto e definitivo, ma al contrario è il risultato di una costante dinamica interiore e ricerca di un equilibrio mai completamente raggiunto."
120 *CIC*, c. 1056.
121 *CIC*, c. 1055.
122 *CIC,* c. 1057.

to the procreation of offspring by means of sexual cooperation. In addition, c. 1061 indicates that this conjugal act by which the spouses become one flesh needs to be performed in a human fashion.

Consequently, in light of the canons reviewed above, this basic minimum canonical maturity assumes a proper development of the fundamental dimensions of the human person, such as a minimum intellectual development so that the person understands what marriage is; a minimum affective development in order to be able to uphold the dignity of marriage; a minimum moral development in order to be able to feel a sense of responsibility for the marriage that is established, for one's spouse, and for one's children; and a minimum sense of self possession of his/her own actions, etc.

Some Factors that May Affect the Maturity of Individuals

a) Culture

It is a widely known fact that cultures differ in their expectations of what constitutes a normal emotional, intellectual, and affective development of the human person. More specifically, cultures differ in their expectations of the period in which a person is considered to have achieved the required degree of maturity to be able to take care of oneself. For instance, in the United States culture, it is normal for a person to finish high-school around eighteen years of age. At this time, the young person is expected to have achieved some degree of maturity (i.e. responsibility, capable of making decisions for oneself, able to work and support oneself, etc.) and to move out of his/her parents' home and become independent. In some instances, one might rely on the support of one's own family to attend college and obtain an apartment. At other times, one might get together with other people undergoing the same experience of leaving home and starting college and choose to become roommates. These occurrences are considered to be very normal in the American culture and it is something that most young adults in this society experience today. They are considered to be important steps into adulthood as one becomes independent, and thus show some signs of becoming mature. This is demonstrated by one's abilities to learn to perform some basic chores around the house and to manage one's money as one learns to survive in society. At the same time, these new experiences help the young person to develop a sense of self-worth as a human being, to make rational decisions as he/she interacts with the world around him/her, and to become aware of himself/herself as he/she realizes that he/she is the owner of his/her own actions.

On the other hand, there are cultures in which it is very normal for a young adult to live in his/her parent's home well into their 20's, 30's and beyond. In this type of culture, it is normal for the young adult to expect one's mother to take care of his/her basic needs, such as cooking, doing laundry, cleaning, etc., and at times, they even rely on their parents for their economic needs. Consequently, for a person from another culture, this type of behavior would automatically classify the person as immature, dependent, and eternally childish. However, it is possible that in this other type of society, people have a different understanding of when a person is considered to be mature.

By the same token, an American young adult who refuses to leave home at an earlier age and become independent, would be considered immature and lacking the necessary skills to survive in society. On the other hand, a young adult whose culture expects him/her to stay at home well into his 20's and 30's but leaves his/her parent's home once he/she turns eighteen years old, might also be considered immature, imprudent, rebellious, or lacking good judgment. Culture, therefore, would appear to have a definite influence on what it means to have the necessary maturity for a person to be able to engage in transactions that require the use of his/her intellectual abilities, such as entering into marriage.

It seems logical to expect that a culture that encourages young persons to be independent and to learn how to make decisions for oneself would have a better influence on that person's intellectual/cognitive development. On the other hand, it appears that a culture that encourages its youth to depend on one's parents well into adulthood might foster some type of psychological immaturity. For these reasons, Aznar Gil (2008) indicates that there are different reasons why a culture experiences a psychological immaturity among its young adults; this immaturity is reflected

> [I]n their insecurity about themselves, lack of confidence or incertitude in interpersonal relationships, incapacity of adaptation and failure to overcome frustrations, emotional lability, kaleidoscopic changes in their affective parameters, scarce sexual integration in their affectivity and in every aspect of one's personality, an ill-defined awareness of self (...).[123]

Consequently, this phenomenon, known as "unending adolescence,"[124] according to Aznar Gil (2008), enables immature behavior well into the 30's and 40's, an age at which one would expect people to have had an adequate degree of maturity. Furthermore, this type of immaturity might have a negative influence on the person's ability to make decisions that require a certain degree of intellectual maturity, i.e. the capacity to use one's reasoning abilities as one makes deci-

123 Federico R. Aznar Gil, "La Inmadurez Psicológica y el Consentimiento Matrimonial en la Jurisprudencia Rotal," in *Anuario Argentino de Derecho Canónico*, 14 (2008) 12. The text in Spanish reads: "(...) como inseguridad sobre sí mismos, desconfianza o incerteza en las relaciones interpersonales, incapacidad de adaptación y de superación de las frustraciones, labilidad emotiva, caleidoscópicos cambios en los ejes afectivos, escasa integración de la sexualidad en la afectividad y en todo el sistema de la personalidad, conciencia de sí mal definida (...)."

124 Ibid., 12. The text in Spanish reads: *"adolescencias interminables."*

sions that will affect one's future life, such as choosing a partner for marriage. Accordingly, Aznar Gil indicates that:

> [T]this psychological immaturity, in fact, is one of the main reasons that cause a high number of matrimonial failures because of the given negative repercussions that some of the more habitual behaviors have on the interpersonal conjugal relationships, such behaviors as selfishness; the scarce or lack of capacity to give or gift oneself to the other; capricious or irresponsible behavior; a life centered around the "me" and not the "you" or matrimonial "us;" the search for one's own pleasure and happiness, forgetting the other spouse; the scarce or lack of capacity to compromise, etc.[125]

b) Abuse

The detrimental effects that negative early childhood experiences have on the psychological development of the human person has been documented by both local tribunals and Rotal jurisprudence. Such negative experiences might cause a person to develop illnesses of a psychic nature that are manifested through distorted perceptions about reality, the self, and others. For instance, the Tribunal of the Archdiocese of Vancouver has documented the negative effects of child sexual abuse in their *c.* Lopez-Gallo of October 29, 1991. In this sentence, the Judges, referring to the issue of sexual abuse of minors, state that:

> Child abuse is one type of tragic occurrence which harms the nature of an individual. The detrimental effects on children who have experienced sexual abuse... lasts for a very long time, sometimes for a lifetime; and the abused individuals suffer from feelings of shame and guilt as well as doubts regarding their own worth.[126]

Consequently, it would be very difficult for a person who experiences the detrimental effects of abuse for a lifetime and learns to doubt oneself to achieve the required canonical maturity to contract marriage.

Unfortunately, these types of negative events during one's childhood are experiences that have the potential to cause detrimental, and sometimes irrevers-

---

125 Ibid., 14. The text in Spanish reads: "esta inmadurez psicológica, de hecho, es una de las causas que provocan un alto número de fracasos matrimoniales dada la negativa repercusión que tienen en las relaciones interpersonales conyugales algunos de sus comportamientos más habituales, tales como el egoísmo; la escasa o nula capacidad de entrega y donación al otro; los comportamientos caprichosos e irresponsables; la vida centrada en el "yo" y no en el "tú" o "nosotros" matrimonial; la búsqueda del propio placer y felicidad, olvidando al otro cónyuge; la escasa o nula capacidad de compromiso; etc."

126 *c.* P. López-Gallo, 29 October 1991, in *Monitor Ecclesiasticus,* 123 (1998) 124, n. 4.

ible, damage to the psychic health of a child. Consequently, throughout life, the child may experience numerous negative long-term effects such as:

> [Incidents of] 'depression, anxiety, tension, nervousness, isolation, negative self-concept, difficulty trusting others, sense of betrayal, inability to enjoy sex, confusion over sex and affection' (W 0047 91, p. 3).[127]

These incidents may render the person incapable of achieving that degree of canonical maturity necessary to express marital consent freely.

Similarly, the Rotal sentence *c.* Verginelli, of 16 March 2007 states that:

> If a person has experienced a very unsettled upbringing as well as economic uncertainty, they will always display inappropriate behavior… This is manifested by putting matters off, primarily seeking the greatest possible freedom.[128]

Consequently, a possible display of such inappropriate behavior would be the person's inability to commit fully and freely to a situation that requires his/her whole self. Such would be the case in matrimony because they might find that their personal freedom is restricted by marriage, rather than finding the matrimonial covenant as a source of growth and self-fulfillment. The reason for this is that they might not have the required affective maturity to fulfill the demands of marriage; because marriage is, in and of itself, interpersonal. This interpersonality, which is essential for matrimony, requires the individual's capacity to accept oneself as he/she is, with all one's own limitations and qualities; as Viladrich states:

> We can say that consensual capacity consists of that degree of possession of self and one's own acts needed to furnish the act of contracting marriage with the freedom of rationality required for the reciprocal donation and acceptance of self, as man or woman, to constitute a lifelong partnership ordered to the conjugal good and the procreation and education of offspring.[129]

Possession of self implies that, in order for the person to be able to express matrimonial consent, the person must be able to form, at least at a basic and imperfect level, meaningful and loving relationships as he/she recognizes and

127 Ibid.

128 *c.* Verginelli, 16 March 2007, in *Studia canonica*, 43 (2009) 555, n. 12.

129 Pedro J. Viladrich, "Commentary to Canon 1095," 1224.

respects the human dignity of the other person as they establish affectional bonds for one another. However, the establishing of affectional bonds of attachment requires the affective maturity of the person to know oneself and to realize that matrimony is a journey that requires the willingness of both spouses to grow in their affectivity for one another, and to learn to confront objectively unpleasant situations that may surface in their marriage and to grasp these situations as a source of growth as they deepen their love for one another. Nonetheless, a successful development of an adequate affective maturity can be affected by many different factors besides culture and abuse; such as psychological and emotional wellbeing of the family environment, exposure to drug and alcohol abuse in the family, education (one's own and one's family), the ability of the same individual to cope with emotional distress and stressful situations, support received by the individual, etc. These factors may contribute to the person's development of a healthy affective maturity.

Effects of the Psychosocial Development of the Person on Internal Freedom

When we reflect upon the vocation of the human person to marriage, it is impossible to dismiss some fundamental components of one's character that enable a human being to establish an interpersonal relationship with a future partner. It is important that these components be adequately developed in a healthy manner because they are necessary in order to establish quality interpersonal relationships between two adult individuals who seek to marry each other. For instance, the person needs to have a clear understanding of his/her personal identity in order to be able to present himself/herself as he/she is without needing to present a false front. It is equally important that the person has developed a good sense of his/her own sexuality because matrimony is ordered to the procreation of children through sexual relationships [can. 1055; c. 1096]. It is also necessary to develop one's intellectual abilities in order to understand and grasp the meaning of marriage and the rights and obligations attained through it. Additionally, a sufficient affective capacity is needed in order to be able to form affectionate bonds of attachment with one's spouse as the partners strengthen the community of life and love established through marriage since marriage is seen as an intimate union "of [the whole of] their persons and of their actions" (*GS*, n. 48). Finally, an adequate sense of morality must be developed so that the individual can understand one's own role and obligations acquired though this juridical partnership.

Even though these components are important, it is not necessary for them to have achieved full maturity in the human person. However, it is necessary for the person to have a sufficient foundation for these elements. Otherwise it would be like building up the community of life and love in a sand castle that is washed away by the waves of chaos created by conflicts that arise in a normal day to day routine and especially when the person is unable to cope with them due to the immature nature of an underdeveloped or neglected dimension of one's character.

The human person, created in the image and likeness of God as a free being, experiences a maturational process from conception to death. This maturational process undergoes a number of developmental stages which are characterized by the individual's transformation from a mere cell into a mature human person and encompasses the psychological, biological, spiritual, intellectual, and affective dimensions of the person. During this transformational process, the biological and psycho-affective elements that bestow the capacity upon the person for engaging in critical thinking and reasoning, as well as the capacity to engage in affective relationships, are formed. The formation of these psycho-affective elements is impacted by multiple factors at any one stage during the maturational development of a human being. Consequently, according to Guiry (1991), maturation can be viewed as "a dynamic process, and as such, there will be a certain amount of unevenness present at any one moment in time... in the individual."[130]

There are some situations in life which require an individual to make a wise choice in regard to one's own future. These choices, in turn, require an adequate development of an individual's maturity so that the individual can understand the nature and object of his/her choice. Otherwise, as some scholars indicate, it would be difficult for an immature individual to achieve:

> The emotional state which will allow the clarity of judgment, ability to discern, and strength to decide. This lack of maturity will result from many factors--physical, environmental, and genetic-- among the most obvious."[131]

However, it is important to point out that, according to Collins & Sroufe (1999), the notion of:

> [W]orking models explicitly includes the possibility that patterns of feelings, expectations, thoughts, and behaviors can change with experience.[132]

Consequently, the mere fact that a person did not experience positive bonds of attachment with his/her primary caregiver does not necessarily mean that the person will be unable to establish a community of life and love in his/her marriage.

---

130 Robert W. Guiry, "Immaturity, Maturity, and Christian Marriage," in *Studia canonica*, 25 (1991) 96.
131 Ibid., 97.
132 W. Andrew Collins & L. Alan Sroufe, "Capacity for Intimate Relationships: A Developmental Construction," in Wyndol Furnam, B. Bradford Brown, & Candice Feiring, (eds.), *The Development of Romantic Relationships in Adolescence* (New York, NY: Cambridge University Press, 1999) 127.

Among some of the factors that affect the maturity of the individual it is well known that the consumption of some drugs and alcohol during pregnancy can have harmful effects on the physical and psychic development of an unborn person. Likewise, the consumption of drugs and cigarette smoking during pregnancy can have similar detrimental effects. Effects from experiences like these can hinder, therefore, the normal development of the intellectual and volitive faculties of a person and might negatively affect that person's capacity to engage in critical reasoning when making choices later in life. The psychosocial and psycho-affective development of a person is critical, therefore, in the formation of that person's intellectual and volitive faculties.

Attachment Theory

In the field of Developmental Psychology, one of the theories that has gained prominent importance for the psychosocial development of individuals is that of attachment theory. According to Simpson, Collins, Tran & Haydon (2007), the fundamental hypothesis established by Bowlby concerning the internal working models of past relationship experiences with the primary caregivers have an effect, either positive or negative, on later relationship experiences. This view has been very influential in the theory of attachment.[133] It must be noted, however, that an individual's past experiences of attachment do not totally determine the manner in which an individual will respond to the formation of affectional bonds later in life. As the authors indicate, the internal working models (or representations):

> [T]end to be modified continuously as individuals enter and leave different types of attachment relationships across successive periods of development.[134]

However, they do, up to a certain point, predict trends of the individual's behavior over time based on their past experiences of attachment. For instance, Simpson et al (2007) indicate that since future relationships are influenced by both familial and social relationships that an individual experiences early in life:

> [A]ttachment relationships with caregivers early in life should have an impact not only on later relationships with caregivers but also on other important relationships with peers, close friends, and romantic partners.[135]

---

133 Jeffry A. Simpson, W. Andrew Collins, SiSi Tran, & Katherine C. Haydon, "Attachment and the Experience and Expression of Emotions in Romantic Relationships: A Developmental Perspective," in *Journal of Personality and Social Psychology*, 92/2 (2007) 357.

134 Ibid.

135 Ibid., 358.

Consequently, the theory of attachment states that attachment relationships with the primary caregivers are critically important during the early years of a person's life. Attachment relationships are important because they:

> [S]et the stage for infant's physiological functioning, their emotional and cognitive interpretations of social- and non-social experiences, their language development, and their acquisition of meaning about themselves and others in complex social situations.[136]

Furthermore, establishing attachment relationships with the primary caregivers enables the child to form affective relationships with others. As an example, Carpendale & Lewis (2003) indicate that:

> [S]ecurity of attachment which is based on the mother's way of relating to the infant, may influence the infant's ability to engage with others... and it is this engagement that is essential... in the development of thinking, especially thinking about the social world.[137]

This view is important because it refers to the fact that the quality of attachment has an effect on the way the child experiences the world and forms relationships as he/she learns to interact with others. As the authors suggest, "(...) infants develop [relationships and] expectations about other people based on primary relationships."[138] Furthermore, they contend that "social interaction is essential in the development of cognitive, social and moral knowledge."[139] Therefore, it can be deduced that the children's psycho-affective development can be affected by the type of attachment that they experience with their primary caregivers as well as by the interactions that they establish with others.

According to Collins and Sroufe (1999), one's capacity for intimacy develops through a series of phases experienced throughout the lifespan of the individual.

136 Karin Grossmann & Klaus E. Grossmann, "The Impact of Attachment to Mother and Father at an Early Age on Children's Psychosocial Development Through Young Adulthood," in Richard E. Tremblay, Ronald G. Barr, Ray deV Peters, & Michel Boivin, (eds.), *Encyclopedia on Early Childhood Development* (Montreal, PQ: Centre of Excellence for Early Childhood Development, 2009) 1-8. [online], http://www.child-encyclopedia.com/documents/GrossmannANGxp_rev.pdf (accessed 10 October 2015).

137 Jeremy Carpendale & Charlie Lewis, "Constructing an Understanding of Mind: The Development of Children's Social Understanding Within Social Interaction," in *Behavioral and Brain Sciences* (Cambridge University Press, 2003) 27. See http://www.psych.lancs.ac.uk/people/uploads/CharlieLewis20030618T085607.pdf (accessed 10 October 2015).

138 Ibid., 27.

139 Ibid., 1.

Each phase builds on the preceding one and is affected by the way in which the individual formed attachments with others. For instance, the quality of the bonds of attachment formed in infancy with one's caregivers lead to either positive or negative expectations about interactions with others. This process is known as the formation of internal working models of self and others and these models have an effect on the way one interacts with others. Furthermore, attachment experiences also provide a context for learning reciprocity which is fundamental in developing relationships later in life. In addition, experiences of attachment have an effect on an individual's sense of self-worth; and as Collins and Sroufe (1999) indicate, "[f]eelings that the self is worthy of respect and care underlie characteristics that are likely to be attractive to future partners."[140]

Similarly, in a longitudinal study, Simpson et al (2007) studied 78 individuals to determine the effect that early interpersonal experiences (attachment) have on an individual's quality of emotional experiences with his/her romantic partner. Their results indicate that people who had experienced secure attachments at the beginning of their lives were more likely to establish secure friendships later in life than those with histories of insecure attachment.[141] Furthermore, they state that:

> [T]he experience and expression of emotion in romantic relationships appear to be tied in significant and meaningful ways to experiences rooted in earlier relationships and stages of social development.[142]

Similarly, Collins & Sroufe (1999) indicate that "children who had been securely attached in infancy tended to form friendships with children who also had secure histories."[143] On the other hand, children who were labeled as experiencing anxious attachment styles:

> [M]ay be less interested in interpersonal relationships, may value them less highly, or may expect negative outcomes in relationships, whereas securely attached children may regard relationships more positively.[144]

As already observed, attachment theory explains a causal relationship between a person's experience with his/her parents or attachment figures and the person's capacity to form and maintain affectional bonds later in life. In other words, when a child experiences positive relationships with his/her primary caregivers:

140 W. Andrew Collins & L. Alan Sroufe, *Capacity for Intimate Relationships*, 127.
141 Jeffry A. Simpson, et al., *Attachment and Experience*, 361.
142 Ibid., 363.
143 W. Andrew Collins & L. Alan Sroufe, *Capacity for Intimate Relationships*, 129.
144 Ibid., 130.

> [S]uch experiences are assumed to a) give the child a sense of worth, a belief in the helpfulness of others and enable the child to explore the environment with confidence; b) be an optimal precondition for mutually supportive, enduring adult partnerships …"[145]

As Simpson et al. (2007) indicate, "the experience and expression of emotions in adult romantic relationships were meaningfully linked to attachment-relevant experiences in social development."[146] The research in the field of attachment indicates that:

> [E]xperiences in and mental representations of relationships earlier in life are likely to influence the types of interpersonal goals, plans, and expectancies that individuals hold for later relationships and, hence, can be facilitated or hindered.[147]

Consequently, researchers in this field state that individuals who had experienced a history of secure relationships may experience more positive emotions in their adult relationships. This is because they may be more accepting of the demands of a relationship, such as accommodating the preferences and desires of one's partner while making important decisions.[148] People with a history of secure attachment experiences:

> [T]ypically strive for 'goal-corrected partnerships' in which each partner's most critical needs and desires are considered before determining which course of action might be best for the relationship.[149]

In addition, research in this area indicates that people with a secure attachment history exhibit a freer psycho-affective maturity, evidenced by being able to engage with their partners in constructive and problem-solving strategies, are more ready to forgive transgressions, and are more willing to adopt and work "toward plans and goals that may be more equitable and more relationship centered."[150] Therefore, the researchers' results illustrate the psycho-affective capacity of individuals with secure attachment histories are more able to establish a community of life and love peculiar to the matrimonial state: a community that requires the individual's capacity to establish, in freedom, quality interpersonal relationships.

---

145 Ibid., 2.

146 Jeffry A. Simpson, et al., *Attachment and Experience*, 363.

147 Ibid., 364.

148 Ibid.

149 Ibid.

150 Ibid.

Adults with negative histories of attachment experiences are typically seen as being more constrained by negative emotions in their relationships. They tend to be more concerned with autonomy, control, and independence, and are less likely to attend to their partner's preferences and desires. This is the result of their unfounded fears of being abandoned or taken advantage of. Furthermore, these types of individuals tend not to establish a goal-corrected partnership. They are more likely to engage in dysfunctional interaction strategies and are less prone to be forgiving.[151] Consequently, it can be concluded that the psycho-affective freedom that these types of individuals experience is of a lesser degree than those with a positive history of attachment experiences.

It is important to indicate, however, that Simpson et al (2007) point out the fact that their results "do not suggest that an individual's past unalterably determines the future course of her or his relationships;"[152] because as they indicate, their findings do not suggest that an individual:

> [C]annot overcome attachment or relationship difficulties encountered earlier in their development or that other factors (such as personality traits…) play trivial roles in generating or sustaining emotions in romantic relationships.[153]

Nonetheless, the literature reviewed above suggests that an individual's psycho-affective development and the person's capacity for developing bonds of affection might be "impacted by the nature and course of their developmental histories."[154] Consequently, an understanding of the history of an individual "may shed novel light on how and why individuals perceive, feel, and behave as they do in their contemporary relationship."[155]

Similarly, understanding the biographical elements that have played a role in the development of an individual's psychosocial maturity may provide some information as to whether a particular individual's manifestation of consent at the time of marriage was free or was the product of internal coercions. Furthermore, given the fact that marriage is an interpersonal relationship, it is important for the spouses to have that internal freedom of mind and the minimum capacity of psycho-affective maturity that allows them to share with each other their very selves, including their feelings, emotions, fears, wants, desires, and insecurities, as they grow in their matrimonial life. According to Collins and Sroufe (1999), these emotionally close interactions become significant because self-disclosing behavior leads the spouses to experience a sense of being understood, validated,

151 Ibid.
152 Ibid., 365.
153 Ibid.
154 Ibid.
155 Ibid.

and loved; and as a result, these individuals become the architects of the relationship as well as the product of the relationship in which they participate.[156]

Obviously, the human person does not grow in total isolation; but rather, one grows in close contact with other human beings who exert some influence on one's developmental and maturational process. One's intellectual and psycho-affective development is shaped and formed by external factors that may help or hinder the person's healthy development. Therefore, it is wise to remember that no individual is completely free of the influence of past events. However, one's ability to cope with that influence may determine the degree of the internal freedom of a person giving matrimonial consent.

It is likewise important to remember that not all difficulties in married life from a person's past imply that the person did not enjoy internal freedom at the time of manifesting matrimonial consent for according to Hettinger (1976):

> [*C*]*ommunion vitae* in our modern vale of tears has to include the frictions inherent in the close, constant contact of two human beings continually in need of being saved from the effects of original sin.[157]

Therefore, it is well-advised to keep in mind the wise words of John Paul II (25 January 1988) who indicates that human nature is internally wounded by sin. Thus, even experts themselves in the fields of psychological and psychiatric sciences find difficulty in defining the concept of normality in a way that satisfies everyone. In any case,

> [T]he concept of normality, that is to say, of the normal human condition in this world, also includes moderate forms of psychological difficulty.[158]

And these mild psychological struggles might influence the choices that people make without taking away their internal freedom.

Concerning Internal Freedom

Reflecting upon the personalistic understanding of marriage presented in *GS*, n. 48 and the *CIC of 1983* (c. 1055), it is normal for the Church to protect the right of individuals to be free from any negative influences in choosing their

---

156 W. Andrew Collins & L. Alan Sroufe, *Capacity for Intimate Relationships*, 134.
157 Clarence J. Hettinger, "Psychic Incapacity for Marrying: Some Theological, Canonical, and Medical Reasons for Uneasiness," in *The Priest*, 32/ 6 (1976) 38.
158 John Paul II, *Roman Rota,* 1988.

state of life.[159] This right, however, can be violated by many different reasons. Sometimes, the reason resides in the very person, such as when there is a psychic anomaly that prevents the person from attaining sufficient knowledge regarding the essential rights and obligations of marriage. At other times, the reason resides in other persons or circumstances, such as when the person feels forced to accept a given spouse because of sociocultural customs (e.g., Force or Fear, c. 1103). This situation is prevalent in cultures in which arranged marriages are common, such as in the Asian culture. For instance, Mendonça (1995) indicates that:

> [R]ecent Rotal jurisprudence maintains that the violation of personal freedom can also happen when, even in the absence of any compulsion from anyone in particular, a person marries according to well-established mores and social customs, but only to avoid injuring the reputation of the family insofar as the injury to the reputation of one's relatives directly offends personal honour and dignity. The element of freedom would be certainly lacking in such human act.[160]

Entering into marriage against one's own will, whether because of a psychic anomaly which deprives the person of the necessary intellectual and volitive faculties to make a conscious, rational, and free choice; or because the person feels constrained to choose the only option presented to him/her, is not only a violation of the personal dignity and freedom of the individual, but it is also a violation of the very nature and essence of matrimony.

As observed previously, marriage is established by the free consent of the engaged. In other words, the engaged, acting in freedom and moved from within, make a conscious and deliberate choice to become a gift for each other out of love. This gift involves all the dimensions of the human person (i.e., emotional, psychological, physical, spiritual, etc.); as such, the engaged must be endowed with the necessary internal freedom to become a true gift for one another. When this internal freedom is lacking, it is impossible to affirm that the matrimonial consent posited by the spouses proceeded from a true human act.

Internal Freedom, therefore, is a crucial element in positing valid matrimonial consent. For this reason, both doctrine and jurisprudence have always upheld the right of the human person to choose marriage as well as one's freedom to choose a suitable spouse. Furthermore, the Church, in order for matrimony to be valid, requires the personal and free consent of the engaged. When these character-

---

159 c. 219.

160 Augustine Mendonça, "Recent Rotal Jurisprudence From a Sociocultural Perspective," in *Studia canonica*, 29 (1995) 52.

istics are missing, it is impossible to establish, from a canonical perspective, a community of life and love.

Brief Analysis of the Data

As mentioned previously, the purpose of this study is to explore the differences between what the Roman Rota has stipulated regarding c. 1095, n.2 and the way in which Tribunals in the United States are using this ground of nullity. What follows, is a very concise summary of these findings.[161] The reader is reminded that in order to obtain some information for this study, a request was sent to 75 tribunals from across the United States asking for their participation by providing two recent decisions regarding grave lack of discretion of judgment or lack of internal freedom. Although the tribunals were assured of strict confidentiality, only six of them provided the information requested.

The following table illustrates the most remarkable differences:

c. 1095: Some Common Differences Between American and Rotal Jurisprudence	
American Conceptions	***Rotal Jurisprudence***
c. 1095 is the easiest ground to prove	c. 1095 is a very difficult ground to prove
Any difficulty can be used to declare the nullity of the marriage	"For the canonist, the principle must remain clear that only a true incapacity not a difficulty" JP, 1987
Every problem that the couple experiences can be placed under this ground	"Only the most severe forms of psychopathology…" JP, 1987
It can easily be proven that the marriage is null because of immaturity	The Rota does not accept immaturity as a ground of nullity. Franceschi, 2011* [full reference below]

161 For a more extensive comparison between Rotal Jurisprudence and American Tribunals regarding this ground of nullity please see Ponce, Jaimes, *Lack of Internal Freedom on Matrimonial Consent: An Analysis of Rotal Jurisprudence and American Decisions*, lulu.com (2012).

Immaturity, the person did not know what marriage entailed	Not any type of immaturity can be the cause of nullity, but only that immaturity which produces grave lack of discretion of judgment** [full reference below]
In cases of psychic incapacity, the problems make the case	In cases of psychic incapacity, the evaluation of an expert is needed, DC, art. 209

* Franceschi, H., "Consideraciones Acerca de Algunas Cuestiones Disputadas Sobre el Canon 1095," in *Ius Canonicum,* 51 (2011) 449-478.

** *c.* Doran. 9 April 1992, in *Decisiones seu Sententiae, LXXXIV* (1992) 171-181.

---

c. Smith-Alpha. 18 March 2003. Canon 1095, 20 – Grave Lack of Due Discretion – On the Part of the Woman. Affirmative.[162]

a) The Case

Joe and Jane contracted marriage in June of 1960 after a dating relationship that lasted for five years. Since both of them were baptized Catholics, the wedding took place in the Church. At the time, he was twenty-two, while she was nineteen. Their marriage lasted nineteen years and, during this time, three children were born of their union. In 1981, a civil divorce was granted. The reasons for the divorce were Joe's infidelity, as well as his mental, emotional, and physical abuse toward Jane. The Tribunal verified its competency and established the doubt as: "Has the nullity of this marriage been proven on the grounds of lack of due discretion on the part of the woman?"[163]

b) The Law

In the analysis of this case, the Judge draws extensively from the *New Commentary on the Code of Canon Law (2000)* which states that:

> A person may possess sufficient use of reason to have a rudimentary and abstract understanding of marriage and its ob-

162 *c.* Smith-Alpha, 18 March 2003. Unpublished Decision provided by Tribunal Alpha.
163 It is disconcerting to observe that although the man Petitioner is the one who was unfaithful and abused the woman Respondent, the Judge decided to place the doubt on the woman.

> ligations and to intend marriage so understood but still be incapable of consent, if he or she lacks the ability to deliberate critically about this choice in the concrete. Canon law calls this incapacity for critical deliberation lack of maturity or discretion of judgment. (*New Commentary on the Code of Canon Law,* 2000, p. 1299).

Even though the Judge rightly indicates that, while a person might have the capacity to understand the nature and obligations of the matrimonial bond, this capacity does not guarantee that the person has the capacity to consent. Consent requires not only that the person understands the nature of the matrimonial bond, but also requires that the person be able to deliberate critically about the object of consent. When the capacity for critical deliberation is absent, then it can be proven that the person is lacking in maturity or discretion of judgment.

Concerning consent, the Judge observes that it must be "informed, prudent,[164] and free" because it is a human act. Therefore, he indicates that: "matrimonial consent must be free from both external coercion and internal compulsion." However, the Judge understands that a human act is never perfectly free because there are both conscious and unconscious influences that move a person toward a given object. He concludes the discussion of personal freedom and consent by stating that:

> [V]alid consent requires freedom 'from immature, obsessive and overpowering ideas, fantasies, instinctual excitations, fear and so forth in the process of choosing the object of consent.' In other words, a person must be able to evaluate his or her motives for marriage and to exercise mastery over impulses and anxieties. (Ibid., p. 1300).

c) The Argument

In this section, the Judge presents the information provided by the partners and the witnesses. This information reveals that Joe was involved with other women before the marriage took place. Apparently, the relationship between Joe and Jane was ended several times; but in the end, they married. The information does not provide any critical situation, such as emotional problems, arguments, etc. The only information presented that hints to the possibility of a problematic relationship is:

---

164 It is important to observe that Rotal jurisprudence constantly states that an imprudent decision to marry does not vitiate matrimonial consent.

> Prior to the parties' engagement at Christmas of 1959 (P26), Jane broke off the courtship (P42-43). Even though Jane could not recall the specific reason for the break-up, she did testify, "she was relieved [that]... it was over, and that was it, and I was going to accept that and just go on" (P42). While Jane could not provide a specific reason for the break-up, her feelings of relief that the relationship was over is consistent with her observations that Joe was inconsiderate to her, and that their relationship was only "adequate." Jane only re-united with Joe after being persuaded to do so by Joe's parents (*Psupp.* 20-21).

On the basis of these observations, which represent a remote possibility of some type of problems between Jane and Joe, the Judge indicates the following:

> Therefore, *serious problems did exist* in the parties' relationship prior to the marriage. Namely, Jane perceived her relationship with Joe to be only "adequate," she considered Joe to be an "inconsiderate" person (probably rooted in the fact that Joe was dating another girl behind Jane's back, and that Joe really did not love her), and Jane broke off their relationship prior to their brief six-month engagement. However, Jane *was incapacitated* from properly evaluating her decision to marry Joe because of two factors: 1) her *lack of self-worth* and personal emotional problems, and 2) her *desire to escape* her parental home.

The Judge seems to be basing his opinion concerning the presence of *"serious problems"* on the fact that their relationship was problematic. However, the problems do not reveal any serious psychic anomaly. They do reveal, nonetheless, a desire for simulating marriage (*"desire to escape her parental home"*), but not an *"incapacity,"* as the Judge states.

The following paragraph, however, does reveal deeper problems:

> Jane felt that she was being *emotionally abused* by her parents during her formative years (P53). "Both of my parents thought that children should be seen and not heard so I didn't get to express opinions very often" (P54). "When I had problems in school or with friends, or socializing, or at work, I couldn't go to [my parents] ... I was supposed to be quiet all the time ... (...) She was *verbally abused* by her mother, and "always was alone so much of the time" (*Psupp.* 25). (...) Jane also was *physically abused* by her mother on several occasions (P55;

> *Psupp.* 25), and was *sexually abused* by a friend of the family when she was three or four years old (P57-63).

On the basis of this testimony, the Judge affirms the following:

> This abusive upbringing experienced and underwent by Jane directly impacted her ability to exercise due discretion of judgment in her decision to marry: "because of the emotional problems that I had, I don't think I ever really trusted my own instincts and my own feelings, I was that unsure of myself... Emotionally I was really young" (*Psupp.* 36).

While there is no doubt that emotional, verbal, and sexual abuse can affect the person's capacity to evaluate, in a critical manner, important decisions in one's life, there is not psychological evaluation to corroborate Jane's statements. She gives the observations regarding her own incapacity to decide to marry. She is the one making an assessment regarding her capacity to posit valid matrimonial consent and the Judge seems to take her statement as that of an expert.

However, evidence shows that Jane made a decision to marry Joe to leave her house. The Judge observes:

> Joe corroborated the fact that Jane looked upon marriage as a means to escape her parental home: Jane "wanted to marry to get away from that situation, and I was the vehicle" (*R30*). This desire to escape her parental home, given the past history of emotional and verbal abuse in her family of origin, would have at least clouded her ability to exercise due discretion of judgment in her decision to marry Joe.

These observations seem to indicate that either *simulation* (she intended to gain something else rather than matrimony) or *fear* (she wanted to escape an adverse situation) could have been better grounds to apply to this case. The Judge mentions the fact that her experiences "clouded" her cognition regarding her decision to marry. However, "clouded" or "confused" thinking does not produce grave lack of discretion of judgment nor does it hinder a person's freedom to determine oneself toward marriage.

Nonetheless, after reviewing the case, the judges found enough evidence to support the claim for the nullity of marriage and arrived at the following conclusion:

AFFIRMATIVE, i.e., the nullity of this marriage on the grounds of lack of due discretion on the part of the woman has been proven in this case.

Personal Observation: The Judge could have tried this case under the ground of simulation or force and fear.

---

c. Burke. 22 July 1991, in Decisiones seu Sententiae, LXXXIII (1991), pp. 500-508. Nullitatis matrimonii ob defectum discretionis iudicii utriusque partis. Pro vinculo.

a) The Case

Aurelius and Joanna were sixteen years old when they began an amorous relationship that lasted for five years. They continued nurturing the relationship even while he was serving overseas because of the war (1943-1945). Once he returned, they married in the Catholic Church in 1945. They both were twenty-one years old. They enjoyed a peaceful married life for thirty years and gave birth to four children. In 1980, they separated because of some serious disagreements. In 1982, they obtained a civil divorce and, subsequently, Aurelius introduced the *"libellum"* to the Metropolitan Tribunal petitioning the nullity of his marriage because of lack of discretion of judgment in both partners. In 1984, the tribunal issued an affirmative decision. This sentence was confirmed by the Appeals Tribunal of the Province, in spite of some objections from the Respondent.[165] Therefore, in 1985 the Judges admitted the case to a full trial in the Second Instance.

In 1985, after the instruction of the cause, a sentence was issued confirming the sentence of First Instance.[166]

The Respondent took recourse to the Roman Rota for a new proposition of the cause. The Acts of the case were requested from the local tribunal on more than one occasion. Finally, they arrived at the Apostolic Tribunal in 1989. Afterwards, the concordance of the doubt was established in 1990 as follows:

---

165 In a recent article, Cardinal Burke expresses his dismay at the fact that in spite of the constant proclamations of the rights of the human person, persons are being denied the right to defense in the Church. Raymond Burke, "Introduzione ai Lavori," in Franceschi, H. & Ortiz, M. A., (eds.), *La Ricerca della Verità sul Matrimonio e il Diritto a un Processo Giusto e Celere: Temi di Diritto Matrimoniale e Processuale Canonico* (Roma: EDUSC, 2012) 13-20.

166 Cfr. *c.* Burke. 22 July 1991, in *Decisiones seu Sententia, LXXXIII* (1991) 500-508, n. 1. An English version of this sentence appears in *Forum* 4 (1993) 107-121. Any direct quotations in English will be taken from this version.

1) an concedenda sit nova causae propositio; et quatenus affirmative;
2) an constet de matrimonii nullitate, in casu.[167]

b) The Law

In paragraph n. 3, the *Ponens* starts the discussion concerning *grave lack of discretion of judgment* regarding the essential matrimonial rights and obligations according to c. 1095, n. 2. He explains:

> The grounds contemplated under n. 2 of c. 1095 on the one hand, and n. 3 of the same canon on the other, are evidently connected, since both relate to consensual incapacity provoked from within. They are also however clearly distinct in that n. 2 relates to *estimative* capacity, in regard to some essential rights/obligations of marriage, while n. 3 relates to *executive* capacity regarding such rights/obligations.[168]

Successively, the *Ponens* reports the words that Pope John Paul II directed to the Rota in 1987 and 1988 in reference to consensual incapacity indicating that it must proceed from a grave, not mild, anomaly:

> (...) "An argument for real incapacity can be entertained only in the presence of a *serious* form of anomaly which, however one chooses to define it, must substantially undermine the capacity of understanding and/or willing of the covenantal partner" (AAS 79 (1987) 1457); "*only the more serious forms of psychopathology* are capable of undermining the substantial freedom of the person" (AAS 80 (1988) 1182). Here we clearly have an authentic interpretation that gives needed and mandatory guidance to all Tribunals on a matter of greatest importance" (Sentence *coram* undersigned of July 18, 1991, n. 3).[169]

As noted, the *Ponens* emphasizes the need for a serious indication of psychopathology in order to establish the incapacity of the person. However, this interpretation of incapacity according to c. 1095, n. 2 is not always followed by the judges of lower tribunals. Concerning the presence of a serious form of psychopathology in cases of grave lack of discretion of judgment, he observes that:

167 Ibid.
168 Ibid., n. 3.
169 Ibid., n. 4.

> This is particularly pertinent to our present case where the Judges of second instance affirm: "One need not be insane or otherwise mentally ill in order to lack due discretion... Lack of due discretion is often caused by some mental malady but not always so" (Acts, II, 67-68). We too hold that a person does not have to be *insane* in order to suffer from a grave lack of discretion. The Judges however go beyond that in suggesting that a lack of due discretion can occur in a person with a perfectly healthy mind; a claim that is scarcely reconcilable with the Pope's words, and with what common sense suggests. The *grave* lack of discretion which alone renders a person consensually incapable must derive from a definite *pathology* or illness of the "psyche" (mind or will; or both together). There may be good reasons – jurisprudential or otherwise – to prefer to speak of a psychic, rather than a mental, malady; but some malady, pathology or illness of the "psyche" must be there, and it must be grave.[170]

As the *Ponens* indicates, in causes of grave lack of discretion of Judgment, the presence of a disturbance of the *psyche* must be grave and it must be documented.

Regarding the person's capacity to understand and accept the essential matrimonial rights and obligations, the *Ponens* remarks that discretion of judgment is not affected by, as the Judges state: "(...) 'the inability to adequately judge the wisdom of a marital consent'."[171] When the judge attributes this inability to discretion of judgment, the *Ponens* indicates that:

> An ecclesiastical Judge loses his juridic perspective and falls into an elementary mistake, if he confuses prudence about the choice of a concrete marriage with a particular person, and discretion about the obligations which are essential to marriage itself.[172]

The *Ponens* explains that the task of the judge is not to determine the capacity of the person to accept one's partner. Rather, the task of the judge is to determine whether the person has the capacity to establish a conjugal relationship (i.e., the capacity is identified as person to institution, not person to person).[173]

---

170 Ibid.
171 Ibid., n. 6.
172 Ibid.
173 Ibid.

The *Ponens* recognizes that sometimes people make imprudent and impulsive decisions to marry; however, he states that imprudence is not a sign of lack of discretion of judgment:

> An impulsive decision to marry is perhaps a sign of a lack of prudence, but not necessarily of a lack of discretion in the canonical sense. In any case, as is evident, the impulsiveness of the decision must be proved. When two persons have had a loving relationship for some years, their eventual decision to marry can seldom be qualified as impulsive.[174]

Clearly, an impulsive decision to marry does not indicate the presence of a grave psychic anomaly that produces grave lack of discretion of judgment, as the Ponens states, it might have been impulsive, but not defective. Therefore, when the person does not show any evidence of a grave psychic anomaly, it is difficult to prove that one lacked sufficient discretion of judgment to understand and accept the essential matrimonial rights and obligations, especially when the marriage in question lasted for three decades and was blessed with several children. For this reason, the *Ponens* indicates:

> Finally we would recall what is written in a Sentence, *coram* Pompedda, of Dec. 16, 1985: "Married life together for many years, and the fact of having had children and of the fulfillment of conjugal duties, while they may not yet create an overwhelming strong presumption for contractual capacity, nevertheless call for the greatest possible caution in asserting a defect of consent" (RRD, vol. 77, p. 586).[175]

Here, the *Ponens* does not discard the possibility that a long married life blessed with children could be declared null due to an incapacity; however, he indicates that the judge must be cautious in asserting and proving a defect in matrimonial consent.

c) The Argument

Concerning the request for the new proposition of the case, the *Ponens* indicates that the Respondent has failed to provide new arguments for a new proposition of the present cause. However, he recognizes that there was an injustice done in the instruction of the case.[176]

---

174 Ibid., n. 10.
175 Ibid., n. 13.
176 Ibid., n. 14.

In the discussion of the facts, the *Ponens* exposes several errors made by the previous Judges and asserts that the facts, witnesses, or experts did not support their conclusions:

> First of all there is the fact of the partners' 35 years of actual married life together, with 4 children (plus two miscarriages). The Appeal Court, in coming to its decision of an incapacitating lack of discretion, comments, "Why they stayed in the union for thirty-five years is unexplainable to the Court" (II, 70). If they suffered from consensual incapacity, the point certainly called for some sort of explanation. The Court was content to advance none.[177]

The *Ponens*, therefore, in the examination of the Acts, does not find any evidence provided by the Appeals Court concerning the alleged consensual incapacity of the partners. The Appeals Court, therefore, failed to support its observations regarding consensual incapacity. Furthermore, the *Ponens* proceeds:

> They had known each other as boy and girl friend for five years before the actual marriage. During war service, she wrote him every day (I, 53). Witnesses bear out that their courtship was close and constant (I, 83/2; 88/2; 92/2; II, 36). The Second Sentence considers that the marriage was an "impulsive decision on the part of both partners that definitely lacked due discretion" (II, 71). The impulsiveness of the decision is not borne out by the Acts.[178]

Once again, the Judges fail to show any indication of an impulsive decision on the part of both partners. Even though this is a claim that they made to support their decision, the Acts, according to the *Ponens*, do not indicate any impulsiveness that might have produced a grave lack of discretion of judgment. The Acts reveal that the partners dated for five years and communicated with each other even when they were far apart. This is an indication of intentionality, not of impulsiveness.

Even when the *Ponens* scrutinizes the statements made by the man, he does not find any strong evidence concerning grave lack of discretion of judgment:

> Even in putting forward his own claim to a possible lack of maturity, his affirmations are very mild: "My present *opinion* of my judgment at the time of my marriage... is that *it was questionable*. The circumstances at the time were certainly

177 Ibid., n. 16.
178 Ibid.

unique. I had returned home as a hero after many months spent in very trying situations, which may have affected my judgment. I do not think that I was able *fully to appreciate* the significance of my decision." (I, 24).[179]

The *Ponens* proceeds to indicate another flaw of the Judges by stating that there were several witnesses that provided testimony; however, this evidence was never considered by the Judges:

> (...) It has to be said in any case that both Sentences totally fail to take the evidence given by witnesses into account. The Judges of first instance admit indeed that their conclusion goes against this evidence, since the witnesses, "paint a different picture: (I, 125); but, like those of second instance, they fail to quote a single word of any witness. One is amazed to find the Defender of the Bond in second instance stating that "support to the allegation has been given by four competent witnesses" (II, 1; II, 60)...[180]

It is clearly perceived that the Judges in the previous Instance failed to provide the necessary proof to support their conclusions. The *Ponens*, in his examination of the evidence provided by the witnesses, does not find any information that may support the alleged grounds of lack of discretion of judgment.[181]

Concerning the reports of the experts, the *Ponens* shows several deficiencies in the Judges' evaluation of the present case. These deficiencies enable the Judges to issue an erroneous decision:

> In the first Sentence the Judges admit that "the psychological evaluations found no psycho-pathology" (I, 125). We find nothing in them that could suggest a grave lack of discretion in either party.[182]

The Judges acknowledge that there was not psychopathology present in the partners; nonetheless, they seem to have found enough evidence, in their own evaluation and way of reasoning, to support a claim for *grave lack of discretion of judgment*. Nonetheless, as the *Ponens* indicates, there was no psychological evidence supporting this conclusion. This is evidenced by the reports of the experts:

---

179 Ibid.
180 Ibid., n. 17.
181 Ibid., n. 18.
182 Ibid., n. 19.

> The opinion of the psychologist is drawn from a reading of the Acts: "In my opinion, the data in this case is not sufficient for a finding of absolute psychic incapacity… There is no evidence of any clinical significant psychopathology within his [Petitioner's] background... The data does not demonstrate any essential psychopathology within the Respondent... it is not possible to form an inference of absolute psychic incapacity" (I, 98).[183]

Furthermore, he provides the following testimony by another expert:

> The second Judgment refers only to the expert called in that instance, Dr. RG, a clinical psychologist. He gave his opinion from a reading of the Acts. He says: "neither the Petitioner nor the Respondent appeared to have had any thought disorder, mood imbalance or tendency to disordered behavior at the time of their marriage."[184]

The *Ponens* concludes the observations of the experts by indicating the following:

> As is evident, these views are totally inadequate to induce moral certainty in a Judge about grave lack of discretion in either party. Yet the Appeal Court comments: "One of the most helpful bits of evidence that point clearly to the lacking of due discretion on the part of both parties, is from the 2nd Instance Court Expert's report" – on which they base their decision (II, 71-72).[185]

For the *Turnus*, this is a complete indication of the lack of competency of the Judges to examine the present case. The Judges ignore the reports of the experts and the testimony of the witnesses[186] while basing their conclusion in unfounded facts. Furthermore, the *Ponens* exposes an attempt, made by the Judge Instructor of First Instance, to persuade the woman to accept that their lack of discretion of judgment was produced by an emotional decision to marry:

> (...) First he argued with her that the Petitioner's lack of discretion was shown in his stubbornness and selfishness, and that hers was shown in her having failed to appreciate the impor-

183 Ibid., n. 20.
184 Ibid., n. 22.
185 Ibid., n. 23.
186 Ibid.

> tance of these defects (I, 66-68). She replied that she realized he had faults but thought she could change them. The Judge then tried to get her to see that her lack of discretion could have consisted precisely in this. "You see, discretion means to separate things, to sort things, to sift things. Now you and he married because well you said you were in love... Were there any motives for *not* marrying?" She replies, "No I can't think of any". And he explained: "When you married with just one point of view, 'I want to get married because I am in love', you disregard all these other things that could make a marriage unhappy and unsuccessful. There is not a perfect freedom in your marriage consent, it's more of an impulse when you married just with one motive... disregarding other motives that could deter you from the marriage. So the matter of the consent is not perfectly free; that is what he's claiming, that there was a lack of due discretion..." (ib. 66-67). The whole of this discourse has nothing to do with discretion in the canonical sense. We would add that such a mode of carrying on an interrogation is not a model of impartial instruction.[187]

Here, the *Ponens* exposes the impartiality of the Judge in instructing the case. This practice is considered unethical and provokes the nullity of the sentence due to procedural violations. Therefore, after having studied the law and the facts, the Auditors of this *Turnus* conceded a new proposition of the cause and upheld the validity of the bond:

> Ad primum: "Affirmative, seu novam causae propositionem concedendam esse, in casu"
>
> Ad secundum: "Negative, seu non constare de nullitate matrimonii, in casu"

---

187 Ibid., n. 25.

c.* Turnaturi. 19 February 1998, in *Monitor Ecclesiasticus, CXXIV* (1999), pp. 14-51.[188] *Nullitatis Matrimonii ob gravem defectum discretionis iudicii in utraque vel alterutra parte circa iura et officia matrimonialia mutuo tradenda et acceptanda (can. 1095, n. 2) et/vel ob incapacitatem utriusque vel alterutriusque partis assumendi onera coniugalia ob causas naturae psychicae (can. 1095, n. 3). Pro vinculo.

a) The Case

This decision examines the validity of the matrimonial bond between John and Jane. John was born in the United States but moved to Poland to continue with his university studies. The Parties met and fell in love. Subsequently, John returned to the United States. However, the Parties kept a long-distance relationship for over 18 months with the intention of establishing a matrimonial bond. In 1984, the Parties married in Poland and, shortly after, Jane moved to the United States. Later in the year, and although the Parties were experiencing some problems because Jane was having difficulties in adapting to the American culture, the Parties married in the Church because Jane was pregnant and they wanted their child "to be born in wedlock."

- In 1989, the Parties separated because Jane continued having problems adapting to the new culture. The civil divorce was granted in 1990.

- In 1992, John submitted his petition for a declaration of nullity without specifying any grounds.

- The Judge did not cite either of the Parties nor notified them of this process.

- The Judge, however, notified the Parties that they had 15 days to petition the Tribunal for a session for the formulation of the grounds.

- The instruction of this cause was completed before the concordance of the doubt; this practice goes against c. 1529 (n. 5).

- Only after the Respondent inquired about the grounds that the Judge notified her that: "the tentative formal grounds according to Canon Law" were "lack of due discretion of both parties" and also "lack of due competence of both parties." (n. 5).

188 This Rotal decision, which is relevant to the issue being studied did not appear in *Decisiones seu Sententiae*; however, appeared in both in Latin and English in *Monitor Ecclesiasticus*.

The Defender of the Bond suggested to the Judge to use *defective consent,* c. 1095, n. 2, as the grounds of nullity (n. 5), because:

> "Brevity of courtship – geographical separation – radical different culture and ethnic background of the couple – profoundly different concepts and expectations regarding marriage and family life – respondent's inability to cope with the sacrifice and adjustment required of her moving from Poland to the U.S. totally separated from family, culture and language" (n. 6).

The Judge established the grounds as:

> "Whether or not it can be established that the marriage of Paul and Maria is invalid by reason that both parties were incapable of contracting marriage due to a grave lack of discretion of judgment (c. 1095, 2); and/or both parties were incapable of assuming the essential obligations of marriage (c. 1095, 3)" (n. 7).

In 1994, the Judge issued an affirmative sentence.

The Respondent appealed the decision to the Apostolic Tribunal, which did not confirm the decision of First Instance, and admitted the cause to the ordinary examination of Second Instance.

b) The Law

The Ponens argues:

> "*grave lack of discretion of judgment* comes about not only if the intellective faculty of the spouse is unable to address the essential rights and obligations of marriage, but also if the faculty of the will is unable by a *free act* to give these rights and obligations as part of the mutual giving and acceptance" (coram Stankiewicz, decision 1 December 1996, no. 8). (n. 10).
>
> "*Discretion of judgment* of itself requires two things: *critical knowledge* or assessment regarding the object of consent, and *internal freedom in choosing marriage*; it is necessary that these be proportionate to the very serious essential rights and duties of marriage: (coram Pompedda, decision 21 November 1983, ib., vol. LXXV, p. 649, no. 5). (n. 10).

The *Ponens* establishes the importance of *internal freedom* in order to posit a human act. Without the adequate *internal freedom*, it is impossible for the engaged to choose marriage in a manner that is both conscious and deliberate and that allows the person to assume the essential matrimonial rights and obligations.

An incapacity, therefore, results from a grave psychic anomaly that renders the person incapable of assuming the essential matrimonial obligations: obligations that they, "*freely* and knowingly, (...) desire." (n. 11).

> "Not every *lack of discretion of judgment* brings about the nullity of the marriage, but only that which is *grave*; and its gravity is to be assessed either subjectively, taking into account the psychic condition of the spouse, or objectively, taking into account the seriousness of the conjugal *rights and obligations* which are included in the mutual giving and acceptance between the spouses (n. 12)."

The *Ponens* concludes this section by asserting that, according to Serrano's jurisprudence of 28 February 1992, whenever there is a cause concerning *lack of discretion of judgment* or incapacity *to assume* the matrimonial obligations, two factors need to be considered with the help of experts:

- There should have been *psychic causes of a serious nature* for many years previously, and certainly existing before the marriage;
- after the marriage there should not have been any other causes of significant weight which in the course of time could have led to the failure of the marriage, so that the breakdown can certainly be attributed to those things which were existing at the moment of consent (R.R. Dec, vol. LXXXIV, p. 136, no. 4) (n. 14).

c) The Argument

The *Ponens* observes the following fact concerning the "normal" practice of some United States Tribunals:

> More than once we have encountered such cases from *North America*, and we have scrupulously, in virtue of our office, encouraged those concerned *to follow the correct procedure*, but alas, it is clear today that what we have said has completely *fallen on deaf ears*.

> The most serious thing is not that these juridical warnings go unheeded, but that over and over again it is clear that there is a *lack of knowledge of procedural laws* and indeed of sacred respect for the Magisterium of the Church. (n. 15).

The *Ponens* identifies an error of the Defender of the Bond. The *Ponens* learns, from reading the Acts, that the Defender of the Bond not only advised the Judge concerning which grounds of nullity to use for the examination of the present case, but she also violated her role by stating "(...) –contrary to her function – that she did not find any 'reasonable objections to propose against the petition of the Plaintiff in this case'." (n. 16). In light of this, the *Ponens* engages in a lengthy discussion of the role of the Defender of the Bond and explains that his/her function is to assist the judge and, relying on c. 1432, he states that he/she is obliged to develop such a task in a serious manner (n. 17).

Additionally, the *Ponens* asserts that whenever there are cases concerning psychic incapacity, the Defender of the Bond must adhere to an anthropological vision of normality so as to prevent "(...) the tensions and difficulties, inevitably involved in the choice and achievement of the ideals of marriage, from being confused with the signs of a serious pathology" (n. 17).

Finally, the *Ponens* argues:

> as the decision *coram* Stankiewicz, 16 December 1994, points out, "the defender of the bond seriously harms the role entrusted to him whenever, having seen the conclusions of the expert, without any attempt at converting them into canonical categories regarding consensual incapacity... he at once dares to declare that he finds no "serious objections to an affirmative decision" (unpublished, n. 10; cf. *coram* Turnaturi, decision 24 April 1997, n. 14).

The Ponens asserted that the difficulties encountered, "(...) 'such as language, culture, distance, and time' (...) could not have affected the consensual capacity of the parties" (n. 19). He explains:

> A *lack of discretion of judgment* can arise form dysfunction in the area of intellect or will, but not from insufficient or non-existent knowledge of every personal family circumstance, unless it is shown that such absence of knowledge in one or both of the spouses resulted from a *disordered psychic constitution* or a *lack of internal freedom* (n. 20).

In the end, the *Ponens* upholds the validity of the bond.

Concluding Remarks

A quick examination of Rotal decisions reveal that numerous Rotal Judges have constantly admonished different American Tribunals and have questioned their practices. For instance:

a) *c.* Turnaturi, 19 February 1998, in *Monitor Ecclesiasticus, CXXIV* (1999), pp. 14-51:
- Asserts that North American tribunal ministers lack knowledge of procedural laws, n. 15
- The Defender of the Bond advises the judges on what ground of nullity to use, n. 16
- The Defender of the Bond does not object to the nullity of the bond, n. 16

b) *c.* Stankiewicz, 26 June 2003, in *Decisiones seu Sententiae, XCV* (2003), pp. 424-438.
- Observes countless violations regarding the procedure by the judges of First Instance, such as:
  1. The Parties were not granted the right to inspect the Acts after the investigation was completed, n. 3
  2. The Respondent was not cited, n. 2
  3. The decision was not communicated to the Respondent, n. 2

c) *c.* Boccafola, 25 June 1990, in *Decisiones seu Sententiae, LXXXII* (1990), pp. 558-571 :
- Indicates that the expert of First Instance composed a report "out of thin air" in order to support his claims for lack of discretion, n. 12

d) *c.* Burke, 22 July 1991, in *Decisiones seu Sententia, LXXXIII* (1991), pp. 500-508:
- Observes that the judge tended to equate impulsivity with lack of discretion, n. 16
- Asserts that the Defender of the Bond supported the allegations against the bond, n. 17

e) *c.* Burke, 7 December 1995, in *Decisiones seu Sententiae, LXXXVII* (1995), pp. 676-684:
- Finds that the judges in lower courts have a defective understanding of discretion of judgment, n. 12
- The judge issued the decision without consulting an expert, n. 17

f) *c.* Serrano-Ruiz, 11 April 1997, in *Decisiones seu Sententiae, LXXXIX* (1997), pp. 265-278:
- Observes that the Defender of the Bond did not sing nor dated the investigations conducted, n. 10
- Asserts that the previous Courts made false assertions concerning the capacity of the Respondent, n. 10

After reviewing the decisions issued by American Tribunals, it seems to me that the problem lies in the fact that tribunal ministers would like to take a more pastoral approach when dealing with the invalidity of the matrimonial bond. This may be the reason why sometimes tribunal ministers provide a declaration of nullity without having any concrete proofs. This issue becomes even more problematic when the tribunal ministers feel a responsibility "to help the faithful to continue in the Church," "to regularize their situation," or "to help them live a sacramental life."

Although these are good intentions, it is important to assert that tribunal ministers must approach the investigation of nullity with a compassionate heart, but with their eyes intent on seeking the truth of the bond. When the tribunal minister is moved solely by compassion, their decisions may be based on a false pastoral sense and their unjust decrees of nullity would lead the faithful to sin.

John Paul II addressed this issue in his speech to the Roman Rota in 1990:

> Such an unjust declaration of nullity would find no legitimate support in appealing to love or mercy. Love and mercy cannot put aside the demands of truth. A valid marriage, even one marked by serious difficulties, could not be considered invalid without doing violence to the truth and undermining thereby the only solid foundation which can support personal, marital, and social life. A judge, therefore, must always be on guard against the risk of false compassion that would degenerate into sentimentality, and would be pastoral appearance alone. The roads leading away from justice and truth end up in serving to distance people from God, thus yielding the opposite result from that which was sought in good faith. (n. 5).

In order to ensure that our decisions are just and merciful, tribunal ministers must keep in mind that according to Rotal Jurisprudence, which serve as a guide to lower tribunals, "grave lack of discretion of judgment":

a) Is a juridical concept (*cfr.* *c.* Civili, 7 November 1996; *c.* Boccafola, 9 December 1999).

b) Must be grave and it must proceed from a psychic anomaly (*cfr.* c. Bruno, 22 July 1988)

c) Must affect, substantially, the capacity of the engaged to understand and to want (*cfr.* John Paul II, Speech to the Roman Rota, 1987)

d) Must be present at the moment of the wedding, at least in a latent stage (*cfr*. c. Boccafola, 25 June 1990).

SEMINAR

TO CARE FOR CHURCH PROPERTY TODAY: CANONICAL RESPONSES TO COMMON CONTEMPORARY CHALLENGES

Reverend Monsignor John A. Renken

Introduction

I begin with a very sincere word of thanks to the leadership of the CLSA for the invitation to share some reflections with you today on canonical responses to some common contemporary challenges in the care of Church property. In the fifty years since the end of Vatican Council II, there certainly have been numerous modifications in the manner of caring for ecclesiastical goods: most of these modifications are expressed in the norms of the 1983 Code. Indeed, I would propose that today's greatest common challenge in caring for Church property is the proper implementation of existing canon law concerning such property.

In today's seminar, we will focus on the following eight topics which, I would suggest, need further consideration in many parts of the Church. These topics identify some challenges in the care of Church property. I hope that our identification of these topics, and some canonical reflections on each of them, will assist the Church in its essential task of evangelization, that is, in proclaiming the Gospel of mercy, in the world today. The eight topics are:

1. the four-fold relationships of the Church to temporal goods (acquisition, retention, administration, alienation);
2. collaboration with others in acquisition, retention, administration, and alienation of goods;
3. the "protective" notion of stable patrimony and its legitimate designation;
4. acts of extraordinary administration *iure universali* and *iure particulari*;
5. canon 1295 transactions;
6. the establishment, modifications, and civil incorporation of public juridic persons;
7. diocesan particular law and special instructions governing the care of Church property;
8. the delict of financial malfeasance.

I propose these topics today in light of my own research over the past decade as professor of temporal goods at Saint Paul University, Ottawa, and on countless discussions with those involved in implementing canon law on ecclesiastical goods. One or two things which I will mention may prompt further discussions among canonists (e.g., what constitutes acts of retention, the nature of the act whereby stable patrimony becomes non-stable patrimony, etc.) Some things may be insights that will help in a more accurate understanding and implementation of the existing law (e.g., the scope of canon 1295). Most of the following, however, may simply encourage a fuller implementation of the *ius vigens* on Church property: this implementation is certainly our noble common task.

The following reflections concern public juridic persons (c. 116) whose temporal goods are assigned the technical term, "ecclesiastical goods" (c. 1257 §1). Much focus will be on dioceses and parishes (which are the most numerous public juridic persons in the whole Church).

1 – The Four-fold Relationships of the Church to Temporal Goods (Acquisition, Retention, Administration, Alienation)[1]

The 1917 Code identified three relationships of the Church to temporal goods: acquisition, retention, and administration (*CIC/17*, c. 1495 §1). The 1983 Code adds a fourth relationship: alienation (*CIC/83*, c. 1254 §1; see c. 1255). On 19 June 1979, by a vote of 5 (for) to 1 (against), the *coetus De bonis Ecclesiae temporalibus* added this precise fourth relationship. One consultative body on the 1975 *Schema* had suggested that alienation be specified as a distinct relationship of the Church to temporal goods, because "*alienatio non est actus*

1 This first section reflects a study entitled "Acts of the Church in Relation to Temporal Goods: The Ordinary and the Extraordinary," to be published in *Studia canonica*, 50 (2016).

administrationis."[2] Under the 1917 Code, alienation had been considered an act of *extraordinary* administration.[3]

Properly, today we speak of four distinct relations of the Church to temporal goods: (1) acquisition; (2) retention;[4] (3) administration; and (4) alienation. Canonical exactness and precision dictate that we be careful to distinguish these four relations properly. "To acquire" means to obtain ownership of goods. "To retain" means to keep goods as possessors. "To administer" means to use goods for their proper purposes, to lead them to bear fruit. "To alienate" means to lose ownership of goods, to convey them to other owners.

These four acts (acquisition, retention, administration, and alienation) are performed by the administrator of the public juridic person to which the temporal goods pertain. Most commonly, all these acts are "*ordinary*," but sometimes an act is "*extraordinary*." An act is *extraordinary* when the administrator[5] needs the

---

2 The report of the meeting explains: "De sententia unius Organi consultationis addi debet in canone: '...administrare *et alienare* valent...', quia alienatio non est actus administrationis. Hanc sententiam avent duo Consultores, dum alii duo sunt contradi, quia alienatio non est nisi actus administrationis etsi extraordinariae. Fit suffragatio an placeat addere verbum 'alienare': placet 5, non placet 1." *Communicationes*, 12 (1980) 396.

3 Interestingly, some commentators in the past (and even a few commentators today still) had identified a canon 1295 transaction as an act of alienation *sensu lato*, although indeed it is not an act of alienation but instead an act of *extraordinary* administration. The commentators had based their terminology in *CIC/1917* canon 1533 (which corresponds to *CIC/1983* canon 1295) which distinguished alienation properly so called (*alienatio proprie dicta*) but and contracts which can worsen the condition of the Church (implicitly, *alienatio sensu lato*). The former was a true act of alienation whereby ownership was passed to another; the latter was *not* an act of alienation but instead an act of *extraordinary* administration *by its very nature*. Such imprecision should be avoided. Alienation always and only involves the transfer of ownership to another; an act of administration never does.

4 Canon 1 (from which developed promulgated canon 1254 §1) of the 1977 *Schema Libri V De iure patrimoniali Ecclesiae* had used the term *retinere*, but canon 2 (from which developed promulgated canon 1254 §2) had used the term *possidere*. On 19 June 1979, the *coetus De bonis Ecclesiae temporalibus* stated its clear preference for the term *retinere*, and said it should replace *possidere* in other canons. *Communicationes*, 12 (1980) 396.

Nonetheless, canon 634 §1 uses *possidere* (not *retinere*) in relation to religious institutes. There is no obvious difference between *retinere* and *possidere*: both intend to convey the same notion.

5 It would be helpful to recall the distinction between terms with the same basic root: administrator, act of administration, and administrative act. An *administrator* is the physical person who acts on behalf of a public juridic person (c. 1279 §1). An *act of administration* is the activity of the administrator which intends to use ecclesiastical goods for their proper purposes, to lead them to bear fruit. An *administrative act* is a singular act issued by a competent person with executive authority in the form of a decree, a precept, or a rescript (c. 35; see cc. 26-93).

involvement of one or more other physical persons, whether as individuals or as members of group, in order to perform the act according to the law.

1.1 – Acts of Acquisition

"Acts of acquisition" are acts whereby a juridic person obtains the ownership of temporal goods through "just means of natural or positive law permitted to others" (c. 1259). If temporal goods are acquired by the universal Church, the Apostolic See, or a public juridic person, these temporal goods are then known as "ecclesiastical goods" (c. 1257). Book V identifies several different kinds of acts of acquisition whereby revenue is obtained, most of which are acts of ordinary acquisition. These acts of *ordinary* acquisition concern:

1. appeals (c. 1262)
2. fees for acts of executive power (c. 1264, 1°)
3. fees for the execution of rescripts (c. 1264, 1°)
4. offerings for the administration of sacraments and sacramentals (c. 1264, 2°)
5. special collections: parochial, diocesan, national, universal (c. 1266)
6. prescription (cc. 1268-1270)
7. diocesan assistance to the Apostolic See (c. 1271)
8. benefices, where they still exist (c. 1272)
9. pious trusts (c. 1302)

Other acts of ordinary acquisition, found elsewhere in the Code, involve:

1. "stole fees" (cc. 531, 551)
2. Mass offerings (cc. 945-958)
3. tribunal fees (cc. 1649)

Interestingly, the Code does not make specific reference to so-called "Sunday collections." Nonetheless, it explains that the diocesan bishop is bound to admonish the faithful to give their temporal goods for the benefit of the Church (c. 1261).

In addition, the Code also identifies some acts of *extraordinary* acquisition. Before one can perform such acts, the involvement of others is required. Acts of extraordinary acquisition are:

1. to impose diocesan taxes, ordinary and extraordinary (c. 1263) – the diocesan bishop must receive the *counsel* of the diocesan finance council and the presbyteral council before imposing a diocesan tax
2. to beg for alms (c. 1265) – one's own ordinary and the local

ordinary must give *written permission* before one begs for alms

3. to accept gifts with a modal obligation or condition attached (c. 1267 §2) – the ordinary must give *permission* before the administrator accepts a gift burdened by a modal obligation or a condition[6]
4. to accept non-autonomous foundation (c. 1304 §1) – the ordinary must give *permission* for the acceptance of a non-autonomous foundation

1.2 – Acts of Retention

While the retention of ecclesiastical goods is mentioned in both *CIC/17* canon 1495 § 1 and *CIC/83* canon 1254 § 1, canonists seem not to identify any specific "acts of retention." Perhaps retention is simply considered the common and constant responsibility of church administrators in the handling of all goods once they have been acquired. Perhaps all acts of administration are so certainly considered as acts intended to hold onto ecclesiastical goods that "acts of retention" and "acts of administration" are almost synonyms: both intend to safeguard all the goods which have been legitimately acquired by the Church.

Nonetheless, it seems to me that there are certain acts, performed by the administrator of a public juridic person, which are performed *precisely* in order that some ecclesiastical goods be safeguarded. Indeed, the Code itself distinguishes "retention" from other acts related to the ownership of temporal goods. We have just seen that the *coetus De bonis Ecclesiae temporalibus* determined that acts of alienation are to be distinguished from the many acts of administration; I would propose that acts of retention should be distinguished similarly.

Some acts of retention are considered *permanent* acts of retention (which intend to assure the retention of an ecclesiastical good perpetually, or at least for a long period of time), and others are *temporary* acts of retention (which intend to assure the retention of an ecclesiastical good for a lesser period of time).

I would hope that dialogue will continue among canonists from which will emerge a consensus on those activities of the administrator of public juridic persons which constitute "acts of retention."

---

6 Robert T. Kennedy distinguishes between a gift with a modal obligation and one with an attached condition: "A modal obligation, according to Roman law whence the term is derived, is an obligation undertaken at the time of accepting a gift which is enforceable against the donee but the breach of which does not result in reversion of the gift to the donor. A conditional gift, on the other hand, conditions transfer of ownership upon fulfillment of the condition; breach results in a reversion of ownership to the donor." "The Temporal Goods of the Church," in John P. Beal, James A. Coriden, and Thomas J. Green (eds.), *New Commentary on the Code of Canon Law*, commissioned by the Canon Law Society of America [= *New Commentary*] (Mahwah, NJ: Paulist Press, 2000) 1469.

1.2.1 – *Permanent* Acts of Retention

One permanent "act of retention" is the legitimate designation of stable patrimony. Stable patrimony, as we will discuss further below, consists of those ecclesiastical goods which form the secure foundation which enables the public juridic person to continue to exist, performing its proper purpose. The legitimate designation of stable patrimony is the preeminent act of retention whereby the administrator clearly, firmly, and permanently retains select ecclesiastical goods in order to ensure the future existence and operation of the public juridic person.

It also seems that other acts, commonly understood to be acts of administration, are indeed permanent acts of retention. Examples of these permanent acts of retention are:

1. to establish the funds for clergy support, clergy social benefits, and other purposes (cc. 1274-1275)
2. to assure that the ownership of ecclesiastical goods is protected by civilly valid methods (c. 1284 §2, 2°)
3. to observe prescripts of canon law, civil law, founders, donors, or legitimate authority, especially so that no damage comes to the Church from the non-observance of civil laws (c. 1284 §2, 3°)
4. to erect an autonomous pious foundation (c. 1303 §1, 1°)

None of these *permanent* acts of retention are *extraordinary* since none require the involvement of others before the administrator of the public juridic person can perform them.

1.2.2 – *Temporary* Acts of Retention

In addition, the Code identifies certain acts of retention which are *temporary*. These acts include:

1. to collect the return of goods and income accurately and on time, to protect what is collected… (c. 1284 §2, 4°)
2. to accept a trust and to safeguard its goods (c. 1302; see c. 1303 §1, 2°, 1302)
3. to reduce Mass obligations, for a just and necessary cause, according to the norms of law (c. 1308)

4. to reduce, moderate, or commute the wills of the faithful for pious causes, for a just and necessary cause, according to the norms of law (c. 1310)

None of these *temporary* acts of retention are *extraordinary* since none require the involvement of others before the competent authority or administrator can perform them. The following *temporary* acts of retention, however, are acts of *extraordinary* retention since they *do* require the involvement of the ordinary before the administrator can act:

1. to invest surplus funds (c. 1284 §2, 6°) – which requires the *consent* of the ordinary
2. to accept a non-autonomous pious foundation (c. 1303 §1, 2°; 1304 §1) – which requires the *written permission* of the ordinary
3. to invest the goods of an endowment (c. 1305; see c. 1303 §1, 1°) – which requires the *prudent judgment (prudens iudicium)*, that is, the direction, of the ordinary after he has heard those concerned and his own finance council

1.2.3 – Acts of Administration Closely Related to Acts of Retention

The Code identifies several acts of administration which are very closely related to acts of retention. These acts of (ordinary) administration are intended to assure the continued safeguarding of ecclesiastical goods which are already retained. These acts of administration include:

1. to exercise careful vigilance over the administration of all goods belonging to public juridic persons (done by the ordinary: c. 1276 §1; see c. 1278)
2. to issue special instructions ordering the entire matter of the administration of ecclesiastical goods (done by the ordinary: c. 1276 §2)
3. to prepare and to retain regularly updated inventories of ecclesiastical goods (c. 1283, 2°-3°)
4. to exercise vigilance so that ecclesiastical goods entrusted to them are not lost or damaged (c. 1284 §2, 1°)
5. to take out insurance policies to take care that ecclesiastical goods are not lost or damaged (c. 1284 §2, 1°)
6. to keep well organized records of receipts and expenses (c. 1284 §2, 7°)
7. to organize correctly and protecting in a suitable and proper archive the documents and records on which the property rights of the Church or institute are based, and depositing authentic copies of them in the archive of the appropriate curia (c. 1284 §2, 9°)

8. to put into writing the establishment of a foundation, and to preserve records of it (c. 1306).

1.3 – Acts of Administration

Book V identifies multiple acts of administration, particularly in its Title II. In fact, the Code identifies more acts of administration than it does acts of acquisition, acts of retention, and acts of alienation.

Indeed, the Code distinguishes three categories of acts of administration: acts of *ordinary* administration; acts of *extraordinary* administration; and, **for dioceses *only***, acts of *ordinary administration more important in light of the economic condition of the diocese.* And, the Code requires that particular law identify the latter two types of acts of administration (the Code does *not* require that particular law identify any acts of acquisition, acts of retention, or acts of alienation).

We will give further consideration to acts of *extraordinary* administration below.

1.4 – Acts of Alienation

The Code provides universal norms for the act of alienation of stable patrimony in canons 1291-1294, 638 §3, and 741 §1. While the acts of acquisition, retention, and administration involve various distinct activities, all acts of alienation involve one thing activity: the conveyance of ownership of ecclesiastical goods to another person, juridic or physical.

We can distinguish between acts of *ordinary* alienation and acts of *extraordinary* alienation.

For all public juridic persons: acts of *ordinary* alienation involve *all* non-stable patrimony which has not been given to the Church by a vow, and which is not precious for artistic or historic reasons.

For public juridic persons other than religious institutes and societies of apostolic life: acts of *ordinary* administration also involve *all* stable patrimony valued below the minimum amount established by law which has not been given to the Church by vow, and which is not precious for artistic or historic reasons. Acts of *extraordinary* alienation involve the alienation of stable patrimony valued above the minimum amount established by law (c. 1292 §1), goods given to the Church by a vow (c. 1292 §2), and goods precious for artistic or historical reasons (c.

1292 §2).[7] Those who must give consent before the administrator can perform an act of *extraordinary* alienation are identified in canon 1292 §§ 1-2.

For a religious institute or a society of apostolic life: acts of *extraordinary* alienation involve everything other than non-stable patrimony which has not been given to the Church by a vow, and which is not precious for artistic or historic reasons. These acts of extraordinary alienation require the *written permission of the competent superior with the consent of the council.* Furthermore, if the stable patrimony is valued beyond the amount defined by the Holy See for the region, or if the property is goods given to the Church by a vow or goods precious for artistic or historic reasons, the *permission of the Holy See* is also (*insuper*) required (cc. 638 §3, 741 §1).

2 – Collaboration with Others in the Acquisition, Retention, Administration, and Alienation of Goods

The Code expects that the Church's proper care of temporal goods involves more than only that single physical person who is the administrator of the public juridic person.

Sometimes, the Code requires the involvement of several physical persons together assisting the administrator of a public juridic person. For example, it requires that a finance council exist in every diocese (c. 492 §1) and parish (c. 537),[8] and in every other juridic person (c. 1280, which allows statutes of a juridic person, other than a diocese or parish, to replace a finance council with at least two financial counselors). Moreover, for the public juridic person of the diocese, the law occasionally requires the diocesan bishop to involve also the college of consultors or the presbyteral council before he performs some specific *extraordinary* acts involving temporal goods.

Sometimes, the Code requires the involvement of a single physical person assisting the administrator of a public juridic person. For example, it requires each diocese to have a finance officer (c. 494 §1) who administers the ecclesiastical goods of the diocese under the authority of the diocesan bishop (c. 494 §3). And, it requires each religious institute and province to have a finance officer distinct

7 Nothing prevents the establishment of other acts of *extraordinary* alienation by particular law. Should such acts be thus established, the particular law will identify the others to be involved before the administrator can perform the act of alienation.

8 Canon 537 says the parish finance council assists the *parochus* in the administration of parochial goods, without prejudice to canon 532 which says that the *parochus* administers the goods of the parish in accord with the norm of canons 1281-1288. Francesco Coccopalmerio observes that the role of the *parochus* as the administrator of parish property involves the entire discipline of Book V, not only that of canons 1281-1288. *De paroecia* (Rome, Editrice Pontificia Università Gregoriana, 1991) 204. Similarly, one would expect that the parish finance council assists him also in the acquisition, retention, and alienation of temporal goods belonging to the parish.

from the major superior; similarly, insofar as possible, a finance officer distinct from the local superior is to be designated even in local communities (c. 636 §1). These requirements also pertain to societies of apostolic life (c. 742 §1). Also, the law occasionally requires the involvement of "those concerned" (cc. 1292 §1, 1305, 1310 §2).

All collaboration with others (whether in groups or as individuals) certainly demands a full transparency: that is, a full disclosure of all related information needed to elicit informed counsel or consent. Such transparency is mandated in canon 1292 §4 of the Code for acts of *extraordinary* alienation of stable patrimony:

> Those who by advice or consent must take part in alienating goods are not to offer advice or consent unless they have first been thoroughly informed both of the economic state of the juridic person whose goods are proposed for alienation and of previous alienations.

There is every reason to expect that this kind of "full disclosure" would be presented by the competent ecclesiastical authority to all groups and individuals who collaborate *also* in the acquisition, retention, and administration of temporal goods. Otherwise, collaborators may have the impression that they are being manipulated or that they are perceived as incapable of responsible assistance. Indeed, one may even suggest that otherwise real collaboration is impossible.

3 – The "Protective" Notion of Stable Patrimony and Its Legitimate Designation

3.1 – The Notion of Stable Patrimony

CIC/1917 canon 1497 had identified several categories of temporal goods: corporeal (immovable and movable), incorporeal, sacred (and non-sacred), precious (and non-precious). An exactly corresponding canon does not exist in the 1983 Code, but the categories identified in the first Code continue to pertain in the current Code (e.g., cc. 638 §3; 1171; 1220 §2; 1270; 1283, 2°; 1285; 1292; 1302, §1; 1305).

The 1983 Code introduces a *new* and *fundamental* category of *all* ecclesiastical goods: all ecclesiastical goods are either *stable patrimony* or *non-stable patrimony*.[9] The development of this fundamental category is rooted in the process

9 For further study of the history of the development of "stable patrimony" in the 1983 Code, and of the meaning of the term as understood by canonical commentators, see John A. Renken, "The Stable Patrimony of Public Juridic Persons," in *The Jurist*, 70 (2010) 131-162.

of the revision in *CIC/1917* canon 1530 §1 (from which developed canon 1291) which had identified the requirements for alienation of "immovable ecclesiastical goods and movable ecclesiastical goods which can be saved by preserving them" (*res ecclesiasticas immobiles et mobiles, quae servando servari possunt*).[10] The first mention of the concept of "stable patrimony" occurred during the afternoon of 13 May 1968 when one consultor of the *coetus De bonis Ecclesiae temporalibus* suggested that these words be replaced with "goods which pertain stably and legitimately to the patrimony of some moral ecclesiastical person." He explained his rationale: the purpose of the law is not to hinder the alienation of those things which can be saved by preserving them, but instead to exercise caution lest the stable patrimony of the Church be imprudently dissipated by administrators. He added that money, for example, is a movable good can be saved by preserving it; nonetheless, it remains alienable without the prescribed solemnities until, through a legitimate act, it becomes part of the stable patrimony of the Church. This proposition was generally pleasing to the other consultors.[11] Thereafter, the *relator*, Hercules Crovella, proposed the following formula: "To alienate goods, which by legitimate designation constitute the stable patrimony of some moral ecclesiastical person, requires...." The *relator*'s proposal was pleasing to all the consultors.[12] That afternoon the *coetus* continued to discuss the revision of *CIC/1917* canon 1530, and completed the formula which had been introduced that morning. The entire proposed formula stated: "To alienate goods which by legitimate designation constitute the stable patrimony of some moral ecclesiastical person, requires the consent of the legitimate superior, without which the alienation is invalid."[13]

The term "stable patrimony" occurs twice in the 1983 Code. Canon 1291, concerning alienation, states:

> The permission of the authority competent according to the norm of law is required for the valid alienation of goods which constitute by legitimate designation the stable patrimony of a

10 The Latin phrase is admittedly difficult to translate. The author is indebted to Dr. Pierre Bellemare, professor of Latin at Saint Paul University, Ottawa, for assistance. Obviously, the phrase "*quae servando servari possunt*" is a reference only to the *res mobiles*. This is consistent with authors, including: F. Wernz and P. Vidal, *Ius canonicum*, vol. 4: *De rebus* (Rome: Gregorian University, 1935) 225-226; S. Sipos, *Enchiridion iuris canonici* (Rome: Herder, 1954) 697-698; Stanislaus Woywood and Callistus Smith, *A Practical Commentary on the Code of Canon Law*, 2 vols. (New York, NY: Joseph F. Wagner, 1948) vol. 2, 207-208.

Some movable goods cannot be saved because they are not preserved: i.e., they are fungible, which means they are consumed in their very use.

11 *Communicationes*, 37 (2005) 120-121.

12 *Communicationes*, 37 (2005) 121.

13 *Communicationes*, 37 (2005) 123; see ibid., 36: "Can. 1530. Ad alienda bona quae alicuius personae moralis ecclesiae ex legitima assignatione patrimonium stabile constituunt, requiritur consensus legitimi superioris, sine quo alienatio invalida est."

> public juridic person and whose value exceeds the sum defined by law.

Canon 1285, concerning donations by juridic persons, states:

> Within the limits of ordinary administration only, administrators are permitted to make donations for purposes of piety or Christian charity from movable goods which do not belong to the stable patrimony.

Further, canon 1295 makes reference to the "patrimonial condition" of a juridic person, which can be threatened by some contracts; this is undoubtedly a reference to stable patrimony. (Canon 1295 will be discussed in more detail later.) And, canon 1283, 3° says that changes in the "patrimony" of a public juridic person are to be identified in regularly updated inventories; indeed, *CCEO* canon 1026 (which corresponds to Latin canon 1283, 3°) makes specific reference to the noting in updated inventories of any changes in the "*stable* patrimony" of each juridic person.[14]

Numerous canonists have offered reflections on the meaning of stable patrimony.[15] To summarize their wisdom, we can responsibly state:

> Stable patrimony consists of those ecclesiastical goods (moveable corporeal, non-moveable corporeal, and non-corporeal) which, through legitimate designation, form a secure basis which provides for the continued and effective operation of the public juridic person.

---

14 Although the *CIC* does not include the adjective *stable* to modify *patrimony* in canon 1283, 3° (unlike the *CCEO* in canon 1026), its implication is obvious.

15 See, for example: Robert T. Kennedy, *New Commentary,* 1495-1496; Mariano López Alarcón, "Book V: The Temporal Goods of the Church," in Ernest Caparros and Hélène Aubé (eds.), *Code of Canon Law Annotated*, 2nd rev. ed. [= *Annotated*] (Montréal: Wilson and Lafleur, 2004) 993; Vittorio Palestro, "La disciplina canonica in materia di alienzatione e di locazione (cann. 1291-1298)" in *I Beni temporali della Chiesa* (Studi Giuridici, 50, Vatican City: Libreria Editrice Vaticana, 1999) 147; Diego Zalbidea, *El control de las enajenaciones de bienes eclesiásticos: El patrimonio estable* (Navarra: Editiones Universidad de Navarra, 2008) 109.

See also Conferenza Episcopale Italiana, "Istruzione in materia amministrativa (2005)," testo approvato dalla 54a Assemblea Generale, Roma (30-31 May 2005), art. 53.

For commentary during the 1917 Code, see: William J. Doheny, *Practical Problems in Church Finance* (Milwaukee, Bruce, 1941) 43; Arturo Araoz Tabera, *Il diritto dei religiosi* (Rome: Commentarium pro Religiosis, 1961) 191.

3.2 – The Methods of "Legitimate Designation" of Stable Patrimony

On 13 May 1968, that day when "stable patrimony" was first introduced among the members of the *coetus De bonis Ecclesiae temporalibus*, one consultor asked the fellow consultor (who had first proposed the phrase "goods which pertain stably and legitimately to the patrimony of some moral ecclesiastical person") his rationale for including the word "legitimately." The proponent replied that *CIC/1917* canon 1523, 4° (as it had been revised by then)[16] required the consent of the ordinary before excess funds are usefully set aside, that is, it required that excess funds be set aside usefully *by a legitimate act*. After this *legitimate* disposition, such excess funds pertain stably to the patrimony of the Church, such that they cannot be alienated without the solemnities prescribed. The secretary of the *coetus*, Raymond Bidagor, supported this reasoning, and mentioned as an example that donated goods can be used either in ordinary administration or extraordinary administration: for extraordinary administration, however, as in the case of increasing patrimony, the consent of the ordinary is required; such is rightly described as being done "legitimately."

Several canonists have identified the legitimate designation of stable patrimony as an act of extraordinary administration. I would imagine that these canonists base their identification in the comment of Raymond Bidagor, immediately above. Leading the contemporary canonists who identify designating stable

16 *1917/CIC* canon 1523, 4° had said that administrators must "with the consent of the ordinary, invest the money of the church which is left over after expenses and can be usefully set aside to the profit of the same church" ("pecuniam ecclesiae, quae de expensis supersit et utiliter collocari potest, de consensu Ordinarii, in emolumentum ipsius ecclesiae occupare"). With minor modifications, it became the new canon 1523, 5° in the preliminary formula proposed by the relator of the *coetus*. Eventually, in the promulgated law, it became canon 1284 §2, 6°, which says that administrators must "with the consent of the ordinary, invest the money which is left over after expenses and can be usefully set aside for the purposes of the juridic person" ("pecuniam, quae de expensis supersit et utiliter collocari possit, de consensu Ordinarii in fines personae iuridicae occupare"). *Communicationes* 36 (2004) 331; see ibid., 317-319.

patrimony as an act of extraordinary administration is Velasio DePaolis.[17] Many others have followed his reasoning, myself included.[18] Upon further reflection, however, it seems that the legitimate designation of stable patrimony is *not* an act of extraordinary administration, but instead an act of retention.

Without doubt an ecclesiastical good can be *implicitly* designated as stable patrimony by reason of its permanent purpose: e.g., the property on which a religious edifice is erected and the building itself. This implicit designation is clearly not an act of extraordinary administration, as the term is properly understood.

---

17 See Velasio DePaolis, *De bonis Ecclesiae temporalibus*, 101; idem, "Negozio giuidico, 'quo conditio patrimonialis personae iuridicae peior fieri possit' (cf. c. 1295)," in *Periodica*, 83 (1994) 523; idem., *I beni temporali della Chiesa* (Bologna, Dehoniane, 1995) 198. Also contending that the legitimate designation of stable patrimony is an act of extraordinary administration are: Nicholas P. Cafardi, "Alienation of Church Property," in Kevin E. McKenna, Lawrence A. DiNardo, and Joseph W. Pokusa (eds.), *Church Finance Handbook* [= *Handbook*] Washington, DC: Canon Law Society of America, 1999) 251, see 249; Francesco Grazian, "Patrimonio stabile: istituto dimenticato?" in *Quaderni di diritto ecclesiale*, 16 (2003) 288; Mariano López Alarcón, *Annotataed*, S997-998; Joaquín Mantecón, "Commentary on Canon 1291," in Ángel Marzoa, Jorge Miras and Rafael Rodrígues-Ocaña (eds.), *Exegetical Commentary on the Code of Canon Law*, Ernest Caparros (Eng. ed.), 5 vols. [= *Exegetical*] ,(Chicago, IL: Midwest Theological Forum, 2004) vol. 4/1, 131; Jean-Claud Périsset, *Les biens temporels de l'Église* (Paris: Éditions Tardif, 1996) 200; Alberto Perlasca, "Commentary on Canon 1291," in *Redazione di Quaderni di Diritto Ecclesiale, Codice di diritto canonico commentato,* 3rd ed. (Milan: Ancora, 2009) 1025; Stefano Ridella, *La valida alienazione dei beni ecclesiastici: Prospettive di diritto canonico e civile* (Estratto della dissertazione dottorate, Rome: Università pontificia salesiana, 2001) 36; idem, *La valida alienazione dei beni ecclesiastici: Uno studio a partie dai cann. 1291-1294 CIC* (Rome, LAS, 2010) 117; Jean-Pierre Schouppe, *Droit canonique des biens* (Montréal: Wilson and Lafleur, 2008) 156; Diego Zalbidea, "El patrimonio estable en el CIC de 1983," in *Ius canonicum*, 47 (2007) 586-587; idem, *El control de las enajenaciones de bienes eclesiásticos. El patrimonio estable* (Pamplona: EUNSA, 2008) 116-119.

Other canonists, however, do not comment that the legitimate designation of stable patrimony is an act of extraordinary administration: e.g., see: Robert T. Kennedy, *New Commentary*,1495-1496; Francis G. Morrisey, "Commentary on Canon 1291," in Gerard Sheehy, et al. (eds.), *The Canon Law: Letter and Spirit* (Collegeville: The Liturgical Press, 1995) 732-733; idem, "The Alienation of Temporal Goods in Contemporary Practice," in *Studia canonica*, 29 (1995) 300; Vittorio Palestro, 147; Jean-Pierre Schouppe, 157.

Indeed, the designation of stable patrimony is not precisely identified as an act of extraordinary administration in Conferenza Episcopale Italiana, *Istruzione in materia amministrativa 2005*, n 53; see nn. 61-62. Available at: http://www.olir.it/areetematiche/86/documents/CEI_Istruzione_materia_amministrativa_2005.pdf

18 See, for example, John A. Renken, *Church Property*, 227; idem, The Stable Patrimony of Public Juridic Persons," 161; idem, "The Statutes of a Parish," *Studia canonica*, 44 (2010) 140.

Moreover, when the administrator of a public juridic person *explicitly* designates some ecclesiastical goods as stable patrimony, it does not seem that the administrator is performing an act of extraordinary administration. The Code itself does not precisely designate the legitimate designation of stable patrimony as an act of extraordinary administration (that is to say, it does not require the involvement of any other authority before an administrator makes this legitimate designation). Indeed, common sense would seem to urge the conclusion that the legitimate designation of stable patrimony does not exceed the manner or limits of ordinary administration: put simply, the legitimate designation is common and routine, not rare and exceptional! Some special faculty (i.e., a power to act) is not needed to perform this protective act (see c. 1281 §1).

My own conclusion (admittedly, a change from my earlier views, and a conclusion rather firmly held by me now) is that the legitimate designation of stable patrimony, whether *implicitly* or *explicitly*, is always an *act of ordinary retention*, performed by the administrator of the public juridic person.

Further, it would seem that making stable patrimony into non-stable patrimony should be considered, by its nature, to be an act of extraordinary administration. After all, the notion of stable patrimony was introduced into the 1983 Code in an effort to safeguard ecclesiastical goods, intended for the long-term existence of a public juridic person, from loss through the irresponsible acts of its administrator through alienation (see c. 1291). *Mutatis mutandis* and by analogy, it follows that, inasmuch converting stable patrimony into non-stable patrimony subjects it to loss through routine acts of administration (e.g., paying bills, making purchases, etc.), the conversion itself should be considered so significant an act of administration that it would require the prior written consent of the ordinary – that is, that it would be an act of extraordinary administration by its very nature. It would be helpful if the universal law would *expressly* require permission of higher competent ecclesiastical authority for the conversion of stable patrimony into non-stable patrimony.

I realize that these thoughts counter positions held by many learned and eminent canonists. I present my opinions here in the hope that perhaps further dialogue will ensue concerning both the concept of stable patrimony and, more significantly, the kind the act by which it is legitimately designated by the administrator of the public juridic person, and the kind of act by which it is converted back to non-stable patrimony.

3.3 – Summary: The Legitimate Designation of Stable Patrimony

In light of the preceding reflections about stable patrimony, even though further reflections would be welcome from scholars of the law as just mentioned, I propose that some conclusions about stable patrimony can be made responsibly and accurately:[19]

1. Every juridic person must have the capacity to possess stable patrimony, as implied in the very wording of canons 1285, 1291, and 1295.[20] This is consistent with the norm of canon 114 §3 which says competent ecclesiastical authority can confer juridic personality only on aggregates of persons (*universitates personarum*) or aggregates of things (*universitates rerum*), which pursue a truly useful purpose and, all things considered, possess the means which are foreseen to be sufficient to achieve their designated purpose." Stable patrimony provides the self-sufficient means to achieve perpetually the designated purpose of the juridic person.

2. Stable patrimony comes into existence by lawful designation (c. 1291), implicit or explicit:
   a. Some stable patrimony is legitimately designated *implicitly* by its obviously intended purpose; such designation is a *permanent* act of ordinary retention.
   b. Other stable patrimony is legitimately designated *explicitly* by the administrator of the public juridic person which owns it; such designation is a *permanent* act of ordinary retention.

3. Goods belonging to stable patrimony must be identified in regularly updated inventories (c. 1283, 3°).

4. Stable patrimony can be alienated; this alienation sometimes requires the consent of others before the administrator can perform the alienation, in which case the act of alienation is *extraordinary* (see cc. 1291-1294).

5. Stable patrimony must be protected in contracts which can threaten it (c. 1295, which will be discussed in greater details later)

---

19 These conclusions reflect a maturation of my earlier thoughts mentioned in "The Stable Patrimony of Public Juridic Persons," 147-162.

20 Yuji Sugawara says that the canons do not explicitly require, but suppose, that every juridic person has stable patrimony. "Amministrazione e alienazione dei beni temporali degli istituti religiosi nel Codice (Can. 638)," in *Periodica*, 97 (2007) 269-270.

Velasio DePaolis comments: "One thing is certain: the new code presupposes that every juridical person has a stable patrimony which can be made up of either movable or immoveable goods." "Temporal Goods of the Church in the New Code with Particular Reference to Institutes of Consecrated Life," *The Jurist*, 43 (1983) 356.

See also Christian Begus, *Diritto patrimoniale canonico* (Rome: Lateran University Press, 2007) 223.

6. Goods belonging to stable patrimony can be transformed from immovable goods to movable goods, and vice versa.[21]

7. Gifts intended by their donors to become part of stable patrimony carry thereby a condition or modal obligation, requiring the permission of the ordinary before they are accepted (c. 1267 §2).

8. Administrators cannot make donations from stable patrimony (c. 1285).

9. Stable patrimony is not subject to diocesan taxation, which is based onlyon income (c. 1263; see also c. 264 §2), although the earnings of stable patrimony would be subject to taxation since they are income.

10. Stable patrimony can be converted back into non-stable patrimony. Inasmuch as stable patrimony is so designated in order to assure the long-term existence of the public juridic person, and inasmuch as sometimes permission from others is needed before some stable patrimony is alienated (see c. 1292), *mutatis mutandis* and by analogy, it seems reasonable to conclude that any conversion of stable patrimony back into non-stable patrimony constitutes, by the very nature of the activity, an act of *extraordinary* administration. Further, it would seem that the same authorities competent to give permission for the alienation of stable patrimony would be competent to give permission for its transfer to being non-stable patrimony.

11. Mass offerings cannot be designated as stable patrimony because, by law, they are held by a public juridic person only temporarily (cc. 954, 956, 958).

4 – Acts of Extraordinary Administration **iure universali** ***and*** **iure particulari**

As mentioned earlier, administration is one of the four aspects of the Church's ownership of temporal goods. Title II of Book V identifies multiple acts of administration. Indeed, Title II distinguishes three kinds of acts of administration: acts of *ordinary* administration; acts of *extraordinary* administration; and, **for dioceses *only***, acts of *ordinary administration more important in light of the economic condition of the diocese.*

The most common acts of administration are "ordinary," performed routinely and rather simply by the administrator of the public juridic person. An act of administration is "ordinary" unless there is certain indication otherwise.

21 See Francis G. Morrisey, "The Alienation of Temporal Goods in Contemporary Practice," in *Studia canonica*, 9 (1995) 308.

An "act of *extraordinary* administration" is an act of administration which exceeds the limits and manner of ordinary administration and which *always* requires the administrator of a public juridic person to receive the consent/permission of one or more other physical persons, whether as individuals or as members of group, in order to perform the act. The competent ecclesiastical authority determines that the act of administration is exceeds the limits and manner of *ordinary* administration (and therefore it is *extraordinary*).

4.1 – Acts of Extraordinary Administration ***iure universali***

The 1983 *Code of Canon Law* does not explicitly identify any specific act of extraordinary administration by that term. Nonetheless, inasmuch as an act of extraordinary administration requires the consent/permission of others before the administrator can perform it, a study of the Code identifies five acts of extraordinary administration *iure universali*. Each of these is an act of administration, not "routine," to perform which the administrator of a public juridic person needs the consent/permission of one or more other identified physical persons. *De facto*, the following are five acts of extraordinary administration established by the Code for the Latin Church:

1. to refuse gifts of greater importance for a just cause and in matters of greater importance (c. 1267 §2) – which requires the *permission of the ordinary*
2. to initiate or to contest civil litigation (c. 1288) – which requires the *written permission of the ordinary*
3. to enter threatening contracts involving stable patrimony

    According to canon canon 1295, if the threatened stable patrimony is valued beyond the minimum amount deignated for alienation of stable patrimony (see c. 1292 §1-§2): If the diocesan bishop, as administrator of diocesan ecclesiastical goods, intends to enter such a contract, he needs the *consent of the diocesan finance council, the college of consultors, and those concerned.* If the administrator of a public juridic person subject to the diocesan bishop intends to enter such a contact, he or she needs the *consent of the diocesan bishop with the consent of his finance council, the college of consultors, and those concerned.* If the administrator of some other public juridic person wishes to enter such a contact, he or she needs the *consent of the competent authority identified in the statutes*. Moreover, if the amount of the threat surpasses the maximum monetary amount established by the episcopal conference for acts of alienation, all the above-mentioned administrators need also (*insuper*) the *permission of the Holy See.*

According to canon 638 §3 (and canon 741 §1): If a religious institute or a society of apostolic life intends to enter *any* threatening contact involving stable patrimony (no matter the amount of the threat), the competent administrator requires the *permission of the competent superior with the consent of the council.* Moreover, if the amount of the threat surpasses the amount defined by the Holy See for each region, goods given to the Church by a vow, or goods precious for artistic or historic reasons, the administrator need also (*insuper*) the *permission of the Holy See.*

4. to lease ecclesiastical goods (c. 1297) – requires *permission from competent ecclesiastical authority* as identified by the episcopal conference
5. to erect a new church building, even by a religious institute (c. 1215) – which requires the *consent of the diocesan bishop*, after he has heard the presbyteral council and the rectors of the neighboring churches.

These five acts of extraordinary administration are identified *iure universali*, although the Code does not employ the technical term "act of extraordinary administration" in relation to any one of them.

It also seems, as mentioned earlier, that the transfer of stable patrimony to be non-stable patrimony is also by its nature an act of extraordinary administration, for the reasons previously proposed. I recommend that this be made clear in law.

4.2 – Acts of Extraordinary Administration ***iure particulari***

In addition to the acts of extraordinary administration *iure universali*, the Code also makes provision for the designation of acts of extraordinary administration *iure particulari*. For dioceses, these are established by the conference of bishops (c. 1277). For public juridic persons subject to the diocesan bishop, these are established by the statutes or by the diocesan bishop after he has received the counsel of the diocesan finance council (c. 1281 §2). For religious institutes (c. 638 §1) and societies of apostolic life (c. 741 §1), these are established by proper law. For other public juridic persons, these are established by the statutes (c. 1281 §2).

It is important to underscore that the conference of bishops establishes acts of extraordinary administration *only for dioceses* – not for parishes or other public juridic persons. Therefore, if a diocesan bishop wants the acts of extraordinary administration pertaining to dioceses *also* to pertain to parishes and other public juridic persons subject to him, he must establish these acts of extraordinary administration for the parishes and the others by diocesan particular law.

Finally, it is helpful to recall that the Code's category of "acts of [ordinary] administration more important in light of the economic condition" pertains *only* to dioceses. The Code makes no reference to such acts in relation to any other public juridic person. (Nonetheless, it is certainly not excluded that particular law or proper law can establish such a category for public juridic persons other than dioceses.)

If an act of administration is not extraordinary *iure universali* or *iure particulari*, it remains an act of ordinary administration. An act of extraordinary administration does not come into existence "accidentally." Some competent ecclesiastical authority must clearly and legitimately define an act of administration as being extraordinary because that competent authority has determined that the act "exceeds the limits and manner of ordinary administration" (c. 1281 §1; cf. c. 1281 §2).

Given the rapid changes in secular society and the Church, it may be prudent for the competent ecclesiastical authority to discern periodically any modification in the listing of acts of extraordinary administration *iure particulari*. Moreover, it would seem entirely prudent that *all* acts of extraordinary administration also be identified in civil legal articles of incorporation of public juridic persons, so that the same discipline will be operative in both the ecclesiastical and the civil fora.[22]

5 – Canon 1295 Transactions

Canon 1295 concerns "threatening" contracts, and identifies an act which by its very nature is an act of extraordinary administration (not alienation) inasmuch as it requires the involvement of others before an administrator is able to enter such a contract involving the ecclesiastical goods of a public juridic person. Canon 1295 identifies an act of extraordinary administration established *iure universali*. The canon states:

> The requirements of canons 1291-1294, to which the statutes of a juridic person must also conform, must be observed not

22 See John A. Renken, "The Statutes of a Parish," in *Studia canonica,* 44 (2010) 99-148.

> only in alienation but also in any transaction which can worsen the patrimonial condition of a juridic person.[23]

Fundamental for the accurate understanding of the discipline of this canon is its reference to canons 1291-1294. This reference reveals that canon 1295 concerns legitimately designated stable patrimony (canon 1291) which is valued above the minimum amount indicated for alienation (c. 1292 §1) or given to the Church by a vow or precious for artistic or historic reasons (c. 1292 §3). This means that the canon identifies as a "transaction which can worsen the patrimonial condition of a juridic person" *only* contractual transactions which involve a threat to a public juridic person involving (1) an amount which surpasses the established minimum amount, (2) votive offerings, and (3) precious goods.

Canon 1295 does *not* concern contracts which can be considered somehow "threatening" due to the subjective factors of a given public juridic person (e.g., a parish with significantly limited resources). To hold that the threatening aspect of a given contract is determined only subjectively does not reflect accurately the wording of the canon nor its intention, as its legislative history shows. [24]

The subject matter of threatening contracts is discussed by Francis G. Morrisey:

> Among the acts which would certainly come under c. 1295, we could list the following: (a) borrowing money; (b) taking out mortgages; (c) entering long-term leases; (d) changing status of ownership (such as turning over certain properties to secular boards).
>
> These acts would be subject to the prescriptions of the canon because, in one way or another, they risk jeopardizing the stable patrimony of the juridical person. Three elements usually enter into account when determining whether there

23 The discipline of canon 1295 is reflected in canon 638 §1, concerning threatening contracts entered by religious institutes. Canon 741 §1 applies the norm of canon 638 §1 to societies of apostolic life. These two canons, however, make reference to "any affair in which the patrimonial condition of a juridic person can worsen," without reference to a monetary amount of the threat to the stable patrimony involved in the threatening contract.

24 For further reflections on the historical development of canon 1295 and canonists' reflections on its discipline, see John A. Renken, "Contracts Threatening Stable Patrimony: The Discipline and Application of Canon 1295," in *Studia canonica*, 45 (2011) 501-519.

is a risk of jeopardy: (a) loss or diminishing of *ownership*; (b) loss or diminishing of *sponsorship*; (c) loss or diminishing of *control*.[25]

In sum: canon 1295 is legislation concerning threatening contracts involving the stable patrimony of a public juridic person valued beyond the minimum amount, or votive offerings, or precious goods. The object of the canon is thus determined "objectively," such that the canon applies identically to all stable patrimony of all public juridic persons within the perimeters listed in canon 1292 §1-§2. Canon 1295 identifies an act of administration which is extraordinary *ex natura sua* and *iure universali*, inasmuch as it requires the involvement of others before the administrator can act.

6 – The Establishment, Modifications, Extinction, and Civil Incorporation of Public Juridic Persons

The Code contains clear discipline on the establishment (cc. 116 §2, 117), union/fusion (c. 121), division (c. 122) and extinction (cc. 120, 123) of public juridic persons.

We all recall the helpful circular letter from the Congregation for the Clergy, issued 30 April 2013,[26] which addresses many issues to assist in the modification of parishes (which are the most numerous public juridic persons in the universal Church). The circular letter is particularly helpful in explaining "extinctive unions," in outlining the process to be followed carefully in modifying parish structures, and in addressing the destination of ecclesiastical goods when parishes are modified in any manner. The circular letter is also helpful in addressing the modification of parishes (as distinct from their closure); the relegation to profane but not sordid use of church buildings; and the alienation of church buildings.

An obvious concern, of course, is that competent ecclesiastical authorities must protect the ecclesiastical goods of public juridic persons with civil methods that correspond as exactly as possible to canon law. This means that parishes (which in canon law are public juridic persons distinct from the juridic person of the diocese: see cc. 515 §3, 373) should be recognized in civil law as structures

25 Francis G. Morrisey, "The Alienation of Temporal Goods in Contemporary Practice," in *Studia canonica*, 29 (1995) 311. See also the reflections of other canonists concerning the kinds of contracts governed by canon 1295: Robert J. Kennedy, *New Commentary*, 1502-1503; Mariano López Alarcón, *Annotated*, 1002-1003; Joaquín Mantecón, *Exegetical,* 142-143; Vittorio Palestro, 149: Jean-Claude Périsset, *Les biens temporels de l'Église* (Paris, Éditions Tardif, 1996) 216-217; Jean-Pierre Schouppe, 163.

26 Congregation for the Clergy, circular letter presenting "Procedural Guidelines for the Modification of Parishes, the Closure or Relegation of Churches to Profane but not Sordid Use, and the Alienation of the Same" (30 April 2013), prot. no. 20131348. Reprinted in, *Roman Replies and CLSA Advisory Opinions 2013* (Washington, DC: Canon Law Society of America, 2013) 5-12.

distinct from, though somehow related to, the diocese. This is very clearly required in the *CCEO*, which states:

> Canon 1020 §1. Each authority is bound by the grave obligation to take care that temporal goods acquired by the Church are registered in the name of the juridic person to whom they belong, after having observed all the prescripts of civil law which protect the rights of the Church.
>
> §2. However, if civil law does not allow temporal goods to be registered in the name of a juridic person, each authority is to take care that, after having heard experts in civil law and the competent council, the rights of the Church remain unharmed by using methods valid in civil law. ...
>
> §4. The immediately higher authority is bound to urge the observance of these prescripts.[27]

Indeed, the circular letter from the Congregation for the Clergy of 30 April 2013 explains that:

> ... when treating the modification of parishes and the relegation or closure of churches, there is a need of much greater clarity in distinguishing the juridic person of a diocese from the juridic person of a parish. Nowhere is this more important than in questions concerning the ownership of churches, and who is responsible for their upkeep.

We all recall that the Sacred Congregation for the Council issued a private letter to the ordinaries of the United States on 19 July 1911 in response to a request from some American bishops on the proper method of civilly incorporating parishes. It explained that the "parish corporation" is the preferred method to hold title to, and to administer, church property:

> 1. Among the methods which now are in use in the United States for holding and administering church property, the one known as Parish Corporation is preferable to the others, but with the conditions and safeguards which are now in use in the State of New York. The Bishops therefore should immediately take steps to introduce this method for the handling of property in their dioceses, if the civil law allows it. If the civil law does not allow it, they should exert their influence with the civil authorities that it may be made legal as soon as possible.

27 This canon corresponds to *CIC* canon 1284 §2, 2° but is very much more detailed.

2. Only in those places where the civil law does not recognize Parish Corporations, and until such recognition is allowed, the method commonly called Corporation sole is allowed, but with the understanding that in the administration of ecclesiastical property the Bishop is to act with the advice, and in more important matters with the consent, of those who have an interest in the premises and of the diocesan consultors, this being a conscientious obligation for the Bishop in person.

3. The method called in fee simple is to be entirely abandoned.[28]

The law of New York, to which the letter refers, provided that an incorporated parish has a five-member board of trustees: three members serve *ex officio* (the bishop, the vicar general, and the rector of the church) and the other two are lay members of the church chosen by the rest for a one-year term. The law states: "No act or proceeding of the trustees of any such incorporated church shall be valid without the sanction of the Archbishop or Bishop of the diocese to which such church belongs, or in case of their absence or inability to act, without the sanction of the Vicar General or of the administrator of such diocese."[29]

This private century-old letter to American bishops presents an unquestionable preference for the civil incorporation of parishes in structures distinct from the corporation of the diocese. It certainly excludes the diocesan-wide corporation sole as the appropriate means for the civil holding of parishes. Indeed, a decade ago, in a communication to the bishops of Ontario, the apostolic nunciature in Canada said the corporation sole is incompatible with canon law:

> Acknowledging that the diocese has an obligation in justice to a victim of abuse, it is nevertheless equally true that the diocese has an obligation in justice to the rest of the faithful of the diocese; these two cannot be mutually exclusive ... Since

28 *CLD*, vol. 2, 443-445. See *Ecclesiastical Review*, 45 (1911) 585- 596. The method of *fee simple* gives ownership of ecclesiastical property to individual persons (e.g., bishops or priests). The corporation sole as a means to hold church property resulted in response to the negative influence of trusteeism. The history of property tenure in the United States, including the background to this private letter from the Sacred Congregation for the Council, is related succinctly by William J. King, "The Corporation Sole and Subsidiarity," in *CLSA Proceedings*, 65 (Washington, DC: Canon Law Society of America, 2003) 107-134. He identifies a number of methods whereby church property is incorporated in the United States today: corporation sole, the charitable trust, the not-for-profit corporation, the corporation aggregate, and aggregates of charitable trusts (123). See also Robert L. Kealy, "Methods of Diocesan Incorporation," in *CLSA Proceedings*, 48 (Washington, DC: Canon Law Society of America, 1986) 163-177; Mark E. Chopko, "An Overview of the Parish and the Civil Law," in *The Jurist*, 67 (2007) 198-202; Mary Judith O'Brien, "Instructions for Parochial Temporal Administration," in *Catholic Lawyer*, 41 (2001) 131-136.

29 *CLD*, vol. 2, 444-445, fn. 1.

> the corporation sole is in fact incompatible with the canonical autonomy of the parish, it appears necessary that all dioceses having their bishop holding the civil status of a corporation sole look seriously at changing it ... This means re-establishing the primacy of Canon Law in the financial structure of the dioceses ... [30]

In light of all this, we rightly conclude that nothing in canon law supports the establishment of civil structures wherein parish property is considered part of diocesan property.[31] It would be entirely appropriate at this present time, wherever such is not the case, to make prudent and steady movement to establish parishes as entities civilly distinct from dioceses. Such an arrangement in civil law reflects canon law. In thus establishing parishes as civilly distinct from the diocese, it would be proper that the same norms govern the operation of a parish both in the ecclesiastical forum and the civil forum. The statutes governing the parish should be identical in each forum,[32] and the civil statutes would reserve certain powers to the superior ecclesiastical authorities in a fashion corresponding to canon law.[33] The administrator of the parish in the civil statutes will be the *parochus*, who is also its administrator in canon law (c. 532).

7 – Particular Law and Special Instructions Governing the Care of Church Property

Subsidiarity is fundamental in Book V, particularly because the Church exists in numerous civil jurisdictions with distinct secular laws governing Church property.[34] In April 1967, a central committee of the Pontifical Commission for

30 Letter of the Apostolic Nunciature of Canada, Prot. No. 6088/05, December 14, 2005.

31 Robert J. Kennedy writes: "In fact, liability considerations in contemporary American society, and the enhanced emphasis on Subsidiarity in the 1983 code, argue strongly for the continued inappropriateness of the corporation-sole method of holding civil title to church-related property. Where such a method remains in use, diocesan bishops and their finance officers and councils should make every effort to see that the Church laws governing the acquisition, retention, administration, and alienation of temporal goods are faithfully fulfilled." *New Commentary* 1457.

32 See John A. Renken, "Statutes for a Parish," in *Studia canonica*, 44 (2010) 99-148.

33 For further reflections on the "reserved powers," see Francis G. Morrisey, *Handbook* 14; Daniel J. Ward, "Temporal Goods," in *Procedural Manual for Institutes of Consecrated Life and Societies of Apostolic Life*, (Washington, DC: Canon Law Society of America, 2001) 199-200; The Catholic Health Association of the United States, *Search for Identity: Canonical Sponsorship of Catholic Healthcare* (Saint Louis, MO: The Catholic Health Association of the United States, 1993) 81; Adam J. Maida and Nicholas Cafardi, in *Church Property, Church Finances, and Church-Related Corporations* (Saint Louis, MO: The Catholic Health Association of the United States, 1984) 167-169.

34 See Phillip J. Brown, "The 1983 Code and Vatican II Ecclesiology: The Principle of Subsidiarity in Book V," in *The Jurist*, 69 (2009) 583-614.

the Revision of the Code of Canon Law had developed ten principles to direct the task of revising the Code. These principles were approved (with a few modifications) by the 1967 Synod of Bishops. Principle 5 on Subsidiarity extolled the importance of particular law, especially concerning temporal goods:

> The importance of these particular laws is to be more accurately described in the new *Code of Canon Law* especially in temporal administration, since the governance of temporal goods must be ordered for the most part according to the laws of each nation.[35]

The Synod of Bishops met September 30-October 4, 1967. They voted in favor of principle 5: 128 *placet,* 58 *placet iuxta modum,* 1 *non placet.*[36]

A cursory study of Book V (and a few canons elsewhere in the Code) identifies multiple opportunities for the establishment of particular law (by the conference of bishops, the provincial bishops, and the diocesan bishop).[37] Moreover, canon 1276 §2 requires ordinaries to issue "special instructions" within the limits of universal and particular law in order to order the administration of ecclesiastical goods. Such establishing of particular law and issuing of special instructions are concrete applications of the subsidiarity mandated by the 1967 Synod of Bishops.

7.1 – Particular Law Established by the Conference of Bishops

The Code requires each conference of bishops to establish particular law governing six issues:

1. Canon 1262 – norms governing appeals to the faithful for Church support
2. Canon 1265 §2 – norms governing begging for alms which are to be observed by all, including mendicants
3. Canon 1272 – norms to govern benefices, where they still exist, in such a way that the income and even, insofar as possible, the endowment itself of the benefices are gradually transferred to the "institute for clergy support" mentioned in canon 1274 §1
4. Canon 1277 – norms defining acts of extraordinary administration for dioceses

35 *Communicationes*, 1 (1969) 81.

36 *Communicationes*, 1 (1969) 99-100.

37 So much of this section reflects: John A. Renken, "Particular Laws on Temporal Goods," in *Studies in Church Law*, 4 (2008) 447-454.

5. Canon 1292 – norms defining the minimum and maximum amounts for alienation of ecclesiastical goods constituting stable patrimony of a juridic person (these norms also govern threatening contracts: c. 1295)
6. Canon 1297 – norms for the leasing of Church goods, especially regarding the permission to be obtained from competent ecclesiastical authority

In addition, canon 1274 §2 requires that the episcopal conference take care that there exists an institute which provides sufficiently for the social security of clerics.

7.2 – Particular Law Established by the Provincial Bishops

The Code requires particular law to be established by the bishops of a province:

1. Canon 1264, 1° – fees for acts of executive power granting a favor, or for the execution of rescripts of the Apostolic See
2. Canon 1264, 2° – limits on the offerings on the occasion of the administration of the sacraments and sacramentals (so-called 'stole fees")
3. Canon 952 – Mass offerings

7.3 – Particular Law Established by the Diocesan Bishop

The Code also mentions particular laws established by the diocesan bishop. In some cases, the diocesan bishop *must* establish particular laws:

1. Canon 537 – norms to guide the operation of the parish finance council
2. Canon 1277 – norms to define acts of ordinary administration "which are more important in light of the economic condition of the diocese"
3. Canon 1281 §2 – norms to identify acts of extraordinary administration for the public juridic persons subject to him (which govern such persons unless their statutes already define such acts)
4. Canon 1287 §2 – norms to determine how administrators render an account to the faithful concerning goods offered by them to the

Church[38]

5. Canon 1303 §1, 2° – particular law to determine the duration of non-autonomous pious foundations

6. Canon 1304 §2 – norms to define conditions, additional to those found in the universal law, for the establishment and acceptance of foundations

In other cases, the diocesan bishop *can* establish particular laws governing Church property:

1. Canon 1263 – norms to impose a "*moderate tax*" for diocesan needs upon public juridic persons subject to him, and to impose an "*extraordinary and moderate exaction*" in cases of grave necessity upon other physical and juridic persons, after he has heard the presbyteral council and diocesan finance council

2. Canon 1266 – norms to determine special collections for specific parochial, diocesan, national, or universal projects[39]

3. Canon 1274 – norms to establish various financial institutes (e.g., for clergy support, for social security of clergy, for non-ordained diocesan personnel, for poorer dioceses, etc.)

4. Canon 1284 §3 – norms to require administrators of public juridic persons subject to him to prepare annual budgets of projected income and expenses[40]

5. Canon 531 – norms to determine the allocation of offerings on the occasion of parochial functions ("stole fees") and the remuneration of the clerics performing these functions, after he has heard the presbyteral council

The canons listed above indicate instances when the Code says the diocesan bishop must or can establish particular law concerning temporal goods. Certainly, there are numerous other particular laws governing temporal goods which

38 Canon 1287 §2 says that norms are to be established by particular *ius* without identifying the competent authority. Clearly, the diocesan bishop can make such a law (see cc. 391 §1; 135 §1). The conference of bishops could also make such a law, but in doing so must have the special mandate of canon 455 §1.

39 Canon 1266 says that the local ordinary (i.e., the diocesan bishop, the vicar general, and the episcopal vicar) can order the gathering of a special collection. A vicar would do this by means of a general executory decree (cc. 31-33) since he lacks legislative power.

40 Canon 1284 §3 says particular law may mandate making annual budgets of projected income and expenses, without identifying the legislative authority. Clearly, the diocesan bishop can make such a law (see cc. 391 §1; 135 §1). The conference of bishops could also make such a law, but in doing so it must have the special mandate of canon 455 §1.

the diocesan bishop can establish: for example, he can establish as diocesan particular law many of the provisions in *Diocesan Fiscal Issues*, prepared by the USCCB's Committee on Budget and Finance.[41]

7.4 – Special Instructions

Canon 1276 §2 requires the diocesan bishop (and other ordinaries) to issue special instructions on the administration of ecclesiastical goods. Instructions clarify laws and elaborate on and determine the methods to be observed in fulfilling them (c. 34). The special instructions required by canon 1276 §2 will assist the *parochus*, as the administrator of parochial property (c. 532), in implementing the laws governing Church property. The following issues, related to the canons of the Code, may be addressed in special instructions on temporal goods:[42]

1. the manner of managing all aspects of Mass offerings (cc. 945-958)
2. the manner of requesting a special parish collection (c. 1266)
3. the manner of obtaining the permission of the local ordinary to refuse a gift of greater importance for a just cause (c. 1267 §2)
4. the manner of obtaining the permission of the local ordinary to accept a gift to which is attached a modal obligation or condition (c. 1267 §2)
5. the manner of obtaining the written faculty from the local ordinary to perform an act of extraordinary parish administration (c. 1281 §1)
6. the manner of taking the oath to administer parochial goods well and faithfully, and before whom the oath is to be taken (c. 1283, 1°)
7. the format for inventories of parochial property, and the frequency with which they are to be updated regularly (c. 1283, 2°-3°)
8. the manner of obtaining adequate insurance coverage (c. 1283 §2, 1°)

41 This document was approved by the USCCB at its November 2002 plenary, revised 2009. Available at: http://www.usccb.org/about/financial-reporting/upload/Diocesan-Financial-Issues-Manual.pdf

This document addresses many issues which, it would seem, could be promulgated as especially helpful particular law to assist in the care of temporal goods in parishes (see Section I-I Parish Financial Management).

See also Renken, "Particular Laws on Temporal Goods," 450-453.

42 This is largely a reproduction of John A. Renken, "The *Parochus* as Administrator of Parish Property," 516-518. See also Judith O'Brien, "Instructions for Parochial Temporal Administrators," in *Catholic Lawyer*, 41 (2001) 113-143.

9. the manner of assuring the civil legal protection of parish property (c. 1283 §2, 2°; see c. 1283 §2, 3°)
10. the manner of collecting and securing parish revenue (c. 1283 §2, 4°)[43]
11. the manner of developing a workable debt reduction schedule (c. 1283 §2, 5°)
12. the manner of obtaining the consent of the local ordinary to invest surplus parish revenue (c. 1283 §2, 6°) or endowed funds (c. 1305)
13. the format for parish records of income and expenditures (c. 1283 §2, 7°)
14. the manner of presenting the annual parish administration report, and its format (c. 1283 §2, 8°)
15. the manner of presenting the annual parish financial report to the local ordinary which he will present for examination to the diocesan finance council, and its format (c. 1287 §1)[44]
16. the manner of maintaining parochial archives on property rights (c. 1283 §2, 9°; see cc. 491 §1, 535 §4)
17. the format for annual parish budgets, if they are mandated by diocesan particular law (c. 1283 §3)
18. the manner of complying with civil employment laws according to the principles handed on by the Church, and of providing a just and decent wage to Church workers (c. 1286)
19. the manner of rendering an account to the faithful about their offerings to the parish, and the format of the report (c. 1287 §2)[45]
20. the manner of obtaining written permission to initiate or to contest civil litigation (c. 1288)
21. the manner of legitimately designating stable patrimony (c. 1292; see c. 1285)
22. the manner of obtaining permission to alienate the stable patrimony of the parish (cc.1291-1294)
23. the manner of obtaining permission to enter a threatening contract (c. 1295)

---

43 This instruction may particularly address how routine parish collections for regular Church support (i.e., "the Sunday collections") are to be secured, counted (by rotating "teams" of "collection counters"), and deposited.

44 See Thomas John Paprocki and Richard B. Saudis, "Annual Report to the Diocesan Bishop," in *Handbook*, 175-183.

45 Royce R. Thomas, "Financial Reports to the Faithful," in *Handbook*, 165-174.

24. the manner of entering a contract to lease property owned by the parish (c. 1297)

25. the manner of informing the local ordinary of the parish's having received a pious will, whether *mortis causa* or *inter vivos* (c. 1301), or a pious trust (c. 1302), and the manner of proceeding

26. the manner of establishing a parish non-autonomous foundation, and all the legal requirements associated with its establishment (c. 1303 §1, 2°; see cc. 1304-1307)

27. the manner of seeking to reduce (c. 1308) or transfer (c. 1309) Mass obligations

28. the manner of seeking to reduce, moderate, or commute pious wills not involving Mass offerings (c. 1310)

29. the manner of determining if a parochial good is sacred (see c. 1269), or precious for artistic or historical reasons (cc.1270, 1292 §2)

30. the manner of conducting an *internal* audit of parish financial records and an *internal* review of parish financial practices, etc.

8 – The Delict of Financial Malfeasance

We are certainly well aware that the Church has faced numerous scandals and embarrassment by the financial misconduct of those charged with caring for church property. The Church, like the secular society, understands the various species of financial malfeasance as delictuous behavior.[46] Book VI of the 1983 Code identifies several delicts which directly (or indirectly) relate to financial malfeasance:

1. invalid alienation of ecclesiastical goods, which is to be punished with a just penalty (c. 1377)
2. impeding the use of ecclesiastical goods (c. 1375)
3. simony (c. 1380)
4. illicit profit from Mass offerings (c. 1385)
5. bribery (c. 1386)
6. the production and use of falsified documents (c. 1391)

---

46 For further reflections on financial malfeasance, see Elizabeth McDonough, "Addressing Irregularities in the Administration of Church Property," in *Handbook* 223-243; Thomas J. Green, "The Players in the Church's Temporal Goods World," 71; Francis G. Morrisey, "Financial Malfeasance and Canon Law," presented to the Diocesan Fiscal Management Conference, Houston, Texas, 25 September 2012 (unpublished); John A. Renken, "Penal Law and Financial Malfeasance," in *Studia canonica*, 42 (2008) 5-57.

All these delicts threaten *ferendae sententiae* penalties (c. 1314) which are indeterminate (c. 1315 §2) and which, as such, cannot be perpetual penalties (c. 1349). One cannot be removed from office for committing these delicts, since removal is a perpetual penalty.

The Code does not make specific reference to embezzlement, theft, misuse of goods for purpose other than those designated, etc. Such acts must be understood as the delict canon 1389 which concerns a rather "generic" abuse of ecclesiastical power or function, perhaps even through negligence. Canon 1389 states:

> §1. A person who abuses an ecclesiastical power or function is to be punished according to the gravity of the act or omission, not excluding privation of office, unless a law or precept has already established the penalty for this abuse.
>
> §2. A person who through culpable negligence illegitimately places or omits an act of ecclesiastical power, ministry, or function with harm to another is to be punished with a just penalty.

This canon permits the removal of office to be the penalty if an administrator commits acts of financial malfeasance with *dolus*. Admittedly, however, a *parochus* can be removed from office administratively for financial malfeasance according to canon 1741, 5°, which mentions "poor administration of temporal affairs with grave damage to the Church whenever another remedy to this harm cannot be found." The Code does not provide specifically for the administrative removal from office of other administrators for their poor administration of ecclesiastical goods.

We are well aware that Book VI of the 1983 Code is currently being revised. We can imagine that the revision will identify financial malfeasance as a delict. Perhaps canon 1377 (which now establishes only the delict of invalid alienation of ecclesiastical goods) would be amplified to establish as delicts also the poor administration, theft, and misappropriation of ecclesiastical goods. Perhaps canon 1386 (which now establishes the delict of bribery) would be reformulated to include also the delict of insisting on an amount higher than that established by law for the performing of some ecclesiastical function. Perhaps the revised law would require that, prior to the remission of *any* penalty, medicinal or expiatory, imposed for any delict of financial malfeasance, the offender would be required to make restitution, or at least to offer a sincerely formulated plan of restitution, to the measure that restitution is possible.

The *praenotanda* of the 2011 *Schema recognitionis Libri VI Codicis iuris canonici*,[47] explains that penal law is intended to be "an instrument of governance which the pastors can have at hand in exercising their responsibilities of governance for the good of the People of God."[48] The use of penal law to counter acts of financial malfeasance by church administrators is unquestionably appropriate. As we await the reform of Book VI, diocesan bishops may find it wise to issue diocesan particular law in order to establish the delicts of poor administration, theft, and misappropriation of ecclesiastical goods by the administrators of public juridic persons subject to the diocesan bishop. Such a particular penal law can establish for these delicts a *determinate* (see c. 1349) and *perpetual* (see c. 1336 § 1) expiatory penalty (other than dismissal from the clerical state: c. 1317). This would provide, at the present time, for the fuller identification of various species of financial malfeasance as delicts in the Church. It may serve as a deterrent for administrators tempted to commit such delicts, and thereby may preclude further scandal in the Church today.

Conclusion

I want to repeat my gratitude to the CLSA for this invitation to offer some reflections on canonical responses to some challenges in the care of church property today. And, I thank all of you for being present here and now. Certainly, there are some few areas where the norms of the Code concerning temporal goods can be improved, and there remain some few issues where the legislation concerning temporal goods may require further consideration by canonists. But, I repeat my informed conviction that the greatest challenge to canonists today concerning the codal norms on temporal goods may simply be their full implementation.

Indeed, I hope that these reflections of mine may assist in some very small way in the realization of that fuller implementation of the *ius vigens*.

47 Pontifical Council for Legislative Texts, *Schema recognitionis Libri VI Codicis iuris canonici (reservatum)*, (Vatican City, Typis vaticanis, 2011). The *praenotanda* is presented in *Communicationes*, 43 (2011) 317-320.

48 This is from the first criteria identified by the PCLT for the revision of Book VI. *Communicationes*, 43 (2011) 318. [Author's translation.]

Seminar

Did Error of Law Concerning Sacramental Dignity Influence a Person's Consent?[1]

Lynda Robitaille

"To act justly and to love mercy"[2]

Introduction

Human beings understand marriage. We are taught that the elements and properties of marriage are 'written in our hearts,' part of the natural law. It is natural for humanity to want to marry for life, in a faithful/exclusive union which is open to new life. John Beal highlights these points:

> From at least the time of Benedict XIV until relatively recently, canonical doctrine insulated itself from the necessity of grappling with widespread errors about the unity and indissolubility of marriage by positing a general will to marry in accord with the dictates of the Creator, which, except in the most extreme circumstances, prevailed over any particular will to enter a marriage in conformity with one's erroneous views.[3]

We are also taught that when a marriage takes place between two baptized persons, that union is a sacrament. It is sacramental by the fact of the parties' baptism and consent to marriage. Not by the fact of their active faith.

The law presumes that people mean what they say when they choose marriage and its properties and elements. Canon 1099 emphasizes this presumption when it notes that "error concerning the unity or indissolubility or sacramental dignity of marriage does not vitiate matrimonial consent provided that it does not determine the will." Thus, if a person's error concerning indissolubility, unity, or sacramental dignity does determine the will, it invalidates consent.

1 Some of this presentation is based on my presentation at the Northwest Regional Canon Law Conference in Alaska, April 21-23, 2015: "Getting at Proofs of Traditional Grounds."

2 Micah 6:8, *New International Version*.

3 J. Beal, "Exploring our Erroneous Zones: Developments in Jurisprudence on Determining Error Since 1983," in *The Jurist*, 69 (2009) 559.

How can people be in error about indissolubility, unity, and sacramental dignity? Not everyone has the same understanding of marriage. Popular culture, the lived experience of divorce and remarriage, and a lack of religious education all contribute to people's differing views of what marriage entails. While the law presumes that people consent to the Church's understanding of the natural law of marriage, what people actually consent to must be evaluated. Judges should delve more deeply into understanding parties' consent to marriage because of the impact that society and culture can have on people's understandings of marriage. It is not that judges presume nullity of consent; rather judges must seek for a better understanding of what people choose. How do these differing views affect the person's decision to marry? Do all people marry as the Church teaches? Judges must be aware of how modern society is diverging from traditional understandings of marriage, and they must be able to evaluate what those differing opinions and intentions about marriage mean canonically.

At the Northwest Regional Convention in April I spoke on the (mis)understanding of permanence in our culture and how that affects error determining the will concerning indissolubility. This was what I expected to focus on in this presentation as well. When Sister Sharon Euart approached me in February of 2014 to present a seminar on the "Ground of Error Determining the Will," I had no idea how interesting this topic would become over the next eighteen months. I originally thought I would reflect on the following questions: "Is a person in error able to recognize his/her error? If not, how does the person speak of it to the Tribunal? How does the Tribunal evaluate it?" I will still touch on these questions, but in relation primarily to error concerning the sacramental dignity of marriage.

Pope Francis has recently emphasized the role of faith in consenting to marriage. In his 2015 address to the Roman Rota, Pope Francis said:

> I would like to reflect on the human and cultural context surrounding the formulation of the marriage intention … Effectively, abandoning a perspective of faith gives rise to a false understanding of marriage, and this is not without consequence in the maturation of an individual's will for marriage.[4]

Francis continues:

> Indeed, at the root of the crisis of marriage is often a crisis of knowledge enlightened by faith – that is, knowledge informed

4 Francis, Allocution to the Roman Rota, January 23, 2015, accessed at: www.vatican.va.

> by the adhesion to God and his design of love realized in Jesus Christ.[5]

The first point, then, is to consider what happens when a person 'abandons a perspective of faith,' when the person does not have or no longer has a faith perspective. How does such abandon affect the person's consent to marriage?

Abandon is not necessarily rejection. If the person never consciously thinks about rejecting his/her faith, but rather simply permits himself to embrace the values of the world, that is "abandon." Rejection is more explicit or conscious. This is reflected in the distinction between error and simulation. If it were a question of 'rejection' of faith, we would be speaking about exclusion or simulation. We also recall that our practice has very clearly stated: "lack of faith does not constitute [a] ground of nullity, which does not result in lack of matrimonial will, as far as it is placed at the intellectual level and not in the will … Hence, faith places itself at the level of efficacy and not as a requisite for the validity of marriage."[6]

How faith affects consent has long been a concern in the Church. A common expression of this can be found in a 1998 statement made by then Cardinal Ratzinger:

> Further study is required, however, concerning the question of whether non-believing Christians – baptized persons who never or who no longer believe in God – can truly enter into a sacramental marriage. In other words, it needs to be clarified whether every marriage between two baptized persons is *ipso facto* a sacramental marriage. In fact, the Code states that only a 'valid' marriage between baptized persons is at the same time a sacrament (cf. *CIC*, c. 1055, § 2). Faith belongs to the essence of the sacrament; what remains to be clarified is the juridical question of what evidence of the 'absence of faith' would have as a consequence that the sacrament does not come into being.[7]

---

5 Ibid.

6 L. Sabbarese, "Faith, Intention and Sacramental Dignity in Marriages Among the Baptized," in *Studies in Church Law*, 3 (2007) 314.

7 Joseph Ratzinger, "Concerning Some Objections to the Church's Teaching on the Reception of Holy Communion by Divorced and Remarried Members of the Faithful," 1998, #4, originally published in Cardinal Ratzinger's Introduction to Volume 17 of the series produced by the Congregation for the Doctrine of the Faith, entitled "Documenti e Studi," *On the Pastoral Care of the Divorced and Remarried*, LEV, Vatican City 1998, pp. 20-29, accessed at www.vatican.va.

More recently, Pope Francis has refocused attention on this question and calls us to a better understanding of the influence of culture on one's faith. His challenges our presumptions and former ways of thinking. He speaks of the influence of popular culture on people's understandings of marriage:

Pastoral experience teaches us that today there is a great number of the faithful in irregular situations, on whose personal stories the diffusion of a worldly mentality has had a hefty influence. There exists in fact a kind of spiritual worldliness 'which hides behind the appearance of piety and even love for the Church' (Ap. Ex. *Evangelii gaudium*, n. 93), which leads to the pursuit of personal well-being instead of the glory of the Lord. One of the fruits of such an attitude is 'a purely subjective faith whose only interest is a certain experience or a set of ideas and bits of information which are meant to console and enlighten, but which ultimately keep one imprisoned in his or her own thoughts and feelings' (ibid., 94). It is clear that for the one who bends under this attitude the faith will always be deprived of its value as a normative force of orientation. This leaves the door open for compromises with one's own egoism and the pressures of the current mentality, a mentality that has become dominant by way of the mass media.[8]

We need to further explore is the 'mentality … dominant by way of the mass media,' described by: worldly mentality, spiritual worldliness, purely subjective faith, compromise with egoism, pursuit of personal well-being, and pressures of current mentality. How can we understand the consent of someone who is 'imprisoned in his or her own thoughts and feelings,' someone who is 'deprived' of faith's 'normative force of orientation'? Francis concludes:

> For this reason the judge, in deliberating the validity of expressed consent, must keep in mind the context of value and faith – or the absence or lack thereof – in which the intention to marry is formed. Indeed, the lack of knowledge of the contents of the faith might lead to what the Code calls determinant error of the will (cf. c. 1099). This circumstance can no longer be considered exceptional as in the past, given the frequent prevalence of worldly thinking imposed on the magisterium of the Church. Such error threatens not only the stability of marriage, its exclusivity and fruitfulness, but also the ordering of marriage to the good of the other. It threatens the conjugal love that is the 'vital principle' of consent, the mutual giving in order to build a lifetime of consortium.[9]

How does it affect consent when a person has a 'lack of knowledge of the contents of the faith,' and is caught up in 'worldly thinking'? Pope Francis speaks

8 Francis, Allocution to the Roman Rota, January 23, 2015.

9 Ibid.

of how 'such error' can affect: 'stability' (indissolubility), 'exclusivity' (unity/fidelity), 'fruitfulness' (procreativity), 'conjugal love/mutual giving.'[10]

Pope Francis calls on judges to "establish the truth in the moment of consent: whether a person was faithful to Christ or instead to the lying paradigm of the world."[11] How can we get at that truth? How can we understand the person's intention at the time of consent?

Even more recently, on September 8, 2015, Pope Francis published the *motu proprio, Mitis Iudex Dominus Iesus*. In Title V, Art. 14, §1 of that document, he speaks about the 'briefer' or 'shorter' process which could include those cases where: "Among the circumstances of things and persons which can allow a case for nullity of marriage to be handled by means of the briefer process according to cc. 1683-1687, are included, for example: the defect of faith which can generate simulation of consent or error that determines the will."[12]

Pope Francis' point that people are choosing the values of the world rather than Christian values is highlighted in a recent song whose refrain is:

> Don't pray for us
> We don't need no modern Jesus
> To roll with us
> The only rule we need is never
> Giving up
> The only faith we have is faith in us.[13]

What are we being asked to consider as canonists? How can a 'defect of faith,' or lack of faithfulness 'to Christ,' or an 'absence' or 'lack' of faith affect consent? Francis has highlighted that this can affect not just consent in general, but consent in relation to error determining the will (c. 1099). Thus, we will consider a

---

10 It is important to note that error concerning all these areas does not necessarily come under canon 1099 which is concerned only with error concerning the indissolubility, unit, or sacramental dignity of marriage. Under the present Code, it would be necessary to study error concerning fruitfulness, conjugal love, or mutual giving under simulation (c. 1011).

11 Francis, Allocution to the Roman Rota, January 23, 2015.

12 From CLSA unofficial translation (September 2015) of Francis, *motu proprio, Mitis Iudex Dominus Iesus*, August 15, 2015. The same language is used in *Mitis et misericors Iesus*. The Latin is: "Inter rerum et personarum adiuncta quae sinunt causam nullitatis matrimonii ad tramitem processus brevioris iuxta cann. 1683-1687 pertractari, recensentur exempli gratia: is fidei defectus qui gignere potest simulationem consensus vel errorem voluntatem determinantem."

13 Portugal. The Man. 'Modern Jesus,' Writer(s): John Baldwin Gourley, Brian Joseph Burton. Copyright: Sweet Science, Approaching Airballoons, WB Music Corp. from the album *Evil Friends* (2013).

lack or defect of faith and a choice for the "lying paradigm of the world" in relation to error determining the will. Or to put it differently: how can we consider a lack or defect of faith and a choice for the 'lying paradigm of the world' or for 'the only faith we have is faith in us' in relation to error determining the will?

People imbued with a 'worldly mentality' could be in error with regard to their understanding of the indissolubility or unity (fidelity) of marriage. A lot of work has been done especially regarding error concerning indissolubility and how a culture which accepts divorce and remarriage necessarily affects people with this error. This work focuses on how one's character, popular culture, lived experience in one's family, and religious education affect the choices one makes in marriage. This, however, will not be the focus here. The focus here will be on the question of how and whether a lack of faith, or to use Pope Francis' words, a person wrapped up in 'one's own egoism and the pressures of the current mentality,' could be in error about the sacramental dignity of marriage, and how that error could determine the person's will?

The focus will then turn to the choice that renders an erroneous consent invalid, namely a choice that 'determines the will.' What does that look like? We will compare it with the positive act of the will required in simulation cases, and especially with an implicit act of the will. Error determining the will and an implicit positive act of the will can look very similar in practice. Finally, we will return to our questions: Is a person in error able to recognize his/her error? If not, how does the person speak of it to the Tribunal? How does the Tribunal evaluate it?

Why is it necessary to stretch our understanding of error determining the will?

We return to Pope Francis' call, as well as to the subtitle of this paper: we are to act justly and with mercy. In introducing *Mitis Iudex Dominus Iesus*, Francis reminds us: "In the course of the centuries the Church, gaining an ever-clearer understanding of the words of Christ, has more completely understood and explained the doctrine of the indissolubility of the sacred bond of marriage, and has developed a system of matrimonial consent."[14] Francis reminds us that the point of the marriage nullity process is "to protect, to the greatest extent possible, the truth of the sacred bond." That marriage is brought into being by the consent of the two parties has not changed; nor has the fact that marriage is indissoluble. We are being called to a greater understanding of what is really happening when a person imbued with the values of the modern world, and not with the values of faith, consents to marriage.

---

14 From CLSA unofficial translation (September 2015) of Francis, *motu proprio*, *Mitis Iudex Dominus Iesus*, August 15, 2015.

How to combine a search for the truth with the practice of mercy? Cardinal Kasper gives us a guide when he speaks of *aequitas canonica*, "canonical fairness": "justice and mercy together are authoritative for the concrete, practical application of church law so that fair and just solutions can be achieved. The *Code of Canon Law* deliberately concludes with the declaration that the highest norm is the salvation of souls."[15] Discussing Benedict XVI's 2012 allocution to the Rota, Kasper states:

> it cannot be the case of a subjective or, indeed, an arbitrary interpretation contrary to the sense of the objective law; nor can it be a matter of a purely situational ethics of justice. On the contrary, the point is to apply the objective sense of the legislation analogously in an often complex concrete situation. It is, therefore, not a matter of an arbitrary reinterpretation but rather a matter of bringing to bear the sense of the objective law in a way that is appropriate to the matter at hand and to the situation. This is not a problem of theoretical, but rather a problem of practical reason; alternatively, it is a problem for the power of judgment, which has the responsibility of applying general principles to concrete situations.[16]

Kasper concludes: "Theologically, the point is to do the truth in love (Eph. 4:15), that is, to do what is right, guided by love. The ecclesial judge … is expected to be a just and merciful judge, following the example of Jesus."[17]

How then can we evaluate the new realities of people being influenced by a non-Christian culture in light of the canonical understanding of consent? How can we evaluate the effect that lack of faith has on consent to marriage? We keep in mind Cardinal Kasper's words: acting with justice and mercy is not subjective, not arbitrary, not purely situational; it is objective, even if that must be analogously understood.

Fundamental question

Lack of faith does not traditionally lead to error determining the will. Pope Francis has emphasized what previous popes have also said, that adherents of modern culture might be in error regarding the sacramentality of marriage. In his 2003 address to the Rota, John Paul II noted: "A relevant fact that emerges from the study of the cases is the diminishing awareness among the partners of the significance in the celebration of Christian marriage of *its sacramentality*,

---

15 W. Kasper, *Mercy. The Essence of the Gospel and the Key to Christian Life* (New York/Mahwah, Paulist Press, 2013) 178.

16 Ibid., 179.

17 Ibid., 180.

a dimension that today is all too often disregarded in its intimate meaning ..."[18] Benedict XVI recalled:

> The indissoluble pact between a man and a woman does not, for the purposes of the sacrament, require of those engaged to be married, their personal faith; what it does require, as a necessary minimal condition, is the intention to do what the Church does. However, if it is important not to confuse the problem of the intention with that of the personal faith of those contracting marriage, it is nonetheless impossible to separate them completely.[19]

In 2001, John Paul II highlighted the traditional approach to the link between the sacramentality of marriage and people's intentions:

> I would like to dwell briefly on the relationship between the natural character of marriage and its sacramentality, seeing that there have been frequent attempts since Vatican II to revitalize the supernatural aspect of marriage which include theological, pastoral and canonical proposals that are foreign to tradition, such as the attempt to require faith as a prerequisite for marriage.

John Paul II concluded:

> to introduce requirements of intention or faith for the sacrament that go beyond that of marrying according to God's plan from the 'beginning' – in addition to the grave risks that I mentioned in *Familiaris consortio* (n. 68, loc. cit., pp. 164-165): unfounded and discriminatory judgements, doubts about the validity of marriages already celebrated, particularly by baptized non-Catholics – would inevitably mean separating the marriage of Christians from that of other people. This would be deeply contrary to the true meaning of God's plan, in which it is precisely the created reality that is a 'great mystery' in reference to Christ and the Church.[20]

18 John Paul II, Allocution to the Roman Rota, 30 January 2003, n. 2, English translation found at: www.vatican.va.

19 Benedict XVI, Allocution to the Roman Rota, January 26, 2013, accessed at: www.vatican.va.

20 John Paul II, Allocution to the Roman Rota, February 1, 2001, n. 8, accessed at: www.vatican.va.

Pope Francis has also reflected on faith and consent and has asked the question: how can we recognize nullity of consent in those who are baptized, yet have no active faith; rather they have embraced the values of the world, not Christian values? Can this choice for the values of the world be argued as error concerning the sacramental dignity of marriage? In this paper I am trying to explore Pope Francis' comments regarding lack of faith leading to error determining the will (c. 1099). This is not the traditional understanding of determining error concerning the sacramentality of marriage.

Herein lies the key: a person who does not have a contrary intention is presumed to consent according to the Code's understanding. In other words, no intention or lack of intention does not affect consent. This is how lack of faith is often interpreted: if a choice is not against marriage or its values, it does not affect consent to marriage. Let us turn our attention away from what is not being chosen – faith – and focus rather on what *is* being chosen: the values of the world. In fact, this choice for worldly values can affect consent. A choice for the world, in the words of the song would reflect: "the only faith we have is faith in us," or in Pope Francis' words: a choice for the "lying paradigm of the world." The question is: is the spirit of the world stronger in some people than their Christianity? In choosing marriage, are people choosing the "lying paradigm of the world" or Christian marriage?

In the traditional understanding of error determining the will, a baptized person who does not have an active faith is presumed to consent validly, as long as he/she has the minimum intention to do what the Church does in marrying. Active faith is not a prerequisite for the sacrament of marriage.

There has long been a recognition that people are marrying without a level of faith, and a question of how this lack of faith is affecting their marriages. At the same time, we are cautioned not to require faith as necessary for the sacrament. What is the happy medium? If we look at the understanding of marriage and its sacramentality through a different lens, we might be able to get at the fundamental recognition of invalidity of consent through error determining the will of sacramentality. To get to that different lens, we will begin by understanding error determining the will and how error concerning the sacramental dignity of marriage has been traditionally understood.

What is error determining the will?

Funghini explains how error affects consent:

> error implies a determined or particular misrepresentation in the judgment of the agent, which is positive in fact, but not at all conforming to reality, because of a false understanding and representation of the object being considered. It is a subjective

> persuasion that the matter is nothing else but what the agent feels it to be, even if in fact he has this feeling for a different reason.[21]

The person in error has no doubt about what he or she believes to be true. If doubt existed, then a different ground of nullity would be involved (i.e. simulation, conditioned consent). Error exists in the intellect, not in the will. However, the will cannot choose something that it does not know. Thus, if the person is in error about what marriage entails, then the will might choose to enter something which is not marriage (c. 1099). If a person's error is so deeply ingrained that the person can only conceive of marriage the way he/she knows it (and that is erroneous), then that error determined the person's will and the person's consent was invalid.

What does this mean? The law of the Church sees as "erroneous" any vision of marriage that does not coincide with the vision outlined in the *Code of Canon Law*. Not only does the Code consider opposite views "erroneous," our culture considers the Church's view to be the ideal of what marriage is held to be. Thus, many people at least give lip service to the concepts that marriage is a lifelong commitment which is indissoluble, faithful, open to children, and for the good of the parties. Yet, the question that must be addressed in marriage nullity cases is whether the people truly accepted this vision of marriage to which they have given lip service. To get a person's true vision of marriage, one has to go deeper than asking if a person was in error about the essential properties and elements of marriage. Instead, you need to understand the person and his or her cultural background, how he or she thinks in order to understand that person's consent to marriage. Remember Francis is speaking of those for whom "the pursuit of personal well-being instead of the glory of the Lord ... for the one who bends under this attitude the faith will always be deprived of its value as a normative force of orientation. This leaves the door open for compromises with one's own egoism and the pressures of the current mentality ..."[22] How does this mentality affect a person's consent to marriage?

What is error concerning the sacramental dignity of marriage?

Mendonça explains the traditional understanding of how error concerning sacramentality affects consent:

> That a marriage between two validly baptized persons is a sacrament represents the firm and explicit teaching of the Church.

21 R. Funghini, "Errore sulla qualità della persona direttamente e principalmente intesa," in *Errore e dolo nel consenso matrimoniale canonico*, 1995, 48.

22 Francis, Allocution to the Roman Rota, January, 23, 2015, accessed at www.vatican.va.

According to this teaching, therefore, the sacramental dignity and the natural reality are so united in a marriage between two baptized persons that they are considered inseparable or identical, leading to the conclusion that in a Christian marriage sacrament is contract or contract is sacrament, a conclusion we often find in the writings of authors and in Rotal jurisprudence ... On a practical level, we are faced with the difficult question as to how can a person without faith or without a sacramental intention celebrate a valid marriage ... According to the prevailing doctrinal and jurisprudential positions on the issue, a person who, for lack or absence of faith, is not properly disposed to receive the sacrament may either explicitly or implicitly exclude the sacramental aspect and thereby cause the nullity of marriage. It is the positive contrary intention, and not the lack or absence of faith per se, which would underlie the nullity. In some cases, lack or absence of faith could amount to radical or deep-rooted error which in turn may lead to the exclusion of sacramentality as an essential element or property of marriage. In this situation, the person concerned would be choosing a marriage (the object of consent) which is bereft of one or more of the essential properties or elements, sacramentality being one of them. This type of error is called determining error implied in c. 1099.[23]

Stankiewicz adds to our understanding:

> The jurisprudence of the Roman Rota has often discussed and continues to discuss juridical consequences which arise from the inseparability of the sacrament and of the contract. Therefore, when it is a question of a marriage celebrated by an unbelieving person, it is often asked whether the defect of *personal faith* in a baptized person who marries could be able to obstruct the valid celebration of a marriage. It must at once be noted that the jurisprudence of the Rota 'directs its consideration to the honesty and the *rectitude of the intention* rather than to the lack of faith itself ...' In other words, 'as often as baptized spouses do with a legitimate form all those things which are necessary by the law of nature, the bond and the sacrament itself become indissoluble. And this depends not on the faith of those contracting marriage, nor even upon their will, but upon the will of Christ ...

---

23 A. Mendonça, "Exclusion of the Sacramentality of Marriage: Recent Trends in Rotal Jurisprudence," in *Studia canonica*, 31 (1997) 47.

> 'Consequently, ... it does not really matter whether the person contracting (marriage) believes in the sacrament of marriage, or in the existence of God, or in the divine institution of the sacraments; as long as he or she does not exclude the contract as it is in its very nature, or positively repudiate whatever involves the essence of this contract.'[24]

Let us turn to a Rotal decision from 2004 which highlights the point that lack of faith does not lead to error concerning sacramentality. In this case both parties were non-practicing baptized Catholics. They married in a Catholic ceremony, had a child together, even had the child baptized. Common life lasted two years. The petitioner "states that both parties, although baptized, never lived religiously, and that while celebrating marriage they neglected to intend the reception of the sacrament. In fact, he maintains that both parties were unaware of the sacred nature of marriage and they did not acknowledge in any manner at that moment the religious dimension of the act which they were celebrating."[25]

Boccafola reflects on the parties' consent: "if a person who marries really wants to enter upon a true natural nuptial pact, he or she does not have to add anything more to his or her natural consent in order to obtain also the sacramental dignity. The only necessary thing one must do is place a true matrimonial consent. Therefore, it follows that faith is not necessary, but only consent."[26] He continues: " ... the 'sacramental dignity' of marriage is nothing other than the very natural bond between the baptized spouses, i.e., the stable covenant between a man and a woman for sharing a partnership of life through an exclusive intimate sexual relationship and which is ordered toward the happiness and mutual help between spouses and for the good of offspring."[27] Boccafola summarizes: "Sacramentality then adds nothing to the natural covenant; nevertheless, it is the essential conjugal covenant raised to the saving sign and font of grace ..."[28] Boccafola considers how marriage becomes a sacrament: "Hence, if a person really wants to contract a true natural pact, he does not have to add anything else to his or her matrimonial consent in order to receive also sacramental dignity. The only

---

24 A. Stankiewicz, "Recent Jurisprudence of the Roman Rota Concerning Total and Partial Simulation," in W. Woestman, ed., *Simulation of Marriage Consent. Doctrine. Jurisprudence. Questionnaires* (Ottawa, Saint Paul University, 2000) 203-204, citing *c.* Doheny, February 18, 1959, in *RRD*, vol. 51, 60, no. 2.

25 *C.* Boccafola, 6 May 2004, in *Philippine Canonical Forum*, 9 (2009) 278, #10. A negative decision was rendered in this case. This case is also discussed in: A. Mendonça, "A Doctrinal and Jurisprudential Approach to the Ground of Determining Error," in *Studies in Church Law*, 3 (2007) 222-228.

26 Ibid., 278-279, #10.

27 *C.* Boccafola, 6 May 2004, in *Philippine Canonical Forum*, 9 (2009) 271-272, #6.

28 Ibid., 272, #6.

necessary thing one has to do is to place a true matrimonial consent. From this it follows that what is necessary is not the faith but only the consent."[29]

Another Rotal decision from 2006, *c.* De Agnelis, outlines the same principles:

> one who contracts marriage should manifest minimum of intention of doing what the Church does. This minimal intention in those who marry is not an intention to confect or to receive the sacrament but only an intention to enter into a conjugal bond. In fact, baptized non-Catholics do not think that marriage is a sacrament, and yet the Church has always considered their marriages as valid and sacramental.[30]

Yet another Rotal decision confirms this understanding, *c.* Turnaturi, of July 21, 2005. Addressing the exclusion of sacramental dignity, Turnaturi states: "Adhering to the magisterium, our jurisprudence has constantly and frequently declared and stated that to contract marriage valid consent is sufficient and faith is not necessary."[31] Citing Cormac Burke, Turnaturi explains:

> However, if one wants to consider the problems from the point of view of minimum of intentionality that is required, one must conclude that the specific minimum intentionality is simply to marry. An intention to receive the sacrament is not necessary. What is necessary is not a conscious sacramental intention, and much less a religious intention, but a simple intention to marry. The Protestants who marry usually do not do so with a sacramental intention; and despite this, the theology and canon law have never contested the validity of their marriages.[32]

Turnaturi continues:

> The Apostolic Exhortation *Familiaris consortio* also presupposes this natural reality, which the spouses should embrace with a right intention, and this does not require faith but a right intention, at least a prevalent one, to accept the conjugal cov-

---

29 Ibid., 273, #7.

30 A. Mendonça, "A Doctrinal and Jurisprudential Approach to the Ground of Determining Error," in *Studies in Church Law*, 3 (2007) 231, citing *c.* De Angelis, March 10, 2006.

31 *C.* Turnaturi, July 21, 2005, in *Philippine Canonical Forum*, 10 (2008) 352, #14.

32 Ibid., 356, #16, citing *c.* Cormac Burke, 'La sacramentalità del matrimonio: riflessioni canoniche,' in *Sacramentalità e validità del matrimonio nella giurisprudenza del Tribunale della Rota Romana*, Città del Vaticano, Libreria editrice Vaticana, 1995, 145.

> enant instituted by the Creator, that is, to consent to a true marriage (cfr. N. 68).[33]

Citing a decision *coram* Pinto from 1971, Turnaturi reflects on a traditional understanding of error concerning sacramental dignity:

> one who, due to an erroneous or contrary mind, 'rejects the sacrament, considering it as an empty ritual, is incapable of willing the sacrament ... And if, only to be allowed to contract marriage, he/she wants an empty ceremony, he/she certainly cannot be said to intend to receive it ... The will to exclude the sacrament is not overturned by the will to go through the ritual, for even if the sacred rite is made available to him/her, it is received by the simulator as not sacred, which in fact is not sufficient for the sacrament.' (decision *c.* Pinto, 28 June 1971, in *RRT Dec.*, 63 [1971], p. 596, n. 15).[34]

Out of this traditional understanding, we note: the intention to marry is sufficient to bring about the sacrament in two baptized people. However, what of those in the situation wherein a sacred rite is not considered sacred (as in the words of Pinto from 1971)? To take that a step further, what of those who choose rather worldly values more than values based on faith? If the rite is not seen as sacred, and worldly values are chosen instead, is that a choice against sacramentality?

The key to understanding the question lies in going beyond the traditional understanding of what is happening when a person who lacks an active faith consents to marriage. Boccafola summarizes the traditional understanding of how lack of active faith does not usually affect consent:

> The Sacrament of Matrimony, or 'the sacramentality' of matrimony consists therefore in the fact that the natural marital covenant or contract itself between a baptized man and a baptized woman has been transformed into a sign and source of grace, i.e. one of the seven sacraments of the New Law. The sacramental dignity is the essential matrimonial convent itself. Sacramentality adds nothing to this natural pact except the fact that for the baptized who have consummated their marriage, this pact, besides being naturally intrinsically permanent, be-

33 Ibid., 358, #18.

34 Ibid., 362-363, #20, citing *c.* Pinto, June 28, 1971.

> cause extrinsically indissoluble because it is also a sign of the union of Christ and His Church.[35]

Is Pope Francis asking us to try for a fuller understanding of error concerning sacramental dignity? An error that is rooted in the person's embrace of popular culture in which there is an implicit rejection of a culture of faith? In that implicit rejection, the person is not choosing marriage as God intended, he/she is choosing an empty ritual. Pope Francis even cautions that the person might have a certain kind of faith, but that the person is affected by the "frequent prevalence of worldly thinking"; that person is affected by "spiritual worldliness 'which hides behind the appearance of piety and even love for the Church' (Ap. Ex. *Evangelii gaudium*, n. 93), which leads to the pursuit of personal well-being instead of the glory of the Lord." How can we recognize this? By the pursuit of personal well-being over anything else.

How can we understanding the choice the person is making?

An error which is so rooted in the personality of the contractant can affect consent if it influences the person's choice to the point that the person can only choose a marriage that is not sacramental. Judges must be aware of the culture of the person alleging marriage nullity, as well as of the background and concrete experiences which could have influenced that person's consent. Boccafola explains:

> To prove that one is no longer dealing with simple error one must demonstrate in some fashion that the error has not remained in the intellect, but has entered the field of operations of the will. This may be done by pointing out concrete deeds, actions or for example, a state of mind perhaps in rebellion against the Church and society etc., which have caused the will to be determined to choose only a non-sacramental marriage. In many Rotal cases the absence of Christian education or an upbringing contrary to the tenets of the faith is often seen as a remote cause of nullity in that absorbed erroneous ideas might possibly have influenced the spouse to limit the object of his consent; but as long as these ideas are only generic and vague, they are not seen to have sufficient force to determine the will. But if a precise reason can be indicated why a spouse would definitely have applied these particular ideas to his own

35 K. Boccafola, "Lack of Faith and Its Effect on the Validity of the Matrimonial Consent of the Baptized," in *The Jurist*, 74 (2014) 65.

specific marriage, this can be a sufficient demonstration that the error has determined the will.[36]

What act of the will proves error determining the will?

Many grounds of nullity require proof of a positive act of the will or something very similar: cases of simulation or exclusion (can. 1101, §2); cases of conditioned consent (can. 1102); cases of error of fact/person (can. 1097, §2); and cases of error of law/error determining the will (can. 1099). All these grounds trace back to a choice. For some grounds that choice is described as a 'positive act of the will.' For other grounds, the choice 'determines the will.' In all cases, the choice/act of the will must enter the level of the will in order for it to affect consent.

There are three elements to an act of the will:

> exclusion takes place in the volitive faculty, that is, an act of the mind (intelligence) is not sufficient, like error – unless it determines the will (cf. c. 1099) … next, there must be an act, since something cannot be decided except through an operation of the will. Thus, an habitual will cannot attain the level of an act of the will because it stays in a place of tendency, as if 'at the entry,' or an interpretative will, which is totally absent at the moment of matrimonial consent. Finally, the act must be positive, that is the positivity is required because inertia of the will – or rather an absence of movement – does not suffice in order to achieve (realize) something.[37]

Stankiewicz explains the positive act of the will in cases of simulation:

> it is necessary that all three elements be present together if the exclusion is to produce an invalidating effect:
>
> a) the *will*, therefore not the intellect, or its specific acts, such as ideas, opinions, errors;
>
> b) *act*, or the transition from inaction to movement, which (act) is clearly distinguished from a mere inclination or a habitual will or a mind set not determining the act at all, and also not from a mere generic or interpretative will, which demonstrates one's disposition of the mind, or a habit; and from hope from

36 K. Boccafola, "Error Concerning Sacramental Dignity. Limits of the Object and Proof," *Forum* 7 (1996) 319-320.

37 C. Caberletti, 21 July 2005, #5.1, in *Recueil canonique d'Arras. Traductions de jurisprudence rotale*, 35 (2008) JU/4107.

a mere foresight and from desire, which things of themselves do not per se affect the consent and can stand together with it;

c) a *positive* (act), not a negative one, or 'to not want," (*velle non*) but not really 'not to want' (*nolle*) ... not, however, actual and explicit, since it is enough for the (act) to be implicit and virtual in the matter in question (namely, still keeping the force of the act expressed and not recalled).[38]

Stankiewicz cautions: "to produce the simulation of marriage a simple absence of the intention of contracting is not sufficient. For consent is manifested externally by a positive act of the will which is only made invalid by a contrary positive act."[39] Lack of the will does not affect consent in simulation cases, nor in cases of error determining the will. Absence of faith in itself is not an act of the will.

The positive act of the will explained differently: a positive act of the will is a choice (an act of the will) that has been made concretely (a positive act) in a person's life. The choice or decision begins theoretically in a person's mind or intellect. When an idea is in the theoretical stage, it does not yet affect the will. For the choice/decision/will act to be 'positive,' it must be concrete or real. It must actually be part of or enter into the person's choice. Provost adds to our understanding:

> What constitutes a positive act of the will admits of a variety of phenomena. Presumed by Bruno is the basic distinction between a positive act, in which something is posited (an act takes place), and a negative act, in which nothing happens (an omission). An omission is never sufficient for simulation; it requires that an act takes place, that something be posited.[40]

Is the act of determining the will the same act as the positive act of the will required for proof of simulation? No ... but it is similar/close. In both cases, the exclusion must enter the level of the will in order for it to affect consent. The starting points between the error and simulation are different. As Beal notes: "Since simulation involves a positive act of the will, simulators must be aware, at least in an inchoate way, of what they are intending, but they need not be aware

38 A. Stankiewicz, "Recent Jurisprudence of the Roman Rota Concerning Total and Partial Simulation," in W. Woestman (*Simulation*, 190, citing *c.* Ferraro, October 16, 1984, in *RRD*, vol. 76, 520, n. 3; *c.* Davino, April 18, 1991, in *RRD*, vol. 83, 269ff, no. 3.
39 A. Stankiewicz, "Recent Jurisprudence of the Roman Rota Concerning Total and Partial Simulation," in W. Woestman, 180.
40 J. Provost, "Simulated Consent: A New Way of Looking at an Old Way of Thinking. Part I," *The Jurist* 55 (1995) 705, where he is citing *c.* Bruno, February 1, 1991.

of the invalidating effect of their intentions."[41] An example: simulation would take place in the person who recognizes that the Church teaches one thing and that he or she believes another. The person whose error determines his or her will sees only one kind of marriage – an erroneous one – and does not acknowledge that the Church sees things differently for his or her own marriage.

How does an act of will become 'positive'?

An act of the will can be: actual or virtual, explicit or implicit.

Actual or virtual act of the will:

"An actual act of the will is accomplished at the moment of consent. A virtual act of the will is emitted before consent, and has never been revoked."[42] The act of the will (choice) might be in the person's mind at the moment of choosing marriage. In other words, as the person is saying 'I do,' he or she is also thinking of this decision. That is an 'actual act of the will.'

"A virtual act is one that has already taken place before the celebration of the wedding, but has never been revoked – thus completely keeping its force/power."[43] If the act is 'virtual,' the choice entered the person's mind and will at a time prior to consent and continues through to consent because it remains in the will. It is commonly accepted that an act once posited is presumed to continue (to not be revoked). For example, canon 1092 of the 1917 Code spoke of "a condition once imposed and not revoked."

Turning to an example of a virtual positive act of the will: A person who sees her mother be beaten by her father as she is growing up. An habitual will is the person who sees it and dislikes it but never makes the connection with herself, never thinks 'I will not let this happen to me.' Such events affect the person's personality, but do not affect the person's decision regarding marriage. If, however, that same person, after a particularly horrible beating that her father gave her mother, said to herself: 'I will never permit that to happen to me. I will never stay in such a relationship.' That person now has made a virtual act of the will, a positive, concrete act. The concrete event of her father beating her mother has entered her will and affected her future choice to marry. As a virtual act, it is presumed to perdure unless it is revoked.

41 J. Beal, Matrimonial Consent, in J. Beal, J. Coriden, T. Green, eds., *New Commentary on the Code of Canon Law* (Mahwah, NJ: Paulist Press, 2000) 1313.
42 C. Caberletti, 21 July 2005, #5.2, in *Recueil canonique d'Arras. Traductions de jurisprudence rotale*, 35 (2008) JU/4107.
43 C. Caberletti, 17 November 2005, #4.B, in *Recueil canonique d'Arras. Traductions de jurisprudence rotale*, 35 (2008) JU/4119.

In cases of error determining the will, a positive act of the will is not required. Mendonça describes what that error determining the will should look like, after comparing simulation (conscious exclusion) and error (unconscious exclusion) cases:

> error becomes the common factor in both conscious and unconscious exclusion of the essential properties of marriage. In conscious exclusion … the contractant in error is somehow aware of his or her error and yet goes ahead and chooses the object infected by the error. Because this exclusion is a conscious act, it is simulation in the strict sense of the word, the error being the motive for simulation. Whereas in unconscious exclusion, the contactant in error is unaware of the dissonance between the true nature of marriage as taught by the Church and the marriage he or she has conceptualized in his or her own mind, and he or she consents to that marriage alone. In this situation, the exclusion of the essential properties of marriage takes place by the conscious choice of an object which does not include those properties. In canonical literature, this has come to be known as exclusion by 'non-inclusion.' This constitutes the ground of 'determining error' of canon 1099 in the strict sense of the word.[44]

Morrisey summarizes:

> A conscious exclusion is an act of simulation … an unconscious exclusion, the contractant, unaware of the dissonance between the true nature of marriage and the particular marriage being conceptualized, consents to that marriage alone. This is sometimes called non-inclusion, but really it is the determining error of canon 1099.[45]

Non-inclusion is different from including something other than marriage in one's consent. Reflecting on the positive act of the will in an earlier article on total simulation and 'invalid convalidation,' I cited an example by Gas i Aixendri which tackles the subject of how an apparent non-choice is, in fact, a choice:[46]

---

44 A. Mendonça, "A Doctrinal and Jurisprudential Approach to the Ground of Determining Error," in *Studies in Church Law*, 3 (2007) 238-239.

45 F. Morrisey, "Error Determining the Will: Canon 1099," paper presented at the annual convention of the Canadian Canon Law Society, October 2011, 17.

46 See my: "Defective Validations Revisited," in V.G. D'Souza, ed., *In the Service of Truth and Justice*. Festschrift in Honour of Prof. Augustine Mendonça, St. Peter's Pontifical Institute, Bangalore, India, 2008, 167-190.

Looking at Rotal jurisprudence and commentaries on total simulation, there is an interesting example raised by Gas i Aixendri,[47] citing R. Ahlers: Mr. X and Miss Y met as children. After completing high school they began living together because they did not want to be alone and because they wanted to fulfill their affective and sexual needs. After some years their friends convince them to marry to *legalize* their situation, *but with the intention of changing nothing in their relationship*. They did not want marriage, but there was no internal act refusing marriage.[48] The question for the understanding of total simulation is that there must be a positive act of the will against marrying. A lack of will is not sufficient. Gas i Aixendri asks the question: how does one demonstrate that the person who has no intention of celebrating marriage before the Church is opposed with a positive act of the will? ...

Gas i Aixendri states that the key to understanding this is in the concept of the positive act of the will. He offers different interpretations of the positive act of the will. Some authors recognize a positive act of exclusion in the fact that the person *positively* seeks an end different from marriage. This is considered as total simulation, and can be considered in terms of 'invalid convalidation.' Other authors seem to accept the possibility of a 'presumed' positive act of the will. This presumed act of the will is found in those cases where there are erroneous beliefs that affect the person's consent. ... Finally, for other authors the requirement of the positive act of the will in cases of a lack of consent has become an insoluble difficulty. It would be impossible to speak of a positive act of the will in such cases because the person does not explicitly exclude marriage.[49]

Gas i Aixendri reflects on cases in which, like the one cited at the beginning of his article, the person has no *intention of contracting*. The difficulty is to find the positive act of the will in this lack of intention because there is no explicit positive act of the will against marriage.[50] Traditional jurisprudence requires proof of the following: a) the will (*voluntas*); b) the transition

47 M. Gas i Aixendri, "L'assenza di volontà matrimoniale tra simulazione totale ed incapacità," in *Ius Ecclesiae*, 16 (2004) 163-181. In this article he is commenting on the decision *c.* Defilippi, 25 July 2002, studying the grounds of total simulation, in *Ius Ecclesiae*, 16 (2004) 135-163.

48 Ibid., 164, note 3.

49 Ibid., 164-165.

50 Ibid., 170-171.

> into action (*actus*); and c) the positivity of the act (*positivus, non negativus*): '*velle non', non vero 'nolle.'*[51] Considering this case, there was no act of the will against marriage, but the person's will was to pose an act that was deprived of any matrimonial intention. In this way the person excluded marriage itself: the person wanted only the external sign, *precisely because* the person had the will not to become a spouse. Simulated consent can consist in substituting the true intention to marry with another will, one which is *positive*.[52] What one must examine precisely is what the person is choosing in going through the ceremony.[53]

This is a very important point in understanding what people are choosing when they are imbued with an error that determines the will concerning the sacramentality of their union. That they do not think about sacramentality in itself seems to indicate that there is no positive act of the will against sacramentality. However, the fact that they chose to live with the values of the world and culture around them demonstrates a positive choice against the sacramentality of marriage because they are making a positive choice to choose something which is not marriage. The fact that they have chosen a world-view that is contrary to the the world-view that accepts the sacramentality of marriage means that their error has determined their will. Turning once again to Pope Francis' words:

> For this reason the judge, in deliberating the validity of expressed consent, must keep in mind the context of value and faith – or the absence or lack thereof – in which the intention to marry is formed. Indeed, the lack of knowledge of the contents of the faith might lead to what the Code calls determinant error of the will (cf. can. 1099).

Explicit and implicit acts of the will:

The distinction between an explicit and an implicit act of the will is also important to this understanding. An explicit act exists "when it appears directly and immediately from its very own words," and an implicit act exists "when it is hidden in the words that are used (for it is contained and hidden in a mass of words)."[54] Caberletti explains: "An act is explicit if the exclusion is manifested by clear words … an act is implicit if it is comprised in the reality of another act,

51 Ibid., 171.

52 Ibid., 173.

53 My "Defective Validations Revisited," 182-183.

54 A. Stankiewicz, "Recent Jurisprudence of the Roman Rota Concerning Total and Partial Simulation," in W. Woestman, 191-192, citing *c.* Palestro, May 16, 1990, *RRD*, vol. 82, 368, no. 7.

without being manifested explicitly."[55] An example from a case of exclusion of the *bonum prolis*: the explicit act is the one where the person states clearly that openness to children is excluded. The implicit act can also be manifested through actions which exclude openness to children in themselves. In another example:

> the act is explicit if the subject excludes an essential element or property directly, or implicit, if the person who marries intends – as an object of the will – something in which the essential property or element is completely absent or removed. A person excludes the *bonum fidei* implicitly who follows or leads a dissolute lifestyle, or who wishes to keep his/her freedom to have sexual relations with another person of either sex.[56]

Remember the Rotal axiom: actions speak louder than words. People's actions and behaviours can explain what they were thinking/feeling/intending. Be open to the fact that what people do is often more clear than what they say. Pay attention to their actions and whether their actions match their words. Also remember: People do not think in canonical terms. They may exclude an essential element or property of marriage yet not realize that that is what they are doing. They may even disagree that that was what they did. They are thinking in 'layman's' terms; the law is working with canonical terms.

Stankiewicz speaks of the implicit positive act of the will:

> Even if the constant and common jurisprudence holds that a positive implicit act is sufficient to nullify consent to marriage, this (positive implicit act) 'has as its direct and immediate object something in which the exclusion of marriage or its essential property is contained'; ... However, it is certain that the presumption of the act of itself is not sufficient. For the so-called *presumed* act is equivalent to a 'more or less probable conjecture' in which 'nothing of a positive reason is to be found.' On the contrary, 'an implicit act remains in the positive order, for, although its substance may not appear directly and immediately in the manifestation of the person who is acting, nevertheless it is found in the same place, again and again, really and not presumably, positively and not interpretatively,

---

55 *C.* Caberletti, 21 July 2005, #5.2, in *Recueil canonique d'Arras. Traductions de jurisprudence rotale*, 35 (2008) JU/4107.

56 *C.* Caberletti, 17 November 2005, #4.B, in *Recueil canonique d'Arras. Traductions de jurisprudence rotale*, 35 (2008) JU/4119.

> although just as it were in the crevices and hiding places of the same manifestation.[57]

Error determining the will often looks like implicit simulation. Simulation/exclusion requires the proof of a positive act of the will. Such an act of the will can be implicit. We could say: implicit simulation would take place in the person who recognizes at some level that the Church teaches one thing and that he/she believes another. The person whose error determines his/her will sees only one kind of marriage – an erroneous one, and does not acknowledge that the Church sees things differently for his/her own marriage. Thus, the starting points between the error and simulation are different.

Error determining the will should not require the proof of a positive act of the will since no such proof is required by law. However, that error determining the will often looks in practice like an implicit positive act of the will.

Exclusion of sacramentality and modern culture:

The common jurisprudence of the Rota reflects on the role of faith in forming consent:

> A personal, conscious and active faith cannot be sought for the validity of Christian marriage, as the personal faith of the spouses *per se* does not constitute the sacramentality of marriage.
>
> According to this, we may conclude that only a firm rejection on the part of the baptized and non-believing spouse to do what the Church does in the administration of sacraments may invalidate the sacrament of marriage.
>
> In spite of some contrary but isolated voices, it may be prudently said that if a baptized person has the intention to marry and to bind in an indissoluble and exclusive love, that person possesses even the personal disposition, faith or at least the *vestigium fidei* that must be presumed in anyone baptized.
>
> To be in line with the prevalent jurisprudence, the lack of faith, then, *per se* does not invalidate the consent, when there is *recta intentio* to celebrate a true marriage. From the point of view of process, in the sphere of proofs, however, the lack of faith, together with the other elements, comes under *causa simulandi*

57 A. Stankiewicz, "Recent Jurisprudence of the Roman Rota Concerning Total and Partial Simulation," in W. Woestman, 191, where he is citing *c.* De Jorio, April 16, 1975 in *RRD*, vol. 67, 311, no. 5; also *c.* De Jorio, June 13, 1979, Valladolid, no. 43, as well as *c.* Sabattani, October 29, 1963, in *RRD*, vol 55, 706, no. 3.

> and constitutes an indispensable probative element of the exclusion of sacramentality.[58]

Pope Francis said in his 2014 Rotal address to judges: "Part of human maturity is also to be able to immerse oneself in the mentality and legitimate aspirations of the community in which one carries out one's service. Like this, he will become an interpreter of the *animus communitatis* which characterizes that portion of the People of God affected by his work. He will also be able to exercise justice in a way adapted to the exigencies of the concrete situation, and not in a legalistic and abstract way. ... he will feel the need to enter more deeply into the situation of the parties involved, studying in depth the documents and every element relevant to the judgment."

How can we as judges understand what parties chose when consenting to marriage? Did the person choose ideals or reality? What the judge instructing the case must discover is whether the person's ideals were what was in the person's mind at the time of consent, or whether the person's character, background, or culture influenced his or her consent to the point that the person was in error. What must be discovered is not the lip-service paid to the teachings of the Church concerning marriage, but what was really in the person's mind and heart at the time consent was exchanged.

Returning to Pope Francis' challenge: how do we understanding those who choose 'marriage,' but

- expect marriage to serve their desires
- expect marriage to permit them to pursue their own wants/needs to the detriment of the other
- live worldly values
- have no active faith
- have a faith according to their own desires

Is there error concerning sacramentality determining the will? Those who are not choosing the sacrament because they do not know it (error), and are choosing something that does not include the sacrament (fulfilment of their own needs, material gain, etc.) could be in the situation of error concerning sacramentality determining the will.

---

58 L. Sabbarese, "Faith, Intention and Sacramental Dignity in Marriages Among the Baptized," in *Studies in Church Law*, 3 (2007) 324-325.

SEMINAR

TRANSITIONING SPONSORSHIP WITH REGARD TO RELIGIOUS INSTITUTES

Brother Patrick T. Shea, O.F.M.

There has been a lot of development since the CLSA issued a booklet on sponsorship in 2006. There is a lot of material out there, especially put out by the Catholic Health Association, who after a meeting, kindly shared materials with me. Most of the CHA journal *Health Progress* is available on line. The National Catholic Education Association (NCEA) also has a number of useful publications.

In the most recent issue of *Health Progress* an article by Panicola and Hamel states that health care in the United States is in a state of major transformation, the likes of which has perhaps not been seen.[1] It seems likely that similar statements have been frequently made over the last number of years.

Concepts/Ideas

Sponsorship

A working definition of "*sponsorship*" is offered in the 2006 CLSA publication *Sponsorship in the United States Context: Theory and Praxis:* "Sponsorship of an apostolate or ministry is a formal relationship between a recognized Catholic organization and a legally formed entity entered into for the sake of promoting or sustaining the Church's mission in the world."[2]

In a 2001 article in *Health Progress*, Sharon Holland says that by "sponsor" she means an entity that is a public juridic person and carries out a ministry or apostolate in the name of the Church.[3] Another discussion of sponsorship observes that sponsorship is a reservation of canonical control by the juridic person

---

1 Michael Panicola and Ron Hamel, "Catholic Identity and the Reshaping of Catholic Health Care," *Health Progress* 96 (Sept.-Oct. 2015) 46.

2 Rosemary Smith, Warren Brown, and Nancy Reynolds, eds. *Sponsorship in the United States Context: Theory and Praxis.* (Alexandria, VA: Canon Law Society of America, 2006) 137.

3 Sharon Holland, "Sponsorship and the Vatican," *Health Progress* 82 (July-Aug. 2001) 32.

that founded and/or sustains an incorporated apostolate that remains canonically a part of the church entity.[4]

In a 2013 article in *Health Progress*, Frank Morrisey says that sponsorship involves use of a church entity's name, exercise of certain stewardship responsibilities, and a relationship that entails quality control or mission effectiveness. He also describes attributes of a sponsored work: it must have a spiritual purpose, it must answer a need, the undertaking must have sufficient means to accomplish its purposes, it must have stability, those persons entrusted with this work must be accountable and be good stewards, and the care or work must be one of quality.[5]

All these sources acknowledge that "sponsorship" is not a term found in the *Code of Canon Law* nor is an applicable usage found in civil law and it is a relatively recent term.[6] In the question-and-answer section of the presentation on which this article is based, Melanie DiPietro said that the term "sponsorship" was developed rather quickly and informally and on reflection, it may be better to avoid the word sponsorship, which a civil court could decide to interpret in a way that it finds appropriate. She indicates that it may be better to not use the term "sponsorship" and simply say what is now meant by sponsorship, something to the effect of: canonical responsibility and accountability to a public juridic person.

The term "sponsorship" is often confused with control and ownership. "Ownership" deals more with holding title to property used by the work or apostolate, and "control" tends to refer to internal governance of the work, while sponsorship deals more with the body under whose name the work operated.[7]

Juridic persons are discussed in canons 113-123 of the *Code of Canon Law*. In *A Guide to Understanding Public Juridic Persons in the Health Care Ministry*, a juridic person is described as an artificial creation of the law, resembling a corporation as found in civil law. It is the subject of rights and duties and can hold property distinctly from the persons who represent it. It can acquire property, sue and be sued.[8]

---

4 Daniel Conlin, "Sponsorship at the Crossroads," *Health Progress* 82 (July-Aug. 2001) 20.

5 Francis Morrisey, "Our Sponsors – Yesterday, Today and Tomorrow," *Health Progress* 94 (July-Aug. 2013) 57.

6 Jordan Hite, Sharon Holland and Francis Morrisey, *A Guide to Understanding Public Juridic Persons in the Health Care Ministry* (St. Louis: Catholic Health Association, 2012) 10.

7 Jordan Hite, Sharon Holland and Francis Morrisey, 9.

8 Ibid., 27.

In *A Guide to Understanding Public Juridic Persons in the Health Care Ministry*, the authors address the question of what factors have motivated religious institutes to request public juridic personality for their sponsored ministries. The authors answer that the main factor seemed to be diminishing numbers of religious to serve the ministries or be involved in administration. They add that the success of laity in participating in the ministries and understanding the charisms of the religious institutes in health care also led them to consider this option.[9]

The authors also noted that the option most frequently chosen has been public juridic personality. Sharon Holland notes that a public juridic person, by definition, carries out its mission in the name of the Church. She added that the Congregation for Institutes of Consecrated Life and for Societies of Apostolic Life (commonly known as "CICLSAL") seems to have a preference for granting petitions to public juridic persons. She notes that in one case the Congregation granted private juridic personality because the particular case demonstrated an unique relationship with the religious institute which had once been the organization's formal sponsor. She adds that institutions like this were probably alienated in an era before reserved powers. She says that the private juridic person at issue involves a ministry and values review process that could serve as a model for Catholic systems of any type.[10]

"Ministerial Public Juridic Person" or "Ministerial Juridic Person" is a term that has recently come into use. The qualifier "Ministerial" is added to the term to distinguish them from other public juridic persons such as institutes of consecrated life which often combine to make up a ministerial public juridic person.[11]

The book on public juridic persons put out by the Catholic Health Association by Jordan Hite, Sharon Holland and Frank Morrisey is a very useful book. It answers a number of questions and is written probably more for lay people than for canonists; it is user friendly. It also has the *canonical statutes* of three public juridic persons as an appendix (Ascension Health Ministries, Mercy Health Ministry and St. Joseph Health Ministry). It is my understanding that Ascension

---

9 Ibid., 59.

10 Holland, Sharon. "Sponsorship and the Vatican," *Health Progress* 82 (July-Aug. 2001) 32.

11 Catholic Health Association, "Ministerial Juridic Person – The Growing Role for Laity in Canonical Sponsorship of Catholic Health Care," *Health Progress* 95 (2014) 60-63; Elias L. Ayuban, "Ministerial Public Juridic Persons: Blessings and Challenges," unpublished article from Catholic Health Association. [Fr. Elias Ayuban, CMF, participated in a panel discussion with sponsors of Catholic health ministries at a Catholic Health Association sponsorship institute in January, 2014 and this article reflects his presentation and he gave this article to the Catholic Health Association.]

Health Ministry is the largest of the Catholic health care systems, but I imagine that such facts can be quickly outdated.[12]

Civil Law Entities

Civil law has a number of recognized structures in statutory law and contract law allows the creation of more creative types of law. These matters can get very complex and selection of the proper legal device will depend on many factors, such as liability, control, tax issues; determination of the proper form is ordinarily a matter of negotiation.

A *corporation* is an artificial person or legal entity created by or under the authority of the law of a state. The law treats the corporation as a person who can, among other things, sue or be sued. It is distinct from the persons who comprise it.[13] This means that the liability is limited to the corporation and does not ordinarily extend to the people or entities that comprise it. It exists perpetually or for a period of years. In this area, people often talk about tiers or levels of governance. Ordinarily a corporation is governed by its board. A non-profit organization may have members which are sort of like shareholders; members have certain powers, often called reserved powers, which can only be exercised by the members and not by the board. This is a useful form and one that is readily understood by Church groups and the civil government.

A *partnership* is business owned by two or more persons that is not recognized as a corporation; it is essentially a voluntary contract between two or more persons to place their money, effects, labor and skill or some or all of them in a lawful business.[14] In this case profits go directly to the partners, as do liabilities. There are also limited partnerships in which there are general partners who can have liability as well as income, and limited partners who get some income but who avoid liability.

A *joint venture* is a legal entity in the nature of a partnership in the joint undertaking of a particular transaction for mutual profit. Generally all parties contribute assets and share risks. There is ordinarily a right to direct and govern the policy in connection therewith, which may be altered by agreement.[15] Unlike a typical partnership, a joint venture does not necessarily entail a continuing relationship among the parties. There is ordinarily a document that sets up a joint venture and this document is often in the form of a contract.

---

12 Jordan Hite, Sharon Holland, and Francis Morrisey, *A Guide to Understanding Public Juridic Persons in the Health Care Ministry* (St. Louis, MO: Catholic Health Association, 2012).

13 *Black's Law Dictionary*, 6th ed. (St. Paul, MN: West Publishing Co., 1990) 340.

14 Ibid., 1120.

15 Ibid., 839.

In each of these entities or arrangements, there may also be canonical issues. Fox notes that if a joint venture is a temporary means of collaboration, it may be a matter of ordinary administration. However, he notes, that when it is a matter of a long standing or permanent formal relationship, then this may be a matter for intervention of competent ecclesiastical authority.[16] One author suggests that one should put one's non-negotiables up front.[17] DiPietro states that an institute should not give another entity control over its "proper works." She notes that a proper work is a concept described in canons 675-677. An institute cannot without permission withdraw from or change its proper work. Proper works are different from the ministries of individual religious or recent undertakings of the institute that are not part of the proper work.[18]

There could be other arrangements based on a contract. For example, an institute of consecrated life which has a health care facility may enter into a *management contract* with a ministerial juridic person which may be the entire relationship or it may ultimately develop into some form of consolidation, affiliation or merger. Often this is done since the institute might have few, if any, qualified administrators available. Obviously, such an agreement would have to be very carefully drafted. It may be that a member of the institute may have some special position like the president of many religious high schools when the institute can no longer provide a principal. Thus, such an institute may have a member as chair of the board or as an executive vice president. This can be important for public perception and development purposes.

Choosing the right entity depends on issues like liability, control, tax issues, public perception, etc. Most entities can be developed to fit needs. As already noted, there are many types of corporations and partnerships. Some entities may be less helpful as a starting point; for example, many religious institutes are familiar with trusts and there may be a need for a trust in some cases, but it is probably a poor starting point since a trust may be better for managing assets and making disbursement, which is a sort of rather passive role, rather than operating a rather active apostolate.

When an institute of consecrated life chooses an appropriate legal entity, it must be careful to follow the process that law or the statutes lay out, e.g., corporations must have meetings and keep minutes. It is also important to pay at-

16 Joseph Fox, "Introductory Thoughts about Public Ecclesiastical Juridic Persons and Their Civilly Incorporated Apostolates, "*Angelicum* 76 (1999) 583.

17 Susan K. Hume, "Relationships with Other Providers," *Health Progress* 74 (Dec. 1993) 40.

18 Melanie DiPietro, "The Apostolate: Is a New Public Juridic Person Next?" *The Legal Bulletin* #75, 4-7; this issue has no date and a date could not be determined from reviewing the website of the Resource Center for Religious Institutes, but 2003 seems to be a fair approximation; see also Marlene Weisenbeck, "Holding Fast to the Mission and Works Proper to the Institute," *Health Progress* 88 (July-Aug. 2007) 13.

tention to the legal entity, to respect it and not ignore it or commingle funds (i.e. keep the economic and financial affairs of the civil law entity and the institute separate). Get expert or professional advice for the civil law entity. See that there is appropriate insurance for the civil law entity. Those involved in the institute of consecrated life should not interfere directly in the affairs of the civil law entity; they should have offices in the latter so they can act as officers in the civil law entity – at times a major superior or similar figure may have to act as head of a civil-law entity rather than as an officer of an institute of consecrated life. Language should not be used or there should not be conduct that is inconsistent with the separateness of the civil law entity; that could create evidence. Do not ignore the stated purposes of the civil law entity, do not ignore signs of financial instability, and do not ignore the civil law. [19] If this advice is not followed, what could happen is that a civil law court could treat the civil law entity as if it did not really exist; for corporations, this is called "piercing the corporate veil." It does not happen often but it can happen and it is not difficult to avoid.

Civil law attorneys will probably dominate this field and will want to use what they have found successful. Other experts like religious, canonists or theologians should not fear to raise concerns about issues from their fields since a civil entity can often be crafted to address other important concerns. An attorney should follow the client's instructions. Good attorneys who have had experience in this area can be quite creative.

Role of Diocesan Bishops

A diocesan bishop is the coordinator of ministry in his diocese[20] which would seem to include sponsored works. He may be asked to erect a juridic person or if another authority is asked, he may be asked for a votum. He is the one to see that the *Ethical and Religious Directives* are implemented in his diocese. It may be imprudent to ignore him. He may likely hear from other sources before the institute contacts him if it delays in contact, e.g., the angry person on the apostolate board who was outvoted. Since a bishop is to have concern for the people of his diocese he should be concerned about the maintenance of effective ministry in his diocese.[21] It would seem that the motu proprio of Benedict XVI which will be discussed in a little more detail later in the article would give a major role to diocesan bishops in the area of in service to charity.

---

19 Joy Flowers Conti, "Liability Issues for Related Church Entities," in *Acts of the Colloquium: Public Ecclesiastical Juridic Persons and Their Apostolates in the Roman Catholic Church in the U.S.A.: Canonical-Civil Aspects* (Rome: Pontifical University of St. Thomas Aquinas, 1998) 178-179.

20 Canon 394.

21 Barbara Anne Cusack, "Bishops and Religious Institutes: Building Collaboration," *Health Progress* 89 (May-June, 2008): 12; Barbara Anne Cusack, "The Role of the Diocesan Bishop in Relation to Health Care," *Health Progress* 87 (July-Aug. 2006) 64.

The liaison for religious in the diocese often represents the bishop in dealing with religious superiors or is the first contact for a major superior. The title of this official can vary from diocese to diocese from Vicar for Religious, to Delegate for Religious, to Liaison for Religious, to other titles. It would seem that this may be a useful person with whom an institute of consecrated life might deal since the liaison or vicar is often a religious and has access to the diocesan bishop, and she or he should have some understanding of the issues that the institute of consecrated life and its apostolate may be facing. Sometimes there may be a delegate for hospitals or a director of Catholic Charities with whom the health care facility normally relates and that may be the best conduit to the diocesan bishop.[22]

Even if a juridic person is to replace the institute of consecrated life, the diocesan bishop is involved in this petition; the statutes will ordinarily delineate the role of the diocesan bishop. The role of the bishop might not change, but what does change is the person to whom he turns if there are questions or concerns. Rather than a major superior, the bishop may be dealing with the chair of governing body of the juridic person.[23]

There is probably more specificity on the role of a diocesan bishop in the field of education since part of the *Code of Canon Law* deals with Catholic schools.

Decision-making by institutes of consecrate life should be based in a multidisciplinary approach, i.e., civil law, canon law, insurance, fund-raising, communications, finance (accounting). If there is a decision being made, be sure to involve all appropriate disciplines. Do not forget public relations. These matters are food for vast misunderstandings, not least inside the religious community. Fear can be a very harmful factor, even if it is unreasonable fear.

Canonists should not forget to speak up in such meetings. I remember a time when I was in diocese and a Catholic high school contacted me about some changes it wanted to make. I checked the file and returned the call, saying as nicely and calmly as I could, "Jim, it seems that technically your high school is not a Catholic school." I quoted canon 803 to him. The school was the product of a merger by two schools sponsored by religious orders and when the dust settled, neither religious order was really in charge, nor was there anything from the bishop recognizing the school. I am sure that there were lots of lawyers and educators involved in this but apparently no canonists. The school operated well as a Catholic school, had a good reputation, and the bishop had gone there for Mass, commencement and other functions. It looked Catholic and acted Catholic. We were able to resolve the matter, but that is not a position in which a school wants

22 Marlene Weisenbeck, "The Bishop's Vicar: How Does It Work?" *Health Progress* 89 (July-Aug. 2008) 14.

23 Sharon Holland, "Vatican Expert Unpacks Canonical PJP Process," *Health Progress* 92 (Sept.-Oct. 2011) 58.

to find itself. A different bishop could have a problem with a certain school and he might refuse to recognize it, he could remove its Catholic status, he could take it out of the *Official Catholic Directory*, the diocesan directory, etc.

Resources

There are resources to which an institute of consecrated life or an apostolate can turn for advice. These resources probably have a lot of experience in this area and can provide more practical advice. Some of these resources include:

- Catholic Health Association
- National Catholic Education Association
- Resource Center for Religious Institutes

There probably is a similar organization for higher education. The Association of Catholic Colleges and Universities may be such an organization.

Ministry

What is done in transitioning sponsored works often depends on its sort of ministry. Different types of ministries or apostolates seem to be in different places and it is hard to evaluate one in the light of another type of ministry. Health care is a very competitive industry and there may be more funds to come up with solutions. Education, especially higher education, has different factors influencing it like alumni, faculty, and development. In higher education tuition is not the concern it is for elementary and secondary education.

Health Care Ministry

There have been many developments in the health care ministry since it is a large and competitive ministry. While dwindling numbers of religious often push for amalgamation of some type, another factor seems to be that a health care system or amalgamation has to have certain assets to be successful; many experts seem to set this figure at $4-5 billion. This sometimes means that money is not so much a problem in doing reorganization where it may be a larger problem in other ministries like education.[24] Since finances are an important consideration, financial experts should keep in mind that the Church often takes a different approach to finances and they would do well to consider the Pontifical Council of

24 John Morrisey, "New Partnerships for a Stronger Mission," *Health Progress* 94 (July-Aug. 2013) 7.

Justice and Peace's brief publication: *The Vocation of the Business Leader: A Reflection.*[25] There are other reasons for combining:

- the Affordable Care Act and its triggering of accountable care organizations;
- the introduction of insurance type strategies, together with increased efforts to serve the poor and the marginalized – an effort that is real and not public relations "window dressing";
- the need to operate more efficiently with less income, while stressing more prevention-oriented models of care;
- the appeal for payers and large employers, who are looking for access to more effective, proactive, and efficient care for their members; and finally,
- the need to capture a share of anticipated new revenue such as fixed fees for bundled payments, expanded Medicaid coverage, and subsidized private insurance for people who are poor or uninsured.[26]

It is useful to look at history in this area. Often developments have not happened by accident but by careful consideration and planning.[27] At first apostolates were simply a part of a religious institute which controlled it and the two were almost inseparable. Then the apostolates began to be formed as separate corporations but were still part of the juridic person of the institute. About this time, the McGrath theory became popular and influential in the wake of the Second Vatican Council and its concern for the laity.

Since many may not know about the McGrath theory, it seems prudent to insert a comment here about it. Monsignor John McGrath was a canon and civil lawyer serving as professor at the Catholic University of America. In 1968 he published an article on the canonical and civil law status of colleges, universities, hospitals, orphanages, and other charitable institutions under Catholic auspices and incorporated under civil law. One thing that influenced this article was the Second Vatican Council and the role of the laity. He concluded that once a Church entity is civilly incorporated it is juridically separate from the Church; it becomes a creature of the civil government under which it was established. It is not a juridic person within the Church with rights and duties. He acknowledged that there may be a relationship between such entities and the Church, but it is not a juridical relationship. McGrath denied that the property used by the entity

25 See generally Pontifical Council for Justice and Peace, *Vocation of the Business Leader: A Reflection,* 4th ed. (Vatican City: Pontifical Council for Justice and Peace, 2014).

26 John Morrisey, 7-8.

27 Morrisey, Francis. "Our Sponsors – Yesterday, Today and Tomorrow," *Health Progress* 94 (July-Aug. 2013) 57-58.

belonged to its sponsor, but rather, it belonged to the civil-law corporation. In 1974, the Congregations for Religious and for Catholic Education referred to McGrath by name, saying that the thesis had never been considered valid nor had it ever been accepted. The Congregations called for a study of this issue and asked sponsors not to make changes without first referring the matter to the Holy See.[28] Adam Maida, a priest of the Diocese of Pittsburgh, a civil and canon lawyer, and later Cardinal Archbishop of Detroit, responded to the thesis contending that an incorporated apostolate still remained a part of the juridic person of the sponsoring religious institute; incorporation did not change an apostolate's status. Some colleges and universities, therefore, influenced by the McGrath thesis, had already acted. Maida, serving as a canonist for many Catholic health organizations and for the CHA, was able to prevent them from following suit. Maida and Cafardi issued a book published by the CHA in 1984 setting forth his position in more detail.[29]

Later, as numbers of religious declined, it was determined that governance of these corporations would be comprised of two tiers: one being a largely lay board, and the other, members who were often the council of the institute who had certain reserved powers. This followed the CHA book authored by Maida and Cafardi.[30] When health care apostolates began to form systems, often the hospitals of one institute would comprise a system. Institutes then began to combine to form ministerial public juridic persons so that an entity would continue to sponsor entities if the religious were no longer able to perform ordinary sponsorship duties.[31]

The main remedy in this area seems to be the ministerial juridic person. There are about twelve or thirteen of these in the United States and the Hite book on juridic person lists them. Morrisey and Ayuban note that there are others in other countries, mainly Canada, Australia and Ireland. There are about 25 worldwide, and Ayuban indicates that CICLSAL has received more requests. Some of these, especially smaller ones, are starting to merge with others.

There may be a cost to joining a ministerial juridic person. Usually a religious institute member must alienate its ministry to the ministerial juridic person which will now sponsor it. This may not always be a requirement and often there is an initial probationary period before there is alienation. However, it does stand to reason that a ministerial juridic person and the other members will expect some commitment. One author describes a situation when one institute did not

28 Robert Kennedy, "McGrath, Maida and Michiels: Introduction to a Study of the Canonical and Civil Law Status of Church Related Institutions in the United States," *The Jurist* 50 (1990) 351.

29 Adam Maida and Nicholas Cafardi, *Church Property, Church Finances and Church-Related Corporations* (St. Louis, MO: Catholic Health Association, 1983).

30 Ibid.

31 Morrisey, "Our Sponsors," 58-59.

think that it was time for a merger, so it entered into an affiliation agreement that allowed its health care institution to get to know the other, that gave it access to the other's purchasing program together with operational and clinical best practices, until they ultimately completed the merger.[32]

The ministerial juridic person was thought to be the solution that would last some time. These are starting to merge and there is concern that declining numbers of religious may begin to affect their ability to carry out sponsorship duties.[33]

Health Progress contains many articles on the experiences of those entities that have consolidated or cooperated with others. In the 1999 article "When Sponsors Become Partners," Sister Maryanna Coyle, S.C., wrote about taking care when choosing a partner. She observed that a Catholic sponsor ought first to look for other Catholic organizations. She notes that even then, it can be hard since Catholic neighboring entities might have old rivalries or might be competitive. She notes that even after that there can be thorny problems such as which partner is to get the administrative jobs and which services are to be shared, transferred, or eliminated. Some, she adds, may oppose a partnership because it seems to threaten their congregation's heritage. She observes that sponsors facing a partnership with other than Catholic partners can face other problems.[34] There will be more discussion of this issue near the end of the talk.

Education

The area of elementary education is pretty much dominated by parochial schools although there are some schools sponsored by institutes of consecrated life. There have been many closures of parochial schools and there seems to be a need for some change. Some dioceses have seemed to address this. The main remedy seems to be in some form of combination, often some sort of *regional schools*. The cost of tuition and declining numbers of students seem to be the driving factors, yet money is often an obstacle for regional systems as well.

The idea of regional schools or consortia may be becoming more familiar. Regina Haney offers examples of parishes that have combined with one or two others and even with other parishes and a high school. She notes that the pastors are usually the authority figures and there are often advisory boards. The book *Design for Success I: New Configurations for Catholic Schools*, of which she is one of the editors, offers a number of examples of consortia, five in chapter one with a brief description of each, and 45 names of others in the appendix. Often the pastors are very active in education and in one case was a former educator.

32 Kathryn Ruscitto, "The Future Has Arrived: Shared, Collaborative and Sustainable," *Health Progress* 96 (Sept.-Oct. 2015) 20.

33 Morrisey, "Our Sponsors," 59.

34 Maryanna Coyle, "When Sponsors Become Partners," *Health Progress* 80 (Nov.-Dec. 1999) 34.

She says that the parish school is an outgrowth of the First Plenary Council of Baltimore in 1852. While parish elementary schools still predominate, there seems to be a move away from this model. Ordinarily the pastor, or a dean, or some Church authority, retained reserved powers; now there seems to be a move toward boards with limited jurisdiction (limited by the reserved powers) with much of the work being done through board committees. These boards are often mainly composed of laity and committees who do work on necessary things like planning and development. The author concludes that Catholic elementary schools should not be abandoned just because many single parish elementary schools must close.[35]

While many of the civil forms used have been two-tiered non-profit corporations with the members having reserved powers, there has also been some use made of *joint ventures*. A joint venture could set up a structure and the parties to it might be two or three parishes and the diocesan bishop. I think that the diocesan bishop will often have a role in these matters since he is the coordinator of all apostolates in a diocese. The old idea of a parish school is now changing as often times there are a number of students in a parish school who come from other parishes that no longer have schools.

Phillip Brown[36] and Deborah Cerullo,[37] both canon as well as civil lawyers, have each authored books published by the National Catholic Education Association discussing how canonical concepts like juridic persons can be creatively used in reconfiguring or better configuring Catholic schools. Brown also wrote a section on this topic in the book *Design for Success I: New Configurations for Catholic Schools,* edited by Haney and O'Keefe. They talk about juridic persons and civil-law corporations and how they might be applied to educational entities. Cerullo in her appendix offers examples of constitutions and bylaws. Both authors stress what Sister Deborah put in her title; that Catholic schools exist in two worlds, that of canon law and that of civil law. Brown notes that it is important to know the canons in this area and to take into account the definition of a Catholic school as found in canon 803. Both look at civil-law structures or actions that can affect canonical entities, and they call for taking both legal systems into consideration. Brown talks about the role of a diocesan bishop and when he might intervene under canon law. It should also be noted that Monsignor William King did a pre-Convention workshop in Buffalo in 2010 on Catholic schools and canon law.

35 Regina Haney and Joseph O'Keefe, eds. *Design for Success I: New Configurations for Catholic Schools* (Washington, D.C.: National Catholic Education Association, 2009); see also Regina Haney, "Design for Success: New Configurations and Governance Models for Catholic Schools," *Catholic Education: A Journal of Inquiry and Practice* 14 (Dec. 2010) 195.

36 Phillip Brown, *Restructuring Catholic School Governance for a New Age: Creativity Meets Canon Law* (Alexandria, VA: The National Catholic Education Association, 2010).

37 Deborah Cerullo, *Catholic Schools in Two Worlds: Governance and Bylaws – Church and Civil Law* (Arlington, VA: National Catholic Education Association, 2011).

Secondary education faces many of the same issues. First, there were corporations with two tiers, with the member/religious institute usually having reserved powers serving as president while there was a lay principal. There have been a number of mergers or closings. Here there seem to be more schools sponsored by institutes of consecrated life than in primary education. Ayuban notes that one of the petitions to the CICLSAL is a network of secondary schools that cater to the needs of poor students in the United States. When he later mentions Cristo Rey, it may be assumed that this is the network to which he makes reference.[38]

In higher education, colleges have often been incorporated, and two tiered corporations do dominate. However, there are still many one tier corporations in which a specified percentage or number of religious serve on the board of trustees and often certain decisions require their approval. Not all colleges appear to have reserved powers. Some have sponsorship agreements to address these issues. A number of colleges have a religious as a sponsorship officer, often serving as a vice president.[39]

Some institutes of consecrated life have set up "mission corporations" to oversee the institutional ministries founded in the institute's name. These new institutions will eventually replace the religious institutes as sponsors. Three institutes seem to be ready to hand over their apostolates to dioceses should they no longer be able to perform sponsorship duties. Others seem open to the institutions becoming secular. Others have some plan to turn over ministries to lay groups, often with some type of formation. Many institutes seem to acknowledge the impending problem but appear to have no plan.[40]

Some religious institutes with several colleges, or some religious institutes that share the same tradition, have set up corporations to run them. Examples include Institutes of the Sisters of Mercy which has a canonical sponsor council that exercises reserved powers for the Conference for Mercy Higher Education. This entity is the corporate member for the individual universities or colleges which each have their own boards and presidents. There is also a conference office that fosters collaboration. The Sisters of St. Joseph of Boston form the juridic person for a corporation for sponsored ministries which is the sole member for each local ministry which include a number of schools and one health care center. The CHA book *One Vine Different Branches*, published in 2007, has not

38 Elias. L. Ayuban, "Ministerial Public Juridic Persons: Blessings and Challenges," unpublished article from Catholic Health Association [Fr. Elias Ayuban, CMF, participated in a panel discussion with sponsors of Catholic health ministries at a Catholic Health Association sponsorship institute in January, 2014 and this article reflects his presentation and he gave this article to the Catholic Health Association], 3, 8.

39 Dennis Holtschneider and Melanie Morey, "Relationship Revisited: Changing Relationships between U.S. Catholic Colleges and Universities and Founding Religious Congregations," *Current Issues in Catholic Higher Education* 21 (Fall, 2000) 15-21.

40 Ibid., 21-22, 26-27.

only articles and models about health care entities, but also for higher education as well.[41]

A 2005 article by Melanie Morey and Dennis Holtschneider summarized the results of a leadership trends study that began in 2002. They noted that most Catholic college and university presidents resemble their peers elsewhere in American higher education. They found that laypersons were emerging as presidents from pools containing members of the founding religious congregation. They found that many presidents lacked formal theological or spiritual formation and often expressed concerns about that lack. They also observed that most of the religious and lay presidents of Catholic colleges or universities found the terms "Catholic identity" and/or "Catholic intellectual tradition" to be "fuzzy" concepts. The authors noted that 54 percent of respondents predicted that there would be fewer institutions in five to ten years through closing or mergers. The authors also suggested that some institutions may simply abandon their Catholic identity.[42]

Higher education may have some unique factors that affect its forms. Many schools have to undergo accreditation approval and this can involve a review of structures as well as teaching. I know secondary schools go through this and I think that colleges and universities do as well. One big issue is academic freedom. Another is the issue of Catholic schools of higher education being expected by the Holy See to follow *Ex Corde Ecclesia* and to give mandates to certain teachers. These can affect an institution's stated relationship with the Church. Commenting on these concepts is beyond the scope of this article. There have been seminars at CLSA Conventions on the issue of *Ex Corde Ecclesia.* This seems to be one area in which history is very helpful and Alice Gallin's article from *The Jurist* is very useful in understanding the background.[43]

---

41 "Practical Components of Sponsorship (Part II)," in *One Vine Different Branches: Sponsorship and Governance in Catholic Ministries – A Collection of Resources for Health Care, Educational and Social Services* (St. Louis, MO: Catholic Health Association, 2007) II-20-26.

42 Melanie Morey and Dennis Holtschneider, "Leadership and the Age of Laity: Emerging Patterns in Catholic Higher Education," in *Lay Leaders in Catholic Higher Education: An Emerging Paradigm for the Twenty-First Century* (Fairfield, CT: Sacred Heart University Press, 2005).

43 Alice Gallin, "On the Road toward a Definition of a Catholic University," *The Jurist* 48 (1988) 536. See also Nicholas Cafardi, "The Higher Education Apostolate in the United States: Canonical and Civil Aspects," in *Acts of the Colloquium: Public Ecclesiastical Juridic Persons and Their Apostolates in the Roman Catholic Church in the U.S.A.: Canonical-Civil Aspects.* (Rome: Pontifical University of St. Thomas Aquinas, 1998) 21-40; Dennis Holtschneider and Melanie Morey, "Relationship Revisited: Changing Relationships between U.S. Catholic Colleges and Universities and Founding Religious Congregations," *Current Issues in Catholic Higher Education* 21 (Fall, 2000) 3.

A number of institutes of consecrated life have other charitable ministries, such as social service agencies, hunger centers, retreat houses, or publication centers. These often already have two-tiered corporations with reserved powers. When an institute can no longer sponsor an institute, the institute often finds another entity to run it, although often it is turned over to another diocesan Catholic agency.

In a number of cases, there may not be what seems like acceptable or appealing remedies. Merger or transfer may not be possible. In some cases after due consideration the only step may be termination of the ministry. It may be impossible to consolidate with someone else; sometimes it may be so late that another entity does not want to have a small entity join it. In some cases, the ministry is not needed, or it has not kept up, or its facilities are outdated. In other cases, the answer may be that it has to transform the ministry into the next service needed. An example might be orphanages. Many orphanages no longer exist; in some cases, the structure, staff and physical plant are transformed to serve a different community, often a different type of youth. Sometimes closing or transforming might be the best decision. Orders have ended. Parishes have closed and schools have closed. It may seem painful, but it also seems to be a part of the order of things.

Recent Documents

Benedict XVI in a *motu proprio Intima Ecclesiae Natura* in 2012,[44] discussed and issued norms on the service of charity in the Church. Many welcomed this since there was little, if anything, in the *Code of Canon Law* on this issue. It appears to pertain to agencies and foundations for charitable purposes promoted by institutes of consecrated life and societies of apostolic life, among other entities. One commentary on this document indicates that most entities founded by an institute or society are private associations rather than formally established public associations. As private associations, they cannot be the object of obligations and rights unless established as a public association by a formal decree with formally approved statutes.[45] Frank Morrisey wrote an article in *Health Progress* on this document.[46]

A major thrust of the motu proprio seems to be to clarify the role of the diocesan bishop in coordinating works of charity. It emphasizes a supervisory role for the diocesan bishop, not one of direct involvement in governance in the work

44 Benedict XVI, *motu proprio Intima Ecclesiae Natura*, November 11, 2012; also titled in English: "In Service of Charity."

45 Resource Center for Religious Institutes, "In the Service of Charity Issued Motu Proprio 11 November 2012 Effective 10 December 2012 – Commentary on Application to Institutes of Consecrated Life and Societies of Apostolic Life," (January 24, 2013).

46 Francis Morrisey. "Benedict XVI's 'Motu Proprio' — What Is Its Scope?" *Health Progress* 94 (May-June, 2013) 82.

of charity. Morrisey notes that *Cor Unum* may issue regulations to see that this motu proprio is properly used.[47]

On February 17, 2014, the Congregation for the Doctrine of the Faith issued a reply but not an official responsum to question that it received from the USCCB in April, 2013 about whether a Catholic health care system could become non-Catholic. The CDF did not respond officially or directly to the question posed to it, but issued seventeen principles for collaboration with non-Catholic health care entities. This seems to be a useful set of principles in dealing with a trend of interaction with non-Catholic health care entities and is discussed in more detail below. There have been useful comments on this document by ethicists when this first was issued.[48]

Cautions/Challenges

St. Louis University Hospital will be discussed as a sort of case study, but first a brief preface is in order. For reasons of liability and operation, and based in part on the thesis offered by McGrath, many Catholic colleges and universities were transferred to lay boards. In 1967, St. Louis University transferred control to a lay board but no indult was sought from the Holy See: It was thought that the university was not Church property and that it was bound to follow the civil law of the appropriate state but not the canon law of the Church. The University of Notre Dame, however, did obtain an indult of alienation when it transferred control of its institution to a lay dominated board.[49]

For St. Louis University Hospital matters seemed to come to a head in 1997, when the university proposed sale of its hospital to Tenet Health System Hospitals, Inc., a for-profit entity. The university claimed that the hospital was a distinct, civilly incorporated entity not subject to canon law. Archbishop Rigali opposed the sale. The Holy See approved the sale with four conditions but said that the hospital was an apostolate of the Society of Jesus and was subject to canon law. The Holy See, in a decision issued by the prefect of the Congregation for Institutes of Consecrated Life and the prefect of the Congregation for Catholic Education, determined that the act of incorporation and control by a lay board in 1967 did not constitute an alienation but a change in structure of the governing body of the university and the owner remained the Missouri Province of the Society of Jesus. The Holy See added that it was the responsibility of the Society

---

47 Ibid.

48 Peter Cataldo, "A Commentary on Collaboration with Non-Catholic Entities in Health Care Services," *Origins* 44 (Nov. 27, 2014) 431-439; this article includes the text of CDF document with commentary interspersed. Another source for this document is the *National Catholic Bioethics Quarterly* (Su. 2014): 337-340.

49 Peter Harrington, "Civil and Canon Law Issues Affecting Catholic Higher Education 1948-1988: An Overview and the ACCU Perspective," *Current Issues in Catholic Higher Education* 20 (Fall, 1999) 63.

of Jesus to put in place a mechanism through which the Society exercised control with regard to the president and board of trustees of the university to ensure that the requirements of canon law as they pertain to the university are followed. This decision was accepted by the university, the Jesuits, the archbishop, and Tenet, and the sale went through. The four conditions on the sale imposed by the Holy See were: 1) Tenet would observe Catholic principles and practices of health care and provide for spiritual needs at the hospital; 2) all students, interns and residents would follow the USCCB *Ethical and Religious Directives* for health care services; 3) Tenet will care for the poor at the same level as the hospital had in the past; and 4) Tenet would continue existing educational programs in pediatrics, obstetrics, and gynecology in accord with those at other Catholic hospitals.[50]

This saga played out in the media for several months. There is some indication that the university and/or the Jesuits may not have kept the archbishop informed as well and as early as they might have. Cardinals Hickey, Law and O'Connor also expressed the same concerns as Archbishop Rigali did. The University contended that it needed the $300 million it was to receive for the continued operation of the university medical school – an offer higher than that of two Catholic health care systems, which had offered $200 million. As an aside, Tenet recently sold the hospital to SSM, a Catholic non-profit system. In accepting the 1997 sale, Archbishop Rigali said that it remained his strong preference that the hospital be owned and operated by a Catholic institution but he accepted the proposal on the condition that all the conditions of the Holy See are fully met.[51]

Some canonists thought that the change in the board's composition could have involved an invalid alienation. One canonist opines that where a canonical steward (i.e., an institute of consecrated life) relinquishes control on a board of trustees so that individuals without knowledge of or commitment to requirements of canon law gain the majority of a board of trustees, the canonical steward may find that it can no longer prevent transactions that violate canon law. If such an action could endanger stable patrimony, then the canonical steward will have placed the patrimony at risk and this could raise a situation in which canon 1295 would apply since it may be argued that the canonical steward had acted to endanger the patrimonial condition of a juridic person, which would then seem to be treated by this canon as a form of alienation.[52]

---

50 Harrington, 64-66; Sean Sheridan, "Catholic Universities and Juridic Persons," *Current Issues in Catholic Higher Education* 30 (Winter, 2011) 35.

51 Archbishop Justin Rigali, "St. Louis University Hospital Sold to For-Profit Corporation," *Origins* 27 (March 12, 1988) 629. See also Harrington, 64-66 and Sean Sheridan, "Catholic Universities and Juridic Persons," *Current Issues in Catholic Higher Education* 30 (Winter, 2011) 35.

52 Jerome Jung, "Property Transactions that May Jeopardize the Patrimonial Condition of a Public Juridic Persons in the Church," *Catholic Lawyer* 41(2001) 85-86, 104.

Continually changing administrations of institutes of consecrated life can create challenges since a chapter could bring in a whole new team. This can have a profound effect on any effort in transitioning sponsorship of an apostolate. This can be frustrating to consultants and it can be troublesome in trying to deal with these complex issues since it can often take a number of years to craft a solution. It would seem that institutes of consecrated life are going to have to deal with this issue in some way. Perhaps a committee that oversees this process could have some ex officio members that include not only present officers of the administrative team but also past officers. This is an area where good minutes can be a big help.

The continual aging of religious members is a real problem. There have already been solutions to addressing the issue of not enough teachers or nurses to serve entities. Now there is a declining number to perform even sponsorship duties. The statutes of current ministerial juridic persons seem to assume that religious institutes will be able to make certain decisions such as appointing members or making certain decisions. CICLSAL already has petitions to amend statutes to relieve members of institutes of consecrated life from performing sponsorship ministries. CICLSAL may face a problem in that it took over this role because of petitions from institutes of consecrate life; it may not feel it has competence when dealing with lay people who now may make up these entities. What entity in the Holy See would deal with health care or charitable entities?[53]

The issue of sponsorship and the duties it entails is a very real concern. These duties or roles can be summarized in four roles:

1. mission integration;
2. mutual accountability among sponsors, boards and administration;
3. sponsorship competencies; and
4. formation and development/succession planning.[54]

Mission integration requires a clear articulation of mission. This must come from the sponsor and may not be easy since religious do not often have an articulated mission; religious hold the leadership and most of the jobs, and mission is what they do. But this has changed as the numbers of religious have declined. This means that those in the ministry of sponsorship must understand the mission, the values, the vision, and the strategic plan. They must develop ways to evaluate them. They should be involved in the selection of board members and key administrators, and be open to the development of succession plans.

---

53 Morrisey, "Our Sponsors" 59-60; Ayuban, 10.

54 "Practical Components of Sponsorship" (Part II), in *One Vine Different Branches: Sponsorship and Governance in Catholic Ministries – A Collection of Resources for Health Care, Educational and Social Services* (St. Louis, MO: Catholic Health Association, 2007) II 27-34.

Mutual accountability among sponsors, boards, and administration means that there must be clear lines of authority. Thus, when these different groups interact and communicate or collaborate, each understands its role.[55] Robert Gibbons notes that in the area of higher education, this need can be heightened when the administrator is getting to an age when his or her successor might no longer be a member of the community that founded the apostolate. There should be some structure to ensure that mutual accountability occurs and that it occupies an important place on the agenda. There should also be a focus on specific and concrete issues and not just abstract concepts. Apostolates must be able to translate the charism into organizational structures and policies. In discussing a college sponsored by an institute of consecrated life, Gibbons posed several questions to sponsors and directors of the board: For whom do the directors hold the college in trust? What do directors expect of the sponsor? What do the sponsors expect of the directors? He got some good and some rather astonishing answers.[56] One matter seems evident: that boards must take up valuable meeting time with these matters; not just during a retreat but in a real discussion.

Sponsors must be involved in, and understanding of, such things as: reserved powers; the ability to express sponsor expectations (religious should be able to hark back to the days when they had to rediscover the charism of the founder as *Perfectae Caritatis* demanded); Catholic identity (*Ethical and Religious Directives*, *Ex Corde Ecclesia*, etc.) An apostolate can be badly hampered if a sponsor controls too much, or if a board is micromanaged, or if the administration runs everything.

Sponsorship is a true ministry. This means that those involved in this ministry act on behalf of the Church and they must be competent. Some ministerial public juridic persons have developed lists of competencies. The religious involved in the ministry of sponsorship must understand the canonical and civil implications of their roles. This means that they may need to talk to others with experience or who are experts.[57] They need to understand reserved powers and why certain powers are reserved. This will mean reading minutes and agendas for meetings, preparing for them in such a way as to not attend in a merely passive manner. It also means that they must understand the ministry or apostolate which is sponsored. Not every religious may be involved with a major apostolate of the institute, so a general or vague awareness might not be enough.[58] This may mean that those involved with the ministry may need to evaluate how well the board or administration fulfills the mission or purpose of the sponsored ministry; this may mean developing some evaluation instrument. All of this may mean not just an individual commitment of time and energy, but a community commitment of

55 "Practical Components of Sponsorship," 27-30.

56 Robert Gibbons, "Sponsors and Directors: An Important Conversation," *Current Issues in Catholic Higher Education* 11 (Winter, 1991) 23-25.

57 "Practical Components of Sponsorship," 32.

58 Rosemary Smith, Warren Brown and Nancy Reynolds, 130.

talented members to whom time is given for this ministry. This may mean that a talented member might be taken from a more traditional ministry or historically useful ministry.

Sponsorship involves a real and active role, not a passive one. It is more than merely holding a veto over an overenthusiastic board or group of administrators. It should exemplify the rich concept of *communio* as King suggests in the CLSA booklet on sponsorship.[59] Beal likens sponsorship of a religious institute to the corporate conscience of the organization.[60]

There is a question as to whether religious involved in the ministry of sponsorship have been really trained or formed for this sort of ministry. It may seem incredible, but there are religious who are not interested in meetings and issues like canon law or finance. There is also the issue of how institutes of consecrated life can form laity to carry on their charisms. Some institutes have done this well, and some still need to develop ways to do this. There is the new issue of whether this can be done as institutes of consecrated life merge in order to carry on an apostolate with other institutes who may not completely share a charism. Some apostolates may end up with a charism more broadly Catholic than having a certain charism based on the spirituality of a founder or foundress.

As noted above, those who currently sponsor must not only be open to further formation for themselves, but for the formation of those who will follow. This must be carefully developed and programmed. An example in education is the Enhancing Catholic School Identity Program, developed by the NCEA. It is a two year program, not merely an afternoon. The CHA has also developed a noteworthy program in Collaborative Formation Program for Public Juridic Persons. Started in 2003, the program trains potential public juridic person sponsors. It consists of four full weekend seminars over eighteen months.[61]

59 Ibid., 49.

60 Ibid., 41.

61 "Practical Components of Sponsorship," 34.

Developments or Trends

In Canada a number of religious institutes presented a joint request to the Holy See for the erection of a new public juridic person to assume some of their responsibilities over church assets. The new juridic person is the Canadian Religious Stewardship. Participation is voluntary and an institute can determine which services it chooses to use and for how long. This new public juridic person has five purposes: 1) to assist religious institutes by managing and safeguarding their ecclesiastical temporal goods and assuring their proper administration in accordance with canon and civil law; 2) to provide personal care programs and services for membership of these institutes; 3) to accept ownership of ecclesiastical temporal goods in those instances in which the institute wishes to divest itself of property in accordance with the requirements of canon law; 4) where appropriate to accept governance responsibilities for any or all health care, educational, religious and social service ministries presently supported by the institute; and 5) with the consent of the diocesan bishop and if appropriate, to accept sponsorship of an institute's ministry. This would allow the public juridic person to accept governance over ministries that do not fit into any of the more traditional categories of health, education, social services, retreat houses, publishing, or similar undertakings. The new public juridic person strives to maintain good relationships with diocesan bishops. An institute can use the services of the public juridic person for only a limited period of time or it will need to become integrated into the public juridic person. The statutes insist on formation for members of the public juridic person and for that of sponsors.[62]

It also seems that in the United States, there may be affiliations that do not involve merger or alienation but something more like cooperation. The entity formed may be able to provide some useful services to its members.

Another trend has been that ministerial public juridic persons seem to be merging and taking on smaller juridic persons set up by institutes of consecrated life. Some thought that this would be the sole future of development.[63]

However, it does not seem that there are either enough or appropriate juridic persons with which to merge, so entities are considering relationship with non-Catholic, profit and not-for-profit entities. At one time Catholic entities would limit themselves to relationships with other Catholic entities. However, because potential Catholic partners are either too small or too old to make some sort of relationship attractive, it means that alternatives are being sought with non-Catholic profit and not-for-profit entities.In some cases, values may be close enough to do this. Others will demand a difficult structuring process with which all might

62 Francis Morrisey, "New PJP Model – 'A Leap of Faith'," *Health Progress* 92 (2011) 68-70.

63 Morrisey, "Our Sponsors," 59.

not agree, but the relationship may be necessary for the continuance of Catholic health care or Catholic education.[64]

The assets needed for a juridic person or a system, the location, the types of services that others in the area offer, together with concern for those whose needs are not being met, may call for a ministerial juridic person or a system to look to others with whom to collaborate or cooperate. This raises ethical or theological concerns. Morrisey notes five general variations or models that are in use and seem to be approved or tolerated by diocesan bishops. One is a model based on control and stewardship, which may be a ministerial juridic person in which the system is Catholic, but some subsidiaries might become involved in activities which may not be in compliance with the ethical and religious directives. This requires evaluating whether or not there is material cooperation. Morrisey notes the responses of diocesan bishops may be mixed as to what they are willing to tolerate for a greater good. Another model may involve stewardship but not direct control of the whole system, so that Catholic entities that relate to the system are realigned: the system might not be Catholic, but reserved powers would be exercised over the Catholic entities and not through the parent corporation. An example of this would be Dignity Health, which will be discussed in a little more detail below. Thus, there can be a statement of common values which applies to the system that may not make reference to sterilizations and related procedures, but otherwise follows the *Ethical and Religious Directives*. In a third model, the system is no longer Catholic, and the public juridic person would only exercise reserved powers over Catholic entities. These powers would involve stable patrimony, compliance with the *Ethical and Religious Directives*, and Catholic identity. A form of common values would apply throughout the system. The public juridic person would lose control over the system board, yet would be a second tier sponsor of the Catholic entities. There could be material cooperation issues if there were two mirror boards with those of the non-Catholic part and the Catholic part being the same. In a fourth model, the system is not Catholic, but a Catholic tradition is continued over at least some entities. The Catholic entities would be alienated but would retain Catholicity by means of an agreement with the sponsor. One term of the contract would be compliance with the *Ethical and Religious Directives*. None of the former Catholic entities would ordinarily be listed in the *Official Catholic Directory*. The last model would involve segregating proscribed procedures, moving these procedures to an entity not related to the Catholic entity, although in the same geographic area. In theory, there would not be material cooperation. This may be hard to achieve in practice. All of these are merely models and may not work well based on differing situations.[65]

Morrisey notes that in these collaborations with non-Catholic entities a major concern seems to be sterilization, while there seems to be less concern with abortion, euthanasia, in vitro fertilization, and the like. He suggests that it may

64 Ibid., 60-66.

65 Ibid., 61-63.

be helpful to look at mission, goals, and consequences. He admits that he is not an ethicist or a moral theologian, but suggests that an interdisciplinary discussion on these issues may be useful.[66]

In an article published this year, "Catholic Identity and the Reshaping of Catholic Health Care," authors Michael Panicola and Ron Hamel note that health care in the United States is in a state of major transformation, the likes of which has perhaps not been seen. They note positive and negative contributing factors, one of which is that financial analysts say that consolidations may be necessary since size and scale are critical for future success. The authors remind us to stay focused on fundamental value commitments, including recent statements by Pope Francis with regard to mercy and hope, care for the poor, and social justice. In one place, they note that while a system may prohibit some action under the *Ethical and Religious Directives*, others may be "carved out" ["carve out" might not be the best term], which may be acceptable as long as the Catholic entity has no more than a minority of seats in the system governance, and that any Catholics on such a board must recuse themselves from decision-making. Furthermore, they argue that the Catholic entity must not derive any revenue or profit from, or provide direct funding for, what is carved out. The management of the Catholic entity must not oversee management of the carved-out medical interventions, while employees and physicians of the Catholic entity must not provide the carved-out medical interventions as a part of their employment agreement (52). This article is useful for offering an analysis and process for these difficult issues.[67]

In a recent (2013) article in *Health Progress*, Doris Gottemoeller looked at the consolidations going on through the lens of the Second Vatican Council, recalling that two documents, the Decree on Ecumenism and the Decree on the Relation of the Church to Non-Christian Religions, saw a positive appreciation of other denominations and other faiths. She gave the example of Catholic Health Partners, which acquired a Jewish hospital but first took care to articulate a "Traditions Agreement" about maintaining a kosher diet, displaying Jewish symbols, and observing holy days. She also discusses *Gaudium et Spes*, noting those sections that talk about inequality of access to the world's goods, and those that refer to working conditions and worker participation. She also discusses the importance of preserving Catholic identity citing par. 43 of *Gaudium et Spes* that speaks of the duty of the lay faithful to cultivate a properly formed conscience and to impress the divine law on the life of the earthly city so that the Catholic identity of a health care entity creates a venue in which the Church's teachings are demonstrated in a public manner. She also notes that par. 42 calls for the

---

66 Ibid., 65-66; Francis Morrisey, "Restructuring Systems: A Call for Dialogue," *Health Progress* 94 (Jan.-Feb. 2013) 66; Jordan Hite, Sharon Holland and Francis Morrisey, 83.

67 Michael Panicola and Ron Hamel, "Catholic Identity and the Reshaping of Catholic Health Care," *Health Progress* 96 (Sept.-Oct. 2015) 46-48.

Church to initiate works of mercy on behalf of all people. She says that Catholic health care is a good example of such a work.[68]

Dignity Health was formed in 2012 as a reorganization of Catholic Healthcare West. As noted above, the system will follow a statement of common values and Catholic entities will follow the *Ethical and Religious Directives*.[69] Archbishop Niederauer wrote a letter to explain the situation and said that Catholic Healthcare West would no longer be a sponsored ministry of the Catholic Church and that "the new system would operate both Catholic and non-Catholic hospitals and the six orders of sisters would, within the new system, continue to sponsor and retain important controls over the Catholic hospitals." The archbishop said that he consulted several moral theologians and a nationally respected health care consultant to examine the matter. He says that he has "determined that the proposed restructuring is consistent with Catholic moral and doctrinal teachings and that the sponsors and their Catholic hospitals are, therefore, free to participate in it." He also noted that his decision does not imply that he believes this to be the best possible arrangement, but only that he found no moral reason to object to it.[70]

In conclusion, I hope that you can see that this is a complex area. I encourage you to review some of the articles that I cite since they deal with complexities that are hard to summarize and probably beyond my skills to abridge in any meaningful way. As Frank Morrisey noted, it is hard for a canonist to discuss adequately delicate ethical issues. There are major changes that have been made, and must be made, and they must be very carefully done. A number of the articles, especially those in *Health Progress,* describe what has been done and how painstaking and perhaps painful a process this has been.

68 Doris Gottemoeller, "The Vision of Vatican II: Alive in Catholic Health Care," *Health Progress* 94 (July-Aug. 2013) 53.

69 Morrisey, "Our Sponsors," 61; Judith Carle, "Dignity Health – New Name, Same Mission," *Health Progress* 94 (July-Aug. 2013) 34; Judith Vanderwater, "Catholic Healthcare West Reorganizes Governance, Changes Name to Dignity Health," *Catholic Health World* 28 (Feb. 2012).

70 Letter of the Most Reverend George W. Niederauer, "Catholic Health Care West Becomes Dignity Health – What Does It Mean?" (February 17, 2012).

Seminar

Models of Shared Responsibility Since Vatican Council II

Most Reverend Charles C. Thompson
Brian B. Reynolds

The election of Pope Francis, on 13 March 2013, was highly touted as being the first pope to have been ordained a bishop since the Second Vatican Council. Thus, his entire episcopacy has been shaped by the actions and spirit of Vatican II. In a similar vein, it should be noted that I was ordained a priest several years following the Second Vatican Council. In fact, having been born in April 1961, I have very little recollection of the Catholic Church prior to Vatican II. In essence, it is all I know in my experience of what it means to be Church, to be Catholic, to be priest and bishop. Servant-leadership and collaboration were prominent themes in my seminary formation at St. Meinrad School of Theology, in southern Indiana. Consequently, I have made very few decisions as a priest or bishop without some form, if not multiple forms, of consultation.

I have had the opportunity to work closely with Dr. Brian Reynolds for several years, in various capacities, under two Archbishops of Louisville; namely, Archbishop Thomas Kelly and Archbishop Joseph Kurtz. Dr. Reynolds and I have held various positions and served together on a number of committees. My governance and pastoral care as a bishop has been greatly influenced by those with and for whom I served as a priest.

As a priest, I relied heavily on three groups in terms of collaborative leadership in the parish; namely, the staff, pastoral council and finance council. I learned from my first pastor the great value of hiring the right persons for the right positions and then letting them do their jobs. As pastor, my role was primarily to provide a sense of direction, collaboration, support and availability/presence. As judicial vicar, I engaged the Tribunal staff with the same philosophy. Having served on the presbyteral council, college of consultors and diocesan planning committee, as well as having served as an agency director and dean, I learned to appreciate the value of being consulted. Of course, effective consultation requires proper transparency and honesty.

We are all familiar with the distinction of consent and consultation, as noted in canon 127. The requirements of counsel as well as consent must be met for the validity of certain juridic acts (cc. 124 f). For instance, members of the presbyteral council must be heard before the bishop formally decides to erect, alter or suppress a parish (c. 515 §2). Of course, we must keep in mind both ecclesiastical and civil norms of law.

In my experience as a pastor, especially of a rather affluent parish, I have encountered some tension in the secular understanding and value placed on the notion of consultation and consent. This is particularly the case when the membership of a pastoral council and/or finance council is made up of doctors, lawyers, business owners, CEOs and upper management personnel. In other words, those who are used to "calling the shots" do not initially take very well to being consulted rather than their consent being required. Evidently, in the secular world, the manner in which consultation is carried out and considered leaves much to be desired. No one wants to be ignored or act as a "rubber stamp." Obviously, no one wants to waste time serving in a capacity that is not taken seriously and properly respected. As we are well aware in this room, consultation is not to be taken lightly.

Key principles for us to keep in mind are the ecclesial notions of leadership as service and authority as primarily being about responsibility. At the heart of *communio,* authentic leadership in the Church must be rooted in the proper balance of rights and obligations in carrying out the triple *munera* of teaching, sanctifying and governance. As Pope Francis has warned, there is no room for arrogance in ecclesiastical leadership.[1] Credible ecclesiastical leadership is predicated on the commitment to virtue and service, especially for the sake of the common good with respect to the dignity of each and every person. In essence, it is only by being Christ-centered rather than egocentric that we are able to embrace a common vision and shared responsibility as *one, holy, catholic and apostolic* Church.

Models of Shared Responsibility are founded on mutual respect, trust, an understood common mission and ongoing commitment to dialogue. Archbishop Kurtz often speaks of the three C's of dialogue – civility, compassion and courage. I dare to add a fourth; namely, competence. Such models of shared responsibility draw upon the Church's sacramental theology, especially as it relates to the Sacraments of Initiation. By the mere fact of baptism, each of us has a role to play in the Church's mission, as entrusted to it by Jesus Christ; "By baptism one is incorporated into the Church of Christ and is constituted a person in it with the duties and rights which are proper to Christians in keeping with their condition, insofar as they are in ecclesiastical communion and unless a legitimately issued sanction stands in the way."

1 Pope Francis, Morning Meditation in the Chapel of the *Domus Sanctae Marthae*, "When the Poor End Up Paying," 16 June 2014.

(c. 96) The fullness of such obligations and rights of the Christian faithful (cc. 208-223) is intricately linked to full initiation, including the reception of Confirmation and Holy Eucharist, age and proper condition (c. 205). Of course, any *Models of Shared Responsibility* must be predicated on the Church's understanding of the power of governance and the Christian faithful as outlined in the following canons:

canon 129:

> §1 Those who have received sacred orders are qualified, according to the norm of the prescripts of the law, for the power of governance, which exists in the Church by divine institution and is also called the power of governance.
>
> §2 Lay members of the Christian faithful can cooperate in the exercise of this same power according to the norm of law.

canon 204:

> §1 The Christian faithful are those who, inasmuch as they have been incorporated in Christ through baptism, have been constituted as the people of God. For this reason, made sharers in their own way in Christ's priestly, prophetic and royal function, they are called to exercise the mission which God has entrusted to the Church to fulfill in the world, in accord with the condition proper to each.
>
> §2 This Church, constituted and organized in this world as a society, subsists in the Catholic Church governed by the successor of Peter and the bishops in communion with him.

With regard to the baptismal call of stewardship that includes the Christian faithful,

canon 212 §3 states:

> According to the knowledge, competence, and prestige which they possess, they have the right and even at times the duty to manifest to the sacred pastors their opinion on matters which pertain to the good of the Church and to make their opinion known to the rest of the Christian faithful, without prejudice to the integrity of faith and morals, with reverence toward their pastors, and attentive to common advantage and the dignity of persons.

Thus, recognizing these inherent obligations and rights of all the Christian faithful, clergy and laity, the Church requires that those capable of carrying out certain juridic acts seek proper consent or counsel before doing so in the spirit of subsidiarity, solidarity and collaboration. With this in mind, we can identify various levels of offices and groups to be considered for *Models of Shared Responsibility*. While some of these are beyond the letter of the law, their inclusion would certainly be in line with carrying out the spirit of the law.

On the universal level, of course, we must keep in mind the nature of Hierarchical Communion (i.e. the Holy Father and Bishops), the College of Cardinals, The Secretariat of State and the Roman Curia. The recent Synods on the Family, restructuring of the Vatican Bank, and Pope Francis's Advisory Council of Cardinals attest to the great value in this regard.

On the national level, we readily call to mind the Conference of Bishops (e.g. USCCB), including the benefits of drawing upon solidarity and discernment among Regions (e.g. Region 7 consisting of Indiana, Illinois & Wisconsin) and Provinces (e.g. Indianapolis Province comprising the 5 dioceses of Indiana).

On the local level, the level of a particular Church, a diocese, we can identify a number of such offices and groups (e.g. councils, committees, boards). Though not meant to be an exhaustive list, I simply take this opportunity to identify several of those that come to mind from my twenty-eight years of priestly ministry, especially including my brief four years of episcopal ministry:

Presbtyeral Council, College of Consultors, Finance Council, Pastoral Council, Agency Directors, Clergy Personnel Board, Deacons, Priestly Life & Ministry Cluster, Review Board, Ad hoc Committees (e.g. Salaries/Benefits, International Priests), Strategic Planning (e.g. Goals, Objective & Action Steps), Parish Reorganization, Pastoral Planning, Deans, Pastors, Parishes, Religious Women & Men, Associations and Apostolates, Quarterly Meetings of Priests & Pastoral Life Coordinators, Senior Priests (e.g. Vicar for Retired Priests), Presbyteral Convocation, Presbyteral Assembly, Vicar General, Judicial Vicar & the Tribunal, Chancellor, Chief Operating or Administrating Officer, and Finance Officer or Business Manager.

Maintaining the proper attitude, perspective and spirit are essential to the effectiveness of any dialogue and discernment related to counsel and consent. If such counsel and consent are to be grounded in faith, hope and charity, then prayer is absolutely essential. While planning and agendas are certainly important in assuring structure, organization, focus/direction and time management, we must always keep before us that it is God's Will, God's Plan, God's Kingdom that we seek to know and embrace. Prayer also keeps us anchored in the realization of God's grace filling up what is lacking in human merit, no matter how good intentioned and seemingly competent. Effective *shared responsibility* necessarily requires that those involved in any given process possess a *shared vision/mission*. This is not to exclude the value of "creative tension." We must be realistic about resources as well as needs, desires as well as concerns, and hopes as well as fears. Again, as Pope Francis has noted, there is no room for arrogance in dialogue and discernment.[2] Rather, each participant, particularly those entrusted with positions of authority at the service of the Gospel and the People of God, must cultivate the virtues of courage, humility (leading to openness and trust) and generosity.

Some of the goals or principles that serve us well in considering *Models of Shared Responsibility* include those of striving to be proactive rather than reactive, of providing for broad ownership and investment, of being mission-driven rather than management-based, and of encouraging full, active and conscious participation. We want to draw from the wisdom, the insights and skills of all those involved. When possible (e.g. when not canonically required to do otherwise), I have found that working toward consensus rather than taking a vote is often more effective in achieving the desired outcome with the broadest sense of success and satisfaction. Although the process of achieving consensus is far more time-consuming, requiring an in-depth engagement of dialogue, it more often results in a sense of win-win rather than a win-lose outcome. Of course, this requires an ability and willingness to act with transparency, respect, trust and conviction. Since human relationships are not necessarily predictable, *shared responsibility* is not always neat and easy. Still, as Church, the Body of Christ, we are most effective and credible when giving witness to such endeavors through prayer, study, discernment and action. All of this, of course, is grounded in the necessity of ongoing dialogue, a theme which permeates Pope Francis's papacy and writings, particularly his Encyclical Letter on the Environment, *Laudato Si'* ("Praise be to you"). Ultimately, we are striving to carry out the **mission** of Jesus Christ, as entrusted to us, by means of ministry and service predicated on the three constitutive elements of the Church's nature; namely, Proclamation of the Word, Celebration of Sacraments and Outreach of Service.

At the heart of the ongoing dialogue permeating *Models of Shared Responsibility* is the process of ongoing formation, education and conversion leading to effective contemplation and action. This process of discernment often involves a tremendous commitment to time, discussion, study, reflection and action. Here, we share the following case studies: Parish Reorganization; (2) Strategic Planning; (3) Diocesan and Parish Councils and Advisory Groups; (4) Priest Initiators; and (5) Welcoming Missionary/International Priests.

---

2 Pope Francis, General Audience, St. Peter's Square, 8 October 2014.

Parish Reorganization

In December 2008, my predecessor, Bishop-emeritus Gerald A. Gettelfinger, formed an *ad hoc* committee to begin discernment of a strategic plan concerning availability of priests and parish vitality. The process progressed very deliberately and carefully, involving various forms of communication, surveys, interviews, committees and timelines. The surveys were made available to everyone in the diocese. Both individuals and parishes were encouraged to participate in response. By the time of my arrival in Evansville (i.e. Episcopal Ordination/ Installation on 29 June) in 2011, two principle sub-committees – one for parishes and one for schools – had been formed. Each sub-committee included representation of clergy (priests and deacons), religious (men and women, of various communities) and laity (including staff and volunteers). I was asked to provide some direction or points of reference. I made the distinction between goals and components. The goals included Catholic Identity, Mission & Presence through vibrant parishes in worship, ministry and service, with the ultimate focus on Encounter with Jesus Christ, the Proclamation of the Gospel, the Kingdom of God and Salvation of Souls. The components included the presbyterate, demographics, infrastructure, technology and Mass attendance. It was very important to maintain this distinction. We set parameters for each deanery (there were seven at the time, now reduced to four), stipulating the number of priests and Sunday Masses to be considered, in the discernment process. While there were already a number of linked parishes in the diocese, both mergers and further links were to be considered. A natural consideration for me was keeping in mind that healthy priests often make for healthy parishes. In other words, one of the best means of pastoral care for the People of God is maintaining proper care of priests. At the end of April 2012, the sub-committees presented their initial proposals. With the assistance of our Diocesan Chief Operating Officer, who is now Chancellor, and other diocesan staff, we then consulted ten diocesan groups over the next couple of months. By the end of August, revised proposals were presented to each deanery, which was instructed to form a Core Committee of representatives from all of its parishes. That group could accept, modify or submit another proposal. However, each core group had to work within the parameters of the number of priests and Sunday Masses determined for that particular deanery. Each deanery core committee had so many months to accomplish this task. When these were returned, a Town Hall Meeting was held in each deanery to share the proposals and listen to feedback. Following this Town Hall process, the proposals were reviewed and modified before being presented to the previous ten diocesan groups for further consultation. Special consideration was given to the Presbyteral Council and College of Consultors, especially in regard to the canonical norms required for proper process of counsel. A number of hours, involving multiple meetings, were involved in this process, with very careful record being kept of the minutes. Following this process, listening sessions were held for sixty-two of the sixty-nine parishes (seven were not directly impacted in the process) throughout the diocese over the course of several months. As bishop, I then made my decision regarding each proposal.

A key aspect in the successful outcome of our process was having our priests "on board,"in support of the plan. Their leadership proved invaluable in helping parishioners to navigate through their emotions amid the changes taking place. It was also important to appreciate the various teaching or catechetical moments throughout the process. Amazingly, some deanery groups ultimately proposed and implemented plans far beyond the scope of what had been presented or suggested for their consideration.

Communication, obviously, was integral to the effectiveness and sensitivity of the process. We held a press conference for secular media, which coincided with our diocesan paper, *The Message*, being sent to every Catholic household on that same day. While no worship site was closed or suppressed, our parish reorganization process reduced the number of parishes from sixty-nine to forty-six. Although there has been some adjustment to the change in Mass times, not a single letter of complaint or appeal was ever submitted apart from complaints about the canonical language in the actual decree. Despite the inevitable grieving often involved with change, especially of this magnitude in one's spiritual life, unity in faith and hope prevailed. Throughout this process, we consistently kept before us the Profession of Faith, particularly the words: *one, holy, catholic and apostolic Church.*

Welcoming Missionary International Priests

When I first arrived as bishop of Evansville, I was quickly apprised of the dearth of priests that existed in the diocese. In fact, we had a couple of parishes without either pastors or pastoral life coordinators. The Director of Clergy Personnel, using a sports metaphor, stated during my first meeting with the Clergy Personnel Board, "Bishop, your predecessor used to talk about having a depleted bench. We're now having trouble fielding a team to cover the bases." In addition to the already ongoing process toward parish reorganization, I mentioned the idea of missionary or international priests. I was immediately and repeatedly told that my predecessor was not in favor of this idea, as he felt that any viable diocese should be able to produce its own priestly vocations. I took the opportunity to consult both clergy and laity about the prospect of missionary priests. This included dialogue at meetings of the Council of Priests, quarterly presbyteral meetings, annual convocations and assemblies. We eventually formed an ad hoc committee to explore a process for inviting, welcoming and engaging missionary priests in the diocese. We set forth to establish a diocesan policy for missionary priests, drawing from recommendations of the USCCB and best practices in other dioceses. We received our first missionary priest, a diocesan priest from Nigeria, in October 2013. In May 2014, we received two Heralds of Good News priests from southern India, and a third one in November of that same year. In

September 2014, we received a priest from Kenya as well as a seminarian from Kenya, both becoming acquainted with the diocese through St. Meinrad Seminary which is less than one hour away. In February of this year, we received two diocesan priests of Imphal, in northern India. A clear diocesan policy, detailed "Agreement of Understanding," required participation in an enculturation program, various meetings with priests as well as programs to facilitate familiarity and cultural sensitivity have enabled us to make this transition without compromise to the integrity and morale of our priests and parishioners. Consequent to the parish reorganization process and receiving of missionary priests, we actually seem to have a bit of a priest-surplus, meaning more priests than assignments. A great deal of our success in this area, in addition to getting some really fine missionary priests, involves the incredible openness of minds and hearts on the part of our priests and parishioners.

Developing a Strategic Plan

No diocese or parish can function properly without an actual vision, a proper vision. Being a canon lawyer, in order not to wonder aimlessly, I am always seeking to be proactive rather than reactive. Given the efforts bringing about our parish reorganization and implementation of welcoming missionary priests, it only seemed appropriate that we develop and implement a deliberate plan for clarity, communication and communion. We formed a steering committee, first meeting in March 2014, toward developing a diocesan pastoral plan. Once again, the committee included the broadest range of diocesan representation – clergy, religious and laity; men and women; staff and parishioners; all seven deaneries. The primary resource for our discernment was Pope Francis's Apostolic Exhortation, *Evangelii Gaudium* ("The Joy of the Gospel"). Our initial discussions involved discerning the following questions: Who are we? Where are we? Where do we want to be? What does it mean to be a diocese? How are we at our best as Church, People of God, the Body of Christ? How do we get to where we want to be? Eventually, inspired by Pope Francis's exhortation to be missionary disciples,[3] we determined that it was necessary to revise our Diocesan Mission Statement to update the language and make it more relevant to our time. This proved to be an exciting and energizing exercise. Once the committee was satisfied with its work, we then took the proposed draft out to various groups – Council of Priests, Diocesan Pastoral Council, Diocesan Staff, Presbtyerate, Deacons, etc. – for feedback. Then, we set out three to five year goals. Once these were established, we again shared our proposals with the various diocesan groups. Next, members of the steering committee were assigned a particular goal to develop objectives and action steps. They were to recruit others in the diocese to form a sub-committee to address their particular goal. From there, we set out to engage clergy and laity throughout the diocese by scheduling a number of listening/dialogue sessions. Our strategic plan, a shared vision, is being pro-

3 Pope Francis, Apostolic exhortation, *Evangelii Gaudium*, nn. 19-21, 24 November 2013.

mulgated by means of a Pastoral Letter. In conjunction with this pastoral plan, we are also considering a shared diocesan-parish campaign and inaugurating an annual signature event in the spring of 2016 toward enhancing our celebration and embrace of Catholic identity and witness. These are already receiving strong support and enthusiasm, hopefully a by-product of the parish reorganization and pastoral planning processes. Grace builds on grace!

Part II: Case Studies

Church structures are not the goal but the means to assist the Church in carrying out its mission. These structures are served well when effective consultation processes are used and when these efforts emphasize common responsibility. The Archdiocese of Louisville, like the Diocese of Evansville, has numerous positive experiences of including effective consultation in church administration. We have chosen five significant administrative activities where the use of effective consultation has proven to be invaluable.

Parish Reorganization. The processes used to merge, cluster, or close parishes has significantly improved over the past twenty years as dioceses have increased consultation with the faithful as plans are being shaped and before decisions are made. Our experiences of reorganization processes in the 1990's seemed to accept hurt and anger as inevitable results of parish planning. Often so-called "blue ribbon" committees drafted parish reorganization plans, announced what would occur and provided opportunities for appeal. This approach fostered distrust and fear of the future rather than build support for a plan. Lessons from previous painful planning processes taught us to employ a different approach in the Archdiocese beginning with our 2005 plan. While likely no perfect model exists, this revised approach led to little resistance and an easy transition as seventeen parishes merged into six new vibrant communities.

1. Study Phase. Early in a planning process we engaged all pastors and their parishes in a study of the present demographics and structure of parishes throughout the diocese. Most parishioners are unaware of data such as the number and size of parishes, the age and ethnicity of parishioners, the number of active priests, details on sacraments celebrated annually, and the financial challenges impacting parishes. Distributing reports on this data and asking Parish Councils and/or other leadership groups to examine this information proved enormously helpful in alerting parishes that some changes were necessary. Having the diocesan Priest Council, Finance Council, and Pastoral Council also study this same information helped ready additional consultation in later steps of the process.
2. Parish or Regional Plans. After a period of study, but prior to

creating a diocesan plan, all parishes (or perhaps regions of deaneries in other setting) were required to prepare written plans as to how they could adjust to the changes in demographics and other data released in the Study Phase. We discovered that once parishes understood that changes would be required they were open to learning about how models such as clusters, mergers, or alternatives to staffing might be implemented.

3. Draft Plan. With parish or regional plans collected, it was easy to prepare a diocesan plan. The draft plan reflected the findings from the Study Phase and included as many alternatives as possible brought forward in the parish or regional plans. The draft plan was widely distributed in order to promote a spirit of transparency.

4. Consultation. Listening sessions were held in every parish impacted by the reorganization plan. The presentation included the rationale for proposed changes, likely timelines, and information on parishioner rights. Proper consultation with the Priest Council must also occurred allowing them to be heard on the plan.

5. Final Plan and Publication of Decrees. After the period of consultation, a publication of the final plan occurred along with the proper decrees.

6. Implementation Process. Each parish identified as part of a merger or cluster was provided a facilitator to assist in preparing an implementation plan. We have had good success in mergers by having a "core team" appointed representing the parishes being joined. This group ability to work out many details can build a good ownership from within the impacted parishes.

Diocesan Strategic Planning. It has become increasingly common for dioceses to create a Strategic Plan to determine priorities for a particular period of time, usually three to five years. These planning processes are a prime example of how the local Church has promoted shared responsibility and built support among the faithful for the work of the Church.

While there is differing nomenclature in various models, these plans usually articulate diocesan mission, goals, objectives, and actions steps. They may also determine how best to allocate diocesan human and financial resources for the implementation of the plan. In the Louisville Archdiocese we have a Planning Commission appointed by the Archbishop to oversee the preparation of the plan. In our experience, this commission works well in part because it is comprised of both diocesan staff and parish pastors. The Archbishop also participates in the committee meetings. The following is an outline of our planning process:

1. Situation Analysis. Good planning is always data driven. The data gathering itself has two values: getting the information to be used to identify needs and providing opportunities for input from a wide range of stakeholders. Evaluations tools, surveys, focus group meetings, and statistics commonly gathered by the Archdiocese about parishes and parishioners, are all used to develop a "State of the Archdiocese" report.

2. Draft Plan. A plan is written by the Planning Commission responding to the priority needs articulated in the "State of the Archdiocese" report.

3. Consultation. The draft plan is widely distributed to parish and diocesan leaders, and even more widely in some instances. Feedback is solicited on the level of goals and even on particular action steps of the plan. More formal consultations occur with Archdiocesan consultative committees or councils with particular emphasis on the Priest Council and Pastoral Council.

4. Final Plan. Using any feedback gathered in the consultation phase, the Planning Commission completes the plan for review and approval by the Archbishop.

5. Publish Plan. Once complete the plan is published and given to Archdiocesan and parish leaders, members of consultative bodies and to key donors to the Archdiocese.

6. Accountability. It has proven very helpful for ongoing planning, building ownership, and for donor relationships, to publish an annual accountability report providing an update on the implementation of the plan. This report also includes the annual financial report of the Archdiocese.

These types of planning processes are an example of building shared responsibility. In addition to serving as a helpful administrative tool, they have also proven useful as a resource of the Quinquennial Report, as an aid to preparing the Archdiocesan budget, and as a model for parish planning.

Diocesan and Parish Councils and Advisory Groups. Over the past fifty years, consultative boards and councils have been integrated into most diocesan and parish structures. The effectiveness of these groups is often dependent on three things: the preparation of the membership, quality of the agenda brought forth to these organizations for review, and the methods used to conduct the meetings.

1. Critical Questions. Many boards and councils waste meeting time listening to reports that can be easily read. A more effective approach, and one that leads to better quality input and meeting dynamics, is the use the critical question method. In this approach the meeting agenda is focused on one key topic or issue. Reports on other matters can still be given but the deliberation is limited to the key topic. After presenting the key topic input is sought but the conversation is limited to no more than three questions. The questions should be fairly open ended and designed to gather this most feedback. For example: "How might we best implement this program" or "What are the strengths and weaknesses of this proposed initiative?" or "How will we know if this program is successful?"

2. Convocation. Another weakness of some councils and committees is found simply in how the membership is determined. While there is no one answer here, rethinking membership may open up new possibilities. For example, about a dozen years ago the Archdiocese of Louisville replaced an ineffective Pastoral Council with a twice annual convocation of all Parish Pastoral Council chairs. The group serves as a consultative body to the Archbishop and provides important feedback using the critical question approach. The agenda from these gatherings often influence Parish Council meetings following these sessions and provide a great connection between the Archdiocese and the parishes. As a bonus, the members network with one another and provide support and encouragement to fellow chairpersons.

Priest Initiators. This approach to consultation is essentially about the engagement of priests in Archdiocesan initiatives. We have often mistakenly assumed that most everyone is ready to begin something new at the same time. Rethinking this concept has led to the creation of Priest Initiator projects.

The Priest Initiators approach invites small numbers of priest who are ready to commit time to a new project without suggesting anyone else is incapable of the same commitment. For example, when attempting to expand our vocation efforts, we asked all priests to participate in an outreach effort to identify young men who might consider priesthood. As this program was underway a number of our priests complained they were being burdened and asked to do "one more thing." This negativity led to frustration and little success.

We changed this approach under the banner of Priest Initiators. Priests were asked to self-identify if they were willing to participate in a special training initiative to promote vocations. A group of highly committed priests volunteered and more was accomplished with a smaller group and no one complained they were being over-taxed. Since that initial project, similar efforts using Priest Initiators have addressed the new evangelization while another group formed to work on programs for the Year of Mercy.

Welcoming Priests. Integrating newly ordained priests, foreign-born priests, and religious order priests, into the life of the parish and Archdiocese has often been challenging. It has been suggested that how welcoming a parish is may be critical to the success of a newly arriving priest. This reality has provided a unique opportunity to practice shared responsibility.

1. Parish welcoming. A more formal process of welcoming has been designed in some parishes whereby the newly arriving priest is provided more than only a welcome reception, but is given the opportunity to work with a special parish committee whose task is to determine what the parish needs to know about the priest and what the priest needs to know about the parish. This group meets regularly with the new priest during his first few months and provides him with the information he needs while introducing him to the parish at gatherings and in written reports. Welcome has been expanded to include a lengthier orientation process. This engagement of parishioners has helped them become more open, helpful and patient with the newly assigned priest.
2. Study materials. New priests are being provided expanded written material on the diocese and on the parish where they will serve.
3. Transition time. Foreign priests have been allowed the option of having a number of months to transition into the diocese prior to receiving an assignment. They live with other priests, but not necessarily where they will be assigned, just to get acquainted with the diocese and get to know some members of the clergy.

Part III: Pastoral Principles

From our experiences in administration, in both diocesan and parish settings, we have grown in our conviction that building shared responsibility through good consultative practices is essential for effective pastoral leadership. We propose five working principles to summarize our presentation.

Effective collaboration leads to shared ownership. Whenever leaders use consultation as a regular part of their planning efforts, and when making important decisions, there is an increase of support for any initiative. In the context of parish life, support for the pastor and other parish leaders is a likely outcome. As parishioners develop a greater sense of ownership and become more engaged in parish life, their personal commitment of time and financial contributions increase as well.

Wisdom lies within the community. Parishioners appreciate opportunities to give input in even simple matters of parish life. Yet, no matter how schooled someone may be in facilitation, and how open they are to the experience of others, the loudest voices may shape the decisions of leaders resulting in disappointed members. That is why employing methods which gather feedback from a wide variety of persons are the most effective. Similar problems exist when even well-intentioned leaders are blinded by their own view of circumstances. Trusting in the power and wisdom of a group can result in leaders considering alternatives they might have otherwise missed.

Dissemination of accurate information provides the formation necessary for good decisions. Consultation works best when the initial steps of the process include the education of those involved. Poor decisions are often made due to decision makers having insufficient or inaccurate information. Likewise, critics of decisions often make judgments based on flawed information. Engaging those most impacted by a decision in the careful analysis of the issues provides for the formation of new understandings. Consultation does not mean conducting straw polls or simple voting, but rather includes study, reflection, and an honest exchange of ideas.

Consultation identifies key goals and focuses the actions of the leader. Good leaders invite the perspectives of others to be heard and allow the insights they hear to shape their own thinking. These more informed leaders are better able to be responsive, set strategic goals, and determine where opportunities exist for the greatest impact.

Consultation is essential to good planning. Planning is essentially an act of prioritizing and effective consultation provides leaders with the insights to understand where there is the greatest need in order to set priorities accordingly. Many leaders prefer to initiate change believing that shared decision making simply delays inevitable conclusions. However, taking time to review alternatives and build support will, in the end, allow plans to be implemented more quickly and easily.

Officer's Report

Report of the President
Rev. Msgr. Michael A. Souckar, JCD

It is my pleasure to offer this summary report on my year as President of the Canon Law Society of America. The year has been marked by both the ordinary work of the CLSA and special projects, culminating in the revision of the canons governing the procedures for marriage nullity cases. Allow me to highlight just a few of the events of the year.

1. Committee Work

I am happy to report that the CLSA committees and task forces continue their work on several projects. Of particular note this year was the work undertaken by the Task Force charged with proposing recommendations to the Special Pontifical Commission on the revision of the procedural norms for marriage nullity cases. Their scholarly work was completed in a timely manner and was well received by the Special Commission. The PAB has continued to promote the Webinar Wednesday series. I wish to thank Eileen Jaramillo for the recent webinar entitled "Erection of a Religious Institute: Process and Praxis." I also highlight the collaborative work done by the Committee on Sacramental Law and the Committee on the Laity to draft a publication on inter-cultural marriage in the United States. It is hoped that their work will soon be completed and a brochure published.

2. Visits to Sister Societies and Schools of Canon Law

As is customary, it was my pleasure this year to represent the CLSA at the annual conventions of the Canadian Canon Law Society, the Canon Law Society of Great Britain and Ireland, and the Antilles Canon Law Society. At each of these gatherings I not only presented greetings from the CLSA but also expressed our interest in working collaboratively with these other societies in our common goal to promote the study and work of canon law. Discussions continue by the presidents of these English-speaking canon law societies to increase our effective collaboration with one another. We have agreed to build upon the initial discussions and to look for ways in which our societies can benefit from one another's experiences and expertise. During the year, I also was able to visit the schools of canon law at Saint Paul University and The Catholic University of America. In both instances I received a most cordial reception by the Dean, faculty and students whom I encouraged to join the CLSA. Several students expressed an interest in joining the CLSA and they thanked me for the work of the CLSA, especially our publications. At Saint Paul University, I delivered a paper on the possibilities of the reception into full communion with the Church of baptized non-Catholics who are in irregular marriages.

3. Rome Trip

I believe that the biennial visit to Rome in March was very successful. Father Viera, Father Keeler and I visited with officials at seven Roman dicasteries (the Roman Rota, Apostolic Signatura, the Congregations for Clergy, Consecrated Life and Societies of Apostolic Life, Eastern Churches, Doctrine of the Faith, and the Pontifical Council for Legislative Texts), as well as three faculties of canon law (Angelicum, Gregorian and Santa Croce). We enjoyed *pranzo* at the *Casa Santa Maria* and following this had a very cordial gathering with the priest-graduate students who are studying canon law to encourage them to join the CLSA. In my assessment, the CLSA is very well respected by the officials at the various Roman Curial offices as well as at the faculties of canon law. All spoke most favorably of our publications and many were receptive to having documents published in *Roman Replies.* General invitations were also extended to officials at the various Curia offices to attend our annual convention and possibly to give a major address or seminar. We also attended a General Papal Audience and were able to greet Pope Francis personally.

I strongly encourage the continuation of these biennial visits and I would suggest that additional Curial offices (e.g. Catholic Education, Causes of Saints, to name only two) be visited. I wish to express my sincere thanks to Father Bob Geisinger, SJ, who most ably guided our preparations and introductions to the various offices we visited. We can be rightly proud of the high esteem with which the Vatican officials and Roman professors of canon law admire the CLSA and its contributions to canonical research and the right application of the law. During our visit in Rome, there also arose the proposal for the CLSA to offer its members occasional working visits to the Roman dicasteries. It is my hope that this proposal will move forward. While in Rome and upon the encouragement of a good friend and canonist, I ran (and completed) the Rome Marathon, my first ever!

4. Board of Governors

I am grateful to the members of the Board of Governors for their continuing service to all of us in the CLSA. The BOG takes its responsibilities seriously and has worked effectively this year for the good of the entire Society. I especially want to thank the BOG for the proposed resolutions on a dues increase, absentee balloting, and the change of the title of the Executive Director. I believe that these resolutions will serve the Society well, both immediately and well into to the future. A special word of thanks is extended to those members of the BOG who are completing their service. I thank Father Phil Brown, *pss*, our Past-President who has been a very able collaborator, as well as Monsignor John Foster and Father Patrick Cooney, OSB, who complete their terms as Consultors. It has been an honor and a joy to work with you on the BOG and in my own name and on behalf of all of us in the CLSA, I thank you most sincerely for your service.

5. Extra Curricular Work

During the course of the year as President, I have had the opportunity to work with the United States Conference of Catholic Bishops on the drafting and implementation of the third edition of the document "Guidelines for Receiving Pastoral Ministers in the United States." The bishops approved the document at their plenary meeting in November 2014 and over the course of the year there have been four regional seminars on its implementation. The Guidelines are especially helpful for chancery officials, seminary rectors and vocation directors, major superiors, and others who assist international ministers coming to serve the Church in the United States. I believe that this collaboration with the USCCB has been a very positive experience and I hope that there will be similar opportunities in the future.

In conclusion, allow me to express my sincere thanks to the members of the Canon Law Society of America for the opportunity to serve as President. When I joined the CLSA in 1993 as a student at CUA, I never imagined that I would one day be called to serve as President of this Society, comprised of such dedicated scholars and practitioners of canon law. It has been a distinct honor to represent the CLSA this year and I hope that whatever small contribution I have made will help the CLSA to continue to achieve its high ideals. I cannot conclude this report without thanking those who have been of special assistance this year. I thank Father Roger Keeler, Colleen Crawford, and Renae Kuettel at the Executive Coordinator's office in Washington, the staff of the Metropolitan Tribunal in Miami, and the priests and staff at Saint Andrew Parish in Coral Springs, where I happily serve as pastor. All of you have been of great assistance this year. Finally, I know that the CLSA is in good hands as Father Manuel Viera, OFM, assumes the office of President.

Officer's Report

Report of the Treasurer
Rev. Thomas E. Cronkleton, Jr., JCD

This is my second report to the Society as Treasurer. I want to thank Father Roger Keeler, our Executive Coordinator, and Colleen Crawford, our Executive Assistant, for the excellent work they have done. They have done an excellent job in managing the funds of the Society. I am also grateful for the assistance of the Resource and Asset Management Committee for their valuable input.

We divide our financial operations into 4 Units: General Operations, Publications, Conventions, and Scholarships. Each unit strives to have a balanced budget, but a positive balance in Publications can be used to be offset a negative balance in General Operations. The Convention Unit seeks to have a balanced budget. The Scholarship Unit and the funds represented are only used for the scholarships and the operational expenses of this Unit. I will highlight below a few items contained in the reports that follow.

General Operations, Conventions and Scholarships finished in the black. Publications, however, finished in the red. Each Unit had unique reasons for these results, which will be discussed below.

General Operations Unit:

In the General Operations Unit, the main source of income is Dues. Our collection of Dues from New Member was $2,700.00 under budget, but Dues from Current Members was $4,700.00 over budget. We, therefore, collected $2,200.00 more in Dues that budgeted ($200.00 from the prior year).

Dividends and interest exceeded expectations. We were also able to use less in Prior Year Net Assets than anticipated. This was due to the extra income, but also some savings in expenses. The fact that we are now using Prior Year Realized Net Assets helps to demonstrate the need for an increase of dues.

We were able to recruit Father Roger Keeler as our new Executive Coordinator. He, however, did not start until August, and we were budgeted for this position to be filled by July 1, 2014. We, therefore, had some savings for salary and benefits.

Our Administrative Assistant, Mary DeBroeck, accepted a teaching fellowship at the Catholic University of America. Renae Kuettel was hired as her replacement, but for fewer hours. We, therefore, realized some savings here.

We experienced some issues with Christian Brothers for both our health care insurance and 403(b) programs. Hence, with the Executive Coordinator position, there were delays in getting Father Keeler covered. This resulted in some additional savings with his benefits. We experienced similar coverage difficulties with the Executive Assistant position, and were able to get things corrected, but we realized some of the expenses in this fiscal year as opposed to the prior year. For this reason, the Executive Assistant benefits are over budget.

We created a new line item for the fees in the 403(b) program, which were unknown at the time we developed last year's budget. They are budgeted in this year's budget.

We incurred more in legal fees than anticipated. These fees were for contract drafting and development.

Both the Office of the Executive Coordinator and the Board of Governors brought their expenses in under budget. For the Board of Governors, this was mainly due to savings in travel expenses. We were fortunate in obtaining some low airfares and some members living close to Baltimore who were able to drive to the meetings.

One of the services we have added for the Membership is the Webinars. These have been very successful and popular. During this last Fiscal Year 2014-2015, webinars were offered at no-cost to members of the Society, and we will continue to fund them at no-cost to members for this current year too.

The Committees overall came in under budget. Only Nominations came in over budget, as they had extra expenses in gathering their members, but the committee put forth an excellent slate of candidates for office. The remainder of Committees were under budget, in part by meeting through electronic means. In the current budget, we provided all the Committees with the funds they requested in order to promote and encourage their activity.

As previously mentioned, we had to use the Prior Year Realized Net Assets to meet our expenses. We have budgeted to do so again this current fiscal year. Because of this, the Resource and Asset Management Committee and the Board of Governors have proposed an increase in dues. The main source of income for the General Operations Unit is dues. For the three prior years, the General Operations Unit was budgeted to use the Prior Year Realized Net Assets in order to balance the budget. While we budgeted to use these funds, we did not have to use them. We did, however, have to use them this past fiscal year.

The Paulists have notified us and their other tenants that they wish to sell the building, and be let out from the lease agreement. We are negotiating for new office space and considering all the connected financial ramifications. We hope to maintain an office in the area.

The Investments in the General Operations Unit have been experiencing generally positive growth the last few years. The decline in the December 31, 2014 balance was due to the $50,000.00 transfer to establish the Doctoral Scholarship Fund. The fund, however, has continued to experience some growth. Below are the quarterly balances for the last three years:

General Operations Investment Fund (CUIT Balance Fund)

Date	Fund Balance
December 31, 2011	$545,113.60
March 31, 2011	$593,318.42
June 30, 2012	$585,252.27
September 30, 2012	$616,230.86
December 31, 2012	$624,659.45
March 31, 2013	$668,626.16
June 30, 2013	$680,025.21
September 30, 2013	$708,690.03
December 31, 2013	$757,643.34
March 31, 2014	$769,264.93
June 30, 2014	$797,237.52
September 30, 2014	$799,740.90
December 31, 2014	$771,084.80
March 31, 2015	$770.355.00
June 30, 2015	$772,070.92

The end of August and the beginning of September have been rough times for the market. We have to see what the end result will be.

The Balance Sheet for the General Operations Unit shows the gains in the market, and a positive balance. This is where the transfer to the Scholarship Fund for the Doctoral Scholarship Fund is recorded.

Publications Unit:

The Publications Unit had a slight negative year of -$8,431.34, because expenses exceeded income. This was due in part to the revenues from publication sales being about 72% of what was anticipated, although we did realize some savings from distribution and warehouse-related fees. The main reason, however, for the deficit was the special authorization by the Board of Governors to provide additional funds for bringing the new Electronic Database online. The Board of Governors wanted the Publication Advisory Board to have all the necessary resources to complete the Electronic Database project.

The Balance Sheet for the Publications Unit shows the inventory we have, as well as some reserves. The Balance Sheet for the Publications Unit is down for the year because of the negative cash flow.

Conventions Unit:

The Conventions Unit had a positive return for last year's Convention and Pre-Convention Workshops in St. Louis, Missouri. This was due to programs that attracted more than anticipated attendance. While some costs were higher than budgeted due to the greater number of attendees, the additional revenue more than offset this expense. Additionally, the expenses for speakers were about $3,200 less than anticipated, resulting in further savings. More and more speakers are using audio-visuals in their presentations: This has resulted in increased, anticipated expenses, yet when audiovisual equipment improves a presentation, it is a worthwhile expense.

The Balance Sheet for the Conventions Unit is positive, and we have some reserves in case our expenses should exceed our income. We also chose to budget this year's Convention using some of this gain.

Scholarship Unit:

The Scholarship Unit operates on a total return basis for the investments in two Scholarship Investment Funds, Licentiate and Doctoral Scholarships. Up to 5% of the total market value of the Scholarship Investment Fund is used to fund the Scholarship Unit. The total market value is computed on the basis of a three (3) year rolling quarterly average, with the ending quarter on the December 31st immediately preceding the January Board of Governors' meeting. This sum is used for scholarship awards, administration, and fundraising efforts. The financial report shows the income and expenses in the unit.

Since the inception of the Licentiate Scholarship Fund through June 30, 2015, $408,437.17 has been donated to the Scholarship Fund. Over the same period, we have distributed $241,749.35 in scholarships to 27 recipients. Five additional recipients are slated to receive scholarship funds in FY 2015-2016.

The Investments in the Licentiate Scholarship Unit have been experiencing generally positive growth the last few years. Below in the quarterly balances:

Licentiate Scholarship Investment Fund (CUIT Balanced Fund)

Date	Fund Balance
December 31, 2011	$434,505.86
March 31, 2012	$472,929.58
June 30, 2012	$466,500.09
September 30, 2012	$491,192.89
December 31, 2012	$497,911.19
March 31, 2013	$532,956.72
June 30, 2013	$542,042.79
September 30, 2013	$564,891.34
December 31, 2013	$603,911.62
March 31, 2014	$613,175.11
June 30, 2014	$635,471.89
September 30, 2014	$637,467.28
December 31, 2014	$657,027.00
March 31, 2015	$656,405.24
June 30, 2015	$657,867.38

This growth has been due both to a positive return in the Market over this period, and from donations to the Scholarship Fund.

We awarded the first doctoral scholarship of $2,500.00 this year. In addition to the $50,000.00 transfer from General Operations, the Doctoral Scholarship received $2,485.19 in donations.

Doctoral Scholarship Investment Fund (CUIT Balanced Fund)

Date	Fund Balance
December 31, 2014	$53,194.96
March 31, 2015	$53,144.65
June 30, 2015	$53,262.98

Since inception, the Doctoral Scholarship Investments have grown too.

Both the Scholarship Investments will be affected by the late August and early September losses in the market.

Christian Brothers Investment Services:

Our investments are with Christian Brothers Investment Services in two of their funds: the CUIT Balanced Fund and the CUIT Money Market Fund (formerly RCT Flex Cash Fund). The CUIT Balanced Fund is 60% equities and 40% bonds. The equities portion is large cap, and the bonds are intermediate term. The bond fund managers have been positioning this portion of the fund for an increase in the interest rate by the Federal Reserve. They anticipated an increase in September, and if not, in December. The CUIT Money Market, like most money market accounts, has less than half a percent return. This will continue until interest rates are raised by the Federal Reserve. All the investments vehicles have performed just below the benchmarks in the last few months, and throughout the last year, but over time, they were at or above their benchmarks.

Accountants' Review:

Linton, Shafer, Warfield & Garrett, PA, did an audit of fiscal years ending June 30, 2015 and June 30, 2014. An audit involves performing procedures to obtain evidence about the amounts and disclosures in the financial statements. The auditor conducts an evaluation of accounting policies used and the reasonableness of significant accounting estimates made by management, as well as an evaluation of the overall presentation of financial statements. Audits are performed every third year, with annual financial reviews conducted in the interim; or when there is a change in the Executive Coordinator. This was the year for an audit, both due the timing and the changes in Executive Coordinators. Next year we are scheduled for a financial review.

Mr. Joseph M. McCathran, CPA, was the principal in the Audit of our financials. We have been given an unqualified audit opinion that our financials are presented in accord with the generally accepted accounting principles. Specifically, the Audit done by Linton, Shafer, Warfield & Garret, PA stated:

> In our opinion, the financial statements referred to above present fairly, in all material respects, the financial position of Canon Law Society of American, as of June 30, 2015, and the changes in net assets and its cash flows for the year then ended in accordance with accounting principles generally accepted in the United States of America.

We have received a positive report. The Independent Accounts' Audit Report follows in this booklet.

Resolution to Increase Dues:

The Resource and Asset Management Committee developed the resolution to increase dues in order to ensure adequate funding for General Operations. The Committee provided two options to the Board of Governors: one with a $50.00 increase in dues for active and associate members and $25.00 increase for student membership, and the second option, with the same increases, but providing a $50.00 discount for active and associate members who were 70 or older by June 30 of the prior fiscal year according to their birthdate in the Society's database. One of the difficulties with the discount for senior members is that only one-third of the membership has disclosed their age in the database. As a result, the financial impact could not be fully measured. The Board of Governors considered carefully both proposals, and after a great deal of discussion and concern over the uncertainty of the financial impact, chose to recommend to the membership the proposal to increase dues by $50.00 for active and associate members and $25.00 for student members, effective July 1, 2016. I wholeheartedly support the resolution to increase the dues and judge it to be a fiscal necessity. Mr. McCathran, who was the principal for our Audit, judges that this would be an appropriate move, given our financials.

Budget and Budget vs. Actual Reports:

The 2015-2016 Budget Report and the 2014-2015 Budget vs. Actual Reports follow.

CANON LAW SOCIETY OF AMERICA

Financial Statements, Supplementary Information and Report of Independent Certified Public Accountants

For the Years Ended June 30, 2015 and 2014

LSWG

Linton Shafer Warfield & Garrett, P.A.
CERTIFIED PUBLIC ACCOUNTANTS

LSWG
Linton Shafer Warfield & Garrett, P.A.
CERTIFIED PUBLIC ACCOUNTANTS

Report of Independent Certified Public Accountants

Board of Governors
Canon Law Society of America

We have audited the accompanying financial statements of Canon Law Society of America (a nonprofit organization), which comprise the statements of financial position as of June 30, 2015, and the related statements of activities and changes in net assets, and cash flows for the year then ended, and the related notes to the financial statements.

Management's Responsibility for the Financial Statements
Management is responsible for the preparation and fair presentation of these financial statements in accordance with accounting principles generally accepted in the United States of America; this includes the design, implementation, and maintenance of internal control relevant to the preparation and fair presentation of financial statements that are free from material misstatement, whether due to fraud or error.

Auditor's Responsibility
Our responsibility is to express an opinion on these financial statements based on our audit. We conducted our audit in accordance with auditing standards generally accepted in the United States of America. Those standards require that we plan and perform the audit to obtain reasonable assurance about whether the financial statements are free from material misstatement.

An audit involves performing procedures to obtain audit evidence about the amounts and disclosures in the financial statements. The procedures selected depend on the auditor's judgment, including the assessment of the risks of material misstatement of the financial statements, whether due to fraud or error. In making those risk assessments, the auditor considers internal control relevant to the entity's preparation and fair presentation of the financial statements in order to design audit procedures that are appropriate in the circumstances, but not for the purpose of expressing an opinion on the effectiveness of the entity's internal control. Accordingly, we express no such opinion. An audit also includes evaluating the appropriateness of accounting policies used and the reasonableness of significant accounting estimates made by management, as well as evaluating the overall presentation of the financial statements.

932 Hungerford Drive, Suite 29B • Rockville, Maryland 20850-1752 • 240-314-7075 • FAX 240-314-7079
ROCKVILLE • FREDERICK
www.lswgcpa.com

We believe that the audit evidence we have obtained is sufficient and appropriate to provide a basis for our audit opinion.

Opinion

In our opinion, the financial statements referred to above present fairly, in all material respects, the financial position of Canon Law Society of America, as of June 30, 2015, and the changes in net assets and its cash flows for the year then ended in accordance with accounting principles generally accepted in the United States of America.

Prior Period Financial Statements

The 2014 financial statements were reviewed by us, and our report thereon, dated August 27, 2014, stated we were not aware of any material modifications that should be made to those financial statements for them to be in conformity with accounting principles generally accepted in the United States of America. However, a review is substantially less in scope than an audit and does not provide a basis for the expression of an opinion on the financial statements.

Other Matter

Our audit was conducted for the purpose of forming an opinion on the financial statements as a whole. The Schedules of Program Services and Supporting Services are presented for purpose of additional analysis and are not a required part of the financial statements. Such information is the responsibility of management and was derived from and relates directly to the underlying accounting and other records used to prepare the financial statements. The information has been subjected to the auditing procedures applied in the audit of the financial statements and certain additional procedures, including comparing and reconciling such information directly to the underlying accounting and other records used to prepare the financial statements or to the financial statements themselves, and other additional procedures in accordance with auditing standards generally accepted in the United States of America. In our opinion, the information is fairly stated in all material respects in relation to the financial statements as a whole.

Linton Shafer Warfield & Garrett

Rockville, Maryland
September 4, 2015

CANON LAW SOCIETY OF AMERICA
Statements of Financial Position
June 30, 2015 and 2014

	2015	2014
Assets		
Current Assets		
Cash	$ 246,025	$ 273,977
Cash - scholarship fund	13,833	17,133
Accounts receivable - other	6,415	2,996
Inventory	76,690	80,318
Prepaid expenses	20,183	19,347
Total Current Assets	363,146	393,771
Furniture and Equipment - at cost		
Furniture and equipment	17,765	17,765
Less: accumulated depreciation	(15,735)	(14,304)
Furniture and Equipment, Net	2,030	3,461
Other Assets		
Investments	772,071	797,237
Investment - scholarship fund	711,130	635,472
Total Other Assets	1,483,201	1,432,709
Total Assets	$ 1,848,377	$ 1,829,941
Liabilities and Net Assets		
Current Liabilities		
Accounts payable	$ 30	$ 30
Deferred revenue	15,235	25,085
Total Current Liabilities	15,265	25,115
Total Liabilities	15,265	25,115
Net Assets		
Unrestricted		
Undesignated	1,022,362	1,058,632
Board designated - publications	79,302	87,733
Total Unrestricted	1,101,664	1,146,365
Temporarily restricted	731,448	658,461
Total Net Assets	1,833,112	1,804,826
Total Liabilities and Net Assets	$ 1,848,377	$ 1,829,941

The accompanying notes are an integral part of these statements.

3

CANON LAW SOCIETY OF AMERICA
Statements of Activities and Changes in Net Assets
For the Year Ended June 30, 2015

	Unrestricted				
	Undesignated	Publications	Total	Temporarily Restricted	Total
Revenue					
Membership dues	$ 234,200	$ -	$ 234,200	$ -	$ 234,200
Convention, workshops	186,762	-	186,762	-	186,762
Sale of publications	-	65,962	65,962	-	65,962
Contributions	-	-	-	11,131	11,131
Interest and dividends	9,003	-	9,003	8,107	17,110
Royalties	-	7,322	7,322	-	7,322
Appreciation on fair value of investments	15,836	-	15,836	17,642	33,478
Net assets released from restrictions	13,893	-	13,893	(13,893)	-
Total Revenue	459,694	73,284	532,978	22,987	555,965
Expenses					
Program Services					
Publications	-	81,715	81,715	-	81,715
Convention, workshops	167,436	-	167,436	-	167,436
Membership services	12,173	-	12,173	-	12,173
Committees	4,896	-	4,896	-	4,896
Holy See and Austrialia	10,945	-	10,945	-	10,945
Scholarship fund	13,893	-	13,893	-	13,893
Total Program Services	209,343	81,715	291,058	-	291,058
Supporting Services	236,621	-	236,621	-	236,621
Total Expenses	445,964	81,715	527,679	-	527,679
Changes in Net Assets	13,730	(8,431)	5,299	22,987	28,286
Net Assets - Beginning of Year	1,058,632	87,733	1,146,365	658,461	1,804,826
Equity transfer	(50,000)	-	(50,000)	50,000	-
Net Assets - End of Year	$ 1,022,362	$ 79,302	$ 1,101,664	$ 731,448	$ 1,833,112

The accompanying notes are an integral part of these statements.

CANON LAW SOCIETY OF AMERICA
Statements of Activities and Changes in Net Assets
For the Year Ended June 30, 2014

	Unrestricted				
	Undesignated	Publications	Total	Temporarily Restricted	Total
Revenue					
Membership dues	$ 263,675	$ -	$ 263,675	$ -	$ 263,67
Convention, workshops	175,956	-	175,956	-	175,95
Sale of publications	-	67,204	67,204	-	67,20
Contributions	-	-	-	12,945	12,94
Interest and dividends	10,876	-	10,876	8,767	19,64
Royalties	-	8,246	8,246	-	8,24
Appreciation on fair value of investments	106,347	-	106,347	84,769	191,11
Net assets released from restrictions	19,362	-	- 19,362	(19,362)	
Total Revenue	576,216	75,450	651,666	87,119	738,78
Expenses					
Program Services					
Publications	-	75,533	75,533	-	75,53
Convention, workshops	157,350	-	157,350	-	157,35
Membership services	8,839	-	8,839	-	8,83
Committees	22,202	-	22,202	-	22,20
Lay Ecclesial Work Group	72	-	72	-	7
Holy See and Austrialia	10,801	-	10,801	-	10,80
Scholarship fund	19,290	-	19,290	-	19,29
Total Program Services	218,554	75,533	294,087	-	294,08
Supporting Services	198,313	-	198,313	-	198,3
Total Expenses	416,867	75,533	492,400	-	492,40
Changes in Net Assets	159,349	(83)	159,266	87,119	246,38
Net Assets - Beginning of Year	902,375	87,816	990,191	568,250	1,558,44
Equity transfer	(3,092)	-	(3,092)	3,092	
Net Assets - End of Year	$ 1,058,632	$ 87,733	$ 1,146,365	$ 658,461	$ 1,804,82

The accompanying notes are an integral part of these statements.

CANON LAW SOCIETY OF AMERICA
Statements of Cash Flows
For the Years Ended June 30,

Increase (Decrease) in Cash	2015	2014
Cash Flows From Operating Activities		
Changes in Net Assets	$ 28,286	$ 246,385
Adjustments to reconcile changes in net assets to net cash provided by (used in) operating activities:		
Depreciation	1,431	1,682
Unrealized (gain) on investments	(33,478)	(191,116)
Change in assets and liabilities:		
(Increase) Decrease in accounts receivable	(3,419)	870
(Increase) Decrease in prepaid expenses	(836)	(533)
(Increase) Decrease in inventory	3,628	19,083
Increase (Decrease) in royalties payable	-	(553)
Increase (Decrease) in deferred revenue	(9,850)	12,025
Net Cash Provided by (Used In) Operating Activities	(14,238)	87,843
Cash Flows From Investing Activities		
Purchase of investments	(67,014)	(19,525)
Proceeds from sale of investments	50,000	-
Net Cash Used in Investing Activities	(17,014)	(19,525)
Increase (Decrease) in Cash	(31,252)	68,318
Cash Balance - Beginning of Year	291,110	222,792
Cash Balance - End of Year	$ 259,858	$ 291,110
Supplemental Disclosures		
Income taxes paid	$ -	$ -
Interest paid	$ -	$ -

The accoompanying notes are an integral part of these statements.

CANON LAW SOCIETY OF AMERICA
Notes to Financial Statements
For the Years Ended June 30, 2015 and 2014

1. Nature of Activities

The Canon Law Society of America (CLSA) is a national, not-for-profit corporation, established in November 1939 in Washington DC to promote canonical and pastoral approaches to significant issues within the Roman Catholic Church. In addition to a publication service, CLSA conducts an annual convention and other symposia to promote a better understanding of church law and its pastoral applications. Major sources of gross income are from membership dues, sales of publications and books and annual convention and workshops.

2. Basis of Financial Statement Presentation

According to Financial Accounting Standards Board (FASB) Codification Standards, CLSA is required to report information regarding its financial position and activities according to three classes of net assets:

(1) **Unrestricted Net Assets** - represents resources that are currently available for support of CLSA's operations.

(2) **Temporarily Restricted Net Assets** - represents resources that may be utilized only in accordance with the restricted purposes established by CLSA's bylaws. When a restriction expires, temporarily restricted net assets are reclassified to unrestricted net assets and reported in the statement of activities and net assets as funds are released from temporary restrictions.

(3) **Permanently Restricted Net Assets** - represents resources for which the principal is to be maintained intact and the income, may only be spent in accordance with the intent of the donor. CLSA currently does not have any permanently restricted net assets.

The financial statements are prepared on the accrual basis of accounting, whereby, revenue is recognized when earned and expenses are recognized when incurred.

3. Summary of Significant Accounting Policies

Cash and cash equivalents – For purposes of the statement of cash flows, CLSA considers all cash accounts and all highly liquid debt instruments purchased with an initial maturity of three months or less to be cash equivalents.

Investments - Investments in marketable securities with readily determinable fair values are reported at their fair values in the statement of financial position. Investment income or loss (including gains and losses on investments, interest and dividends) is included in the statement of activities as an increase or decrease in unrestricted net assets unless the income or loss is restricted by donor or law.

CANON LAW SOCIETY OF AMERICA
Notes to Financial Statements
For the Years Ended June 30, 2015 and 2014

3. Summary of Significant Accounting Policies (Continued)

Investments consist principally of two mutual funds. Fair value of investments in securities is based on the latest reported sales price at June 30, 2015 and 2014.

Accounts receivable - Accounts receivable are stated at the amount management expects to collect from outstanding balances. The provision for uncollectible accounts is based on management's evaluation of the collectability of accounts receivable. CLSA considers accounts receivable to be fully collectible; accordingly, no provision for doubtful accounts is required. Books and publication receivables are considered uncollectible if not collected within 90 days after the sale.

Inventory – The inventory of books and publications is valued at cost, on the first-in, first-out method.

Property and Equipment - Purchases of furniture and equipment are recorded at cost. CLSA's policy is to capitalize expenditures for equipment purchased in the amount of $1,000 or more. Depreciation is calculated over an estimated useful life of five to ten years using the straight-line method. Depreciation and amortization for the years ended June 30, 2015 and 2014 totaled $1,431 and $1,682.

Fair Value – Financial Accounting Standards Board (FASB) Codification Standards defines fair value, establishes a framework for measuring fair value, and expands disclosures about fair value measurements and establishes a hierarchy for valuation inputs.

Fair value is the price that would be received to sell an asset or paid to transfer a liability in an orderly transaction between market participants at the measurement date. A fair value measurement assumes that the transaction to sell the asset or transfer the liability occurs in the principal market for the asset or liability or, in the absence of a principal market, the most advantageous market. Valuation techniques that are consistent with the market, income or cost approach are used to measure fair value.

The fair value hierarchy prioritizes the inputs to valuation techniques used to measure fair value into three broad levels:

- Level 1 - inputs are based upon unadjusted quoted prices for identical instruments traded in active markets.

- Level 2 - inputs are based upon quoted prices for similar instruments in active markets, quoted prices for identical or similar instruments in markets that are not active, and model-based valuation techniques for which all significant assumptions are observable in the market or can be corroborated by observable market data for substantially the full term of the assets or liabilities.

3. Summary of Significant Accounting Policies (Continued)

- Level 3 - inputs are generally unobservable and typically reflect management's estimates of assumptions that market participants would use in pricing the asset or liability. The fair values are therefore determined using model-based techniques that include option pricing models, discounted cash flow models, and similar techniques.

Revenue Recognition - CLSA bills membership dues annually on a basis which conforms to CLSA's fiscal year-end. Dues, workshop and convention registrations received in advance of the next fiscal year are deferred and recognized as revenue in the subsequent year.

Contributions are recognized when the donor makes a promise to give to the Society that is, in substance, unconditional. Contributions received are recorded as unrestricted, temporarily restricted, or permanently restricted support depending on the absence or existence and nature of any donor restrictions. Contributions restricted by the donor are reported as increases in unrestricted net assets if the restrictions are met or expire in the fiscal year in which the contributions are recognized. When a restriction expires, temporarily restricted net assets are reclassified as unrestricted net assets. Revenue from convention and workshop registration fees are recognized when the events take place.

Tax Status - CLSA is exempt from federal income tax under Section 501(c)(3) of the Internal Revenue Code. CLSA has not been classified by the Internal Revenue Service as a private foundation. Income which is not related to the exempt purpose, less applicable deductions, is subject to Federal and state corporate income tax. CLSA is covered under a group religious exemption and is not required to file Form 990.

Expense Allocations - Directly identifiable expenses are charged to programs and supporting services. Overhead and expenses related to more than one function are not allocated but are included in supporting services.

Estimates - In preparing financial statements in conformity with generally accepted accounting principles, management is required to make estimates and assumptions that affect the reported amounts of assets and liabilities, the disclosure of contingent assets and liabilities at the date of the financial statements, and the reported amounts of revenues and expenses during the reporting period. Actual results could differ from those estimates.

Financial Instruments – CLSA's financial instruments consist of investments, accounts receivable, accounts payable and accrued expenses. It is management's opinion the CLSA is not exposed to significant interest rate or credit risk arising from these instruments. Unless otherwise noted, the fair values of these financial instruments are market values of these financial instruments, and approximate their carrying values.

4. Investments

Investments in balanced funds at June 30, 2015 and 2014, which are all considered level 1, consist of the following:

	Cost	Market
Total Investments 6/30/2015	$ 1,033,533	$ 1,483,201
Total Investments 6/30/2014	$ 1,016,520	$ 1,432,709

By fund type at June 30, 2015 and 2014:

	2015		2014	
	Cost	Market	Cost	Market
Unrestricted	$ 513,806	$ 772,071	$ 554,809	$ 797,237
Restricted	519,727	711,130	461,711	635,472
Total Investments	$ 1,033,533	$ 1,483,201	$ 1,016,520	$ 1,432,709

CLSA invests in a professionally managed portfolio that contains balanced funds. Such investments are exposed to various risks such as interest rates, market and credit. Due to the level of risk associated with such investments and the level of uncertainty related to changes in the value of such investments, it is at least reasonably possible that changes in risks in the near term would materially affect investment balances and the amounts reported in the financial statements.

Investment income, which is included in the Statement of Activities for the years ended June 30, 2015 and 2014 is comprised of the following:

	2015		2014	
	Unrestricted	Temporarily Restricted	Unrestricted	Temporarily Restricted
Net unrealized gains	$ 15,836	$ 17,642	$ 106,347	$ 84,769
Interest and dividends	9,003	8,107	10,876	8,767
Net Investment Income	$ 24,839	$ 25,749	$ 117,223	$ 93,536

CANON LAW SOCIETY OF AMERICA
Notes to Financial Statements
For the Years Ended June 30, 2015 and 2014

5. Concentration of Credit Risk

CLSA maintains its cash in bank deposit accounts, which at times, may exceed federally insured limits. CLSA has not experienced any losses in such accounts and believes it is not exposed to any significant financial risk on cash.

6. Commitments

Office Lease
CLSA leases office space in Washington DC for a 10 year period ending December 31, 2017. Monthly rent payments were increased during year 2013 from $1,564 to $1,743. Monthly rent payments for the sixth through the tenth year will be increased by the CPI each July 1st. Rent expense for the years ended June 30, 2015 and 2014 was $20,916 for each year. Minimum future rental obligations are: 2016 – 20,916; 2017 - $20,916; 2018 - $10,458.

Postage Lease
CLSA entered into a fifty-one month lease for a postage machine ending April 30, 2018. The lease payment is $184 per quarter.

7. Board Designated Funds

The Board has designated that net income from the sales of publications and books be set aside for use only in the publication activities. As reported on the statement of activities, the net assets from publications decreased in fiscal year 2015 by $8,431 from $87,733 to $79,302. In fiscal year 2014 the publications net assets decreased by $83.

8. Temporarily Restricted Net Assets

The activity in temporarily restricted net assets for years 2015 and 2014 is as follows:

	Scholarship Fund	Ministry Grant	Total
Balance June 30, 2013	$ 571,270	$ (3,020)	$ 568,250
Income	106,481	-	106,481
Expenses	(19,290)	(72)	(19,362)
Transfer from undesignated	-	3,092	3,092
Balance June 30, 2014	$ 658,461	$ -	$ 658,461

	Scholarship Fund	Doctorial Scholarship	Total
Balance June 30, 2014	$ 658,461	$ -	$ 658,461
Income	33,617	3,263	36,880
Expenses	(13,893)	-	(13,893)
Transfer from undesignated	-	50,000	50,000
Balance June 30, 2015	$ 678,185	$ 53,263	$ 731,448

The $50,000 transfer made from undesignated net assets into a doctorial scholarship investment account in accordance with a resolution passed at the year 2013 convention.

9. Annual Meeting Site Reservation Agreements

CLSA has reserved hotel space for future annual meetings. The terms of these reservation agreements provide that a fee will be assessed to CSLA if the reservation is canceled due to site change, within a specified period prior to the meeting dates.

10. Executive Coordinator's Contract

CLSA has contracted with the Executive Coordinator beginning August 1, 20148 and ending August 1, 2017, unless renewed or terminated in accordance with the terms of the employment agreement..

11. Subsequent Events

Management has evaluated subsequent events through September 4, 2015, the date that the financial statements were available to be issued. There were no significant events to report.

Supplementary Information

CANON LAW SOCIETY OF AMERICA
Schedules of Program Services
For the Years Ended June 30,

	2015	2014
Publications		
Cost of publications sold	$ 14,281	$ 21,194
Executive coordinator office	11,927	11,693
Royalty expense	2,248	1,977
Advertising	10	-
Electronic data base initiative	12,048	-
BrightKey	41,201	40,668
Total Publication Expenses	81,715	75,533
Convention and Pre-convention Workshop		
Coordination	116,747	108,992
Food service	3,130	2,418
Honoraria	8,700	9,200
Speakers' travel	1,212	-
Printing	4,322	4,688
Freight	749	678
Other	21,127	18,890
Postage	595	572
Convention chair	1,241	1,091
Liturgy	1,450	2,293
Supplies	5,954	5,973
Convention planning	1,554	1,946
Convention company	655	608
Total Convention and Pre-Convention Workshop	167,436	157,350
Membership Services		
Postage	5,847	3,373
Printing	4,615	4,025
Newsletter	11	39
Platform service webinar	1,700	1,402
Total Membership Services	12,173	8,839
Visit to Holy See and Australia Trip	10,945	10,801

Continued

CANON LAW SOCIETY OF AMERICA
Schedule of Program Services
For the Years Ended June 30,

		2015		2014
Committees				
Church governance	$	670	$	337
Resource & asset management		98		91
Nominations		2,511		2,143
Clergy		-		165
Laity		1,166		-
Other		451		19,466
Total Committees		4,896		22,202
Lay Ecclesial Ministry Work Group		-		72
Scholarship Fund				
Scholarships paid		11,972		17,959
Scholarships expenses		1,921		1,331
Total Scholarship Fund		13,893		19,290
Total Program Services	$	291,058	$	294,087

The accompanying notes are an integral part of this schedule.

14

CANON LAW SOCIETY OF AMERICA
Schedules of Supporting Services
For the Years Ended June 30,

		2015		2014
Board of Governors				
Rental housing	$	13,837	$	12,508
Travel		6,903		4,843
Food service		5,581		5,732
Other expenses		682		450
President		3,258		4,634
Vice President		223		552
Executive Coordinator Office		183,790		146,997
Depreciation expense		1,431		1,682
Rent expense		20,916		20,916
Total Supporting Services	$	236,621	$	198,313

The accompanying notes are an integral part of this schedule.
15

Account Summary
Fiscal Year 2015-2016 Budget

GENERAL OPERATIONS	
Income	$ 324,239
Expenses	$ 324,239
Excess/(Deficit)	-
PUBLICATIONS	
Income	$ 76,925
Expenses	$ 76,925
Excess/(Deficit)	-
CONVENTIONS	
Income	$ 190,245
Expenses	$ 190,245
Excess/(Deficit)	-
Subtotal Gen. Ops., Pub. & Conv. *	**$** -
SCHOLARSHIP FUND	
Income	$ 37,620
Expenses	$ 29,375
Excess/(Deficit)	**$ 8,245**
Grand Total *	**$ 8,245**

Note: Since Scholarship income by definition belongs to the Scholarship Fund, it cannot be used to balance the overall budget. Hence, the first three CLSA "companies" as a whole need to achieve a balance independently, and the number labeled as "Grand Total" is not a simple "operational" profit. An "Excess" in the Scholarship Fund represents an increase in the fund, which is needed for the fund to grow.

General Operations Unit Summary *(by fiscal year)*

		Budget 15-16	Actual 14-15	Budget 14-15	Actual 13-14	Budget 13-14
INCOME						
Investment Income						
Interest/RCT	$	-	6	-	10	-
Dividends/CUIT	$	8,720	8,998	6,000	10,865	6,000
Sub-total	$		**9,004**	**6,000**	**10,875**	**6,000**
Portion of Prior Year Realized Net Asset Increase (Note 1)	**$**	**58,519**	**21,432**	**48,815**	-	**26,429**
Dues Income						
New Member Dues	$	12,000	9,300	12,000	13,500	11,000
Previous Year Member Dues	$	-	200	-	-	-
Current Year Member Dues	$	220,000	224,700	220,000	226,800	215,000
Sub-total	**$**	**232,000**	**234,200**	**232,000**	**240,300**	**226,000**
Intensive Workshop Registration	**$**	**25,000**	-		**23,375**	
TOTAL INCOME	**$**	**324,239**	**264,636**	**286,815**	**274,550**	**258,429**
EXPENSES						
Staff Compensations and Benefits (Note 2)	**$**	**175,961**	**153,291**	**178,907**	**112,065**	**152,098**
Service Charges						
Bank Service Charges/Wells Fargo	$	700	839	600	696	400
Flex Fund/RCT	$	-	-	50	-	50
Credit Card Fees	$	3,600	3,248	4,000	3,557	4,500
Sub-total	**$**	**4,300**	**4,087**	**4,650**	**4,253**	**$ 4,950**
OEC Expenses (by account number)						
Postage Meter Lease	$	900	788	900	852	900
Postage Meter Supplies	$	175	184	175	106	150
Insurance & Workers Compensation	$	1,100	1,071	1,100	1,057	2,200
Hospitality	$	600	465	600	484	500
Postage/UPS/FedEx	$	500	432	500	628	600
Office Supplies	$	2,300	2,079	2,500	2,122	2,500
Telephone/ISP/DSL	$	3,320	3,379	3,000	2,943	3,000
Travel	$	1,000	872	1,000	317	500

General Operations Unit Summary *(by fiscal year)*

		Budget 15-16	Actual 14-15	Budget 14-15	Actual 13-14	Budget 13-14
Continuing Education (EC)	$	1,000	938	1,000	-	-
Taxes	$	80	-	130	80	100
Furniture & Equipment	$	1,000	693	1,000	1,309	1,000
Books and Periodicals	$	300	285	300	215	400
Professional Collaboration w/ Nat'l Orgs	$	500	50	500	-	500
Rent	$	20,916	20,916	20,916	20,916	20,916
Copier Lease	$	-	-	-	-	-
Copier Maintenance	$	800	800	800	800	800
Sub-total	**$**	**34,491**	**32,952**	**34,421**	**31,830**	**34,066**
Professional Services						
Accountant/Auditor (Note 3)	$	6,750	5,700	6,000	5,700	5,000
Web Design & Maintenance	$	6,237	6,237	6,237	6,237	6,237
Legal Services	$	1,500	1,500	500	-	500
Sub-total	**$**	**14,487**	**13,437**	**12,737**	**11,937**	**11,737**
Member Services						
General Postage	$	1,600	1,032	1,800	897	1,800
Newsletter Postage	$	50	11	50	39	50
Proceedings Printing	$	5,000	4,615	5,300	4,025	5,000
Proceedings Postage	$	5,000	4,816	5,000	2,476	4,500
Sub-total	**$**	**11,650**	**10,474**	**12,150**	**7,437**	**11,350**
Board of Governors, Meetings						
Food	$	6,000	5,581	6,000	5,732	6,000
Lodging	$	13,500	13,836	13,000	12,508	14,000
Meeting Space	$	1,000	675	1,000	450	1,200
Postage/UPS	$	-	-	-	-	50
Supplies	$	50	7	50	-	50
Telephone	$	-	-	-	-	-
Travel	$	9,000	6,903	9,000	4,843	9,000
Rome or Australia Trip	$	11,000	10,495	10,000	10,801	10,000
Regional Canon Law Society Meetings	$	2,000	-	-	-	-
Sub-total	**$**	**42,550**	**37,974**	**39,050**	**34,335**	**40,300**
Board of Governors, Officers						
President	$	4,000	3,258	4,000	4,634	5,000
Vice President/Past President	$	500	223	500	552	500

General Operations Unit Summary *(by fiscal year)*

		Budget 15-16	Actual 14-15	Budget 14-15	Actual 13-14	Budget 13-14
Treasurer/Secretary	$	500	-	500	-	500
Sub-total	$	**5,000**	**3,481**	**5,000**	**5,186**	**6,000**
Intensive Workshop Expense	$	**20,000**	**-**		**18,801**	
Committees						
Constitutional Committees						
Nominations Committee	$	2,600	2,511	1,800	2,143	1,800
Resolutions Committee	$	100	-	100	-	100
Resource & Asset Management	$	500	99	500	91	500
Professional Responsibilities Committee	$	-	-	-	-	-
Standing Committees						
Church Governance Committee	$	2,000	670	2,000	337	500
Clergy Committee	$	500	-	500	165	500
Institutes of Consecrated Life Committee	$	150	-	150	-	150
Laity Committee	$	3,000	1,166	2,500	-	2,500
Research & Development	$	1,500	-	1,500	314	1,500
Sacramental Law Committee	$	1,000	-	1,000	-	1,000
Committee Chair Orientation	$	450	450	350	629	
Approved Cmte. Work Contingency	$	1,000	-	1,000	36	1,000
Sub-total	$	**12,800**	**4,896**	**11,400**	**3,715**	**9,550**
Miscellaneous						
Platform Service Expense - Webinar (Note 4)	$	3,000	1,700	3,200	1,402	1,000
Depreciation	$		1,431		1,682	
Sub-total	$	**3,000**	**3,131**	**3,200**	**3,084**	**1,000**
Staffing Transition	$	**-**	**940**	**2,500**	**7,516**	**-**
Lay Eccl. Work Group	$				**72**	**-**
TOTAL EXPENSES	$	**324,239**	**264,636**	**304,015**	**240,231**	**271,051**
EXCESS/DEFICIT	$	**-**	**-**	**(16,200)**	**34,319**	**(11,622)**

General Operations Unit - Notes

Note 1: Use of a portion of prior year realized net asset increase to help offset projected General Operations Deficit. This was suggested by the Accountant/Auditor.

Note 2: This expense includes salary, benefits, and retirement for the Executive Coordinator and Executive Assistant, as well as wages and benefits for te administrative assistant. Included in this expense are FICA payments, payroll service fees, and retirement fund service fees. As in previous years, the EA salary is apportioned between General Ops and Publications.

Note 3: This line item is apportioned between General Operations and Publications.

Note 4: This expense is the cost of the platform subscription that supports webinars. No grant is attached to this project, so the funds will come from the General Operating account.

Publications Unit Summary *(by fiscal year)*

		Budget 15-16	Actual 14-15	Budget 14-15	Actual 13-14	Budget 13-14
INCOME						
Publication Sales	$	61,295	54,377	75,000	56,855	75,000
Reprint Permissions	$	-	-	-	-	500
Royalty Income	$	4,000	7,322	5,000	8,246	4,000
Shipping/Restocking - BrightKey	$	11,000	11,585	15,000	10,349	20,000
Database Resolution	$					
TOTAL INCOME	$	**76,925**	**73,284**	**95,000**	**75,450**	**99,500**
Cost of Goods Sold	$		14,281		21,194	
GROSS PROFIT	$	**76,925**	**59,003**	**95,000**	**54,256**	
EXPENSES						
Compensation & Professional Services						
Staff Salary (Note 1)	$	5,300	4,937	4,950	4,514	4,368
Accountant (Note 1)	$	2,250	1,900	1,875	1,900	2,500
Publications Advisory Board	$	2,500	1,854	2,500	2,456	2,200
Sub-total	$	**10,050**	**8,691**	**9,325**	**8,869**	**9,068**
Royalties Paid						
Royalties/*CCEO*	$	250	181	300	166	200
Royalties/*CIC*	$	2,000	1,839	1,600	1,534	1,600
Royalties/*Dignitas Connubii*	$	250	147	400	203	400
Royalties/*Selected Issues*	$	100	81	100	73	50
Royalties/*R&C*	$	25	-	25	-	25
Sub-total	$	**2,625**	**2,248**	**2,425**	**1,977**	**2,275**
Publication Expenses						
Advertising - Printing	$	100	-	100	-	500
Advertising - Electronic	$	50	10	50	-	100
Book Production	$	10,000	204	15,000	-	20,000
Copyright Applications	$	100	-	100	-	150
Outsourcing - BrightKey	$	38,000	41,202	46,000	39,175	51,000
Sub-total	$	**48,250**	**41,416**	**61,250**	**39,175**	**71,750**
Office of the Executive Coordinator						
Postage	$	250	168	150	74	100
Supplies	$	150	149	150	91	150
Sub-total	$	**400**	**317**	**300**	**165**	**250**
Service Charges						
Bank Service Charges	$	600	676	500	555	400
Credit Card Fees	$	3,000	2,040	4,000	2,104	5,000
Sub-total	$	**3,600**	**2,716**	**4,500**	**2,659**	**5,400**

Publications Unit Summary *(by fiscal year)*

		Budget 15-16	Actual 14-15	Budget 14-15	Actual 13-14	Budget 13-14
Miscellaneous						
Publications Contingencies	$	500	-	-	-	500
Sub-total	$	**500**	-	-	-	**500**
Database Resolution	$	11,500	12,047		1,494	-
TOTAL EXPENSES	$	**76,925**	**67,435**	**77,800**	**54,338**	**89,243**
EXCESS/DEFICIT	$	-	**(8,432)**	**17,200**	**(83)**	**10,257**
Self-Funded Project (Note 2)						
Canon Law Digest Resolution						
Income	$			2,517		4,011
Expenses	$			278	1494	
Total Excess/(Deficit)	$			2,239	2,517	

Note 1: This line item is apportioned between General Operations and Publications.

Note 2: These lines are for the Resolution approved by the membership at the 2010 convention. Since it includes designated funds and could stretch across many fiscal years, it is not included in the annual budget.

CONVENTIONS UNIT SUMMARY *(by fiscal year)*

		Budget 15-16	Actual 14-15	Budget 14-15	Actual 13-14	Budget 13-14
INCOME						
Convention Fees (Note 1)	$	128,000	134,575	122,000	132,850	122,000
Pre-Convention Workshop 1 Fees (Note 2)	$	11,000	17,975	10,450	12,575	9,625
Pre-Convention Workshop 2 Fees	$	11,000	14,000	10,450	10,775	11,000
Exhibitors' Fees	$	2,800	4,500	2,500	2,725	2,375
Sponsors' Donations	$	-	750	-	1,200	-
Additional Banquet Fees	$	420	1,260	420	480	420
Guest Registrations	$	300	150	500	200	500
Hotel Room Commission (Note 3)	$	13,000	13,553	13,000	15,151	13,000
Surplus from Previous Year (Note 4)	$	23,725		6,070		
TOTAL INCOME	$	**190,245**	**186,763**	**165,390**	**175,956**	**158,920**
EXPENSES						
Professional Services						
General Convention Chair	$	1,300	1,241	1,300	1,091	1,500
Convention Liturgy Chair	$	500	-	500	-	-
Convention Planning Cte	$	2,000	1,554	2,000	1,946	2,000
OEC	$	2,200	1,249	2,200	2,233	1,500
Convention Company	$	900	655	250	608	700
Sub-total	$	**6,900**	**4,699**	**6,250**	**5,878**	**5,700**
Pre-Convention						
Honoraria	$	6,000	3,000	3,000	3,000	3,000
Liturgy	$	500	-	500	500	500
Printing	$	100	-	100	-	100
Shipping	$	100	89	50	42	50
Speaker's Travel & Lodging	$	2,000	-	2,000	-	2,500
Supplies	$	250	242	150	148	150
Hospitality/Speaker Dinner (Note 5)	$	500				
Sub-total	$	**9,450**	**3,331**	**5,800**	**3,689**	**6,300**
Convention						
Convention Company/Nix	$	44,345	42,640	42,640	42,249	41,000
Convention Hotel (Note 6)	$	76,000	74,107	69,500	66,743	63,000
Audio Visual	$	17,000	15,430	13,000	12,695	12,000
Food	$	3,500	3,130	2,000	2,418	2,300
Honoraria	$	11,400	5,700	6,100	6,200	6,500
Liturgy	$	2,000	1,450	2,000	1,793	2,000
Postage	$	700	595	1,000	572	1,500
Printing	$	4,200	4,322	4,000	4,688	4,000
Shipping	$	700	660	700	637	700
Speaker's Travel	$	2,500	1,212	2,500	-	3,000

Conventions Unit Summary *(by fiscal year)*

		Budget 15-16	Actual 14-15	Budget 14-15	Actual 13-14	Budget 13-14
Supplies	$	6,000	5,712	6,000	5,826	6,000
Telephone/Internet	$	-	-	-	-	100
Hospitality/Speaker Dinner (Note 7)	$	1,000				
Other/Contingency	$	500	250	-	-	
Sub-total	$	**169,845**	**155,208**	**149,440**	**143,820**	**142,100**
Service Charges						
Bank Service Charges/Wells Fargo (Note 8)	$	450	615	400	451	400
Credit Card Fees	$	3,600	3,583	3,500	3,512	3,000
Sub-total	$	**4,050**	**4,198**	**3,900**	**3,962**	**3,400**
TOTAL EXPENSES	$	**190,245**	**167,436**	**165,390**	**157,350**	**157,500**
EXCESS/DEFICIT	$	-	**19,327**	-	**18,607**	**1,420**

Note 1: FY 2015-2016 Budget assumes 320 attendees @ $400 each.

Note 2: FY 2015-2016 Budget assumes 80 pre-convention attendees (40 per workshop) @ $275 each.

Note 3: This line represents the hotel room commission we receive as a result of the work of NIX.

Note 4: This line item reflects surplus in the convention unit from 13-14 and 14-15, used to balance the overall budget for FY 15-16.

Note 5: This is a new line item, allocated for in-room hospitality and one dinner outing for Pre-Convention speakers.

Note 6: This line item reflects general convention expenses with the contracted hotel, including one lunch for attendees.

Note 7: This is a new line item, allocated for in-room hospitlaity and one dinner outing for Major/Keynote speakers.

Note 8: These lines reflect an overall adjustment to convention speaker honoraria; rates have been doubled.

SCHOLARSHIP UNIT SUMMARY *(by fiscal year)*

		Budget 15-16	Actual 14-15	Budget 14-15	Actual 13-14	Budget 13-14
INCOME						
Investment Income						
(Reinvested in Fund)						
Interest Income/Wells Fargo	$	120	91	100	107	100
Dividends/CUIT	$	7,000	8,016	5,000	8,660	5,000
Sub-Total	$	**7,120**	**8,107**	**5,100**	**8,767**	**5,100**
Designated Funds (Note 1)						
Previously Designated Funds	$	14,000	14,000	14,000	14,000	14,000
This Year Designated Funds	$	7,000	7,000	7,000	7,000	7,000
Sub-Total	$	**21,000**	**21,000**	**21,000**	**21,000**	**21,000**
Sch. Donations Income						
Donations Accompanying Dues	$	2,000	2,390	2,000	1,550	2,000
Donations from Appeal	$	6,000	5,951	6,000	9,145	6,000
Donations from Convention	$	500	300	500	1,250	500
Donations from Regional Meetings	$	1,000	1,815	1,000	1,000	1,000
Previous Year Donation			675			
Sub-Total	$	**9,500**	**11,131**	**9,500**	**12,945**	**9,500**
TOTAL INCOME	$	**37,620**	**40,238**	**35,600**	**42,712**	**35,600**
EXPENSES						
Service Charges						
Money Market Fees/Wells Fargo	$	1,500	1,200	1,200	1,084	1,200
Sub-total	$	**1,500**	**1,200**	**1,200**	**1,084**	**1,200**
Postage						
General Postage	$	25	21	25	-	25
Appeal Postage	$	750	590	950	247	700
Sub-total	$	**775**	**611**	**975**	**247**	**725**
Printing						
General Printing	$	100	-	100	-	150
Appeal Printing	$	500	111	500	-	200
Sub-total	$	**600**	**111**	**600**	**-**	**350**
Scholarships						
Current Awards	$	26,500	11,972	21,000	17,959	21,000
Sub-total	$	**26,500**	**11,972**	**21,000**	**17,959**	**21,000**

Scholarship Unit Summary *(by fiscal year)*

		Budget 15-16	Actual 14-15	Budget 14-15	Actual 13-14	Budget 13-14
TOTAL EXPENSES	$	29,375	13,894	23,775	19,290	23,275
EXCESS/DEFICIT	$	8,245	25,669	11,825	23,423	12,325

Officer's Report

Report of the Executive Coordinator
Rev. Roger H. Keeler, JCD

As I re-read the brief report I offered to you in St. Louis last year – a report of "beginnings" – I find myself echoing the thought that our Society is "on a fine administrative footing, a solid financial position, engaged in myriad initiatives, and with tack set to the wind." A reading of the reports offered by our President, Msgr. Michael Souckar, our Treasurer, Fr. Tom Cronkleton, the audit prepared by *Linton Shafer Warfield and Garrett*, the report presented by the Chair of the Publications Advisory Board, Sr. Sharon Euart, RSM, together with those of our Constitutional and On-going Committees, affirms this. I need not repeat their findings in detail here. However, I do want to bring to the fore several matters, largely arising from offerings in the December, March, June and September *eNewsletter*'s, which I believe are significant for all of us.

The Office of the Executive Coordinator continues to operate efficiently and with an eye toward sound financial stewardship.

Colleen Crawford, with her consummate professionalism, attention to detail, and graciousness, remains a wellspring of insight and experience upon whom I rely each day. Renae Kuettel, who came on board with us this past winter, has shown herself to be a capable collaborator, whose efforts have borne good fruit. I know I speak for all of us when I express our gratitude to both of them for all they do.

The 76th Annual Convention in St. Louis was, despite several challenges, a success. Evaluations praised the facility, programme and speakers. Both attendance and income increased, leaving us with a modest surplus as we look forward to our gathering in Pittsburgh. Once again, I express thanks to Msgr. Victor Finelli, General Convention Chair, Sr. Ann Rehrauer and Msgr. Eskind, Liturgy Chairs, Fr. Nicholas Kastenholz, and the entire staff of the Metropolitan Tribunal of St. Louis, for so much done behind the scenes to make it all appear worry-free and seamless. I look forward to working once again with Msgr. Finelli, with our new Liturgy Chairs, Msgrs. Michael Cariglio and Peter Polando, and with Fr. Thomas Kunz and Fr. Dennis Yurochko, and all who minister with them in the department of Canonical Services for the Diocese of Pittsburgh.

We reached out this year to invite colleagues from other societies of canon law to join us in Pittsburgh: the Antilles, Argentina, Belgium, Brazil, Chile, India, Kenya, Mexico, Nigeria, Peru, the Philippines, Slovakia, South Africa, Spain and Venezuela. Once completed, the office will ensure that copies of *Proceedings* are sent to them.

On-going effort is needed in liaising with organizations and groups whose apostolates and aims intersect with ours. One concrete step was taken with my participation in a symposium entitled "Toward Canonical Consideration for Lay Ecclesial Ministry," in Collegeville, MN, in May. The resolution passed at that gathering is being distilled with a view toward concrete engagement on our behalf.

The same can be said for enhancing our relationship with schools of canon law, here in Washington at The Catholic University of America, in Ottawa at Saint Paul University, and, as driven home during the biennial visit to the Holy See, with the schools of canon law at the Gregorian, Angelicum, Santa Croce, and the students at the Casa Santa Marta. The visits made by our President, Msgr. Michael Souckar, to CUA and SPU were very well received. This office co-hosted an event with Fr. Phillip Brown and his Sulpician community at Theological College for canon law students living in the house during the summer session. On our part, we hosted a reception for students and faculty in early July that was well received. Twenty-eight new student members have been added to our roster this past year, bringing the total number of student members to 101.

As I wrote in June: "Supporting students of canon law is something all of us would do well to keep before ourselves: some are already ministering with us in our vineyard; others will eventually be our colleagues; among their number are future leaders of the Society; there will be those we will call upon to teach us during our Conventions, and there will be those who will assume the writer's mantle."

A significant expression of members' support for students is found in the $10,455 given during our annual scholarship appeal. The *eNewsletter* posted in June reported that the Subcommittee on Scholarship awarded the first ever CLSA Doctoral Scholarship to Sr. Karla Felix-Rivera, VDMF, together with four Licentiate Scholarships to each Dcn. Michael Forbes, Mr. Luis Guzman, Mr. John Vizza and Mr. James Zahler.

The most significant time of liaison must certainly have been the biennial visit to the Holy See with President Msgr. Michael Souckar and President-Elect/Vice-President Fr. Manuel Viera, OFM. As Msgr. Souckar reports: "… the CLSA is very well respected by the officials at the various Roman Curial offices as well as at the faculties of canon law."

Arising from those meetings was the suggestion that "it might be valuable for our members to meet with representatives from the curial offices and courts affording them the opportunity to share with us the nature of their service to the Church." Efforts planning a trip such as this are ongoing and, please God, information will be made available in the near future.

The June *eNewsletter* indicated "[a] second Tribunal survey was launched a short while ago seeking to learn something about tribunal fee structures, an issue that has been in the news of late." This initiative, at the behest of the Board of Governors, enjoyed a favourable response rate. With thanks to Renae for her fine efforts in this regard, I am pleased to offer the following "Polaroid Snapshot":

146 Tribunals responded to the survey sent out in late May, 2015.

In response to the question:

Does your Tribunal charge a fee to examine a marriage case?

For an ordinary process YES/NO

YES 105

NO 40

For a documentary process including lack of form YES/NO

YES 97

NO 45

If yes, how much is charged?

For an ordinary process

less than $100.00 (42); $100-200.00 (1); $200-300.00 (10); $300-400.00 (19); $400-500.00 (23); $500-600.00 (25); $600-700.00 (9); $700-800.00 (3); over $800.00 (3).

For a documentary process

Several reported a flat fee

less than $100.00 (42); $100-200.00 (10); $200-300.00 (5); $300-400.00 (1); $500-600.00 (1); $600-700.00 (1).

Others reported according to type

Lack/defect/absence of form

less than $100.00 (33); $100-200.00 (3); $200-300.00 (1); $300-400.00 (1); $600-700.00 (1); more than $800.00 (1).

Ligamen

less than $100.00 (13); $100-200.00 (14); $200-300.00 (6); $300-400.00 (1).

Pauline

less than $100.00 (6); $100-200.00 (9); $200-300.00 (5); $500-600.00 (1).

Petrine

less than $100.00 (2); $100-200.00 (1); $400-500.00 (2); $500-600.00 (1); $600-700.00 (1); more than $800.00 (1).

Other (*Nihil obstat*; presumed death, *sanatio*, declaration of separation, *ratum non consummatum,* appeal to the Rota)

less than $100.00 (5); $100-200.00 (3); $200-300.00 (2); more than $800.00 (2).

If you are currently charging a fee, is there any thought being given to dropping it?

YES	27
NO	70

There was a broad range of comments including 14 Tribunals that will waive all fees for those in need; "Hardship cases are given discounts and are asked to make small payments until fully paid"; "Fees ensure that people will take the process seriously"; "Collection of fees is not a significant source of revenue for the Tribunal/Diocese"; "Since charges were eliminated, the number of formal cases has doubled"; "Since our Tribunal was founded … we have never charged a fee. We accept donations to defray our expenses"; "We are waiting to see what Pope Francis does next"; "We need to cover our administrative expenses somehow"; "Often parishes underwrite or cover the fee. It allows our process to operate at a fairly high level"; "No one is denied access to justice because of an inability to pay."

There has been a considerable buzz around the OEC since the 8th of September when the Holy Father gave the Church his *motu proprios Mitis Iudex Dominus Iesus*, and *Mitis et misericors Iesus*. In presenting English-language translations of the norms on Monday, the 21st of September, the Board of Governors expressed their gratitude to Meg Romano-Hogan, Rev. Bruce Miller, Msgr. John Renken and Msgr. Girard M. Sherba for their collaboration on *Mitis Iudex Dominus Iesus*, and to Chorbishop John D. Faris, and Rev. W. Becket Soule, O.P., for their work on *Mitis et misericors Iesus.* Theirs was a single-minded, time-consuming, daily back-and-forth, which has yielded fine results; results that have been shared among friends and colleagues around the world. The hope expressed by the Board that "these unofficial translations will assist all who exercise the Church's juridic ministry in studying and implementing the new norms," will surely be realized. Let's all be sure to extend our personal thanks to these two teams.

I echo the thanks expressed by our President, Msgr. Michael Souckar, to the members of the Task Force on Matrimonial Procedures that was constituted this past December in response to the resolution passed at last year's Convention. Given a mandate "To reflect upon and make recommendations concerning possible changes to facilitate and expedite the process for discerning the validity or invalidity of marriage in the Spring of 2015 to the Special Commission created by the Holy See," the Task Force began its work in earnest the first week of January. With Fr. Bruce Miller serving as its Chair, Diane Barr, Fr. John Beal, Fr. John Griffiths and Sr. Victoria Vondenberger, RSM, worked with efficiency, professionalism and thoroughness, producing a list of recommendations that were hand-delivered to Msgr. Vito Pinto, the Chair of the Special Pontifical Commission and Dean of the Roman Rota, on the 16th of March by Msgr. Michael Souckar. Msgr. Pinto expressed his profound gratitude for their findings, indicating that the Commission hoped to present its recommendations to the Holy Father during Eastertide. Copies of the Task Force report were given to other members of the Commission in the days that followed. All expressed similar gratitude for this fine work.

So just as we will do for those who have translated the *motu proprios*, please be sure to express your thanks to the members of the Task Force for the work they offered to the Commission.

There is a change on the horizon that will surely present new challenges and opportunities for us in the OEC: all of the tenants of the Hecker Center have been advised by the Paulist Fathers of their intention to sell this property. We have been asked to vacate our offices by the end of June, 2016. The Board of Governors agrees that remaining in this area is of importance to the Society, despite the dearth of space. We are currently engaged in negotiations with the Associated Sulpician's of the United States for a suite in the McCormick Pavilion, attached to Theological College, which will require some renovation to make it fully useable. A move to that new space could well take place before Christmas.

We receive many calls and emails posted via our "Contact Us" point on the CLSA website. Some want general information, others are looking to connect with a member, some need a reference to a publication, some just to let off steam, and others are seeking the help of a canonist for all manner of issues. We have a list of members willing to assist those seeking counsel. However, that list is not large and the demand seemingly increasing. If you are willing to be of service in this regard, will you contact the OEC, please?

When I spoke at the Annual Meeting in St. Louis last year, I expressed the belief that ours were exciting times and that we, as members of the Canon Law Society of America, were well situated to respond to, and to inform, our times. I remain convinced of that, and am profoundly grateful for the year of learning and exploring, of stretching horizons, and of becoming acquainted with so many of you. It has been a pleasure to work with Colleen and Renae, with the members of the Board of Governors, and with those serving on committees. At the time of this writing, 1,025 membership renewals have been received, generating $197,900 in revenue. Maintaining sound services for our members a top priority for the OEC. I – we – welcome your suggestions and comments on how to better meet your needs and those of the Church we all serve.

Constitutional Committee Reports

Committee: Nominations
Constituted: Constitution, Article X
Charge: This is a standing committee of the Society. Its mandate is:

1. To submit to the active members, at least one month prior to the date of election, the names of nominees as provided for in Article IX of the Constitutions; (and)
2. To formulate and recommend to the Board of Governors plans for maintaining and increasing the membership of the Society.

This committee's current composition is as follows:

Members: Meg Romano-Hogan, *chair* (2016)
Very Rev. Phillip J. Brown, *ex officio* (2015)
Mr. Jay Conzemius (2017)
Rev. Msgr. C. Michael Padazinski (2017)

ANNUAL REPORT

This committee met on February 9-10, 2015, at the Hecker Center in Washington, DC, to propose a list of candidates for election to various offices at the CLSA Annual Business meeting in October 2015. After deliberation regarding appropriate persons to ask to run, prospective candidates were called by members of the committee and questioned about their willingness to serve. The following persons were nominated and agreed to run as candidates and serve if elected:

For the Office of Vice-President/President-Elect:

- Dr. Diane Barr, a laywoman serving as Chancellor of the Archdiocese of Baltimore
- Rev. Bruce Miller, a presbyter of the Diocese of Alexandria, LA, serving as Judicial Vicar

For the Office of Consultor:

- Rev. Anthony Bawyn, a presbyter of the Archdiocese of Seattle serving as Judicial Vicar
- Sr. Deborah Cerullo, SSND, a School Sister of Notre Dame serving in the Diocese of Providence, RI
- Dr. Marie Hilliard, a laywoman serving at the National Catholic Bioethics Center in Philadelphia

- Rev. Kenneth Riley, a priest of the Archdiocese of Kansas City-St. Joseph, MO, serving as Chancellor

The committee found very helpful and fruitful the fact that members came from or had experience in widely diverse parts of the country, and thus knew many canonists in various regions who might be appropriate for nomination and willing to serve on the BOG.

We also discussed the possibility of offering the knowledge and the experience of the committee members to the President and President-Elect as they search for members to serve on various committees, as committee membership is a usually a stepping stone to BOG service. We would be quite willing to serve the Society leadership in this capacity, either officially or unofficially.

There was no further activity of this committee this year, as we fulfilled our mandate with the presentation to the BOG of a slate of candidates for election. The names of these candidates, along with a brief *curriculum vitae* for each, have been published in the announcement of the 77th Annual Convention of the Society, which will take place October 12-15, 2015, in Pittsburgh, PA.

Respectfully submitted,
Meg Romano-Hogan

Committee: Resolutions
Constituted: Constitution, Article X
Mandate:

1. To solicit, develop and draft proposed resolutions which will express the concerns of the Canon Law Society of America;
2. To consult with the membership at large and, in particular with the Board of Governors the standing and ad hoc committees of the Society, and the organizers of the convention;
3. To formulate resolutions on given points in response to requests of the members of the Society;
4. To compose differences in the formulation of similar proposals and to revise all the proposals so the meaning of each is clear; (and)
5. To encourage resolutions which authentically express in a positive way the activities and concerns of the Society.

Members: Ms. Susan Mulheron, *chair* (2015)
Rev. Langes Silva (2015)
Rev. Jamin David (2016)

ANNUAL REPORT

The Resolutions Committee will hear and process resolutions during the 2015 Convention.

Respectfully submitted,
Susan Mulheron

Committee: Resource and Asset Management
Constituted: Constitution, Article X, as last amended in 2008 and 2013
Old Committee Structure: Committees on Budget, Investment and Scholarship Fund.
Charge: The functions of the Committee on Resource and Asset Management shall be:

1. To develop a comprehensive budget for all the activities of the Society and report on the funding available for projects;
2. To submit the proposed budget for the coming fiscal year to the Board of Governors for approval at its spring meeting;
3. To conserve, invest and disburse the monies of the Scholarship Fund in accord with the criteria established by the Society; (and)
4. To advise the Treasurer on all matters pertaining to the Society's investments (Article X, 7).

Membership: The Committee of Resource and Asset Management shall consist of the Vice-President, the Treasurer, and a senior consultor and two additional members appointed by the President. The Treasurer shall act as Chair of this committee (Article X, 2).

Members: Rev. Tom Cronkleton, *chair; treasurer* (2016)
Rev. Manuel Viera, OFM (Vice-President; *ex-officio* 2015)
Rev. Thomas C. Anslow, CM (2015)
Msgr. Charles V. Antonicelli (2015)
Ms. Catherine A. Gilligan (2015)

The Resource and Asset Management Committee met via conference call on March 5, 2015. At this meeting, the Proposed Budget for Fiscal Year 2015-2016 was prepared, approved and recommended to the Board of Governors.

The RAM discussed via email, from March 24 through April 7, a Proposed Spending Policy for General Operations Investments and a Resolution for Increasing Dues.

The RAM reviewed the "Fiscal Policies," which can be found on page 36 of the *Board of Governors Handbook.* The recommendation was given to the Board of Governors to amend the "Fiscal Policies" to utilize a "Total Return Approach" with the investments for the General Operations instead of using an "Income Approach." When investing for income, the investing is done to maximize interest and dividends. There is no use of capital gains. When investing for income, investments are made in instruments which produce interest and/or dividends. When budgeting, investing for income has been used, because interest and dividends from investments have been used to finance General Operations. The investments, however, have been in a Balanced Fund, which is meant to achieve a return through the production of interest and dividends and capital gains. This manner of investing is best suited for producing a Total Return. The Total Return Approach reinvests interest and dividends, which then are not available for funding expenses. Instead, a percentage of the total value of the investments on a certain date is used to fund expenses. The proposed amendment recommended that "up to 5% of the total market value of the General Operations Investments, computed on the basis of a three (3) year rolling quarterly average, as of the December 31st immediately preceding the budget meetings of the RAM and the Board of Governors may be used for the General Operations of the Society." This is the same investment policy as for the Scholarships Investments.

The RAM, in preparing the Spending Policy and the Budget, noted that an increase in dues was necessary to meet future expenditures. The RAM developed two options for the consideration of the Board of Governors, one with a discount for those 70 and older, and one without the discount. The RAM noted that it could not determine the full effect of a discounted rated because only a third of the membership have disclosed their birthdays. A discount would also require an additional increase in dues in a shorter period than would no discount.

Upon review of investments, the RAM recommended up to $24,000 in licentiate scholarship awards over the next 3 years and up to $2,500 in doctoral scholarship awards. The licentiate award can be in scholarships paid to one or more recipients over a period of up to three years in any combination that does not exceed the total allotted amount. The doctoral scholarship is a 1 year award, but can be given to one or more recipients.

Respectfully submitted,
Rev. Thomas E. Cronkleton, Jr.

Please see the Report of the Treasurer on page 19. The proposed budget for fiscal year 2015-2016 may be found on page 24.

Committee: Professional Responsibility

Constituted: Constitution, Article X, as last amended in 1995, and the Code of Professional Responsibilities, canon 9c(1), d(1)

Charge: The mandate of the Committee is:

1. Regarding complaints:
   a) To receive complaints of any party aggrieved with respect to provisions of the *Code of Professional Responsibility* originally adopted by the CLSA in October, 1983, and its can. 9d(i);
   b) To make an initial finding that the complaint is not frivolous but is serious in character; (and)
   c) By majority vote to refer the matter to the hearing officers.
2. To issue advisory opinions and decisions on the application of the *Code of Professional Responsibility*; (and)
3. To advise on all other questions concerning the professional responsibility of canonists (can. 9d(i) of the PR Code).

Members:
Rev. James Conn, SJ, *chair* (2015)
Rev. Patrick Cooney, OSB, *ex officio* (2015)
Msgr. John J. Foster, *ex officio* (2015)
Rev. Paul Hartmann, *hearing officer* (2015)
Msgr. John Alesandro, *hearing officer* (2016)
H. Roberta Small, *hearing officer* (2017)

ANNUAL REPORT

This year the committee successfully intervened in the case of a financial dispute between a member and a member's client. The dispute was settled to the satisfaction of the complaining party. No disciplinary action against the member was deemed appropriate.

Respectfully submitted,
Rev. James Conn, SJ

ON-GOING COMMITTEE REPORTS

Committee: Church Governance
Constituted: 2009
Mandate: It is the function of the Committee on Church Governance:

1. To initiate as needed any projects pertinent to the study of canon law pertaining to Church structures and governance or the implementation thereof, including but not limited to the following: (a) diocesan and parish temporalities; (b) consultative bodies; (c) diocesan and parish structures; (d) power of governance; (e) comparative law issues; (f) Eastern canon law and institutions
2. To oversee projects referred to the committee by the BOG;
3. To oversee its subcommittees working on projects concerning Church governance; (and)
4. To collaborate with national organizations and other groups dealing with issues of Church governance.

Members: Ms. Barbara Bettwy, *chair* (2016)
Rev. J. Patrick Reynolds (2015)
Msgr. William King (2016)
Rev. Francis Marini (2016)
Sr. Nancy Reynolds, SP (2016)

ANNUAL REPORT

The Committee on Church Governance published its report on the Survey of Diocesan Finance Councils at the 2014 CLSA Convention. Copies of the Report were sent to all diocesan/eparchian bishops in the Fall of 2014. The Diocesan Fiscal Management Conference then published the findings to its membership as well.

The Report made the following recommendations:

- The Canon Law Society of America contact the Diocesan Fiscal Management Conference to discuss the possibility of providing a series of workshops at the annual DFMC convention on key canonical issues related to finance councils.

- In addition, the Canon Law Society of America offer its assistance to the DFMC to review and perhaps re-publish the DFMC's *Diocesan Financial Issues* to incorporate finance council issues.
- The Canon Law Society of America publish a handbook/orientation manual for finance council members.

Regarding the first recommendation, Monsignor William King, a member of this committee, will be presenting a major address at the annual DFMC convention in Atlanta in September 2015. The title of Monsignor King's presentation is "Diocesan Finance Councils: Value, Vision, and Variety." He will present the findings of this committee's survey, compare these findings to the provisions in canon law, and derive a set of best practices for arch/dioceses and arch/eparchies.

The Committee continues to work on the other two recommendations. We have offered our assistance to the DFMC to review and perhaps re-publish the DFMC's *Diocesan Financial Issues* to incorporate finance council issues. The DFMC is still considering that offer. Finally, work on the handbook/orientation manual for finance council members is in the early stages of planning and will be the main focus of the Committee for the next year.

Respectfully submitted,
Barbara A. Bettwy

Committee: Clergy
Constituted: 2008
Mandate: The mandate of the Committee is:

1. To initiate as needed any projects pertinent to the study of canon law pertaining to the life and ministry of bishops, priests and deacons or the implementation thereof, including, but not limited to, the following:
    a. canonical issues related to the sexual abuse of minors
    b. clergy personnel issues and resources
    c. advocacy for clergy in penal cases
2. To oversee projects referred to the committee by the BOG;
3. To oversee its subcommittees working on projects concerning clergy; (and)
4. To collaborate with national organizations and other groups dealing with clergy issues.

Members: Rev. Msgr. Tomás Marín, *chair* (2016)
Sr. Maureen McPartland, OP (2015)
Rev. Kenneth Riley (2015)
Rev. Georges F. deLaire (2017)

ANNUAL REPORT

E-Mail conversations in March 2015: A topic I think most helpful for our reflection – to aid the society and chancery offices – continues to be letters of suitability, in our mind at least. We are spending a great deal of time preparing letters and responding to letters. I know that due to Office of Child and Youth Protection protocols and processes, these letters are needed, but I'm hopeful a more electronic and/or conducive manner might be explored, proposed and facilitated.

We are discussing how to best meet the needs of the Society without changing the Handbook for Clergy.

We would like to have a conference call at some point to hash out the recommendations on these issues, possibly in May.

Respectfully submitted,
Msgr. Tomás M. Marín

Committee: Convention Planning Committee
Constituted: 1971
Previous Committee Structure: Committees on Convention Planning (constitutional) and Convention Liturgies
Mandate: It is the function of the Committee on Convention Planning:

1. To receive from the Board of Governors the approved general theme of the next Convention as well as any suggestions from the Committee on Research & Development for the development of the theme;
2. To recommend to the BOG, in accord with the general theme, topics for major addresses, seminars or other presentations at a future Convention, as well as a list of potential speakers and the honoraria for such speakers;
3. Following BOG approval, to arrange for the speakers, addresses and seminars for the annual Convention;
4. To plan all Convention liturgies and prayer services;
5. To review the evaluations of the most recent Convention and assist the Convention Chairperson in planning future arrangements, as needed.

Membership: A chair and three active members of the Society, appointed by the President, each with staggered three year terms, the Executive Coordinator *ex officio*, and the Past President *ex officio*.

Members: Rev. Michael Joyce, CM, *chair* (2015)
Rev. Paul Counce (2015)
Sr. Sharon Euart, RSM (2016)
Rev. Phillip J. Brown, *ex officio*
Rev. Roger Keeler, *ex officio*

ANNUAL REPORT

The committee met in January of 2014 at the Office of the Executive Coordinator to plan the Convention program for the 2016 Convention. The Board of Governors approved the proposed theme, program, speakers, and presenters for the 2016 Convention to be held in Houston, Texas. There were several revisions of the program because proposed presenters were unable to accept the invitations extended to them.

Proposed Program for the 2016 CLSA Convention
Prepared by the Convention Planning Committee
Convention Theme: Collegiality and Synodality

Keynote Address

Topic: *Collegiality and Synodality*
His Eminence Donald Cardinal Wuerl, Archbishop of Washington

Major Addresses

Marriage in Light of the Synods on the Family
Rev. Msgr. John Alesandro, Diocese of Rockville Center

The Status of Lay Ecclesial Ministry Ten Years after the Publication of ***Coworkers in the Vineyard***
Bishop Gerald Kicanas, Bishop of Tuscon

Seminars

1. Separation of Members from Religious Institutes or Societies of Apostolic Life
Rev. Michael Joyce, CM (Archdiocese of St. Louis)

2. Non-Degreed Laity Assisting Judges in Resolving Cases (Usually these members of the lay Christian faithful do not have canonical degrees and

they may or may not have advanced degrees.)
Ms. Zabrina Decker (Archdiocese of Milwaukee)

3. Reflections on the 2015 Synod on the Family
Rev. Patrick Lagges (Archdiocese of Chicago)

4. Canon 1680 (This seminar will focus on the use of canon 1095, 2° without availing the use of an expert witness.)
Ms. Catherine Gilligan (Diocese of Little Rock)

5. An Exegesis of Canon 1055 (The seminar will examine the canon in light of recent developments in secular society's understanding of marriage.)
Rev. Roger Keeler (Archdiocese of Edmonton)

6. The Challenge of the Definitive Sentence by the Defender of the Bond in Causes of the Nullity of Marriage
Mr. William Daniel (Diocese of Winona)

7. Interaction between the Civil and Canonical Spheres in Human Resources Issues
Ms. Rita Joyce (Diocese of Pittsburgh)

8. Responding to New Allegations of Sexual Abuse of Minors after Resolution of Previous Allegations
Rev. Msgr. Frederick Easton (Archdiocese of Indianapolis)

9. New Approaches to Advocacy in Helping the Accused (Often enough, an accused cleric even if he is not guilty must adjust to a new way of living. Advocacy now frequently must help the accused come to this realization. It also must work cooperatively with diocesan or provincial administrations to develop ways in which the accused can live with his new condition.)
Rev. Msgr. Ricardo Bass (Archdiocese of Detroit)

10. Canonical Issues in Psychological Assessment, Counseling, and Psychological Treatment of an Accused Cleric
Rev. Paul Golden, CM (Archdiocese of Denver)

11. The Rights and Responsibilities of a Bishop in Inviting New Religious Communities into His Diocese
Dr. Barbara Anne Cusack (Archdiocese of Milwaukee)

12. Canonical Issues in Codes of Conduct for Clerics and Male Religious (Dioceses and provinces have developed codes of conduct to protect clerics from potential allegations of the sexual abuse of minors. These codes have

canonical issues especially involving the rights of the Christian faithful and the rights of clerics that can be explored.)
Rev. Lawrence Jurcak (Diocese of Cleveland)

13. Canonical Dimensions of the Organization and Maintenance of Chancery Archives
Mr. John Treanor (Archdiocese of Chicago)

Respectfully submitted,
Michael Joyce, CM

National Convention Chair Report 2015

Presented by: Reverend Monsignor Victor F. Finelli, J.C.L.
Convention Chair

2015: Pittsburgh, Pennsylvania
Welcome to Pittsburgh! Our Convention this year has all the makings to be another wonderful event for all our members. Hard to believe but this is our 77th Annual Convention and we're happy to be back once again in Pittsburg. I hope you find the hotel and meeting space up to what we have come to expect. We have all worked hard to make this event both a time to further our canonical education but also build those ties of friendship between us. Both are important. Outside of the hotel you will experience a large variety of restaurants, bars, and entertainment venues to meet everyone's needs. Be sure to take some time to walk around the downtown and enjoy Pittsburgh! I hope you enjoy your stay and find our Convention rewarding. I think you will.

2016: Houston, Texas
I traveled to Houston in August of 2013 to begin the planning for the 78th Annual Convention which will be held from October 10-13, 2016. We will be gathering at the Houston Marriott Westchase. Houston is a wonderful town of fine eateries ranging from Tex-Mex, wonderful steakhouses, and of course many bar-b-que establishments. The hospitality of the people in the city was excellent. Houston will be yet another great location for us to visit.

2017: Indianapolis, Indiana
Work has already begun for our 79th Annual Convention which will be held in Indianapolis, Indiana from October 16-19, 2017. We will be residing at the Westin Hotel in Indianapolis. I will be visiting this site soon enough but until then, I thank Father John Vaughn, our past President, for making the initial contact for this venue.

2018: Denver, Colorado

Plans are just beginning to unfold for the 80th Annual Convention which will be held in Denver, Colorado. Although nothing is confirmed with a hotel, it looks like the dates will be October 6 – 12, 2018. Denver should be a great city to visit and hold our Convention…something to look forward to.

I'm most thankful to Fr. Roger Keeler, our Executive Coordinator, for his immeasurable assistance in planning this year's Convention. I'm also thankful to Colleen Crawford of the Office of the Executive Coordinator and to Kimberly Ritter of NIX Associates for their assistance in planning this gathering. It's a real corporate work with everyone sharing the load. In the end, it's our goal to make these days truly a benefit to your canonical ministry, in whatever capacity that may be. Personally, it's an absolute pleasure to assist in this endeavor and to work with these fine, dedicated people. Thank you for allowing me to do so.

Respectfully submitted,
Rev. Msgr. Victor F. Finelli

Committee: Institutes of Consecrated Life and Societies of Apostolic Life

Constituted: 2010

Mandate: The mandate of the Committee is:

1. To initiate as needed any projects pertinent to the study of canon law pertaining to the life and ministry of Institutes of Consecrated and Apostolic Life or the implementation thereof, including but not limited to the following: (a) sponsorship; (b) mergers and restructuring institutes; (c) governance; (d) membership; (e) new forms of consecrated life.
2. To oversee projects referred to the committee by the Board of Governors;
3. To oversee its subcommittees working on projects concerning Consecrated and Apostolic Life;
4. To collaborate with national organizations and other groups dealing with issues of Consecrated and Apostolic Life.

Members: Sr. Amy Hereford, CSJ, *chair* (2015)
Sr. Catherine Darcy, RSM (2015)
Sr. Lynn McKenzie, OSB (2016)

Sr. Karla Felix-Rivera, VDMF (2016)
Dr. Eileen Jaramillo (2017)

ANNUAL REPORT

The committee met at the Convention in October in St. Louis and discussed ways of celebrating the Year for Consecrated Life. In addition to a seminar on Consecrated Life at the next Convention, we discussed the possibility of presenting a pre-convention workshop on issues related to Consecrated Life.

Pre-Convention Workshop

Purposes:

1. Celebrating the Year of Consecrated Life with the whole Church.
2. Offering educational presentations to members of the CLSA who are facing are assisting Institutes and Societies and their members.

Title: New Institutes and Forms of Consecrated Life Emerging in Your Arch/ Diocese: A Pastoral–Canonical Approach

Presenters: Sr. Amy Hereford, CSJ, JD, JCD; Sr. Karla Felix-Rivera, VDMF, JCDc-Cand.; Christina Hip-Flores, JCD-Cand.

This workshop, offered during the celebration of the Year of Consecrated Life, will explore the various ways in which the Life of the Spirit is stirring anew in the Church today through new religious institutes, diocesan hermits and consecrated virgins, new forms of consecrated life, and the lay ecclesial movements that may give rise to new institutes.

Each of these movements calls for a response that is both open to the Spirit and is canonically precise.

The workshop will explore:

- the new ways religious are sharing their lives and spirituality with the laity,
- special concerns of autonomous monasteries,
- religious who move into a diocese for ministry or fundraising,
- ecumenical communities,
- civil issues that may arise in this context, etc.

Chancery staff who advise their bishop on these matters will benefit and are encouraged to attend.

The Committee will meet during the 2015 Convention.

Respectfully Submitted,
Amy Hereford, CSJ

Committee: Laity
Constituted: 2009
Mandate:

1. To initiate as needed any projects pertinent to the study of canon law pertaining to the life and ministry of lay persons or the implementation thereof, including, but not limited to, the following:
    - α. Lay ecclesial ministry;
    - β. Collaboration with clergy;
    - χ. Rights of the lay family.
2. To oversee projects referred to the committee by the BOG;
3. To oversee its subcommittees working on projects concerning the laity, (and)
4. To collaborate with national organizations and other groups dealing with the role of the laity in the Church.

Members: Dr. Marie T. Hilliard, *chair* (2015)
Mr. Timothy Cavanaugh (2015)
Ms. Amy Tadlock (2016)
Ms. Anne Bryant (2017)
Mr. Stephen Garbitelli (2017)

ANNUAL REPORT

A. The COL members met a total of three times over the last year: in October 2014 at the CLSA Convention in St. Louis; and twice by conference call (May 18, 2015 and June 30, 2015). All but one committee member was able to attend the October 2014 meeting. All committee members participated in the conference calls, and all meetings/calls were attended by the Chair of the Committee on Sacramental Law, due to the collaborative nature of the project in which COL is engaged.
B. Despite the turnover of COL membership due to term limits, COL has been

successful in completing, for review by the Publications Advisory Board, the project described, below. COL wishes to thank the past members who contributed significantly to this project (Msgr. Steven Callahan, Ms. Anna Marie Chamblee), and to congratulate COL's new members (Ms. Anne Bryant and Mr. Stephen Garbitelli), who immediately provided excellent contributions to the project.

C. The project focus remains as it was reported in the October 2014 report, which will be recapped in an abridged form below:

   I. The project focus (approved by Publications Advisory Board) was narrowed to marriage preparation of persons when one or both persons are from a non-dominant culture from those dominant in the United States, and was done in collaboration with the Sacramental Law Committee.

   II. The goal was not to alter the decision to marry but to increase awareness of how differences can impact the relationship. Critical areas to address were: theology of the Sacrament of Marriage; marriage consent (re: c. 1055); primordial sacrament tied to culture as no other sacrament; family as Church; issues framed positively (presumption that couples want what Church envisions); importance of seeking counsel.

   III. COL reviewed existing diocesan/canonical literature and resources and gaps were identified and addressed. A brief abridged recap of those results follows:

      a. Culturally relevant themes are addressed: faithful life-long partnership; spirituality: marriage enriched by grace; intimacy; children as gift; domestic life; family expectations; potential conflicts, including universal challenges and "red flags."

      b. Resources specific to five non-dominant cultures were identified: Vietnamese; Filipino; Hispanic, African; and Native American.

      c. COL recommends sponsor/mentor couples from the non-dominant culture.

      d. Potential pro bono translation resources, skilled in canon law, have been identified for a Vietnamese and Hispanic translation.

   IV. Pricing policies for printing and distribution were developed, with budget resources identified (see COL Budget 2015 – 2016, attached).

An on-site Convention meeting is planned for October 2015, to consider brochure translations, e.g., Spanish; Vietnamese.

COL focus for 2015-2016: Continue with plans for marketing, distribution, and translation of brochure, as well as an evaluation mechanism to determine if there is a need (market) for more detailed documents, as well as other cultures to be addressed.

Respectfully Submitted,
Marie T. Hilliard, Chair

Committee: Publications Advisory Board
Constituted: 2007; revised in 2008
Mandate: The mandate of the Committee is:

1. To advise the Board of Governors about all aspects of current, periodic and proposed CLSA publication projects, including financial, literary, educational and marketing issues.
2. To monitor the progress of all CLSA publication projects.
3. To implement the procedures for peer review of CLSA publications.
4. To make the final recommendation to the Board of Governors regarding specific publications.
5. To review the coordination and management of the CLSA's publications activity on the part of the Office of the Executive Coordinator.
6. To provide a written report to the CLSA membership at the annual convention.

Members: Sr. Sharon Euart, RSM, *chair* (2019)
Rev. Patrick Cogan (2017)
Rev. Patrick Cooney, OSB (2015)
Msgr. Thomas Green (2015)
Rev. Paul Hartmann (2018)
Chorbishop John Faris (*ex officio*)
Msgr. John Alesandro, consultant

ANNUAL REPORT

Meetings

The 2014-2015 year has been a very busy one for the Publications Advisory Board. During the past year, the members of PAB followed their usual pattern of meetings. The board met in person at the October 2014 Convention in St. Louis, Missouri, and at the CLSA office in Washington, D.C., on June 15-16, 2015. The chair of PAB also participated by conference call in the BOG meetings in January and April, 2015, to offer progress reports on publications. The members also communicated by conference call and e-mail throughout the year.

Publications Budget

The actual revenue and expenditures for CLSA publications for FY 2014-2015, as of May 31, were below the budgeted estimates; the decrease in sales income is due primarily to the lack of new publications. The sales of our current titles were generally in line with previous years. The PAB discussed the challenges of publishing (e.g., fewer members interested in writing or lacking time for writing, others choosing to write for other publishers, etc.) and identified it as a Society concern that needs to be addressed by the Board of Governors as well as the PAB.

The expenditures for PAB itself have been in line with the approved budget for FY2014-2015. The assumptions and estimate for FY2015-2016 for both publications in general and for PAB itself seem to be accurate.

New Publications

Though PAB remains concerned about the lack of publications, it is very pleased to report that during 2015 several new publications have been completed and, at the time of this writing, are in the process of being prepared for printing. These include the first of the CLSA Pastoral Resources, *Pastoral Councils: Parish and Finance* by Rev. James Coriden and Dr. Mark Fischer; *Proceedings of the 2014 Penal Law Workshop* by Msgr. John Alesandro, Very Rev. Larry DiNardo, Msgr. Fred Easton, and Msgr. Thomas Green; a brochure on *Marriage: Many Cultures – One Sacrament* prepared by the CLSA Committee on Laity. In addition, the 2014 *CLSA Proceedings* and *CLSA 2014 Roman Replies and CLSA Advisory Opinions*, both of which are primarily member services, were also published during the past year. We are most grateful for those who responded positively to our request for new publications and are confident that each of them will be well received by CLSA members and other pastoral ministers.

The PAB has been in contact with several CLSA members regarding the possibility of new publications. At this time we continue to discuss topics and possible authors. PAB welcomes your suggestions on ways the Society might move forward to increase our inventory. Besides being a source of income to the Society, English-language canon law resources are immensely important to our membership, especially our international members. It continues to be critical for the future of the Society that we look at ways to address this concern.

The PAB continues to assess the feasibility of scheduling a Spring 2016 workshop on Temporal Goods. Due to time constraints for 2016 scheduling for key presenters, the workshop may need to be postponed until 2017. The outcome of the workshop might be a Church finance publication and/or a pre-convention workshop.

Inventory

PAB continues to monitor and manage the CLSA inventory, reducing it when there is little likelihood of additional sales of any significance, particularly for older publications, in order to consolidate the volumes into fewer pallets and thereby reduce monthly storage expenses at BrightKey. This is an ongoing task, which involves collaboration with the Office of the Executive Coordinator and the staff of BrightKey, the company that provides fulfillment services (sales, handling and shipping) on behalf of the CLSA. For example, due to the large number of volumes in the inventory and the low number of annual sales of certain publications, the PAB decided to offer complimentary copies of a few publications (e.g., *CLSA Proceedings*, *RRAO* 2006-2009, *CLD* 6-9) to canon law students while retaining a few copies of each in the OEC or a specified number of copies at BrightKey.

Webinars

The main challenge regarding CLSA webinars is finding presenters who are interested in preparing a 40-45 minute presentation. During the past year PAB identified several potential topics and presenters for future webinars and welcomes suggestions from members as well as volunteers to be presenters for future programs. The chair of PAB contacted the CLSA committee chairs for assistance both in identifying topics and presenters. Currently we have webinars planned by Deacon Jerry Jorgensen on the use of experts, Jeannine Moreno on the canonization process, diocesan finance councils by Msgr. Bill King, and one on how to use the new database. We would also like to include some regional presentations as webinars. The OEC staff provides an orientation for presenters on the technique of webinars and is available to assist with the preparation of PowerPoint slides.

Roman Replies and CLSA Advisory Opinions

The Index on the CLSA website continues to be a valuable research tool for canonists. It is maintained by the Office of the Executive Coordinator, including uploading the titles of new advisory opinions. This method refers the reader to both the original volumes of *RR&AO* and to the printed *Collections*, both of which contain the entire article. The entire text of all advisory opinions will eventually be available in the *CLSA Resource Database* for all those who hold a subscription. *Roman Replies and CLSA Advisory Opinions* was published again this year in time for the Pittsburgh convention.

CLSA Research Database

Significant progress has been made on making the *CLSA Research Database* (CLSA RD) operational. The consultant, Alexander Padmos, demonstrated the end-product to the members of PAB at their June 2015 meeting. The members were able to view it on computer, tablet and smartphone. The search function was sophisticated and speedy and met with the approval of the members of PAB. Meanwhile, with the help of members of PAB as well as other CLSA members who volunteered their time, Msgr. Jack Alesandro, the project director, has incorporated into the CLSA RD the later volumes of *Canon Law Digest* (CLD), which cover the years after the 1983 promulgation. In addition, Msgr. Jack Alesandro, Msgr. John Renken and Colleen Crawford met during the summer to iron out the protocol for adding new documents into the database, beginning with those issued after the completion of *CLD* Volume XIV. This ongoing enhancement will be the future of the CLSA RD, constantly updating it, literally day by day. It is anticipated that the CLSA RD will be available to the public at or very near the 2015 Convention in Pittsburgh. Once it is launched, the volumes of *CLD* prior to the 1983 Code (which are currently available on a CLSA CD) will be incorporated into the database itself, completing this first phase of the project. The project will then move forward with the incorporation of many other kinds of research materials, making the CLSA RD the most valuable canonical research tool possible.

The Publications Advisory Board is most grateful to Msgr. Jack Alesandro and Alex Padmos for their tireless work on developing and testing the new *CLSA Resource Database*. We appreciate their expertise, patience and generosity and are most grateful for their service to the PAB and the CLSA. We are also grateful to the PAB members and CLSA members who have assisted in working with the project and those who will continue to oversee the *CLSA Research Database*.

Respectfully submitted,
Sister Sharon Euart, RSM

Committee: Research and Development
Constituted: 2008
Mandate: The mandate of the Committee is:

1. To initiate or cooperate in all CLSA research projects such as seminars, symposia and special studies;
2. To design and implement Think Tanks that will allow for diverse views on issues of ecclesial life having canonical implications;
3. To develop and recommend themes for the annual conventions for submission to the BOG for approval and subsequent referral to the Convention Planning Committee for implementation;
4. To maintain close communication with all the committees
5. To interact with the Publications Advisory Board in order to assess the current and contemplated publications of the CLSA and offer suggestions and guidance for publication planning.

Members:
Chorbishop John D. Faris, *chair* (2015)
Dr. Michael Nobel (2015)
Rev. Msgr. F. Stephen Pedone (2015)
Sr. Rose McDermott, SSJ (2015)
Ms. Rita Joyce (2016)
Rev. Manuel Viera, OFM, *ex officio* (2015)

ANNUAL REPORT

John Faris was re-appointed as Committee Chair of the Research and Development Committee on December 30, 2014, for a one-year term.

The committee met by conference call only once on January 9, 2015. All participated with the exception of Michael Nobel.

2016 Convention Theme

Manuel informed the committee that, in the absence of a proposal from R & D, Michael Joyce had been asked to work with the Convention Planning Committee to propose a theme. He recalled that theme proposed had been *Collegiality and Subsidiarity*.

The members of the R & D Committee suggested that the proposed theme be used in 2017 and that the theme for the 2016 Convention focus on *Consecrated Life* in consideration of the current year dedicated to consecrated life. (The Year of Consecrated Life will end February 2016.) Manuel further noted that the 2015 Convention had no seminars treating consecrated life.

2009 Convention Resolution on Changes in the *CIC*

John Faris noted that there does not seem to have been any movement regarding the 2009 Convention resolution and the proposal submitted to the BOG by R & D. He recalled for everyone that this was a resolution unanimously accepted during the CLSA general meeting; neither the BOG nor any committee can set it aside. Perhaps the CLSA can decided to create a "think thank" that would produce a study.

Future Directions

The proposal was that that there is a need for some kind of canonical formation for non-canonists involved in child protection programs.

Respectfully submitted,
Chorbishop John Faris

Committee: Sacramental Law
Constituted: 2009
Mandate:

1. To initiate as needed any projects pertinent to the study of canon law pertaining to the sacramental life of the Church or the implementation thereof;
2. To oversee projects referred to the committee by the BOG;
3. To oversee its subcommittees working on projects concerning the sacramental life of the Church;
4. To offer suggestions to the BOG for marriage topics for pre-convention workshops;
5. To collaborate with national organizations and other groups dealing with the sacramental life of the Church.

Members: Rev. Bruce Miller, *chair* (2015)
Dr. Chad Glenndinning (2015)
Mr. Jay Conzemius (2016)

Mrs. Heather Jo Eichholz (2017)
Rev. Robert Sinatra (2017)

ANNUAL REPORT

Pending Items:

- Dr. Chad Glendinning and Rev. Bruce Miller come to the end of their terms of service on the Committee on Sacramental Law. It is indeed time for a new name to be surfaced for a successor to Father Miller. On the other hand, Doctor Glendinning has only served one term; it seems appropriate that he would be reappointed.
- The CSL is pleased to note that the Pre-Convention Workshop by Father Paul Counce this year will cover the topic "Instructing Marriage Nullity Cases," a subject suggested by the CSL. Also, "Elements in Writing a Sentence" in Matrimonial Cases by Father Thomas Cronkleton will be a Convention presentation, another topic that the CSL has encouraged. Finally, Monsignor Roch Pagé will present on a topic at the Convention similar to one suggested by the CSL.
- For a future webinar, the committee suggests the question of faculties/the drafting of *pagella*. The name of a canonists has been surfaced as a presenter. A dialogue with the PAB has ensued.
- Depending on developments in the procedural law of marriage that may come about as a result of the Pontifical Commission or the Synod on the Family, many opportunities for seminars or webinars may become immediately available.
- The entire CSL had an opportunity in July to give to the Committee on the Laity a review of their forthcoming brochure on "Marriage Preparation Enriched by Cultural Heritage."

Worthy of Continued Study:

- At the recommendation of the CLSA Committee on the Laity to this committee:
    - Revision of the *Tribunal Handbook* on *Dignitas Connubii* (now that there is 10 years of experience)
    - Support Eastern Church Laity re: Marriage
    - Issues re: *Omnium in mentem*
    - Webinar Addressing Use of Expert: What Should Be Requested of an Expert and How Should Opinions Be Interpreted?

Respectfully submitted,
Rev. Bruce Miller

Committee: National Penal Tribunal Study Commission
Constituted: 2014
Mandate:

Following upon a resolution of the Canon Law Society of America approved at its annual business meeting on October 16, 2013, the President of the Society offered to the Most Reverend Joseph Kurtz, President of the United States Catholic Conference of Bishops, the assistance of the Society to study and make recommendations including but not limited to structure, personnel, education, and finances of a regional/ national tribunal to achieve the expeditious resolution of causes and controversies concerning ecclesiastical delicts. In a letter dated March 7, 2014 to Very Rev. Phillip J. Brown, *pss*, the CLSA President, Archbishop Kurtz expressed openness to receiving from the CLSA a more detailed study of such a structure for addressing penal cases which would also include a realistic assessment of the human and financial resources which would be necessary to achieve the goal. Therefore, by June 9, 2014 this CLSA Study Commission was established and the members were appointed by the President of CLSA.

Members:

Msgr. Frederick Easton, *co-chair*
Msgr. John A. Alesandro, *co-chair*
Very Rev. Lawrence A. DiNardo
Very Rev. Mark O'Connell
Msgr. Michael Padazinski

ANNUAL REPORT

Since the constitution of this Commission, the members have conversed only by way of conference calls. However, the Commission was able to meet in person on Monday, October 13, 2014 at the site of the 2014 Annual Convention of the Society. Only one of our members was not able to be present, Very Rev. Lawrence A. DiNardo. We managed during that meeting and also afterward during that week to prepare a report to the Chair of the Committee on Canonical Affairs of the United States Catholic Conference of Bishops. The final version of that report was sent on October 27, 2014 to Archbishop Timothy P. Broglio, J.C.D., who, by that time, was the outgoing Chair.

Unlike other committee reports, the report of this Commission belongs to the Committee on Canonical Affairs of the United States Catholic Conference of Bishops. Nevertheless, this Commission did strongly urge the constitution of a first and a second instance national penal tribunal. In our report we made some rather specific recommendations for the beginning of a practical implementation thereof.

Since the submission of our report to the Committee on Canonical Affairs of the United States Catholic Conference of Bishops, there has been no further word or directions given to this Commission.

Respectfully submitted,
Rev. Msgr. Fred Easton (co-chair)
Rev. Msgr. John Alesandro (co-chair)

Varia

Seventy-Seventh Annual Business Meeting
Pittsburgh, Pennsylvania
October 14, 2015

MINUTES

Call to Order and Opening Prayer

Reverend Monsignor Michael Souckar, President, called to order the Seventy-Seventh Annual Business Meeting of the Canon Law Society of America (CLSA), on October 14, 2015 at 11:00 a.m., at The Westin Convention Center Hotel in Pittsburgh, Pennsylvania. He presided over the meeting as Chair.

The Chair then led the assembly in an opening prayer.

Following the opening prayer, it was announced that Brother Patrick Shea, OFM, would serve as Parliamentarian for the Business Meeting, and that *Robert's Rules of Order* would resolve matters not provided for in the CLSA's *Constitution* or *Bylaws*.

The Chair then gave instructions on the voting procedures to be observed for the election of Vice-President/President-Elect, and Consultors during the Business Meeting. The procedures were adopted as described by the Chair.

The Chair then reviewed the procedures for addressing the assembly, and the CLSA's practices for presenting resolutions. The procedures and practices were adopted as presented by the Chair.

The Chair then entertained a motion that Associate Members present at the meeting have the opportunity to address the assembly, as called for in Article 5.3 of the CLSA's *Constitution*. The motion was seconded and approved unanimously by the assembly.

The Chair then called upon the Secretary, Ms. Mary Gen Blittschau, to read the Minutes of the Seventy-Sixth Business Meeting of the CLSA, unless there was a proposal to accept the Minutes as published in the 2014 CLSA *Proceedings*. A motion to accept the Minutes was presented. The motion was seconded and approved by the assembly with two objections.

The Chair called upon Ms. Meg Romano-Hogan, Chair of the Nominations Committee, to present the slate of nominees for Officers and Consultors. Ms. Meg Romano-Hogan announced the candidates for Officers and Consultors.

Additional nominations from the floor were added to the slate, as is provided for in Article 9.5 of the CLSA's *Constitution*. Following motion made and duly seconded, Rev. Msgr. Jason Gray was nominated as a candidate for the office of Vice-President/President-Elect; he accepted the nomination, and his name was added to the slate of candidates. Following motion made and duly seconded, Anna Marie Chamblee was nominated as a candidate for the office of Consultor; she accepted the nomination, and her name was added to the slate of candidates.

The Chair then read the provisions of the CLSA's *Bylaws* regarding elections. The active members of the CLSA were instructed to cast their votes. The tellers collected the ballots and retired to a separate room to count them. Later in the meeting, Ms. Meg Romano-Hogan returned to the Business Meeting and informed the Chair of the election results. The Chair then announced that:

For the Office of Vice-President/President-Elect:

252 valid ballots were cast, with 127 votes needed for election. There were no invalid ballots or abstentions. The votes cast were:

Dr. Diane Barr: 95
Rev. Msgr. Jason Gray: 45
Rev. Bruce Miller: 112

The Chair reported that a run-off election will occur since none of the three candidates was elected.

For the Office of Consultor:

251 valid ballots were cast, with 126 votes needed for election. There were no invalid ballots or abstentions. The votes cast were:

Reverend Anthony Bawyn: 121
Sr. Deborah M. Cerullo, SSND: 70
Ms. Anna Marie Chamblee: 50
Dr. Marie T. Hilliard: 126
Very Reverend Kenneth A. Riley: 117

The Chair declared an election with Dr. Marie T. Hilliard selected as Consultor. The election was received with applause.

The Chair reported that a run-off election for the second Consultor will occur since none of the remaining candidates was elected.

Later in the meeting, Ms. Meg Romano-Hogan returned to the Business Meeting and informed the Chair of the run-off election results. The Chair then announced that:

For the Office of Vice-President/President-Elect:

240 valid ballots were cast in the run-off election. There were no invalid ballots or abstentions. The votes cast were:

Reverend Bruce Miller: 150
Dr. Diane Barr: 90

The Chair declared an election with Reverend Bruce Miller selected as Vice-President/President-Elect. The election was received with applause.

For the Office of Consultor:

227 valid ballots were cast in the run-off election. There were no invalid ballots or abstentions. The votes cast were:

Very Reverend Kenneth A. Riley: 126
Reverend Anthony Bawyn: 101

The Chair declared an election with Very Reverend Kenneth A. Riley selected as Consultor. The election was received with applause.

Reports

President's Report

The Chair referred the assembly to pages 17-18 of the *2015 Annual Reports Booklet,* distributed at the convention registration, for the full text of the President's Report. Since the membership had the opportunity to read the Report in advance of the Business Meeting, he called for any questions or observations on the Report. There were none.

The President noted that the CLSA is considering the arrangement of a trip for the membership to visit the dicasteries, and the recommendation was for this to occur during either May or November. The assembly was then polled and asked to exhibit a show of hands so as to indicate a preference for either month. The result of the poll clearly manifested a preference for such a proposed visit to the Vatican during the month of May as opposed to November.

Work accomplished by the committees was highlighted, and the chairs and members were commended. In particular, the Task Force on Matrimonial Procedures was recognized for its contributions and recommendations which were forwarded to the Special Pontifical Commission. Collaboration occurred between the Committee on Sacramental Law and the Committee on the Laity regarding intercultural marriage, and a brochure may be published soon.

The biennial visit to Rome was a successful one, and the CLSA representatives were well-received by the dicasteries. All spoke most favorably of the CLSA publications, and many were receptive to having documents published in *Roman Replies*. The faculties of canon law of the Angelicum, Gregorian, and Santa Croce were also visited.

The President had the opportunity to work with the United States Conference of Catholic Bishops regarding the drafting and implementation of the third edition of the document *Guidelines for Receiving Pastoral Ministers in the United States*. Throughout the year, four regional seminars regarding its implementation were provided, and the President was one of the presenters.

The President expressed his gratitude for the opportunity to have served the CLSA.

Executive Coordinator's Report

The Chair then explained that due to a family emergency, Reverend Roger Keeler was not able to be present at this meeting. Therefore, the President referred the assembly to the written Report from the Office of the Executive Coordinator, found on pages 53-55 of the *2015 Annual Reports Booklet*. The membership acknowledged the service of Rev. Roger Keeler with applause.

Treasurer's Report

The Chair next invited Reverend Thomas E. Cronkleton, Jr., Treasurer, to the podium to provide the Treasurer's Report. He noted that the written report was found on pages 19-52 of the *2015 Annual Reports Booklet*.

The Treasurer thanked Rev. Roger Keeler, Colleen Crawford, and the Resource and Asset Management Committee for all of their assistance.

The CLSA operates out of four units. The financial auditor of the Society has provided a positive financial report. It is anticipated that the Society will have a "break-even" budget for the next fiscal year.

General Operations Unit

The Investments in the General Operations Unit have been experiencing generally positive growth the last few years. The decline in the December 31, 2014 balance was due to the $50,000 transfer to establish the Doctoral Scholarship Fund. The fund, however, has continued to experience some growth. The Balance Sheet for the General Operations Unit shows the gains in the market and a positive balance.

Webinars have been added as a membership service and have proven to be very successful and popular. They were provided at no cost for the members during the past fiscal year and will continue at no cost for members for the current fiscal year as well.

In order to meet expenses, it was necessary to use Prior Year Realized Net Assets, and we have budgeted to do so again for the current fiscal year. Due to this, the Resource and Asset Management Committee and the Board of Governors have proposed an increase in dues which is the main source of income for the General Operations Unit. For the three prior years, the General Operations Unit was budgeted to use Prior Year Realized Net Assets in order to balance the budget. While we budgeted to use those funds, we did not have to use them. We did, however, have to use them this past fiscal year which helps to demonstrate the need for an increase in dues.

The Paulists have notified us that they wish to sell the building and to be let out from the lease agreement. We are negotiating for new office space and are considering all of the connected financial ramifications.

Publications Unit

The Publications Unit had a slight negative year because expenses exceeded income. This was due in part to the revenues from publications sales being about 72% of what was anticipated. The main reason, however, for the deficit was the special authorization by the Board of Governors to provide additional funds for bringing the new Electronic Database online; the concept of publications is changing dramatically from print media to electronic.

Conventions Unit

The Conventions Unit had a positive return for last year's Convention and Pre-Convention workshops in St. Louis, Missouri due to programs that attracted more than anticipated attendance. More speakers are using audio-visuals for their presentations which results in increased expense, but when the quality of the presentation is improved, it is worthwhile.

The Balance Sheet for the Conventions Unit is positive, and we have some reserves in case our expenses should exceed our income.

Scholarship Unit

The Scholarship Unit operates on a total return basis for the investments in two Scholarship Investment Funds: Licentiate and Doctoral Scholarships. Five recipients are slated to receive scholarship funds in fiscal year 2015-2016. The investments in the Licentiate Scholarship Unit have been experiencing generally positive growth for the last few years. Since inception, the Doctoral Scholarship investments have experienced slight growth.

Resolution to Increase Dues

The Resource and Asset Management Committee developed the resolution to increase dues in order to ensure adequate funding for General Operations. The Board of Governors carefully considered the proposal to increase dues, and after discussion, chose to recommend the increase of dues by $50.00 for active and associate members and $25.00 for student members, effective July 1, 2016.

No questions were posed for the Treasurer.

CLSA Research Database

Msgr. Jack Alesandro, project director, addressed the assembly and noted that significant progress has occurred in bringing this database to fruition. Alex Padmos, the technology consultant, provided an onscreen demonstration for all to view. The search function was sophisticated and speedy and met with the approval of the members of the Publications Advisory Board. The later volumes of *Canon Law Digest* which follow the promulgation of the 1983 *Code of Canon Law* have already been incorporated, and the volumes prior to that will follow at a later date. It is anticipated that this database will be available to the membership for a reasonable subscription fee in the near future.

Resolutions

The Chair read the applicable CLSA *Bylaws* that govern proposing resolutions from the floor and asked if there were any such resolutions to be presented. There being none, he called upon Mrs. Susan Mulheron, Chair of the Resolutions Committee, Reverend Langes Silva, and Reverend Jamin David, time-keeper, to approach the podium and present the resolutions previously submitted to the Resolutions Committee.

Three resolutions were previously submitted, and two resolutions were presented at the convention.

The full texts of the resolutions were projected onto screens in the hall. In addition, printed copies of the resolutions were accessible to those in attendance.

Resolution 1

The Resolutions Committee moved the resolution.

PROPOSED BY: Board of Governors

TITLE: Dues Increase Resolution

STATEMENT OF RATIONALE:

WHEREAS, the *Constitution*, "Article IV – Dues," number 1 states:

> Any change in the amount of the annual dues of active, associate, and student members shall be proposed by the Board of Governors but shall be determined by a majority vote of those active members present and voting at a General Meeting at which the proposal is made.

WHEREAS, the "Financial Policies" of the Board of Governors state that operating costs for the Society are to be covered by revenue from the dues of the membership (*2013 Board of Governors Handbook*, p. 36).

WHEREAS, despite the efforts of the Executive Coordinators to reduce expenses by various cost saving measures and by providing various services in-house that had previously been outsourced, budgeted expenses in the General Operations Unit have increased every year;

WHEREAS, the expense providing salary and benefits to the Executive Coordinator, the Executive Assistant, and the Administrative Assistant have increased every year;

WHEREAS, operational expenses in the General Operations Unit is anticipated to continue to increase and exceed projected income;

WHEREAS, the use of interest and dividends alone from the General Operations Unit Investments is insufficient to cover expenses that dues do not;

WHEREAS, the Resources and Asset Management Committee has only been able to provide the Board of Governors and the Membership with a Balanced Budget for the General Operations Unit for the last four years and for the upcoming year by utilizing "prior years realized net assets;"

WHEREAS, the "prior years realized net assets" used to balance the budget for the General Operations Unit came from the years in which the General Operations Unit took in more income than expenses and from a positive gain in the value of the General Operations Unit Investments, and the continued use of a growing amount of "prior year realized net assets" will exceed the capital gains of investments and exhaust the prior year profits in the near future;

WHEREAS, the Publications Unit continues to provide less and less Ordinary Net Income which has been used in the past to help offset projected deficits in the General Operations Unit;

WHEREAS, the Board of Governors desires to provide Webinars forums for discussing relevant issues in Canon Law and to provide these to members as a membership benefit without additional fees;

WHEREAS, there has not been an increase in dues since 2003, twelve years ago;

WHEREAS, according to the United States Department of Labor, Bureau of Labor Statistics, CPI Inflation Calculator the inflation rate from 2003 to 2014 has been 28.5% and if the active and associate membership dues had been increased according to the inflation rate they would now be $257;

AND WHEREAS, the Resources and Asset Management Committee supports the need for a dues increase;

BE IT RESOLVED that the Board of Governors proposes an annual dues increase of $50.00 per year for active and associate members and an annual dues increase of $25.00 per year for student members, thereby making active and associate members' dues to be $250.00 per year and student members' dues to be $125.00 per year. The increase is to be effective July 1, 2016.

IMPLEMENTATION BY MEANS OF: Annual dues collection.

COST: $0.00

Rev. Thomas Cronkleton, Jr., of the Diocese of Cheyenne and a member of the Resource and Asset Management Committee and the Board of Governors spoke in favor of the resolution. He noted that continuing to use prior year realized net assets may eventually exhaust the savings of the CLSA; the dues increase is recommended for the financial benefit of the Society.

Rev. Michael Boccaccio of the Diocese of Bridgeport inquired whether the increased attendance at conventions would have an effect on dues.

Rev. Thomas Cronkleton, Jr., responded that the convention unit is self-contained and that if the number of convention attendees increases, overall cost would decrease.

The Chair called the question on the resolution. The resolution was adopted by the membership with a small minority opposed.

Resolution 2

The Resolutions Committee moved the resolution.

PROPOSED BY: Board of Governors

TITLE: Title Change Resolution

STATEMENT OF RATIONALE:

WHEREAS, Article VIII of the *Constitution* of the Canon Law Society of America (CLSA) creates the office of Executive Coordinator defined as follows:

Article VIII -- Executive Coordinator

1. The Executive Coordinator shall work under the President and the Board of Governors and shall be responsible for the general implementation of their policies and decisions as well as the fulfillment of specific duties as mentioned in the By-Laws.

2. The Executive Coordinator shall be appointed from the active membership by the Board of Governors for a three year term of service. Such service may be renewed by the consent of the Board of Governors.

3. Financial provisions for the position of Executive Coordinator, including office and secretarial expenses, shall be made by the Board of Governors.

And,

WHEREAS, the Executive Coordinator as so created is also referred to in a number of places in the By-Laws of the Society, and

WHEREAS, the responsibilities of the Executive Coordinator are the equivalent of the Executive Director of an American civil corporation, and

WHEREAS, the Canon Law Society of America is a duly organized charitable corporation under section 501 (c) (3) of the United States Internal Revenue Code, and

WHEREAS, the office of Executive Coordinator functions in essentially the same manner as that of the Executive Director of an American civil corporation, and

WHEREAS, the title "Executive Coordinator" was adopted rather than "Executive Director" for reasons that are not entirely clear today, and

WHEREAS, use of the title "Executive Coordinator" in an entity that is both an ecclesiastical association and an American civil corporation could lead to misunderstandings and ambiguities with respect to the responsibilities, rights and privileges inhering to the office, and

WHEREAS, greater clarity can be given to the nature and role of the office in both its ecclesiastical and civil aspects, and potential misunderstandings better avoided, if it is given a title more readily familiar in civil law and common parlance, creating as much consonance as possible between the ecclesiastical and civil aspects of the CLSA's organization and governance,

NOW THEREFORE BE IT RESOLVED that Article VIII of the Constitution of the CLSA be amended in its title and content changing the name of "Executive Coordinator" to that of "Executive Director" and that all references to "Executive Coordinator" in the Constitution and By-Laws of the Society and elsewhere in relation to this office be changed to "Executive Director;" and that henceforth the former office of "Executive Coordinator" shall be officially known as the office of "Executive Director." The intent of this Resolution is to change the title of "Executive Coordinator" to "Executive Director" and not to change in any way the responsibilities, rights and privileges inhering to said office.

IMPLEMENTATION BY MEANS OF: Constitutional amendment.

COST: $0.00

Rev. Phil Brown, rector of Theological College, Washington, DC, and a member of the Board of Governors, spoke in favor of the resolution and noted that the title of executive director is more recognizable in civil law.

Rev. Pat Cogan of the Diocese of Arlington requested clarification regarding the nature of the role of the Executive Coordinator over the past years.

Sr. Sharon Euart, of the Resource Center for Religious Institutes responded that the Board of Governors governs the CLSA while the Executive Coordinator serves under the Board of Governors; an Executive Director would have more autonomy than an Executive Coordinator.

Rev. Thomas Franciscus of the Diocese of Reno commented that since this would entail a Constitutional amendment, the membership needed to have been properly notified ahead of time.

The Chair responded that the membership was indeed notified, and the resolution was properly filed.

The Chair called the question on the resolution. The resolution was not adopted by the membership.

Resolution 3

The Resolutions Committee moved the resolution.

PROPOSED BY: Board of Governors

TITLE: In Support of Absentee Ballots

STATEMENT OF RATIONALE:

WHEREAS, Article IX of the *Constitution* of the Canon Law Society of America (CLSA) describes the election of officers is by the membership of the CLSA during its Annual General Meeting, and

WHEREAS, Section 17 of the By Laws outlines the method by which those elections are to take place, and

WHEREAS, no provision is made for every member of the CLSA to have an opportunity to vote for the officers of the CLSA because of their absence from the Annual General Meeting,

NOW THEREFORE BE IT RESOLVED that Article IX of the Constitution and Section 17 of the By Laws be amended as shown below in boldface to make provision for absentee voting by CLSA members in the election of officers of the CLSA during the Annual General Meeting.

CONSTITUTION
Article IX – Elections

1. The election of the Vice-President, the Secretary, the Treasurer, and the Consultors shall take place during the Annual General Meeting.

2. The person elected Vice-President thereby becomes President-elect and will succeed to the office of Presidency at the conclusion of the next Annual General Meeting. However, if by the time of that next Annual General Meeting the elected Vice-President is unavailable to serve in the office of Presidency, no fewer than two nominations shall be made for the office of Presidency by the Committee on Nominations.

3. The President, Vice-President shall hold office for one year; the Secretary, Treasurer and the elected Consultors shall hold office for three years. Terms of office shall end at the close of the Annual General Meeting at which new officers are elected. The terms of the Secretary and Treasurer shall end in different years so that both do not go out of office in the same year.

4. Insofar as it shall be possible, the Consultors shall be from different regions.

5. Nominations for the elective offices shall be communicated to all active members by the Committee on Nominations not less than one month before the Annual General Meeting. Active members present at the Annual General Meeting have the right to nominate candidates for each office from the floor. In every case, the nomination is subject to the consent of the nominee.

6. For all offices no fewer than two nominations shall be made by the Committee on Nominations.

7. It shall be a necessary qualification of any nominee, whether named by the Committee on Nominations or from the floor, that the nominee be an active member of the Society.

8. The electoral body of the Society shall be all active members who are present at the General Meeting at which the voting takes place **and any active member who has requested an absentee ballot from the Office of the Executive Coordinator forty-five days prior to the election, and returned it on or before the fifteenth day prior to the election. Such Absentee Ballots shall be counted in the vote tally in the first ballot at the Annual General Meeting and will not be included in any voting subsequent to that.** Voting by proxy is prohibited.

9. The election shall be by secret ballot according to the rules set down in the By-Laws.

10. Elected officers shall assume their office at the close of the Annual General Meeting at which the respective officers are elected. If an office is actually vacated, the one newly elected shall assume that office immediately upon election.

11.

12. If either the Treasurer or the Secretary becomes unable to fulfill the term of office, the President, after consultation with the Vice President and Past President, will appoint an interim Treasurer or Secretary who will hold office until the next Annual General Meeting, at which time there will be an election to fill the unexpired term of office, if any.

BYLAWS

17. The elections of officers of the Society will be carried out in accordance with Article IX of the Constitution. The method of election follows:

For the election of single offices:

1. The results shall be determined by an absolute **majority of the active members present and voting and the active members voting by official Absentee Ballot** and voting. If an absolute majority is not reached on the first ballot, the names of those receiving the two highest number of votes shall again be proposed to the **electorate present at the Annual General Meeting.** In case of a tie for any of the offices, one more ballot shall be taken for that office in which the tie resulted.

For the election of the Consultors:

1. There shall be at least four nominees for the office of Consultor, plus any others who may be nominated from the floor. Members shall, on one ballot, vote for two Consultors. If anyone names the same Consultor twice, that vote for this office shall be considered invalid. **In the first ballot, an election shall be determined by an absolute majority of the active members present and voting and the active members voting by official absentee ballot.**
   a. If an absolute majority is not reached by anyone on the first ballot, the names of the top three candidates shall again be proposed to the electorate. The active membership present at the AGM, shall vote for two candidates. The two with the highest number of votes are considered elected.
   b. If in the first ballot only one person receives an absolute majority, the other top two candidates shall be placed on the second ballot. The two with the most number of votes are considered elected.
   c. If on the first ballot there are three or four persons who have a majority of the votes, the two with the most votes shall be considered elected.

2. Any ties not taken care of in the above procedure shall be resolved by lot.

3. The ballot for the election of all Officers and Consultors shall be prepared by the Office of the Executive Coordinator before the Annual General Meeting. Extra nominations for all offices shall take place before any office is voted on. After all the nominations have taken place, the members will mark their ballots, thereby voting for all offices at one time. The run-off elections, if necessary, shall be held by using unprinted ballots, but again all at one time.

19. To amend these By-Laws there is needed the approval of the Board of Governors and the consent of a majority of the active members present and voting at the Annual General Meeting at which the amendment is proposed. Without the approval of the Board of Governors, these By-Laws may be amended in the same manner as the Constitution itself in accordance with the provisions of Article XII:

1. That the proposal to amend the Constitution has been filed by an active member with the Secretary at least three months prior to the Annual General Meeting of the Society at which that member intends his proposal to be submitted.

2. That notice of the proposed amendment has been sent to each active member of the Society at the last known mailing address not less than one month in advance of that Annual General Meeting mentioned in No. 1a of this Article.

IMPLEMENTATION BY MEANS OF: Board of Governors

COST: Printing and postage.

Patricia Dugan of Canon Law Books, Inc. in Philadelphia and a member of the Board of Governors spoke in favor of the resolution and noted that 620 active members are not able to be present at this annual convention for a variety of reasons. Absentee ballots would be beneficial for the senior members who are unable to travel.

Brother Pat Shea of the Diocese of Springfield in Illinois spoke against the resolution and recommended voting by mail instead of absentee ballots.

Anna Marie Chamblee of the Diocese of Fort Worth spoke against the resolution and stated that absentee ballots would preclude nominations for office from the floor.

Cherry Clark of Baltimore commented that she is a self-employed canonist who takes her membership very seriously and prefers to retain the voting process as it currently is.

Rev. David Szatkowski of the Diocese of Jackson spoke against the resolution and stated that absentee ballots do not provide the opportunity to vote if nominations from the floor occur.

Rev. Michael Boccaccio of the Diocese of Bridgeport noted that if someone has an emergency arise and is called away from the annual meeting, that person is not able to vote.

Deacon Jerry Jorgensen of the Archdiocese of Dubuque spoke against the resolution and recalled that this issue was discussed at a previous canon law convention where it was determined that support for absentee ballots was lacking. He suggested that it would be best to have all voting handled by mail or to continue with the same procedure which is now in place.

The Chair called the question on the resolution. The resolution was not adopted by the membership.

Resolution 4

The Resolutions Committee moved the resolution.

PROPOSED BY: Board of Governors

TITLE: Resolution on Persecuted Christians

STATEMENT OF RATIONALE:

WHEREAS, the civil war in Syria and the violence in Iraq have brought suffering, persecution and martyrdom to religious minorities, especially affecting untold numbers of Catholics, Orthodox and other Christian faithful.

WHEREAS, the scourge of war has resulted in millions of Syrian refugees – including families and children – within Syria, in neighboring countries and as far away as Europe.

WHEREAS, this year marks the twenty-fifth anniversary of the promulgation of the *Codex Canonum Ecclesiarum Orientalium* by Pope Saint John Paul II so that the Catholic Church might "breathe with two lungs".

WHEREAS, the Canon Law Society of America was established to promote justice in the Latin and Eastern Catholic Churches.

BE IT RESOLVED that the Canon Law Society of America, gathered in Pittsburgh, Pennsylvania for its seventy-seventh annual Convention, stands in prayerful solidarity with the Catholic, Orthodox and other Christian faithful of Syria and Iraq as they bear witness to the Gospel of Jesus Christ and share in His sufferings for the salvation of the world.

We further commit ourselves as individuals to do what we can to raise awareness of this concern, to provide for humanitarian relief, to promote a peaceful and just resolution of the crisis, and to undertake acts of prayer, penance and solidarity with and on behalf of our fellow Christians and all those suffering as a result of this armed conflict.

IMPLEMENTATION BY MEANS OF: A letter from the President of the CLSA sent to the Melkite Patriarch Relief Fund.

COST: Postage.

Rev. Manuel Viera of the Diocese of Tucson and a member of the Board of Governors spoke in favor of the resolution and stressed the need for prayerful support of those Christians who are being persecuted for their faith.

Msgr. John Sekellick of the Byzantine Eparchy of Passaic spoke in favor of the resolution and reiterated that many have suffered tremendously for their faith.

Rev. Andres Ligot of the Diocese of San Jose spoke in favor of the resolution and stressed the importance of publishing it in *Proceedings*.

The President called the question on the resolution. The resolution was adopted by the membership with one opposed and one abstention.

Resolution 5

The Resolutions Committee did not move the resolution.

PROPOSED BY: Kurt Martens, Roch Pagé, Robert J. Kaslyn, William L. Daniel, Sean Sheridan, R. Paul Beach, James Goodwin, Peter O. Akpoghiran, Nicholas Kastenholz, Richard Welch, William Elder, James F. Pereda, Mark Steffl, John Boyle, Ramil E. Fajardo, Ed Condon, Jason Gray, Anna Marie Chamblee, Shane Kirby, Jason Asselin, Eileen Magdalen Ross, Brian T. Austin, Daniel Quinan, Sean T. Doyle, Albert A. Della Russo, Raphael Lee, Anthony Omenihu, Matthew Glover, Benedict Nguyen, Nwazi Nyirenda, Rob Graffio, Joseph V. McCabe, Jonathan Wisneski, Silvana Usandivaras, Robert Zilliox, Joseph Arsenault.

TITLE: Proper Implementation of the Motu Proprios on Marriage Procedures

STATEMENT OF RATIONALE:

WHEREAS, Pope Francis has recently promulgated two motu proprios to reform the canonical process for the declaration of nullity of marriage, whereby on the one hand the requirement for a double conformity of affirmative sentences was abolished, and on the other hand an abbreviated briefer procedure before the diocesan Bishop was introduced;

WHEREAS, while the procedural requirements to arrive at the declaration of nullity of marriage have been lessened, the presumption of validity of the marital bond remains nevertheless intact;

WHEREAS, the removal of the procedural safeguards which have been in place for centuries may jeopardize the rights of all involved and may give rise to an erroneous misunderstanding of *the processus brevior* as a means for granting a "no-fault Catholic divorce", as has been already demonstrated in comments made in the secular press by those lacking any canonical training;

WHEREAS, the motu proprios mentioned above introduce the possibility of the testimony of one party constituting "full proof" in particular circumstances;

WHEREAS, the Canon Law Society of America recalls the many valuable lessons learned from the practice of the American Procedural Norms concerning the maintenance of a credible standard of proof and the centrality of moral certitude to every decision;

WHEREAS, the instructor and assessor in the *processus brevior* are not explicitly required by the text to be well-trained, properly degreed canon lawyers or even expert or knowledgeable about canon law;

WHEREAS, in the absence of formalities and rigors of the procedural law of the ordinary process, it is essential that all those assisting the diocesan Bishop be truly expert in the law itself and in the jurisprudence of the Roman Rota, which can most easily be met by utilizing degreed canon lawyers;

WHEREAS, given the immediate and personal involvement of the diocesan Bishop in the *processus brevior* and the increased scrutiny to which his decisions will be subjected, it is essential that decisions reached in his name, for his signature, conform to the highest standards of probity and justice and represent an earnest and humble seeking of the truth;

BE IT RESOLVED, that the Canon Law Society of America underscores the centrality of the teaching of the indissolubility of the bond of marriage to the entire process for a declaration of nullity, urges all involved in the work of tribunals to guard jealously the teaching on indissolubility, and recommends the involvement of well-trained, properly degreed canonists in the new procedures, to help safeguard and serve the essential ministry of justice;

BE IT FURTHER RESOLVED, that the Canon Law Society of America recommends to all ecclesiastical tribunals of the United States that, in implementing the reforms of the two motu proprios, they carefully regard the clear intention of the Roman Pontiff that the full process for determining causes of nullity is, and remains, the ordinary process and that the *processus brevior* is intended as an exceptional means for processing cases of an unusual nature;

BE IT FURTHER RESOLVED, that the Canon Law Society of America observes that full probative value to the testimony of the parties be assigned only after considering other indications and supporting factors including consistency or inconsistency, uncertainty or vacillation, and corroboration;

BE IT FURTHER RESOLVED, that the Canon Law Society of America notes that a foundational principle of justice is the preservation of the right of defense; as such the *processus brevior* is suitable only for those cases where both parties actively consent to its use;

BE IT FURTHER RESOLVED, that, in the implementation of the provisions of the motu proprios, ecclesiastical tribunals are strongly encouraged to make a renewed commitment to the dignity of the office of the defender of the bond and to take all measures possible and proper to safeguard their freedom of conscience in their exercise of the right of appeal;

BE IT FURTHER RESOLVED, that the President of the Canon Law Society of America convey the contents of this resolution to the President of the United States Conference of Catholic Bishops;

IMPLEMENTATION BY MEANS OF: A letter from the President of the CLSA to the President of the USCCB.

COST: Less than $25.00

The Chair asked if one of the authors wished to move the resolution; Dr. Kurt Martens moved the resolution, and this was duly seconded.

The Chair indicated that the Board of Governors does not support the resolution and called for discussion.

Rev. Tom O'Donnell of the Diocese of Pittsburgh spoke against the resolution. Though he does not have a JCL degree, he has many years of experience as well as a certificate in related canonical studies and therefore opposes the resolution as presented since he and others would not be able to work on such possible cases in the Tribunal.

The Chair reminded the attendees not to applaud or otherwise indicate support or opposition to what a speaker states.

Dr. Kurt Martens, professor of canon law at The Catholic University of America, spoke in favor of the resolution and indicated that not all of those who are supportive of it are present at this meeting. He stated that Pope Francis has given us a great instrument and has given us the "what", but we need the "how" and believes that the resolution provides that. He commented that it is not a resolution in opposition but is a positive resolution.

Rev. John Porter of the Diocese of Grand Rapids opposes the resolution and specifically objects to the "Whereas" clause which refers to the "failed practice of the American Procedural Norms"; he believes that those were not a failure. He and others have worked in Tribunals both before and throughout the time of the American Procedural Norms which provides perspective for both periods of time.

Rev. Mark O'Connell of the Archdiocese of Boston spoke in opposition to the resolution since he considers it as too premature to make a statement.

Rev. Michael Boccaccio of the Diocese of Bridgeport spoke against the resolution. Though he is not a canonist, he has other degrees and much experience in canon law, as well as has been a member of the CLSA for thirty years and feels that the resolution does not respect those who have that experience which has been gained over many years.

Rev. Phil Brown, rector of the Theological College and member of the Board of Governors, noted a point of order for speakers to address the Chair and not others who are present.

Rev. Michael Boccaccio accepted that point of order.

Timothy Olson of the Diocese of Fargo read a portion of the response from the Pontifical Council for Legislative Texts regarding the required consent of the respondent in using the *processus brevior*.

Jeffrey Staab of the Diocese of Richmond believes that the resolution is too wordy and offered a friendly amendment to delete the second, fourth, fifth, sixth, and seventh "Whereas" clauses as well as the third, fourth, and fifth "Be it Resolved" clauses. The Chair inquired of the authors whether the friendly amendment was accepted; the authors replied that the friendly amendment was not accepted.

Silvana Usandivaras of the Archdiocese of New York spoke in favor of the resolution. She indicated that she is originally from the Holy Father's hometown in Argentina and believes that the intention of the motu proprios is to provide a simpler procedure for places in the world such as Argentina and remote areas, and is not issued primarily with the USA in mind. Canonists are in the process of making recommendations to the bishops.

Rev. Greg Luyet of the Diocese of Little Rock spoke against the resolution. He is concerned that the tone may appear to be arrogant in places, especially since it attempts to remind bishops of what their job is. He believes that the language seems to have an inflammatory tone and that it would be inopportune to support this resolution.

Most Rev. Thomas John Paprocki of the Diocese of Springfield in Illinois and member of the Canonical Affairs and Church Governance committee of the USCCB, rose to speak in favor of the resolution and stated that the wording is respectful of the Holy Father and the bishops. He does not consider the resolution as making demands or being critical, but believes it to be canonically sound and helpful as it offers suggestions.

Anna Marie Chamblee of the Diocese of Fort Worth spoke in favor of the resolution and believes that no dissent is present in it. She indicated that the authors support the motu proprios and hope for uniformity of implementation. She stated that the information contained in the letter from the Pontifical Council for Legislative Texts in regard to the required consent of the respondent in the *processus brevior* is important since it provides clarity that simply citing the respondent without receiving any response is not sufficient for the respondent's consent.

Msgr. Jack Alesandro of the Diocese of Rockville Centre spoke against the resolution and considers it to be presumptuous since no practice has taken place yet.

Bonnie Landry of the Diocese of Lake Charles opposes the resolution and considers the word "abolished" in the first "Whereas" clause not to reflect the respondent's right to lodge a personal appeal against an affirmative decision.

Rev. James Goodwin of the Diocese of Fargo stressed the importance of proper implementation of the motu proprios so that they are used in the manner in which Pope Francis intended.

Rev. Thomas Cronkleton of the Diocese of Cheyenne and a member of the Resource and Asset Management Committee and the Board of Governors offered a friendly amendment. In the fifth "Whereas" clause, strike "failed". In the seventh "Whereas" clause, strike "degreed canon lawyers and" and insert "which can most easily be met by utilizing degreed canon lawyers" after "Rota". In the first "Be it resolved" clause, strike "calls for" and insert "recommends"; strike "only"; strike "without having recourse to non-canonists"; strike "better" and insert "help". In the second "Be it Further Resolved" clause, strike "when assigning" and strike "such testimony must be manifestly disinterested and above suspicion and ordinarily cannot come from a party with an obvious interest in a decision of nullity, including those who have already entered a second merely civil union".

The Chair informed Rev. Thomas Cronkleton that the time had expired. Then, the Chair inquired whether the new wording was accepted as a friendly amendment by the authors. The authors did accept the new wording as a friendly amendment, and it was duly seconded.

Rev. Thomas Cronkleton came forward to integrate his changes into the text. The changes will be made to the text.

The Chair then inquired whether the amended resolution was ready to read, but work still continued on the revision of the text.

A point of order was questioned regarding the ability to amend "Whereas" clauses as opposed to amending the "Be it Resolved" clauses. The parliamentarian responded that "Whereas" clauses may be amended, though the vote is for the "Be it Resolved" clauses.

The Chair expressed that the new language will be projected onto the screens for all to view.

The Chair then continued discussion regarding the resolution since the new wording was still being written into the text.

Rev. Robert Kaslyn, SJ, dean of the School of Canon Law at The Catholic University of America spoke in favor of the resolution. He noted that Archbishop Tobin opened this convention with his talk on the practical applications of *communio* in the Church, and Fr. Kaslyn stated that the resolution reflects that ecclesiology. Only the Holy Spirit is able to bring order and unity from different charisms in the Church. Division is created when we remain closed to our own particular way of doing things. If we let ourselves be led by the Holy Spirit, conflict will not be present.

Rev. David Szatkowski, of the Diocese of Jackson spoke in opposition of the resolution which he believes rushes too far too fast.

The Chair indicated that the question before us is whether the authors would now allow Rev. Thomas Cronkleton to complete the formulation of his friendly amendment; the authors of the resolution accepted that, and this was duly seconded. The changes will be made to the text.

The Chair indicated that another comment would be made, and then, the amended resolution would be read to the attendees.

Rev. Oliver Angel of the Diocese of Brownsville spoke against the resolution and commented that it is unlikely for non-canonist bishops to choose non-canonists to instruct the *processus brevior*. If a bishop has a canon law degree, three degreed canonists do not need to instruct the case.

The new wording of the resolution was then completed.

The Chair requested that the amended resolution be read. Mrs. Susan Mulheron read the entire amended resolution to the attendees.

The Chair inquired whether the assembly was ready for the question, and several people answered in the affirmative.

An inquiry was posed regarding whether the question is on the amendment. The Chair replied that the question is on the resolution.

The Chair then asked whether the body was ready for the question on the amended resolution, and a few people replied in the affirmative.

As the Chair then began to ask the question by stating, "Those who are in favor of the amended resolution as read, please indicate by …", another question was posed regarding whether the vote is on the amendment or the resolution, and the Chair replied that the assembly is voting on the amended resolution.

Several at once again inquired whether the vote is on the amendment or the resolution. The Chair replied that the vote is on the amended resolution which was accepted as a friendly amendment.

Another friendly amendment was offered. It was recommended that in the second "Be it Further Resolved" clause, to strike "when assigning" and to add "be assigned" after "parties". The Chair asked whether that change is accepted as a friendly amendment by an author, and an author replied that it was accepted as a friendly amendment.

The Chair then asked the body whether they were ready for the question. Several answered in the affirmative.

The Chair began to ask the question, and an attendee then inquired regarding the continuation of the discussion. The Chair stated that the body is ready for a vote.

Many attendees together stated, "Call the question."

Having heard the many interventions, the Chair called the question. Those who were in favor of the amended resolution were asked to raise the green card. The vote was inconclusive, and so, the Chair then requested a hand count.

Those who were opposed to the amended resolution were asked to raise the red card. The vote was inconclusive, and so, the Chair requested a hand count.

Those who were abstaining from voting on the amended resolution were asked to raise the yellow card. The Chair requested a hand count of the abstentions.

The Chair then announced that after counting the votes, the resolution was not adopted.

The results of the votes by hand count were as follows:

In favor: 71
Against: 129
Abstentions: 4

The resolution was not adopted by the membership.

The Chair then thanked all attendees for the discussion and the contributions which were provided. A special word of thanks was given to the Resolutions Committee which was received with applause.

Old Business

The Chair then opened the floor to discuss any Old Business of interest to the assembly. There was none.

New Business

The Chair opened the floor to discuss any New Business of interest to the assembly. There was none.

Varia

Greetings by Officials of Canon Law Societies

The Chair then invited visiting officials of other Canon Law Societies to the podium to address the assembly.

Sister Maria Casey, President of the Canon Law Society of Australia and New Zealand, brought the cordial greetings of the CLSANZ to the attendees of this convention. 2016 will mark the 50th anniversary of the CLSANZ, and its annual convention will be held in Queensland. The CLSA was thanked for all of its work and contributions to the field of canon law.

Monsignor Gordon Read, President of the Canon Law Society of Great Britain and Ireland, extended the good wishes of the CLSGB&I and is thankful for the warm welcome he has received. The attendees were invited to the annual conference which will be held in Galway. Though the website has been under construction during the past year, it is being redesigned and will launch in the near future.

Rev. Eric Dunn, President of the Canadian Canon Law Society, shared the greetings of the CCLS. Appreciation for the invitation to attend this convention was expressed. The 2015 convention, which will be held in Gatineau, marks the 50th anniversary of this Society. He is appreciative for the collaboration which has occurred over the years between the CLSA and the CCLS.

Rev. Totti of the Canon Law Society of the Antilles represented Rev. John Persaud who was not able to be present at this convention. Theirs is a small society, and many do not have degrees in canon law but graciously offer their services to the Church. He appreciates the hospitality which has been extended to him at this meeting.

Adjournment

There being no further business, the Chair entertained a motion to adjourn the meeting. The motion was seconded, and passed unanimously.

At 1:30 p.m., Reverend Monsignor Michael Souckar thanked many and formally closed the Seventy-Seventh Business Meeting of the Canon Law Society of America.

Respectfully submitted,

Ms. Mary Gen Blittschau
Secretary

Varia

Convention Mass Homily

Reverend Monsignor Michael A. Souckar

It could be said that we have gathered for this annual convention of the Canon Law Society of America in the wake of the recent apostolic visit of Pope Francis to the United States of America (and Cuba). The Holy Father's visit has generated much enthusiasm among Catholics and non-Catholics alike. It reminded me of the second pastoral visit to the United States by Pope Saint John Paul II in 1987, a visit that started in Miami. As a fourth year seminarian, I had the opportunity to serve the Papal Mass. You might remember that the Mass in Miami was suspended due to torrential rains and terrible lightning, something that can be typical of South Florida. Some eight months later, I was ordained a priest by Archbishop Edward McCarthy and assigned to Holy Family Parish in North Miami, a parish with increasing ethnic diversity and decreasing financial income. I vividly recall that for my first year as a priest, every once and a while – but with regularity – someone would come to Confession who had been away from the Church for many years. The penitent would say that the visit of Pope John Paul II so many months before was the reason why he or she was returning to the sacraments.

I am confident that the same will happen for months to come in the wake of Pope Francis' visit. It will happen in the confessional. Will we priest-confessors be merciful judges? It will happen at Mass, when someone who has been away from the sacraments for a long time decides one Sunday morning to give it another try. Will that person simply be a nameless stranger to ushers and the regular parishioners? It will happen at parish and school offices. Will the first question the receptionist asks be, "Are you a registered member of our parish?" It will happen at chancery and tribunal offices when e-mail messages, phone calls and letters arrive from people who only know what Pope Francis said as redacted by the media. When all these encounters happen, what will our response be? Will we be agents of *communio* to welcome those who have lived on the periphery? Will we turn to the structures of the Church to correct and discipline, or use these same structures with integrity to promote reconciliation? How will we as canonists and ministers of the Gospel maneuver in the wake of the Papal visit and recent developments in canon law?

As someone who was born and raised in Fort Lauderdale, I am comfortable in a city like Pittsburgh with water on so many sides. If you have ever been out on the water, you know that boats can create a lot of wake. Should you be out on the Allegheny, Monongahela, or Ohio River on a beautiful spring day with many other boaters, you know that the waters can get turbulent. The wake from each boat moves out, and as it hits the river bank, the energy bounces back, creating even more waves moving in opposite directions. When the waves are turbulent like this, the boat captain has to make a choice as to how to navigate the waters. One option is to give greater power to the engine and plow through the waves. If he does this, the captain risks damaging the boat and possibly tossing the passengers overboard. Alternatively, the captain can pull back on the engine's power and drift cautiously through the waves. If the captain does this, there is the risk of the waves crashing over the boat, soaking the passengers and even possibly capsizing the boat. In such a turbulent situation, a captain must exercise good judgment, knowing just how much to push the boat so as to fight the waves and how much to pull back and ride them out.

My friends, we are not captains of the Bark of Peter but we have been called to be assistants. We must be wise and prudent in our judgments as canonists, knowing when to plow ahead and when to pull back. We must allow the breath of the Holy Spirit to fill the sails of the boat and allow the same Spirit to determine its course. We are merely servants.

Before I conclude, allow me to say a few words about the Gospel selection which often is read during our annual convention. As we heard, Jesus castigates and scolds the Pharisees and the scholars of the law for their hardness of heart and their unwillingness to help others with the burdens of the law. However, we should not forget the context of this encounter. Jesus was invited by a Pharisees to his home for dinner, an invitation that he accepted. It seems that our Lord was rather non-discriminate in accepting invitations to meals. He dined with the Pharisees who hardly were his fans. He ate in the homes of Matthew and Zacchaeus and their friends, who were not held in high esteem by their fellow Jews. He was a guest of Martha, Mary, and Lazarus, where he appreciated their hospitality but taught the importance of having an open and docile heart to listen to the Teacher. Finally, there was the Last Supper with his Apostles, where he who was Master washed their feet and at which he gave us the Eucharist, that greatest encounter of *communio* which we can experience in this life.

This evening, it is the Lord who invites us to this Eucharistic banquet to enter into *communnio* with the Blessed Trinity and with one another. As we do so, may I suggest that we, like the Apostles, need to have our feet washed. In fact, like Peter, we need to have not only our feet washed, but our hands and our heads washed as well. We need to be transformed by the sacraments, the wisdom of the Holy Spirit, and the guidance of the Church, to be canonists who prudently engage ecclesial structures for the good of souls. Let us pray that we will maneuver the wake of the recent Papal visit, the *motu proprios* changing marriage nullity procedures, and the Synod on the family presently under way in Rome, as agents of *communio* and faithful disciples of Jesus Christ, the merciful judge.

VARIA

ROLE OF LAW CITATION
Reverend Monsignor Michael A. Souckar

Since 1973, it has been the practice of the Canon Law Society of America to confer its highest honor on someone who has contributed in a particularly positive manner to the high ideals of this scholarly society, at service to the Church's mission to preach the Gospel of Jesus Christ and to exercise justice in accord with the truth and tempered by mercy.

As the Universal Church observes the Year of Consecrated Life, this year's Role of Law recipient has given faithful witness to the evangelical counsels of poverty, chastity and obedience for 49 years.

Our honoree, a native of Pawtucket, Rhode Island, was taught by religious sisters in secondary school and later entered religious life with the same community. Her vocation has led her to roles of service in the Church that she never could have anticipated, even after earning both the licentiate and doctorate in canon law at The Catholic University of America. Going beyond the usual works undertaken by women religious, our honoree was repeatedly called upon to serve the Church in ever more challenging and significant roles. Becoming the first woman religious to have "this" or "that" job became so common that it was, I dare say, no longer exceptional. Her talents, skills, knowledge and dedication to the mission of the Church were her credentials. And that was enough.

As a teacher, our honoree has been a professor of canon law at CUA (where she taught religious law to my JCL class, the class of 1994). We were only one small group of many whom she has taught, whether in the classroom, at convention seminars for the CLSA or other Societies – canonical and non-canonical – in published scholarly articles, or simply by a friendly word of instruction, guidance or counsel.

As an executive, our honoree has held roles of responsibility at the diocesan level, within her religious community, for groups of religious communities, and for the Conference of Bishops. With determination and with grace she has guided these respective authorities, even during turbulent times, to make decisions in accord with the Gospel and the law of the Church, and she has most ably assisted in the implementation of those decisions. She has been a loyal and active member of this society since 1984, and has served on several committees, the Board of Governors, and in the role of Executive Coordinator and President.

Dear friends, during this Year of Consecrated Life, please join me in congratulating the 2015 recipient of the Role of Law Award, a Sister of Mery and a daughter of the Church, **Sister Sharon Euart, R.S.M**.

VARIA

ROLE OF LAW RESPONSE
Sr. Sharon A. Euart, R.S.M.

There really are no words to express adequately my deep appreciation to the Board of Governors and Msgr. Michael Souckar for the honor you have given me by adding my name to the list of recipients of the Role of Law Award. I am humbled and privileged to join such renowned company. I am grateful to the Society and to all of you with whom I wish to share this honor, for I have been blessed to witness your profoundly good and generous spirit in your dedication and devotion to canonical ministry in our Church. I am also indebted to the Sisters of Mercy and the Archdiocese of Baltimore for the canonical education I received from some of the most distinguished canonists in the Church, and for the opportunity to play a small part in the educational experience of some of you who are developing into fine canonists as the next generation of leaders of the Society.

In thinking of what I might reflect upon this evening, I was drawn to the Society's Constitution and its description of the intent of this award – "to choose someone in our midst who best exemplifies the ideals spelled out in the preamble of the Society's *Constitution*." The preamble proclaims "our desire to promote the use of every method of serving God's people that comes under the concept of law," always "mindful that church laws ought to be pastoral in character and made only to serve the people of God." If in some small way I have been able to exemplify this ideal, I am truly grateful, for it is also a fundamental Christian ideal.

We are disciples of Jesus, who defined his own ministry as that of one who seeks to serve and not to be served, so it is essential always to recall this self-definition, in whatever circumstances we have been granted to serve Jesus and his Church. Especially in such a specialized field as canon law, in which only comparatively few of us among the faithful have had the opportunity to become educated practitioners of the law, it is crucially important to recall Jesus' reminder to his disciples that those among them who would be first must be the servants of all.

Happily, reflecting the Second Vatican Council's *communio* ecclesiology, the Code of Canon Law incorporates the sense of Jesus' teaching when it states in canon 208, "From their rebirth in Christ, there exists among all the Christian faithful a true equality regarding dignity and action by which they all cooperate in the building up of the body of Christ according to each one's own condition and function." This common existence of the Christian faithful precedes all differences of function, charism and office (*LG* 32).

In my own varied experience as a canon lawyer, I have found among the most gratifying elements of the revised code its fidelity to the conciliar notion of the Church as a community of great diversity whose members, within the universal community, make up other communities within the whole which have their own dignity, rights and responsibilities. Recognizing the Church's unity in diversity, the council's teaching on ecclesial communion describes well the nature and the mystery of the Church.

We have all experienced within the Church as a hierarchical communion moments when it appears to be more hierarchy than communion. Yet, our law accepts the existence of, and defends the importance of, diversity, as well as unity for the common good and the orderly character of ecclesial life.

Of special interest to me as a woman religious, especially in my current ministry, is the body of law within the Code dealing with Institutes of Consecrated Life and Societies of Apostolic Life that respects the rich diversity that exists among religious institutes and societies. Women and men religious are united in their desire to follow Christ (c. 573 §1), yet challenged by the diverse ways and multiplicity of forms in which this common desire can be realized. The Final Report of the Apostolic Visitation of Women Religious in the United States and the Joint Final Report of the Doctrinal Assessment of the Leadership Conference of Women Religious highlight the importance of mutual relations between bishops and religious as a service to ecclesial communion through what Pope Francis describes as experiences and interactions of "encounter and dialogue." During this Year of Consecrated Life, Pope Francis invites women and men religious to become "experts in communion, witnesses and architects" of communion, creating a model of community built on the dignity of all persons and respect for each one's gift. He urges religious to listen to the Spirit in seeking ways to respond to the challenging realities facing many institutes in the United States and Europe as they "embrace the future with hope."

While serving the United States Conference of Catholic Bishops, I became familiar with a then-newly developing area of law necessitated by the emergence of episcopal conferences in the wake of Vatican II. Their incorporation into the revised Code was only the beginning of a struggle on the part of both the Holy See and the individual episcopal conferences to understand their roles vis-à-vis each other in strengthening ecclesial communion around matters calling for unity or unity in diversity.

Both religious institutes and the episcopal conference provide experiences of the splendid diversity of the Church. The institutes with their differing charisms, and apostolates and dioceses with their responsibility to respond to variegated Catholic populations with wide spectrums of needs, call forth Christian activity of sometimes bewildering complexity. In whatever ways canon law can serve the living of these charisms and the response to these needs, it is our duty and our blessing to be of assistance.

On a more local level, the implementation of the structures which provide opportunities of shared responsibility for laity, religious, and clergy in diocesan and parish governance of the Church has only been partially achieved in many places, and in other places hardly achieved at all. These participative structures are a means of pastoral revitalization assisting the Church in carrying out its mission. This is an important area of church life in which we as a Society have made valuable contributions over the years. Today, we might look for new and fresh ways to promote the fuller use of these means of participation as instruments of dialogue and experiences of community.

The strength of the Church is found in communion, which is the real source for witnessing the mutual relations among the disciples of Jesus Christ. Given "our desire [as a Society] to promote the use of every method of serving God's people that comes under the concept of law," it is incumbent upon us to serve our dioceses, religious institutes, and all the faithful in a way that reflects the image of the Church we find in the Code as a universal community made up of many communities, and individuals as well, working together "until [in the words of St. Paul] all of us come to the unity of the faith and of the knowledge of the Son of God, to maturity, to the measure of the full stature of Christ" (Ephesians 4.13).

As we approach the opening of the Extraordinary Jubilee of Mercy – a proclamation of Pope Francis close to my heart as a Sister of Mercy – I believe that we, as canon lawyers, have a special obligation to demonstrate how law within the Church functions in the service of the God of Mercy. Law is usually considered ideally to act objectively and impartially and not as a "respecter of persons" in a way that distorts justice. Yet, in declaring the Jubilee Year of Mercy, Pope Francis has called the Church to act in a profoundly personal way, exhorting us "never to stop at the surface of things, especially when we are dealing with a person…to look beyond, to focus on the heart to see how much generosity everyone is capable of." Francis tells us that the "appeal to a faithful observance of the law must not prevent attention from being given to matters that touch upon the dignity of the person." May we as a society and individuals in both teaching the law and applying it assist the faithful in knowing and responding to the God of Mercy.

Thank you for the confidence you have placed in me with this extraordinary honor. I am truly blessed by the people God has placed and continues to place in my life. I humbly accept this award and acknowledge with gratitude, mercy and love all those whose guidance and support made this possible. Thank you!

VARIA

U.S. TRIBUNAL STATISTICS
2014

Since 1975, the CLSA has published Tribunal Statistics annually in *Proceedings*. These statistics are provided voluntarily by participating tribunal offices in the United States. This year's statistical report was compiled by means similar to last year's report. Tribunals were asked to submit a copy of the report sent annually to the Apostolic Signatura, as well as some basic financial information. Submissions came by mail to the Office of the Executive Coordinator or by on-line entry via clsa.org. This change, implemented three years ago, has resulted in a more accurate comparison of statistics among U.S. tribunals.

Participation in the survey increased in comparison to last year. This year, the CLSA received information from 171 tribunals, compared to 165 last year. Included again in this year's report is the number of decisions found contrary to nullity from each reporting tribunal, with the percentage of negative decisions out of the total calculated. Following the same gradual trend as indicated in the past several years, the number of cases introduced and decisions made in American tribunals continues to decline, while expenses continue to rise.

Number of Tribunals Represented

2010	135
2011	130
2012	164
2013	165
2014	171

Documentary Cases Introduced					
Year	**2010**	**2011**	**2012**	**2013**	**2014**
Cases	4147	3774	3692	3581	4007

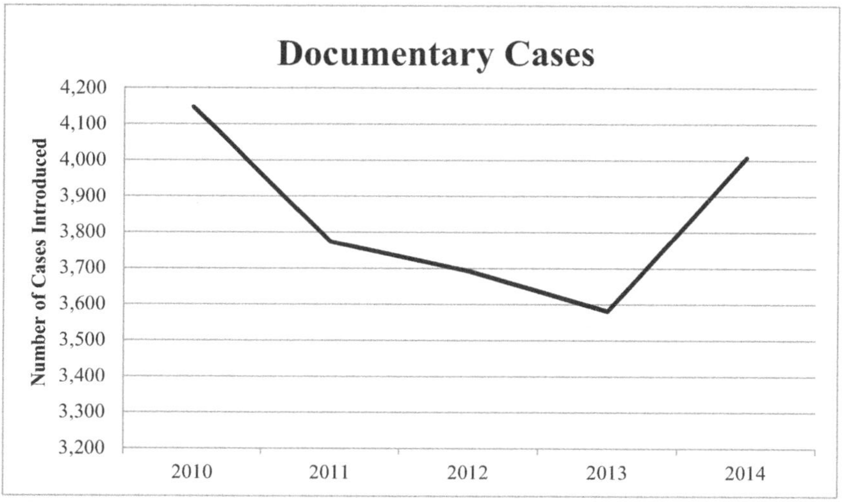

Formal Cases					
Year	**2010**	**2011**	**2012**	**2013**	**2014**
Decisions	14360	14314	14781	14045	15357
Introduced	16787	15589	16191	16462	14953
Abated	1284	1515	1593	1463	1434

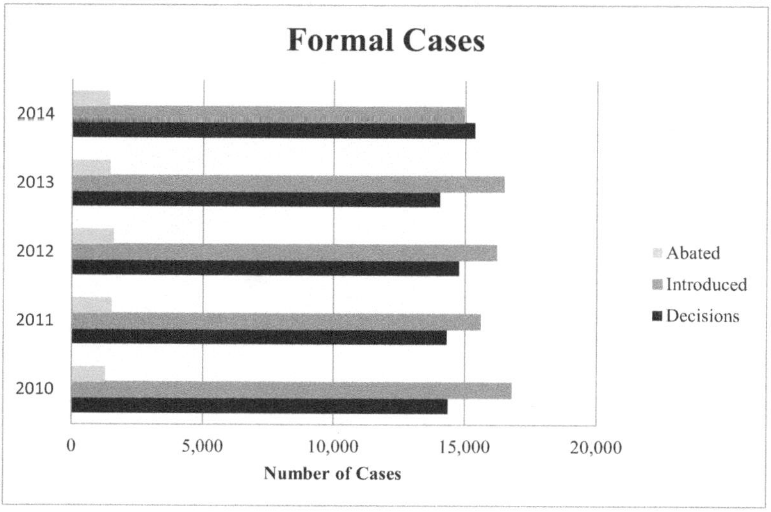

Fees and Expenses					
Year	**2010**	**2011**	**2012**	**2013**	**2014**
Fees Received	$5,193,872	$4,569,371	$4,824,170	$4,925,213	$5,079,797
Diocesan Subsidy	$6,477,648	$25,211,816	$45,148,059	$28,397,617	$29,796,433
Total Expenses	$31,612,970	$30,372,513	$30,073,434	$32,233,606	$30,736,442

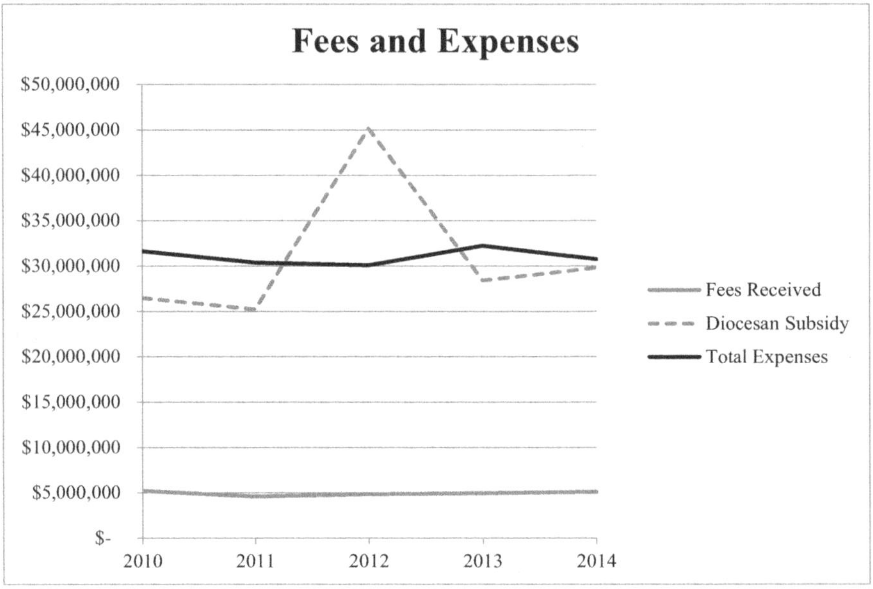

First Instance Tribunal Statistics 2014

(Arch)Diocese	Documentary Cases Closed	Formal Cases Held Over	Formal Cases Introduced	Sentence in Favor of Nullity	Sentence Contrary to Nullity	Total Formal Decisions (affirmative & negative)	% of Total Decisions Found Contrary to Nullity	Peremption/Renunciation	Total	Total Fees Received	Amount of Diocesan Subsidy	Total Annual Expenses
Albany		83	810	70	3	87	3%	8	81	$10,375.00	$104,586.00	$114,961
Alexandria	9	40	51	41	1	45	2%	3	45	$15,950.00	$180,010.00	$195,960
Allentown		99	115	121	0	126	0%	3	125			
Altoona-Johnstown	1	36	162	100	0	111	0%	11	111	$300.00	$73,000.00	$60,000
Anchorage		31	48	43	0	43	0%	4	47	$10,072.81	$88,329.59	$98,402
Atlanta		294	332	360	60	425	14%	5	425			
Austin	14	253	120	99	9	114	8%	6	114	$54,505.00	$337,273.00	$396,829
Baker	26	27	16	22	0	22	0%	5	27	$7,850.00	$106,682.24	$114,532
Baltimore	8	121	172	140	1	141	1%	5	146			
Baton Rouge	14	173	116	110	2	112	2%	18	130	$43,480.00	$220,184.35	$263,664
Beaumont	10	170	50	37	5	42	12%	0	42	$21,092.00	$111,981.00	$133,073
Belleville	13	107	58	57	0	63	0%	6	63	$11,150.00	$51,216.87	$62,366
Biloxi		108	43	41	0	51	0%	10	51	$4,435.00	$135,000.00	$162,092
Birmingham	5	112	62	70		70	0%	9	79	$26,605.00	$182,220.00	$213,707
Bismarck		50	42	29	0	29	0%	3	32	$10,328.00	$184,658.00	$194,986
Boise	14	233	112	119	2	130	2%	9	130			
Boston	3	211	117	158	1	170	1%	11	170			
Bridgeport	2	55	39	50	0	55	0%	5	55			
Brooklyn	3	130	86	87	2	103	2%	14	103	$106,038.00	$288,016.00	$340, 223
Brownsville	222	73	69	44	2	52	4%	6	52	$33,100.00	$37,976.00	$71,076
Buffalo	81	28	67	70	0	70	0%	0	70	$61,211.00	$272,290.00	$333,501
Burlington	3	39	45	32	3	35	9%	0	35	$0.00		
Camden		73	66	28	2	35	6%	5	35	$33,955.00	$289,169.13	$323,124.13
Charleston	11	72	96	59	12	106	11%	35	106	$76,266.00	$296,209.08	$372,475.08
Cheyenne	13	86	146	127	3	133	2%	3	133	$60,495.00	$333,232.00	$393,727
Charlotte	7	47	42	40	1	44	2%	3	44	$22,925.00	$100,055.00	$122,980
Chicago	9	194	333	302	1	306	0%	3	306	$237,290.00	$985,812.00	$1,223,103

First Instance Tribunal Statistics 2014

(Arch)Diocese	Documentary Cases Closed	Formal Cases Held Over	Formal Cases Introduced	Sentence in Favor of Nullity	Sentence Contrary to Nullity	Total Formal Decisions (affirmative & negative)	% of Total Decisions Found Contrary to Nullity	Peremption/Renunciation	Total	Total Fees Received	Amount of Diocesan Subsidy	Total Annual Expenses
Cincinnati		176	202	201	11	229	5%	17	229	$61,816.00	$400,884.00	$483,387.67
Cleveland	173	269	237	204	2	228	1%	22	228	$113,468.00	$587,601.00	$717,616.00
Colorado Springs		39	13	15	6	29	21%	8	29	$10,365.00	12, 171.96	280, 892.02
Columbus	9	125	182	180	2	182	1%	5	187	$0.00	$468,526.00	$575,951.00
Corpus Christi		147	57	102		102	0%	0	102	$21,016.00	$161,356.00	$182,372.00
Covington	10	42	57	64	0	67	0%	3	67			
Crookston	0	46	37	23	0	29	0%	6	29	$0.00	$161,620.00	$164,238.00
Dallas	41	215	279	148	0	248	0%	100	248	$46,810.00	$477,229.00	$524,039.00
Davenport	3	92	75	70	2	80	3%	8	80	$30,775.00	$118,588.00	$150,478.00
Denver	0	369	137	176	3	186	2%	7	186	$136,626.00	$0.00	$102,755.00
Des Moines	50	71	62			53	0%	0		$36,350.00	$57,590.00	$93,940.00
Detroit	9	163	277	239	4	281	1%	38	281	$25,375.00	$609,897.36	$635,272.36
Dodge City	1	15	32	31	0	37	0%	6	37	$2,750.00	$77,478.00	$80,228.00
Dubuque	7	153	112	126	4	138	3%	8	138	$46,711.00	$185,285.00	$232,146.00
Duluth		30	22	9	5	20	25%	6	20	$6,330.00		
El Paso		97	64	63	2	67	3%	2	67			
Erie	3	68	105	118	0	124	0%	6	124	$29,755.00	$330,273.00	$358,993.00
Evansville	3	3	60	37	0	51	0%	14	51	$14,130.00	$201,735.00	$215,865.00
Fairbanks		12	8	5		5	0%	0	5			
Fall River	64	92	48	48	0	54	0%	6	54			
Fargo	38	33	41	34	0	36	0%	2	36	$1,550.00	$237,832.53	$241,478.69
Fort Wayne-South Bend	79	94	101	32	13	56	23%	11	56	$5,185.00	$363,229.00	$358,044.00
Fort Worth	17	430	133	147	6	173	3%	20	173	$5,500.00	$1.00	
Fresno	215	157	140	118	0	118	0%	19	137	$87,903.00	$87,628.00	$275,500.00
Gallup		14	24	8	6	15	40%	1	15	$4,650.00	Total	$21,376.14
Gary	2	103	63	50	0	59	0%	0	50	$24,160.00		
Gaylord	0	52	36	38	3	43	7%	2	43	$0.00	$89,561.00	

First Instance Tribunal Statistics 2014

(Arch)Diocese	Documentary Cases Closed	Formal Cases Held Over	Formal Cases Introduced	Sentence in Favor of Nullity	Sentence Contrary to Nullity	Total Formal Decisions (affirmative & negative)	% of Total Decisions Found Contrary to Nullity	Peremption/Renunciation	Total	Total Fees Received	Amount of Diocesan Subsidy	Total Annual Expenses
Grand Island	32	75	38	39	0	43	0%	4	43	$7,100.00	$179,147.10	$186,247.10
Grand Rapids	79	152	118	137	1	155	1%	17	155	$0.00	$131,775.69	$131,775.69
Great Falls-Billings	26	17	25	11	0	14	0%	3	14	$825.00	$64,408.86	$65, 233.86
Green Bay		52	85	81	4	87	5%	0	85	$30,935.00	$125,690.00	$156,625.00
Greensburg	5	27	77			62	0%	0				
Harrisburg		312	158	163	6	175	3%	6	175	$81,184.00	$370,089.00	$451,273.00
Hartford	0	78	81	58	14	81	17%	9	81			
Honolulu	2	18	45	43	2	47	4%	2	47	$24,350.00	$78,043.00	$102,393.00
Houma-Thibodaux		37	38	46	0	46	0%	0	46	$12,665.00	-$59,361.00	-$72,026.00
Indianapolis	23	137	77	83	0	91	0%	8	91			
Jackson	10	28	34	41	0	56	0%	15	56	$0.00	$101,213.00	$101,213
Jefferson City	14	137	85	80	0			6	86	$0.00	$147,461.00	$147,461
Joliet	16	42	124	161	1	184	1%	22	184	$68,447.50	$473,567.67	$542,015
Kalamazoo		50	61	56	0	56	0%	0	56			
Kansas City - St. Joseph	14	138	85	72	0	74	0%	2	74			
Kansas City in Kansas	128	390	224	186	0	196	0%	10	196	$66,194.00	$227,000.00	$293,194
La Crosse								0		$41,935.00	$120,919.00	$149,134
Lafayette in Louisiana	10	174	127	82	24	109	22%	3	109	$44,240.00	$118,625.00	$8,738
Lafayette-in-Indiana	55	81	64	38	5	55	9%	12	55			
Lake Charles	6	84	57	47	1	50	2%	2	50	$14,412.00	$153,588.00	$167,999
Lansing	12	72	142	118	0	118	0%	15	133	$26,400.00	$434,213.30	$460,613
Laredo	56	33	32	19	0	19	0%	0	19	$14,323.00	$38,000.00	$39,364
Las Cruces								0		$19,480.00	$82,094.13	$101,574
Las Vegas		46	61	40	7	53	13%	6	53	$40,718.96	$193,888.43	$234,607

First Instance Tribunal Statistics 2014

(Arch)Diocese	Documentary Cases Closed	Formal Cases Held Over	Formal Cases Introduced	Sentence in Favor of Nullity	Sentence Contrary to Nullity	Total Formal Decisions (affirmative & negative)	% of Total Decisions Found Contrary to Nullity	Peremption/Renunciation	Total	Total Fees Received	Amount of Diocesan Subsidy	Total Annual Expenses
Lexington	9	22	67	49	0	56	0%	7	56	$0.00	$225.91	$225.91
Lincoln	0	57	37	40	0	45	0%	5	45			
Little Rock	38	88	142	127	7	161	4%	27	161	$28,675.00	$181,531.00	$210,206
Los Angeles								0		$65,247.50	$771,493.27	$836,740.77
Los Angeles, Eparchy of OLL	11	10	19	14	1	15	7%	0	15	$11,900.00	$3,350.00	$15,000
Louisville	23	14	116	111	0	111	0%	0	111	$18,827.00	$253,126.00	$271,953
Lubbock	48	85	51	45	0	47	0%	2	47	$6,535.00	$38,811.27	$54,846.27
Madison	4	86	21	25	23	55	42%	7	55	$13,270.00	$320,282.27	$333,552.27
Manchester								0		$27,350.00	$4,180.00	$31,530
Marquette	37	10	36	26	0	28	0%	2	28	$4,200.00	$0.00	$40,356.20
Memphis	0	81	60	65	1	68	1%	2	68	$1,850.00	$136,628.00	$138,070
Metuchen	1	112	80	75	1	80	1%	4	80	$48,535.00	$310,259.42	$358,794.42
Miami	3	191	217	198	8	233	3%	27	233			
Military Services	4	242	100	108	2	216	1%	106	216	$61,395.00	$155,636.00	$217,031
Milwaukee	3	241	184	185	0	185	0%	19	204	$50,762.00	$530,345.26	$581,107.26
Monterey		48	41	26	0	28	0%	2	28	$14,725.00	$89,674.00	$104,449
Nashville	20	138	114	49	14	76	18%	13	76	$0.00	$361, 631.00	$361, 631
New Orleans	15	198	122	102	18	123	15%	3	123	$59,350.00	$437,928.00	$497,278
New Ulm	11	43	18	22	0	27	0%	5	27	$1,000.00	$154,942.00	$155,942
New York	2	218	171	191	36	227	16%	14	241	$326,000.00	$973,894.00	$1,299,894
Newark	0	80	94	65	1	66	2%	14	80	$44,400.00	$432,474.00	$476,874
Newton, Melkite Eparchy	23	6	14	12	0	22	0%	1	13			
Norwich	0	43	37	32	0	32	0%	0	32	$7,600.00	$311,587.73	$319,187.73
Oakland	155	256	61	40	6	46	13%	17	63	$60,223.00	678, 421.00	$738,644
Ogdensburg		32	41	27	2	38	5%	9	38	$15,121.72	$50,932.26	$66,053.98

First Instance Tribunal Statistics 2014

(Arch)Diocese	Documentary Cases Closed	Formal Cases Held Over	Formal Cases Introduced	Sentence in Favor of Nullity	Sentence Contrary to Nullity	Total Formal Decisions (affirmative & negative)	% of Total Decisions Found Contrary to Nullity	Peremption/Renunciation	Total	Total Fees Received	Amount of Diocesan Subsidy	Total Annual Expenses
Oklahoma City	141	157	216	183	12	216	6%	21	216	$0.00	$138,000.00	$138,000
Omaha	1	276	114	92	11	110	10%	7	110	$38,629.00	$283, 983	$322,612
Orange		97	220	168	0	180	0%	12	170	$137,140.00	$784,700.00	$921,840
Orlando	0	68	277	236	55	291	19%	15	306			
Owensboro	12	93	62	57	0	63	0%	6	63	$10,125.00	$238,826.00	$248,951
Palm Beach	19	54	92	88	3	93	3%	2	93	$31,000.00	$3,558,844.00	$388,884
Parma, Byz. Eparchy	1	2	3	2	0	3	0%	1	3			
Passaic, Byz-Ruth Epar		17	6	6				1	7	$4,800.00	$18,000.00	$24,000
Paterson	0	152	43	34	6	40	15%	10	50	$40,370.00	$262,562.00	$302,932
Pensacola-Tallahassee	84	46	54	35	4	45	9%	6	45	$7,750.00	$60,682.00	$68,432
Peoria	10	111	124	129	0	129	0%	3	132	$61,597.00	$453,085.00	$510,610
Philadelphia Ukrainian Archepar	3	0	7	5	2	7	29%	0	7	$2,125.00	$0.00	$2,585
Phoenix	6	318	127	113	37	161	23%	11	161			
Phoenix, HPM Byz. Eparchy		3	3	3		3	0%	0	3			
Pittsburgh Byz. Archepar	8	4	5	9	0	9	0%	0	9	$4,865.00	$9,882.33	$10,062.33
Portland in Maine	82	90	114	120	0	120	0%	8	128	$35,000.00	$258,760.00	$293.76
Portland in Oregon	9	137	131	116	0	118	0%	2	118	$37,456.00	$0.00	$167,621
Providence		83	77	56	20	83	24%	7	83	$57,300.00	$259,178.00	$316,478
Pueblo	2	26	31	27	0	31	0%	4	31	$4,140.00	$165,933.00	
Raleigh	150	101	113	92	0	103	0%	11	103	$37,097.00	$231,780.00	$258,090

First Instance Tribunal Statistics 2014

(Arch)Diocese	Documentary Cases Closed	Formal Cases Held Over	Formal Cases Introduced	Sentence in Favor of Nullity	Sentence Contrary to Nullity	Total Formal Decisions (affirmative & negative)	% of Total Decisions Found Contrary to Nullity	Peremption/Renunciation	Total	Total Fees Received	Amount of Diocesan Subsidy	Total Annual Expenses
Rapid City	12	51	19	10	1	13	8%	2	13	$1,610.00	$59,278.00	$60,888
Reno	82	51	19	25	2	32	6%	5	32	$13,595.00	$149,751.34	$163,346.34
Richmond	12	128	155	158	5	173	3%	10	173	$0.00	$523,108.68	$523,108.68
Rochester	0	44	115	54	1	58	2%	3	58	$38,245.00	$139,416.00	$177,661
Rockford	98	69	99	130	1	135	1%	4	135			
Rockville Centre	8	436	235	194	67	292	23%	31	292	$212,725.00	$216,624.00	$429,349
Sacramento	9	195	98	103	32	193	17%	58	193			
Saginaw	49	29	72	62	0	66	0%	4	66	$2,075.00	$100,430.51	$102,580.51
Salina		54	52	58	0	62	0%	4	62	$14,000.00	$27,000.00	$41,100
Salt Lake City	32	8	75	62	3	69	4%	4	69	$11,735.00	103.123.05	114,858.05
San Angelo		48	50	38		38	0%	0	38	$8,200.00	$172,223.81	$180,423.81
San Antonio	23	127	250	242	5	250	2%	3	250	$130,350.00	$242,208.00	$372,558
San Bernardino	8	170	178	110	11	134	8%	13	134	$0.00	$0.00	$0.00
San Diego	3	257	240	123	3	144	2%	18	144	$56,866.00	$260,713.00	$317,579
San Jose	146	97	101	86	0	86	0%	11	86	$69,644.50	$438,532.14	
Santa Rosa	3	13	33	26	2	33	6%	2	30	$17,490.00	$72,719.00	$90,209
Savannah	8	24	54	44	4	61	7%	13	61	$16,661.63	$216,225.00	$188,029.90
Scranton	1	51	125	100	2	114	2%	12	114	$62,803.00	$257,721.00	$320,524
Seattle	27	207	180	147	1	152	1%	4	152	$84,687.00	$400,533.00	$549,751
Shreveport	8	34	21	42	0	42	0%	0	42	$17,050.00	$215,763.00	$232,813
Sioux City	1	50	71	51	0	57	0%	6	57	$210,003.00	$169,130.67	$190,133.67
Sioux Falls	0	36	58	42	0	46	0%	4	46	$17,300.00	$68,167.10	$85,467.10
Spokane	5	8	46	49		49	0%	0	49	$10,900.00	$14,499.00	$25,399
Springfield, IL	74	128	104	96	3	100	3%	1	100	$42,412.50	$131,029.73	$173,442.23
Springfield, MA	62	60	56	65	1	71	1%	5	71	$23,685.00	$169,097.00	$192,782

First Instance Tribunal Statistics 2014

(Arch)Diocese	Documentary Cases Closed	Formal Cases Held Over	Formal Cases Introduced	Sentence in Favor of Nullity	Sentence Contrary to Nullity	Total Formal Decisions (affirmative & negative)	% of Total Decisions Found Contrary to Nullity	Peremption/Renunciation	Total	Total Fees Received	Amount of Diocesan Subsidy	Total Annual Expenses
St. Augustine	146	209	130	127	5	155	3%	23	155	$57,395.00	$207,244.00	$248,544.19
St. Cloud								0		$40,000.00	$144,000.00	$173,000
St. Louis	13	272	185	129	15	170	9%	26	170	$122,211.00	$336,745.00	$458,956
St. Paul and Minneapolis	153	242	114	69	5	87	6%	13	87			
St. Petersburg		199				185	0%	0				
Stamford, Ukrainian Eparchy								0		$300.00	$0.00	$50.00
Steubenville	5	17	44	39	1	42	2%	2	42	$8,400.00	73,168,72	$81,568.72
Stockton	0	49	30	31	1	38	3%	6	38	$45,436.00	$99,668.00	$145,104
Superior		18	41	43		43	0%	0		$10,450.00	$92,004.85	$102,254.85
Syracuse		20	94	93	2	95	2%	3	98	$59,578.00	$17,339.00	$76,917
Toledo	125	86	138	146		162	0%	16	162			
Trenton	3	179	95	90	0	90	0%	5	95	$55,836.00	$276,137.00	$331,973
Tucson	2	112	43	38	0	52	0%	14	52	$28,921.00	$102,098.00	$130,389
Tulsa	74	17	69	73	3	73	4%	8	84	$940.00	$66,311.96	$67,251.96
Tyler		51	41	42	3	56	5%	11	56			
Victoria	5	10	43	36	0	36	0%	0	36	$0.35	$0.65	$45,000
Washington, DC	9	148	156	139	17	162	10%	6	162			
Wheeling-Charleston	66	126	82	94	11	109	10%	4	109	$0.00	$0.00	$0.00
Wichita	106	326	187	183	5	199	3%	11	199	$75,000.00	$55,000.00	$130,000
Wilmington	4	91	50	44	0	44	0%	0	44	$29,655.00	$167,346.00	$197,002
Worcester	2	46	50	30	0	30	0%	2	30	$17,812.00	$154,424.00	$172,235
Yakima								0		$20,355.00	$170,010.00	$154,860
Youngstown	8	109	65	63	0	68	0%	5	68	$17,252.92	$291,826.00	$305,020.62

Second Instance Tribunal Statistics 2014

(Arch) Diocese	Second Instance Pending at Beginning of Year	Introduced	Closed	Decree Confirmation	Sentence in Favor of Nullity	Sentence Contrary to Nullity
Baltimore	5	364	364	351	12	0
Boise	0	83	83	82	1	0
Boston	11	169	174	166	5	1
Bridgeport	13	28	32	25	3	2
Camden	20	34	41	35	1	5
Cleveland	11	321	313	0	313	1
Columbus	15	63	59	59	3	1
Covington	12	56	50	49	0	0
Davenport	0	47	47	47	0	0
Denver	10	81	86	86	86	0
Denver	10	81	86	86	86	0
Denver	10	81	86	86	86	0
Des Moines	0	39	39			
Detroit	46	462	434	432	0	2
Dubuque	24	188	188	181	0	2
Evansville	0	49	49	49	0	0
Fargo	3	14	13	13	0	0
Fort Wayne-South Bend	12	39	30	16	1	12
Fresno	10	53	60	60	0	0
Gary	7	48	50	50	50	0
Grand Rapids	22	190	189	189	0	0
Green Bay		203	203			
Hartford	6	73	77	75	1	1
Indianapolis	22	34	49	35	35	6
Kansas City in Kansas	11	215	200	200	200	0
Lafayette in Louisiana	4	46	49		48	1
Lafayette-in-Indiana	8	98	94		94	0
Lake Charles	9	50	45	47	47	0
Lexington	1	48	42	41	0	0
Louisville	28	103	123	123	0	0
Lubbock	0	0	0	45		

Second Instance Tribunal Statistics 2014

(Arch) Diocese	Second Instance Pending at Beginning of Year	Introduced	Closed	Decree Confirmation	Sentence in Favor of Nullity	Sentence Contrary to Nullity
Memphis	4	65	60	0	59	1
Metuchen	5	40	40	39	1	
Miami	79	730	731	716	1	8
Milwaukee	9	271	272	272	261	11
Nashville	26	78	104		102	2
New Orleans	15	403	397	380	11	5
Newark	5	170	170	170	0	0
Norwich	1	37	38	38	0	0
Oakland	33	143	105	105	20	0
Omaha	3	80	80	80	77	3
Orlando	0	0	0	0	0	0
Owensboro	19	66	65	47	2	0
Paterson, New Jersey	15	31	33	33	0	2
Philadelphia, Ukrainian Archeparchy	0	2	2	2	2	0
Phoenix	49	113	126	116	7	3
Portland in Maine	0	154	154	154	0	0
Portland in Oregon	9	203	197	197	0	0
Richmond	27	137	164	164	164	0
Rockford				131		
Saginaw	2	94	96	93	3	0
San Bernardino	19	88	107	107	0	1
San Diego	15	215	233	229	0	4
San Jose	16	94	85	85		1
Seattle	16	219	219	215	3	1
Sioux City	4	29	29	29	0	0
Sioux Falls	2	14	14		14	0
Springfield, Massachusetts	11	214	208	206	2	0
St. Paul and Minneapolis	269	240	285	260	13	10
Steubenville	4	56	54	0	54	0
Stockton	13	150	149	149	0	0

Second Instance Tribunal Statistics 2014

(Arch) Diocese	Second Instance Pending at Beginning of Year	Introduced	Closed	Decree Confirmation	Sentence in Favor of Nullity	Sentence Contrary to Nullity
Toledo	25	140	150	150		
Trenton	0	44	43	43	0	0
Washington, DC	39	200	229	226	0	3
Wheeling-Charleston	11	75	84	80	3	1
Wichita	0	256	256	256		
Youngstown	16	93	93	93	93	0

Varia

Contributors

Rev. Jobe J. Abbass, OFM Conv., JCD, Tenured Full Professor, Saint Paul University, Ottawa, ON, Canada

Very Rev. Anthony E. Bawyn, JCD, Judicial Vicar, Archdiocese of Seattle, Washington

Timothy J. Cavanaugh, JCL, Defender of the Bond, Diocese of Madison, Wisconsin

Rev. Thomas E. Cronkleton, Jr., JCD, Judicial Vicar, Diocese of Cheyenne, Wyoming

Very Rev. Lawrence DiNardo, JCL, Vicar-General/General Secretary, Diocese of Pittsburgh, Pennsylvania

Sr. Sharon Euart, RSM, JCD, Executive Director, Resource Center for Religious Institutes, Silver Spring, Maryland

Most Rev. Bernard A. Hebda, JCL, JD, Coadjutor Archbishop of Newark, New Jersey

Very Rev. Anthony Kerin, JCL, Episcopal Vicar for Marriage, Life & Family; Adjutant Judicial Vicar and Pastor, Archdiocese of Melbourne, VIC, Australia

Rev. Ronald Knott, D.Min, Founding Director of the Institute for Priests and Presbyterates, Saint Meinrad Seminary, St. Meinrad, Indiana

Michael Nobel, JCL, PhD, Professor, Saint Paul University, Ottawa, ON, Canada

Kelly E. O'Donnell, JCD, Judge/Canonical Consultant, Diocese of Fresno, California

Rev. Jaimes Ponce, JCD, Defender of the Bond, Diocese of Colorado Springs, Colorado

Rev. Msgr. John Renken, M.A. (Civil Law), STD, JCD, Vice Dean and Director of Graduate Studies, Faculty of Canon Law, Saint Paul University, Ottawa, ON, Canada

Brian B. Reynolds, Ed.D, Chancellor, Archdiocese of Louisville, Kentucky

Lynda Robitaille, JCD, Dean of Theology, St. Mark's College, Vancouver, BC, Canada

Brother Patrick T. Shea, OFM, JD, JCD, Vice-Chancellor, Diocese of Springfield in Illinois

Rev. Msgr. Michael A. Souckar, JCD, Adjutant Judicial Vicar and Pastor, Archdiocese of Miami, Florida

Most Reverend Charles C. Thompson, DD, JCL, Bishop of Evansville, Indiana

Most Rev. Joseph W. Tobin, C.Ss.R., MRE, M.Div., Archbishop of Indianapolis, Indiana

Varia

2015 Convention List of Participants

Jobe Abbass
Ottawa, ON
Wendy Abraham
Atlanta, GA
Peter Akpoghiran
New Orleans, LA
John Alesandro
Rockville Centre, NY
Timothy Alkire
Lafayette, IN
Anna Amato
San Diego, CA
Krystyna Amborski
San Francisco, CA
Daniel Andree
Chicago, IL
Oliver Angel
Brownsville, TX
Thomas Anslow
Los Angeles, CA
William Anton
Lubbock, TX
Charles Antonicelli
Washington, DC
Christopher Armstrong
Washington, DC
Das Arockia
Lexington, KY
Joseph Arsenault
Kansas City, KS
Kathleen Asdorian
Bethesda, MD
Anne Asselin
Ottawa, ON
Ronald Aubin
St. Petersburg, FL
Joseph Augustine
Charleston, WV

Jeffery Bacon
Cincinnati, OH
Diane Barr
Baltimore, MD
Nancy Barshick
Marianna, PA
Andrew Bartell
Sioux Falls, SD
Michael Barth
Covington, KY
Mary Ann Bartolac
Overland Park, KS
Virginia Bartolac
Kansas City, KS
Mariana Bartolillo
Venice, Florida
Carlotta Bartone
Philadelphia, PA
Nancy Bauer
Washington, DC
Anthony Bawyn
Seattle, WA
R. Paul Beach
Louisville, KY
John Beal
Erie, PA
John Bell
Plano, TX
Joseph Bellerive
Orlando, FL
Iden Bello
Laredo, TX
Matthew Bergschneider
Rockford, IL
Vincent Bertrand
Springfield, MO
Barbara Bettwy
Harrisburg, PA

Maria Bianco
Boston, MA
Rita-Mae Bissonnette
Portland, ME
Mary Gen Blittschau
Evansville, IN
Michael Boccaccio
Bridgeport, CT
Celeste Boda, OSB
Owensboro, KY
Douglass Bond
Chicago, IL
James Bonke
Indianapolis, IN
Marvin Borger
Toledo, OH
Paul Bouchard
Manchester, NH
John Boyle
Portland, Oregon
Michael Bradley
Chicago, IL
Sean Bransfield
Philadelphia, PA
Marie Breitenbeck
Atlanta, GA
Dexter Brewer
Nashville, TN
R. Richard Brickler
Rochester, NY
Timothy P. Broglio
Washington, DC
Steve Brown
Cincinnati, OH
Phillip Brown
Washington, DC
Anne Bryant
Houston, TX

Janette Buchanan
Nashville, TN
Michael Burchfield
Fresno, CA
Jeffrey Cabral
Fall River, MA
Jesus Cabrera
Milwaukee, WI
Steven Callahan
San Diego, CA
Luis Capacetti
Atlanta, GA
Giovanni Capucci
Denver, CO
Michael Cariglio
Youngstown, OH
John Caronan
Garden Grove, CA
James David Carter
Knoxville, TN
Maria Casey
Croydon, Australia
David Castronovo
Savannah, GA
Timothy Cavanaugh
Madison, WI
Martin Celuch
Youngstown, OH
Pablo Cepeda
Atlanta, GA
Deborah Cerullo
Providence, RI
Charles Chaffman
San Antonio, TX
Krikor Chahinian
San Antonio, TX
Margaret Chalmers
Greenville, SC
Anna Marie Chamblee
Fort Worth, TX
Paul Clark
Harrisburg, PA
J. Michael Clark
Owensboro, KY

Cherry Clark
Baltimore, MD
John Cody
Columbus, Oh
Oscar Coelho
Santa Fe, NM
Patrick Cogan
Sterling, VA
Edward Condon
Washington, DC
James Conn
Boston, MA
Jay Conzemius
Pittsburgh, PA
Patrick Cooney
Indianapolis, IN
James Coriden
Washington, DC
Paul Counce
Baton Rouge, LA
Derek Covert
Lake Charles, LA
John Crerand
Columbus, OH
Thomas Cronkleton
Cheyenne, WY
Joachim Culotta
Lafayette, IN
Barbara Anne Cusack
Milwaukee, WI
Vincent Cushnahan
Belfast, Nor. Ireland
William Daniel
Washington, DC
Catherine Darcy
Merion, PA
Jamin David
Baton Rouge, LA
Georges de Laire
Manchester, NH
Robert Deeley
Portland, ME
Jesus Del Angel Leon
Fresno, CA

Robert DeLand
Saginaw, MI
Louis DeNinno
Pittsburgh, PA
John Dermond
Trenton, NJ
James DeViese
Wheeling, WV
Melanie Di Pietro
Alexandria, VA
Javier Diaz
Trenton, NJ
Paul DiGirolamo
Philadelphia, PA
Anthony Dill
Harrisburg, PA
Lawrence DiNardo
Pittsburgh, PA
Francis Dolan
Chicago, IL
John Donovan
Syracuse, NY
Robert Duesdieker
Jefferson City, MO
Patricia Dugan
Philadelphia, PA
Eric Dunn
Charlottetown, PEI
Brian Dunn
Antigonish, NS
Frederick Easton
Bloomington, IN
Heather Eichholz
Owensboro, KY
William Elder
Yonkers, NY
Timothy Elmer
Syracuse, NY
Martins Emeh
Geneva, IL
Sharon Euart
Silver Spring, MD
Ramil Fajardo
Chicago, IL

Eric Fasano
Rockville Centre, NY
Thomas Feeney
Corpus Christi, TX
James Ferguson
Alexandria, LA
Thomas Ferguson
Arlington, VA
Christopher Ferrer
Austin, TX
Victor Finelli
Allentown, PA
Daniel Firmin
Savannah, GA
J. M. Fitzgerald
Richmond, VA
Kassandra Flores
Garden Grove, CA
Efrain Flores
Garden Grove, CA
Kenneth Fortener
New Hope, KY
Shannon Fossett
Portland, ME
John J. Foster
Washington, DC
Joseph Fox
Scranton, PA
Raphael Frackiewicz
Chicago, IL
Thomas Fransiscus
Reno, NV
Matthew Frisoni
Albany, NY
Canuto Fuentebella
Aruba
Matthew Furgiuele
Gaylord MI
Mark Gantley
Honolulu, HI
Stephen Garbitelli
Denver, CO
Esau Garcias
Orlando, FL
John Gargan
Dallas, TX
Paul Gargaro
Glasgow, UK
Joe Gehret
Indianapolis, IN
Elpidio Geneta
Wheeling, WV
John Giel
Orlando, FL
Karen Giffin
Seattle, WA
J. Fernando Gil
Orlando, FL
M. Margaret Gillett
Dallas, TX
Catherine Gilligan
Little Rock, AR
Garry Giroux
Ogdensburg, NY
Chad Glendinning
Ottawa, ON
Matthew Glover
Little Rock, AR
Paul Golden
Denver, CO
James Goodwin
Fargo, ND
Mary Ellen Goverts
Rochester, NY
Robert Graffio
San Francisco, CA
William Graham
Baltimore, MD
Jason Gray
Peoria, IL
Thomas Green
Washington, DC
Bradley Greer
Steubenville, OH
Janice Grochowsky
Dodge City, KS
David Gross
Grand Rapids, MI
Ralph Gross
Milwaukee, WI
Paul Hachey
Atlanta, GA
Mary Haddad
St. Louis, MO
James Hagel
Calgary, AB
Edward Hankiewicz
Grand Rapids, MI
Joseph Hannawacker
Trenton, NJ
Paul B. Hartmann
Milwaukee, WI
Leo Hausmann
Rapid City, SD
Robert Hayes
San Jose, CA
Bernard Hebda
Newark, NJ
Amy Hereford
Saint Louis, MO
Ryan Hilderbrand
Evansville, IN
Marie Hilliard
Overbrook, PA
Christina Hip-Flores
Camden, NJ
Jordan Hite
Harrisburg, PA
Viet Peter Ho
Garden Grove, CA
Thuan Hoang
San Francisco, CA
Michael Huszti
Pittsburgh, PA
Robert Hyde
Syracuse, NY
Francisca Igweilo
Denver, CO
James Innocenzi
Trenton, NJ
Eileen Jaramillo
Lansing, MI

Jolene Jasinski
Beaver Falls, PA
Chanel Jeanty
Miami, FL
Gerald Jorgensen
Dubuque, IA
Rita Joyce
Pittsburgh, PA
Michael Joyce
Perryville, MD
Lawrence Jurcak
Parma Heights, OH
Thomas Kadera
Wheatland, WY
Christopher Kadrmas
Bismarck, ND
Samuel Kalu
Lafayette, IN
Robert Kaslyn
Washington, DC
Connie Kassahn
Cheyenne, WY
Nicholas Kastenholz
St. Louis, MO
Roger Keeler
Washington, DC
Anthony Kerin
Melbourne, Australia
Elaine Kerscher
Joliet, IL
Daniel Ketter
Atlanta, GA
Rita Killackey
Kansas City, MO
Adela Maria Kim
Peoria, IL
Shane Kirby
Scranton, PA
Wayne Kirkpatrick
Toronto, ON
David Klein
Camden, NJ
Lee Kneipp
Alexandria, LA

Daniela Knepper
Muskego, WI
Ronald Knott
St. Meinrad, IN
Jose Kochuparambil
Lubbock, TX
Feliks Kosat
Bordentown, NJ
Thomas Kunz
Pittsburgh, PA
Victor Kynam
Grand Rapids, MI
Patrick Lagges
Chicago, IL
Bonnie Landry
Lake Charles, LA
Daniel Laurita
Athens, AL
Raphael Lee
Newark, NJ.
Richard Lelonis
Pittsburgh, PA
William Leser
Northridge, CA
Andres Ligot
San Jose, CA
Judene Lillie
New Orleans, LA
John List
Lexington, KY
Douglas Loecke
Dubuque, IA
Douglas Lucia
Ogdensburg, NY
William Lum
Feura Bush, NY
Paul Luniw
Cherryville, CT
Vinh Luu
New Orleans
Gregory Luyet
Little Rock, AR
Paula Lynn
Orange, CA

Corey Lyon
Salina, KS
John Lyttle
New York, NY
Peter Mangum
Shreveport, LA
Wilfredo Manrique
San Jose, CA
Wojciech Marat
Chicago, IL
Francis J. Marini
Scranton, PA
Jeannine Marino
Washington, DC
Kurt Martens
Washington, DC
Ricardo Martin
Milwaukee, WI
Rogelio J. Martinez
Las Cruces, NM
Paul Matenaer
Madison, WI
Reynaldo Matunog
Los Angeles, CA
Alberto Maullon
Houston, TX
Herbert May
Creole, LA
Robert McBride
Newark, NJ
Joseph V. McCabe
Maryknoll, NY
Jeremiah McCarthy
Columbus, GA
Rose McDermott
Trenton, NJ
James McDonough
Coraopolis, PA
Wendy McGrath
Manchester, NH
Kevin McKenna
Rochester, NY
Linda McKinney
Fort Worth, TX

Maureen McPartland
Dubuque, IA
Abel Mena
Santa Rosa, CA
Gerard Mesure
Philadelphia, PA
George Michalek
Lansing, MI
Ken Mikulcik
Owensboro, KY
C. Thomas Miles
Charleston, SC
Bruce Miller
Alexandria, VA
Donna Miller
Arlington, VA
Richard Millette
Houston, TX
Bernard Mohan
Newark, NJ
Christopher Moore
Brooklyn, MD
Francis Morrisey
Ottawa, ON
Susan Mulheron
Saint Paul, MN
Matthew Muller
Newcastle, Australia
Martin Mwongyera
Peoria, IL
James Nall
Belleville, IL
Luis Navarro
Stockton, CA
Luis Navarro
Rome, Italy
Martin Nelson
Sour Lake, TX
Dennis Nesser
Dunbar, WV
Joseph Newton
Indianapolis, IN
Steve Nguyen
Honolulu, HI
Kevin Niehoff
Grand Rapids, MI
Michael Nobel
Ottawa, ON
Aaron Nord
St. Louis, MO
Mary Judith O'Brien
Saginaw, MI
Mark O'Connell
Boston, MA
Thomas O'Donnell
Pittsburgh, PA
Kelly O'Donnell
Fresno, CA
Timothy Olson
Fargo, ND
Thomas Olszyk
Milwaukee, WI
Jude Onogbosele
Sisters, OR
Michael Onyekuru
Atlanta, GA
Jose Opalda
Baltimore, MD
Greg Osburg
Covington, KY
Sinclair Oubre
Orange, TX
William Palladino
Boston, MA
Duaine Pamment
Laingsburg, MI
Thomas Paprocki
Springfield, IL
John Payne
New Orleans, LA
F. Stephen Pedone
Worcester, MA
James Pereda
Rockville Centre, NY
Thomas Petro
Scranton, PA
Anthony Pileggi
Kansas City, MO
Peter Polando
Youngstown, OH
Jaimes Ponce
Colorado Springs, CO
Stanley Pondo
Indanapolis, IN
John Porter
Grand Rapids, MI
Mark Porterfield
Jefferson City, MO
Frank Pugliese
San Diego, CA
George Puthusseril
Miami Shores, FL
Daniel Quinan
Saint Paul, MN
Kevin Quirk
Wheeling, WV
Nicholas Rachford
Parma, OH
Steven Raica
Gaylord, MI
Margaret Ramsden
Orange, CA
Lawrence Rasaian
Tyler, TX
Michael Ravenkamp
San Diego, CA
Catherine Mary
Raymond
Newark, NJ
Gordon Read
Brentwood, England
Ann Rehrauer
Green Bay, WI
Richard Reidy
Worcester, MA
Charles Renati
San Francisco
John Renken
Ottawa, ON
Brian Reynolds
Louisville, KY

Nancy Reynolds
Louisville, KY
Joseph Richard
Crookston, MN
Thomas Richstatter
Tell City, IN
Kenneth Riley
Kansas City, MO
J. Michael Ritty
Feura Bush, NY
Carmine Rizzi
Newark, NJ
Giovanni Rizzo
Newark, NJ
Lynda Robitaille
Vancouver, BC
Carolyn Roeber
Seattle, WA
Marie Roldan
San Jose, CA
Meg Romano-Hogan
Frisco, TX
Lee Roos
Manassas, VA
Eileen Ross
New York, NY
Charles Rowland
Charleston, SC
Patricia Ruiz
Fresno, CA
Adam Rust
Memphis, TN
Mark Rutherford
Williamston, MI
Carlos Sacasa
Fort Worth, TX
Mary Santi
Seattle, WA
John Santone
Notre Dame, IN
Noel Sanvicente
Los Altos, CA
Alessio Sarais
Rome, Italy

Mary Schaumber
Alma, MI
Joseph Scheib
Pittsburgh, PA
J. Gerard Schreck
Savannah, GA
Tait C. Schroeder
Madison, WI
Phillip Schweda
Venice, FL
Gilbert Seitz
Baltimore, MD
John Sekellick
Passaic, NJ
John Shamleffer
Saint Louis, MO
Donetta Shaw
Kansas City, MO
Patrick Shea
Springfield, IL
Sean Sheridan
Steubenville, OH
Richard Shewman
Erie, PA
Richard Siegel
Joliet, IL
Langes Silva
Salt Lake City, UT
Bill Simon
Muskegon, MI
Louis Sirianni
Rochester, NY
Christopher Siuzdak
Portland, ME
Jaroslaw Skrzypek
New Madrid, MO
H. Roberta Small
Seattle, WA
Daniel Smilanic
Chicago, IL
Rosemary Smith
Atlanta, GA
Patricia Smith
Aston, PA

Nathaniel Sokol
Lansing, MI
Michael Souckar
Coral Springs, FL
Anthony St. Louis-Sanchez
Colorado Springs, CO
Jeffrey Staab
Richmond, VA
Ronald Stake
Chicago, IL
Margaret Stallmeyer
Covington, KY
Susan Stankis
Orange, CA
Sahaya Stanly F
Grand Rapids, MI
Richard Stansberry
Oklahoma City, OK
Ryan Stenger
Covington, KY
Charles Strebler
Cleveland, OH
Therese Sullivan
Cleveland, OH
David Szatkowski
Olive Branch, MS
Andrew Szymakowski
Redmond, OR
Amy Tadlock
St. Paul, MN
Gerard Tartaglia
Oslo, Norway
Michael Taylor
Manchester, NH
Charles Thompson
Evansville, IN
Nancy Thompson
Indianapolis, IN
Mathew Thundathil
Miami Shores, FL
James P. Tobin
Newark, NJ

Joseph Tobin
Indianapolis, IN
Margaret Toole
Portland, OR
Allison Townley
Kansas City, MO
Luong Tran
Beaumont, TX
Gregory Trawick
Cadiz, KY
Ann Tully
Indianapolis, IN
Ted Tumicki
Norwich, TC
Robert Turner
Pomeroy, WA
Daniel Ulishney
Greensburg, PA
Silvana Usandivaras
New York, NY
Louis Vallone
Pittsburgh, PA
Kelly Vandehey
Portland, OR
John Vaughan
Madisonville, KY
Lucy Vazquez
Orlando, FL
Therie Velasco-Gonzales
San Jose, CA
Carlos Venegas
Denver, CO
Siobhan Verbeek
Washington, DC
Manuel Viera
Tucson, AZ
Adam Voisin
Hamilton, ON
Victoria Vondenberger
Cincinnati, OH
Michael Vuky
Portland, OR
Richard Wahl
Houston, TX
A. David Warriner
New Orleans, LA
Rick Wells
St. Petersburg, FL
Daniel Welter
Chicago, IL
Adam Westphal
Des Moines, IA
Paul Wienhoff
Belleville, IL
Jonathan Wisneski
Greensburg, PA
Thomas Wisniewski
Darby, PA
Geri Woodward
New Orleans, LA
Gary Yanus
Cleveland, OH
Dennis Yurochko
Pittsburgh, PA
Dariusz Zielonka
Bridgeport, CT
Robert Zilliox
Buffalo, NY

Made in United States
Cleveland, OH
05 November 2026

47673393R00268